Theory of Self Relativity

How to relate to your "self" and everything else

Dr. Vahé Ohanessian

Se#1f

Disclaimer

This book is not a substitute for professional advice. The views, information, or opinions expressed in this book are that of Dr. Vahé Ohanessian (the author) and Self Relativity, Inc. (the Company) only and they are simply opinions and cannot be guaranteed to be correct or concise. Dr. Ohanessian is not a licensed psychologist, psychotherapist, mental-health professional or any other licensed medical doctor, and his opinions are not to be construed as professional or expert advice. The author and the company do not verify for accuracy any of the information contained in this book or its affiliated prints, online or voice and media publications. The primary purpose of this book is to share opinions and information and to educate and inform. This book does not constitute medical and/or other professional advice or services. Neither the author nor the company assume any liability for any activities in connection with this book or for the use of this book in connection with any other books, publications, websites, and computer or playing devices. The information and data used in the book is based on common knowledge that is openly shared and found via online search engines and other publicly available forms of publications. No information or data is directly or specifically extracted from specific sources, therefore, no references or citations are necessary for claims made and for information shared in this book.

Mission Statement

To live this improbably rare gift of life to its fullest possible potential.

Foreword

If you are looking to reinforce your desired-feelings by getting peptalked into feeling good and getting a pat on the back; you might want to look somewhere else. However, if you have heard enough empty-motivation and you are now ready for true-transformation, you have come to the right place. You have one life to live. Life is precious and life is short; cherish every moment of life. It is your self-given-right and your self-responsibility to live the best life possible. You are your best friend; improve your Self constantly and consistently so that you can make each day a better day than the day before. Stop being shackled to the outside and start freeing your Self from within.

To feel good…you must think well.

Dr. Vahé Ohanessian

About The Author

Dr. Vahé Ohanessian is a self-aware, empathetic person interested in self-improvement and living a content and fulfilling life. Dr. Ohanessian's personal experiences and general curiosity led to continual research in concepts and principles entailing psychology, philosophy, and physics where he conceived of the concepts of factual-thinking and the Theory of Self-Relativity. Professionally, Dr. Ohanessian is a USC graduate dentist with decades of experience. He is also an entrepreneur and inventor of the Airigation treatment system for halitosis which is a primary socio-biological concern in personal interactions and relationships. Dr. Ohanessian's life goal is to share his teachings with others so that others can also experience living a fulfilling life.

Table of Contents

Preface

We often think things and we do things not because they are good for us, but because we want to feel good.

The truth is often uncomfortable and when forced to face the dislikeable-truth, our emotional tendency is to ignore, deny, and deflect in order to avoid getting in touch with the dislikable-truth; and to create, support, and preserve the preferred-thoughts that make us feel good. We ignore, deny, and even attack the truth or the messenger because the truth does not match our preferred comforting perspective; even though that perspective might be incorrect, fallacious, and nonfactual. According to Theory of Self-Relativity:

The need to avoid pain, to feel good, or at the minimum, to feel less-bad; is the main cause of our bad decisions, our incorrect actions, and our inability to change and improve.

In other words;

The need to feel good versus the necessity to think well is a core factor that inhibits change and blocks self-improvement.

We feel because feelings enable us to quickly identify, connect, act and react relative to internal and external stimuli. This quickness and impulsivity of acting on feelings is intended to be a protective-mechanism for safety and survival; because in urgent situations such as in primitive-times that our ancestors lived in, they did not have time to think if the data that they were getting was factual or not. They acted on feelings and impulse instead of evaluating the facts and data of the circumstance, because being wrong was not as detrimental as being killed or eaten; hence, humans developed more ways of feeling negative in order to stay protected and safe, because negative-feelings force us to take action to resolve or eliminate the causes of those negative-feelings.

For example, fear is a negative-feeling that our ancestors felt, because fear was intended to keep them safe by getting them to react to potential danger; either by facing the danger or by running away from it. It is because of this primitive programming of our mind that we have developed more negative-feelings than positive-feelings, because negative-feelings notify us that there is a possible threat or a potential for danger; and since negative-feelings are unpleasant, they force us to take quick "corrective" action in order to increase our safety, and in-turn, to eliminate the unpleasant negative-feeling.

Since we strive to minimize negative-feeling, hence, most self-help systems focus on motivation as the core requirement for transformation and improvement; because motivation functions by improving our feelings. However, the problem with such motivational teachings is that motivational programs incorrectly, and sometimes deceptively, try to elevate our emotions in order to get us excited to change and improve. Through peptalking and chest-pounding sessions, seminars, write-ups and messages, most motivational programs create false-hope which quickly fades out without producing any results.

Unrealistic motivation and peptalk is the perfect setup for failure and hopelessness.

Most motivational teachings are made of implied purpose and reason for life's negativities and failures, as if the failure or the negativity happened for a purpose or a reason; thus, if we uncover the "secret" purpose or reason, we will make our life better. Negativities do not happen with a mystical purpose or a reason in order to get our life to transform; negativities happen because we, "our Self," either caused the negativity by doing something wrong, or because we refrained from taking an action to improve or to prevent an unfavorable outcome. Regardless of how we look at it, negativities and setbacks happen because we "our Self" are a factor in the situation.

Motivational programs make us feel good and tell us what we want to hear rather than be honest to tell us how we are often responsible for the things that happen in our lives. Instead of telling us how reality is, regardless of its unpleasantness, and instead of showing us how to change so that we can improve our reality; most motivational-programs focus on telling us what we want to hear, rather than what we should hear. Furthermore, even when motivational programs try to tell us what we need to do to change, they often fall well short of showing us how to make the change. Empty-motivation without implementation of follow-through action is like knowing we need to eat to stay alive but we don't know how to find the food.

We all know we need to eat to stay alive; the question is how to find the food.

Motivation is a state-of-mind that creates the desire or willingness to do something; however, motivation alone cannot lead to change and transformation. It is easy to get motivated, but motivation dies out if we don't follow through with proper action. To take proper action, we must learn to think and reason based on facts so that the feelings that we create as a result of our thoughts can lead us to make proper decisions for action. We cannot just think positive-thoughts in order to create positive-feelings so that we feel good; we must create feelings that are based on reality and facts. This is why, motivation is easy, but the difficult part is how to turn motivation into results.

Motivation is easy; it is dedication and implementation that requires effort.

In order for motivation to lead to change and improvement, proper decision-making and behavior is necessary. Proper behavior can only happen if we learn to think properly. Thinking generates feelings and feelings lead to behavior. Although behavior is commonly associated with taking an action, behavior could also be inaction or not taking any action; thus, behavior is comprised of action or inaction. Therefore, our behavior is as a response that we take based on a feeling that we feel, and if our feelings are not generated by factual-thoughts, our response would be incorrect.

Theory of Self-Relativity defines "behavior" as "an action or an inaction as a response to a feeling that is caused by an underlying thought."

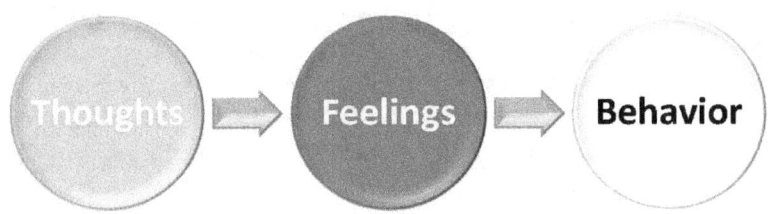

The disconnect between motivation and transformation happens when we directly go to our feelings to behave. Feelings are irrational and feelings by themselves are not reliable to lead to proper behavior. In order for feelings to properly lead us into taking proper action or inaction, we must generate the feelings as a result of proper thoughts. Although our thoughts generate our feelings; as stated above and throughout Theory of Self-Relativity, we often think things and we do things in order to avoid pain, to feel good, or at the minimum, to feel less-bad. This means we think thoughts to feel good but not necessarily to do the right thing. This is why, motivation without knowing how to take action fails consistently. Although motivation creates positive-feelings, if these feelings are only created to make us feel good; we will either do the wrong thing or we will not proceed to responding with the correct behavior. Because:

Our behavior does not represent how we are thinking; it only represents how we are responding.

This is why, many self-help and self-improvement systems end up being empty peptalks that get people worked-up and motivated but do not result in transformation. Many tell us what we need to change but they don't show us how to make the change. In order for motivation to lead to proper action, motivation must be based on, what Theory of Self-Relativity refers to as, *"Factual-Thinking;"* and not based on thoughts that make us feel good, or thoughts that help us feel less-bad. Subsequently, feelings which are produced as a result of factual-thinking, will then lead us to making sound decisions and taking proper actions.

Theory of Self-Relativity defines "factual-thinking" as "thoughts that are supported by facts and reason."

According to Theory of Self-Relativity:

Facts are evidence in support of reality.

And:

Facts are evidence sufficient to reach a conclusion.

Therefore:

Factual-thinking is about having reasonable confidence in the facts; unless or until falsified.

Factual-thinking creates feelings which are based on facts and not based on how we want to feel. Feelings created by factual-thinking are based on the truth and facts of how reality is; not based on how we want reality to be. As uncomfortable and difficult as the feelings that are generated from factual-thoughts may be; these feelings will force us to take proper action to correct and improve the uncomfortable facts which are causing our negative-feelings. Factual-thinking forces us to behave correctly by taking an action or inaction in order to improve our Self and the reality which we are dealing with.

Factual-Thinking teaches us "how" to think, not "what" to think.

Therefore:

To modify our behavior and to self-improve, we must change and improve how we think.

We are more in touch with our feelings than we are with our thoughts; this is why, we often behave based on how we feel rather than behave based on what we think. Our thoughts cannot directly create our behavior; our thoughts lead to our behavior through our feelings. Since feelings are much more accessible, yet because feelings are irrational; to make our feelings rational, we must generate these feelings via factual-thinking. Factual-thinking is the system of checks and balances of our feelings, our behavior, and our existence as a whole. Although Theory of Self-Relativity places utmost importance on factual-thinking; it also insists that the feelings generated as a result of our thoughts lead us to expressing our Self as the person that we are. Factual-thinking does not make us into robotic creatures who have no feelings; on the contrary, factual-thinking filters out unnecessary feelings which disable us from improving and living a quality life.

Factual-thinking is the system of checks and balances of our mind.

Our feelings are what separates us from one another and from entities which have no feelings; however, as discussed, our feelings have no rationality, therefore, in order to feel the truth and to be in sync with reality, we must generate our feelings based on factual-thinking. We should not create thoughts and beliefs in order to feel good; we must think factually so that our true feelings will enable us to change and adapt to the way reality is, and not to the way we want reality to be. Thus, to have the purest and most rational feelings, and to live a frictionless life, we must learn to think factually.

Although René Descartes has stated of the relationship between thinking and existing as "I think, therefore I am;" his philosophy is based on the thinking process creating doubt which is a form of cognitive analysis. Just because we can create doubt by thinking does not make us into the complex individuals that we are. Descartes states "I think I am, because I doubt, therefore I exist," which is a philosophy that is relevant to existentialism. Our existence is not in question; the issue-at-hand is the understanding of our existence relative to our own Self, relative to reality, and relative to everything and everyone else.

Thinking is made up of multiple thoughts and each thought generates a feeling or an emotion that we feel; therefore, Theory of Self-Relativity defines the relationship between our thinking and our existence as:

I think…therefore I feel…therefore I am

Since our existence is a confluence of our thoughts and their resulting feelings and behavior; thus:

Self-Relativity is the fact that we exist, and Theory of Self-Relativity is the best explanation of how we exist.

Introduction

We are our thoughts; and how we think determines how we feel and how we behave.

Cognition is traditionally defined as the process of acquiring knowledge and understanding through thought, experience, and the senses. Cognition is important for our thinking, reasoning, and analytical abilities which enable us to make decisions and take actions to deal with our life and to relate to our existence.

Theory of Self-Relativity defines "cognition" as "awareness and understanding through mindfulness, thoughtfulness, and thought-management."

Since our thinking and cognition are the basis of our self-identity and who we are; our incorrect thinking is the main cause of why we are unhappy and why we are not able to change and improve.

1. **The Problem:** The mystery of the "Self," and its interactions and relationships with itself and with everything and everyone else, in order to live a content, fulfilling, and happy life; is one of the oldest human existential questions. Although understanding of how we interact with other-things in The-Universe is important; however, the commonly noticeable challenges and difficulties which we experience relative to our self-identity and our sense of Self are our interactions and relationships with our own Self and with other-people. According to Theory of Self-Relativity, lack of self-awareness and a weak or negative sense of Self due to flawed, emotional, and nonfactual-thinking is the main cause of our personal and interpersonal challenges in life.

2. **The Solution:** According to Theory of Self-Relativity, facts and evidence are the basis of understanding, learning, and knowing how everything, including we exist and relate to each other. To be able to self-improve and to live a content, a fulfilling, and a happy life, we must learn to think factually because facts and evidence are the only verifiers of reality. Facts are the only verifiers of reality because only one fact exists per situation and facts are not open to interpretation; therefore, facts are not open to manipulation. Factual-thinking enables us to live our life in the most effective way possible, and it safeguards us from external and internal lies and deceptions. Factual-thinking enables us to live our life based on facts and evidence and not based on subjective-perspectives, preferred-interpretations, and comforting-emotions. By thinking and by living our life based on facts and evidence, we not only protect our Self from external-negativities, but we also protect our Self from our own self-created fallacies and deceptions. Instead of living our life based on unproven comforting hope,

faith, and beliefs; facts enable us to live our life based on knowledge and factual-reality, regardless of how dislikable or uncomfortable factual-reality may be. By dealing with reality based on facts, we can take action to change the dislikable reality to become more favorable for us.

3. **The Approach:** Theory of Self-Relativity bases its approach on what it has coined as the principle of *"Psychophysosophy."* Psychophysosophy is described as a system that is a confluence of the scientific principles of Psychology, Physics, and Philosophy.

I. Psychology: Relates to matters of thoughts, feelings, and behavior, and their interactions and relativities to each other.

II. Physics: Relates to matters of matter and energy, and their interactions and relativities to each other.

III. Philosophy: Relates to matters of the mind, thinking, and existence, and their interactions and relativities to each other.

Philosophy is where we formulate ideas; science is where we prove the ideas.

Theory of Self-Relativity focuses on how our thinking makes us who we are and how we interact and relate with everything and everyone else. Theory of Self-Relativity considers everything to be physical and matter-based in its origin, and this material nature of things is what gives rise to the psychological aspect of sentient-beings and the philosophical aspect of intellectual-existence. Since everything is physical; therefore, everything can be understood, resolved, and improved by understanding the facts and evidence associated with it. This is how science advances; by looking, by discovering, and by understanding the facts and evidence associated with matter and nature.

Science is not absolute. Science is about having reasonable confidence about the evidence.

System of Self-Relativity, through its *"Cognitive-Cognition-Technique,"* provides the tools to develop skills of self-improvement; and to learn how to filter out cluttering and nonfactual-thoughts, and to only keep thoughts that are based on facts and evidence. By streamlining thinking and decision-making abilities into a simple, quick, and repeatable format; System of Self-Relativity enables and assists the mind to unclutter as it guides the mind to think based on how reality is, and not based on how we want reality to be.

Theory of Self-Relativity defines the "Cognitive-Cognition-Technique" as "The ability to use our feelings, to access and identify our thoughts, in order to take proper action.

Since we are more aware of and more in touch with our feelings; by understanding and by applying Theory of Self-Relativity's Cognitive-Cognition-Technique, our mind and our thinking-system will learn to develop and enhance its thinking-skills in order to identify, resolve, or eliminate cluttering thoughts quickly, cleverly, and consistently. The Cognitive-Cognition-Technique teaches us to use our feelings as symptoms in order to identify their underlying causal-thoughts, so that we can then take proper action.

The Cognitive-Cognition-Technique is our mental-algorithm for proper thinking.

Since each person is the entity that spends the most time with one's Self, Theory of Self-Relativity gives the individual person the ability to become one's own primary support-system. As many of us have experienced, the more support we need during difficult times, the less support we get, and the more people walk-away from us. Although this is because many are too self-centered to want to attend to other-people's difficulties; it has also been demonstrated that many do not want to be around susceptible people because they are concerned that the person's weaknesses and negativities could affect themselves negatively.

Therefore, while a good support-system can be helpful; instead of solely relying on other-people's availability as a support-system, it is better to primarily rely on our own Self so that we can resolve our own difficulties. System of Self-Relativity is one of the few systems that teaches us how to become our own coach and our own primary support-system; at our own time and moment of need. System of Self-Relativity is effective in doing so because:

System of Self-Relativity treats the causal-thoughts, not the symptomatic-feelings.

Spirituality

Many, broadly claim to be spiritual without knowing and without having a definition for what their ambiguous identification with spirituality actually represents. Just because spirituality can be vague; vagueness and ambiguity should not make spirituality mysterious and mystical.

Because:

Although something might feel or might be experienced as being mystical; personal-experience does not mean that thing is mystical.

Spirituality has broad definitions and has been practiced in different forms throughout centuries in all cultures of the world. Spirituality is commonly associated with religious and other forms of comforting-beliefs; however, in the modern-times, spirituality is also considered to refer to personal qualities such as one's mind, thoughts, and feelings.

Theory of Self-Relativity defines "spirituality" as "the emotional experience associated with a thought, a belief, or a mindset."

Theory of Self-Relativity, itself, could be considered as a spiritual system, under the definition of spirituality as a means of dealing with personal thoughts and feelings; however, Theory of Self-Relativity does not subscribe to immaterial or supernatural-based beliefs such as souls, ghosts, personal-energy, chakras, auras and other immaterially assumed ways of existence. Likewise, Theory of Self-Relativity does not subscribe to other new-age spiritual-beliefs such as positive-thinking, good and bad personal-energy, or personal frequencies and vibrations; and neither does it accept superstitions, miracles, and other religious or tradition-based theories, which in order for them to be true, they would have to violate the laws-of-physics that govern The-Universe.

According to Theory of Self-Relativity, spirituality does not have to be mythical or mystical; it is how we experience the natural world and how we make our experiences special. Since spirituality is based on emotional-experience associated with a mindset; therefore:

We are all spiritual about something.

However, spirituality, for example, relative to the supernatural, does not necessarily mean it is based on facts; although when spirituality is based on factual-reality, such spirituality will actually lead to the confidence of experiencing the spirituality more intensely. This is why, science, the natural-world, and how we think, are the best sources for our spirituality.

True spirituality is not believing in something mystical or mythical; true spirituality is to use the awareness of our emotions, to improve our thoughts, and to strengthen our behavior.

Since something might feel or be experienced personally as mystical but does not necessarily mean that things is mystical; Therefore:

Personal-experience is subjective and cannot be demonstrated factually to others.

Hencey why:

Personal-experience is not a reliable way of demonstrating reality.

Theory of Self-Relativity is founded upon its unique principle of psychophyso-sophy, which deals with the material-products and the immaterial-byproducts of the brain and The-Universe associated with human existence. Theory of Self-Relativity is based on factual-thinking and evidence-based scientific principles that are directly as a result of the material Universe that we live in; and the laws-of-physics that govern The-Universe, which in-turn, govern our existence.

True spirituality is increasing knowledge by learning, and by applying it to one's existence.

Existence

Human-beings have been searching for the elusive answers to questions about the "Self" and existence. This yearning for answers has embarked us on a long journey that has only made finding the answers even more complicated. We have looked everywhere, and we have tried to understand how things work so that we can answer questions such as:

- What is life?
- Why am I here?
- Who am I?

We not only have not found the answers, but we have managed to confuse ourselves even more. As our technology, knowledge, and intelligence have advanced, the answers to the most basic Self and existence questions have become even more complicated. We have looked farther into The-Universe, we have looked further back into time, we have delved deeper into the subatomic world of quantum-mechanics, and we have thought harder and harder to learn about how we think and what makes us tick. The harder we have looked everywhere and the more questions we have asked about everything, the further we have moved away from our own Self. We have tried to look for answers anywhere and everywhere, yet we have individually failed to look within our own Self. We have focused too much on why we are here and what will happen after we die, than to focus on how to live the best life possible. We keep looking into the past or into the future yet what we miss is the passing present-moment of life which will never come back. We have failed in answering and resolving the most important question of all time:

How can I feel good and live a better life?

The reason we have failed to find answers to these questions is because as intelligent-sentient animals we have focused more on sensing and observing reality as we want it to be, rather than sensing and observing how reality truly is. When we choose to interpret reality to the way that we would like it to be rather than accepting reality to be the way that it really is; we open our Self up to misunderstanding, manipulation, and deception of the truth. Although we use logic, reason, and rationalization about how we observe reality; we are often not aware that what we believe to be logical and reason-based is often nonfactual and preferential at its core. Although we believe that the logic and reasons that we use are *"valid;"* what we feel and believe as being valid might not necessarily have factual *"value."*

Validity is not necessarily a verification of factual-value.

There is a big difference between validity and value, just as there is a big difference between what is factual and what is real. Although value is often perceived, and this perceived value could vary and change; unlike perceived-value, factual-value or existential-value is always consistent and never changes. Factual-value or existential-value could only change if the underlying facts associated with the value of that thing change.

Therefore, even though something is valid, it does not necessarily mean that it has factual-value. For example, we might feel and believe that we are the smartest person in the world. What we feel and believe is valid to us because we are feeling it; however, what feels real to us might not have factual-value. In other words, what we feel to be true, might not be the factual-truth. Therefore:

There is a big difference between what is factual and what is real.

There is a big difference between factual-truth, which is almost absolute, and reality, which could be subjective and based on interpretation. The reason factual-truth is as close to absolute as possible but not absolute, is because only one fact exists per situation, and facts are not open to interpretation; however, facts are open to examination and if necessary, facts are open to replacement. The reason reality is not absolute is because in the absence of factual or evidence-based verification, reality is open to subjective-interpretation. When something is open to interpretation or subjective-experience, it will also be open to misunderstanding, manipulation, and deception. According to Theory of Self-Relativity:

"Interpretation" is often an attempt to adapt to the absence of evidence, or an attempt to adapt to contradictory evidence.

Therefore:

Interpretation, absent of facts, could lead to misunderstanding.

Facts are facts, and only one form of fact exists for every situation; therefore, facts are not open to interpretation, hence, facts are not open to manipulation. Although facts can be open to examination, facts cannot be open to interpretation. Furthermore, facts are not completely absolute and could be examined, and if necessary, facts could be replaced; therefore:

Factual-thinking is about having reasonable confidence in the facts, unless or until falsified.

Since facts are not open to interpretation; therefore, facts are the only dependable criteria that could be used for our personal and universal system of checks and balances.

Facts create truth and facts verify reality.

Because:

Factual-truth is real, but reality is not necessarily factual.

This is why, truth, which is always supported by facts, remains the undisputed-truth, until and unless the supporting facts change; or until the supportive facts are proven to be incorrect, as new facts emerge or are discovered.

Although facts are not open to interpretation, facts are open to examination and they are open to replacement. Since the space that a fact occupies could only house one fact; hence, the strongest evidence and best supported fact fills the gap in that space. However, if we cannot find the facts to fill the gap, we should not be obligated to fill-in the knowledge-gap with nonfactual or perceived facts, causes, reasons, purpose or meaning.

Interpretation to our liking is one of the main causes of "self-deception;" because interpretation could affect us to see reality the way we want it to be, rather than seeing reality the way reality truly is.

The problem and the confusion associated with our existence arises when we incorporate reality or realities that are not factual-reality into our life. For example, mermaids and dragons in an amusement park are part of the reality of the park, but mermaids and dragons do not actually exist. Although mermaids and dragons are real in amusement parks, they are not factually-true; therefore, if we try to incorporate mermaids and dragons as realities into our life, the factual-truth will clash with this false-reality. Of course, this is an extreme example, but this is what children do as they create their own reality; yet, this is no different than when many adults do similar iterations of reality, such as twisting the truth or misrepresenting reality which is also known as "lying," which in-turn, could have severe life's implications.

The truth is always real and factual; but a lie, although real, is not the truth nor is it factual.

Although many consider lying as an act performed against others, the biggest lies we hear are the lies we tell our Self; and we do so in order to avoid pain, to feel good, or at the minimum, to feel less-bad. Our ability to lie and deceive our own Self in order to feel better or to feel less-bad, is one of the main causes of our inability to understand our own Self and our "existence" in The-Universe. While one would think that advancements of intelligence, information, and knowledge should have made the knowing of our Self and the understanding of our existence easier and clearer; on the contrary, such progress and evolution has enabled us to self-deceive with more complicated schemes of how we want reality to be, versus how the factual-reality truly is.

We self-deceive by thinking "if it conflicts with what I want to be true, therefore it must be false."

Modern technologies and communication tools such as social-media, dating-apps, and even a multitude of popular reality-TV shows, although real, are often deceiving in their representation of reality. These communication mediums and their contents have distorted reality and have caused alterations of reality for those observing and interacting with these realities from the user's perspective. Through exaggeration and creation of false façades, which have a tendency of creating a false field of comparison for others; many participants deceptively represent a much happier and more successful portrayal of their life. The ease of fabricating a false-reality often has a significant effect on the most susceptible and insecure individuals in thinking their reality is sub-standard to the realities presented in these social platforms.

Likewise, virtual-reality, just like reality-TV and social-media, is based on the sub-jectivity of the creator of the content; which itself, is often an altered or non-exis-tent reality. This is why, according to Theory of Self-Relativity, virtual-reality could become a form of mind-control. Virtual reality, reality-TV, and the internet could distort factual-reality, and in-turn, distort one's perception of reality.

To live in factual-reality and not just in any reality, we must check and verify everything with facts and supportive-evidence. Furthermore, for us to begin to find the answers to the existential questions that we, as humans, have been asking, yet have not been able to answer; we must live in harmony with not just reality, but with the factual-truth. When we use facts to support our existence, we will then be able to live in harmony with our Self and with everything and everyone else; therefore, our existence and our relativities will be based on solid and uns-hakable foundation. When we live our life with the confidence of knowing that everything we think, everything we feel, and everything we do is based on facts; we will then have the confidence and security of establishing a positive self-identity and a strong sense of Self.

To know who I am, I must know how I am.

Such personal-strengths will, in-turn, enable us to use the sword of facts to cut down negativities and to increase positivities. Factual-thinking will purify our feelings and will enable us to make good decisions and to take proper actions for living a content, fulfilled, and a happy life.

To feel good, we must think well.

Feelings

All feelings are valid but not all feelings have factual-value.

We feel, because feelings enable us to quickly identify, connect, and act or react relative to internal and external information and stimuli. This quickness and impulsivity of acting on feelings is intended to be a protective mechanism for safety and survival; because in urgent situations such as in primitive-times that our ancestors lived in, they did not have time to think if the data and information that they were getting was factual or not. They acted on feelings and impulse because being wrong was not as detrimental as being killed or eaten; therefore, humans developed more ways of feeling negative in order to stay protected and safe, since negative-feelings force us to take action so that we resolve or eliminate the causes of those negative-feelings.

For example, feeling fear is intended to keep us safe by making us quickly run from a potential threat. When we minimize or eliminate the potential threat; our feeling of fear subsides or disappears. It is because of this primitive programming of our mind that we have developed more ways to feel negative than positive, because negative-feelings notify us that there is a potential for danger; and since negative-feelings are unpleasant, negative-feelings force us to take quick action, so that by increasing our safety, we can eliminate our unpleasant and undesired negative-feelings. Therefore, negative-feelings must be resolved and eliminated only by resolving or eliminating the causes of the negative-feelings.

When we resolve or eliminate the cause of a negative-feeling; the negative-feeling automatically improves or disappears.

When we feel discomfort, threat, or danger, we feel negative and not positive; because undesired and uncomfortable negative-feelings force us to take action in order to resolve or eliminate the causes of our negativity. This, in-turn, eliminates our negative-feelings so that we can feel better. Nature has programmed us to get rid of the causes of our negative-feelings because those causes could be bad for us; hence, nature has defaulted us with negativity. Therefore, we are programmed to minimize, resolve, or eliminate what makes us feel negative so that we can feel better. Nature has not programmed us to feel good or to feel happy; nature has only programmed us to feel better than the worst negative. In other words, nature has programmed us to attempt to feel less-bad. This is why:

If you feel negative more often than you feel positive, and if your negativities arise faster and last longer than your positivities; you are simply a normal human-being.

As commonly understood, our behavior is as a result of our feelings, and our feelings are generated by their underlying thoughts; therefore:

To do the right thing, we must think the right way.

Although this order of Thinking - Feeling - Behavior is well known and taught in all aspects of human related sciences, Theory of Self-Relativity has termed this sequence as the *"Absolute-Order;"* because regardless of our awareness of our underlying thoughts, or our awareness of our feelings, our behavior is as a result of this sequence.

We cannot take an action without feeling something, and we cannot take an action without having a thought that directed us to take that action. The absolute-order is the fundamental sequence of our existential interactions with our Self and with everything and everyone else. Additionally, there is also an intermediate state of "decision-making" involved before we take an action; because when we think and as we feel, it is then that we make a decision to behave.

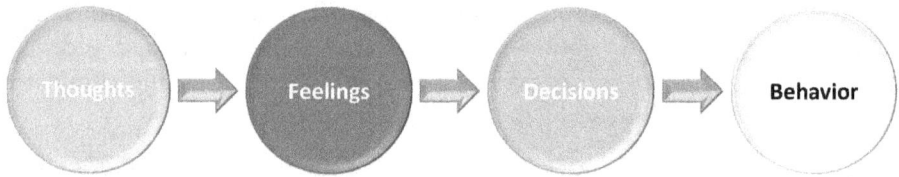

This sequence of including decision-making could also be referred to as the absolute-order; however, to simplify referencing our three most important components of thoughts, feelings, and behavior, Theory of Self-Relativity considers "decision-making" as an implied constant that bridges our thoughts to our behavior. Decision-making is simply an intermediate stage that leads us to taking an action or to abstain from taking an action (inaction). It must be noted that behavior does not necessarily mean only taking an action, because part of our behavior could be inaction or not taking an action; hence, our behavior is a response relative to our thoughts.

Although there are extensive references to decision-making throughout the field of psychology, Theory of Self-Relativity considers decision-making as a stage which leads to action or inaction; because it is as a direct result of our passed-through thoughts. Therefore, when discussing thoughts, feelings, and behavior throughout Theory of Self-Relativity, the role of decision-making is implied and not referenced as regularly as the other three stages. Theory of Self-Relativity's focus is primarily on the two stages of thoughts and feelings, because these two reliant yet often conflicting stages are the components that define our self-identity and create our sense of Self.

Behavior does not represent what we are thinking; behavior represents how our brain has responded.

We are more aware of our feelings than we are aware of our thoughts; yet, our feelings are created by our thoughts. Although we often believe that our feelings are independent of what we think; our feelings and our emotions could not exist if we were not able to think. To be able to feel the most basic feelings, our mind must become aware of and it must evaluate the causal-stimulus so that it can create the sensation of feeling something. When our mind becomes aware of the stimulus, that is when we think and generate our feelings and emotions. Therefore, without our mind creating our thoughts, we would not be able to feel or have emotions; and if we cannot think or feel, we would not be able to make decisions, hence, we would not be able to interact.

Our feelings are a symptom of our thoughts.

Since our feelings are a symptom of our thoughts; therefore, our feelings are a manifestation of what we are thinking. Likewise, since we are sentient-beings who are also intelligent; we are generally more in touch with our feelings than we are with our thoughts. We sense our feelings more strongly than we are cognizant of our thoughts; and since our feelings are at closer proximity to our behavior, we act much quicker based on our feelings than we do based on our thoughts. As discussed, the reason we act and react quicker based on feelings is so that in threatening and dangerous situations, we can act quickly to get away from danger in order to stay safe and alive.

Feeling-awareness is easy, but thought-awareness is not.

This is why, especially in the modern-times where we do not have as many life-threatening natural dangers as our ancestors did in the primitive-times, instead of quickly behaving on feelings, we must learn to become aware of our thoughts in order for us to behave and interact properly and effectively. A feeling is never the initial trigger of a thought, a feeling is always triggered as a result of a mental-process and a thought; however, because we are usually not aware of our initial thoughts which create our feelings, we tend to believe our emotions arise independently, or that our feelings lead to our thoughts. A feeling does and could result in a thought, but that feeling itself had an initial thought and a mental-process that created the feeling. It is awareness, identification, and understanding of those initial thoughts responsible for our feelings which will help us engage in proper decision-based behavior. Although feelings could result in the creation of new thoughts, that is a violation of the absolute-order; therefore, when feelings create thoughts, these thoughts are often irrational and incorrect, because such thoughts are commonly concocted in order to rationalize, justify, and support a desired or a comforting feelings. Therefore:

Our emotions must make us feel what we must feel; not make us think how we want to feel.

As stated throughout Theory of Self-relativity:

Feelings are for feeling; not for thinking.

When the absolute-order gets disrupted and when we create thoughts to rationalize a desired-feeling, Theory of Self-Relativity refers to this incorrect sequence as the *"Emotional-Order."*

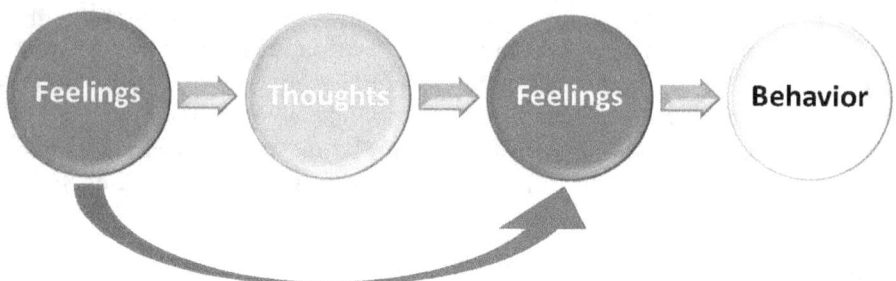

The emotional-order represents the sequence where we create thoughts in order to justify and rationalize our desired-feelings. For example, when we feel bad because we lost money gambling, instead of taking the longer but more stable way of changing our gambling tendencies, we talk our Self into believing that the next time by doubling down our wager, we will bring all our losses back. This rationalization and justification of allowing our Self to continue gambling is how people engage in self-deception, in order to feel better at that moment. Instead of accepting that we might have a gambling problem, and instead of taking the longer way of working harder to earn back the money; we convince our Self to abstain from changing by rationalizing without any evidence that the next time, we will achieve a better result. Since we felt bad after losing money, we justified to our Self that what happened was alright; hence, we created a false-thought to rationalize our desired comforting-feeling in order to not feel as bad. Therefore, we used our feelings to create a supportive false-thought in order to recreate the absolute-order. Although now, the feeling is supported by an underlying thought; in this case, fallacy recreated the absolute-order to justify taking an action that supported our desired-feeling, but the action was not necessarily the right thing to do.

When we self-deceive, we recreate the absolute-order based on how we want to feel, and not based on how we should think.

As discussed throughout Theory of Self-Relativity, feelings are irrational; hence, feelings have no independent rationality. Feelings are only as rational as the thoughts that create them; therefore, only correct thinking can generate proper feelings. Although proper thinking generates proper feelings; proper thoughts are not always desirable, because reality is not always to our liking. Thus, in order to experience comforting-feelings, instead of feeling the feelings that our correct thoughts are generating; we often violate the absolute-order by creating false-thoughts and fallacious-beliefs so that we could rationalize and support our desired-feelings. When we create thoughts based on how we want to feel, rather than feeling based on what our thoughts are indicating; we create our own desired reality and that is when we violate the absolute-order by engaging in the emotional-order, which ultimately will place us on a collision-course with factual-reality. This is why, Theory of Self-relativity designates "Self-Deception" as one of the 10-Enemies of Self-Improvement.

Even though our feelings have no rationality on their own, our feelings are just as valid as our thoughts are; because we feel the feelings and we think the thoughts as they are both mental-processes. Although what we think and what we feel are valid, this does not mean they have factual-value; therefore:

Validity is not an indication of value.

In order to establish value, we must qualify our thoughts and feelings, and the only way that we can consistently qualify our thoughts and feelings as having value, is based on verifying them with supportive facts and evidence. This is why, Theory of Self-Relativity is founded upon the principle of factual-thinking. When we get our thoughts in proper order and when these thoughts are generated and supported by existing facts; our thoughts will have a much higher potential for being correct and in parallel with factual-reality. When our thoughts are factually supported, our thoughts will then be rational; and when our thoughts are rational, the feelings that we feel will be more genuine and rationality-based, thus, the actions that we take will be better positioned to produce favorable results.

"Think" before you "Feel" to "Act."

Matter of Mind

Life is not mysterious, mythical, or magical; because all the underlying laws-of-physics that govern our existence are known.

Thus:

We are what we think.

According to Theory of Self-Relativity, our consciousness and our mind are as a result of our physical-brain's activities; and without our brain and its estimated 86 billion neurons and 100 trillion neural-networks, our consciousness, our intelligence, our self-identity, and our sense of Self would not exist.

We are our brain.

Therefore, without our brain, our mind, which is a metaphor for where our thinking takes place, would not exist.

We are our brain therefore we are our mind.

Our consciousness, our mind, and our thoughts are derivatives and emerging-properties of our physical-brain's activities; therefore, without our physical-brain, our "Self" would not exist. The evolution of our brain is the main cause of our survival and intellectual progress. Our brain is an information-processor which adapts and evolves as the human species adapts and evolves and becomes more intelligent.

Theory of Self-Relativity defines "intelligence" as "the ability to acquire, process, and apply information and knowledge."

Intelligence is the modern component for natural-selection, and the more intelligent a species becomes, the better will be the chance of its adaptation and survival to its environment. The evolution of our brain and its ability to process information is the primary natural-selection component which has caused our continuous existence and our advancement as a species. As humans progressed and as they became more intelligent, the human brain size, especially the prefrontal-cortex grew, causing us to become even more adaptable to our environment and to have a better chance of survival. This growth in the size of the prefrontal-cortex enables humans to acquire, process, and apply information and knowledge more quickly and efficiently.

According to Theory of Self-Relativity:

Intelligence could be increased not necessarily by increasing the measurement of intelligence, but through the efficient and pragmatic application of intelligence.

Advancements in science and technology now clearly show how our physical-brain creates our intelligence. Due to our understanding of the brain, its neural-networks, and its neural-circuitry, we can now disregard theories and claims of non-physicality causing our intelligence, consciousness, and our self-identity. Although the method of the emergence of such mental attributes is still up for debate, we now know that our physical-brain creates its *"non-physical-processes"* and *"immaterial-byproducts"* such as our intelligence, our language, our thinking, and even our consciousness. By understanding the physical nature and activities of the brain's neural-circuits, we do not need to assign spirits, ghosts, or souls to our Self in order to define our existence; because we now know that everything relating to our existence is matter-based.

As a natural information-processor, our physical-brain creates our non-physical characteristics such as intelligence, consciousness, and thinking-ability. Our brain also evolves and becomes a stronger and faster information-processor as it creates more intelligence, and as it gathers and analyzes more information. The evolution of our brain and the advancement of our intelligence is apparent in the growth of the size of the human brain throughout our evolutionary period. A larger brain size allows for bigger data and information storage capacity, as well as faster data and information processing ability. This increase in information processing ability is directly related to the evolutionary increase in human brain size. By increasing brain size through evolution, humans were able to increase memory and information processing and computational abilities via analytical-thinking. This repetitive cycle of faster processing leading to a larger brain size, and a larger brain size leading to an increase in faster processing ability, is responsible for the intellectual advancement of human-beings. Theory of Self-Relativity refers to this intellectual-advancement as *"Intellectual-Selection."*

Theory of Self-Relativity defines "intellectual-selection" as "the accelerated progress of a species through intelligence, knowledge and technological advancements."

Unlike many new-age spiritual or ancient unscientific motivational programs that advocate not-thinking, or tout slowing down thinking; it is this evolutionary increase in thinking-ability that reflects Theory of Self-Relativity's cognitive self-improvement style. Because, in the modern-era, to improve and succeed, we must think quicker and cleverer.

The anatomy of our physical-brain is segmented and categorized into multiple sections. Although all sections are important, Theory of Self-Relativity places special importance on the prefrontal-cortex which is primarily responsible for our cognitive and thinking abilities. The prefrontal-cortex, in simple definition, is the region of the brain, which is in front of the brain, as it sits behind our forehead. The human brain has tripled in size in its 5 million years of evolution; yet the prefrontal-cortex has increased six-fold in size, or twice as much as the brain itself. The primary activities of the prefrontal-cortex are:

- Cognition
- Planning; especially complex cognition-based planning
- Decision-making
- Thinking organization and orchestration
- Executive-Function

The collection of these activities and functions of the prefrontal-cortex are knows as our "Executive-Function." Executive-function is our "mental" ability to differentiate between different or conflicting thoughts. The prefrontal-cortex is also responsible for differentiation of opposites and extremes; for example, differentiating between good and bad. According to and as discussed throughout Theory of Self-Relativity, our mind is most comfortable when it evaluates each fundamental-thought in its simplest *"binary-format;"* therefore, for quick and clever implementation of its executive-functions, the prefrontal-cortex becomes least stressed when it deals with binary options, because binary options minimize complexity, which in-turn, creates simplicity and efficiency in processing. Therefore, if we can filter and address our cognitive and thinking processes at their simplest fundamental level, we could have a more efficient, yet quicker way of thinking. For example, it is easier and more efficient when we address individual-thoughts, rather than addressing complex thinking. When we learn to address, analyze, and resolve individual "building-block-thoughts," our macro thinking will consequently become a sounder "building-shape-thinking." Simply stated, when we address and treat each thought as a building-block of our thinking; the resulting shape of our "thinking-building" will automatically take its correct shape. Thus, individual-thought-processing optimizes the information processing tasks of the prefrontal-cortex.

Additionally, the prefrontal-cortex plays an important role in our personality expressions and in regulating our social and emotional behavior. The human prefrontal-cortex occupies a larger percentage of the human brain in comparison with other animals; consequently, the size and number of connections in our prefrontal-cortex is directly related to our *"Sentience."* Classically, sentience is defined as "the ability to have subjective experience." Since subjectivity is personal and subjective-experience is commonly associated with emotions and perceptions, Theory of Self-Relativity defines sentience in a more comprehensive manner.

Theory of Self-Relativity defines "sentience" as "the capacity to have individual-feelings, intrinsic-perceptions, and subjective-experiences."

Because the larger human prefrontal-cortex is more sentient, this could also be why humans commonly engage in *"emotional-thinking."* Theory of Self-Relativity recognizes a potential relationship between our prefrontal-cortex's ability to think cognitively and to perform executive-functions relative with its sentience capacity; hence, causing us to think emotionally. The prefrontal-cortex is also the region of our brain which enables mindfulness and thoughtfulness, and it is instrumental in orchestrating our thoughts and actions relative to our internal goals. These characteristics of the prefrontal-cortex make it one of the most important and crucial regions of our brain for enabling self-regulation and self-improvement.

Although science has proven that without our brain there will be no consciousness or mental-activities; regardless of what gives rise to our consciousness, our mind, and our thoughts, what is obvious is that we are conscious creatures with a mind, and we can think. Whether it is the firing of our neural-network synapses or some quantum level sub-atomic processes that gives rise to our consciousness; as long as we are conscious and sentient and we can think, we should manage our thoughts based on their factual-value and not based on how they make us feel.

Just as the discovery of the Higgs Boson did not change the way we interact with The-Universe; the discovery of exactly how consciousness arises will not change how we, as conscious beings, think and function. Unless the physiology or the anatomy of a person's brain is modified or affected, according to Theory of Self-Relativity, proper everyday thought-management should be based on conscious evaluation of the factuality of those thoughts. In other words, as long as we are cognitively functioning normally and we do not have a medical or mental condition which takes objectivity and true sense of reality away from us; we should learn to manage our thoughts and we should live our life based on the factual-value of those thoughts.

Therefore, in the grand scheme, Theory of Self-Relativity focuses on how to apply our consciousness, our thinking, and our analytical abilities to our life, in order for us to change and improve the quality of our existence as we move through life.

Theory of Self-Relativity defines "Thought-Management" as "the process of eliminating nonfactual-thoughts and only retaining factual-thoughts."

While the mind and consciousness are highly debated scientific and pseudoscientific subjects; Theory of Self-Relativity, true to its foundation of factual and evidence-based thinking, categorizes our consciousness, our mind, and our thoughts, as *"immaterial-byproducts"* or *"immaterial-processes"* of our *"material-brain's"* or *"physical-brain's"* activities. According to Theory of Self-Relativity, our physical or matter-based brain's activities and processes not only produce our immaterial-consciousness, our immaterial-mind, and our immaterial-thoughts; but, they also produce other immaterial-byproducts such as our feelings, our emotions and our behavior.

Therefore, our material-brain, via its immaterial-byproducts and processes, communicates with and connects us to all material-things and immaterial-byproducts in The-Universe. It must be noted that although immaterial-byproducts are generally invisible and have no shape, weight, or any other physical or material characteristics; immaterial-byproducts are not capable of existing independently, thus, immaterial-byproducts are not immaterial-things.

Immaterial-byproducts only exist as emerging states of the functions of their underlying material-entities.

As stated throughout Theory of Self-Relativity, immaterial-byproducts are not the same as immaterial-things, because no immaterial-thing could ever exist. However, even if we were to assume that an immaterial-thing could exist, which according to the laws-of-physics it cannot, we would not be able to detect nor interact with it; because in order for things to interact with each other, they must be made of matter.

Hence, as stated:

Life is not mysterious, mythical, or magical, because all the underlying laws-of-physics that govern our existence are known.

According to Theory of Self-Relativity, if our brain is damaged or dies, so would our consciousness, our mind, and our thoughts. Same holds true for our feelings and emotions, because our emotions are caused by our thoughts; hence, our feelings are generated as a result of our physical-brain's activities. Therefore, our behavior and our interactions with our Self and with The-Universe are as a result of our physical-brain's activities. When our brain dies, so does our consciousness, our mind, our thoughts, our feelings, and our behavior and interactions. In other words, when our brain dies; our "Self" dies.

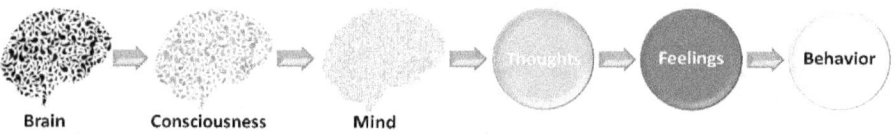

Brain   Consciousness   Mind   Thoughts   Feelings   Behavior

Theory of Self-Relativity defines "Self" as "the collection of the material and immaterial aspects of one's existence."

Likewise:

Theory of Self-Relativity defines "Self-Relativity" as "the interactions and relationships of the Self internally and externally with the Self and with everything and everyone else."

As long as we have a healthy and functioning brain; our mind, our thoughts, and our thinking-system remain the nucleus of our Self-identity. To address how our mind and our thoughts affect our existence and our interactions within our Self and with everything and everyone else; we need to first become aware of and to understand how our mind and our thoughts shape and influence our Self, Our-Universe, and our existence. Furthermore, we need to understand how our Self and everything and everyone else are all relative to one another.

Contrary to certain popular beliefs, Theory of Self-Relativity advocates that our mind is not separate from our body and our brain. As stated, according to Theory of Self-Relativity, our mind and our thinking are as a result of our physical-brain's activities. If our brain is damaged, severed, or removed; so would our conscious-ness, our mind, our thoughts, and our Self. Although there are a multitude of assu-med theories of how consciousness arises; no spiritual or immaterial concept has ever been able to factually demonstrate the independent existence of consciousness and the Self, without the underlying operations and activities of a physical-brain.

Spirits, souls, energy, karma, aura, chakras, and all other immaterial assumptions regarding human existence have remained as beliefs, assumptions, and human imaginations, and none have been proven with facts and evidence to exist. The only aspect of human existence that has proven to affect self-identity and personal-existence is the matter-based aspects of a person's body which includes the brain. If the brain, which is a part of our body, is damaged, our brain's immaterial-byproducts of existence such as our mind, our thoughts, and our personality will also be affected, or will cease to exist. We can either make our Self feel good by assuming comforting-thoughts that there is more to us than our physical-existence, which gives rise to the "Self;" or we can get on the path of dealing with the evidentiary truth of what we are made of, by making the changes needed to improve our existence.

Since damaging our physical-brain has proven factually to affect our existence negatively, and since no other immaterial or supernatural theory of existence independent of a properly functioning physical-brain has proven to factually exist; therefore, we should focus on operating our mind based on the evidence and the facts of how we exist.

Spirits, energy, souls, and all other supernatural assumptions of the human existence have been around for millennia and not once have they been proven by evidence or scientific experiments to be true. If and when such evidence emerges, we can then adjust our approach relative to such findings. However, since these immaterial and supernatural-assumptions and comforting-beliefs have existed for a very long time, and since they have never been demonstrated or proven factually; at this point and after so long, it is quite safe to realize and accept that they will never be proven to be true, because in order for the supernatural to exist, it must be able to interact with the natural. Simply stated, the supernatural could never exist.

If and when supernaturality is proven, it will no longer be supernatural; it will simply become natural.

Therefore, we must focus on living and improving our life based on what is factually true, and not based on what we want to be true, because it makes us feel good. This is why, Theory of Self-Relativity is founded upon the principle of evidence-based and factual-thinking.

The biggest lies we hear are the lies we tell our own Self; and we lie to our Self in order to avoid pain, to feel good, or at the minimum, to feel less-bad.

Facing facts is often an emotionally difficult task because facts that require change are often uncomfortable to deal with; however, factual-reality always catches up and further affects our lives negatively, if we do not deal with facts properly. It is better to face facts and evidence, as uncomfortable as they might be, in order to change and improve the reality around us; than to alter our thinking about reality in order to temporarily feel-better. Reality-distortion via denial, ignorance, delusions, and other forms of defense-mechanisms such as positive-thinking, is a significant contributor to our inability to self-improve. Factual-thinking prevents reality-distortion and self-deception.

We self-deceive by thinking "if it conflicts with what I want to be true therefore it must not be true."

We can learn to minimize negativity and increase positivity by improving the quality of our life in the actual and fact-based real Universe. However, we must make actual changes based on what facts are showing us, rather than change our thoughts based on how we want our preferred reality to be. We must learn to adapt our thoughts, our feelings, and our behavior to evidence and factual-reality; we must not try to ignore reality by altering our perception of reality in order to feel good.

Our mind is a powerful tool yet a dangerous tool; because our mind can make us believe what feels good rather than make us recognize what is true.

As stated, although there is a possibility that consciousness might be created and affected by currently unexplained physical-processes in the brain and in our neural-networks; finding out how our consciousness emerges will not affect the fact that our resulting macro-level thinking should be based on facts and evidence. Just as the discovery of quantum-mechanics and its strangeness does not affect the macro and larger scale of The-Universe that our life interacts with; the discovery of how our consciousness arises will not influence the fact that when we think, these thoughts must be based on facts and evidence, and not based on preferred-perceptions, feel-good assumptions, or comforting manmade beliefs.

This is why, no matter how much science and technology advance, human critical-thinking and skepticism becomes even more important in questioning everything. Skepticism is a cognitive trait and a skill that Theory of Self-Relativity recommends cultivating in order to be able to look for supportive facts, reason, and logic for a proposition; and especially for a thought. Since Theory of Self-Relativity is founded upon the foundation of what it has termed as factual-thinking; thus, to be able to seek facts, we must have a skeptical mindset.

Regardless of the source of information and data, be it another person or through scientific and technological advancements; factual-thinking will enable us to sort out through disinformation, misinformation, and other potentially biased information and data that, for example, artificial-intelligence could bring about. While as a productivity tool, artificial-intelligence or AI will significantly improve human thinking and information-processing; the value of artificial-intelligence still relies on the quality of the information and data that it uses to provide its output and to reach its conclusions. Therefore, AI could be biased based on the information and the data that it uses to achieve results; hence why, humans need to have critical-thinking ability to ensure that the results achieved are constructive and based on how reality is.

This is why, critical-thinking must be prescriptive by the human mind, but only descriptive or predictive by AI; which means, we do not want AI to do the thinking for us. Thinking, especially creative and critical-thinking, must still be done by the human mind; because, innovation and reasoning is the result of pragmatically applying information, data, and knowledge to reach a conclusion. But if the data or the information that humans, or even AI, rely on is incorrect or corrupted; the conclusion reached will also be faulty. Just as calculators streamlined daily calculations and allowed for the human mind to focus its time and energy on efficiency and innovation, and just as cell-phones took away the need for us to use our memory to remember phone numbers; artificial-intelligence will also enable other ways of efficiency that will allow the human mind to create and innovate new ways of improving our lives. However, technological productivity tools such as calculators, cell-phones, and even AI are simply tools, and they should not replace our ability to think critically and to make sound decisions.

Therefore:

When it comes to thinking, we must do the thinking for our own Self; we do not want artificial-intelligence or any other entity to do the thinking for us.

This is why, as conscious entities, our thinking must be prescriptive; and other manmade tools, such as artificial-intelligence, should only be descriptive or predictive in aiding and facilitating our cognitive-processes. This is where the fine line of consciousness separates a data processing thinking being such as a human, from other nonconscious and non-thinking data-processing entities such as computers and artificial-intelligence.

Our consciousness, our mind, and our thoughts are not separate entities that join our body when we are born, and which separate from our body when we die. We do not have a body that has a mind; we have a body which includes our brain; and, our physical-brain creates our mind, our thoughts, our feelings, our behavior, and our sense of "Self."

Our mind is our "Self-Identity" which is produced by our brain.

Therefore:

Our mind is a metaphor for where our thinking takes place.

Mind & Consciousness

The mind is a metaphor for where thinking takes place.

As discussed, according to Theory of Self-Relativity, our "mind" is as a result of our material or physical-brain's activities. Additionally, according to Theory of Self-Relativity, our mind is as a result of our consciousness, which itself, is as a result of our physical-brain's activities.

Theory of Self-Relativity defines the nature of our consciousness and our mind as "the immaterial-byproducts of our material-brain's activities."

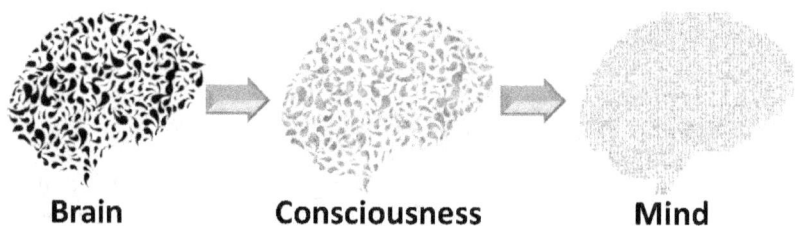

Brain   Consciousness   Mind

Theories of the mind and consciousness have been debated for centuries and there have been disagreements about what defines consciousness and the mind, how they develop, and how they affect our existence. Yet, according to Theory of Self-Relativity, the most important consideration is that regardless of the differing opinions and theories about the emergence of consciousness and the mind; the mind and consciousness are states-of-existence. Although knowing the emergence of our mind and consciousness is important scientific knowledge; at the human interactive level, how mind and consciousness arise is irrelevant to how we use our mind and consciousness to interact with The-Universe and to live our lives.

As long as we are conscious and we have a mind, knowing their emergence properties is not as important as knowing how to apply them to our everyday life. Furthermore, Theory of Self-Relativity persists that neither our mind, nor our consciousness, nor our self-identity would be possible without the existence and the proper functioning of our physical-brain. While Theory of Self-Relativity is always open to consider evidence and facts for differing points of view; however, until and otherwise such evidence is presented, Theory of Self-Relativity considers the physical-brain as the core of our mind, our consciousness, and our *"Self-Existence."*

According to Theory of Self-Relativity, our physical-brain is part of our body, while our consciousness and our mind are as a result of our physical-brain's activities;

therefore, there is no separation of mind and body, or separation of mind and brain. Our mind and thinking are as a result of our physical-brain's functions, and our brain is a part of our physical-body. According to Theory of Self-Relativity, our mind is our self-identity and our individual sense of Self. It is this immaterial-byproduct known as the "mind" that shapes and operates our thoughts, our thinking-processes, and our cognition; and in-turn, our thinking creates our feelings, and our feelings lead to our decision-making and behavior.

We are our mind, we are what we think; therefore, we are our brain.

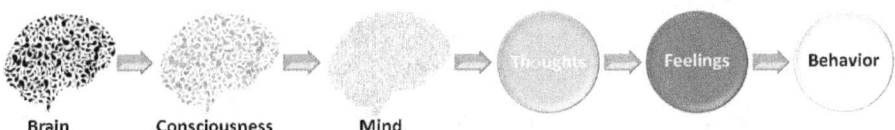

As disheartening as it may be to realize, all evidence and facts indicate that our consciousness, our mind, and our thoughts are not separate entities that join our body when we are born, or separate from our body when we die. In other words, according to Theory of Self-Relativity, the immaterial-byproducts of our material-brain's activities such as our consciousness, our mind, our thoughts etc., which define our individual Self, are not spiritual, energy, or other pseudoscientific or supernaturally defined entities. Sometimes, in popular culture, these immaterial-byproducts of our material-brain's activities are also referred to as our "soul." According to Theory of Self-Relativity, no such a thing as a soul could exist, because its existence would be outside of the laws-of-physics which define the natural world. We do not have a body and a soul; we are a material-body whose functions gives rise to its immaterial-byproducts. When the body dies, so do its immaterial-byproducts and functions such as consciousness and the mind

There are a multitude of popular and scientific categories about the levels of the mind, such as the conscious-mind, the subconscious-mind, and the unconscious-mind. Since the mind is not a defined material-entity, any references to the mind, including those made by Theory of Self-Relativity, are purely metaphorical for visualization and for better understanding. Unlike popular classification, Theory of Self-Relativity categorizes the mind binarily:

1. **The Conscious-Mind:** Is the state-of-mind that we are more-aware of and one which we can access directly. The conscious-mind is used for logic and reasoning as well as analytical and critical thinking. The conscious-mind is where many of our more-aware thoughts take place.

2. **The Nonconscious-Mind:** Is the state-of-mind that we are less aware of and one which requires deeper levels of awareness and understanding to access. The nonconscious-mind is not as directly accessed, and, in Theory of Self-Relativity's categorizations, it includes the subconscious-mind and the unconscious-mind. Although the nonconscious-mind could carry out analytical and critical thinking functions, especially when these thoughts are repeated or are associated with a skill; the nonconscious-mind is where

many of our less-aware emotional-thinking or our emotional-reactivities takes place.

As indicated in the aforementioned categorization, Theory of Self-Relativity links consciousness and the mind inseparably because they are undefined metaphors; hence, for the purpose of self-improvement, where one ends and where the other begins is irrelevant. Additionally, our consciousness and our mind which lead to our thoughts, our feelings, and our behavior are all interconnected and overlapping; thus, references to distinct separation of these states are for visualization and understanding purposes. However, to reiterate, according to Theory of Self-Relativity, consciousness is needed for the emergence of the mind; and the mind is what leads to our thoughts, our feelings, our behavior, and our sense of Self.

Our physical-brain generates our consciousness, and our consciousness gives rise to our mind.

Therefore, consciousness is the prerequisite for thinking, feeling, decision-making, and behavior; and as discussed, behavior consists of either taking action or inaction. In order for an entity to be conscious, a certain number of neurons, and more so for complex animals, having a brain, which itself is a collection of millions or billions of neurons, is necessary.

As discussed, our consciousness is a state of our existence that is the result of our physical-brain's activities and processes. Consciousness is one of the building-blocks of our self-identity. Consciousness is difficult to explain, especially when most attempts try to define consciousness as to what consciousness is or what it isn't. This debate has created disagreements about the definition of consciousness as it is impossible to have a well-defined or legal definition of consciousness. Since consciousness is an immaterial-byproduct of brain activity, the variability of this activity makes it impossible to draw a line to pinpoint a starting position for consciousness. This is why, after so many decades of debate and neuroscience advancement, it is still difficult to classify, and more importantly determine, if for example, a worm has consciousness, if a bird has consciousness, or if an unborn child has consciousness.

Regardless of these inconsistencies, Theory of Self-Relativity defines our physical-brain as the *"non-negotiable"* requirement for us to have consciousness; therefore, without our brain and its activities we would not have consciousness. Although what consciousness is and how it emerges is up to questioning; by moving onto the next conditions required to develop and define consciousness, one thing that is certain is that as intelligent creatures we do have consciousness. Thus, for the purpose of self-improvement, what matters is for us to use our consciousness to define our self-identity and to create and to improve our sense of Self. Therefore, for everyday life:

How consciousness and the mind emerge is not as important as how we apply them.

According to Theory of Self-Relativity, in order for consciousness to lead to the emergence of other properties such as mental-activity, emotions, intelligence, and behavior; consciousness, relative to living organisms, must have certain properties which leads to the emergence of these states. Additionally, since Theory of Self-Relativity conditions individual consciousness as a result of one's physical-brain's activities; it additionally concludes that there cannot be a well-defined comprehensive and singular definition of consciousness. However, as a collective:

Theory of Self-Relativity defines "consciousness" as "the awareness to perceive and to interact with the Self and with other things."

Theory of Self-Relativity categorizes and collectively defines consciousness in the following three overlapping states:

1. **Simple-consciousness**
2. **Specific-consciousness**
3. **General-consciousness**

1. **Simple-Consciousness:** According to Theory of Self-Relativity, simple-consciousness is the minimum requirement for consciousness to exist in a living organism. Simple-consciousness is also the minimum core requirement for all other states of consciousness. Although awareness in more complex organisms could be intellectual or knowledge-based; in simple-consciousness, Theory of Self-Relativity describes "awareness" as the minimum required condition for consciousness.

Neural-Activity ✚ Awareness ═ Simple-Consciousness

Theory of Self-Relativity defines "awareness" as "an entity's ability to sense separation of Self from others". For example, separation of Self from its environment, from other organisms, or from other things.

2. **Specific-Consciousness:** According to Theory of Self-Relativity, specific-consciousness, in addition to "awareness," also includes "perception." In specific-consciousness, an entity or an organism is not only capable of sensing a separation of Self from others, but it is also able to distinguish the differences between the Self and the things that it is separate from.

Neural-Activity ✚ Awareness & Perception ═ Specific-Consciousness

Theory of Self-Relativity defines "perception" as "an entity's ability to identify and recognize others from the Self." For example, the Self is able to distinguish the difference between Self and its environment, other organisms, or other things.

3. **General-Consciousness:** According to Theory of Self-Relativity, general-consciousness is the ability of an entity or an organism to not only be able to sense and recognize separation of Self from others via awareness and perception; but it is also capable of interacting with them. For example, the Self is able to interact with its environment, with other organisms, or with other things. In general-consciousness, the entity is capable of interacting with and experiencing its interactions with things which it is separate from. In humans, general-consciousness is the resulting state of our brain's activities which makes us capable of sensing, perceiving, experiencing, and interacting with our environment, with other-people, and with other-things. Simple-consciousness and specific-consciousness are inherent to general-consciousness.

$$\text{Neural-Activity} + \begin{matrix}\textbf{Awareness} \\ \& \\ \textbf{Perception} \\ \& \\ \textbf{Interaction}\end{matrix} = \text{General-Consciousness}$$

Theory of Self-Relativity defines "interaction" as "an entity's ability to engage and experience with the Self and with others." For example, the Self is capable of experiencing interactions with its environment, with other organisms and with other-things.

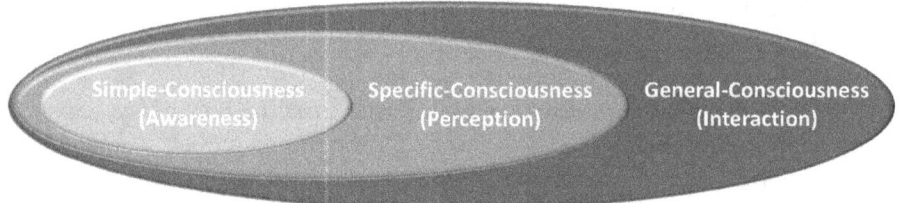

To truly be considered a "cognitively" conscious entity, Theory of Self-Relativity requires the following conditions:

1. **Awareness.**
2. **Perception or recognition of the awareness.** (Whereas in higher intelligence levels, this recognition will be in the form of comprehension and understanding of the awareness.)
3. **Interaction with the perceived or recognized awareness.**

The alternative to consciousness is lack-of-consciousness or nonconsciousness, where there is no awareness, no comprehension, no experience, and no interaction of the mind with one's own Self, with other-organisms, or with other-things. Therefore, according to Theory of Self-Relativity, as conscious-beings, we are either in a state of consciousness, or we lack consciousness. Thus, for personal-development and for everyday interactions in life, Theory of Self-Relativity recommends considering personal-consciousness binarily, because by being conscious we can either be aware of, perceive, and interact with our Self and with everything and everyone else; or if we cannot, regardless of what stage of nonconsciousness we might be in. This is why, Theory of Self-Relativity considers consciousness to be an emergent property of our material-brain's activities.

Theory of Self-Relativity categorizes the state of personal-consciousness binarily:

1. **Consciousness:** Is the ability to sense, recognize, comprehend, experience, and interact with the Self and with other-things or other-organisms. For example, being awake or being alive.

2. **Nonconsciousness or Lack-of-Consciousness:** Is the inability to sense, recognize, comprehend, experience, and interact with the Self and with other-things and other-organisms. For example, anesthesia or death.

Although there can be other altered or in-between states of consciousness; Theory of Self-Relativity is most interested in consciousness whereby we are capable of awareness, comprehension, and interaction with our Self and with everything and everyone else.

Theory of Self-Relativity defines "personal-consciousness" as "the ability of a person to comprehend, experience, and interact, with the Self and with everything and everyone else."

This is why, consciousness is the prerequisite for having a mind; hence, consciousness overlaps with our ability to have mental-activities such as thinking and cognition.

As consciousness allows for the mind to take shape, we then become capable of thinking, problem-solving, decision-making, feeling, and behaving (action or inaction). According to Theory of Self-Relativity, consciousness, regardless of how it emerges, is the condition which enables an animate-physical-entity, such as a human-being, to interact independently and at somewhat free-will with other-things and with other-people. Theory of Self-Relativity identifies our mind and our thinking-ability as an integral component of our self-identity and who we are. Therefore, our consciousness and our mind, which arise as a result of our physical-brain's activities, and which enable us to think; are the basic necessities for us to exist as an individual Self.

Our "Self-Existence" begins with and continues as long as our physical-brain generates our consciousness and our mind.

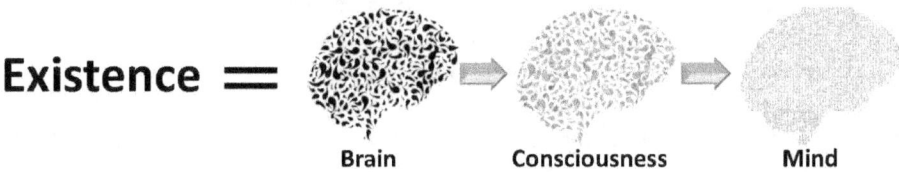

Existence = Brain → Consciousness → Mind

Although we must be conscious to think, our thinking is not synonymous with our consciousness. Our thinking-ability is as a result of us being conscious, because without consciousness we would not be able to think; however, to also be aware of our consciousness, we must be able to think. Therefore, our consciousness, our mind, and our thinking, which are the foundation for our self-existence, are interrelated and overlapping.

Since no one else has been able to factually and with evidence prove that the physical-brain is "not" the necessary entity for consciousness; Theory of Self-Relativity considers our brain as the cause of our consciousness, our mind, our thoughts, our feelings; and therefore, our self-existence. Our brain is our personal-hard-drive, our mind is our personal-software, our consciousness is the coming alive of our computer when the power switch is pressed on; and our thoughts, our feelings and the other immaterial-byproducts of our material-brain's activities are the operations of our *"Self-Computer."* It is because of this overlap, that consciousness, as a well-defined and bordered entity, has been difficult to explain.

Our consciousness is analogous to turning on a computer, where it allows the connection of the physical hard-drive with the non-physical software to initiate and expand its operations. Therefore, consciousness, just like our feelings, cannot exist on its own; hence, it is not self-sustainable. Consciousness, just like our feelings, is the result of a cause. As discussed in detail throughout Theory of Self-Relativity, our feelings are caused by our thoughts and our consciousness is caused by our brain. Our brain creates our consciousness, our consciousness creates our mind, our mind creates our thoughts, and our thoughts create our feelings which lead to our behavior.

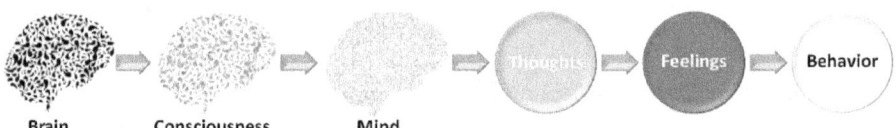

Brain   Consciousness   Mind   Thoughts   Feelings   Behavior

Our mind, our consciousness, and our thinking end when our brain dies or when our brain stops functioning. Just as the functions of a personal-computer ceases when the computer is turned off or when it runs out of energy; our self-existence and consciousness cease to exist when our brain dies or stops working. That's because our brain is made of atoms, and we know how atoms, as particles, function and interact. Therefore, after we die, there are no other particles or forces that exist which could move the immaterial-byproducts of our brain, such as our consciousness, our thoughts, our feelings, and our sense of Self, from our brain into another immaterial state.

As stated, although there will be further discoveries in science and physics; nevertheless, we have already discovered all the particles and forces in nature which affect our physical existence. There are no other new particles or new forces that we can discover that could interact with and affect our existence which we do not know about. Any new discoveries of particles or forces in nature would be too weak or too unstable to interact with the atoms that make us up. Every other sensationalistic explanation of duality or quantum existence of consciousness and mind, is just that; sensationalism and mysticism in order to try to stand out from the crowd, and for the financial gains of the entity pitching the nonsense. Unless, otherwise proven factually that our consciousness could exist separate of our brain's activities, Theory of Self-Relativity considers our material-brain as the cause of our immaterial-functions of consciousness, mind, thinking, feelings, behavior, and our sense of Self.

Although it is comforting to think that our consciousness, and even our mind and our Self, could exist separately from our material-body; the laws-of-physics which govern The-Universe do not allow for such a reality. The laws-of-physics which govern the existence of nature and the interactions of everything in it, define that when our material-brain dies, so do its immaterial-byproducts. By understanding and by accepting this simple yet dislikable fact about our brain, our mind, and our existence; only then, we can learn to begin our fact-based personal-transformation. By learning to deal with reality based on how reality is, rather than based on how we would like for reality to be; we will get on the path of facing, resolving, and improving the difficulties of our lives more cleverly and more efficiently. The only way to deal with reality as reality is, rather than to deal with reality as we would like it to be, is to think factually, instead of thinking emotionally. Facts and reality don't care about our feelings or our likes; hence, we must learn to generate feelings that are based on factual-thoughts, rather than generate nonfactual-thoughts to rationalize and support our desired-feelings.

We must learn to adapt our feelings to facts, and not to force facts to adapt to our feelings.

For existential discussion, whether the mind or consciousness still exists for minutes after clinical death, doesn't matter; because, what matters is what is the quality, value, and effectiveness of that consciousness. Even if we are somehow conscious for a period of time after death, we cannot think to function; which means, consciousness without the ability to engage in thinking is not a quality-consciousness. The most important aspect of consciousness, which seems to get overlooked in heated discussions of the emergence of consciousness, is the quality and value of our consciousness and our mind while we are alive. Regardless of what the definition of consciousness is or how consciousness emerges, what matters is how effectively do we use and apply our consciousness; and how does our consciousness provide us with a fulfilling-existence.

Thoughts are non-physical or immaterial, but our thoughts are as a result of our physical or material-brain's activities. Our material-brain can only be active when we are alive; therefore, a normal-functioning person that is alive can think, feel, and engage and interact, but a person that is dead cannot do so. Although it is culturally and even personally common to think that, at the time of death, something immaterial separates from the body; no such thing is factually true. The reason a dead person cannot think, feel, or interact is because the dead person's physical-brain has stopped functioning; and as a result of its lack of function, no consciousness exists, hence, no mind exists, therefore, no thoughts, no feelings, and no actions could be generated. Thoughts, information, and knowledge stop existing after death, if not shared with others, or if not preserved or stored in a physical or material format such as writing, audio, video, etc. If Shakespeare, DaVinci, and Darwin did not record their thoughts in a preservable format; we would not be able to now call upon their immaterial separated souls to learn of their thoughts and findings. Therefore, when a person dies, so does the Self, because the *"Self-Cycle"* stops.

Theory of Self-Relativity defines the "self-cycle" as "the chain of events that transfer the activities of our physical-brain into the expressions of our self-existence."

The stages of self-cycle: Our brain, via its consciousness, connects to the external world through awareness, perception, and interactions as it shapes our mind and our thoughts. Subsequently, our thoughts create our feelings which influence our reasoning and decision-making; in-turn, leading to our behavior and further interactions with our Self and with everything and everyone else. Our brain processes the information received from these new internal and external interactions and repeats the self-cycle. This repetition of the self-cycle and its stages is what drives us forward in life and through the passage-of-time as we age.

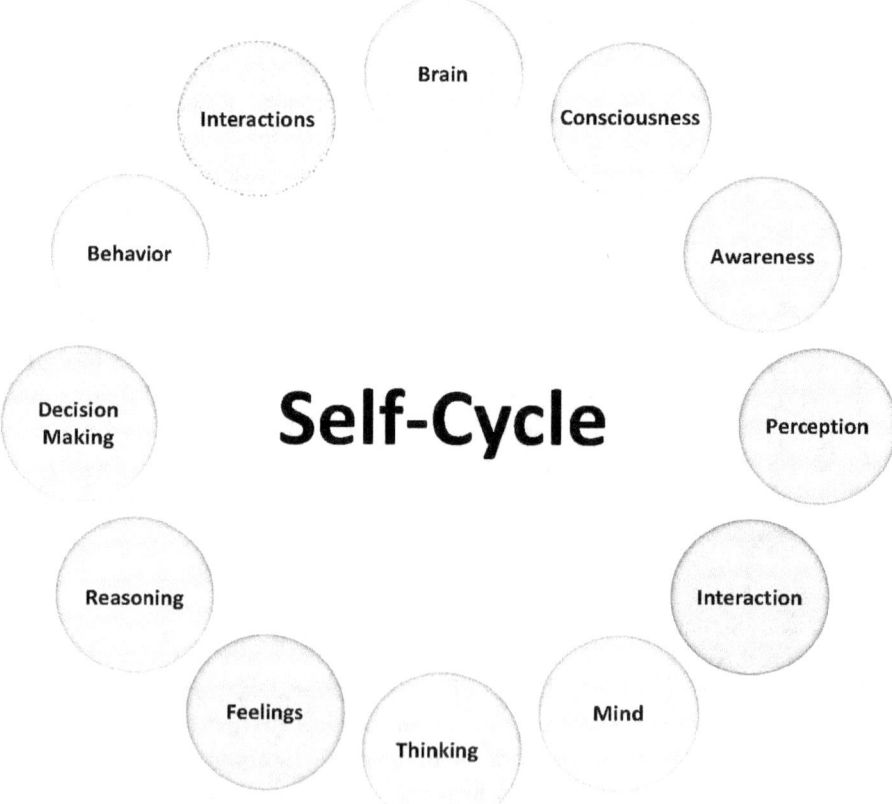

Humans make functioning "things" that are not only structurally and ergonomically similar to the way humans themselves have evolved; but the components of the things that humans create have similar functions to the way humans operate. The reason humans have certain anatomical characteristics and intellectual abilities that have changed and improved over time is not by accident; it is as a result of evolution to better adapt and more efficiently function with The-Universe. It is for this reason humans make things that are similar to themselves. These similarities are not because humans like to duplicate themselves; but they take shape because nature and The-Universe require functioning things to have certain characteristics in order to compatibly function with The-Universe, and with the laws-of-physics that govern The-Universe.

This human creativity became most evident as human-beings began to incorporate science and technology into their existence. Technology requires an energy source and physical-housing of components which produce advanced or intelligent immaterial-functions that result in improved outcomes. Whether it is our personal-computer or the car we drive, they are made of a body-type structure which store their operational components, and they use energy to run their operations.

For example, when compared to a personal-computer, we recognize the following parallels and similarities with humans:

1. Being alive is like having the power-source turned on. As long as we are alive and we can consume food and get energy to our body, and especially to our brain, we are like a computer that is on by being connected to an energy source.

2. Our physical-body, which contains our brain, is like the computer's physical casing, keyboard, and outer-shell, which contains its hardware such as the hard-drive.

3. Our physical-brain is similar to the computer's hard-drive.

4. Our consciousness, our mind, and our thoughts are similar to the computer's software and operating systems.

5. Our memories and experiences are like the documents and files created and stored in a computer.

6. Our decision-making and behavior, where we reach conclusions and take action or inaction, are like the computer's functions and processes. As our mind thinks and creates new experiences and memories, these experiences and memories get filed away in our brain's memory storage as new files; which in-turn, increases the information and knowledge base of our mind.

1.	Life	1.	Power-Source
2.	Body	2.	Computer Casing, Keyboard, etc.
3.	Brain	3.	Hardware & Hard-Drive
4.	Consciousness, Mind & Thoughts	4.	Software & Operating-System
5.	Memories & Experiences	5.	Documents & Files
6.	Decision-Making & Behavior	6.	Computer's Functions & Processes

When the computer is turned on, within seconds, its functions come together and load for operation. The operations and functions of a computer cease when the computer is turned off. When the computer is off, these operations do not go into another state or dimension; they just turn off and cease to operate. Simply stated, when we turn off the computer's hardware, the software ceases to function; but the software, its memory, and its files do not go anywhere.

Same thing is true with our brain. When our brain stops functioning, our memories, experiences, consciousness, mind, and thinking ability will all turn off and will cease to exist. Our life, which continues as a result of the energy in the food we consume, is the power-source for our brain and consciousness; just as electricity is the power-source for a computer. Without life and without energy, neither us nor the computer could operate. Similarly, our memories and experiences stay imbedded in our brain just as documents and files stay imbedded in a computer's memory; neither could be accessed if no life or power goes into it.

This is the dislikable and uncomfortable truth about the realities of our Self; the fact that we are mortal, and at some point, when the power-source to our brain goes out, our life will end. Since mortality is and has been a difficult and dislikable factual-truth for humans to accept; we, as humans, have devised delusional and nonfactual ways to not only try to deny and ignore this uncomfortable reality, but we have attempted to create an alternate nonfactual-reality by believing that we will exist in an immaterial-state or supernatural-form after we die. It is uncomfortable and scary to think that when life ends, all that is our Self will also end; however, all facts and evidence point to this dislikable reality. When we die and when our brain dies; so do our consciousness, our thoughts, and our self-existence.

Immaterial-byproducts cannot independently exist without the activities of their underlying material-causes.

Immaterial-byproducts are intangible and completely reliant on the existence and function of their underlying material-causes. For example, the wind which is invisible, is formed as a result of differences in atmospheric pressures in different areas. When the atmospheric pressures of air changes, as the air molecules in an area become more active or hotter than the air molecules in another area; this differential in temperature or molecular activity causes the air molecules to move from higher pressure areas to the lower pressure ones. Thus, the movement of the "material" air-molecules in the atmosphere creates the "immaterial" wind. The wind is the immaterial-byproduct of the material air-molecules' activities. When the material-molecules of air slow-down their movements and enter into a more stable state or equilibrium; the immaterial-wind simply "dies-out." This stabilization occurs when the temperature of the air molecules become more uniform. Same holds true for our consciousness, our mind, our thoughts, our feelings, and our self-existence. Just like the wind, when the material-brain stops its activities, its immaterial-life's functions "die-out." Neither the wind, nor our consciousness, or our thoughts go anywhere; they simply cease to exist.

The formation of the invisible-wind is an analogy that demonstrates how consciousness, mind, thoughts, and feelings arise. Although immaterial-byproducts are invisible and have no physical characteristics; it is important to note that "immaterial-byproducts" are not "immaterial-things." No such thing as an immaterial-thing could exist, because an immaterial-thing, unlike immaterial-byproducts or immaterial-processes, would not have to be reliant on the existence of an underlying causal material-entity. Although non-existent, immaterial-things could hypothetically be self-sufficient and without reliance on an underlying cause; but, immaterial-byproducts or immaterial-processes could only exist because of an underlying material-cause.

Theory of Self-Relativity defines an "immaterial-thing" as "something that is not made of matter, and which could exist independent of matter."

Since The-Universe is matter-based, everything in The-Universe can only be matter-based, hence, everything is made of atoms; therefore, everything in The-Universe is governed by and follows the laws-of-physics. The only way that an immaterial-thing could exist would be for it to exist outside the laws-of-physics; which means it would have to defy the nature of existence by not being made of particles or atoms. Therefore, an immaterial-thing would be something that is not made of matter, which means it is not made of atoms; thus, it would not be able to interact with matter.

Because of science and physics, we now know that it is the behavior of atoms and their components such as electrons and their interactions together which create everything including our brain's activities. Likewise, it is atoms that are particles that make up everything in The-Universe including our body, our brain, the chair we sit on, and the stars and the planets that make up The-Universe. Existence and interaction between existing things are processes that happen as a result of the interactions of the particles or atoms of things, and the forces of nature. Although there will be further discoveries in science; all matter, all particles, and all forces that make us who we are, and how we interact with nature at the human macro-level, are already known and have been discovered. No new particle or force discovery will change our understanding of how atoms that make up matter operate. We have all the formulas to know how atoms behave and how matter interacts; therefore, there are no more new discoveries that would change that knowledge. As stated, any new discovery of particles or forces will be the discovery of particles and forces that are either too weak to interact with the atoms in our brain, in our body, and with The-Universe; or they are too unstable to exist long enough to interact with the atoms of our brain, our body, and everything else in The-Universe. Therefore, no immaterial-thing could exist that could react with the atoms of The-Universe which could influence our mortal existence or could create an immaterial form of existence after we die. For something to be an immaterial-thing and for it to exist outside the laws-of-physics which govern nature; this immaterial-thing would have to be *"Supernatural."*

A supernatural-thing or a cause is something that is outside the applicable laws-of-physics which govern The-Universe and everything in it. Supernatural things such as ghosts, spirits, souls; or mysterious-energies such as personal-energy, vibrations, and other immaterial-things and unprovable causes are as a result of human imaginations and fabrications, or as a result of human ignorance and lack of knowledge about how the laws-of-physics govern nature. Although scientific and material-based hypothesis are similarly thought of and originated by humans in the mind; unlike supernatural claims, material-based hypothesis can actually be tested, falsified, and even proven.

As discussed further in Thery of Self-Relativity, humans have the intrinsic need to find purpose and meaning for things by finding an answer for them. These answers could either be factual as science attempts to provide, or they could be in the form of assumed comforting-thoughts and nonfactual-beliefs. Finding factual answers could be a lengthy process as evidenced by scientific experiments and empiricism. Even when the factual answers and evidence are found, these conclusions are often not the most comforting or likeable answers one would hope for. Since facts do not necessarily mean likeable answers; human-beings have a tendency of either denying the dislikable facts, or they tend to fabricate comforting purpose, meaning, or reason, to alter the perception of the evidence at hand. But more commonly, instead of searching for and discovering the factual-evidence; humans often create an imaginary likeable cause or agent, in order to fill-in the reason or knowledge-gap. This knowledge-gap can be filled with a feel-good imaginary and often supernatural cause or agent, as humans have done for multi-millennia; or one can attempt to fill the knowledge-gap by not only hypothecation, but by testing and by discovering the underlying natural causes.

Science works through the process of falsification, because only one form of fact can exist per situation. Falsification allows for the process-of-elimination, which means science filters-out and eliminates the bad or the not-good answers, until it filters-in the single best remaining answer which is supported by the facts; or at the minimum, which is not falsified by existing information and knowledge. However, simply imagined thoughts and especially long-term held unproven beliefs cannot be tested or falsified through experiments, empiricism and falsification.

Although imagination and the desire to feel good can concoct immaterial-thoughts, beliefs, and agents such as souls, spirits, energies, and even gods; thoughts and beliefs created as a result of desired-feelings or personal-experiences are not necessarily factual-thoughts, therefore, they are not reliable. To prove the factuality of a thing or a thought we must approach it in the same manner that we do in science; by finding and by knowing the supportive evidence for that thing or that thought. If supportive evidence could not be found for that thing or that thought, especially after a lengthy period of time; then that thing or that thought must be considered to be nonfactual, or simply stated, to be untrue. Consequently, if something is supernatural, it cannot be tested or proven to exist; thus, if something cannot be proven to exist, therefore, that something must be considered non-existent.

If we knew of or if we could detect a supernatural-entity; such entity could not be supernatural, it would be natural, because it would have to interact with matter.

Therefore:

If and when supernaturality is proven, it will no longer be supernatural; it will simply become natural.

This is why, Theory of Self-Relativity is founded upon the concept of factual-thinking. Just because something such as consciousness and the mind might be difficult to explain and we might not have the answers for how they emerge; this does not mean that consciousness, the mind, and most importantly, the Self, are supernatural. For the purpose of self-improvement and living the best life possible, we must consider our existence as a mortal and material-based entity; because that is what the facts indicate. Regardless of where and how consciousness emerges, it would be an awful waste of a precious life if we lived our life based on imaginary supernatural or nonfactual-beliefs. The only thing that works best with reality is for us to think factually so that we can transform our Self and improve our life parallel with how reality is, and not as how we would like reality to be. Our life, and therefore our existence, should be based on facts, so that it can harmoniously relate to and interact with The-Universe.

Our self-identity, our sense of Self, and as a whole, our Self begins with our material-brain, and from there, it branches out into its emerging immaterial-byproducts that make us who we are and how we relate to everything and everyone else. By understanding how nature functions and how we function in nature, we can improve our Self by keeping our brain healthy and functioning at its most efficient and clever capacity possible. It is only then that our brain can generate the most factual-thoughts and our most genuine-feelings. Since:

Our mind and our thoughts are the first personally-accessible thing that our brain produces.

Therefore, we must learn to base our thoughts and our thinking on facts. Although we might not be able to modify our physical-brain and we have no control over our consciousness; we can certainly modify and improve how we think. This is how our Self-Relativity is established, because this is how we go through the self-cycle.

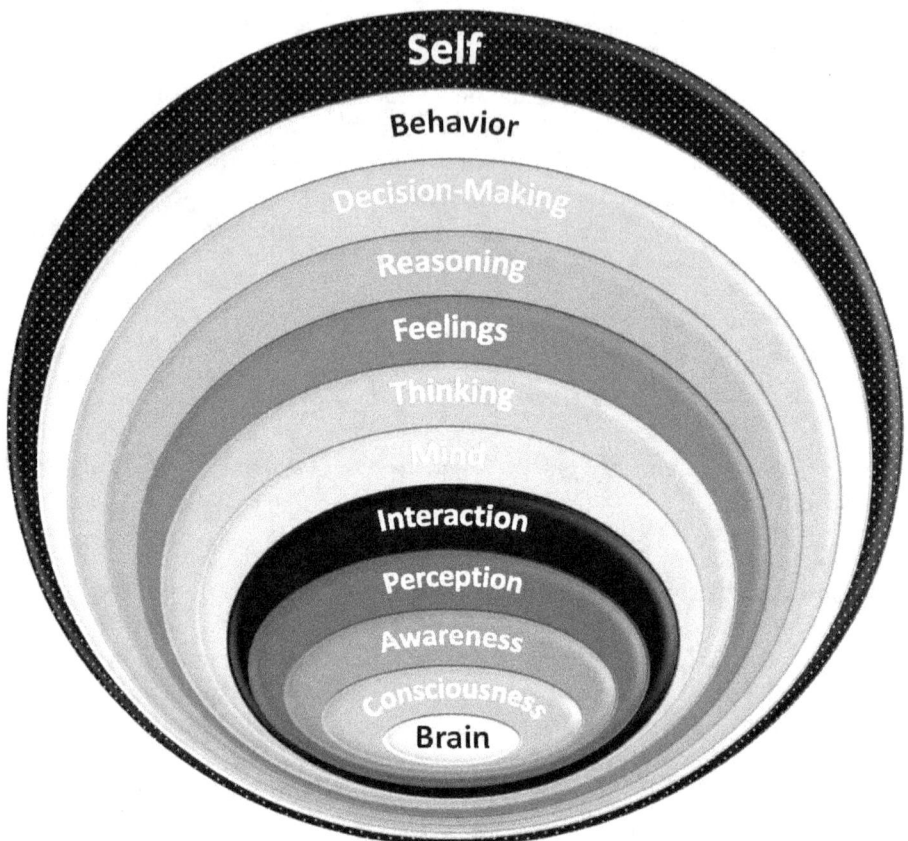

It is important to note that although reasoning is a cognitive-process that leads to decision-making and our behavior; according to Theory of Self-Relativity, reasoning does not immediately follow thinking, but it takes place after feelings. This is why, we have a tendency to commonly deploy emotional-thinking, motivated-reasoning, and rationalization, in order to justify making decisions based on what makes us feel good, rather than based on what is the truth. Therefore, to think properly, in order to generate the proper feelings that lead to our sound decisions and correct actions, we must think based on facts and how reality is, and not based on what we believe or how we feel reality should be.

Our thinking is what makes us who we are and how we live life. Our thoughts not only direct us into making decisions and doing the things that we do; but they are also responsible for how we feel. Our thoughts create our self-identity, and our thinking creates our sense of Self and our self-identity.

I think…therefore I feel…therefore I am

Mindfulness & Thoughtfulness

We spend almost half of our wake time in a state-of-mindlessness or lack of awareness of our thoughts. The rest of the time we are somehow mindful and aware of our thoughts, but we are not fully understanding our thoughts. Being mindful or being in a state-of-mindfulness is commonly referred to as being conscious or aware of something; especially being aware of our thoughts. Popular definition of mindfulness is being aware of our thoughts and being able to observe them without judging them or reacting to them.

Theory of Self-Relativity defines "mindfulness" as "the ability to be aware of one's thoughts."

In many ancient, spiritual, and eastern teachings; mindfulness, through techniques such as meditation, includes the act of observing our thoughts, slowing down our mind, and minimizing our thinking, via patience and focused concentration. Many also suggest getting in touch with our thoughts as well as getting in touch with our feelings. So, we perceptually try to slow-down time by just sitting and by trying to not think at all, or by trying to think of simple things in order to become mindful. Okay, and then what? While these techniques, which are very time and skill intensive "may" help to temporarily minimize some of the effects of our cluttering-thoughts; they do not in anyways resolve or eliminate these cluttering and unnecessary thoughts. Mindfulness alone is like diagnosis without resolution. It is like being a deer in a headlight; it observes and understands that the car is coming, but it doesn't do anything to resolve or eliminate the danger.

To truly be mindful and aware of our thoughts, we need to not only recognize our thoughts, but we must also understand what our mind is doing. Additionally, recognizing and understanding our thoughts by recognizing what our mind is doing is not going to resolve or eliminate our incorrect thoughts. As stated throughout Theory of Self-Relativity, the "why" and the "what" are important first steps in diagnosing an issue; however, the more important aspect of dealing with issues is "how" to resolve or eliminate them. This is why, many self-help and personal-development systems can motivate us by getting us excited about change and transformation, but they fall short of showing us how to do it consistently and with long-term constructive effects. Same applies to our thoughts, which are the core of our self-identity. To be able to put mindfulness into constructive use; mindfulness must be followed by what Theory of Self-Relativity describes as *"Thoughtfulness."*

Theory of Self-Relativity defines "thoughtfulness" as "the ability to be aware of and to understand the factualities of one's thoughts."

According to Theory of Self-Relativity, thoughtfulness is comprised of:

1. Awareness of our thoughts (or mindfulness).
2. Understanding of our thoughts.
3. Verification of our thoughts for their factuality.

Unlike standalone mindfulness, which at best tries to observe our thoughts; thoughtfulness, which should always succeed mindfulness, allows us to not only be aware of and to understand our thoughts, but it uses our thought-awareness to organize, resolve, or eliminate our cluttering, our repetitive, and most importantly, our nonfactual-thoughts. Mindfulness allows us to become aware of and to observe our thoughts; however, thoughtfulness allows us to evaluate and understand our thoughts so that we can then properly act on those thoughts.

As discussed, we are generally more in touch with and aware of our feelings than we are with our thoughts; hence, we are more aware of how we feel rather than how and what we think. This is why, our instantaneous, impulsive, and immediate reaction is inclined to minimizing negative-emotions, so that we could feel better. Although our feelings, which are caused by our thoughts, should always take a back-seat to our thoughts when it comes to decision-making and behavior; we are rarely able to slow-down our feelings in order to get in touch with our thoughts. Therefore, when we feel something, especially something dislikable, we want to act or react quickly so that we can minimize or eliminate that negative-feeling. We intuitively focus on making the feeling better; instead of addressing, resolving, or eliminating the cause of the feeling. However, this is incorrect, because, as discussed throughout Theory of Self-Relativity:

A feeling is a message or a symptom of an underlying cause.

Theory of Self-Relativity categorizes the causes of our feelings binarily:

1. **Tangible-Feelings:** Theory of Self-Relativity describes tangible-feelings as feelings which are triggered by a tangible cause. For example, a tooth-ache, a tickle, a hug, etc. Tangible-feelings are commonly associated with a physical cause, and they are generally experienced through our five senses.

2. **Intangible-Feelings:** Theory of Self-Relativity describes intangible-feelings as feelings which are triggered by an intangible cause. For example, jealousy, sadness, happiness, etc. Intangible-feelings include and are synonymous with our emotions, and they are _always_ associated with the same immaterial-cause. This immaterial-cause of our intangible-feelings or our emotions is always a "thought."

Since our emotions or our intangible-feelings are always caused by an underlying-thought; therefore, our feelings themselves can lead us to identify their underlying causal-thoughts much faster than any old-fashioned mindfulness or mediation technique could. Theory of Self-Relativity defines this quick way of using our feelings to become aware of our causal-thoughts as *"Modern-Mindfulness."*

Theory of Self-Relativity defines "modern-mindfulness" as "the ability to become aware of and to recognize one's thoughts through one's feelings."

Theory of Self-Relativity's *"Cognitive-Cognition-Technique,"* which is described in detail throughout its teachings, enables us to implement modern-mindfulness in an intuitive and structured format. The Cognitive-Cognition-Technique teaches us that instead of using our feelings to quickly behave (act or inact); we use our feelings to evaluate and understand the thoughts which are causing those feelings. When we evaluate our thoughts, the only criteria that is used to understand our thoughts is their factual-value. If a thought is based on facts and evidence, then that thought is what Theory of Self-Relativity defines as a *"Factual-Thought."* However, if a thought could not be supported by facts and evidence, then according to Theory of Self-Relativity, that thought is a *"Nonfactual-Thought."* If a thought is a factual-thought, we will then accept that thought and proceed to taking an action or we will abstain from taking action (inaction). However, if the thought is a nonfactual-thought, we will then proceed to dismiss the thought, which means we would not take any action. When we dismiss the thought that is causing our feeling, our feeling will automatically disappear; hence, we would no need to take any action. It must be noted that dismissing a thought should only occur if the thought is determined to be nonfactual; therefore, dismissing a thought is not the same as ignoring or denying an uncomfortable factual-thought.

How we think is important to what we do.

Therefore, to make best decisions and to take proper action or inaction, we must become aware of our thoughts, and we must ensure that our thoughts are based on facts, and not solely based on feelings.

Our behavior does not represent, nor does it tell us what we are thinking; our behavior tells us how our brain has responded.

Sometimes the evidence for a thought might not be readily available; therefore, we must take some time to find the facts behind our thoughts. However, if after a certain amount of time we cannot find the supporting facts for a certain thought, we should then consider that thought to be potentially nonfactual, and we should proceed to dismiss it, or at the minimum, we should put less value on it. Nonfactual-thoughts are often assumed, perceived, or imagined; and commonly, such thoughts are created in order to support, rationalize, or reinforce a desired-feeling. Feelings are not supposed to create thoughts; thoughts are supposed to create feelings. Therefore, by understanding the factual-value of our thoughts, we can then parallel our thinking and our existence with how reality is, instead of how we would like reality to be.

Since we behave based on how we feel and since our feelings are created by our thoughts; when we feel something negative, our first instinct is to do something to feel better, or at the minimum, to do something to feel less-bad. However, as discussed, if we cannot identify the causal-thought of a feeling, we should not take action until we find the causal-thought. This need to constantly intervene and take quick action in order to correct an uncomfortable situation or a dislikable-feeling is one of the main reasons we make so many mistakes. Intervening and taking action gives us a sense of being in control; hence, the need to do something to quickly feel better is like an instinctual urgency. Theory of Self-Relativity describes this need to act as *"Self-Interventionism."*

Theory of Self-Relativity defines "self-interventionism" as "the urge to take an action in order to improve a dislikable-feeling or an uncomfortable-situation."

Instead of needing to intervene and act, by recognizing the underlying thought which is causing our feeling; we can often realize that the thought is faulty and nonfactual, thus, we can abstain from taking an action and making a mistake. As discussed in detail throughout Theory of Self-Relativity, we have more negative-feelings than positive-ones; therefore, our natural and desired tendency is to do something to minimize the negativity immediately. Often, these negativities result because of an incorrect and nonfactual-thought that we are thinking, which itself could have been falsely fabricated because of a previously uncomfortable feeling. Therefore, instead of having to take an action to try and feel better, we should routinely evaluate our thought, and if proven to be nonfactual, we should dismiss the faulty thought. When we dismiss our faulty thought because of its nonfactuality; our negative-feeling will automatically disappear. By dismissing the faulty or nonfactual-thought and by removing our negative-feeling, there would be no need to take any action. Since we have more negative-feelings and more nonfactual-thoughts which are causing our negative feelings; this means we should more frequently consider taking inaction, instead of having to continuously take action.

Sometimes, the hardest thing to do, is to do nothing.

According to Theory of Self-Relativity, we not only have more negative-feelings than positive ones; but we also have more nonfactual-thoughts than we do factual ones. The reason we have more nonfactual-thoughts is because many of our thoughts and beliefs are self-generated as a defense-mechanism to make us avoid pain, to make us feel good, or at the minimum, to make us feel less-bad. In other words:

The need to feel good versus the necessity to think well is a core factor that inhibits change and self-improvement.

When we feel negative, we try to quickly come up with thoughts and actions that help us feel better. However, doing things to feel better quickly does not mean doing the right thing. Since action to improve takes time, we try to quickly feel good by creating comforting-thoughts and beliefs; yet, we often end up feeling worse, because, since we didn't correct the cause of the negativity, the negativity returns after the cover-up effect of the comforting-thoughts dissipate. However, when we use modern-mindfulness to recognize our thoughts, and when we use The Cognitive-Cognition-Technique to filter out the nonfactual-thoughts; that is when we act properly, because our thinking-system becomes simpler, more focused, and more efficient. This is why, just being mindful does not resolve anything. Mindfulness must be followed by thoughtfulness; and furthermore, it must be followed by action or inaction, in order to resolve or eliminate the causes of our troubling-thoughts.

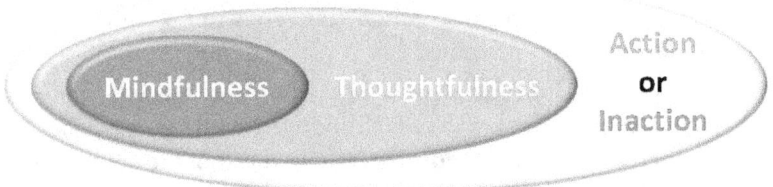

Being only mindful is to be conscious, and to observe and to gain information about something; however, being thoughtful is to be able to understand, process, and apply the observed and gained information. Since we now live in a faster moving technology and information-based society, it is only natural that we need to process information quicker, faster, and with less-clutter. This could only be achieved by being able to "quickly" identify thoughts and problems that need to be resolved or eliminated. Although modern-mindfulness will get us to recognize and sort out our thoughts faster; as stated, simply recognizing our thoughts is not enough. We must learn to understand our thoughts so that we can take proper action or inaction based on the factual-value of those thoughts. Modern-mindfulness could only become effective if it is followed by a similar quick and clever thoughtfulness mindset. Theory of Self-Relativity defines this form of thoughtfulness as *"Modern-Thoughtfulness."*

Theory of Self-Relativity defines "modern-thoughtfulness" as "the ability to quickly and cleverly recognize, analyze, and act upon the factualities of one's thoughts."

Modern-thoughtfulness allows us to understand and evaluate our thoughts quickly, cleverly, and with less-clutter. This analysis and understanding is simply done by evaluating the factualities of our thoughts; and nothing else. The purpose of modern-mindfulness, followed by modern-thoughtfulness, is to identify the factualities of our thoughts in order to quickly and cleverly eliminate or resolve the nonfactual-thoughts. When we eliminate or resolve our thoughts, the genuine feelings generated as a result of addressing our remaining thoughts will lead us to take proper action; or the elimination of our nonfactual-thoughts and their resulting feelings will cause us to not act. As discussed, feelings are generated by thoughts, while action or inaction are as a result of feelings. When there is no thought, there will not be a feeling, and when there is no feeling, there will not be the need to take action.

Theory of Self-Relativity defines the difference between ancient and modern mindfulness and thoughtfulness techniques as follows:

1. **Ancient Mindfulness and Thoughtfulness** (Minimally-effective but mostly ineffective):

   o **Ancient-Mindfulness:** Attempts to slow-down the mind in order to create awareness, through time-consuming and skill-intensive, yet ineffective methods.

   o **Ancient-Thoughtfulness:** Focuses on observing thoughts, and it attempts to slow-down thinking. Majority of mainstream and ancient techniques do not give us the tools to develop our skills necessary to resolve or eliminate our thoughts; instead, they attempt to do the impossible task of slowing down our thoughts, or in extreme and unrealistic cases, they try to teach us to not think.

2. **Modern Mindfulness and Thoughtfulness** (Effective):

   o **Modern-Mindfulness:** Quickens the mind by creating awareness of our thoughts, through the quick and easily accessible gateway of our feelings.

   o **Modern-Thoughtfulness:** Quickens the mind by understanding the observed thoughts through evaluation of their supportive facts and evidence. Factual-thinking enables quick and efficient filtering of our thoughts, and in-turn, factual-thinking guides us to behave based on the factual-value of our thoughts.

Contrary to ancient techniques and majority of mainstream teachings of slowing down our mind; according to Theory of Self-Relativity, the correct way of dealing with our thoughts must enable the quickening of our mind and our thinking-system, not slowing it down. Our mind is a thinking-machine and its job is to think and to process information. Slowing down our mind or getting our mind to think less is completely contradictory to the nature of how our mind operates. This is why, ancient techniques such as meditation and other mind-slowing techniques are ineffective, frustrating, and they leave more unimproved and depressed people behind than they actually help them. Meditation is simply a relaxation or retreat method that requires lots of commitment and down time in order for us to try to extract some of its inefficient thought-management benefits.

The mind is a thinking machine, and its job is to think quickly, cleverly, and efficiently.

Mindfulness should not be an arduous and time-consuming method of observing our thoughts; or not thinking of our thoughts. Mindfulness, in the modern-era, must be achieved quickly in order for it to get us to resolve or eliminate cluttering, repetitive, and nonfactual-thoughts; on-the-go. To implement them properly, both modern-mindfulness and modern-thoughtfulness require awareness; which means, they require conscious attendance. Although initially, when learning how to implement modern-mindfulness and modern-thoughtfulness, we will have to do it consciously; the uniqueness of learning to be mindful through our feelings and to be thoughtful through factual-thinking is that, in due time and with proper practice, the conscious effort should become more intuitive and nonconscious. Mindfulness is the awareness and observation stage; and thoughtfulness, which follows mindfulness, is the understanding and implementation stage of what mindfulness has uncovered.

Modern-Mindfulness	Modern-Thoughtfulness
1. Consciousness	1. Consciousness
2. Awareness	2. Mindfulness
3. Observation	3. Understanding
4. Identification	4. Cognition
5. Information-Stage	5. Knowledge-Stage
6. Analytical-Thinking	6. Critical-Thinking

This is why, the key to becoming self-aware is not to try to think less or to not think at all. The key to self-awareness and self-improvement is to think faster, cleverer, and more efficiently. This could only be accomplished by training our mind to evaluate our thoughts factually, and to resolve or eliminate our thoughts based on their factual-value.

Millennia ago, in ancient civilizations, be it in the mountains of Tibet or in the deserts of the Middle-East, people did not have much to do, and they did not have much to think or worry about. People had lots of down-time to commit to just sitting there and observing their few thoughts and concerns. They did not have their end of the month obligations such as rent, car-payments, credit-card payments, and other recurring financial-commitments; hence, most of the thoughts that they tried to observe without resolution did not lead to any actual repercussions if left unresolved. However, in the modern-times, no matter how much we sit in silence and try to count our breathing and observe our thoughts; our bills are going to be due, and our problems are still going to exist. While meditation and ancient-mindfulness might be good relaxation and unwinding practices; meditation and ancient-mindfulness are not going to solve the problems and concerns that are on our mind.

This is why, according to Theory of Self-Relativity, meditation, especially long-term meditation, when used primarily as a mindfulness technique instead of simply a relaxation method; becomes impractical, inefficient, and it has minimal benefit-to-cost ratio. Contrary to popular belief, meditation cannot put us in a state of not-thinking; because our mind is a thinking-machine and it is an impossibility to try to get our mind to not think. To slow-down our thinking or to try to get our mind to not think is like trying to get a lion to become an herbivore; it simply cannot happen.

Our mind is a thinking machine, and its job is to think.

Meditation or ancient-mindfulness, relative to modern-mindfulness and modern-thoughtfulness, is similar to what homeopathy and other pseudoscience-based healing techniques are to modern-medicine. Homeopathy, which is a form of ancient alternative-medicine and a branch of pseudoscience, claims if we dilute substances or medicines, they will become more effective in healing. Not only there has been no evidence for this claim; but all evidence is contrary, as it demonstrates that homeopathy is nonsensical and could endanger a person's health, and even life, when used instead of science-based modern-medicine.

If homeopathy and other pseudoscientific healing methods were truly medicine, and if they were truly effective; they would not be categorized as alternative-medicine or as pseudoscience. When alternative-medicine is proven with facts and evidence to be effective, it will no longer be categorized as alternative-medicine; it will simply become medicine.

Alternative-medicine treats the symptom via the placebo-effect, instead of treating the cause, which is what modern-medicine does via the alteration of disease at the molecular level. Alternative-medicine and other pseudoscientific methods are popular as a result of us wanting to believe the impossible, because it feels good; which reverts us back to the placebo-effect. Therefore, pseudoscience and the power of placebo-effect is often associated with some kind of deception; either inflicted by others, or self-inflicted in the form of self-deception. Pseudoscientific claims are abundant in the fields of motivation and personal-development, because such claims capitalize on the susceptibility of those who are desperately seeking to find answers for their difficulties and who are hoping to live a more fulfilled and happier life.

Same holds true for ancient methods of mindfulness and meditation. According to Theory of Self-Relativity, meditation is actually a mechanism of "distraction" of our thinking; because, what is the most common suggestion at beginning of a meditation session? Close your eyes and "think of":

- Your breathing, or
- Being in space, or
- Being on a quiet beach, or
- Being on a mountain top

Therefore, meditation is a form of distraction through the power of suggestion; because in order to meditate, we are actually advised to "think" of something!

This something is usually peaceful, non-chaotic, and singular; hence, true meditation is not disengaging from thinking, but it tries to make us think of alternative and easy on the mind thoughts. Meditation, when effective, works by attempting to interrupt and distract our repetitive thoughts; not to abstain us from thinking. We do not need meditation to interrupt our thoughts; we can also interrupt our repetitive-thoughts through dissociation, distraction, and denial, which are all unhealthy forms of avoiding reality. Or, we can choose to interrupt our repetitive-thoughts through healthier routines such as working out, reading a book, or watching television. Assuming that we could even succeed in interrupting our thoughts with meditation and other healthy and unhealthy practices; those thoughts return as soon as we pick up our life's routines after the meditation session ends. The key to thought-management should not be to interrupt and pause our thoughts; but it should be to understand and act upon them so that our distracting and unnecessary thoughts resolve or eliminate without returning.

In the modern-times, meditation might be somehow more effective for ultra-wealthy people who have the luxury to dedicate their time and resources to such trendy luxuries; however, for the majority of people, such time and money would be better spent in learning on-the-go thought-management and improvement skills. When we have modern-day obligations and responsibilities, it is impossible on a consistent and sustained long-term basis, to disengage from cluttered-thoughts and to become a singular thinker. Regardless, no matter how hard we try to slow-down our thinking-machine, also known as our mind; we are not going to succeed in resolving our issues and problems. Because when we come out of our meditation-zone, our body-massage session, our workout class, or our substance-induced state-of-mind; we will still have to deal with resolving or eliminating our problems and obligations.

This undermining of meditation as the secret to fulfillment is not in anyways intended to undermine the role of meditation teachers and coaches. Meditation coaches are no different from the position that a therapist is in. Their job is to be the catalyst and the outer voice to help one focus on one's thoughts and to try to minimize one's mental clutter. Most industry professionals, even though they get paid to advocate these services, also believe in the field which they are promoting; but that does not necessarily mean they understand what they are advocating. This takes us back to Einstein's infamous quote, which states: "If you can't explain it simply, you don't understand it well enough." Most promotors of such mystical and mysterious programs either do not understand these subjects themselves and advocate them based on memorization and their own reliance on other-people's hype and advocacy; or they do so intentionally because it is easy to make money by tapping into people's susceptibilities by selling them a bill of goods that requires continuity without reaching any finality.

It is up to us to factually and objectively look at the effectiveness of such programs and services, and to not just accept them because they are difficult to understand, because they sound mystical, or because of their appeal-to-popularity fallacy. Just because our consciousness and our thoughts are immaterial-byproducts of our brain and they are difficult to explain materially; this does not mean that the potential solution to address our thoughts should also be mysterious and difficult to understand. To truly be able to meditate, we must have minimal to no obligations or worries in life. In our modern and fast-paced society; that is almost an impossibility. Meditation is extremely inefficient and impractical, especially in our modern-fast-paced multitasking cultures. To be able to meditate and limit the number of thoughts, we need to invest a great deal of time and effort to be in the right undisturbed environment and to focus our mind to it. This is why, many do not commit to meditation, or they simply give up on it. Meditation is frustratingly similar to other non-cognitive therapy sessions. They are inefficient and impractical; because to get a slight positive result, they need to be repeated continuously. Additionally, the requirements of our lives, such as the need to go to work, interrupt the continuum needed. Thus, most meditation or non-cognitive therapy sessions end with "see you next week."

According to Theory of Self-Relativity, meditation, as a form of self-improvement, simply does not work, or is at best, extremely inefficient; because:

- Meditation takes a long time to achieve any results.
- Meditation is costly when practiced commercially with an instructor or in a class.
- Meditation is costly because of loss of time and productivity.
- The benefit-to-cost ratio of meditation is minimal to non-existent.
- Most who try to practice meditation continuously, spend more time in trying to convince themselves and others of its effectiveness.
- Meditation has a high initial phase of excitement but an even higher churn and drop off rate; not to mention an even higher rate of disappointment and hopelessness associated with its ineffectiveness and failure.

This is why, meditation, living in the moment-of-now, and other new-age spiritual and nonfactual techniques are, at best, simply relaxation and retreat methods which deviate our mind from our real and factual-thoughts and other life's obligations. It is the misleading cultural and social grandiosity of such practices that has left many broken and unimproved individuals behind. Making meditation and similar mystical practices the magical gateway to solving our problems of life leads to nothing but failed attempts of change and improvement. It is one thing to not want to self-improve; but it is a severe emotional and psychological blow when people commit to changing and improving, yet they end up becoming even more hopeless because what they signed up for did nothing but waste their time and money.

Meditation, like working out and massage-therapy, could function as a supportive role to cognitive self-improvement; but not as a primary-solution. Although physical-exercise and healthy diets cannot be compared to meditation, because unlike meditation, they drastically improve one's physical health, and in-turn, one's ability to think effectively; even physical-exercise or healthy living alone will not create proper mindfulness, thoughtfulness, and thinking ability to inherently transform and change the Self. Meditation, just like other calming and retreat techniques, is a method of breaking our continuation of thoughts. Although meditation and other supportive means of relaxation and retreat could help with the process of mindfulness; the main means of making mindfulness effective should be to follow it up with thoughtfulness. The correct approach to focused-thinking for controlling clutter and for bringing the focus onto our thoughts, is to have a cognitive and pragmatic system that can be applied broadly, systematically, and on-the-go. To do so, we need to learn to control and unclutter our thought-processes faster; not to slow-down our thinking.

In the modern multitasking era, efficient and focused thinking is what we need. Meditation, and even certain forms of therapy, attempt to slow-down thinking in a controlled environment by minimizing external influences so that we can get in touch with our thoughts. Ancient practices such as meditation, when compared to modern quick and clever thinking strategies, is like riding a mule to get to a destination, instead of using a car or other means of modern motorized transportation. Unlike the modern-times, in the older-times when meditation originated, life was much simpler and much slower-paced. Additionally, the human population was fewer, metropolitan areas were not as large, and most importantly, technology was not as advanced; therefore, the pace of life itself was much slower.

The slower pace of life, the fewer technological achievements, and the lack of scientific knowledge, limited people's thinking and understanding to be based on perception, rather than based on cognition and evidence. This slow pace of life and lack of understanding of how humans functioned and how they related to everything else allowed for imaginary beliefs and associated rituals to become widely accepted practices. However, since times have changed and humans have exponentially advanced their pace of activities and their level of knowledge; using meditation to deal with thoughts is outdated, inefficient, and most of all, impractical.

Just as modern urbanites rarely use a mule to commute from one place to another, people should also not be using meditation to get in touch with their thoughts or to try to resolve them. We can use a mule to ride on a beach when on vacation as a fun activity, just as we can use meditation for relaxation and retreat when we need to downtime; but to make either our primary means of dealing with the modern-times would be inefficient, to say the least. Meditation, like other culturally accepted traditional-beliefs or trendy popular-practices, tends to become an incorrectly accepted fact without its factuality ever being tested for evidence. Just because they have been passed on from generation-to-generation, the acceptability of traditional-beliefs or the popularity of societal-practices does not make them practical or effective. Just because many believe in something, that does not make that thing factually-real.

Fallacy of traditions: It's been always done that way therefore it must be true.

For example, the traditionally accepted association of colored-eggs and the Easter-bunny relative to Jesus Christ and Christianity. Other than biblical hearsay writings of a few individuals from millennia ago, not only there have been no significant evidence about Jesus or the Easter event elsewhere; there is also no mention or association of bunnies and colored-eggs with Easter in the Bible. Yet, the Easter-bunny and colored-eggs have, throughout, time become incorrectly assumed cultural-beliefs as facts regarding Christianity.

To use meditation or other inefficient and nonfactual rituals to address our modern-era daily thinking requirements would be no different than using a mule to commute regularly, or to think that bunnies and eggs are a part of Christianity. Although according to Theory of Self-Relativity, slowing down our thinking or living in the moment-of-now is nothing but a fallacy; regardless, we do not need to slow-down our thinking in order to address our current modern-age faster-paced living requirements. On the contrary, we need to do just the opposite. We must quicken our thinking by addressing our thoughts factually; because an efficient-mind operates best when it is uncluttered and as it is riding the momentum. Mental-efficiency is not achieved when the mind is on standby trying not to think, or trying to think less. A true and applicable modern-day analogy to efficient, quick, and clever thinking is the fact that:

Cars and planes operate most efficiently when they are cruising at faster speeds; not when they are parked idling.

So, the next time we criticize our Self as to why we could not embrace meditation, we must realize that our mind is not programmed to benefit from meditation or other ideological and imaginary rituals; because, such practices are not based on factual-reality, they are simply the imaginary illusions of one or more ancient individuals who did not have much to do in life, and who did not understand how science, nature, and The-Universe actually worked. Therefore, we must realize that our inability to adapt and adhere to meditation is not an indication that there is something wrong with us; it means we are simply normal and not delusional, and what others often advocate for us to do is not in tune with how factual-reality operates.

People who claim highly of the positive and direct transformational benefits of meditation are either:

- Newbies to meditation who are excited to have just committed to this inefficient program; only to abandon the practice in frustration and despair at a later time.
- People who have the financial and time luxury to try to adapt to meditation as another luxurious means of relaxation and retreat, without expecting any life changing resolutionary outcomes.
- Monks and other individuals living downsized lifestyles who have the luxury of dedicating time to just sit there, relax, and not do much.

In conclusion, to deal with and to transform through modern life, we must learn to think quickly, cleverly and efficiently; instead of trying to slow-down our thinking. Factual-thinking, through modern-mindfulness and modern-thoughtfulness, allows us to filter out nonfactual-thoughts and to only allow factual-thoughts to pass through our mind's *"Binary-Filter."* The binary-filter, which is discussed in detail and is a term introduced by Theory of Self-Relativity, is a metaphoric mental-filter which helps us understand how to retain only thoughts which are based on evidence and facts, while minimizing and dismissing nonfactual-thoughts and unsubstantiated ideas, opinions, and beliefs.

Since only one form of fact exists per every situation, and since facts are not open to interpretation; therefore, facts are not open to manipulation. Although facts are not absolute and could be examined, and if necessary, replaced; factual-thinking is about having reasonable confidence in the facts, unless or until falsified. Factual-thinking allows us to effortlessly minimize the effects of cluttering-thoughts by enabling us to focus on addressing only thoughts that truly apply to our life and to our existence. However, it must be noted that:

Facts are not absolute; the only absolute are the laws-of-physics that govern The-Universe.

Theory of Self-Relativity's Cognitive-Cognition-Technique is intended to provide individuals with the tools to develop their thinking-skills for understanding and for implementing their factual-thinking abilities. Therefore, the next time we hear someone praise meditation or living in the moment-of-now as a lifechanging event; we should give it some time and see how long they will stay committed. We will undoubtedly see the same quick drop-off rate as we experienced and witnessed with other nonfactual rituals and practices. When we realize that our inability to understand or implement such nonfactual and fad rituals is not an indication of something being wrong with us; we will then be able to proudly learn to adhere our Self to living our life via factual-thinking and evidence-based reasoning.

Consider this! How come the same cultures that invented and implemented meditation and other ritualistic-practices are some of the least advanced societies in the modern-era? Since they were the discoverers and early implementers of meditation and other ritualistic practices that are touted to be lifechanging; isn't it only logical that these older cultures should currently be the most advanced societies on Earth?

We must use facts and evidence as our only guiding-light in life; because facts and evidence do not lie, distort, or misrepresent the truth. Only one form of fact exists per situation; hence, facts are not open to interpretation,   therefore, facts are not open to manipulation to our liking. Facts are open to examination and facts are even open to replacement should new and stronger facts emerge; however, facts are not open to interpretation. Facts are the only true pathway to being in touch with the factual-reality.

Be mindful through thinking; not through not-thinking.

The Universe & Life

Theory of Self-Relativity makes reference to a multitude of different Universes. These references to different Universes are not the same as the "Theory of The Multiverse" which hypothesizes the potential existence of multiple Universes as described in astrophysics. Different Universes in Theory of Self-Relativity refers to the metaphorical perspective-references to the one and only Universe which we live in. These different relative-perspectives of The-Universe are:

1. **The-Universe:** Is the classic Universe that we are familiar with, which is the physical and matter-based Universe in which everything exists; for all of time.

2. **Our-Universe:** Is referred to "The-Universe" during our lifetime. Our-Universe also consists of how we relate to everything that exists within our lifetime. Our-Universe refers to our local environment as well as objects, beings, and people that we interact with during our lifetime. Our-Universe is local and relative to our lifetime. Our-Universe is sometimes referred to as *"Your-Universe"* when the description is in a second-person "you" reference, instead of a first-person "I or we" reference. Collectively, ours and yours is represented as Our-Universe so that it can encompass singular references to The-Universe relative to the "Self."

3. **Others'-Universe:** Refers to other-people's Self-Universes. Others'-Universe consists of how other-people relate to everything that exists within their lifetime. Others'-Universe also refers to other-people's local environment, objects, and people that they interact with during their life-time. Others'-Universe is local and relative to their lifetime. For example, Jack's Universe relative to us is an "Other-Universe;" and likewise, Our-Universe relative to Jack is an "Other-Universe." Others'-Universe is also sometimes interchanged with "Their-Universe" when the description is in third-person "they" reference.

Theory of Self-Relativity focuses on the two most important Universes which are:

1. **The-Universe:** Everything and everyone that exists relative to one another in all of time.

2. **Our-Universe:** Everything and everyone that exists relative to one's Self in one's lifetime; including one's own existence. Our-Universe is a tiny slice of The-Universe and when we die, it will become a tiny history of The-Universe. Our-Universe includes the events, memories, experiences, places and times we occupy and interact with during our lifetime relative to The-Universe and relative to everything and everyone else.

Our lifetime is a small component of all of time. For now, time, as we know, has existed for about 13.8 billion years. Although science does not know if time began with the Big-Bang, which is when the observable Universe came into existence; for all intents and purposes, we can measure time going back to the Big-Bang which is estimated to be about 13.8 billion years. If we consider our lifespan to be about 80 years, our individual lifetime would be 5.8×10^{-10} or 0.00000000058 of all time that The-Universe has existed. Furthermore, our individual lifetime, and therefore, Our-Universe, will become an even smaller slice of the history of The-Universe and all of time; as time and The-Universe continue to exist well after we die. The-Universe is a continuum and regardless of where and when it started and what will happen to it, our lifetime and Our-Universe is a miniscule and finite segment of that continuum. Our lifetime begins when we are born, and it will end when we die; it's that simple. The-Universe only matters to us when Our-Universe exists as a part of The-Universe; which means when we are alive.

The-Universe is made of matter and matter is made of atoms. All atoms behave the same way regardless of what matter or "thing" they occupy. Although we are human; we are also a "thing" because we are made of matter. Whether the atoms that make up matter are in a rock or they are in our brain, principles of physics apply the same way to all atoms; therefore, everything in The-Universe including humans are atomic, elementary, and natural-based, hence, they are governed by the laws-of-physics that govern The-Universe. Since everything is made of atoms and so are we; thus, The-Universe does not care more about us and our atoms, than it does for anyone or anything else and their atoms.

Although The Big-Bang might not necessarily be the point when The-Universe began, The Big-Bang is the point where our current understanding of The-Universe ends; thus, The Big-Bang is when our current understanding of the origins of The-Universe begins. Initially, the only elements that were present were hydrogen, helium, and a minute amount of lithium. The rest of the elements were created from these initial elements during stars formation, and most importantly, from when the stars exploded. Elements such as oxygen, carbon, and nitrogen, which are the necessary ingredients for biochemistry and for biological life such as humans and other organisms to exist; were all formed as a result of stars formation, but especially as a result of stars explosions. When stars exploded, these elements were spread throughout The-Universe and some ultimately ended up on Earth and in our bodies as the building-blocks of life.

Therefore, every atom in our body was formed and is derived from an exploding star; hence, we are literally star-children. If stars didn't explode, we would not exist; therefore, we are directly connected to the stars and to The-Universe. We are connected to The-Universe and we are relative to everything in The-Universe not in a mystical, mythical, or supernatural way; but we are connected to The-Universe in an atomic, material, and physical way. Every physical thing, including humans exist as a result of the existence of the "physical" or "material" Universe. Thus, The-Universe did not come into existence so that we could exist; we came into existence because The-Universe already existed.

The-Universe does not exist for us to exist; we exist because The-Universe exists.

Although this factual perspective could make us feel not so special in The-Universe; we can make our Self the most special entity that ever lived in Our-Universe, and we can do so by creating our own purpose and by giving our own meaning to our own life. Thus, our purpose and meaning in life should not come from The-Universe or from other externally real or imaginary sources; our purpose and meaning in life must come from within our own Self.

Your purpose is neither found nor given by someone or something; your purpose is created, cultivated, and realized from within.

We are not special to The-Universe because we are nothing but another object made of atoms and particles; however, in Our-Universe, which only exists during our lifetime, we should be the most special entity. As termed by Theory of Self-Relativity, by living a *"centered-self"* life and by making our "Self" the center of Our-Universe; we will learn to cultivate and improve our sense of Self and our self-purpose from within, so that we can be in control and in charge of our own self-created destiny.

Theory of Self-Relativity defines "centered-self" as "placing our self-first before others, but not at the expense of others."

Centered-self is not the same as self-centered or selfish. Both centered-self and self-centered people put themselves first before others; but unlike self-centered people, those who live a centered-self life do not do so without consideration for others, or at the expense of others. Living a centered-self life means to make our Self the most important and most special entity in Our-Universe during our lifetime; because, in order for us to be caring and considerate of others, we must first know how to be caring and considerate of our own Self.

If you can't be good to your own self, you won't know how to truly be good to others.

In order for us to be able to help others, we must first be on sound ground in our own life, so that we don't fall or crumble when attempting to help others. Likewise, in order for us to be able to love others, we must first love our own Self, so that we can love others not as a reason for others to love us back, but to love others because we know how to love our own Self.

When you know how it is to feel something; you will then have a better understanding of how others feel about the same thing.

To treat others and to interact with them in the best way, we must first make our Self strong and special. To truly be special to our own Self means we must look at life with an objective and rational perspective. Objectivity and rationality could only be achieved via evidence-based living. We must learn to think factually so that we can deal with The-Universe based on how The-Universe is and not based on how we want The-Universe to be. We must understand "the fact" that we are not special to The-Universe and that our "life" is simply the process that arises as a result of biochemical reactions. Theory of Self-Relativity's simplest definition of life is:

Life is the byproduct of biochemical reactions.

Therefore, the only thing that is truly special, is our lifetime; which we must deal with from our own factual-perspective, from within the center of our own Self. Our lifetime can be special in The-Universe only if we make it special in Our-Universe and in our lifetime. Since we are not special to The-Universe, hence, it is up to us to make our lifetime special in Our-Universe. Thus, as stated in Theory of Self-Relativity's "Mission-Statement," our mission in life should be:

To live this improbably rare gift of life to its fullest possible potential.

Event vs Process

Self-improvement can only be achieved by making a change. Change is not an "event;" it is an ongoing "process."

Change and improvement are not singular events; they are continuum of events in the process of life.

One of the main reasons self-improvement and personal-transformation have been challenging is because most people seek quick-fixes and instantaneous-gratification, rather than seeking to achieve longer-term and stable results. As described throughout Theory of Self-Relativity, our immediate need and quest to feel good, or at the minimum to feel less-bad, is so strong that we will do anything, including lying to our own Self in order to quickly minimize negativities, and to try to increase positivity. In other words:

The need to feel good versus the necessity to think well is a core factor that inhibits change and blocks self-improvement.

Since facing facts is often an emotionally difficult task because facts that require change are often dislikable and uncomfortable to deal with; the amount of time that we waste in trying to reach quick feel-good results, collectively, adds up to a much larger amount of time wasted without achieving any improvement, than if we would've spent the time to make changes. One of the main difficulties in trying to achieve stable and constant improvement is to learn to commit to an ongoing improving process with a definitive final result, rather than trying to achieve a big-bang result from a temporary event. Although rare, unique, and grand outcomes are hallmarked with an event; such outcomes rarely take shape as a result of a singular event.

An event is a distinct moment which occurs as a result of an ongoing process.

Even The-Universe that we currently live in, which occurred as a result of the Big-Bang, did not take shape at the time of the Big-Bang. The-Universe has gone through a 13.8-billion-year process to be the way it is currently; and The-Universe will continue evolving through this process as it transforms into the future. Similarly, our life began with the event of our conception; however, for us to become the cognizant living being that we are, the event of our conception had to go through the process of our birth, childhood, adulthood, and as it will, our eventual death. Even the moment of our conception was an identifiable event which required other processes to get the egg and the sperm to meet and conceive. We are who we are not because of an event, but because of a process; and we will keep changing and evolving as the process continues. Therefore, an event is simply an identifiable moment or a timestamp which cannot occur on its own without an underlying and an ongoing process.

Theory of Self-Relativity defines an "event" as "a defined moment in the continuum of a process."

Although the events that standout in our lifetime are memorable or identifiable as moments in time; they all resulted and will continue to result because of an ongoing process. For example, our high school graduation was an event that was in the making for over a decade which started when we first entered kindergarten. Therefore, even though we can identify many good and bad events in our life; our life is not simply a collection of events, but it is a continuation of a process.

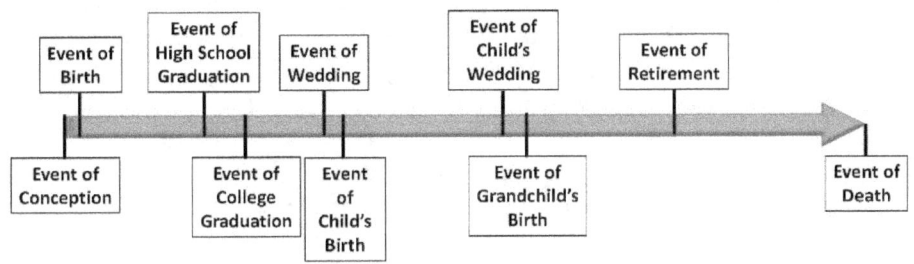

Process (Events) of Life

Human-beings have an easier time reflecting on a certain moment in history as a representation of memory or as a point of change, because timestamping a moment in the past makes it easier to remember that moment than it does to remember the intricate details that it took to get to that moment. We timestamp cyclical recurrences such as birthdays as events, just as we timestamp non-cyclical occurrences such as graduations, weddings, funerals, and other memorable positive and negative moments as events in time. We remember the events with our feelings and based on how they made us feel at that moment; however, what we fail to recognize is that events are easily identifiable moments in time which occurred as a result of a lengthier underlying process. Unless an event somehow occurred as a result of a miracle or a supernatural cause, which science has proven to be impossible; events are simply timestamped moments in the continuum of an ongoing process.

Events do not just happen; they require a prior event and a connecting process to lead to the event. Furthermore, events that directly affect our lives not only require a process, but they also require taking action to initiate the process. Even an event as rare as winning the lottery requires the effort and the process of buying tickets; often for weeks, months, and even for years. Without going through the process of buying a ticket a person will not be able to experience the event of winning the lottery. Although the probability of us winning the lottery is very small, when millions of people simultaneously buy tickets, the probability of someone winning the lottery increases. On an individual basis, that probability for each person is as small as it is for everyone else; however, the collective probability of someone winning the lottery increases as the number of players increase. The more tickets are bought, the higher the chance is for someone to win. Therefore, the occurrence of such a truly unlikely event should not be categorized as luck or a miracle, but it should be considered as a low probability event which arose as a result of the process of many individuals taking action and buying tickets.

Same holds true with other personal-events such as birth, wedding, selling a company for big profit, and so on. They are all events in the timeline of an ongoing process; and that personal-process is our individual lifetime.

Every event is as a result of a previous event in the continuum of the process; thus, to experience favorable and positive events, we must learn to guide the process ourselves, so that the continuum of the process will get us to that event faster, and further. Since events are as a result of a previously initiated event and as a continuum of the process, and since every event is a timestamp in the continuum of the process; therefore, an event, when properly built upon, will get us to the next event in the continuum of the process. As long as we do not accept an event as finality, every event is an *"opportunity"* to build on, so that we can reach a stronger and more favorable next event. Opportunities which lead to change or success are created "by us" as a result of the continuation of events; regardless of the nature of the event.

Opportunities are created by the opportunist.

Success is a process that results from many events of failures and prior successes. As long as we do not accept a failure or even a success as a finality, all we have to do is to learn from the failure or from the success, and to use that failure or success to move along the process to the next successful event. However, when we accept an event, for example a failure as finality; that is how we get our mind stuck in the past and that becomes one of the main reasons that we cannot move forward with time.

Mistakes and failures are simply events in the process of progress and success.

There are no final-events in The-Universe, but there is only one final-event in Our-Universe; and that final-event is our death. Any other event in our lifetime should be viewed as a timestamp or a steppingstone that is used to guide us to the next better event in the process of our lifetime.

As stated, the majority perceive events as standalone occurrences, and because the majority want things to change quickly so that they can feel better quickly; they often chase after quick-fixes in order to experience a favorable event. The reason many cannot reach significant events in their lifetime is because they do not consider events as a timeline in the continuum of a process; they incorrectly believe that events are standalone occurrences and that these occurrences often happen as a result of chance, luck, or even as a result of mythical-origins or actions of supernatural-agencies in the form of a miracle. Since a miracle could never occur;

Theory of Self-Relativity considers a miracle to simply be an unexpected or a low probability event which could also be classified as luck. However, as discussed in later sections, according to Theory of Self-Relativity, there is no such thing as luck, because what seems to be luck, is a matter of a decision, an action, or a positioning by an entity that created an opportunity.

Theory of Self-Relativity defines "luck" as "when determination and action create opportunity."

Therefore:

Theory of Self-Relativity defines a "miracle" as "an unexpected or an improbable event which occurred when action met chance."

Due to the lack of conscious awareness of the relationship between events and processes, many waste their lives hoping and wishing for extraordinary events, such as praying for a miracle, to solve their problems and to make a change in their life. A true-miracle, which is actually an oxymoron, is an extraordinary supernatural-event that is supposed to have occurred or is strongly prayed for or wished for to occur; often involving intervention of a divine, supernatural, or spiritually imagined agency. For this unexpected or strongly wished-for event to occur, such an occurrence would need to suspend and violate the laws-of-physics that govern The-Universe. What many fail to realize, for example, in the event of miracles; is that the bigger the wish or the desire for an extraordinary event is, the more exceptional or extraordinary the process leading to that event would need to be.

Extraordinary events require extraordinary processes.

Therefore, in order for an extraordinary event of a miraculous nature to occur; it would either require an extraordinary process to lead to it, or it would require an extraordinary agent to create it. Since miracles are supposed to be instantaneously standalone events; therefore, by Theory of Self-Relativity's definition of an event and its relationship to a process, a miracle could never take place under the governing laws-of-physics. Additionally, since all events are timestamps in the timeline of a process; in order for a miracle to spring out of nowhere and present itself as an event, the continuum of time, itself, would need to get suspended. Therefore, claimed miracles either never happened, or if a miraculous-looking unlikely event occurred; such a low probability event occurred because of an underlying action and a prior event in the continuum of the process that led to it. If and when a personal miraculous-looking event occurs; such event is simply the result of action taken by the person, or action taken by others, which transpired into the favorable outcome. What often gets labeled as a miracle, would not have been possible if an underlying action was not taken in order for that particular event to occur.

Theory of Self-Relativity considers miracles as stories or illusions that are fabricated by humans as a form of belief; because humans are conditioned to believe that they are special, and that miracles happen especially for them. Case and point, the belief that The-Universe was especially created for humans to exist. Due to this unique but fallacious existential-belief, humans also believe that a supernatural-agent who created The-Universe for humans to exist; is also watching over them and at the most critical time, this supernatural-agent would provide them with a dramatic and much needed miracle.

Outcomes and events do not occur as a result of the intervention of an intentional supernatural-agent; outcomes and events occur as a result of the actions of an intentional natural-agent.

Life's events occur because, us, or something or someone around us, initiated a process that lead to that event. When examined in detail, our behavior, which occurs as a result of our thinking, causes an event, or places us in the path of an event; therefore, to experience favorable events, we must put in effort to start the process of changing things in our favor.

Stop praying and hoping for a miracle, and start by taking action.

Because:

When we pray, we are simply talking to our Self; and if others are present, when we pray, we are trying to influence their emotions through words.

By believing, wishing, praying or waiting for an extraordinary event such as a miracle to occur; all we do is to waste our precious lifetime away with false-hopes, by waiting for something good to happen for us. Instead of hoping, wishing, and waiting for a miracle; we can use our precious time to initiate the process required to lead us to our desired event. As discussed, hope, faith, and beliefs, although in the short-term could be comforting; in the long-term, they have no influence on the outcome of a process. Facing facts is often an emotionally difficult task, because facts that require attention are generally dislikable. Feelings, as important and as integral as they are to our existence, can be destructive if they control our thinking. By continuously wanting to immediately feel good, or at the minimum, to quickly feel less-bad; we could, as we often do, influence our thoughts against facts, evidence, and objective reality.

We self-deceive by thinking "if it conflicts with what I want to be true therefore it must be false."

When we understand that change, improvement, and transformation are not events, but they are parts of an ongoing process; we can then learn to initiate the action necessary to launch the process of change and transformation. However, if we are surrounded by ignorant, false, and intentionally-fallacious motivational teachings that use our feelings to manipulate us into believing in effortless-transformation and overnight-enlightenment; we will then end up wasting a great deal of time, money, and resources in trying to follow these fallacies.

In many motivational teachings, enlightenment is incorrectly, and often intentionally, portrayed as a lightbulb-moment or a magical-event. Just as many do not conceptualize that change and improvement are not momentary events, but they are ongoing processes; most also incorrectly believe that enlightenment is an event that could be traced back to a particular moment in time. Contrary to popular belief, enlightenment and improvement, just like other positive personal occurrences, are not events; they are processes. By portraying enlightenment and improvement as events, many create false-hope that enlightenment and improvement could happen quickly if they wished for it hard enough and if they thought positive-thoughts. We want to believe in enlightenment as an event because quick-fixes feel good, and in theory, they require minimal input; hence, they are preferred over long-term solutions, thus, they are easy to sell. However, comforting-beliefs and false-hopes are not only useless in the long-term; but they quickly lead to severe disappointments and withdrawals when they fail to yield results.

Since true enlightenment, just like true improvement and betterment, is not defined by a moment in time; therefore, enlightenment, just like many other personal-development attributes, is a process and not an event.

Theory of Self-Relativity defines "enlightenment" as "the process of conscious transformation by taking action based on evolving knowledge."

Although on the collective scale, enlightenment is marked by historical timelines where philosophy, science, and reason transformed the way humans began to think; enlightenment, on a personal-level, has incorrectly been portrayed as a light-bulb miraculous moment where something magical or spiritual changed and transformed a person. Unlike sensational and unsubstantiated personal stories, personal-enlightenment does not happen with the strike of a lightning bolt, nor does it suddenly happen overnight after the enlightened wakes up from sleeping on a park-bench. Enlightenment is not an instantaneous event; enlightenment is a process of transformation and change that begins with a person's or people's conscious decision to initiate and to make that change.

Enlightenment and transformation begin and continue to evolve as we open our Self up to learning and gaining knowledge. Since enlightenment happens as a result of learning and gaining knowledge, and since learning is not an overnight event but it is an ongoing process; therefore, enlightenment and transformation are also ongoing and evolving learning processes. The only true form of learning is to seek and find the facts and evidence associated with the subject that we are learning about, and to use these facts to base our thinking and problem-solving abilities upon them. Enlightenment only leads to true transformation when our thinking-system is based on facts and evidence. When we learn to evaluate situations and events factually, we will then become enlightened to not accept baseless-beliefs and nonfactual-traditions.

Factual-thinking minimizes distortion of judgment by uncluttering our thinking, as it enables us to have an objectively-factual perspective of our life and our existence.

Factual-thinking is of utmost importance for living a life in sync with reality and in harmony with The-Universe. To truly succeed in personal-transformation and to truly experience a fulfilling life; we must stop thinking emotionally and we must begin by disallowing our unsupported feelings and emotions to rule our existence. We must learn to become aware of and understand our thoughts that are causing our dislikable and uncomfortable feelings. To control our emotions and to minimize the influence of our feelings on our thoughts, we must do so by identifying the validity and factuality of our thoughts. When we allow only fact-based thoughts to lead to our emotions, we can then make proper decisions and take effective actions.

Changing and improving our thoughts will help to change and improve our feelings; which in-turn, will improve our behavior so that we can create a high-quality life for our Self and for others. Through thoughtfulness and factual-thinking, we can begin the process of change for improving our life and for improving the quality of our emotions.

Factual-thinking enables us to begin the process of creating sequences of favorable events so that our life's process will continue to improve.

Don't wait for an event; begin the process.

Success or failure are events which occur in the process of life. Only death is a final event; hence, everything else is simply an event in the process of life.

Stop waiting for events to happen and begin enjoying the process.

Primitive-Mind vs. Intelligent-Mind

The mind is a metaphor for where thinking takes place.

The-Universe and everything around us changes continuously. Time changes constantly and continuously. Our physical body and brain change continuously as time moves forward. Yet, when it comes to change, which requires mental-input, we tend to resist such change.

The only thing that can resist change is our mind.

Any change that requires active-input by the mind is difficult, because maintaining the status-quo is familiar and comforting. Resistance to change is the primary reason people cannot improve. Change requires action and proper action requires rational and analytical thought-processes. Change, especially changing the routines is difficult, because routines minimize uncertainty; while in contrast, change increases uncertainty. Constancy creates comfort and change creates discomfort, because change exposes us to new unfamiliar variables which could potentially increase the possibility of something going wrong; hence, change could increase the potential for exposure to threats and danger, which in-turn, could compromise our safety. Therefore, by trying to keep things constant, our mind resists change so that it can try to keep us safe.

The reason humans and other intelligent animals prefer routines and they resist change is because routines create familiarity and comfort, while change creates variables, uncertainty, and discomfort. This discomfort, especially in the modern-times, is often perceived rather than it being factual; because our mind wants to minimize new variables which could expose us to negativity, threats, danger, and even pain or death. We create routines, habits, and even rituals because routines, habits, and rituals create familiarity and comfort-zones by minimizing variables and diversities. Although routines are important in creating discipline and efficiency; nonconscious-routines are often created and implemented by our mind in order to keep us safe. Routines that are based on analytical-thinking and which streamline repetitive tasks into efficiency are commonly used to create and increase efficiency and even discipline. For example, getting up every morning at 7 a.m. to be at work at 9 a.m. is a constructive-routine which creates discipline and efficiency, in order to accomplish a task. However, when routines are implemented nonconsciously or when routines are based on nonfactual-thoughts, beliefs, or traditions; such routines often turn into bad-habits and rituals. For example, praying before an exam or a game, or rubbing a rabbit's foot before taking an action, are examples of nonfactual and comforting routines that have turned into rituals.

When routines turn into rituals, that is when we have a higher possibility of creating and adopting bad-habits. We engage in habits because habits are repetitive; however, when habits limit our progress or continuously cause us to make mistakes, such habits are bad-habits.

Mistakes are something we can improve; bad-habits are mistakes we repeat.

Our mind's comfort-level and its primary basic responsibility is to keep us safe. As discussed throughout Theory of Self-Relativity, the mind is referred to as the immaterial-byproducts or the immaterial-process of our material-brain's activities. Since the "mind," itself, is a metaphorical reference to the activities of the brain; Theory of Self-Relativity, for ease of reference, metaphorically categorizes the mind binarily:

1. **The "Primitive-Mind":** *Theory of Self-Relativity defines the "primitive-mind" as "the mental activities that our brain undertakes in order to keep us safe."*

2. **The "Intelligent-Mind":** *Theory of Self-Relativity defines the "intelligent-mind" as "the mental activities that our brain undertakes in order to adapt, change, and progress."*

In primitive-animals, the primitive-mind tries to keep the animal safe by minimizing its tasks to basic needs of finding shelter, finding food and not becoming food, and for procreation. Therefore, the less the animal does and the less the animal exposes itself to the environment, the lower its chances of being exposed to danger would be. This is why, most animals do not evolve intellectually; because their instinctual-need for safety overrides their natural-need for change and progress.

According to Theory of Self-Relativity, the primary reason most animals do not evolve intellectually is because their instinctual-need for safety overrides their natural-necessity for change and progress.

Although humans also have a primitive component to their mind; due to their increasing intelligence and understanding of knowledge, humans can intellectually realize that they must commit to change in order to progress and to improve. Humans can use their intelligence, their planning abilities, and their technology, which is as a result of their intelligence, to minimize danger and to increase safety; hence, they can override their instinctual-need for safety. When the primitive-mind feels safe and as it notices that its basic needs are met, it can then allow the intelligent-mind to take control in order to change and evolve.

The primitive-mind and the need for safety is the main reason we create comfort-zones.

Humans have minimized danger as they have changed, progressed, and evolved through advancements in science and technology. Our intelligent-mind, through these advancements in sciences and technology, has minimized the primitive-mind's safety concerns, by allowing the primitive-mind to take a backseat so that the intelligent-mind could guide and drive forward our thinking. Our primitive-mind's safety concerns have been reduced because we have reduced our exposure to *"Primitive-Dangers,"* by reducing our exposure to the *"Primitive-Agents,"* which are the causes of these dangers. Theory of Self-Relativity refers to primitive-dangers as agents, elements, and situations which have been around as part of the natural-world and the environment around us that could endanger our existence. Primitive-dangers could be wild-animals, lack of food, lack of shelter, lack of reproductive-mate, and other natural and environmental dangers which could cause us harm, or endanger our existence. Primitive-agents could be non-living or living things, including wild-animals and other humans which could harm us or endanger our existence.

Despite the fact that human intellectual advancements have minimized primitive-dangers, such as wild-animal attacks; the primitive-mind is innately programmed to always lookout for danger and negativity, regardless of intellectual, societal, and cultural advancements. To increase our chances of survival, our primitive-mind, which is constantly looking out for negativity, threats, and danger, feels safest when dealing with routines and familiarities; hence why, our primitive-mind resists change. Yet, our intelligent-mind knows that change and progress are necessary for advancement and evolution as they increase our chance of safety and survival. Although the goal of our primitive-mind and intelligent-mind are parallel, which is to improve our chances of safety and survival; they operate in conflict with each other. The primitive-mind is protective, while the intelligent-mind is progressive.

While our-primitive-mind tries to keep us safe by not wanting us to change; our intelligent-mind wants to increase and cushion our safety by creating change.

Although our primitive-mind could ease-up when it senses less danger and negativity; due to its default position, our primitive-mind is always a quick-trigger away from taking over the activities of our intelligent-mind. Therefore, our primitive-mind is always on standby to kick into action. Even when fear and danger are minimized or eliminated; instead of looking for threats and danger, our primitive-mind begins treating lesser negativities as potential threats and danger. The way that the primitive-mind engages in this role of looking out for negativities, instead of danger, is by it engaging in "worry and anxiety." Being in a state of worry and anxiety, places the primitive-mind in a state of standby, instead of it completely turning itself off; because the primitive-mind must always be ready to jump into its safety and protective role to help us react to danger. Since the primitive-mind can never turn itself off, and since the least active state that it could be in is the standby mode; therefore, the primitive-mind constantly interjects itself to ensure safety by inhibiting our attempts to change things.

It is this tendency of our primitive-mind to lookout for danger through fear, and to look for negativities through worry and anxiety, that is causing us to feel more negativities and even more sadness, than we feel positivities and happiness. It is this "safe-keep" innate default-position of our primitive-mind that makes our human innate default-nature of existence to be "negative." Since human-beings are animals, and the primitive concern of all animals is to be safe; animals need to constantly be on the lookout for negativities and danger. Therefore, the default-state-of-existence of all animals, including humans, is to be negative. As discussed in detail throughout Theory of Self-Relativity, we, as humans, are negative by nature and our default-state-of-existence is to be negative; because by being negative and by being worried, anxious, and even fearful, we can be on the lookout to react quickly to any and all dangers that could threaten our safety and survival.

Our primitive-mind does not care if we are happy; all it cares about is if we are safe.

Hence why, as discussed in detail throughout Theory of Self-Relativity:

Negativity is a default state-of-existence, but positivity is only a temporary state-of-experience.

Since modern-humans have minimized exposure to primitive-dangers by reducing fear and concerns for safety; therefore, our primitive-mind is more engaged in the standby state of negative-feelings such as worry and anxiety, than it is for fear. Due to the advancements in science, medicine, and technology, and due to the reduction of primitive-dangers; in the modern-times, we feel more episodes of negativities such as dislike, worry, and anxiety, rather than fearing for our safety. Since it is much easier to trigger negative-feelings of dislike, worry, and anxiety; when these feelings remain unresolved for a period of time, they commonly evolve into fear and concerns for safety. Therefore, if our negative-feelings remain open and are not resolved or eliminated; our primitive-mind will elevate these longer-term negative-feelings to be treated as fear of danger, in order for it to force us to resolve or eliminate them. Theory of Self-Relativity refers to our modern causes of our negative-feelings such as dislike, worry, and anxiety, which trigger the primitive-mind into action, as the *"Modern-Dangers."*

Modern-dangers, just like primitive-dangers, could make quality of life less than optimal and they could also cause a multitude of negative-feelings and outcomes for us. Although primitive-dangers could be directly caused as a result of a primitive-agent; modern-dangers are caused by the scarcity or the absence of the *"Modern-Agent." "Money"* is the modern-agent, which its scarcity causes an increase in modern-dangers; which in-turn, increases our feelings of worry, anxiety, and fear. This increase in worry and anxiety that is being treated as danger, constantly triggers our primitive-mind into action and dominance. While in the primitive-times, the presence of primitive-agents caused our primitive-mind to kick into action; in the modern-times, lack of the modern-agent, or money, causes our primitive-mind to kick into action.

Money's universality has replaced the bow-and-arrow, the cave, and the cowhide stone-age outfit with its buying-power for shelter, food, clothing, and other goods and services. In the primitive-times, humans made their own shelter in order to minimize danger, and they found their own food in order to increase their chances of survival; but in the modern-times, we work and do business, to create income and to increase our financial strength, so that we can use money as a universal-tool in exchange for goods and services. Therefore, the more money we have, the less potential we will have for fear of being exposed to modern-dangers. Although our primitive-mind is by default fear and safety based; in the modern-times, our primitive-mind is more worry and anxiety based. However, as discussed, when worry and anxiety become persistent and unresolved, and as they get elevated to uncontrolled levels such as stress; they trigger fear and safety concerns.

In the modern-times, in order to minimize our primitive-mind's fear and safety concerns; we must find ways to lower the levels of our worry and anxiety. For example, becoming homeless, not having food to eat, and not being a qualified mate who could ensure the surviving and thriving of our offspring are common causes for worry and anxiety. In the modern-times, to minimize such outcomes, we must have and we must increase our access to money. When we have money, we will be able to have the basic necessities that minimize our worry and anxiety from elevating into stress, fear, and concerns for safety. This, in-turn, minimizes the dominance of our primitive-mind.

Although money, or lack of money, is not necessarily the only cause of worry and anxiety; lack of money will unquestionably cause worry, anxiety, and even stress. For example, if we do not have enough money by the end of the month, worry and anxiety begins to kick in, because we will not be able to make rent or mortgage payment. If we do not make rent or mortgage payment, then worry and anxiety turn into stress and even fear as we could be evicted and become homeless, and even go hungry. Therefore, having access to money can minimize the modern causes of worry, anxiety, stress, and fear; which in-turn, could relax our primitive-mind from intervening and kicking into action. Access to money for basic necessities is different than chasing money as a means of self-validation and creating an externally-derived self-identity. This appetite for excess money as a means of self-validation and creating a self-identity façade is discussed throughout later sections of Theory of Self-Relativity.

Money can save you lots of misery, but it can't buy you lasting happiness.

In general, other than not having enough money, the modern-times have significantly minimized our exposure to other agents that could create danger. This decrease in danger in the modern-times is as a direct result of our intelligent-mind's ability to change, innovate, and evolve. Change and innovation are further accelerated by incentivizing change and innovation through financial rewards; thus, money facilitates and accelerates change, innovation, and the evolution of the modern-human. However, even though change, innovation, and evolution lead to progress and improvement; inherently, our primitive-mind does not like change, because change creates variables and uncertainties. Variables and uncertainties increase the potential for things to go wrong, and any such increase in the possibility of things going wrong causes our primitive-mind to take over our intelligent-mind's activities, so that it can try to minimize these variables and uncertainties, in order to keep us safe.

Therefore, while our intelligent-mind wants to continuously change and improve; our primitive-mind is trying to resist change; thus, the battle between the two minds continues. Since the primitive-mind who wants to keep us safe is inherently dominant to our intelligent-mind who wants us to change; if the thoughts that make our primitive-mind increase its activities are not resolved or eliminated quickly, we begin to feel an increase in our negative-feelings. When we begin to feel this negativity, we can resolve and eliminate our negativities in one of two ways. We can either continue changing and making our primitive-mind cause chaos, unless this change can quickly materialize into a favorable outcome; or our primitive-mind will overwhelm our intelligent-mind to the point where our intelligent-mind will give up and will abstain from changing so that our primitive-mind can feel safer. Hence why, most of us have difficulty embracing change, and why instead of taking action to resolve and eliminate the causes of our negativities, many of us choose to create nonfactual-thoughts in order to quickly, yet, temporarily make our Self feel better.

Add to this inherent need for safety, the fact that getting in touch with the causes of our negative-feelings is often a difficult and painful process; consequently, we now have the two main "personal" reasons as to why change and improvement is such an arduous undertaking. As discussed in later sections, the "universal" reasons that change and improvement are difficult are different than the "personal" reasons that make change and improvement difficult. Therefore, the two primary "personal" reasons we do not like to change are:

1. **Introspection:** Which is synonymous to self-inspection, means to look within our Self in order to identify our personal deficiencies and shortcoming; so that we can change, improve, or eliminate these weaknesses. As discussed throughout Theory of Self-Relativity, for many, self-reflection and introspection is an emotionally difficult task to undertake because introspection exposes us to face and accept our dislikable and often painful personal-shortcomings that require change and improvement. Introspection, through self-reflection, requires us to become conscious of our deficiencies and shortcomings by bringing them up from our non-conscious state to the higher-levels of our consciousness.

2. **Primitive-Mind:** As discussed throughout Theory of Self-Relativity, our primitive-mind, which is always on the lookout for negativity and danger, is the default program of our mind. Our primitive-mind does not care if we are happy; all our primitive-mind cares about is if we are safe. Therefore, the primary role of our primitive-mind is to keep us safe and it tries to do so by minimizing our exposure to threats and danger. Change, by-nature, creates variables and uncertainties, which in-turn, could lead to something going wrong; therefore, change itself could increase danger. Consequently, change makes our primitive-mind get worried, anxious, stressed, and even fearful; thus, the primitive-mind kicks into action in order to minimize and prevent any change. Change is inherently contradictory to how our primitive-mind likes for things to be, because our primitive-mind is instinctually programmed to seek constancy and certainty.

The intelligent-mind cannot force itself to take control; it is up to the primitive-mind to allow the intelligent-mind to be in control.

This is why, factual-thinking is instrumental in learning to change and to self-improve. Factual-thinking enables the intelligent-mind to learn to evaluate facts and evidence and to override the primitive-mind's domination through feelings of fear and concerns for safety. By learning, by practicing, and by instinctualizing factual-thinking as the primary means of our thinking and evaluation of the world around us; we can subsequently learn to calm down our primitive-mind's fears.

As we learn to think factually and as we base our decision-making and actions on facts; we will then begin to see positive-change take place, because we will be aligning our Self with the way reality is and not the way we want reality to be. As we solidify the foundation of our actions by basing them on facts, and as we increase the frequencies of positive-outcomes; our primitive-mind will begin to have more confidence in our intelligent-mind, that our intelligent-mind can analyze properly and can make sound decisions. As our primitive-mind learns to trust our intelligent-mind, our primitive-mind will take a less active role in preventing change; thus, it will create less change inhibitive-thoughts in order to try to keep us safe.

Both the primitive-mind and the intelligent-mind have the same objective of minimizing negativity; however, the primitive-mind tries to do so via prevention, while the intelligent-mind tries to do so via progress.

Primitive-Mind	Intelligent-Mind
• Minimize-Negativity	• Increase-Positivity
• Safe-Keep	• Safe-Keep
• Protective	• Progressive
• Anti-Change	• Pro-Change
• Default State	• Controlling State via Thought-Management
• Passive	• Active then Passive via Practice
• Nonconscious	• Conscious then Nonconscious via Practice
• Instinctual	• Intuitive
• Impulsive/Reactive	• Analytical
• Instant-Gratification Based	• Stability Based (not Delayed-Gratification)
• Feeling-Based (Emotional)	• Evidence-Based (Cognitive)
• Fear and Safety Based	• Anti-Worry & Anti-Anxiety Based
• Fight or flight	• Problem-Solving

The intelligent-mind's focus and responsibility is to deal directly with and to resolve the worries and anxieties of the primitive-mind, in order for it to prevent the fear and safety concerns of the primitive-mind from emerging and overpowering our mental-processes. In the modern-times, the intelligent-mind strives to enable us to have access to money so that we do not worry about food, shelter, and other goods and services. Although our primitive-mind is protective versus our intelligent-mind, once we learn to use our intelligent-mind to comfort and resolve the issues concerning our primitive-mind, the primitive-mind will take a backseat; hence, the intelligent-mind will not worry as much about the negative-effects of the primitive-mind.

Our intelligent-mind comforts and calms down our primitive-mind in one of the following two ways:

1. **Deceptive-Thinking (Bad):** The intelligent-mind, through rationalization, can create false-thoughts and fallacious-beliefs to make us avoid pain, to feel good, or at the minimum, to feel less-bad quickly. When we self-deceive by creating nonfactual-thoughts, we might improve how we feel in the short-term, and this might calm down the primitive-mind temporarily; however, when reality clashes with our nonfactual-thoughts as the causes of our negativities still remain unresolved, it is then that the primitive-mind will lose trust and confidence in the intelligent-mind's thinking and decision-making abilities. Once the primitive-mind goes haywire and loses its trust in the intelligent-mind, the primitive-mind is going to take back full control of the situation and it will begin treating even minor negativities such as worry and anxiety as danger; because it simply will not trust the intelligent-mind's decision-making abilities to keep us safe.

2. **Factual-Thinking (Good):** Instead of concocting false-thoughts and fallacious-beliefs in order to try to rationalize our desired-feelings so we can feel better quickly; we can learn to think factually by looking for the facts that are causing our negativities, therefore, we can make changes so that we can resolve or eliminate these causes. Once we think factually and as we resolve or eliminate the causes of our negative-thoughts, we can then truly change and improve our situation and move to correcting the next negativity. As we minimize negativities, we will then become available to experiencing more positivities, and ultimately, experiencing more happiness. By thinking factually, we can put our primitive-mind at ease by making it realize that our intelligent-mind is making safe and sound decisions. By thinking factually and by making sound decisions, our intelligent-mind can create stability and higher levels of certainty; so that our primitive-mind will lessen its reactivities and interventions.

Since our primitive-mind's primary role is to keep us safe, by reacting quickly and often impulsively to minimize danger and negativity; majority of our quick and hasty actions are undertaken without the ability to verify their underlying facts. To react quickly, we use pattern-seeking, pattern-recognition, and other quick-thinking strategies to get away from potential danger; hence why, we often make mistakes in recognizing reality. During the primitive-times, getting away from danger was more important for our ancestors than being right; because if we got away from danger, we lived another day, but if we tried to verify the facts, we could have become a pray. Thus, we have learned to engage in pattern-seeking and pattern-recognition, rather than fact-seeking and fact-verification, as a first line of thinking in order to stay safe and feel better. Because, feeling safe reduces our negative-feelings, hence, it makes us feel better.

However:

Pattern-seeking and pattern-recognition often lead to errors in cognition.

For example, in the primitive-times, when humans heard a noise in the trees, they could either think that the noise was a potential predator or the noise was the wind. If they considered the noise to be an animal and it happened to be the wind, despite making an error in judgment, the mistake did not cause them any harm; but if the noise was caused by a predator but they chose to believe that it was the wind, they could have become pray to the predator. Therefore, our primitive-mind has instinctually learned to "seek and trust" patterns in order for us to stay safe; regardless of how often these patterns might be incorrect. Because, when we feel safe, we remain protected, and consequently, we feel less-negativity. When we feel less-negativity, we feel better; hence why, we continuously seek and even concoct imaginary patterns in order to feel better.

Seeking and recognizing patterns is a cognitive and thinking process; therefore, our mind has learned to make mistakes in recognizing facts and reality for the benefit of keeping us safe. We feel negative in the presence of real or perceived threat and danger, because negativity is a protective-mechanism. Since negativity is undesirable, nature has programmed us to feel negativities such as fear, in the presence of threats and danger, so that we would react to reducing these negativities by getting away from potential threats and danger. When we are safe, we minimize fear and other negative-feelings; therefore, seeking and creating patterns, even though they might be nonfactual and perceived, could make us feel better, or at the minimum, it could make us feel less-negative. It is this tendency of humans to create false-thoughts to feel less-negative, that has evolved into our current practices of fallacious-thinking in order to avoid pain, to feel good, or at the minimum to feel less-bad.

In the primitive-times, in the face of potential danger, we did not have time to stop and evaluate the facts whether we were dealing with an animal or the wind; therefore, we trusted patterns. However, in the modern-times, we do not face the same primitive-dangers which our primitive-mind reacted to in order to minimize danger and negativity. In the modern-times, although our primitive-mind does not have primitive-dangers to react to; it still reacts to the strongest negativities just as strongly.

Since negativity feels undesirable and uncomfortable, in the presence of prolonged and unresolved negativities, we react to them in the same way that we would have reacted to primitive-dangers; by trying to get away from the negativity caused by the danger. Therefore, whatever we do not like, we treat it as if it were dangerous, in order to quickly avoid the negative-feelings associated with it. We do so, quickly and impulsively, without verifying the facts associated with it because we want to avoid feeling bad, and to feel better quickly. As described throughout Theory of Self-Relativity, in the modern-times, the quickest way to feel better is to rationalize our desired-feelings by creating false-thoughts, fallacious-beliefs, and other comforting nonfactual mindsets and practices. In other words, we try to feel better by changing our perception of reality.

Since in the modern-times, we do not have the urgency of dealing with primitive-dangers; therefore, we have the time to verify the factualities of our thoughts in order to evaluate the causes of our negative-feelings. Thus, to feel good, or to feel less-negative, and to minimize the dominance of our primitive-mind, we must place our intelligent-mind in the controlling position so that it can evaluate the data and information associated with our thoughts. When we place our intelligent-mind instead of our primitive-mind in the driver's seat, we can then begin to think and make decisions based on facts. This can only be done by us thinking factually. Factual-thinking enables us to slow-down and balance our thinking so that we can base our thinking on facts and evidence, and not based on creating feel-good and comforting fallacious-thoughts. When we learn to think only based on facts, our factual-thinking abilities will quicken, and it will enable us to think efficiently and effectively.

Factual-thinking enables us to slow-down our emotional-thinking and impulsive behaviors, by placing a system of checks and balances on our emotionally desired thoughts.

The human brain is a thinking machine. In order for it to learn to continuously change and improve, we must learn, practice, and intuit analytical mental processing, over impulsive and emotional mental activities. In other words, we must learn to empower our intelligent-mind over our primitive-mind so that we can resolve negative-feelings through fact-based cognitive processes; rather than through emotional and impulsive threat-avoiding behavior. While our primitive-mind works off instincts and emotions, our intelligent-mind must operate via factual-thinking, reason-based analysis, and rationality. The only way to untangle this battle of the intelligent-mind and the primitive-mind is to have our intelligent-mind become dominant over our primitive-mind. The way to make our intelligent-mind become the dominant one is by minimizing the effects of our primitive-mind, and this could only happen by facing, by analyzing, and by resolving our negative-thoughts. When our primitive-mind feels safe with the decisions that our intelligent-mind makes, our primitive-mind will naturally begin to take a backseat and our intelligent-mind will consequently take control of our thinking processes.

Self-improvement via factual-thinking creates a layer of cushion and protection around our primitive-mind in order for our primitive-mind to feel safe. When we feel safe, we can then focus on minimizing negativities, and we can begin to increase positivities. In the modern-era, this personal stability is achieved by having access to money and by creating basic financial security. As we stabilize and improve our financial position, we can begin to increase focus on improving our other personal attributes that enhance and strengthen our self-identity and our sense of Self. For example, we can begin working on our physical appearance, we can strengthen our personal and business interactions, and we can improve our societal and cultural standings. This, in-turn, will improve our success, progress, and relationship potentials, and it will enable us to strengthen our self-confidence and our sense of Self. This is why, true self-improvement could only happen by increasing the strengths of our intelligent-mind; and the way to strengthen our intelligent-mind is to train our mind to think factually. The more factual we think, the more genuine and purer our feelings will become, and the sounder our actions will be. The sounder our actions are, the more secure our primitive-mind will feel; which in-turn, will allow our intelligent-mind to guide our life forward even further.

Factual-thinking and proactive-change are the "basic" requirements for self-improvement and personal-transformation.

This concept is discussed in further detail in subsequent sections of Theory of Self-Relativity. As stated, due to the instinctive nature and constant presence of our primitive-mind; our mind is programmed to first consider danger and negativity. This negativity for recognizing and reacting to danger has evolved from looking out for basic stone-age dangers, to by worrying about modern lifestyle consequences. For example, the stone-age fear of getting exposed to a predator when looking for food or when sleeping out in the open because we did not have a cave; has now been replaced with the fear of not having a job or not having enough money to be able to afford food and rent. This constant need to have enough money, is why, worry, anxiety, fear, and as a whole, negativities, are more prevalent and more dominant in our modern-times than positivities and happiness are.

However, unlike the survival urgencies of the primitive-times; our modern worries and anxieties do not need to be dealt with instinctively and impulsively. Through rational and factual-thinking and planning processes, the intelligent-mind can help to make the primitive-mind less fearful and less impulsive. By strengthening our factual-thinking, we can minimize the instinctive and often unnecessary effects and disruptions of our primitive-mind. For example, instead of panicking because we lost our job, our intelligent-mind can proactively and in advance of being fired, recognize rather than deny the evidence that is pointing to the potential of us being fired. Instead of falling in the lap of routine and comfort and exposing our job to external factors; by learning to change constantly, we would then proactively change our job, rather than waiting for us to get fired and then panic to immediately find another mediocre replacement job. Therefore, by using experience and knowledge, our intelligent-mind can act to improve, instead of reacting to do damage control.

Instead of wishing and hoping that things will be fine on their own; by learning to think factually and by facing facts, we can make changes by taking actions to improve our life in advance of potential negativities. Additionally, factual-thinking will also help us to not ignore, deny, or alter the truth, because we would not want our primitive-mind to kick in. A factually-thinking intelligent-mind will keep our primitive-mind from dominating and over functioning, without it shutting down our primitive-mind from protecting us in cases of real danger. Factual-thinking, combined with awareness and understanding of our thoughts can become intuitive with enough practice and enhancement of our cognitive-skills. A strong and factual-thinking intelligent-mind will help us change and transform, while keeping our primitive-mind controlled to only act instinctively for protecting us from true danger. Although factual-thinking cannot stop our primitive-mind from constantly triggering protective-thoughts; our intelligent-mind, through factual-thinking, can stop the protective-thoughts from becoming overpowering.

By increasing awareness of our thoughts, and by evaluating and understanding the factualities of our thoughts, we can then take action in response to these thoughts, in order to minimize the constant obstructions caused by our primitive-mind. Our primitive-mind cannot distinguish if we still live in the stone-age where a predator could kill us, or if we are living in an advanced society where we are much safer. Our primitive-mind reacts to prolonged and unresolved negativities the same way that it would react to primitive-dangers. Awareness, rationality, and factual-thinking stabilize the battles within our mind by minimizing the effects of our primitive-mind and by increasing the control of our intelligent-mind. Although our primitive-mind does not care if we are happy and all it cares for is if we are safe; by thinking factually and by making sound decisions, our primitive-mind can learn to trust our judgment and decision-making abilities and to allow us to enjoy more frequencies of positivity and happiness. This is why, Theory of Self-Relativity advocates, that the way to be positive and to feel happy can only be achieved from the way we think.

To feel good…we must think well

Centered-Self vs. Self-Centered

According to Theory of Self-Relativity we must make our Self the most important and the most special entity in in Our-Universe and in our lifetime. As termed by Theory of Self-Relativity, this could only happen if we learn to live a *"Centered-Self"* life.

Living a centered-self life does not mean being self-centered and selfish. Although being centered-self and self-centered sound similar as they both prioritize the Self before others; being centered-self, unlike being self-centered, does not do so at the expense of others, or without consideration for others. In addition, centered-self means we do not sacrifice our Self for others; especially for approval-seeking and for social-acceptance.

Centered-Self ✓		✗ Self-Centered	
1.	Self-First	1.	Self-First
2.	Self-Focused	2.	Selfish
3.	Not at the Expense of Others	3.	What Happens to Others Doesn't Matter
4.	Not Sacrifice for Others	4.	Others are Irrelevant
5.	Others after "Self"	5.	Others Don't Matter

Living a centered-self life means our life and our existence is balanced as we live our life from the inside-out; with our Self being the core of our existence. Self-centeredness means being selfish by living one's life without consideration for others, or at the expense of others. When we learn to place the absolute importance in our Self and as we realize that everything and everyone else is relative to us; we will then begin to first think, feel, and act based on what is good for us. *"Self-First"* is how we are able to create an internally derived self-identity and a well-defined sense of Self. Since everything else and everyone else is relative to us, without a healthy sense of Self and a central self-first approach, we will not be able to have a healthy perspective on life or healthy relationships with others.

We cannot be good to others if we do not know how to be the best for our own Self.

Self-first does not mean not-caring, being rebellious, or doing anything we want impulsively and without considering the consequences of our actions on others. Self-first is actually just the opposite. Self-first means to learn to view our Self from a personal-perspective, by improving our Self through self-reflection and personal-awareness. A positive self-image and a strong sense of Self are core indications of an improved Self. Without first improving our Self and without first recognizing, eliminating, and strengthening our weaknesses; we will not be able to have healthy relationships with others. For example, even in a passenger air-craft emergency, it is recommended that we put our oxygen mask on first before securing the mask for our child. No matter how much we have the urge to save our child first; if we do not secure our own oxygen mask first and we pass-out, our child will not survive. However, by first securing our Self, we will have a better chance of saving both of us. Therefore, if we cannot be the best Self that we can be for our own Self, we cannot be and we cannot do our best for others. We must be healthy first before we can take care of others.

If we don't know what is good for us, how can we be good to others?

To be able to live a centered-self life, we must first learn to bring the focus onto our own Self. Centered-self life is best accomplished by living our life from the inside-out, rather than living it from the outside-in. When we learn to live a cen-tered-self life by putting our Self in the center of Our-Universe; our existence will emanate from the inside-out, and not from outside-in. Just as centered-self does not mean self-centered; being the center of Our-Universe does not mean being the center of The-Universe. Being the center of Our-Universe means placing our self-first in the core of our existence during our lifetime. When we learn to focus on our Self, we will then be able to recognize our weaknesses and deficiencies that need to be improved; because, the first thing that being centered-self exposes is our self-deficiencies and personal-weaknesses. By bringing the focus onto our Self, we will then be able to live a quality and fulfilling life as we improve our weaknesses and as we resolve our deficiencies.

Without knowing what needs to change, we won't know how to improve it.

Inside-Out vs. Outside-In

Living our life from the inside-out rather than from the outside-in is to have self-awareness by being in touch with our inner Self and by focusing on our self-first, before focusing onto others. Living inside-out enables us to live a centered-self life, and as described throughout Theory of Self-Relativity, centered-self does not mean being self-centered. To learn to live our life from the inside-out, we must first learn to observe our Self from the outside-in. Introspection, which is simply self-inspection and self-reflection, enables us to see our Self from the outside-in and to recognize our feelings, our thoughts, and our deficiencies and weaknesses which need to be changed and improved.

Our thinking, which generates our feelings, is the core of who we are. Being mindful and aware will help us to recognize our thoughts and it will enable us to thoughtfully make changes and improvements to our thinking; from the inside-out. Self-reflection, self-awareness, and a clear and strong sense of Self, will enable us to have transparency and to recognize these personal traits and characteristics that need improvement. To create a strong self-identity and to develop a strong sense of Self:

1. We must observe our Self from the "outside-in"
2. We must change our Self from the "inside-out"

Thinking and living from the inside-out places our Self in the center of our thoughts and decision-makings, while it minimizes our dependency and reliance externally. Society, culture, and even our families often influence and distort our sense of Self and our self-identity, by teaching us to place others before our Self. For example, our empathy and compassion are often used to manipulate us by placing a guilt-goblin on our shoulder that any time we choose our Self before others, we are being selfish. Such guilt-ridden inability to put our self-first is one of the main causes for many, becoming codependents and people-pleasers. Additionally, societal, cultural, and religious teachings which focus externally on placing others first and by teaching us to do for others before doing for our own Self, gives society and the people whom we interact with the ability to control us.

Centuries old terminologies like "turn the other cheek" or "do unto others as you would have them do unto you" are prime examples of cultural influences of how we are taught to place others before our own Self. These principles create unfairness in the name of forgiveness; and courtesy, at the expense of our own self-interests. Such social standards ensure our loyalty and contribution to the community by making us feel guilty, and even bad, about our Self if we choose our personal-interests before others. Just as living a centered-self life does not mean putting our self-first at the expense of others; living from the inside-out will similarly prevent us from placing others first, at the expense of our own Self. As stated by Theory of Self-Relativity, a truly caring, symbiotic, yet self-interest preserving way of stating "do unto others as you would have them do unto you" should be:

Do unto others as you do unto your Self.

This means we do no harm to others, because we would not harm our own Self; and we are kind and empathetic with others, because we are kind and empathetic with our own Self. To do to others as they do to us is more of an an-eye-for-an-eye approach; however, to treat others as we would treat our own Self, is based on self-reflection and self-awareness. The best possible way to treat others should not be the way that we would want them to treat us; but, it should be the same way that we treat our own Self. Therefore, if we treat our own Self unkindly or anything less than the best; we should first improve how we care for our Self and how we treat our Self, so that we can then improve how we care for and treat others. When we live a centered-self and inside-out life, we don't ignore our Self and we don't give something up in order to pay attention to others. We first pay attention to our own Self and we take care of our own Self, so that we would then know how to be available for others.

By placing our self-first, we do what is right for our own Self and we pass on the same values and interests to others. Instead of guilt-ridden principles or fear-based beliefs; centered-self and inside-out approach creates personal-standards that are good for our own Self, and which will consequently be good for others. When we learn to place our interests first, we will likewise become more aware of other-people's interests. Instead of placing others first, at the expense of our interests, we will recognize how to prioritize our interests relative to other-people's interests. By preserving our self-interests, we will be more cognizant of the balance needed between our self-interests and that of others. When we know how to prioritize and preserve our own self-interests; it is only then that we will know how to prioritize other-people's interests without sacrificing ours. Theory of Self-Relativity defines the relativities of our Self with others as the *"Self-Equation,"* which is discussed in detail in subsequent sections.

Theory of Self-Relativity defines "self-equation" as "the dynamic balance of the Self, relative to the Self, and to others."

Living inside-out not only places our self-first, but it allows us to change and improve our Self before we attend to others. Living centered-self and inside-out is important in placing our self-first because if we cannot think, feel, and do the best for our own Self; how could we do our best for others? We need to be healthy and strong first before we can help make others healthy and strong.

To be good to others, we must first learn to be good to our own Self.

By placing our Self in the center of Our-Universe; we emanate thoughts, feelings, and actions from within to the outside. When we become the center of

Our-Universe, everything else flows around us relative to this core position. Instead of us constantly focusing externally onto others; by focusing on our self-first, we live our life from the inside-out and we require others to adapt to us from the outside-in. By living from the inside-out; we dictate the rules of personal-engagement, and we play to our own home-court advantage. Unlike traditional, cultural, and societal teachings and expectations, there is absolutely nothing wrong by engaging with others based on our preferences. If others don't meet our preferences, we should be self-sufficient enough to simply choose to not deal with them; thereby, we can choose to move on.

When our self-identity and personal-values are internally-defined, we will then operate based on our self-sufficiencies and without having expectations from others. Furthermore, such internally well-defined parameters and values will enable us to set our borders and boundaries so that we know how much and how far we can be available for others; and reciprocally, it will signal to others how they would be required to interact with us.

Living a centered-self and inside-out life does not mean being rigid. Living a centered-self and inside-out life means we are aware of our Self, and we know how we relate to our own Self; therefore, we would also know how to relate to others, and in-turn, we would know how we would want others to relate to us. If others cannot or do not relate to us according to our well-defined values and preferences; we would either make changes and modifications to adapt to others, or we would require others to make changes to adapt to us accordingly. However, if adaptability is not possible, we will not remain in an interaction or in a relationship with incompatible or disrespectful people. Self-reliance and living inside-out allows us to define our borders and boundaries. The more self-aware and the more self-reliant we become, the less we will be dependent on others, and the more we will rely on our Self; therefore, the more control and certainty we will have in our life. Consequently, such personal-independence, in-turn, minimizes neediness and expectations from others.

Everything in The-Universe is relative; hence, to have the most balanced relativity, we must remain unbiased and adaptable, but well-defined.

Although everything is relative, *"Self-Relativity"* or *"Personal-Relativity"* should not be just two-dimensional. As discussed:

Theory of Self-Relativity defines "Self-Relativity" as "the interactions and relationships of the Self internally and externally with the Self and with everything and everyone else."

Therefore, true Self-Relativity could be viewed from not just two, but from three different perspectives. *"Trilateral-Relativity"* is a perspective that is coined and defined by Theory of Self-Relativity which enables us to observe and recognize our relativities and characteristics with our own Self, with others, and others' relativities with our Self from a three-sided perspective.

Theory of Self-Relativity defines "trilateral-relativity" as "the three-sided connections, interactions, and relationships of one's Self with the Self and with others."

Representation of our relativities with everything and everyone else in a trilateral-format enables us to recognize how much more focused most of us are externally rather than internally. Recognizing our trilateral-relativities enables us to visualize why living a centered-self life from the inside-out enables us to become aware that our Self-to-Self relativity is the most important aspect of our relativities, and why, our relativity to others should be the less important one.

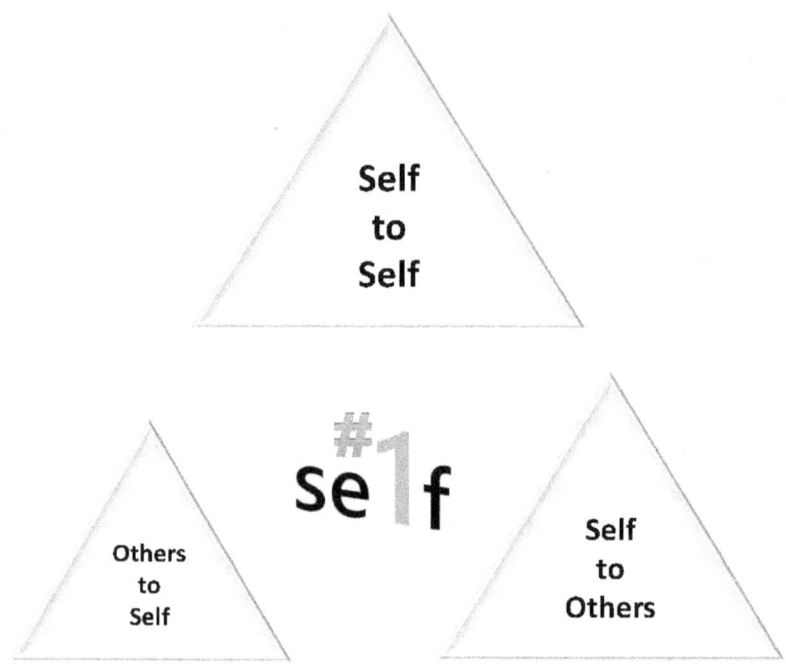

Trilateral-Relativity consists of:

1. **Self-to-Self Relativity:** Is how we relate to our own Self and how we view, perceive, understand, feel, and value our own Self. This is the most important, yet often the most ignored of all Self-Relativities.

2. **Self-to-Others Relativity:** Is how we relate to our own Self and how we view, perceive, understand, feel, and value our Self relative to others. This is the second most important of all Self-Relativities.

3. **Others-to-Self Relativity:** Is how others relate to our Self and how others view, perceive, understand, feel, and value our Self relative to their own Self. Although significant, according to Theory of Self-Relativity, other people's relativity to us should take a back seat to our own personal-perspective of our own Self; because if we cannot be aware of how we relate to and how we view, perceive, understand, feel, and value our own Self, we will not be able to properly relate to how others view, perceive, understand,

feel, and value us. This is why, Theory of Self-Relativity insists on living a centered-self life, from the inside-out.

When we place our Self in the middle of Our-Universe and when we realize that we are the most important entity in Our-Universe; it is only then that we will recognize that in order for us to be in actual equilibrium and harmony with everyone and with everything else in The-Universe, we must live a centered-self life from the inside-out. Being in the center of Our-Universe brings the focus onto our own Self so that we learn to do more for our own Self, while we learn to expect less of our Self; and most importantly, we learn to expect less from others.

Expecting more of your Self decreases self-worth; doing more for your Self increases self-worth.

Through living a centered-self life and by living life from the inside-out, we will learn to:

1. Do more for our Self and not expect more of our Self.
2. Do more for our Self and not expect more from others.
3. Do more for our Self and expect less from others.

Expecting less lowers our expectations, and when we expect less, we lessen our disappointments; especially when our expectations are reliant on other-people's participation and performance. Thus, when we expect less, especially from others, we increase our self-reliance. Likewise, instead of expecting more of ourselves or expecting more from others, we should do more for our Self and we should expect less of our Self and less from others. Doing more for our Self and expecting less from others does not mean being selfish or antisocial; but it means to prioritize our self-interests first before others, but not at the expense of others. It also means to learn to become self-sufficient; because:

Expectations often lead to disappointments, especially when reliant on others.

Therefore:

Don't expect more…Do more!

In other words:

1. Do more for your Self.
2. Expect less of your Self.
3. Expect less from others.

Having no self-expectations does not mean having no drive. Instead of expectations, we should set realistic goals for improving our life. Achieving these goals is accomplished by "doing," which means putting effort to change and improve. When we set goals and when we put in effort in order to achieve the goals; we are therefore changing our expectations to *"anticipation."*

Expectation means waiting for something to happen; anticipation means influencing something to happen.

Expectation gives us no sense of certainty or control; but because anticipation is based on an objective and an action to reach that objective, anticipation gives us a better potential for reaching a desired goal. When we set goals and when we put effort into it, we anticipate for our goals to be achieved. Expectations are open-ended and speculative; however, properly set realistic-goals are defined and achievable. As further discussed in later sections, same applies to hope versus optimism, because hope is often based on a wish or faith without the necessity for action; however, optimism is based on effort and action anticipating a positive outcome.

Goals are accomplished by meeting objectives; not by having expectations.

An expectation is to believe something will happen; a belief is not a formula for certainty.

As stated, expectations often lead to disappointments; especially when the expectation is reliant on someone or something else. This is true in all aspects of our interactions, whether the expectation is from our own Self-to-Self interactions, or from our interactions with others.

Expectations and disappointments are relative to one another. Although expectations can be viewed as *"Trilateral-Expectations;"* to understand this relativity and why expectations often lead to disappointments; Theory of Self-Relativity categorizes expectations binarily:

1. **Internal-Expectations or (Self-Expectations):** Are our expectations of our own Self. We have more control over expectations from our Self than we do from others; however, to have most control, we should set goals for our Self instead of having expectations of our Self. Regardless, by being self-aware and self-reliant, we will have the ability to turn self-expectations into personal-goals.

2. **External-Expectations:** Are our expectations relative to others. External-expectations are not in our control; they are reliant on others' performance or involvement. Theory of Self-Relativity further categorizes external-expectations binarily:

   a. **Our expectations from others:** Us having expectations from others could happen because we choose to do things for others, such as acts of kindness; and in return, we were consciously or nonconsciously expecting something from others. *This is the classic form of expectations which often leads to disappointments.*

      ● To minimize disappointments, when we do something for others, unless previously defined and agreed upon, we should not do so based on expecting something in return; we should do so without having any expectations. If we want something in return, we must have an agreement, or at the minimum, we must have an understanding with the other person, in advance of our interaction.

b. Others' expectations of us: Likewise, we should not allow others to do things for us and to expect something from us; unless understood or agreed upon in advance. If others choose to do something for us and then they give us guilt feelings because they expected something from us; we should not feel guilty nor should we feel responsible for their disappointment because they expected something of us. *Do not carry a guilt-goblin on your shoulders because of someone else's expectation.*

- Whether someone choses to do something for us, by choice or by a request from us; unless a conditionality was pre-defined, we should not allow others to guilt-trip us because of their own expectations. In other words, we should not allow our Self to be emotionally blackmailed by someone else because they did something for us; even if that act or favor was requested by us. *This is the classic form of expectation which often leads to disrespect, control, and abuse.*

As a rule of thumb:

- *We should have no expectations from others so that we will not get disappointed.*
- *We should not allow others to have expectations from us so that we won't be controlled.*

To truly self-improve, we must learn to live a centered-self life. This is best accomplished by putting our self-first before others, but not at the expense of others; and we should live our life from the inside-out, rather than from the outside-in. Furthermore, we must learn to minimize and eliminate expectations by learning to set goals, and in order to achieve our goals, we must learn to put in effort to create positive-change. By becoming self-reliant and by changing our Self, rather than by expecting others to help change us; we can thus live a true centered-self life. Self-reliance allows us to place our self-first ahead of others, but not at the expense of others; and this could only be accomplished through awareness, objectivity, and factual-thinking.

To consider others without having to sacrifice one's Self is the mark of a truly self-secure and self-confident person.

The Most Important Word…Ever!

When asked "what is the most important word ever;" the majority of people focus on emotions, or they focus on a word or an action which is directed externally. Some of the most common answers are love, fear, kindness, family, friends, etc. What most ignore, is the common-factor in everything, everyone, and every action that they considered. The most important word ever is the common factor associated with everything that we feel, think, do, and, with everyone and everything that we interact with; and this common factor is the only entity that is with us at every moment of our existence. This common factor is our "Self."

Self is the most important word…ever!

Although Theory of Self-Relativity defines "Self" as "*the collection of the material and immaterial aspects of one's existence;*" our self-identity and our sense of Self are not only as a result of our material existence, but more importantly, they are as a result of our immaterial attributes. Our immaterial-processes such as our thoughts and our emotions are as a result of the immaterial-byproducts of our material-brain's activities. As discussed, these immaterial-byproducts are our consciousness, our mind, and as a whole; our thinking-system which make us who we are, and which give us our "sense of Self." Therefore:

Theory of Self-Relativity more specifically defines "Sense of Self" as "the collective combination of our consciousness and our thoughts."

As discussed, as material objects, we are not anymore special to The-Universe than any other object is; and the only reason that we feel or we think that we are special is because we have the ability to think and understand our existence. What sets us apart from other living and non-living things is our ability to think, feel, and behave, as a result of our intellectual and critical-thinking abilities.

We are what we think.

Our existence is relative to how we think, feel, and behave with our Self, with others, and with Our-Universe. As stated, Our-Universe is everything and everyone that we deal with in our lifetime; therefore, our "Self" is the most important component of our existence. Everything else and everyone else is only relative to our Self and only relative to us while we exist. Since we are the most important entity in Our-Universe and in our lifetime; therefore, we should bring the focus onto our Self by learning to live a centered-self life, which is directed from the inside-out. As discussed, centered-self does not mean self-centered; it means to prioritize our self-first before we do others, but not at the expense of others.

Centered-self living teaches us to pay attention to our Self before we do so with others, and it places our Self at the core of Our-Universe. By living life from a core central position, we connect to and interact with everything and everyone else relative to our existence. Centered-self existence makes us the most important entity in Our-Universe, but not the most important entity in The-Universe.

We shouldn't make our Self the center of The-Universe; but we should make our Self the center of Our-Universe.

Self-first and living a centered-self life should be our core principle of existence. Self is the most important word because what is relative to us and what really matters to us is everything that exists while we are alive. Whether the Sun and the Earth have been around for 4.6 billion years, or the fact that they will cease to exist in the next 5 billion years, makes no difference to our "Self" existence. In Our-Universe, the only thing which directly affects us is if the Sun and the Earth are going to be around during the time that we are alive. Although The-Universe, the Sun, and the Earth coming to existence allowed us to exist; what they did or what they will do makes no difference to us when we are not alive. What matters is the relativity of the Sun and the Earth and everything else to us during our lifetime. While the knowledge of the past and the predictions and anticipation of the possible future are important for human advancement; what matters is the relativity of everything to our "Self" during our few decades of lifetime.

Self-first does not mean focusing on our Self by being selfish and only caring for our Self. Self-first means focusing on our Self to make the best out of this almost improbable gift of life that we have received. By us focusing on our Self, we can not only make the best for our Self during our lifetime; but our self-contributions and self-improvements will allow next generations to continue building on our personal-achievements. Theory of Self-Relativity advocates placing the utmost importance on our Self because when we learn to value our own self-first, we can then properly value everything and everyone else.

If we want to be of value to others, we must first learn to be of value to our own Self.

For example, in an airplane emergency, it is recommended we put our own oxygen mask on first, before securing our child's mask; because if we pass out, so would our child, since children do not know how to take care of themselves. As much as we would have the urge to take care of our child first; the logical and unemotionally correct thing to do would be to secure our self-first. Likewise, if we are not healthy and safe on our own, we will not be able to keep others healthy and safe either. When we help our self-first, we have a better chance of helping others.

To have a strong "we" mindset, we must first have a strong "me" mindset.

Since our Self must be the most important entity in our life; consequently, our thoughts and our thinking-system must be clear, well-defined, and central to our existence. Our thoughts and thinking-system make us the individuals that we are; therefore, our thoughts and thinking-system create our sense of Self and our self-identity. Thus, to have a balanced and minimally chaotic life, we must manage our thinking-system to be uncluttered, quick, and realistic.

To quicken our thinking, and to minimize clutter and distractions to our thinking-system, we must learn to think factually. Facts are facts and only one form of fact exists per situation. Facts do not lie, and facts are not open to interpretation; therefore, facts are not open to manipulation. Facts are open to examination and facts are open to replacement should new facts emerge; however, facts are not open to interpretation. Although facts are not absolute and facts could and should be examined, and if necessary, replaced; factual-thinking is about having reasonable confidence in the facts, unless or until falsified. When we learn to think factually and as we evaluate everything based on evidence, we will then create the most balanced and stable "Self." Factual-thinking filters-out clutter and gets rid of baseless beliefs and biases.

Factual-thinking is about having reasonable confidence in the facts, unless or until falsified.

Majority of our cluttering thoughts are perceived, imaginary, and as a result of emotional-thinking; because we often create thoughts, we justify behavior, and we fallaciously reason with our own Self so that we can quickly feel good, or at the minimum, so that we can quickly feel less-bad. Therefore, even our logic, our rationality, and our reason could be faulty and false; if that logic, rationality, and reason is based on beliefs, and if it does not use facts to verify or discredit the basis of the logic. We can believe to be logical and rational because we are convinced that what we believe feels reasonable and valid to us; however:

Believing is not knowing.

Just as believing is not knowing; feelings are not rational. Even though we might believe, or we might feel what we are thinking is rational; our logic and rationality could be flawed if it is not supported by facts and evidence. This is why, to live the best life; we must live our life based on factual-thinking. Factual-thinking is the system of checks and balances that keeps us on the fact-paved path of living a stable and fulfilled life.

Factual-thinking is the system of checks and balances of our mind.

Nonfactual and unproven beliefs and ideologies, at some point must be proven valid via their underlying evidence; or they should be discarded if supportive evidence could not be found. More importantly, we should abstain from acting strongly upon nonfactual-thoughts until supportive evidence is found. As long as facts and evidence needed to verify the factuality of an idea, a thought, or a belief is not found, we should not place much reliance on that mindset; because such ideas, thoughts, and beliefs could actually be fabricated by our mind in order to rationalize and support our desired-feelings. As human-beings, we are very good at deceiving our own Self in order to avoid pain, to feel good, or at the minimum, to feel less-bad. Since we are good at fooling our Self; this is why, we should become the primary guardian of our own Self.

The easiest person to fool is your "Self".

Our Self is the most important entity in Our-Universe and no other entity should be placed above our Self. Our religious, spiritual, and other beliefs should only exist as supportive tools to our Self; because when we don't exist, none of these beliefs matter. As long as spirituality, which could arise from many forms of emotionally satisfying sources such as religion, meditation, or even science, affects our lives as a supportive and calming tool; spirituality and beliefs could have relaxation, unwinding, and satisfactory benefits. However, no spiritual or super-natural belief or state-of-mind should act as a primary thinking-system for us to base our decision-making, behavior, and existence upon. Therefore, Theory of Self-Relativity states:

True spirituality is not believing in something mystical or mythical; true spirituality is to use the awareness of our emotions, to improve our thoughts, and to strengthen our actions.

The value, perception, and influence of our beliefs are only relevant to us in their uniqueness when we are alive. When we die, these beliefs and doctrines still exist for others, but they make no difference for our dead "Self." While many could argue about reincarnation and life after death; if one must insist on believing in them, such beliefs should only come in as supportive tools to our factual-existence when we are alive, and not as mindsets that lead us to our thinking, decision-making, and behavior. Since there has been no factual-evidence that our life or the quality of our existence continues after death; therefore, we should live our mortal life to the best quality that we can as a sentient human-being, thus, irrespective of ideologies, doctrines, or beliefs. Although beliefs such as the after-life are comforting; living our short and precious mortal existence for the hopes of an unproven-belief such as the afterlife, could be a complete waste, if what happens after death is simply nothing. Instead of having empty-faith and instead of believing in things that we cannot prove; we can learn to improve our Self so that we can provide the best quality of life for our Self and for our loved-ones based on things that are provable and factual. If and when we can factually prove the existence of the afterlife; we can then accept that fact as knowledge, and live our life accordingly.

We, as human-beings, strive to advance healthcare and to cure diseases so that we can increase our lifespan. Deep within our consciousness, we want to live a healthy and prolonged mortal-life. We have an innate tendency to stay alive and prolong our life; therefore, because of this inherent and instinctual natural characteristic, we do not easily succumb to the idea of dying. Although human-beings are the only living-things who are aware of their mortality; just like other living-things, we are innately programmed to keep safe, stay away from danger, and to try to avoid death by surviving for as long as we can. Likewise, nature has not programmed living beings to want to die so that they can get to experience the afterlife. As humans, just like other living things, we naturally do all that we can to stay alive; because our survival instincts want to keep us alive. Hence why:

We have "survival" instincts; not "dying" instincts.

While many believe there could be afterlife, no one knows if there is one. Currently, all evidence and natural laws that govern The-Universe indicate that no such state-of-existence is possible. Since other than social-construct and personal-hearsays, there has never been any evidence to prove the existence of the afterlife; instead of making our Self feel hopeful that life continues after we die, we should use the lack of evidence as indication that there is no afterlife, therefore, we should focus on making the best of our current one-and-only life. Until and unless evidence is presented that there is afterlife; we should consider where we go after we die, to be the same place as where we were before we were born. Despite our beliefs and ideologies, there is only one certainty; this life that we live, will end at some point. Our-Universe will end, but The-Universe will continue. Does The-Universe continuing really matter to us after we die; or should we try to make Our-Universe the best it could be when we are alive?

The afterlife paradigm example is how Theory of Self-Relativity recommends applying factual-thinking neutrally and non-judgmentally to our existence and towards our self-improvement. Theory of Self-Relativity does not take sides with religious, political, or subjective beliefs that many hold. Theory of Self-Relativity advocates factual-thinking to be our primary driver for existence; and it recommends for us to dismiss nonfactual-beliefs, if evidence for such beliefs could not be found. This means, we should approach life and our existence with skepticism. Skepticism means to question the validity of things until the validity is verified with facts, reason, and logic. Skepticism does not mean cynicism, whereby the cynic continuously looks to find fault with things. Skepticism, unlike cynicism, looks to find answers that are based on facts.

Skepticism is a cognitive trait and a skill that Theory of Self-Relativity recommends cultivating in order to be able to look for supportive facts, reason, and logic, for a proposition; and especially for a thought. Since Theory of Self-Relativity is founded upon the foundation of what it has termed as factual-thinking; thus, to be able to seek facts, we must have a skeptical mindset. As stated, skepticism does not mean being cynical, because those who are cynical are generally not interested in finding facts; they are more interested in finding faults, especially in others, as a means of validating their own stance and intellect, regardless of what the facts indicate. Cynics often argue not because they are debating to learn the truth; cynics often argue because they want to prove someone else wrong, or at the minimum, they argue in order for themselves to not be proven wrong.

Cynics don't debate to learn the truth; cynics argue to prove others wrong.

Skepticism cultivates critical-thinking, while cynicism tries to maintain a competitive mindset based on emotional-reasoning. Therefore, a skeptical mindset does not simply believe; a skeptic attempts to know.

Skeptics looks for facts; cynics looks for faults.

This is why, according to Theory of Self-Relativity, nonfactual-thoughts are synonymous with beliefs until the supportive facts to the belief are found. Because, as described by Theory of Self-Relativity:

A belief is simply a thought that has not been verified by evidence.

As we train our mind and as we improve our Self with quick and clever analytical-thinking; we will intuitively begin to qualify, modify, or eliminate our beliefs relative to our existence. Nonfactual-thoughts and beliefs are commonly concocted in order to make us avoid pain, to make us feel good, or at the minimum, to make us feel less-bad at the moment. We do so because facing facts is often an emotionally difficult task, and facts that require attention, are often dislikable and uncomfortable to deal with. We can choose to seek facts and evidence in order to stop our Self from self-deception; or we can numb-up reality by continuously seeking unfounded-beliefs and by concocting false-thoughts in order to feel good. Theory of Self-Relativity has termed this form of emotional-thinking or rationalization as *"Placebo-Thinking."*

Theory of Self-Relativity defines "Placebo-Thinking" as "thoughts that we concoct regardless of their factuality, in order to support our desired feelings."

According to Theory of Self-Relativity:

- Placebo-thinking is creating and rationalizing thoughts based on how we want to feel.
- Placebo-thinking is thinking based on feelings, instead of feeling based on thinking.
- Placebo-thinking is a form of emotional-thinking or emotional-reasoning.

One should not feel to think; one should think to feel.

For example, the thought of the afterlife is a form of placebo-thinking, and despite the fact that it feels good and it gives hope to believe that there is afterlife; the only self-certainty that exists is that we are alive now and that we will die sometime in the future. Therefore:

The question is; do we just want to be alive, or do we want to live life?

It is important for us to factually validate reality because our feelings, our perceptions, and our beliefs could be incorrect, biased, and factless. For example, in ancient-time, humans perceived and believed without facts that the Earth was flat, and that the Sun actually went around the Earth, and that the Earth was the center of The-Universe. This perceived-reality was based on nonfactual-thoughts and false-beliefs that had not been verified nor validated with evidence. In this example, the tools of understanding the facts did not exist in the ancient-times; therefore, societal-beliefs and lack of accessibility to facts created a reality which was perceived, false, and nonfactual. However, with the progress of science, when the facts and the evidence were discovered and understood, this incorrect belief about the Earth's centrality was discarded. This is why, nonfactual-thoughts are nothing but factless-beliefs which need to be verified and supported with facts; or they need to be dismissed when supportive facts could not be found, and to be discarded when contradictory facts are found.

Similarly, in personal situations, reality could be primarily based on personal, societal, or cultural nonfactual-thoughts and beliefs. Often, we or one or more members of society think or imagine of an idea, an opinion, or a belief; and without seeking or verifying the underlying facts, these ideas, thoughts, and beliefs become personally and socially accepted standards, traditions, and sometimes, even, ethics and rules of existence.

Similarly, personal-experiences seem real and convincing to the person having an experience; however, a personal-experience does not necessarily make the experience real or factual. For example, many believe that the holy-spirit talks to them, and that it has touched them; but when asked to demonstrate the reality of their experience, they cannot, because they claim it is a personal-experience.

Personal-experience is subjective and is a first-person experience; hence, to everyone else, personal-experience is simply hearsay. Since the mind can create fallacious-beliefs, especially when these beliefs are based on faith and comforting-thoughts; this is why, hearsay or personal-experience is not acceptable as evidence in a court-of-law. As another example, we might have dreamt that someone killed another person in our dream. Just because we had that dream, we cannot report the person to the law-enforcement and have that person arrested; nor will society punish the person because of a dream that we had. This is why, we must verify our personal-experiences with supportive facts and reason in order to be able to validate our experiences as factually-real, or to discard them because they are unreal and nonfactual.

Hence, factual-thinking is the only way for us to be able to live the most balanced, stable, and best quality life possible. By bringing the attention to our Self, we will be able to become more self-aware and we will be able to get directly in touch with our thoughts. Our Self is what matters, irrespective of our religious, cultural, and societal or new-age spiritual beliefs; or even our scientific orientation. By bringing the focus to our Self, we will not only learn to take accountability and responsibility for our decisions and actions; but we will also learn to take credit for our accomplishments and good deeds. Although many lack the ability to take responsibility for incorrect decisions; many more have difficulty giving themselves credit for correct decisions and favorable outcomes.

By bringing the attention to our Self and by living a centered-self life from the inside-out; we will be able to become more aware of our thoughts. By becoming aware of our thoughts, and by learning to analyze and evaluate them on-the-go, we will then be able to have more quality self-time in our life, and we can enjoy different experiences. Likewise, we will learn to recognize unhealthy and faulty-thinkings of other-people; hence, we will be able to adjust our interactions and relationships with them accordingly. Factual-thinking gives our primitive-mind the peace and safety that it is looking for in order for it to allow us to focus on enjoying a happy life. When our primitive-mind feels safe, it will then have the confidence to allow our intelligent-mind to make constructive decisions and to take advancing actions.

Self-confidence is established and improved when our primitive-mind backs off and allows our intelligent-mind to lead our thinking. When we become self-confident, we, in-turn, become more self-reliant; and, we will have less dependency on others. By minimizing our neediness and reliance of others, we will consequently enjoy more of our Self and more of our self-time; thereby, others will become an additive factor in our life. When we put our self-first because we are the most important entity in Our-Universe; our lifetime will become our *"Self-Time."*

What time is it? It's self-time!

The 10-Enemies of Self-Improvement

As discussed throughout Theory of Self-Relativity, to live a fulfilled and happy life, we must minimize and eliminate negativities first, before we reach for positivities. Without addressing the difficult negative issues in our lives, we cannot jump into trying to feel good and live a fulfilled and happy life. Minimizing negativities is a process which requires awareness, understanding, and taking action; in other words, we must learn to change in order to improve, and to do so, simply being motivated is not going to accomplish the task. To properly change and improve, we must not only make an effort to change, but we must also know what we need to change. Therefore, awareness and understanding of what we need to change is just as important as committing to and making the change.

To change and improve, we must find the cause in order to alleviate the symptom.

As will be discussed in detail in subsequent sections, the two non-negotiables for change and self-improvement are:

1. **Desire** = Wanting to improve
2. **Introspection** = Knowing what to improve

If we do not have the desire to change and improve and if we do not have the ability to look within our Self to see the deficiencies and weaknesses that we need to change and improve; consequently, we also will not be able to look around our Self and see what externally derived factors need to be resolved, eliminated, or improved. Some of these attributes that need improvement are personal to us, therefore, they require self-reflection and introspection; and some are relative to others which require extrospection. Regardless, we must have the ability to internally and externally inspect our relativities so that we can find the negative and troubling causes that are preventing us from change and improvement.

As discussed, introspection could be an uncomfortable and even a painful task to undertake, because self-reflection and introspection could reveal many personal-shortcomings that we have been avoiding, ignoring, and even denying. Likewise, extrospection could reveal difficult and even painful realities about our relationships with others and about the unhealthy ways that we have been engaged in such interactions.

Theory of Self-Relativity has identified the following ten internal and external contributors, labelled as *"The Enemies of Self-Improvement,"* as the primary reasons change and improvement have been difficult. The identification of these enemies also demonstrates how awareness and understanding of these contributors could put us on the path of resolution and elimination of negativities in our lives. Without awareness, understanding, and relating to how these factors influence our existence negatively, we will not be able to move to the next stage of changing and improving our life positively. Before we try to motivate our Self to change and to improve, we must first become honest with our Self to identify and diagnose the major contributors in our life that prevent us from improvement.

Theory of Self-Relativity has termed the following negative-influencers as the *"10-Enemies of Self-Improvement."*

10 Enemies

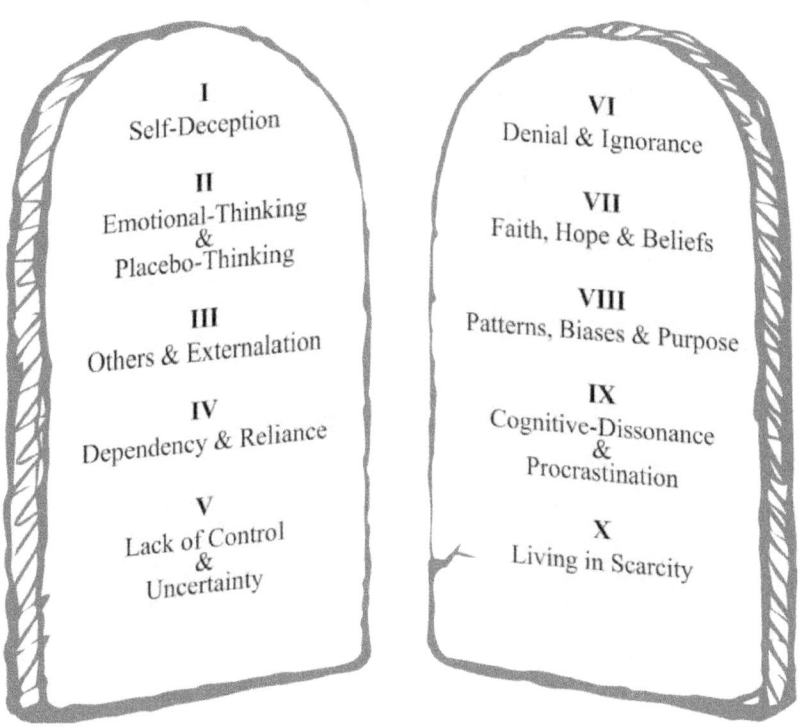

I
Self-Deception

II
Emotional-Thinking
&
Placebo-Thinking

III
Others & Externalation

IV
Dependency & Reliance

V
Lack of Control
&
Uncertainty

VI
Denial & Ignorance

VII
Faith, Hope & Beliefs

VIII
Patterns, Biases & Purpose

IX
Cognitive-Dissonance
&
Procrastination

X
Living in Scarcity

I. **Self-Deception:** Thou shalt not lie to thy Self.

- **Solution:** Thou shalt live life based on facts and evidence.

II. **Emotional-Thinking & Placebo-Thinking:** Thou shalt not create feel-good and comforting-thoughts in order to deny or ignore the dislikable facts.

- **Solution:** Thou shalt think and reason based on facts and evidence; not based on emotions.

III. **Others & Externalation:** Thou shalt not prioritize others over thy Self; and thou shalt not distract and preoccupy thy Self with others.

- **Solution:** Self-First; before others, but not at the expense of others.

IV. **Dependency & Reliance:** Thou shalt not rely on or become dependent on others.

- **Solution:** Thou shalt remain independent and self-reliant.

V. **Uncertainty & Lack of Control:** Thou shalt not become susceptible and helpless by not having control.

- **Solution:** Thou shalt be in control by seeking facts and by gaining knowledge.

VI. **Denial & Ignorance:** Thou shalt not deny and ignore facts and evidence.

- **Solution:** Thou shalt seek facts and evidence regardless of how inconvenient, dislikeable, or painful such facts may be.

VII. **Faith, Hope & Beliefs:** Thou shalt not "believe" in something without reason, facts, and evidence.

- **Solution:** Thou shalt "know" by relying on facts and evidence.

VIII. **Patterns, Biases & Purpose:** Thou shalt not create false-thoughts and baseless-beliefs to comfort thy Self.

- **Solution:** Thou shalt think based on facts and evidence.

IX. **Cognitive-Dissonance & Procrastination:** Thou shalt not rationalize falsehood nor delay action.

- **Solution:** Thou shalt think factually and put in effort to minimize negativity and to increase positivity.

X. **Living in Scarcity:** Thou shalt not live with few options or without many choices.

- **Solution:** Thou shalt live in abundance by increasing personal-value.

I.
Self-Lies & Self-Deception

The biggest lies we hear are the lies we tell our Self; because the easiest person to fool is our Self.

The truth is often inconvenient and when forced to face the dislikeable truth, our emotional tendency is to deny, ignore, and deflect the facts, in order to preserve our preferred-thoughts that make us feel good. We deny, ignore, and even attack the truth or the messenger because the truth does not match our preferred feel-good perspective; even though that perspective might be incorrect, fallacious, and nonfactual.

If the message of the truth conflicts with how I want to feel, I must attack the truth or the messenger.

We lie, especially to our own self, because we want to avoid pain and we want to feel good. Lying allows us to avoid pain, to feel good, or at the minimum, to quickly feel less-bad about something. We lie to our Self because facing facts is often an emotionally difficult task, as facts that require change and improvement are often uncomfortable to deal with. We do so by denying, ignoring, and altering the facts, in order to alter the perception of reality to our liking; instead of dealing with reality, the way reality truly is. Changing our thoughts and perceptions of reality to how we want it to be is much easier and quicker than actually facing the uncomfortable reality; because recognizing and changing the unfavorable reality requires time and effort. Hence why, we often fool our Self because we don't want to get out of our comfort-zone, no matter how unfavorable, inhibiting, and even dangerous our comfort-zone might be.

We often think things and we do things not because they are good for us, but because we want to feel good.

The power of self-deception is so strong that many of us go through life without recognizing we are engaged in chronically and even pathologically lying to our own Self.

We lie and self-deceive so that we can cover-up negative-feelings.

In other words:

Our need to feel good versus the necessity to think well is a core factor that inhibits change and blocks our self-improvement.

Instead of correcting the cause, we choose to cover-up the symptom; because facing reality via self-reflection and introspection is a difficult and painful task. The power of self-deception is so strong that we end up believing our own lies by choosing to live our life based on hope, faith, and wishful-thinking. We'd rather lie to our Self via false-hope, instead of taking action to change the undesired-reality. However, the problem remains, because when we self-lie and self-deceive, we only delay facing the consequences of avoiding the uncomfortable truth, and we complicate the effort needed to correct the negativities.

Self-lies and self-deception is one of the main causes of our inability to self-improve and to live a better life.

Although we often self-lie nonconsciously, we also know that we will have to face the consequences of our self-deception at some point in the future. In the short-term, self-deception is intended to minimize the discomfort of facing the undesired-reality; but in the long-term, the avoidance consequences of self-deception create other problems which deepen our chronic negative-feelings of anxiety, stress, and unhappiness.

The stink of self-deception cannot be covered-up; it will eventually rise to the surface.

Feelings and emotions are the main problem for self-improvement. Our feelings, especially our need to avoid feeling negative and the need to feel positive, is the main culprit that prevents us from self-improvement. The reason feelings, especially negative-feelings, are the main problem for self-improvement, is because our instinctual and immediate reaction to negative-feelings is to quickly think of something, or to quickly do something, in order to instantly improve our feelings.

We self-deceive by thinking "if it conflicts with how I want to feel, therefore I must attack it, or I must run from it."

We do things or we abstain from doing things, regardless of their long-term consequences; just so that we can avoid short-term discomfort and pain.

The need to avoid pain, to feel good, or at the minimum, to feel less-bad, is the driving force behind why we make bad decisions, why we take incorrect actions, and why we cannot change and improve.

Hence, as stated:

Our need to feel good versus the necessity to think well is a core factor that inhibits change and blocks our self-improvement.

This short-term desire to avoid pain, to feel good or at the minimum, to feel less-bad, is the primary driving force behind how we nonconsciously live our lives. It is this nonconscious need to feel good and to avoid negativity which causes us to lie to our Self and to deny and ignore dislikable-facts and uncomfortable-truths. Facing facts is often an emotionally difficult task because facts that require change are often uncomfortable to deal with.

We self-deceive by thinking "if it conflicts with what I want to be true, therefore it is not true."

Theory of Self-Relativity commonly refers to feelings and emotions interchangeably. Theory of Self-Relativity defines emotions as a collection of similar feelings; for example, being emotionally depressed as a result of a romantic-relationship break-up is often due to a collection of feelings such as feeling sad, heartbroken, jealous, angry, hurt, etc. Although a feeling describes a singular reference to the way we feel; emotions often occur in groups of two or more. For example, when we are feeling angry, we might also be feeling sad or scared simultaneously.

As discussed, according to Theory of Self-Relativity, the unaware human thinking and behavior is nonconsciously driven by the instinctive need to stay safe and to avoid danger; which is commonly associated with negative-feelings such as pain, or even death in extreme cases. This need to avoid pain and negativity is rooted in our nonconscious default-based primitive-mind so that by staying safe we can avoid discomfort, pain, negativity, and even death. Normally, a thought gets triggered which makes us feel a certain way and that feeling subsequently leads us to take action; however, we are often not in touch with the underlying causal-thought as much as we are in touch with the symptomatic-feeling that the thought generated. This is because we are more easily in touch with our feelings than we are aware of our thoughts; hence, we immediately know how we are feeling but we cannot quickly recognize what caused us to feel that way. The reason for this is because our feelings enable us to fight-or-flight quickly in order to subside threats and danger. This reactionary behavior to our negative-feelings is carried-over from the dangerous primitive-times that our ancestors lived in. In the primitive-times, our ancestors did not have enough time to gather data to cognitively evaluate if the threat or danger they felt was real or not. They needed to act quickly to be safe. Because once they resolved, eliminated, or got away from the cause of the threat they felt; consequently, they felt safer, thus, they felt less-bad, and, they felt better.

For survival, being safe is more important than being right.

Since our primitive-mind's job is to keep us safe, and since negative-feelings are intended to be protective mechanisms to warn us that our safety or our comfort might be in jeopardy; our mind often reacts quickly to the negativity in order to get away from the perceived danger, so that we will remain safe. By minimizing negativity, our primitive-mind thinks it is minimizing danger; and therefore, our primitive-mind thinks it is keeping us safe. Since getting away from danger minimizes negative-feelings; therefore, minimizing danger by reacting quickly to negativity makes us feel better. Although during the primitive-times such instinctive and nonconscious actions were necessary for survival; in the modern-era, where continuous fight-or-flight requiring instinctive thinking and behavior is not as necessary, treating any and all negative-feelings as threatening or dangerous becomes counter-productive. This is why, emotional-thinking, which is intended to make us feel good without resolving the root cause of the problem, is so prevalent in the modern-times; hence why, emotional-thinking is another one of Theory of Self-Relativity's 10-Enemies of Self-Improvement.

Self-deception occurs when we hold thoughts and beliefs that are comforting but not necessarily factual.

II.
Emotional-Thinking & Placebo-Thinking

When feelings instead of "facts" drive our thoughts and actions, we end up engaging in *"Emotional-Thinking."*

Theory of Self-Relativity defines "emotional-thinking" as "thinking based on how we want to feel."

Although all feelings that we feel are valid, not all feelings have rational value. As discussed, our intangible-feelings or our emotions are always caused by an underlying-thought, and if the thought that is causing our feeling is not factual or rational, our resulting feeling will also be irrational. Emotional-thoughts form as a result of how we want to feel; and not as a result of how we should feel.

Emotional-thinking is a form of thinking which is intended to make us feel good without resolving the root cause of the problem.

According to Theory of Self-Relativity, all feelings, no matter what we feel and no matter how we describe them, can be categorized under two major binary categories:

1. **Positive-Feelings:** For example, happiness, pleasure, satisfaction; etc.
2. **Negative-Feelings:** For example, unhappiness, sadness, depression, loneliness, fear, anger, jealousy, heartbreak, pain, suffering, worry, anxiety; etc.

Feeling positive is what we strive for; however, it is negative-feelings which are undesirable & troubling.

As discussed, our mind is negativity defaulted because negativity is intended to be protective. This is why, our mind does not care if we are happy; all it cares about is if we are safe. As further discussed, since feelings are symptoms of a cause, negative-feelings are intended to indicate that there is a problem that we must attend to; therefore, negative-feelings are symptoms of underlying problems, threats, and even danger. We feel negative because negativity is dislikable, hence, nature has programmed us to feel negative in the presence of problems, threats, and dangers, so that we would take corrective action in order to resolve the problem, or to eliminate the threat or the danger; and in-turn, to eliminate our negative-feeling. When we resolve or eliminate the cause of the negative-feeling, the negative-feeling, itself, automatically disappears; which means, we are safer, therefore, we feel better.

Although there are differing opinions as to the ratio of negative-feelings to positive-feelings, human-beings experience many times more negative-feelings than positive ones. The *"Negative-Differentiation-Principle,"* which is a part of the *"Negativity-Bias,"* has shown that conceptualization of negativity is more complex than that of positivity. Negative-differentiation also indicates that there are more terms and definitions associated with negative-feelings than there are with positive feelings; therefore, there are more ways for us to feel negative, than to feel positive. And as discussed, the primary reason we have more ways of feeling negative than positive is because negative-feelings are intended to be protective; thus, safety-first.

The following list of our common emotions compiled by Theory of Self-Relativity demonstrates this imbalance between the ratio of negative-feelings versus positive-feelings.

List of Emotions

Sad	Bad	Fear	Anger	Pain	Happy
Bored	Indifferent	Hesitant	Frustrated	Confused	Content
Abandoned	Embarrassed	Worried	Disrespected	Irritated	Fulfilled
Isolated	Ashamed	Cautious	Bitter	Disappointed	Relieved
Distant	Guilty	Anxious	Critical	Deprived	Relaxed
Withdrawn	Regretful	Uncertain	Disgusted	Betrayed	Peaceful
Lonely	Inadequate	Nervous	Dismissive	Weak	Comfortable
Victimized	Insignificant	Insecure	Defensive	Powerless	Confident
Fragile	Tired	Shocked	Offended	Pressured	Trusting
Despair	Fragile	Frightened	Jealous	Shocked	Loving
Remorseful	Rejected	Scared	Judgmental	Overwhelmed	Joyful
Hopeless	Inferior	Horrified	Hate	Hurt	Elated
Grief	Worthless	Helpless	Rage	Stressed	Ecstatic
Depressed	Empty	Vulnerable	Hostile	Awful	Euphoric

We experience more negative-feelings than positive ones because negative-feelings exist as a protective-mechanism, whereas positive-feelings are intended to be constructive. Furthermore, negative-feelings are triggered quickly; yet, positive-feelings take time to build up. Additionally, if unresolved, negative-feelings linger on; however, for positive-feelings to last, we must put in effort to replenish or create new catalysts to keep positivity going.

Negativity-Bias, also known as the negativity-effect, is the notion that negativity affects us more than neutrality or positivity does. Even when of equal intensity, things of negative nature, such as unpleasant-thoughts, uncomfortable-emotions, or traumatic-events, have greater effects on one's psychological state than neutral or positive events do. Thus, positive things affect us less, than equally negative things do; hence, we are more affected by negative-feelings, such as sadness, than we are with positive-feelings, such as happiness. For example, the intensity and the negative effects of losing something such as money or a relationship-partner, is far greater than the positive-effects of gaining the same things. Therefore:

According to Theory of Self-Relativity, negativity is the default-state of our existence.

We do not have to put in effort to feel negative; however, to feel positive, we almost always must put in effort. To simplify, positivity requires effort and input; negativity does not. Another metaphorically popular but not-factual way to describe this relativity is to view negativity as a low-energy state, while considering positivity as a high-energy state. As described throughout Theory of Self-Relativity, to make a favorable or positive-change we must put in active-effort; however, if left alone, passive-change will almost always result in unfavorable and often negative outcomes.

A similar principle applies to negative-feelings versus positive-feelings. To feel good, we must put in active-effort; but feeling bad, does not necessarily require any effort. Although there are no high-energy or positive-energy states of mind, just as there are no low-energy or negative-energy states of mind; references to energy here is to metaphorically demonstrate the necessity for effort. The feeling of energy is simply a change in our hormonal activities that make us feel good or bad. When we feel high-energy or good-energy we are simply feeling a rush or higher levels of dopamine; we are not suddenly emanating mystical energies between our Self and others. Therefore, if we want to feel good, we must do something to increase the levels of our dopamine. This could be something quick, yet short-lasting, which will subside after the effects of the dopamine goes away; or it could be done slowly to make it last longer.

Regardless, when dopamine subsides, our positive-feelings subside as well. We cannot have a rush of dopamine continuously because reaction and mood hormones are there to make us take action. To continuously try to get a rush out of dopamine, we will burn ourselves out quickly; thus, why we get addicted, and why we need more of a dopamine producing agent to match the initial rush we experienced. This is often referred to as *"chasing the dragon."*

Since our thoughts generate our emotions, through thinking and by creating positive-thoughts and beliefs, we can also create a rush of dopamine to get a shot-in-the-arm in order to feel good. This is how emotional-thinking or positive-thinking makes us feel good temporarily, without actually making any long-term positive-changes. Therefore, when popular motivational and new-age spiritual teachings fallaciously suggest for us to think positive and positive-things will happen to us; they are deceptively getting us to experience a rush of dopamine without us actually making any positive-change. Furthermore, because the effects of dopamine subside after a while, hence why, we need another motivational quote or another feel-good belief to uplift us for further brief period of time.

As stated, according to Theory of Self-Relativity, our mind is default programmed to be negative. We are inherently and instinctively programmed to be negative because negative-feelings are defensive in nature and they are intended to protect us and to keep us safe. Our mind's primary and primitive role is to keep us safe and alive; hence why, we have so many negative-feelings as compared to positive ones. Negative-feelings are dislikable; therefore, negativity forces us to take protective or corrective action in order to stop feeling negative.

Don't blame your Self for being too negative; blame mother nature.

Since our primitive-mind does not care if we are happy, and all it cares about is if we are safe; this is why, negative-feelings onset quickly, yet they linger on. Negative-feelings not only last longer, but to reduce or eliminate negative-feelings, effort and corrective action is required. This is the essence of our fight-or-flight mechanism, which is intended to keep us safe and alive.

Therefore:

If you feel negative more often than you feel positive, and if your negativities arise faster and last longer than your positivities; you are simply a normal human being.

On the contrary, to onset positive-feelings, effort or action is almost-always required. Positive-feelings are not as instantaneously onset as negative-feelings are, because positive-feelings generally require intent and action. It is this intent and the need for action which causes their delayed onset. For example, even when we laughed joyfully in a comedy club, we had to plan and intend on going to the comedy club in order to experience that laughter. However, an accident on the way to the comedy club, which could prevent us from going and enjoying the comedy, would not need to be planned or intended. Such negative event as the accident could and would dominate our effort and action to experience positivity. Since negativity is a default-state-of-existence, we are surrounded more by negativity than we are with positivity; hence, we have more ways of feeling negative than positive. Consequently, since negativity is the default-state of our existence, and as further discussed, since negativity is the default-state of The-Universe; negativity will happen without effort or action, however, to have neutrality or positivity, we must have intent and we must put in effort and action.

When left alone, there are more ways for things to go wrong than for things to go right.

Negative-feelings can come on at any time and they can even override our positive-feelings; however, in order for positive-feelings to emerge and remain, we must have no lingering negative-feelings.

Positivity is contingent on the absence of negativity.

As demonstrated throughout Theory of Self-Relativity, to experience positivity and happiness, we must first minimize and control negativity. Unlike negative-feelings which are dominant and can replace positive-feelings instantaneously; positive-feelings are dependent on the non-existence or absence of negative-feelings. We can begin to feel negative even if we were experiencing something positive; however, in order for us to feel longer-lasting positivity, we must first eliminate or resolve our negativities. This is why, positive-thinking or other peptalking motivational states of mind do not and could not have lasting positive-effects, unless active-effort is placed to make positive-change.

Since in the presence of negativity, lasting positivity or happiness will not be possible; therefore, in order to experience more frequencies of positivity and happiness, we must first resolve and eliminate the causes of our negative-feelings.

Negative-Feelings	Positive-Feelings
• Default-Based	• Effort-Based
• Protective	• Constructive
• Safety	• Pleasure
• Dominant	• Dependent & Contingent
• Outnumber Positive-Feelings	• Outnumbered by Negative-Feelings
• More-Intense	• Less-Intense
• Triggered Quickly	• Slower Onset
• Linger On	• Terminate Quickly
• Onset requires no Intent or Effort	• Onset requires Intent and Effort
• Termination Requires Effort	• Termination Requires No Effort

Since creating positivity takes intent, action, and time; therefore, impulsive thinking and behavior rarely leads to positive results. However, our need to feel less negativity and to feel more positivity is so strong that we concoct feel-good thoughts at the snap of a moment in order to release some dopamine so that we can feel better temporarily. It is this feelings-based emotional-thinking which is the root cause of self-deception; because human-beings, by nature, are dopamine junkies, hence why, dopamine is also known as the "feel-good" or "happy" juice.

As discussed, all feelings are symptoms of an underlying cause; therefore, Theory of Self-Relativity categorizes the causes of our feelings binarily:

1. **Tangible-Feelings:** Theory of Self-Relativity describes tangible-feelings as those feelings which are triggered by a tangible cause. For example, a tooth-ache, a tickle, a hug, etc. Tangible-feelings are commonly associated with a physical cause, and they are generally experienced through our five senses.

2. **Intangible-Feelings:** Theory of Self-Relativity describes intangible-feelings as those feelings which are triggered by an intangible cause. For example, jealousy, sadness, happiness, etc. Intangible-feelings include our emotions, and they are _always_ associated with the same immaterial-cause.

This immaterial-cause of our intangible-feelings or our emotions is always a "thought."

Although tangible-feelings could have different causes, identifying the cause of a tangible-feeling is usually easier than identifying the causal-thought of an emotion or an intangible-feeling. For example, it is easier to identify which part of our body is hurting and why we are experiencing that pain, than it is to identify why we are sad or unhappy. When our tooth hurts, the toothache is a symptom of an underlying problem. The toothache is "pain," which is a protective negative-feeling that is making us realize that there is something wrong with our tooth. This negative-feeling is a symptom of an underlying cause which is coming from our tooth. This negative-feeling of pain forces us to pay attention so that we can do something to our tooth, in order to resolve or to eliminate the cause of our pain.

Negativity is intended to force us into corrective action.

Pain and negative-feelings force us to take action to correct something that is wrong; hence why, disease, threats, and dangers are associated with negative-feelings. The reason symptoms needing correction feel negative is because negative-feelings are dislikable and nature wants us to feel negative so that we would be forced to do something to resolve the disease, the threat, or the danger. If our diseased tooth did not hurt, we would not do anything about it. For example, if instead of pain we felt a tickle or a giggle, we would not make an attempt to get our tooth checked out. However, because our toothache causes us uncomfortable-pain, the dislikable-feeling of pain forces us to take action in order to resolve or eliminate the cause of that pain; so that in-turn, our unpleasant negative-feeling of pain would go away.

Nature has programmed us to feel negativity, so that in order to get rid of our negativity, we are forced to resolve or eliminate the cause of the negativity.

Therefore, the negative-feeling of pain was a symptom of an underlying cause which forced us to find the cause, and to either resolve the cause by getting our tooth fixed, or to eliminate the cause by getting our tooth pulled. Regardless of the action that we took; the diseased tooth was addressed; hence, our negative-feeling of pain was resolved or eliminated. By resolving or by eliminating the cause of our pain; our negative-feeling of pain consequently disappeared.

Be it tangible or intangible, negative and positive feelings are there for a reason; and the reason for our feelings is that they are messengers that force us into action. When we feel negative, we are getting a message that something needs to be fixed, corrected, changed, or eliminated; which means, we need to take action. If we don't take corrective-action, the negativity will continue. Negative-feelings give us the message that there is something wrong that needs to be fixed; while positive-feelings give us an incentive to do something. This is why, happiness, unlike negativity, is almost always reached as a result of a reward for an effort. As stated:

Negativity is intended to be protective while positivity is intended to be constructive.

Since a feeling is the symptom of an underlying cause, a symptom cannot exist without a cause; which means, a feeling cannot exist without a cause. Since a feeling cannot exist without an underlaying cause; therefore, our emotions cannot exist on their own and without their underlying causal-thoughts. Since emotions are always reliant on their underlying causal-thoughts; therefore, our emotions will also change or disappear accordingly if their underlying causal-thoughts are resolved or eliminated. Although to resolve or eliminate a feeling we must take action so that we can resolve or eliminate the cause of the feeling; the problem with our negative-emotions arises when we take impulsive action based on how we are feeling, rather than what the feeling is representing.

When we feel a negative-emotion, we often want to do something to get rid of that negativity quickly; instead of looking to fix the cause of that feeling so that the feeling will truly go away and not return. We often do things that cover-up the negativity of the feeling, rather than doing something that resolves or eliminates the cause of the negative-feeling. We do so because we are more focused on avoiding pain, feeling good, or at the minimum, feeling less-bad; with whatever quick-fixes we can deploy to minimize negativity. Instead of looking for and fixing the cause of our negative-feeling, we often try to fix the feeling by just dealing with the feeling. Instead of fixing the cause, we often cover-up the symptom by convincing our Self that things are not as bad as we feel; or we simply try to wish the negativity away. However, just as we could not wish for our toothache to go away, we cannot wish for our negative-emotions to go away; because, unless we find, resolve, or eliminate the thought that is making us feel bad, the negativity will resurface again. Since a feeling is a symptom of an underlying cause; therefore, our emotions, which are intangible-feelings, are also caused by their own underlying causes. Although tangible-feelings could have differing causes, for example, a headache could be caused by high blood pressure or a tumor, and a toothache could be caused by a cavity or an infection; all intangible-feelings or emotions are *"always"* caused by the same universal cause.

The cause of an intangible-feeling or an emotion is always a "thought."

Since, in the toothache example, fixing or pulling our tooth caused our negative-feeling of pain to disappear; similarly, resolving or eliminating our thoughts that makes us feel, for example, sad or scared, will make those feelings improve or disappear. This is why, Theory of Self-Relativity is founded upon the principle of thought-management via factual-thinking. Since our emotions are caused by and are dependent on our thoughts; therefore:

By changing or by eliminating our thoughts, we can change or eliminate our feelings.

As discussed, we are easily in touch with our feelings; because feelings are easy to feel, identify, and access. Since feelings are easy to identify, we often react by taking action based on how we feel, which means, we try to resolve the symptom without understanding the cause. Since emotions, just like feelings are symptoms; therefore, our emotions cannot exist independently on their own, hence, our emotions cannot have their own independent identity. The identity of our emotions is reliant on the identity of their underlying thoughts; thus, the rationality of our emotions are also reliant on the rationality of their underlying thoughts.

Be it negative or positive, our emotions are directly related to and are as a result of our thoughts that are generating these feelings; therefore, to improve or eliminate an undesired emotion, we must improve or eliminate its underlying thought. To change our thought, we must look at the facts associated with that thought; therefore, we must take action based on the facts so that we can change the circumstances which are causing our thoughts. When we learn to think factually, our thoughts will then become rational and parallel with reality; thus, our feelings will be generated as a result of rationality.

Change your feelings, change your thoughts.

This is why, in order to feel balanced and content, and to have stable yet succinct emotions; we must first learn to think factually.

To feel good…you must think well.

To think factually and to generate rationality-based feelings does not mean for us to have no feelings and to become like a robot. On the contrary, when we generate our emotions based on factual-thoughts, our emotions will then be in sync with reality; because we would be generating feelings that are based on how reality is and not based on how we want reality to be. Consequently, when our feelings are in sync with reality, we will make better decisions and we will take better actions to have more favorable outcomes.

When you think factually, you're not going to feel how you want to feel; you're going to feel how you should feel.

In the analogy of the toothache, by using the symptom of the negative-feeling of pain associated with our tooth, we identified the tooth that was causing the pain; and by fixing or by pulling that tooth, we resolved and eliminated the negative-feeling of pain. By fixing the cause, we fixed the symptom; we did not take other unrelated actions to ignore, deny, or wish for the pain to go away. Likewise, we did not take endless number of pain killers to mask the pain, nor did we get drunk in order to numb the pain. We knew better, that doing anything other than getting our tooth treated or pulled would've prolonged our agony and pain. As a matter of fact, not choosing to treat or pull our tooth could've led to more serious implications such as infections and even death; because one of the leading causes of death among primitive-humans was tooth infections. Since a tooth infection could lead to death, nature has programmed us to feel pain when there is something wrong with our tooth, so that the pain forces us to take corrective-action. Elimination of the undesired feeling of pain is nature's incentive for us to act.

Therefore, our intangible-feelings and emotions should be treated similarly to our tangible-feelings. Since our emotions, just like our toothache, are also symptoms of underlying causes; we should use our negative-feelings and emotion that we feel, to identify, resolve, or eliminate their causal-thoughts, so that our negative feelings will adjust and improve accordingly.

The cause of an intangible-feeling or an emotion is always a "thought."

This is the basis of Theory of Self-Relativity's Cognitive-Cognition-Technique. The Cognitive-Cognition-Technique teaches us how to identify our causal-thoughts via awareness of how we feel; and how to resolve or eliminate those thoughts by taking action so that we can feel better and we can experience better outcomes. What we feel is valid, and in case of negative-feelings and emotions, they are truly undesired, uncomfortable, and sometimes even, painful. As discussed, our feelings and emotions, as irrational or as nonfactual as they may be, are always valid; but being valid because we feel them, does not mean they have rational value.

There is a big difference between validity and value of an emotion.

According to Theory of Self-Relativity, validity of an emotion means a person is feeling that emotion, but the value of that emotion is whether the emotion is generated as a direct result of a factual-thought or as a result of a faulty or nonfactual-thought. If the underlying thought that generates the feeling is factual and as a direct result of how reality is, then that feeling is not only valid, but it is also valuable; which means, it is based on rationality. However, if the underlying thought that is generating the feeling is nonfactual or as a result of a previous emotion; then that thought does not have value, which means it is irrational. When our thoughts are rational, then our emotions will be based on rationality, hence, our decisions and actions will be based on how reality is; therefore, our outcomes will be more favorable.

According to Theory of Self-Relativity, majority of our thoughts are unnecessary, as they are nonfactual, irrational, ruminating, repetitive, cluttering, or useless. Therefore, by recognizing the feelings that these thoughts are producing, we can objectively evaluate these underlying thoughts and we can accordingly choose to take action or abstain from taking an action. Since majority of our thoughts are unnecessary thoughts, majority of our actions in response to our thoughts are also unnecessary; therefore, until we learn to think factually, our behavior for negative-feelings should more often be inaction rather than action that is intended to quickly and impulsively mask the emotion. This is why, in the modern-times, as long as we are not dealing with a fight-or-flight situation; it is commonly recommended to pause and evaluate before reacting to a negative-emotion.

Sometimes, the best thing to do, is to do nothing.

This means, when we realize that majority of our thoughts are nonfactual and unnecessary; instead of trying to resolve these thoughts, we would choose to eliminate or dismiss the bulk of our negative-thoughts. By dismissing our thoughts, hence by not having to think of these cluttering and repetitive nonfactual-thoughts again; we will subsequently eliminate or not generate the feelings that these thoughts were producing. It is important to note that dismissing or eliminating our thoughts does not mean, denying, ignoring, or deflecting them; because those are defense-mechanisms implemented by individuals who want to avoid the truth. Dismissing or eliminating our thoughts means to discard and eliminate those thoughts after evaluation for their nonfactuality.

Additionally, as we learn to dismiss and eliminate these cluttering or repetitive nonfactual-thoughts, we will also learn to not allow those thoughts to return because we now "know" that we already eliminated those thoughts based on critical-thinking and factual-reasoning. After we have eliminated our unnecessary and nonfactual-thoughts; we will then be left with fewer thoughts which are factual and applicable to our existence. By recognizing the applicability and value of the remaining thoughts, we will then take action or inaction as the facts associated with those thoughts indicate and require.

It is estimated that we have between 60 to 70 thousand thoughts per day. By filtering out the noise, the disorder, and the nonfactuality of our thoughts; we can subsequently calm down our mental-clutter and we will be able to more objectively address only those thoughts that matter. As described in modern-mindfulness, by using our feelings to become mindful of our thoughts, and by evaluating our thoughts thoughtfully to become aware of their factuality; we can clear out clutter, and in-turn, we will open up ample processing and storage space in our mind. When we clear out clutter, we will then become a more focused and more efficient thinker; thus, we will not be controlled by our emotions, instead, we will be in control of our emotions.

Don't be controlled by your emotions; take control of your emotions by thinking factually.

Being able to be in touch with ours and other people's emotions is referred to as having *"Emotional-Intelligence."* Emotional-intelligence is commonly defined as the capacity to be aware of, control, and express our emotions, and to use this emotional-awareness to handle interpersonal-relationships. However, just being in touch with our emotions or being empathetic to other-people's emotions is not going to resolve our difficult emotions.

Theory of Self-Relativity defines "emotional-intelligence" as "one's ability to be aware of and to understand one's own and others' emotions, and consequently, their thoughts."

Generally, emotional-intelligence helps people get in touch with theirs and with other-people's feelings; however, since Theory of Self-Relativity is focused on the Self, it also takes specific interest in *"Personal-Emotional-Intelligence."*

Theory of Self-Relativity defines "personal-emotional-intelligence" as "putting factual-thoughts behind one's own feelings."

Most motivational, self-improvement, and psychology teachings do state the importance of our mental and emotional awareness; however, majority of them fail to show us how to use that awareness to move past our problematic thoughts and negative-feelings. This is why, Theory of Self-Relativity insists that being only mindful is not simply enough. Mindfulness without thoughtfulness, which enables us to understand the thoughts that are causing our troubling emotions, is like knowing that a train is approaching yet we simply watch the oncoming train without taking any action to get out of its way. Hencey why, emotional-intelligence, especially personal-emotional-intelligence, is actually an oxymoron; because emotions are not intelligent, and as a matter of fact, emotions are irrational. To increase our emotional-intelligence and to make our emotions rational, we must use facts to put rationality into the thoughts that cause our emotions. This is why, Theory of Self-Relativity considers emotional-intelligence through mindfulness and thoughtfulness to be one of the requirements for its Cognitive-Cognition-Technique; as thoughts and feelings are inseparably connected and relative to each other.

When we address the thought behind a feeling; the feeling itself will change, improve, or disappear.

This is why, factual-thinking is the only way to self-improve, because when we allow for factual-thoughts to generate our feelings, our feelings and emotions become aligned with reality; and instead of our feelings guiding our thoughts, our thoughts create our feelings.

Making sure that our feelings are caused by factual-thoughts requires awareness, understanding and practice. Likewise, recognizing what is factual is a skill that we would need to develop. As stated throughout Theory of Self-Relativity, the "factual" truth is often inconvenient, dislikeable, and sometimes, even painful; because facts associated with a dislikable-truth that requires corrective-action, make us feel-bad, or they make us feel not as good as we would like to feel. It is this nonconscious desire to feel good which is causing us to lie to our Self by avoiding, by denying, or by ignoring the facts. Since we, as human-beings, are intelligent yet emotional; our mind can manipulate us to use faulty-logic and flawed-reasoning to convince our Self that we are thinking factually. Emotional-thinking or emotional-reasoning can actually make us avoid, deny, or ignore facts; and it can even make us fabricate fallacies as facts, in order to make us feel better quickly.

Theory of Self-Relativity defines "emotional-thinking" as "thinking based on how we want to feel."

Emotional-thinking causes us to use faulty-logic and flawed-reasoning to fool our Self to "believe" that we are being factual. This is why, any uncertainty such as a "belief" can be a dangerous mindset.

A belief is not knowledge, and to believe is not to know.

Emotional-thinking and placebo-thinking are the main causes of our bad decisions, because when we make decisions based on what we believe to be true or based on what feels good to us; we are not doing so based on how reality is, we are doing so based on how we want reality to be. Therefore:

Decisions must be based on best evidence; not based on what one feels, likes, or believes.

To create certainty, we should not just "believe;" we must "know." Many, incorrectly think or assume that because a thought, an opinion, or an idea is convincing or because it feels good to them; therefore, that thought, opinion, or idea must be true. Many are not aware that a feel-good thought or comforting-belief is often, at best, a belief and not factually proven knowledge; therefore, it is integral that we distinguish between beliefs and knowledge.

When you believe, you assume that you know, but you don't know that you know.

In order to feel good, we often want to find a reason to justify how we feel. Even though we might "believe," or we might even "think" that our reason or logic can justify how we are feeling; we regularly fail to recognize that what we believe or think to be sound reason is actually a fallacy we fabricated because it makes us feel better. What we might "believe" to be logical, rational, and based on sound reason; could very well be fallacious and fabricated by our own mind. We should not "believe" in our reason and logic; we must "know" that our reasoning, rationality, and logic is not only real but it is factually-supported. Being convinced of our belief is not the same as knowing that our mindset is factually supported.

The only way that we can know of the validity of our reason, logic, and rationality, is for us to verify them with facts. This is why, Theory of Self-Relativity is not content with reason, logic, and rationality alone; unless they are factual-reasoning, factual-logic, and factual-rationality. Facts and evidence are the only means of "knowing" that something is "truly" real.

Theory of Self-Relativity defines "factual-logic" as "thinking, reasoning, and processing based on facts and evidence."

As discussed throughout Theory of Self-Relativity, we often try to fit facts to our feelings, instead of fitting our feelings to facts. The reason we try to fit facts to our feelings is because we are trying to create falsehoods and fallacies, in order to support and rationalize our feelings; or simply stated, we are engaging in self-deception so that we can get some dopamine boost and feel better. Facing facts is often an emotionally difficult task because facts that require change and improvement are generally uncomfortable to deal with. This is why, *the biggest lies we hear are the lies we tell our Self;* because by creating fallacious-thoughts, we try to fit these thoughts to our feelings. Theory of Self-Relativity has termed this fitting of thoughts to feelings, instead of generating feelings based on factual-thoughts, as *"Placebo-Thinking."*

Theory of Self-Relativity defines "Placebo-Thinking" as "thoughts that we concoct regardless of their factuality in order to support our desired feelings."

According to Theory of Self-Relativity, placebo-thinking is a form of emotional-thinking or emotional-reasoning, because placebo-thinking convolutes the separation of thought from feelings. Simply stated:

Placebo-thinking is "to think based on how we want to feel."

Since human-beings are more feelings-aware than thoughts-aware, we frequently act and make decisions based on our feelings rather than based on our thinking; therefore, we clash with reality. Thinking emotionally rather than thinking factually is like trying to fit the square-peg of feelings into the round-hole of facts; it simply will not work.

Placebo-thinking is fitting facts to feelings.

Placebo-thinking is thinking based on feelings, instead of feeling based on thinking.

Emotional-thinking creates a false-realty based on how we want reality to be; however, it is factual-thinking that makes us see reality the way it actually is. If our actions are based on emotional-thinking, this might make us feel good temporarily; but factual-reality will eventually catch up with our false-reality and it will disrupt our life. Emotional-thinking cannot overpower factual-thinking because sooner or later facts and evidence will clash with our emotions. Facts don't care if we like what they represent or how they make us feel; facts represent how things are, not how we want them to be. Emotional-thinking cannot replace critical and factual-thinking; it will never work, and if we try to force it, it will eventually break. Since emotional-thinking creates false or alternate realities, emotional-thinking is one of the main causes of self-deception. Emotional-thinking causes us to be out of sync with factual-reality.

If it conflicts with what I want to be true, therefore it is not true!

Factual-Thinking	Emotional-Thinking
• Fact-Based	• Feeling-Based
• Cognitive	• Emotional
• How things are	• How one wants things to be
• Factual-Reality	• Alternate-Reality
• Rational	• Irrational
• Fits Feelings to Facts	• Fits Facts to Feelings

To minimize self-deception and emotional-thinking, we must learn to seek facts and evidence, and we must learn to think factually.

We must always fit feelings to facts; not facts to feelings.

- Facts will not adapt to our feelings; we must adapt our feelings to facts.
- Facts don't have to be compatible with our feelings; our feelings must be compatible with facts.
- In order for our feelings to be compatible with facts; our thoughts must be factual.
- Facts don't care if our feelings don't like the facts.
- Facts exist because of the laws-of-physics and the way nature is.
- Facts, reality, and The-Universe don't exist because of our existence.
- We exist because of the existence of facts, reality, and The-Universe.
- We must adapt to factual-reality.

If we want to live happily and with less friction with reality, we must learn to adapt our feelings to facts, and not to try to deceptively convince and justify to our Self that facts can adapt to our feelings. Feelings are not self-sustainable without thoughts, and although feelings are real and what we feel is valid; this does not mean what we feel has factual-value. For our feelings to connect us to reality, our feelings must be generated as a result of rationality and supported by factual-thinking; because, although a feeling is valid:

The value of a feeling is only as good as the value of its underlying thought.

This means, we must abstain from placebo-thinking; which is rationalization through the creation of comforting-thoughts in order to support our desired-feelings.

The-Universe creates facts, and everyone and everything else must abide by the laws of The-Universe that represent these facts; therefore, to adapt to the realities of The-Universe, we must adapt to how The-Universe works. We must adapt our thinking to how factual-reality is so that our feelings can be generated as a result of factual-reality. Our feelings must become compatible with reality based on how reality is; not based on how we would like reality to be. Imagine if people were truly able to change facts to match their feelings; The-Universe would have been unstable, and nothing would exist. Because nature would have to continuously change itself to adapt to different people's feelings and preferences.

The-Universe is as is, and it will never adapt to us; we must adapt to The-Universe.

For example, in a sports match, all members and fans of one team want their team to win over the other team. For either team to win, they must prepare and improve, in order to become better than the other team; that is how The-Universe rewards a winner. The winner will not emerge based on which team's members and fans wished and prayed harder and longer for their team to win. The winning team is usually the one that was able to best adapt and perform with the realities of the game. Thus, The-Universe will not adapt to the stronger feelings of the players and the fans; The-Universe will reward the team that adapted the best to The-Universe.

The-Universe rewards those who adapt to factual-reality.

Since nature operates based on the laws-of-physics, if we want to live a harmonious, content, fulfilled, and a happy life, we must learn to adapt to nature; and to not expect The-Universe to deliver us our wants, desires, and needs. Once we become aware of facts and as we begin to think factually; our feelings will automatically adapt to our factual-thinking, and in-turn, factual-thinking will harmonize us with factual-reality. When we get in sync with factual-reality, our fact-based generated feelings will then lead us to take proper action that best fits reality the way reality is, and not based on how we want reality to be. To be in touch with factual-reality, our fact-based generated feelings will guide us to consistently go through active-change to adapt and to improve. When our feelings are generated by underlying factual-thoughts, instead of wishing for miracles to improve our life; our feelings will continuously guide us to take control by actively changing and improving our circumstances and our existence.

To remain in harmony with The-Universe, we must remain unbiased and adaptable.

Furthermore, we must also become aware and learn that what we think or believe to be rational, reason-based, or logical; might not be "factual." We must use factual-thinking as a system of checks and balances to make sure that we are not trying to avoid painful reality through avoidance, ignorance, or denial of facts. Factual-thinking will also eliminate our tendency for fabricating fallacious thoughts and beliefs that are intended to make us abstain from facing dislikeable factual-reality. It is because of our mind's tendency to reason, logic, and believe fallaciously, that we must learn to think factually. Such logical-fallacies are often associated with placebo-thinking, which through rationalization tries to change and influence our thoughts so that we could feel better.

According to Theory of Self-Relativity:

Only humans rationalize via logical-fallacies; because it takes intelligence to manipulate reality.

As stated throughout Theory of Self-Relativity, only one form of a fact exists per situation. Facts do not lie and facts are not open to interpretation; therefore, facts are not open to manipulation. We must ensure what we believe to be a fact; is actually a fact. The only way to do this is for us to "know" and not just believe what we consider as fact, is actually a fact. Because beliefs, as described in detail in later sections; are highly intertwined with feelings.

True factual-thinking is fitting feelings to facts; not fitting facts to feelings.

By truly thinking factually, we will then see reality as is and we will avoid fooling our Self from seeing reality as we want it to be. Placebo-thinking, which is the fabrication of comforting-thoughts through rationalization and creation of false-realities, is as a result of nonfactual-thinking. Since thoughts could be nonfactual, unreal, or perceived; such corrupted value of our thoughts makes it even more difficult to address our emotions. By becoming aware of our feelings and by understanding the factuality of our thoughts behind our feelings, we can then adjust or eliminate our feelings by resolving or by dismissing our thoughts. Once we learn to address the thought behind a feeling; the feeling itself will change, improve, or disappear.

Factual-thinking frees us from the grasp of uncertainty and the fear of the unknown.

When we learn to think factually, we will not need to react to our feelings in order to feel good, or to feel less-bad. We will just need to recognize the thought behind our feeling, hence, resolve or eliminate that thought, and the correct feeling will emerge; or the incorrect feeling will improve or disappear. By evaluating our thoughts and by only allowing factual-thoughts to remain; instead of rationalizing by engaging in logical-fallacies or in emotional-reasoning and placebo-thinking, we will then generate feelings which are as a result of factual-thinking. Such pure feelings will then lead us to make sound decisions, take constructive actions, and create positive-change.

As discussed, since majority of our thoughts are nonfactual, repetitive, and cluttering; by eliminating nonfactual and cluttering thoughts and by only keeping thoughts that are based on facts that actually apply to us, we can subsequently eliminate the majority of our negative and uncomfortable feelings. This, in-turn, minimizes impulsivity and the need to do something quickly in order for us to feel good, or at the minimum, for us to feel less-bad, at that moment. By eliminating unnecessary thoughts, we will then take action only on the remaining thoughts that are factual; because there will be no need to take action on thoughts which we eliminated. By eliminating cluttering and nonfactual thoughts, we will need to act less frequently; but when we act, our actions will be based on factuality.

Factual-thinking also allows us to base our logic, reasoning, and rationality on facts and not on perceptions or assumptions. Although assumptions, perceptions, and predictions are necessary initial mindsets to seek and find facts and evidence; without facts and evidence, our logic, reasoning, and rationality could be flawed.

As discussed, we are generally driven by our feelings more than we are driven by our thoughts; especially in the short-term and in on-the-go situations. Many of our emotions are the core reason for our unhappiness, our inability to improve, and our failure to live the most fulfilled life possible. Our feelings and emotions are also the main problem for self-improvement because we are consciously, non-consciously, and constantly driven by our desire to avoid uncomfortable-feelings so that we can feel better. We will often think of anything and we will do anything to quickly feel good, or at the minimum, to quickly feel less-bad at that moment. We are not only constantly trying to minimize negativity and increase positivity, but we want to do so as quickly as possible. However, when we seek comfort via fallacious-thinking, even if we succeed to achieve instant-gratification in the short-term; since the underlying negative cause was not addressed, the temporary comfort fades away and our negativity resurfaces again.

Our desire and quest for gratification, especially instant-gratification, is our mental Achilles-heel.

In other words:

Our need to feel good versus the necessity to think well, is a core factor that inhibits change and blocks self-improvement.

This intangible weakness of our existence is what creates the path that our life's journey takes. We want to continuously feel good quickly, despite the fact that the default state of nature, and our default state-of-existence is negativity. As discussed, there are more adjectives that describe negative-feelings than there are ways to describe positivity and happiness. Additionally, there are more ways that things could go wrong on their own and very few ways that things will go right without active-input or intentional action. This is why, positive-thinking or any other form of thought that is intended to quickly improve how we feel without correcting the underlying cause of why we feel bad, rarely yields positive results.

The main reason we do things that we do and we have difficulty transforming for the better is because instead of making long-term changes, we try to avoid discomfort and pain through immediate-gratification. We sacrifice long-term change for short-term gratification; and we often do so without consideration for the longer-term consequences of our emotional actions.

We often think things and we do things not because they are good for us, but because we want to feel good.

133

Just as our thoughts are reliant on brain-processes, so are our five senses. To properly experience the most positive and the least negative tangible or intangible feelings, we must learn to implement thought-management. Our feelings can be so overpowering on our mind that we can confuse or even corrupt the value of facts that are causing our feelings. Because of the *"Recency-Bias,"* as human-beings, our most recent emotions tend to feel stronger than our previously experienced identical emotions. How many times have we:

- Felt or said that we've never felt anything like this before?
- Believed that we've never seen anything like this before?
- Admitted that this is the best we've felt about something or someone in a long time?

These extreme feelings could very well be equal or even weaker than the same identical feelings we felt before; however, because these feelings are happening real-time or because they happened recently, the memory or the effect of these feelings feel much stronger than those that happened before. The main reason for this is because:

We remember things with our feelings, and we remember people based on how they made us feel.

If we compare the factual-value of the events which caused these recent feelings, with similar feelings from the past; we will then realize which event was more significant and which associated feeling was actually stronger. For example, when we broke up with our first romantic-relationship partner, we were truly heartbroken, because that was the first time that we felt the discomfort and the pain of breaking up. However, the sadness and pain of our most recent breakup seems to have made our first breakup pale in comparison. Yet, should we factually evaluate and compare the facts and the circumstances of both breakups, we would realize that during the first breakup, we probably had less resources and less experience to know that our breakup would pass and that we would fall in love again. But no matter how painful our recent breakup was, when we evaluate the situation and its associated negative-thoughts factually, we would have enough knowledge and experience to know that this too shall pass; because we went through it before, and we have also seen others go through it. In this example, by factually evaluating the thoughts behind our recent feeling of breakup; we were able to prevent the impulsive need to call our ex back, or to rebound onto someone else, or the need to find short-term unstable gratification by taking other distracting measures.

Although memories are cognitive, we remember and recall memories with our feelings, rather than with our thoughts.

We remember certain moments, people, and events with our emotions rather than with our thoughts; hence, the memories that we recall easily are those that have emotions associated with them, and those that we don't remember or that we forget, are the ones that we did not assign emotions to them. We assign emotions to a memory because we give it importance, yet, those that we do not think are as important, we do not assign emotions to them. The reason we retrieve memories with emotions faster is because emotions make them seem more important; therefore, we recall memories of things, places, and people with our feelings.

We remember people by how they made us feel, and people remember us by how we made them feel.

Likewise, we do not forget things because they are out of our memory; we forget them because those memories got filed away without much emotional-attachment. When memories get filed away without emotions, this means those memories did not have as much significance; therefore, access to that information is not as easily available as it is with memories that we assigned emotions to them. Although we might not remember certain memories, those memories are still there; but because they are filed away deeper without any emotional significance, they are not easily accessed. However, if someone or something else reminds us of that memory, we then begin to remember it. Even though we might not remember a memory, we can still use the memory to go through our actions. For example, when running on a sidewalk that we usually run on, we avoid certain uneven areas that might twist our ankle; and we do so without consciously remembering why we avoid and go around those spots.

This is why, unless we have recognized and mastered awareness and understanding of how our feelings are generated and how they interact with our thoughts; we will have difficulty taking "the best" action. As discussed in the "absolute-order" section, we commonly feel and then take action, and we often take such action to improve the feeling that caused us to take the action. After we experience a negative-feeling, in order to minimize negativity and to try to increase positivity, we often have the urge to take action immediately because we just want to feel better quickly. How many times have we heard or uttered the phrase:

I just want to be happy!

We do so because we are fallaciously conditioned to believe that we will reach long-lasting, if not eternal-happiness, at some point in our life. What we fail to recognize is that unlike negativity, lasting positivity, and especially lasting happiness, is not sustainable.

Eternal-happiness is like an elusive dragon that we chase; but one that does not exist.

Because, in trying to achieve lasting and sustainable happiness, instead of changing from the inside, we often look for other-things or other-people to make us happy. We falsely believe that, for example, making more money, attaining more material goods, or popularity, are the secrets to happiness. Yet, even the rich, the famous, and the popular people become unhappy, sad, and sometimes even suicidal, when the external effects of their happiness fades away.

Money, power, fame, and popularity might rent a person sporadic periods of happiness; however, neither can buy anyone eternal-happiness.

Longer lasting and more frequent happiness could only be achieved via internal self-improvement, not via external sources. The more we try to reach external-based happiness, the harder the withdrawal from those happy and euphoric levels becomes, because those levels are unsupported by an internal-foundation. And the next time we try to reach similar levels of happiness, a larger dose of the same catalyst is needed in order to achieve a smaller percentage of the previous level of happiness that we experienced.

Trying to achieve happiness externally and without self-improvement, is no different than an addict who is trying to get a temporary high by using addictive substances. Without a solid internal-base, larger doses of external-stimuli are needed to reach an even smaller level of happiness than the previous one; let alone, that the newly reached happiness will fade-away even quicker than the previous one. Happiness, just like positive-feelings, requires intent, effort, and input. Although emotionally we strive to achieve happiness; by the inherent nature of our mind's safety orientation, we are default-programmed to focus on the negativities, instead of easily achieving happiness.

Babies, toddlers, and animals demonstrate these effects clearly. When hungry, babies cry, toddlers get cranky, and dogs go to a corner with their tale tucked in. Sadness and negativity are protective-mechanisms that force us to do something to stay alive and safe. Negativity forces us to fight-or-flight in lieu of danger, and negativity in the case of hunger, forces us to eat in order to intake energy; because if we don't eat, we will starve and die. When babies, toddlers and dogs are fed, babies stop crying, toddlers wiggle from side-to-side, and dogs wag their tale. For babies and dogs to get hungry and sad no effort is needed; however, for a human or a dog to survive, they must put in intentional-effort to find food or to hunt for food.

Happiness or positivity requires intent, effort, and action; unhappiness or negativity requires none.

Despite the fact that being fed creates contentment, temporary satisfaction, and even happiness; the effects of contentment and happiness subside when the person or the animal begins to feel hungry again. Thus, if food is not readily available for subsequent consumption, the negative-feelings associated with hunger will begin to resurface again. One will stay in this state of negativity indefinitely and the feelings of negativity will continue to increase in intensity; until and unless the catalyst of contentment and positivity, in this case food, is found and consumed. Therefore, according to Theory of Self-Relativity, negativity or unhappiness are states-of-existence; however, positivity or happiness are not states-of-existence, they are states-of-experience.

Negativity is a state-of-existence; however, positivity is a state-of-experience.

The key to reaching more frequent and longer lasting happiness is to minimize, control, and eliminate the negativities; however, the reason reaching happiness has been difficult is because most people want to jump from negativity straight to happiness, without first reducing and eliminating the underlying causes of their negativities. If we jump from negativity to happiness without minimizing negativity first, we will relapse back to negativity even harder because we have not raised our fallback level. Furthermore, once negativity is minimized and controlled, and before we attempt to experience happiness; we must first reach the *"Contentment-Zone."*

The contentment-zone, or zone of contentment, is a neutral area that buffers positivity from negativity. Positivity, and even happiness, could be achieved easier if we learn to live in the contentment-zone and to not allow our Self to fall back into the negativity-zone. Although contentment is commonly defined as a mild form of happiness which is based on satisfaction of one's state-of-existence; Theory of Self-Relativity views contentment as a much narrower "dependent" state-of-existence which is not characterized as having mild positivities, but it is a state which is characterized as having minimal to no negativities.

Theory of Self-Relativity defines "contentment" as "a satisfactory state of neutral existence which is reached and maintained by minimization of negativities."

According to Theory of Self-Relativity, contentment is the most important state-of-existence; because contentment is the zone of balance, equilibrium, and neutrality.

The goal of any self-improvement should be for us to change enough to get out of the negativity-zone and get into the contentment-zone; and to continue changing, in order to remain in the contentment-zone, or to fall back into the contentment-zone from higher positivity and happiness experiences. Once we learn to keep our Self in the contentment-zone, we will then be able to reach positivity, and even happiness, more easily and more frequently. Contentment is integral to maintaining happiness, and this too, requires intent, active-effort, and active-change; if not, we will begin to be pulled back down from the contentment-zone into the lower levels of underlying negativities.

Contentment does not mean indifference or a lack of motivation; contentment means to be in a neutral state of equilibrium and harmony from which reaching positivity and happiness becomes easier and more achievable. Contentment, in the absence of lingering negativities, also provides a higher level of fallback when the effects of positivity and happiness begin to fade away.

As discussed, positivity and happiness are states-of-experience; and unlike negativity, they are not states-of-existence. Since positivity and happiness are states-of-experience, this is why, the effects of positivity and happiness fade away after a while. Living in the contentment-zone minimizes our withdrawals from positivity and happiness by cushioning our decent from the experiential states of positivity and happiness. The contentment-zone minimizes extreme emotional gyrations of going from happiness quickly into negativity, unhappiness, and even sadness; thereby, contentment creates a base-level state of neutral existence.

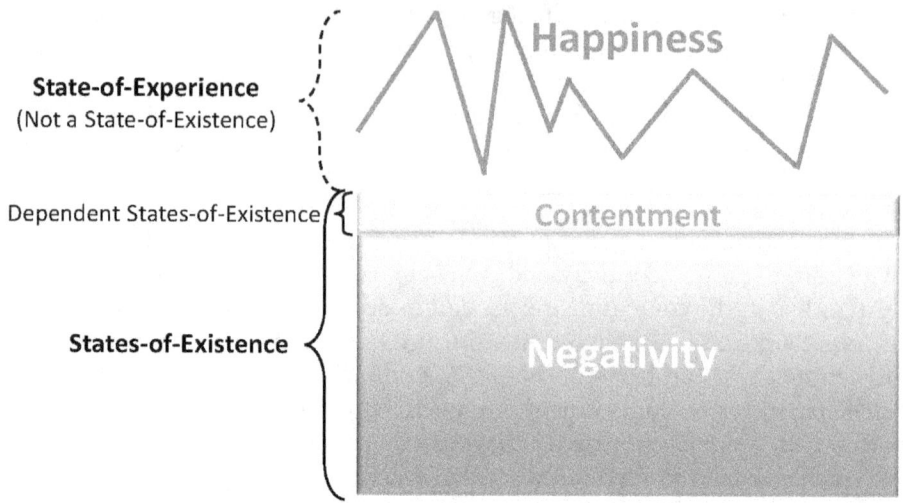

State-of-Experience
(Not a State-of-Existence)

Happiness

Dependent States-of-Existence

Contentment

States-of-Existence

Negativity

Phrases such as *"In pursuit of happiness"* are actually unachievable oxymorons because happiness cannot be achieved unless negativity is first minimized and controlled; therefore, the correct and realistic phrase for reaching happiness must be:

In pursuit of less-negativity.

To become happier, we must first address negativity, which is the default-program of our mind's operating system. Negativity is like a computer's registry, and it cannot be modified or deleted; because negativity is a protective-mechanism which is intended to keep us safe. It is for this reason that our primitive-mind does not care if we are happy, all it cares about is if we are safe; and the way that it attempts to create safety, is by it detecting less-negativity.

The mind feels safer when it detects less negativity, or when it feels less negative.

Since there are more ways for things to go wrong than to go right; the human mind, naturally and instinctively, likes being in an "effort-minimizing state" in order to stay safe. Less-effort means less-variables and less-uncertainty; hence, less chance of something going wrong. Our mind will allow us to enjoy positivity and happiness, only after it feels safe that our negativities are under control, minimized, or eliminated. This is why, Theory of Self-Relativity persists that:

True-happiness is contingent to the non-existence of underlying negativities.

As a survival instinct, our mind tends to focus on resolving negativity rather than reaching for positivity; because we are safer to avoid something bad rather than in trying to achieve something good. Once our mind feels safe that something bad won't happen, it can then allow us to reach for positivity and even happiness. This is why negativity requires no effort, but positivity requires effort; thus, positivity is contingent on the non-existence of negativity.

Consequently, positivity does not last, hence, positivity or happiness requires maintenance; because our primitive-mind's innate default setting always tries to revert back to the state of negativity or protectiveness in order to keep us safe. Once we understand and accept that negativity is intended to keep us safe and this is the main personal-reason why experiencing positivity and happiness cannot be achieved without intent, effort, and action; we can then begin to take matters in our own hands in order to minimize and eliminate negativities, so that we can remain in the contentment-zone.

Therefore:

- *Negativity is a "state" of default existence.*
- *Contentment is a "state" of dependent existence.*
- *Positivity is a "state" of experience.*
- *Happiness is a "form" of reward.*

To abstain from sinking into a negative state, we must learn to change continuously in order to adapt to and be in sync with the constantly changing Universe; therefore, to make positive-change, we must put in active-effort. Active-effort does not mean an exhausting and never relaxing life. Active-effort means to implement favorable "change" as an ongoing and integral part of our existence. This is why, changing a negativity requires effort, because, as discussed in subsequent sections, without effort, things will become more disorderly and more negative. Since change occurs constantly, passive-change is often unfavorable for our existence; hence why we must put in effort to change things in our favor. Furthermore, once we make favorable change, we must continue putting in effort to maintain the positive-changes achieved. This is why, change is an integral constant to self-improvement and for living a fulfilled and happy life.

	Negativity	Contentment	Positivity	Happiness
Format	(Default) State of Existence	(Dependent) State of Existence	(Dependent) State of Experience	(Reward-Based) Form of Experience
Stability	Stable	Semi-Stable	Variable	Unstable
Duration	Long-Term	Mid-Term	Short-Term	Sporadic
Shape	Linear	Wave	Curvy	Spikes
Input	No-Effort	Effort-Based	Effort-Based	Effort-Based
Maintenance	No-Maintenance	Some-Maintenance	Maintenance	High-Maintenance

As represented in the previous diagram created by Theory of Self-Relativity, positivity and happiness are less-stable and more fragile. In order for positivity and happiness to exist, they are contingent on lack of negativity and on a stable level of contentment. Happiness, which is what everyone desires to achieve and experience, is not "a state-of-existence;" it is an unstable "form" of sporadic reward "experience." To achieve and to sustain positivity, and especially to experience happiness, effort is required; and to prolong positivity and happiness, maintenance is necessary. Therefore, to reach positivity and to experience happiness, change, especially positive and active-change is required. On the other hand, negativity is our "default" state-of-existence; hence, in order for negativity to take control, no-effort is required. Negativity self-sustains and requires no-effort because it is our default protective set-back state-of-existence.

Negativity is a state-of-existence; however, positivity and happiness are states-of-experience.

Likewise, unhappiness, which includes sadness, depression, and other deeply negative feelings, is much easier to fall back into than experiencing happiness; because unhappiness is imbedded deeply in the area of negativity. Thus, prolonged negativity could result in lingering feelings of unhappiness, sadness, and depression. Since the severity of unhappiness could vary, hence, unhappiness is wavy in nature; and this variable waviness of unhappiness always remains in the negativity-zone. It is because of this variable nature of unhappiness, that sadness and depression can have manic or depressive gyrations.

When dealing with our feelings and emotions, the continuous battle is how to minimize and eliminate negative-feelings, while achieving and maintaining positive-feelings. And since, there are more ways to be negative than to be positive; therefore, there are more ways to be unhappy than to be happy. To minimize stress and anxiety, and to reach more repeatable positivity and happiness, we need to minimize the swings between positivity and negativity, in order to stabilize the sporadic nature of happiness. By elevating and by maintaining our general mental and emotional state into the contentment-zone, the extremes of our swings will be minimized and controlled, while the continuity and predictability of our positivity and happiness will be more frequently achievable.

According to Theory of Self-Relativity, in order to reach equilibrium between negativity and positivity, we need to Implement many-times more active-effort to induce positive-change, for every negative occurrence. Hence why, it is so much harder to achieve positivity or happiness; and it is even more difficult to maintain them once achieved. Negativity usually occurs when we have less-control and less-certainty about something. Until lack of control and uncertainty are minimized, negativity cannot be minimized or eliminated. Lack of control and uncertainty, in-turn, create unpredictability, anxiety, and feelings of susceptibility. This is why, negativity sets-in effortlessly and pulls-down like gravity; however, positivity, like a rocketship, requires active-effort and energy in order to escape the gravitational pull of negativity. Theory of Self-Relativity refers to this metaphoric pulling down effect of negativity as *"Negativity-Gravity."*

Statements such as "you pull me down," or "that sinking feeling," are analogies that have been around in defining the perceived heavy-weight and downward pull of negativity. This pull of negativity, just like the pull of gravity, does not require any effort; however, positivity or happiness, just like the rocketship trying to escape the gravitational-pull of a planet, requires effort. Hence, another perspective as to why, many, feel and relapse into negative-emotions much easier than they do with positive ones. Even our physical gestures represent the weight and pull of negativity and the effort needed to represent positivity. When we are sad, we don't have to put in any effort for our eyes, cheeks, and mouth to droop down; gravity simply takes care of it. But to smile and be happy, we have to actually put in effort and burn energy so that we can create a smile, by engaging and by lifting up our facial muscles. This is best represented in arts and theatre by the "comedy and tragedy masks."

Most people are not necessarily negative or pessimistic; there is a big difference between *"Natural-Negativity"* versus being pessimistic or negative as a whole. It is important to distinguish that natural-negativity is not the same as negativity-bias, which represents that when of equal intensity, we feel the effects of negativity more than those of positivity.

Theory of Self-Relativity defines "natural-negativity" as "the negativities that we feel and experience as a result of our default negative mindset."

By understanding that negativity is our default-state-of-mind, and for us to feel negative does not necessarily mean that there is something wrong with us, or that we are pessimistic; we can then appreciate the fact that to begin to feel more positive, we must first minimize negativity. Minimization of negativity, in order to experience more positivity and happiness, is why we need to actively and constantly "change" so that we can live a better and happier life. Negativities that we feel and try to prevent are normal, because as discussed, these negativities and uncertainties that we constantly experience are as a result of the inherent default-system of our primitive-mind trying to keep us safe.

For many of us, our life's purpose, goals, and mission is to feel good and to feel happy. We are constantly battling to float within positivity and happiness against the constant gravitational pull of inherently primitive and protective negativity. Although nature has made negativity the default-state of our existence; nature has also given us reward mechanisms to entice us into survival and progress. To survive, continue, and to move forward, nature has programmed us to actively strive for rewards that will distance us from our core of negativity and unhappiness, and would move us towards the direction of positivity and happiness. True positivity and happiness are rewards that need to be actively achieved; therefore, they also need to actively be maintained. This is why, eating, sleeping, and reproduction are human traits associated with the reward of positivity and happiness. However, unlike negativity, which could be constantly present, positivity and happiness are sporadic experiences associated with the good feeling of a reward or accomplishment.

If eating or sex did not feel good, we would eat less, reproduce less, and potentially endanger our own survival and the survival of our species. The positive effects of the inherent reward associated with these human attributes are so strong that not having food to eat, not having shelter to sleep in, and not being able to have sex to reproduce, makes us feel unhappy, sad, and even depressed. It is this inherent dislike of negativity and the reward of positivity that keeps us advancing and succeeding as a species. Nature has programmed staleness and lack of change with negativity, while it has programmed progress and improvement with positivity and reward. Despite the fact that nature has programmed us with negativity in order to stay safe; nature has also programmed us with the rewards of positivity and happiness so that we can have additional incentives of getting away from negativity. This is why, for example, failure does not feel good; but success or positive outcomes feel great. As discussed:

The primitive-mind minimizes negativity via prevention; the intelligent-mind minimizes negativity via progress.

Although negativity is supposed to be protective; sustained negativity can be destructive and detrimental. Contrary to the passive protective default-state of human existence, the emotional goal of human existence is all about attaining positivity and happiness, while avoiding negativity and unhappiness. Yet, to achieve and maintain these parallel emotional states, active-effort is necessary. This is why, less-negativity, contentment, and happiness require effort; yet, the only state that requires no-effort is our default-state of negativity. While everyone is in pursuit of eternal-happiness; getting to contentment and happiness requires awareness, understanding, and management of our thoughts. This means, we must put in constant effort, and we must continuously attempt to make positive-change based on proper thinking, in order to experience more frequencies of happiness.

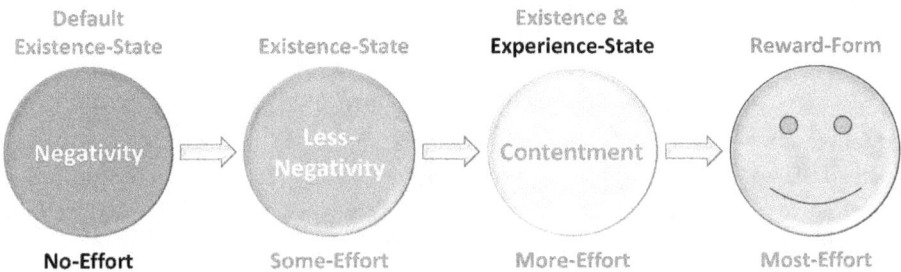

As stated, happiness is unsustainable spikes of reward that fade out. The key to becoming happy more frequently is to stay out of the negativity-zone and to remain in the contentment-zone. Contentment, just like negativity, could be a state-of-existence; the difference is negativity is a state of default-existence, but contentment is a state of dependent effort-based existence. Once we learn to *"Self-Regulate"* by bringing our negativities under control; we can then try to become content and get on the path to more frequent experiences of happiness.

Theory of Self-Relativity defines "self-regulation" as "one's ability to manage, regulate, and control one's thoughts, in order to experience better emotions and more favorable outcomes."

The goal and path to happiness is to make our default throwback become the zone of contentment, so that we require less-effort to reach more frequent experiences of happiness. This is why, contentment is an integral state of self-regulation. Minimizing-negativity, maintaining-contentment, and increasing positivity and happiness requires awareness, understanding, and implementation of change via factual-thinking. By learning to change and improve, we can escape the gravitational pull of negativity and we can float through life with less effort. Since most methods of controlling negativity with the hope of achieving positivity are generally very labor, thought, and behavior-modification intensive; by learning to think factually, we can learn to achieve happiness and positivity more frequently and more consistently, with less effort; as factual-thinking becomes the intuitive mindset of our existence.

To change the quality of our life; we must change the quality of our thoughts.

Since our behavior is as a result of our feelings, and our feelings are as a result of our thoughts; by learning to think factually and by resolving and by eliminating the causes of our negativities, we can put our Self on the path of longer lasting positivity and more frequent experiences of happiness. Self-regulation is further discussed in subsequent sections.

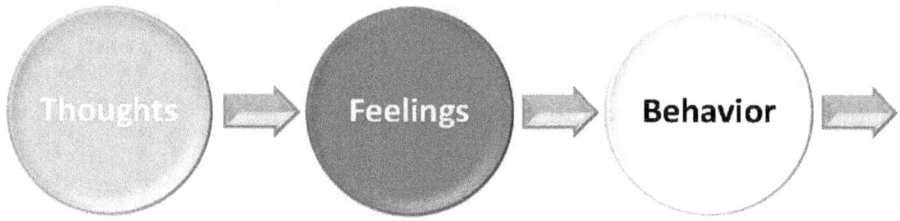

Since most people want to avoid pain, to feel good, or at the minimum, they strive to feel less-bad; commonly, instead of understanding why they feel negative and instead of changing the causes of their negativities, they try to convince themselves that they are not negative. In other words, they try to see things the way they want them to be rather than to see things the way they really are. A common baseless analogy which represents many people's inclination to justify and convince themselves that they are not negative is by claiming that they are a "glass half-full" type of person." People rarely claim that they are a "glass half-empty" person because that would insinuate a negative and unpopular mindset.

Instead of convincing our Self through unactionable words that we are a "glass half-full" type of person, or that "things will work themselves out;" we must learn to change our thinking so that the constructive actions that we take will truly begin to make us feel less-negative, and in-turn, allow us to experience more positivity. While most people focus on whether the level of water in the glass is half-empty or half-full; factual thinking enables us to objectively evaluate the level of the water and to take proper action to reach a definitive and favorable result.

Factual-thinking enables us to recognize that the glass is not half-full or half-empty, but the glass is only filled halfway. By recognizing that the glass is half-filled, we can take action and put in effort to change, by emptying the current

144

water into a smaller glass, to have a full glass of water; or we can add water into the current glass to make the larger glass truly full. When we have a full glass of water, we would not need to debate whether the glass is half-full or half-empty. Although emptying the water into a smaller glass will not give us more water; however, our sense of fullness or positivity will be accomplished. Likewise, by putting in effort and filling the glass with more water; we will not only have a full glass, but we will also have more water. Therefore, instead of trying to make our Self feel good with placebo-thinking; when we take action and make a change, we truly transform reality to the way that we want reality to be.

As discussed, because negativity is our mental default-state; the natural tendency of our mind is to go back to negativity. This is why, negativity requires no effort; however, to reach and maintain less-negativity, contentment, or positivity, requires constant effort. To truly achieve and maintain positivity, we must learn to change in a two step-approach. First, we must minimize the cause and then we must maintain the result achieved. We must first minimize and eliminate negativity, which is the cause of why we cannot reach positivity; then, we can increase positivity, by maintaining contentment and by building on it.

To analogize differently, consider negativity is like body-odor. Body-odor is caused by bacteria breaking down sweat. Our body-odor increases if we do not make an effort to bathe in order to remove the causal-bacteria. The bacteria will keep on multiplying and causing more odor, unless we first bathe to remove the body-odor causing bacteria. Bathing kills and removes the odor causing bacteria. Bathing is an effort-based action that we undertake in order to minimize negativity; we don't take the easy way out of not bathing by spraying perfume on our dirty body. If we don't bathe, which means if we do not take action to eliminate negativity; we will just keep covering up our body-odor with perfume. If we cover-up odor and not remove the odor causing bacteria; the stink will keep on rising up, because the underlying cause still exists. However, if we really want our body-odor to be minimized and controlled, we must first bathe with soap and water in order to remove the smell causing bacteria; and once we have removed the cause, we can then apply perfumes in order to smell good. Additionally, as the days go on, we continue bathing in order to maintain the minimized bacterial level we achieved; we don't just bathe once and stop. Once we maintain the bacterial level at a minimum, we are then able to truly achieve fresh smelling body, more frequently, and with longer lasting effects.

Constant bathing is an effort-based continuous "change" that we undergo routinely in order to:

1. Remove the negative (in this case bacteria) and to achieve less negativity or neutrality.
2. Maintain the neutrality by bathing regularly.
3. Achieve positivity (in this case smelling-good) by using a perfume.

We don't avoid bathing by taking the easy path of continuously trying to cover-up our body-odor with perfumes; because we know that the stink of body-odor or negativity will rise to the surface no matter how much perfume or positivity we use to cover up the negativity.

Reaching emotional-positivity and personal-happiness is no different. We must first undergo an effort-based action of change to minimize or eliminate negativities; and then, we must continue the effort to reach positivity and happiness. If instead of taking action to make a change, we continue peptalking our Self into feel-good beliefs, comforting-hope, or baseless positive-thinking; all we will be doing is covering up the stench of negativity with positive-thinking perfumes. Trying to feel positive in the short-term without taking corrective action is no different than covering up our body-odor with perfumes, without taking shower.

The stink of negativity cannot be covered-up; it will eventually rise up to the surface.

Furthermore, once we have taken action to remove the negativity, we must continue our efforts to maintain the contentment and neutrality that we achieved; because if we don't maintain it, the negativity, just like our body-odor, will return. Therefore, once we learn to change, it is easier to continue to change in order to maintain and improve the results achieved. Additionally, just as the good smell of the perfume goes away after a while, so does the positivity that we have achieved. This is why, positivity not only requires the constant control and maintenance of its underlying negativity, but it also requires constant effort in order to maintain the positive results achieved. Furthermore, when dealing with nature:

When left alone, there are more ways for things to go wrong than for them to go right.

This is how nature operates, because negativity and disorder are the default-state of The-Universe and they are continuously increasing in nature. This fact of increasing disorder, also known as the *"Law of Entropy,"* is discussed in detail throughout subsequent sections of Theory of Self-Relativity. In summary, when left alone, personal-negativity increases because of:

1. **Primitive-Mind**: because our personal mindset is defaulted to detect negativity.
2. **Entropy:** Because The-Universe is continuously increasing in disorder.

Since this section focuses on the "personal" aspect of why we are prone to negativity; in order to achieve positivity and to experience happiness, we must learn to:

1. Minimize and eliminate negativity.
2. Achieve and maintain less-negativity.
3. Achieve and maintain contentment.
4. Create more stable positivity.

While this sounds like an arduous task, it actually is not. A streamlined and easy to repeat system of awareness and understanding, which could only be achieved via factual-thinking, will enable us to minimize negativity and help us increase the frequencies of positivity and happiness. Hence why, we should think of our negativities as our *"Mental-Odor."* Minimizing and eliminating body-odor is best achieved and maintained via *"rinse and repeat;"* therefore, we should do the same with our mental-odor.

Factual-thinking is the mental-soap that cleanses mental-odor.

Since our body-odor cannot be cured because it is as a result of our natural bacterial-flora and our existence; hence, as long as we are alive, the bacteria that cause our body-odor will always be present, as they repopulate, even after bathing. Since these bacteria are a natural part of our existence; therefore, we cannot cure body-odor, we can only treat and maintain it, and we do so by making bathing a normal part of our daily routines.

We should have a similar approach to self-improvement and to dealing with negativities. Self-improvement is a repetitive-process which can become streamlined as a routine part of our daily existence. Instead of covering-up our negative-thoughts and feelings through perfumes of lies and deceptions; we should resolve or eliminate them so that we can experience longer-lasting positivity and happiness. To achieve lasting and stable happiness, we must first minimize and control our underlying negativities. Without minimizing, resolving, and controlling negativities; we would simply be covering up the stench of our negative-feelings with perfumes of positive-thinking.

Factual-thinking is the bathing process that cleanses the "stink" of our negative-emotions.

Factual-thinking enables us to incorporate constant and continuous improvements into our everyday life, and it helps maintain the results achieved. Instead of covering up the stink of negativity via perfumes of lies and self-deception; we resolve and eliminate negativities via the cleansing power of factual-thinking.

Bathe your thoughts; don't cover them up.

Since feelings are created and guided by thoughts; therefore, in order for us to "feel good" we must first "think well." Trying to feel good by focusing on external things and other-people only covers-up our negativities. To truly feel good, we must look inside our own Self and we must change from within. This can only be achieved by us becoming aware of our thoughts and by understanding the thoughts that are creating our feelings. Hence, without a proper thinking-system, we will not be able to reach sustainable happiness. To attain proper thinking, we must learn to evaluate, understand, and change the real facts which are causing our thoughts; regardless of how uncomfortable or painful these facts may be.

To "feel good" you must "think well;" and to "think well" you must "think factually."

Although actions follow feelings; the goal of Theory of Self-Relativity is to make us use our feelings to get in touch with their underlying thoughts, before we take action. While this sounds like a difficult and slow process, and it could even appear as if it is being suggested for us to become a robotic thought-machine; it is not so. Through proper awareness and understanding, we will be able to quickly and cleverly evaluate the factual-value of our thoughts that generate our feelings. We will learn to either accept or dismiss our thoughts, which in-turn, will consequently regulate our feelings and our subsequent actions.

To regulate your feelings; you must first regulate your thoughts.

As described, according to Theory of Self-Relativity, emotional-intelligence is our ability to identify our own emotions and those of others; and to use that information to identify our thinking and to guide our behavior. Theory of Self-Relativity's Cognitive-Cognition-Technique guides our behavior by using our emotions so that we can identify their causal-thoughts. The Cognitive-Cognition-Technique teaches us to identify our thoughts by identifying our feelings. By identifying, modifying, resolving, or eliminating our thoughts based on their factuality; we subsequently modify, improve, or eliminate our feelings, and in-turn, we improve our behavior.

Factual-thinking unclutters your mind and purifies your feelings.

Factual-thinking allows us to feel better through changing our thoughts, rather than by changing our feelings. We must learn to change our feelings by first changing our thoughts, and not to change our thoughts based on how we want to feel. Resolving, accepting, or dismissing our thoughts based on facts and evidence will automatically create our proper feelings. Rational-thoughts lead to rationality-based feelings, which in-turn, lead to rational-decisions so that we can behave rationally.

Feelings run your life; factual-thinking guides your life.

By using our feelings to become aware of our thoughts, instead of allowing our feelings to influence our thoughts; our thoughts will generate our proper feelings. Factual-thinking will prevent our feelings from manipulating our thoughts.

Put a factual-thought behind how you feel.

Since feelings are irrational, our underlying factual-thoughts are the only way to support our feelings rationally. Properly and factually addressed thoughts will lead us to having pure and genuine feelings which are based on how reality is, and not based on how we want reality to be. In-turn, our rationally supported feelings will lead us to taking sound and rational actions.

To feel good; you must think well.

As discussed, one of the first steps to minimizing and eliminating self-deception is to have introspective ability. Introspection or self-inspection allows us to self-reflect by identifying our nonconscious desire to avoid uncomfortable-facts. For example, if we have gained weight, we can either acknowledge the fact that our clothes have gotten tight on us because of having gained weight; or we can deceive our Self by justifying that we are bloated, hence why, the clothing is tight. We can further choose to use a scale to see the evidence that we have gained weight; or we can ignore, avoid, or deny the fact that we have gained weight by avoiding the scale. Additionally, we can self-deceive and convince our Self that we will begin dieting and working out next week or we will do so as a New Year's resolution; in an attempt to avoid and delay the dislike and discomfort of having to make a change now.

Avoiding negative-feelings is the main reason we self-deceive and we can't self-improve.

Facing facts is often an undesired and an unpleasant task because the factual-truth can be dislikable and even painful; thus, facing facts makes us feel negative, or at the minimum, it makes us feel less than good. To minimize self-deception, we must think factually by learning to seek, evaluate, and act based on facts and evidence, and not based on our emotions. As difficult as it is to experience negative-feelings, negative-feelings exist as a protective-mechanism. As discussed throughout Theory of Self-Relativity, a feeling is a symptom of an underlying cause, and the underlying cause of an intangible-feeling or an emotion is always a thought; therefore, our feelings are symptoms of our thoughts. Additionally, our feelings and emotions are more accessible to us than are our thoughts; hence why, our nonconscious and immediate inclination to feel better is to want to alter reality based on how we feel. Because of this ease of access to our feelings, we tend to react quickly and impulsively based on what we feel, rather than to act based on what we should be thinking.

Since our intangible-feelings are caused by their underlying thoughts, every emotion that we have is caused by a thought. Additionally, our emotions, although valid and real, are actually irrational, because they do not have a mind of their own; therefore, the only way to rationalize our feelings, is to address, change, and rationalize their underlying causal-thoughts. Since feelings are caused and supported by their underlying thoughts, feelings cannot exist on their own. Although what we feel is real and valid, this does not mean our feelings have factual-value; therefore, if our thoughts are flawed, our feelings will also be flawed. In order for us to generate feelings that match reality, we must first address and change our thoughts.

To regulate your feelings; you must first regulate your thoughts.

Hence, to generate the correct feelings, we must learn to think correctly. Correct thinking can only come from evidence-based and factual-thinking. Unfortunately, facts and the truth are often inconvenient, dislikeable, and even painful. As discussed, to minimize this pain, we often engage in self-deception by allowing our feelings to create false-thoughts so that we can feel better. However, to reason properly and to think effectively, we must always look for facts. We cannot create new facts to fit our feelings; we must learn to fit our feelings to existing facts. The way to fit our feelings to facts is to think factually.

Since our feelings are always caused by our thoughts; when we learn to think factually, our feelings will adjust accordingly and automatically. Therefore, to truly feel good, we must change the circumstances which are causing us to have undesirable and uncomfortable thoughts. This means, we need to change, resolve, or eliminate the causes of our difficult and undesired thoughts. The only way to change our thoughts is to put in active-effort to make a positive-change with the circumstances that are causing our thoughts. When we improve our circumstances, the facts that are affecting our thoughts will become more favorable; therefore, we will consequently feel better.

Lying, is the epitome of defense-mechanisms which is intended to ignore the truth, or is intended to change reality in order to make us avoid uncomfortable feelings and to feel better. Since factual-reality can only be changed or influenced with proper action, and since actions are as a result of thoughts; unless we think properly and we follow our thinking with proper action to make a change, we will not be able to avoid the truth forever. As human-beings, we are often not deeply cognizant of the causes of our feelings. Instead of changing, resolving, or eliminating the cause, we often do things to quickly avoid pain, to feel better, or at the minimum, to feel less-bad at that moment. As discussed, Theory of Self-Relativity defines this form of rationalization through emotional-thinking as "placebo-thinking."

Placebo-thinking is "thinking based on how we want to feel."

Our innate desire for feeling less-negative and for wanting to feel positive is so powerful that it makes us lie to our own Self, by concocting comforting-thoughts in order to justify our feelings, so that we can feel better at that moment. For example, rather than taking a difficult action to make a change, we instead pray or wish for a miracle to fix the situation. By praying, we make our Self feel better through self-deception that the situation will get better because we have faith. Although believing in false-hope, having empty-faith, and thinking fantastical and improbable thoughts will not lead to an actual positive outcome; we engage in such activities just so that we can feel good at that moment and so that we can avoid facing the difficult reality. It is this need for short-term, instant, and immediate gratification that is one of the primary causes of our inability to change, improve, and transform.

The need to feel good versus the necessity to think well, is one of the main causes of our inability to change and improve.

To truly transform, we need to take action, and to take action, we must create motivation; however, motivation alone does not lead to action if the motivation is intended to just make us feel good. Empty-peptalk and chest-pounding motivational thoughts and speeches are worthless unless they are followed by effort and action to make the change. Getting motivated is easy; but motivation fades away if it is not followed by action to make a change. To stop lying to our Self and to begin facing the dislikeable-reality, we must learn to accept reality as reality is, rather than to try to ignore facts by concocting comforting-falsities. To truly transform, progress, and feel better, we must learn to see facts as they are, rather than as we would like them to be. Once we learn to always seek evidence, especially facts regarding every thought and belief that we have, we can then learn to only retain thoughts that are based on real facts. Factual-thinking prevents us from fooling our Self and it forces us to learn to tackle problems immediately, effectively, and with long-lasting results.

Factual-thinking is the system of checks and balances for the mind.

Furthermore, the desire to lie in order to make reality less painful is why people lie to others. By lying to others, liars try to present a better than true image of themselves or of reality to others. Most liars know that they are lying; however, they often bury this knowledge by ignoring the facts of what they are lying about. For those who have not self-transformed, in order to present a better than truth reality; it is easier to lie than it is to put in effort to change reality to their favor. It is easier to lie to temporarily feel good than it is to put in effort to change the circumstances associated with the need to lie. Although lying to others will eventually fail by the exposure of the truth; such lies temporarily comfort the liar. Liars are generally good at deceiving people, because liars tell people what people want to hear.

Liars do unto others as they often do unto their own Self.

Similarly, self-lying will also fail eventually. Self-liars feel good temporarily by justifying and by convincing themselves of the lie they're thinking; but in the long-run, they will pay the price for not taking action to change the circumstances of the lie.

To minimize self-lies and self-deceptions, or to minimize being lied to by others, we must learn to change and improve our Self by taking action to change. Taking action causes change, and proper action based on factual-thinking causes positive-change. However, proper action takes time to produce proper results, because change takes time. Change and transformation are not events; lying and deception to misrepresent the truth are events. True change, improvement, and transformation is a process, not an event; and the sooner we learn to commit to change by considering the facts and the evidence, the sooner we will make the change.

Change and improvement are not events; they are lifetime processes.

Facing facts is often an emotionally difficult task because facts that require change are often uncomfortable to deal with. People lie because they want to avoid pain, they want to feel good, or at the minimum, they want to feel less-bad. People also lie to themselves or to others because if they considered the factual-truth, the truth would not be as favorably representative of how they want things to be. People lie because avoiding the truth, or denying the truth temporarily, makes them feel better. To stop lying, we must recognize and evaluate the factual but often dislikable truth, and we must put in the effort to change the dislikable truth to a more likable one. When a person's dislikable truth is changed to a likable truth; the person referencing to the truth will not be lying anymore.

151

To stop lying to our Self or to others, we must change and improve our circumstances positively.

As discussed, our feelings, especially our need to avoid feeling negative and the need to feel positive; are the main culprits that prevent us from self-improvement. If we are truly ready to self-improve, we must demand facts and evidence no matter how unpleasant or painful facts may be. This includes factual-thinking and evidence-based living with our Self and with others, so that instead of trying to feel good through self-deception, we can try to change our Self so that we can improve our circumstances.

The biggest lies we hear are the lies we tell our Self because the easiest person to fool is our Self.

Emotional-thinking, which is when our feelings affect our thoughts, prevents us from proper thinking. We undertake emotional-thinking and fallacious-reasoning because we want to feel good, or at the minimum, we want to feel less bad. In order to satisfy our comforting-feelings, our mind not only ignores dislikable-facts, or interprets facts to our liking; but more often, our mind can do the opposite, it can convince us through rationalization that something which is not factual, to actually be true, or more commonly, something that is true, to not be true.

If it conflicts with what I want to be true, therefore it must not be true.

This is why:

Our need to feel good versus the necessity to think well, is a core factor that inhibits change and blocks self-improvement.

Therefore:

Theory of Self-Relativity defines "rationalization" as "using intelligence for deceptive reasoning."

We create false and fallacious thoughts by engaging in faulty-thinking and flawed-reasoning, in order to minimize the pain of facing the dislikeable and often painful reality. This is sometimes referred to as a *"Logical-Fallacy."* A logical-fallacy is simply flawed-reasoning associated with faulty-thinking; and according to Theory of Self-Relativity, logical-fallacies are often undertaken in order to see things the way we want to see them, rather than to see them the way they are. This is why, what we think to be as logic, could be completely wrong and against factual-reality. Since logic is based on information and reason; if one's reasoning is flawed or if the information or lack thereof that the person relies on is incorrect; consequently, the logic would be flawed.

Theory of Self-Relativity defines "logic" as "the application of information and reason to reach a conclusion."

Therefore, flawed-logic is commonly associated with logical-fallacies. Logical-fallacies can also be arguments that are directed towards others, in order to get others to see things the way that the arguer wants them to see. Although logical-fallacies are commonly recognized as arguments directed towards others; according to Theory of Self-Relativity, the most damaging of logical-fallacies are the ones that we deploy against our own Self, to avoid introspection.

Theory of Self-Relativity defines "introspection" as "one's awareness, observation, and understanding, of one's own mental-processes and emotional-traits."

A fallacy is rooted in deception, and it is intended to make something appear better than it really is. A fallacy is commonly used in place of valid reasoning in order to communicate a point, with the intention to persuade. This persuasion could either be directed towards others or it can be self-directed. Logical-fallacies are commonly associated with an appeal to a justification, and they are generally associated with an interpretation rather than an objective evaluation of the facts. Fallacies appear to have logic, reason, and facts behind them; but when examined closely, the logical foundations of fallacies begin to fall apart. Although logical-fallacies could be rooted in ignorance, Theory of Self-Relativity recognizes logical-fallacies as a means for conscious but more commonly nonconscious deception. Fallacies are generally arguments and reasonings that are intended to support an already preferred conclusion; instead of using fact and reason-based arguments in order to reach a conclusion.

Logical-fallacies are intended to make sense of the nonsense.

Logical-fallacies are common in self-deception, as well as in relationships with others; and they are commonly based on emotional-reasoning rather than factual-thinking. Such fallacies are also the foundation of many ideological groups such as cults, religions, and motivational teachings; because it is easier to persuade and win over the weak and the susceptible via emotions, especially when facts would contradict what is being touted.

Theory of Self-Relativity categorizes fallacies trilaterally. *Trilateral-fallacies* are the ways that we engage in fallacies relative to our Self.

1. **Fallacy from others:** This is when others try to justify, convince, and persuade us of an intentional or unintentional flawed and faulty logic and reasoning. The objective of others using fallacy against us is commonly self-serving for them; because they are either trying to gain something from us, or they are trying to convince themselves of something by getting us to validate their flawed-reasoning.

2. **Fallacy against others:** This is when we try to justify, convince, and persuade others of our intentional or unintentional flawed and faulty logic and reasoning. The objective of us using fallacy against others is commonly self-serving for us, because we are either trying to gain something from others, or we are trying to convince our Self of something by getting others to validate our flawed-reasoning.

3. **Self-Fallacy:** This is when we try to justify, convince, or validate our own Self of our own intentional or unintentional flawed and faulty logic and reasoning. The cause of self-fallacy is generally emotional and it is commonly nonconscious. The objective of self-fallacy is also self-serving because we are trying to convince our Self of something in order for us to avoid pain, to feel good, or at the minimum, for us to feel less-bad. Although self-fallacy has a self-serving purpose behind it, the self-serving purpose of self-fallacy does not commonly result in personal-gains. The self-serving component of self-fallacies is usually for the purpose of feeling better despite contrary or non-existent supportive facts. Self-fallacies allow us to fool our own Self. As in other trilateral-relativities, self-to-self relativity, or in this case, self-fallacy is the most important form of fallacy for us to become aware of. Theory of Self-Relativity considers self-fallacy or fallacy against our own Self as the least aware, the most dangerous, yet the most important form of fallacy to recognize.

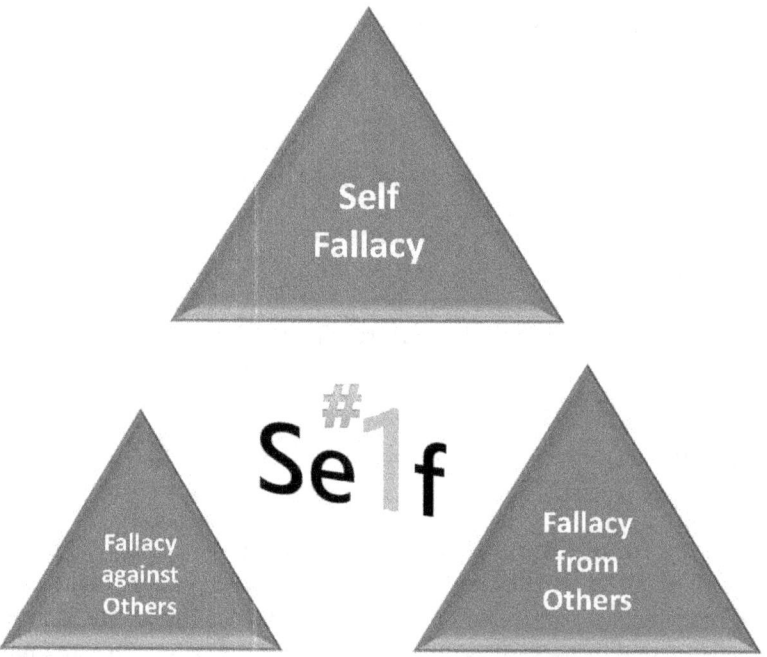

As stated, logical-fallacies are more obvious when deployed by others to persuade, confuse, or defraud us; however, logical-fallacies are more common as most people deploy them as a form of fallacious-thinking against their own Self. Logical-fallacies are a major reason for self-deception. We do this because logical-fallacies tend to make us temporarily feel good, and they enable us to abstain from facing dislikeable truths as they help us abstain from dislikable change. Although logical-fallacies are commonly arguments or justifications that a person presents to or against another person; Theory of Self-Relativity focuses on self-fallacies, which are justifications that we present to our own Self, in order to rationalize and justify our desired feelings. Some of the more common forms of logical fallacies are:

- **Appeal-to-ignorance:** An appeal-to-ignorance is a form of thinking or an argument that the logic is true because there is no evidence against it; or because the evidence is being ignored. For example, "Because I can't find a good reason for it; therefore, God did it." An appeal-to-ignorance is also common in myths, superstitions, and religions.

- **Appeal-to-tradition:** An appeal-to-tradition is adhering to false reasoning because it has always been so, although there are no facts or supportive evidence for it. For example, "It's always been done this way therefore it must be true." An appeal-to-tradition is also common in myths, superstitions, and religions.

- **Appeal-to-authority:** An appeal-to-authority is adhering to false reasoning because a real or perceived authority claimed it as true; without any reason or supportive fact. For example, "4 out of 5 dentists recommend using a particular brand of toothpaste." An appeal-to-authority is also common in myths, superstitions, and religions.

- **Appeal-to-popularity:** An appeal-to-popularity is a form of factless or incorrect reasoning because many individuals believe in it. For example, "It might be against the law to buy cigarettes under the legal age, but many teens do it, therefore it's okay." An appeal-to-popularity is also common in myths, superstitions, and religions.

- **Appeal-to-emotion:** An appeal-to-emotion is incorrect thinking that creates false reasoning, in order to feel good. For example, "Because it feels good, therefore it must be true." An appeal-to-emotion is also common in myths, superstitions, and religions.

- **Strawman-Fallacy:** This is a type of argument in which the real subject of the discussion was not addressed or refuted; and instead, it was replaced by a false one. For example, "a person asks, do you like dogs or cats better?" and the other person responds, "I like dogs more". In further response, the questioner then concludes by stating that "Oh so you hate cats!" Strawman-fallacy or strawman-argument is often used in intentionally misleading interactions and relationships such as politics, or in relationships involving high-conflict and toxic-personality individuals.

- **Ad-Hominem:** This is another form of logical-fallacy, in the form of personal-attack strategy that uses blame-shifting, deflection, rabbit-holing, and gaslighting, in order to avoid challenging or arguing the substance of the topic in discussion; and instead, it attacks the character, motive, or other attributes of the person involved in the argument. Simply stated, ad-hominem is commonly name-calling, usually in the form of a personal-attack. Similar to other fallacious arguments and personal-attacks, ad-hominem is intended to gain something from someone else or to avoid losing something to someone else via intimidation, persuasion, and by creating confusion. Ad-hominem is common in toxic-relationships such as in dealing with bullies, in dealing with jealous people, and most importantly, when interacting with insecure people. Hence, ad-hominem is prevalent in relationships with personality-disordered individuals such as narcissists and borderline-personality-disorders; where gaslighting and crazy-making are common occurrences. For example, instead of discussing why the partner in a relationship cheated; when asked, the cheater attacks the cheated by saying "stop eating when you're talking to me; can't you see how much weight you've gained!"

Personal-attacks are the only refuge of a weak-person with no answers or arguments.

Theory of Self-Relativity recognizes logical-fallacies, especially "appeals to emotions," alongside emotional-thinking, as constant nonconscious influencers of human thoughts. In order to satisfy the way that we want to feel, rather than the way that we should feel; we try to influence and justify our desired-feelings by engaging in logical-fallacies, emotional-thinking, emotional-reasoning, biased-thinking, and other forms of nonfactual-thoughts such as faith, hope, and beliefs. We additionally seek to find false-patterns, as well as purpose and meaning, in order to justify and rationalize how we want to feel. As discussed, Theory of Self-Relativity defines a combination of these practices as Placebo-Thinking.

Placebo-thinking is to allow our feelings to influence our thinking, in order for us to avoid pain, to feel good, or at the minimum, to feel less-bad.

Placebo-thinking is almost always associated with logical-fallacies; especially with "appeal-to-emotion." An appeal-to-emotion is a logical-fallacy that is intended to win an argument or to be convincing by justifying a thought through emotions and feelings, without any factual evidence. Placebo-thinking is what we engage in, in order to rationalize and fit fallacious-thoughts to our feelings; by creating a thought to support the appeal-to-emotion argument.

- **Appeal-to-Emotion:** If I feel it, therefore it must be true.
- **Placebo-thinking:** If I feel it, therefore I'm going to reason and justify that it is true.

Theory of Self-Relativity defines "Placebo-Thinking" as "thoughts that we concoct regardless of their factuality in order to support our desired feelings."

This is why, placebo-thinking and emotional-thinking often overlap with the logical-fallacy of an appeal-to-emotion. Appeal-to-emotion and placebo-thinking are also commonly deployed in times of extreme emotional discomfort and desperation, when a person really needs to avoid pain, to feel good, or at the minimum, to feel less-bad. Although feelings are valid and what we feel is real; this does not mean what we feel is based on factual-reality or it has factual-value. Feelings are not facts but we often create false-facts based on how we want to feel; therefore, we mislead ourselves that what we feel is factual. To stay with factual-reality, we must create feelings based on factual-thoughts; not creating thoughts based on how we want to feel.

Facts don't care how we feel; we should feel what facts dictate.

If we don't like how a fact makes us feel, we should change and improve the circumstances associated with the fact; and in-turn, our negative-feelings will accordingly change, improve, or disappear. Therefore, it is important to recognize that:

Our emotions are not built in our mind; they are built by our mind as we need them.

Our emotions are malleable, and they are created based on what we perceive and sense from reality. When reality is uncomfortable or unfavorable, our mind builds negative-feelings so that we can become aware of our surrounding; and in-turn, we can take corrective action in order to minimize the negativity, hence, to get away from any potential threat or danger. However, in the modern-times, since primitive-dangers are not as prevalent; instead of taking corrective action to minimize the negativity, we often engage in logical-fallacies in order to change the feeling associated with the dislikable reality. Instead of reading the message of reality that our mind is giving us, we change the message of the mind so that reality feels better.

Read the message of reality that your mind is giving you; instead of changing the message of the mind so that reality feels better.

Because:

Feelings are the message of our mind but not necessarily the message of reality.

Although logical-fallacies can seem convincing, they are unacceptable in a court-of-law or in a legal setting. Since logical-fallacies are not acceptable in a legal setting; therefore, our mind must also learn to not deploy or accept perceived and fallacious-thinking. Our mind must learn to think factually, even though facts might not be to our preference or to our liking. Factual-thinking leads to feelings that are generated by sound-thoughts; which in-turn, lead to sound-action. By seeking and by finding the facts associated with a thought, we can then base our behavior on the facts, rather than on what we like.

Facts keep our feelings in check.

Factual-thinking is the only way for us to truly be in touch with reality and to stop fooling our Self that reality is otherwise. When we think factually, we will learn to see reality as it is, rather than to see reality as we want it to be. Factual-thinking, as dislikeable or as uncomfortable as it might be in the short-term, will enable us to have a more balanced and stable future as it enables us to recognize and tackle the negativities in our lives. When we minimize negativities, we can then proceed to increase positivities in our lives.

Once we master factual-thinking, it is only then that we will be able to remove the clutter caused by our nonfactual-thoughts. By eliminating nonfactual-thoughts, which according to Theory of Self-Relativity make up the majority of what we think about, and especially what we duel upon; we will then be left with only the thoughts that have factual-value. When we remove the clutter and as we only keep our factual-thoughts, we will then realize how much more capacity and time we actually have to dedicate to our own Self as well as to others. When clutter is filtered-out and only factual thoughts remain, we will have more than enough time to address new things and to improve our Self.

Factual-thinking unclutters your mind and purifies your feelings.

Additionally, as a positive side-effect of this filtering-out of clutter; we will consequently become calmer and more balanced, because we will be able to have the self-confidence to know that we are in control of our life. Factual-thinking minimizes chaos and drama from our life; because when we think factually, we can confidently know that we are dealing with things in a factual-manner.

Factuality minimizes uncertainty.

Furthermore, through factual-thinking and elimination of cluttering thoughts, we will create so much more mental storage space that our mind would want to look for new things to learn and for new things to resolve.

Factual-thinking defragments and organizes the mind.

Consequently, our focused-mind and clear vision will also spot other-people's weaknesses and chaos. This will either give us an advantage over others, or it will make other-people realize how peaceful and comfortable it is to deal with us. People like balance and positivity, and although many do not know how to master such balance, they are always attracted to people who are capable of being balanced and controlled. While others rev their mental-engines out of control, factual-thinking will help us find our optimal and most effective performance-zone; without wasting mental-fuel and without redlining our mental-engines.

Factual-Thinking teaches us "how" to think, not "what" to think.

Because, if we allow our feelings to generate our thoughts, we will be attempting to incorrectly fit facts to our feelings, instead of fitting our feelings to facts.

Factual-thinking fits feelings to facts; not facts to feelings.

As stated, emotional-thinking or thinking based on feelings which often triggers logical-fallacies, can fool us into faulty-thinking by creating false, fallacious, and flawed thoughts and logic. To minimize the effects of feelings on our thoughts, we must learn to have our thoughts create our feelings; not for our feelings to create our thoughts. The only means of accomplishing this is for us to learn to think factually.

Factual-thoughts must generate fact-based feelings; emotions should not generate feelings-based thoughts.

When we allow our Feelings to influence our thoughts in order for us to Feel less-bad, we are allowing our Feelings to Fool us by creating False, Fallacious and

Faulty-thoughts and Flawed-reasoning. The only means of minimizing Faulty-thinking and Flawed-reasoning is to learn to become a Factual-thinker.

The "F" Words

Feelings	**F**acts
• **F**ool you	
• **F**alse-thoughts	
• **F**allacious-thoughts	**F**actual-Thinking
• **F**aulty-thoughts	
• **F**lawed-reasoning	

Although facts should be evaluated objectively; it must be noted that the subjective-experience of facts and evidence is real and personal. However, the subjective experience of facts cannot alter the objective value of the facts. While facts and evidence should be applied objectively; facts and evidence are often experienced subjectively by different people.

Facts are objective, feelings are subjective.

Therefore:

Facts can be experienced subjectively but must be dealt with objectively.

This subjective experiencing of facts and evidence is what distinguishes people's personal feelings, relationships, and their existence. Although facts are facts and they apply the same way to each and every person; it is the subjectivity of experience and interactions, alongside individual-perspective of reality which makes each person relatively different from another. Subjective-experience of facts and evidence is acceptable and personal; however, for a person to be able to properly experience facts subjectively, the person must accept the objective value of the experienced facts, regardless of how dislikable or painful such experience with facts may be.

Although facts are experienced subjectively, facts must be evaluated and applied objectively.

This is why, it is important to recognize the effects of the "F" words when dealing with "Facts" versus "Feelings." Because if instead of dealing with factual-thoughts, we deploy false-thoughts and fallacious-beliefs; we then expose ourselves to affecting our thoughts based on our feelings, rather than affecting our feelings based on our factual-thoughts.

As stated throughout Theory of Self-Relativity:

- Facts are facts…and
- Only one form of fact exists per situation…therefore,
- Facts are not open to interpretation…hence,
- Facts are not open to manipulation…however,
- Facts are open to examination…thus,
- Facts are open to replacement…furthermore,
- Although facts are experienced subjectively…nevertheless,
- Subjective experience of facts cannot alter the objective value of said facts.

Facing facts is an emotionally difficult task because facts that require change are often uncomfortable to deal with. Hence, self-deception, which is intended to make us avoid pain, to feel good, or at the minimum, to feel less-bad, is the main cause of our inability to change and to improve. Therefore, in order to minimize the effects of self-deception, we must learn to think factually.

Although our experiences are subjective, our understanding must be objective.

A person that thinks factually and receives arguments which are based on facts, data, and statistics, would be open to learning; however, dealing with those who think emotionally is like "walking on eggshells." Since what one says could hurt the emotional-thinker's feelings; hence why, emotional-reasoners are not open to evaluating new or better evidence that could falsify their comforting-thoughts and fallacious-beliefs.

To feel good…you must think well.

Because:

Although we feel things subjectively, we must learn to think objectively.

III.
Others & Externalation

Our-Universe is comprised of our "Self" and "Others." Theory of Self-Relativity commonly refers to others as "everything and everyone else" or "other-things and other-people."

Your-Universe

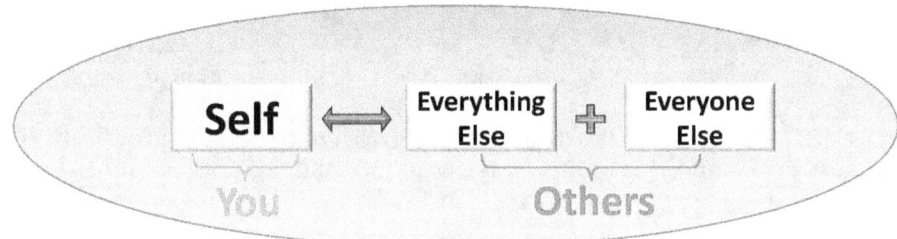

"Self-Equation"

Since we are we, and everything and everyone else is not us; by nature, and as a way of life, we can only focus on one side of our *"Self-Equation,"* at any given moment. The self-equation is a concept developed by Theory of Self-Relativity whereby our "Self" is one side of the equation and everything and everyone else is on the other side of it.

Theory of Self-Relativity defines "self-equation" as "the dynamic balance of the Self, relative to the Self, and to others."

As discussed, Theory of Self-Relativity recognizes "Self" as the "most important word ever;" and as discussed below, Theory of Self-Relativity recognizes "others" as the "most dangerous word ever." Theory of Self-Relativity defines "others" as everything and everyone that is separate from our Self; therefore, references to others often collectively includes other-people and/or other-things.

According to the self-equation, the most optimum value is when both sides of the equation are balanced and in equilibrium; because such balance places our Self in harmony with everything and everyone else. The dynamic nature of keeping our Self in balance with others is how we can keep a continuous system of checks and balances to ensure that healthy relativities exist between our Self and others. It is this dynamic nature of maintaining the equilibrium that, according to Theory of Self-Relativity, makes self-improvement a process and not an event. However, due to personal, cultural, societal, religious, and other factors; achieving and maintaining this dynamic-equilibrium is often difficult.

People, relative to their own Self or relative to others, are generally either too selfish or too selfless. When others have more weight than the Self, the balance and the focus of the self-equation shifts away from the Self; hence, the person becomes a selfless person. People-pleasers and codependents are a good example of selflessness. Conversely, when Self is the only point of focus, the equilibrium shifts towards the Self, without much consideration for others. Selfish-people and psychopaths are a good example of such unhealthy self-focus.

Selfless   **Selfish**

Although Self is the most important word for self-improvement, prioritizing our Self does not mean being selfish; just as being self-focused does not mean being self-centered.

Theory of Self-Relativity defines "Self-Focus" as "to bring focus and attention to one's Self-first, but not without consideration for, or at the expense of others."

Just as in living a centered-self life, being self-focused brings the focus onto one's self-first, before focusing onto others. The reason most people have difficulty being self-focused is because of familial, societal, and cultural upbringings and prioritization of values; as being focused onto others and concerning our Self with others is commonly praised as being good and righteous. Therefore, the Self gets ignored, as the focus and attention is directed towards pleasing, and even serving others. Conversely, focusing onto our Self is often portrayed and viewed as being selfish or even bad. However, the best way for us to develop and improve our Self and to live a life of balance with others, is for us to be in equilibrium between our Self and others. This means, we should try to reach and maintain a dynamically-balanced self-equation.

In order for us to keep our self-equation in balance, we must learn to evaluate both sides of our self-equation dynamically and on an ongoing basis. Dynamic-balance means for us to become aware of and to understand the relativities between our Self and others, so that we can objectively keep the balance between our Self and others in a healthy state. This balance must be dynamic, because reaching equilibrium between our Self and others, just like other aspects of self-improvement, is not a one-time event, it is an ongoing life-long process. This is best accomplished by learning to seamlessly, continuously, and intuitively shift the focus between our Self and others. Therefore, to be able to shift focus between the two sides of the self-equation in an objectively balanced manner, we must become aware of our thoughts and their external influencers.

According to Theory of Self-Relativity, the human mind operates most comfortably and most efficiently when it deals with individual-thoughts in a fundamental binary-format. This is why, Theory of Self-Relativity emphasizes on what it has termed as the *"Binary-Approach."* Likewise, the mind feels most comfortable when it focuses on one thing or on one side of the self-equation, rather than focusing on multiple things or on multiple thoughts simultaneously.

As discussed throughout Theory of Self-Relativity, the "Binary-Approach" does not mean to think binarily; but it means to evaluate each fundamental-thought individually, and to take action or inaction based on each individual-thought's merits, before moving onto the next thought. This is why, for example, no one can truly multitask. Multitasking is a good metaphor; however, in reality, the human mind cannot attend to more than one thought or more than one task at any given moment. What is described as multitasking is not actually thinking multiple thoughts or attending to multiple tasks simultaneously. Those who seem to be able to multitask are actually able to shift their focus dynamically and quickly between multiple thoughts and multiple tasks. Dynamic-equilibrium and dynamically-shifting between thoughts, tasks, or between both sides of the self-equation requires active-effort and action; which is also the basis for positive-change. Once we learn to initiate and continue dynamic-shifting, the effort needed for such fluidity will become more intuitive.

Effort and action are the requirements for positive-change.

The binary-approach, which is discussed in detail in subsequent sections, enables us to become aware of and to evaluate each individual-thought or each issue at its basic fundamental or micro level; rather than to approach it as a whole from the macro level. In other words, we should approach our thinking-system from the bottom-up, rather than from top-down. The binary-approach, or as also referred to as the *"Binary-Thought-Process,"* enables us to evaluate and process individual-thoughts binarily; however, this does not mean our collective thinking should be binary. The binary-approach, for any situation, including our thinking, should be applied at the fundamental level of a system or a hierarchy. For example, our thinking is a collection of our individual-thoughts and when we approach each thought individually and deal with each individual-thought in a binary format, our thinking automatically becomes the collection of our properly addressed individual-thoughts. According to Theory of Self-Relativity:

All things at their fundamental level are binary; all other variations are simply derivatives.

Although it is accepted that one must think in shades-of-gray and not engage in black and white thinking; according to Theory of Self-Relativity, the human mind cannot think in a shade-of-gray. Thinking in shades-of-gray is similar to observing and approaching from the outside-in. Just as building the whole building requires to build it one brick and one component at a time; building our thinking also requires building it one thought at a time. The analogy or metaphor that we should think in shades-of-gray is actually an oxymoron. The reason we cannot think in a shade-of-gray is because gray is not actually a color; gray is a collection of black and white pixels. Thinking in shades-of-gray is to approach our thinking from the outside-in, or from the top-down. As stated, according to Theory of Self-Relativity, we should not think from the top-down, we should think from the bottom-up; therefore, in order to achieve the right shade-of-gray-thinking, we must collect the correct number of individual black and white pixels of thoughts to form that correct shade-of-gray. When we approach each individual-thought in a metaphorical "0 and 1," or "on and off," or "black and white" format; our collective macro thinking will automatically take on the right shade-of-gray. Therefore, when we address our individual-thoughts binarily, our collective thinking becomes stronger, quicker, and cleverer.

Our thinking-system is a collection of all our individual-thoughts. Instead of thinking in a shade-of-gray, when we learn to address each individual-thought in a black or white format; our macro thinking will automatically take on the right shade-of-gray. Additionally, as we color each new individual-thought in a black or white format; our macro thinking's correct shade-of-gray will dynamically adjust to the collection of its black and white individual-thought components. Therefore, the shade-of-gray associated with our macro thinking will not be rigid, hence, it would be able to change continuously; depending on the emergence of the different number of individual black and white thoughts that we hold at any given moment.

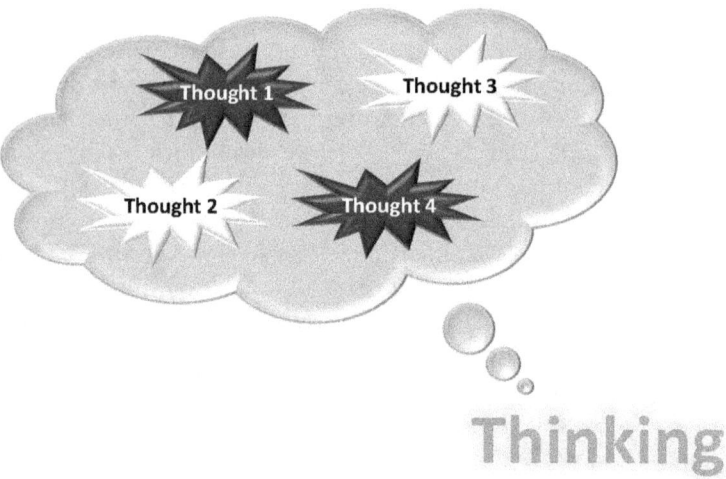

Since everything is dynamic and everything in The-Universe changes constantly; therefore, our thinking-system should also be dynamic and should be changing continuously, which means, we should change constantly and continuously. This is why, Theory of Self-Relativity states:

To change and to improve, you must remain unbiased and adaptable.

Although the black and white analogy makes understanding our thought-processes easier; Theory of Self-Relativity's analogy to black and white is to simplify the understanding that we should binarily resolve or dismiss each individual-thought. As discussed, majority of our thoughts are unnecessary and nonfactual; therefore, by attending to each thought and by accepting (keeping) or by dismissing (eliminating) these individual-thoughts, we will then be left with only the right number of applicable-thoughts in our thinking-system. Consequently, by uncluttering our thinking-system from unnecessary and wasteful thoughts, this binary-filtering of our individual-thoughts will release ample processing and storage space in our mind.

Similar approach should apply to the self-equation. To keep the best balance and equilibrium in Our-Universe, we can only focus on one side of the self-equation at any given moment; however, collectively, we should learn to operate from both sides of the self-equation in a dynamically interchangeable manner. Once our mind learns to observe, identify, and act on each thought individually; our mind will then learn to fluidly move between the two sides of the equation as it dynamically creates and maintains the balance, by addressing each task, each issue, or each situation, individually.

We will not be able to create the proper equilibrium by approaching everything in our life in a collective and whole format, from the macro-perspective; which is mostly what unaware people do. Most people who are unaware of the relativity between their Self and others are incapable of consciously observing both sides of the self-equation; hence, they do not know how to dynamically create checks and balances between the two sides. This is why, majority of people who focus on others become people-pleasers and self-sacrificers; because they live their lives by trying to get validation and self-identity from others. Conversely, those who are self-centered and selfish can only focus on their own Self; thereby, they have minimal to no consideration for others. Just as one's thinking should not be binary, but each individual-thought should be approached and addressed binarily; one's self-equation cannot be binary either, each individual situation that deals with the Self or with others must be approached binarily. This is because our mind feels most comfortable by approaching, by observing, and by addressing each individual-thought or each individual-task binarily.

According to Theory of Self-Relativity, not only there isn't anything wrong by observing and by approaching individual-thoughts or tasks binarily, but Theory of Self-Relativity recommends dealing with individual-thoughts and tasks binarily; because, we best problem-solve when we observe and focus on each fundamental-component individually. Therefore, in dealing with the self-equation, we should only focus on our Self or on others at any given moment. When we focus and resolve or eliminate each thought or task individually, we can then move onto the next thought or task while maintaining the best balance between the two sides as a whole. This focus is best initiated via observation. Observation does not just mean looking, seeing, or visually observing; but it also means to be aware of and to understand the observed via any means of observation, including evaluation and measurement through science and technology.

Theory of Self-Relativity defines "observation" as "the awareness to identify and evaluate information, facts, and knowledge."

This observation and focus can be short-term or long-term. According to Theory of Self-Relativity, for self-improvement purposes; long-term focus is more important than short-term. Short-term focus is usually a singular event that requires us to direct our attention to it. Long-term focus usually encompasses multiple short-term focuses; but more importantly, long-term focus indicates our default conditioning of which side of the self-equation we prioritize and pay attention to. For example, due to familial, cultural, and societal influences, more and more people have been conditioned to place importance on others before their own Self. As a child, we get conditioned based on what we learn from our family, and later on from our culture and society. Prioritizing others usually begins with our family structure as we are growing up. The family unit commonly teaches a child to respect and even obey parents and elderly members; and this respect or obedience is usually not questioned. Respect is often comingled with obedience and control in order for the child to be how others, especially how the parents want the child to be. Since children do not have a fully developed sense of Self; the child takes the parents', teachers', pastors', and other members of society's teachings as the way things ought to be. Thus, the child develops a sense of Self based on what the child learns from others; or quite often, the child develops a self-identity that is reliant externally onto others.

What parents and other members of society teach a child, which often shapes the child's sense of Self, is not necessarily the truth or what is good for the child's long-term independent development and self-identity. Parents and members of society often dictate the ways that a child should be, based on their own perspectives on life, and based on their own perceived and adopted traditional, cultural, and even religious values of how a "good" child should be. It is noteworthy to consider that in many families and cultures "good" is often synonymized with "validation of likability," or with "acceptance" by others, and even with "obedience". This obedience and external-validation are often intentionally or unintentionally instilled as respect; hence, the child learns to adopt and adapt to such demands from parents, teachers, and other members of the society, in order to be accepted, to be validated, to be liked, and to be considered as being "good." Additionally, obedience and the need for validation disguised as respect allows those who want to control a person to do so without the person's awareness.

Obedience is not synonymous with respect, nor is it synonymous with being a good person. Obedience is a disguise for being controlled.

By teaching a person to focus on others, the person will not be able to focus on one's own Self. By focusing on others, self-awareness, self-worth, and as a whole, one's self-identity gets minimized and becomes reliant on others; rather than it being developed internally from within one's own Self. This is because we are more comfortable to only focus on one side of the self-equation; and the more conditioned we are or the more vested we are on a particular side of the self-equation, the more difficult it becomes for us to dynamically shift between the two sides. Additionally, according to Theory of Self-Relativity, the more a person focuses on one side of the self-equation, especially as a learned skill and habit starting from childhood; the more that focus becomes a dominant personality trait.

Childhood and early-life skills and habits often become personality-traits as we age.

Respect and courtesy are important attributes for establishing and maintaining healthy interactions and relationships; thus, interactions and relationships are discussed in detail in subsequent sections. However, when respect, courtesy, and focus are dominantly directed externally and become reliant on others and at the expense of one's own Self; such respect, courtesy, and focus become disguised tools for selflessness as one lives life by prioritizing others. The long-term implications of focusing on others creates dependency as well as validation and approval-seeking from others; instead of the person learning to develop and cultivate those characteristics from within one's own Self. Focusing onto others is the primary cause of neediness, codependency, and people-pleasing characteristics; as well as it is one of the main reasons for one's inability to become independent and self-reliant.

According to Theory of Self-Relativity:

It is not necessarily what others do to a person that makes others the most dangerous word ever; but it is how a person prioritizes others over one's own Self that shifts the focus over to others, and at the expense of one's Self.

Being loved and accepted is an important attribute for social and group-animals such as humans. Although humans are social-animals, humans are also capable of being on their own. Yet, despite the fact that people can be on their own, the ability to interact with others is important for a balanced development and healthy functioning. However, when the majority or all of a person's attention is directed towards getting confirmation, validation, approval, and even love from others; such interpersonal interactions become unhealthy for the individual. Such externally-focused way of life could even be more damaging than being alone, because the individual's self-identity and sense of Self becomes fully reliant externally on others.

Individuals such as codependents and people-pleasers, who are focused on others, learn from early in life that if they continuously focus onto others and if they do things for others, others will like them and will give them the love and the sense of validation that they are continuously seeking. Unfortunately, when others realize that a selfless person does not value and respect one's own Self and is continuously seeking approval and validation externally; such selfless person naturally becomes less important and less valuable to others. Consequently, others learn that externally-focused individuals, such as people-pleasers, are always willing, waiting, and available to please others to receive attention, validation, and praise.

When a person focuses onto others, the balance of the self-equation shifts unfavorably from the Self towards others. Focusing onto others takes the focus away from the Self and places the Self in a position of living one's life from the outside-in, rather than from the inside-out. This diversion of focus away from the Self and onto others creates dependency, reliance, and self-doubt; because the individual becomes dependent on others, rather than relying on one's own Self. By becoming reliant on others and by getting validation, sense of self-worth, and even self-identity externally; the person has no choice but to instinctively become a people-pleaser and a codependent.

Although it is a good feeling to get other-people to compliment us, to like us, and to even love us; it is more important that we value our own Self by learning to establish our self-worth and our strong self-identity from within. This could only be done if we learn to like, love, and value our own Self from within, and by living a centered-self life from the inside-out. Dependency and reliance are discussed in detail as one of Theory of Self-Relativity's 10-enemies of Self-Improvement in subsequent sections.

Approval from others and pleasing others are learned and adaptive-traits that are developed and carried over from early childhood. It becomes a learned characteristic when the child realizes that in order to be cared for, to be liked, and to be loved, and to not be criticized; the child must make mother, father, and others happy. As is common with many people-pleasers, they generally experienced family structures and childhoods that required pleasing their parents. Similarly, and on a larger scale, society places expectations on us for becoming a people-pleaser. In most cultures and societies, being a people-pleaser or sacrificing our priorities for others is guilt-riddenly characterized as being a "good" person.

Being self-focused is not selfish; but being selfless and self-sacrificial is self-abuse.

Approval-seeking and people-pleasing is an inhibiting characteristic for developing a healthy sense of Self and a strong self-identity. Instead of focusing on making their Self as a priority, people-pleasers and approval-seekers focus on making others a priority. They do so by trying to fulfil others' needs and wants ahead of themselves and at the expense of their own Self's needs and wants. When people-pleasing and approval-seeking becomes chronic, people-pleasers automatically volunteer to please others based on their own conditioning; even though some others might not be expecting anything from the people-pleaser. This is because approval-seekers are used to prioritizing others intuitively; even when they come across others who are not looking to be prioritized.

Such pleaser characteristics are similar to a dog that rolls-over as a sign of submission, which is as a direct reflection of internal-weakness, dependency, and insecurity. This is why, when individuals place too much focus on others, they tend to become people-pleasers; and as they do so, they lose their sense of Self and they come across as a weak person. The dilemma is that the harder such individuals try to please others, the more their self-worth diminishes; this is further reason for Theory of Self-Relativity considering "others" as the most dangerous word for self-improvement. Consequently, dependency and reliance on others, combined with approval-seeking and people-pleasing, leads to *"Codependency."*

Theory of Self-Relativity defines "codependency" as "one's excessive reliance on others for approval, validation, and confirmation of one's own self-identity."

According to Theory of Self-Relativity, codependency is a characteristic commonly associated with people-pleasers and approval-seekers. As discussed, such personality traits focus on others instead of focusing on one's own Self. Despite the praise that selflessness receives from others, Theory of Self-Relativity considers selflessness as one of the biggest self-inflicted wounds. Although others, such as family, culture and society commonly praise selflessness to be a superior and even heroic characteristic; encouraging selflessness is generally intended as a means of controlling and using a person. Theory of Self-Relativity considers selflessness as the ultimate form of self-abuse and self-treason.

Theory of Self-Relativity defines a "selfless" as "a person who sacrifices one's own Self for others in exchange for validation, approval, and gratification."

Since selflessness sacrifices one's Self and mostly benefits others at the expense of one's own Self, and while others such as family, society, and culture often encourage and praise selflessness as a high-value trait; selfless people commonly learn to ignore what is good for them by placing their focus on keeping others happy. By categorizing selflessness as the opposite of selfishness, others use and exert control over the selfless person via guilt or praise by portraying selflessness as righteousness. This is why, codependents and people-pleasers who seek approval and validation externally and unconditionally, commit to pleasing others continuously in order to receive attention, praise, approval; and even a shred of love.

Selflessness is the biggest form of self-abuse.

As stated, dogs are the epitome of selflessness, because their main goal is to please people in order to get approval and to be taken care of. The term "unconditional-love," which is what a dog offers, exists not because the dog naturally loves others; but it exists because the domesticated dog is unconditionally dependent and reliant on others for food, shelter, and safety. Since domesticated dogs are mostly focused on others for their survival, dogs also rely on people to be validated; this is why, dogs give their unconditional dedication in order to get some attention, praise, and love. Conversely, the non-domesticated ancestor of the dog, the wild wolf, who is self-reliant and knows how to hunt and shelter on its own; has no reason to provide unconditional-love to humans. On the contrary, the wolf might very possibly attack and kill humans in order to protect itself and its family from perceived or real potential danger.

Dogs have become dependent on humans by completely being domesticated via getting food and shelter; rather than by seeking food and shelter as wild-wolves do. Dogs are not only tangibly-dependent on humans for food, shelter, and safety; but they are also dependent on humans intangibly for praise, for validation, and for love. As dogs became domesticated and dependent on humans, dogs lost their inner wolf self-identity by becoming reliant on humans for their safety, survival, and self-identity; this is why, dogs are the epitome of people-pleasing, selflessness, and unconditional-love. Therefore, contrary to popular belief:

Unconditional love exists not because one loves another unconditionally; unconditional love exists because one is dependent on another conditionally.

The reason dogs give unconditional-love to humans is not because that is their nature; they do so because their acceptance, safety, and survival is "conditional" to their owners' desires, authority, and even pleasure. According to Theory of Self-Relativity, if left alone or if not conditioned with the potential consequences of reward and punishment; no sentient-being would voluntarily provide another with unconditional-love or unconditional-companionship.

Theory of Self-Relativity defines "conditionality" as "the placement of conditions or the enforcement of consequences for acceptance and/or for compliance."

Although most love should not be a blank-check unconditional-love; love itself should be without-condition. There is a big difference between unconditional-love, which is what occurs in imbalanced-relationships; and love without-condition, which is to have a desire and a choice to love someone without any conditions. Conditionality is discussed in detail in subsequent sections, and it demonstrates why the only true unconditional-love should be *"self-love."*

As discussed, tangibility and intangibility refers to the source of the described characteristic. For example, *"Tangible-Dependency"* refers to a person's dependency and reliance on others for material things such as money, food, shelter etc.; whereas, *"Intangible-Dependency"* refers to a person's dependency and reliance on others for immaterial things such as attention, approval, love, and other emotional interactions. Additionally, dependency and reliance on others lowers personal-value relative to others, which in-turn, leads to others viewing the person with diminished value; thereby, mistreating, controlling, and even abusing the person.

This is why, people such as codependents and people-pleasers who live their lives by focusing on others have difficulty loving their own Self, as they are looking for love in the wrong places. Such individuals often have no bottom limit of when to stop focusing on others; because people-pleasers and codependents, just like a dog, will do all that it takes to get a shred of affection and attention from others. At some point, this need for validation, attention, and love, becomes so demeaning and disabling for the selfless, that they just go on wasting their life waiting for someone or something else to give them validation and self-identity.

Codependents and people-pleasers who lack self-focus not only seek validation from other-people, but they also often seek validation and self-identity from other-things. Buying more stuff, buying bigger stuff, and even cheating or having sex with multiple partners in an addictive manner are all signs of lack of self-worth and self-focus, because such person is trying to get validation and self-worth from other-things or other-people. Therefore, "more" other-things and "more" other-people become a false external means of trying to increase self-worth and trying to get personal-validation. This is why, Theory of Self-Relativity defines others, namely other-people and other-things, as the most dangerous word ever.

We are all people-pleasers and codependents to some extent, as by being a pack-animal and a social-being, we are all interdependent and interactive with one another. Since humans live in social-packs, social-acceptability is an important part of an individual's societal belonging. Social-acceptability creates stability for a person and it is also a major part of social-safety. Social-safety is primarily achieved through courtesy and by doing things for others. By doing things for others, we not only seek and receive validation and love from others; but we also establish social-favor pathways in order for others to be there for us whenever we need them.

However, there is a big difference between being interdependent and being excessively dependent. Constant people-pleasing as an excessive dependency on others in order to feel loved and validated destroys one's sense of Self and prevents the independent establishment of self-identity. Any form of thinking and behaving which first puts the focus onto others, especially at the expense of one's own Self, is destructive to the quality of one's own existence. When our focus is to the outside, we cannot focus on our Self; and when we cannot focus on our Self, we cannot improve our own deficiencies and shortcomings. This is why, Theory of Self-Relativity recognizes and designates *"introspection"* as one of the two non-negotiable attributes for self-improvement.

Theory of Self-Relativity defines "introspection" as "one's awareness, observation, and understanding of one's own mental-processes and emotional-traits."

Theory of Self-Relativity's simple definition of introspection is *"self-inspection."*

According to Theory of Self-Relativity:

Introspection is a person's ability to "self-inspect," in order to "self-improve."

Since introspection and focusing onto one's own Self is integral for self-improvement; excessively focusing externally onto others can be destructive for self-improvement. As described in the self-equation, one can only focus on one side of the equation at any given time. Those who learn to focus externally and ignore the Self also find it difficult to introspect; because the longer one focuses onto the outside, the more internal deficiencies build up, and the more difficult and even painful it becomes to self-inspect. However, the main reason many have difficulty introspecting is because introspection exposes uncomfortable and even painful personal-deficiencies and shortcomings.

Therefore, to avoid the discomfort and pain of looking within their own Self, many choose to constantly focus their attention externally onto other-people or other-things. Since we can only focus on one side of the self-equation at any given moment; by focusing externally onto other-things and other-people, we intentionally but often nonconsciously manage to avoid observing our own painful and uncomfortable self-deficiencies and personal-shortcoming. In other words, we actively, but often nonconsciously, engage and preoccupy our Self externally with other-things and other-people, in order to avoid introspection.

Introspection-avoidance is implemented through mechanisms that distract us away from our own Self and place the focus onto the outside; namely onto other-people and other-things. This is why, Theory of Self-Relativity identifies others as the most dangerous word ever. The reason "others" is the most dangerous word ever is not because others are dangerous; but "others" is considered as the most dangerous word ever because shifting focus onto others enables us to abstain from introspection and from self-improvement. When we put too much focus externally onto other-people and other-things, the self-equation shifts and tilts to the outside and this takes the focus away from our own Self. Although for proper self-improvement we must bring the focus onto our own Self; we often, nonconsciously, try to shift the focus away from the Self so that we will not have to pay attention to our personal-weaknesses and shortcomings. On one hand, we should bring the focus onto our Self in order to improve our weaknesses; however, on the other hand, self-inspecting our weaknesses is dislikable, uncomfortable, and even painful.

In mainstream psychology, such ways of dealing with discomfort and stress is commonly labeled as defense-mechanisms, which are "psychological strategies that are nonconsciously used to protect a person from anxiety arising from unacceptable or dislikable thoughts or feelings." If defense-mechanisms are deployed constantly and continuously to avoid uncomfortable-feelings, they become "unhealthy" avoidance-coping-skills, which in-turn, is defined as "nonconscious psychological responses that prevent us from feeling any anxiety or upset that can arise from a difficult or harmful stimulus." Similarly, Theory of Self-Relativity has specifically termed the defense-mechanism coping-skill that enables us to avoid and abstain from introspection as *"Externalation."* Externalation reflects any conscious, but mostly nonconscious, mental and behavioral activities that we deploy and engage in, in order to distract and preoccupy our mind externally with other-things or with other-people, so that we can avoid the difficult process of self-reflection and introspection.

Theory of Self-Relativity defines "externalation" as "one's focus and preoccupation with external things and events, in order to avoid and distract one's Self from observing and recognizing one's own deficiencies."

Externalation, for simplicity purposes, can be viewed as the antagonist of introspection. Theory of Self-Relativity, more specifically, views externalation as a collection of defense-mechanisms and avoidance-coping-skills which enable a person to avoid introspection by shifting the focus to external distractions and preoccupations. The primary mode of deploying externalation is by shifting the focus away from the Self onto others, and this focus could be in a positive way, such as excessive over-caring and concern, or even altruisms towards others; or it can be in a negative way, such as excessive gossiping and anger, or even ill-wishing towards others. Therefore, as long as the shift and the preoccupation with others are primarily intended to avoid introspection; it can be classified as externalation.

The key takeaway words form the definition of externalation are:

- Focus
- Avoidance
- Preoccupation
- Distraction

Since we can only focus on one side of the self-equation at any given time, by chronically learning to focus on the others' side of the self-equation, we learn to avoid the painful task of introspection. We do so by distracting us and by preoccupying our Self with other-people and with other-things. This distraction and preoccupation caused by externalation enables us to avoid the uncomfortable and often painful task of focusing on our own Self, in order to observe, inspect, discover, and eventually, resolve our own internal shortcomings and deficiencies. The power of externalation is so strong that it makes externalation one of the main reasons we have difficulty changing and improving. By focusing, by distracting and by preoccupying our Self externally with other-people and with other-things, we nonconsciously excuse our Self from self-improvement. Externalation, which is rooted in distraction and preoccupation, is also the main cause of procrastination and our inability to change. Focusing on other-people and other-things creates a self-deceiving justification as to why we cannot change at this moment. This is why, Theory of Self-Relativity additionally defines:

"Externalation" as "focusing onto anything and anyone else other than our own Self, and at the expense of our Self."

Theory of Self-Relativity recognizes externalation as the antagonist of introspection because externalation is intentional, although often nonconscious, and it enables us to avoid self-inspection by distracting and by preoccupying our Self with others. The reason externalation is an "intentionally" destructive personal-trait is because by focusing onto the outside, we intentionally avoid focusing onto the inside. And the reason externalation is "nonconscious" is because by engaging in chronic externalation as a way of life; it gives us a deceptively-legitimate reason to avoid the discomfort and dislike of recognizing our own shortcomings.

By pushing avoidance, distraction, and preoccupation into our nonconscious; we have learned that by focusing onto the others' side of the self-equation, we can self-deceptively avoid the discomfort and pain of facing our own self-deficiencies. Although the externally focused nonconscious justifications deceptively give us reasons as to why we cannot focus on our Self; these justifications and rationalizations are nothing but invalid and fallacious forms of reasoning. This is why:

The biggest lies we hear are the lies we tell our Self.

Externalation and its components can occur in many forms; for example, gossip. By focusing externally onto other-people or other-things, we give our Self a deceptive-justification to avoid making personally positive-change. By focusing on other people's comments or actions directly or indirectly, we deceptively shift the focus onto the outside so that we can avoid identifying and recognizing our own internal-deficiencies. By preoccupying our mind with what other-people are saying or doing; we shift the focus away from our own Self and onto others, so that we can avoid looking at our own dislikable and difficult weaknesses that need change and improvement. Gossiping, arguing, and focusing onto others, takes the focus away from our own Self and gives us a deceptively-legitimate reason to distract our Self by avoiding the uncomfortable process of introspection; and by procrastinating the changes that are needed to improve our own weaknesses.

Gossip, in all shapes and forms, is a form of externalation that enables us to deflect and distract attention and focus away from our own Self, onto someone else. The reason we gossip is because gossip primarily enables us to ignore and deny our own personal-weaknesses, by shifting the focus onto others. Gossip, for example, is at the core of gossip-magazines, reality-shows, soap-operas, social-media, and even news. By preoccupying, by distracting, and by shifting the focus away from our own Self, gossip enables us to avoid pain, to feel better, or at the minimum, to feel less-bad. Although gossip is commonly considered as statements that are unverified in their factuality; as a self-improvement system, Theory of Self-Relativity is more interested in the reasons people gossip, than the actual quality and value of the content of the gossip.

Theory of Self-Relativity considers the nature of gossip binarily:

1. **Positive Gossip:** Is designated as externalation through distraction and preoccupation with other-people's positive-attributes and accomplishments.
2. **Negative Gossip:** Is designated as externalation through distraction and preoccupation with other-people's negative-attributes and difficulties.

Positive-gossip is a form of externalation in which by associating one's Self with someone else's success, wealth, fame or other positive-attributes and accomplishments; one avoids, ignores, and covers-up one's own personal weaknesses. Positive-gossip is often intended to present the Self positively through association with someone else, all awhile dissociating the person from one's own self-deficiencies.

When we engage in positive-gossip, we often do so in order to create a positive self-image; and instead of focusing on our own weaknesses in order to improve them from within, we attempt to do so by focusing and by associating our Self with others whom we believe have more positive-attributes and better accomplishments. By associating with someone else's positivities, we falsely make our Self and others believe that we have a higher personal-value than we actually do. Despite the fact that nonconsciously we know that we have deficiencies that we must change and improve, we try to mask these deficiencies by associating and by identifying with others. We engage in positive-gossip just to feel good at that moment, despite the fact that positive-gossip does not in any way improve our personal-value and self-identity. For example, by positive-gossiping about having briefly met a famous or successful person, we attempt to bring importance to our own Self by showing association with someone else's accomplishments. Positive-gossip is a form of externally-derived confirmation and validation.

Similar to positive-gossip, negative-gossip is intended to shift the focus away from personal-weaknesses, by focusing on other people's real or perceived faults and deficiencies. However, unlike positive-gossip, negative-gossip, which is the more common form of gossip, is intended to make the gossiper feel better, or to feel less-bad, by lowering someone else's value, and by focusing on others' weaknesses, shortcomings, or misfortunes. Negative-gossip is rooted in the principle of "misery loves company." By fault-finding with others, gossipers nonconsciously justify their own faults by belittling or by lowering others in order for them to feel better; thus, to abstain from introspection and self-improvement. Instead of focusing and improving their own self-deficiencies and weaknesses; negative-gossipers focus on distracting and preoccupying themselves on other-people's perceived or real deficiencies. All forms of gossip are forms of externalation intended to avoid seeing one's own personal-shortcomings, by shifting the focus onto other-people. Gossiping is intended to make the gossiper feel good, or feel less-bad, by focusing on other-people's deficiencies, shortcomings, or mishaps. Conversely, individuals who live a self-focused life and are capable of introspection and self-improvement; will not have the time or the need to preoccupy and distract themselves with gossip.

In the modern-era, social-media, which is a readily available platform for gossip and externalation, has eased and facilitated our abilities to avoid introspection and to instantly distract ourselves away from our own "Self." Social-media, by instantly and limitlessly exposing us to what others are doing, gives us immediate ability to distract and preoccupy our Self from staying on the Self side of the self-equation. As long as we can use any notification or other forms of distractions to break the process of staying focused onto our own Self and to abstain from introspection and self-improvement; we can deceptively cover-up our externalation attempts. However, to truly minimize externalation and to maximize introspection, we must learn to focus on our own Self and make the necessary changes that introspection reveals.

According to Theory of Self-Relativity, externalation is also a means of attempting to find one's purpose and meaning in life externally. As discussed in detail in later sections:

Purpose and meaning are not found nor are they given by someone or by something. Purpose and meaning must be created, cultivated, and grown from within.

This is why, minimization of focus onto others and increasing focus onto the Self, although initially uncomfortable, is integral to self-improvement. Additionally, and as explained in detail in other sections, externalation, which inherently includes avoidance via distraction and preoccupation, is also a major cause of procrastination. According to Theory of Self-Relativity:

Procrastination is commonly associated with performing an undesired, uncomfortable, or even a painful task that leads to change.

Although the change that we often procrastinate is generally a positive-change, the process of changing a negativity associated with our Self, itself, is a dislikable and often difficult task. This is why, we avoid, preoccupy, and distract in the form of procrastination, despite knowing that when we accomplish the task or when we make the change, our actions should lead to improvement. Since procrastination is a post-introspection state-of-mind; procrastination is discussed in detail in subsequent sections.

According to Theory of Self-Relativity, the primary causes of externalation are:

1. **Defense-mechanism:** Externalation could be as a result of a person intentionally, although often nonconsciously, focusing externally onto other-people or other-things, in order to abstain from seeing one's own self-deficiencies and personal-weaknesses. In other words, we externalate so that we do not remain with our own negative-thoughts. This is the classic and primary reason for people engaging in externalation. By distracting and by preoccupying our Self with external things, we engage in externalation; and we do so by shifting the focus and attention away from our own Self, in order to avoid the uncomfortable and often painful task of facing our own internal-weaknesses and deficiencies. We engage in externalation despite being intuitively aware that introspection, which enables us to face our weaknesses and difficulties, is the only means for us to begin changing our circumstances and improving our life.

2. **Social-Acceptance:** As a result of external personal-validation and confirmation of self-worth, one learns to focus on others instead of focusing onto one's own Self in order to feel worth and validation. People who engage in externalation do not develop self-worth and self-validation from within, because they rely on others. Since such people's sense of worth and validation is not achieved from within, a person who engages in externalation must develop people-pleasing and codependency characteristics in order to maintain this externally dependent self-identity. Externally reliant self-identity is unstable because it is not created and strengthened from within. All personal-attributes such as self-worth, self-identity, and sense of Self must come from within; they cannot be created nor validated from the outside by other-people or through other-things.

Externalation is not the same as *"Externalization."* Externalization is a nonconscious defense-mechanism by which one "projects" one's own internal characteristics onto the outside; particularly onto other-people. Externalization is intended to create or find realities which support one's projections onto others. Externalation does not project, it rather focuses on other-things and other-people external to one's own Self, in order to avoid self-reflection introspection.

Additionally, externalation is not the same as *"Extrospection,"* which is defined as "observation of things external to one's own mind."

Theory of Self-Relativity defines "extrospection" as "one's awareness, observation, and understanding of other-things and other-people external to one's own Self."

Although both externalation and extrospection observe things external to one's own Self; externalation focuses and concerns itself onto others, in order to avoid observing within one's own Self. Externalation is an intentional but often nonconscious means of avoiding the uncomfortable task of introspection. Extrospection is an external observation and information gathering system, while externalation is a distraction mechanism to avoid observing internal-weaknesses. Extrospection can actually lead to positive outcomes; however, externalation is a self-deceptive practice intended to avoid observing, identifying, and improving self-deficiencies.

Theory of Self-Relativity identifies externalation as a significant contributor to one's inability to change and improve; because, externalation is an intentionally, although often nonconsciously, engaged tactic to abstain from the uncomfortable task of introspection. In other words, we externalate so that we don't remain with our thoughts. Therefore, as a defense-mechanism:

Theory of Self-Relativity additionally defines "externalation" as "to distract and preoccupy one's Self with external things and events, in order to abstain from introspection."

Extrospection is the opposite of introspection, while externalation is the antagonist of introspection; however, extrospection does not counteract with introspection but externalation is intended to counteract with and replace introspection. Simply stated, introspection is *"self-inspection"* and externalation is *"avoiding self-inspection."* Although externalation is intentional and nonconscious, it can also be a learned form of avoidance and distraction.

Extrospection	Externalation
1. Opposite of Introspection	1. Antagonist of Introspection
2. Complementary with Introspection	2. Replaces Introspection (Contradictory)
3. Neutral to Positive for Self-Improvement	3. Negative for Self-Improvement
4. External to one's mind	4. External to one's mind and one's Self
5. External Observation & Examination	5. External Focus, Distraction & Preoccupation
6. Does not Shift Focus away from Self	6. Shifts Focus Away from Self
7. Not at the Expense of Self	7. At the Expense of Self
8. Neutral to Positive for self-awareness	8. Minimizes self-awareness
9. Sometimes for Personal-Improvement	9. Sometimes for Social-Acceptance
10. Non-Defensive	10. Intentionally Defensive
11. Conscious & sometimes Nonconscious	11. Mostly Nonconscious

As discussed, external focus-shifting or externalation minimizes self-awareness and it causes a person to focus one's attention on other-things and other-people in order to avoid self-reflection and introspection; hence why, introspection is an integral requirement for self-awareness and self-improvement, and why externalation is the enemy of self-improvement. As further discussed, according to Theory of Self-Relativity, introspection is one of the two *"non-negotiables"* for self-improvement. The other non-negotiable is *"Desire."* The reason these two characteristics are non-negotiable is because if one does not have the desire to self-improve and if one does not have the ability to recognize what needs improvement, even System of Self-Relativity will not be able to help the person improve.

Desire and introspections are the two non-negotiables for self-improvement.

As further discussed, introspection could be uncomfortable and even painful as it often causes a person to become aware of covered-up personal weaknesses and shortcomings. Because of the discomfort associated with introspection, many, instead of focusing on their own personal-weaknesses, often cover-up their deficiencies by distracting and by preoccupying themselves with other-things and with other-people. Many, abstain from introspection by focusing and by preoccupying themselves with others in order to continue avoiding and ignoring their own weaknesses and deficiencies. This focus and preoccupation with others is quite apparent in high-conflict and argumentative individuals. By continuously creating friction and drama with others, high-conflict and difficult people focus externally onto other-people and other-things, in order to avoid from the difficult task of introspection. For example, high-conflict and difficult people's most common means of externalation is blame-shifting. By shifting the blame for their own frustration, anger, and inability to improve; high-conflict and difficult people distract and preoccupy themselves with others, in order to avoid introspection. By focusing on others and by intentionally, but often nonconsciously, shifting the focus away from their own issues and shortcomings which need to be addressed and improved; externalation enables these individuals to abstain from observing, understanding, and improving their own weaknesses. Hence why, self-reflection and introspection is often an uncomfortable and painful process.

Since most humans do things or avoid doing things in order to not feel pain and to feel good; they'd rather refrain from self-awareness and discovery of self-deficiencies, in order to avoid the negative-feelings associated with recognizing their own shortcomings.

Theory of Self-Relativity categorizes externalation binarily:

1. **Positive-Externalation:** Is the type of externalation that focuses on other-people or on other-things, with a positive intent. Positive-externalation is commonly associated with prioritizing others over one's own Self. For example, people-pleasing, attention-seeking, and even being excessively empathetic or excessively altruistic could turn into a form of externalation. Focusing excessively on doing good for others, instead of doing what is necessary to improve one's own Self, is a form of distraction to avoid addressing and improving one's own personal-weaknesses; and

for trying to validate and to improve one's own self-image and sense of Self through external means.

2. **Negative-Externalation:** Is the type of externalation that focuses on other-people or on other-things with a negative intent. For example, gossiping, blame-shifting, and even excessive activism and tribalism are often rooted in externalation. Instead of recognizing one's own faults and negativities; by focusing on others, especially in the form of fault-finding and negativity, negative-externalation causes people to avoid addressing and improving their own personal-weaknesses.

When deployed as a defense mechanism, tribalism and altruism antagonistically enable externalation.

Externalation is a powerful yet self-destructive negative trait and its effects are more apparent in the modern-era. Many engage in externalation because focusing on others, especially on others' negativities, makes them feel better. Concerning one's Self with others as a means of externalation is the root cause for the popularity of social-networks, reality-TV shows, gossip-magazines and News programs. Millions of people follow and concern themselves with what a famous person is doing or wearing, while ignoring their own personal-problems that need to be improved. They do so because focusing on other-people shifts the focus away from their own Self, as it distracts and preoccupies their mind from having to self-reflect. This is why, self-awareness and introspection, alongside factual-thinking, are key to self-improvement.

When we feel the need to criticize others, find-fault with others, be mesmerized by others, or when we put our priorities and personal-existence on the backburner by focusing onto others; we are denying our Self from living a fulfilled life. However, when we learn to shift the focus back onto our own Self by first recognizing our own shortcomings, and then by making an effort to change and improve our weaknesses; we can then become aware of our feelings that cause us to avoid introspection, in the name of interest, caring, or hate for others. When we recognize these feelings, be it in the name of caring for others, or as misery-loves-company; we can then dig deeper to get in touch with our thoughts that are causing these feelings. When we enable our Self to get in touch with our thoughts, that is when our introspection abilities will increase, and consequently, our need for externalation decreases. According to Theory of Self-Relativity, introspection and externalation are inversely-proportional to one another; therefore, the more we focus onto others, the less we can pay attention to our own Self.

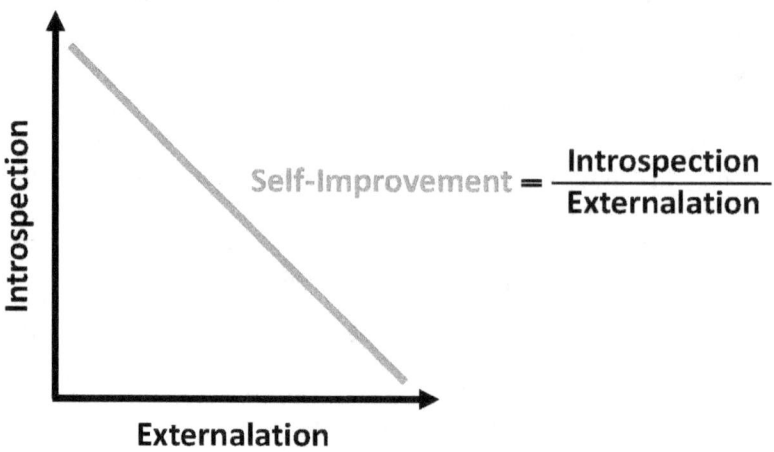

$$\text{Self-Improvement} = \frac{\text{Introspection}}{\text{Externalation}}$$

To truly self-improve, we must learn to pay attention to our Self before doing so to others. More importantly, we must first learn to focus on our Self and to stop focusing onto other-people or other-things, so that we can begin focusing on our weaknesses. Therefore, the more we introspect and the less we engage in externalation, the better we can self-improve.

Don't try to change others…Improve your Self.

This is why, Theory of Self-Relativity views "Self" as the most important word ever, and "others" as the most dangerous word ever; and this is why, Theory of Self-Relativity places strong emphasis on bringing the focus first onto our Self, rather than onto others. As discussed throughout Theory of Self-Relativity, we must learn to first live a centered-self life from the inside-out, rather than by prioritizing others over our Self from the outside-in. Living a centered-self life does not mean being self-centered or selfish; living a centered-self life means to prioritize our Self before we prioritize others, but not without consideration for, or at the expense of others. This could only happen if we can be honest with our Self by objectively and factually observing our own thoughts. However, no matter how we try to approach self-improvement and what methods we use to motivate our Self to change and improve; as stated, there are two non-negotiable requirements for self-imrpovement that without them change, improvement, and transformation will not be possible.

The two necessary and "non-negotiable" requirements for self-improvement are "Desire and Introspection."

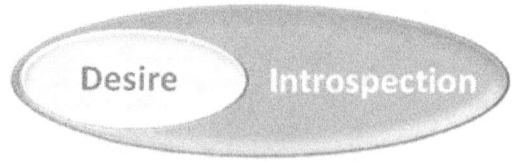

Without the desire to change and to improve, and without knowing what needs to change and improve; no motivation, coaching, or therapy system could help us with self-improvement and personal-transformation. Even "The System of Self-Relativity" will be ineffective if a person does not want to change and improve, or if the person does not see the need to change and improve. No matter who we are, how wealthy we are, and what we have or have not accomplished in our life; we must learn to change and improve constantly and consistently. Everyone could and should improve and transform for a better quality of life, a stronger self-identity, and a higher value sense of Self. However, if we don't want to improve or if we don't see the need to improve, then we cannot self-improve.

The good news is, if one is reading Theory of Self-Relativity, one has the desire to self-improve; and when one has the desire to improve, one will then be more open to being introspective, so that one can find out what needs improvement. As discussed:

Theory of Self-Relativity defines "introspection" as "one's awareness, observation, and understanding of one's own mental-processes and emotional-traits."

Theory of Self-Relativity's simple definition of introspection is *"self-inspection."* Awareness, observation, and understanding are essential to identifying and diagnosing problems. Unless we can identify and diagnose a problem, we will not be able to find a solution for that problem. Introspection gives us the ability to observe, identify, understand, and diagnose our problems, our personal-weaknesses, and our self-deficiencies.

Introspection is the antonym to extrospection, but more importantly, it's the antidote to externalation.

Therefore, introspection is a necessary requirement for all aspects of our mental and emotional existence; including mindfulness, thoughtfulness, and happiness. While extrospection and externalation are related to our external-surveillance system; introspection is our self-analysis or our internal-surveillance system. Introspection allows us to observe, inspect, and visualize our Self, by seeing and by observing our thoughts and feelings. Introspection allows us to live our life from the inside-out rather than from the outside-in. Introspection allows us to focus on our self-first before we focus onto others and on external things. Although extrospection is important in establishing social, cultural, and environmental comparative and competitive yardsticks; introspection is more important for self-improvement. Without self-awareness and a healthy sense of Self, we will not be able to properly relate to and connect with others.

It must be noted that introspection should be engaged as a means of identifying our inner-deficiencies and personal-weaknesses, so that we can then use our findings to improve our Self. Introspection should be used as a means of awareness and understanding so that we can then take action to improve our Self. Introspection should not be used as a means of self-criticism, self-bashing, and dwelling on our weaknesses. Likewise, once we learn to master introspection for identifying our weaknesses and deficiencies, we can also learn to use introspection to identify our strengths and unique attributes. Although introspection is primarily important in identifying negativities; introspection can also be an important tool in the awareness of our strengths.

As discussed, externalation is the enemy of introspection. Theory of Self-Relativity designates externalation as one of the 10-Enemies for Self-Improvement because externalation causes a person to focus and preoccupy one's Self with others and on external things, in order to abstain from facing and observing one's own personal weaknesses and deficiencies. The reason externalation is so prevalent, silent, yet so destructive, is because externalation preoccupies our mind and prevents us from the often difficult and painful task of introspection; which itself, is intended to expose us to our personal weaknesses and shortcomings that are often unknown or buried in our nonconscious.

To identify and recognize personal-deficiencies is often a difficult and painful task; hence why, most people will fight tooth and nail to abstain from discovering their personal-weaknesses. This is why, self-improvement, when not approached with awareness and understanding, becomes a difficult process. A true self-improvement system should encourage and teach us how to learn to introspect so that we can observe and become aware of our personal-shortcomings; a good self-improvement system not to just peptalk or motivate us. Empty-motivation without follow through, actually, encourages placebo-thinking and bad decision-making; because:

We often think things and we do things in order to feel good; not because they are good for us.

As stated throughout Theory of Self-Relativity, most people focus on and do things that gets them to avoid pain, makes them feel better, or at the minimum, makes them feel less-bad. Most will avoid facing up to anything that will make them feel bad, especially if that thing comes from within themselves. Many, not only have difficulty facing these traits, but it is even more uncomfortable for them to actively and intentionally seek to discover their faults and deficiencies. It is this difficulty of observing and recognizing one's buried shortcomings which leads to abandonment of self-improvement and personal-development. Facing facts is often an emotionally difficult task because facts that require change are often uncomfortable to deal with. If a fact is comforting and constructive, that fact would not need to be changed. Facts that need to be changed are always undesired and uncomfortable because they are negative.

By shifting our interests and focus externally, we often preoccupy our self with other-people or other-things, in order to avoid introspection. Externalation, which is our preoccupation with anything else but our Self, is the distractive process by which we shift our attention away from our self-deficiencies and our personal-weaknesses. Preoccupying our mind by focusing on external things is the primary way that we avoid self-awareness and the pain of introspection. Addictions, gambling, shopping, sex, daydreaming, and even certain positive-attributes such as overachieving, fame-pursuit, power-seeking, and excessive altruism, are a few examples of focus and behavior which could be rooted in externalation and self-awareness avoidance.

Additionally, externalation can be in the form of criticizing, gossiping, judging, and even sometimes over-caring with what others are doing; especially when we have problems of our own to address. This is quite apparent with the advent of social-media. Before social-networks and their interactivity with instant notifications, externalation was slower to onset and required some effort to engage in. For example, we would've had to call someone or to come face-to-face with them in order to engage them, so that we could distract our Self through others. However, in the modern-era, new instant communication platforms such as social-networks and other addictive social contents such as reality-TV shows and even the News have become the dominant mediums for externalation. Social-networks and other means of instantaneous and especially visual communication methods draw our attention to them quickly by taking the focus and attention away from our own Self. Every time that we need to get away from an uncomfortable feeling or a thought, or any time that we want to distract our Self away from a responsibility; we take a quick social-network break on the device that is in our hand. Additionally, instant-messaging and notifications continuously break our trains of thought by taking the focus and attention away from our Self or from what we are doing. These notifications become the modern "excuse" that help us justify our externalation attempts.

Social-networks and their interactive nature are the modern-day enablers of externalation.

This advent and increase in use of modern communication mediums, such as social-networks, has complicated and has made achieving self-confidence and a stronger sense of Self even more difficult. Social-media, where everyone is richer, more accomplished, younger, and prettier than they appear, could alter reality; especially for those who are susceptible to externalation and those who don't have a strong internally-derived self-identity. Representations of beauty, success, and happiness, alongside pretentions and misrepresentations of reality are fast-moving common themes with social-networks which can negatively influence an observer's sense of self-worth. Hence why, social-networks increase feelings of jealousy and envy. Jealousy and envy are rooted in externalation because they are negative-feelings which are triggered by comparatively focusing on others against one's own Self.

Regardless of what is pictured and represented, even though it might be a misrepresentation of factual-reality; social-networks are like poison to many who lack a strong self-identity and who are susceptible to externalation. According to Theory of Self-Relativity, social-networks reduce the ability to introspect, and instead, they increase external-focus and comparison with others. Keeping up with the Jones' has reached an epidemic due to the existence and adoptability of social-networks. This is why, nowadays, it is even more important than ever that one must minimize externalation and must increase self-awareness via introspection in order to bring the focus back to the Self. Social-media, to the insecure and the low self-esteemed person, is like drugs are to the addict. In contrast, self-secure people do not have the constant need to be on social-networks, because they are more focused on their own Self rather than onto others.

Although social-media and virtual-interactivity, to some degree or another, is now a part of our lives; once we learn to improve our Self by minimizing externalation and by increasing introspection, we will then be able to interact with social-media in a more harmonious manner, rather than as a form of externalation. Therefore, similar to other addictive or externally focused behavior, when we learn to introspect and bring the focus back to our Self, we will consequently have less desire to be on social-networks and we will be less interested in concerning our Self with what others are doing. Social-media and other communication formats, which take the focus away from one's Self, have a tendency of distracting reality for those who live in denial or ignorance, and who are incapable of introspection. In such situations, social-media and interactive social-networks are no different than alcohol, gambling, or other addictive-agents; because, they shift the focus externally onto something or someone else. The distractive power of electronic-communication and social-media is so effective that these mediums are often referred to as "weapons of mass distraction." Social-media has become a primary agent for externalation; because, it facilitates introspection-avoidance by shifting our focus externally and by preoccupying us with what others are saying and doing.

This is why, Theory of Self-Relativity recognizes introspection as a non-negotiable attribute for self-improvement. Introspection allows us to live life from the inside-out rather than from the outside-in. Introspection, as it might initially be uncomfortable or even painful, is an important attribute for us to be able to shift our focus back onto our Self, rather than to keep it pointed onto the outside. By keeping our surveillance cameras pointed outwardly, we avoid looking within; therefore, by us focusing onto others, we take the focus away from our own Self. This is often done to avoid recognizing our own shortcomings. If the mind sits still and has nothing to think about, it often starts looking inward and begins seeing self-deficiencies. Our innate tendency to abstain from pain and to feel better is so strong that we will do anything to preoccupy our mind from sitting still and looking within our own Self.

Despite knowing that we must look for our shortcomings and deficiencies to change and to improve; we nonconsciously distract and preoccupy our Self with other-people and with other-things in order to avoid observing and fixing our own weaknesses. For example, in order to avoid and distract our Self away from having to face the reality of our obligations; we'd rather occupy our mind and waste our time by concerning our Self about someone else's vacation pictures, or by watching a wealthy housewife's marital drama. We do so, in order to buy our Self a few hours of avoiding our uncomfortable reality; and to distract our Self from putting in the effort and action necessary to meet our responsibilities for improving our weaknesses.

This is why, Theory of Self-Relativity designates self-deception and lying to our own Self as the biggest lies we ever hear; because, we'd rather kick the painful can of personal-responsibility down the road by looking to the outside and by preoccupying our mind with other-things and with other-people. Doing something to improve requires us to make a change, and changing something requires self-reflection by facing facts. Facing facts is often an emotionally difficult task because facts that require change are often uncomfortable to deal with; hence why, introspection is often difficult and uncomfortable. Despite knowing that reality will ultimately catch up with us, we'd rather keep our mind busy with other-things or with other-people, in order to avoid painful feelings and discomfort. Therefore, we engage in externalation; and if unaware, we would fight tooth and nail to avoid introspection. As stated:

The need to feel good versus the necessity to think well is a core factor that inhibits change and blocks self-improvement.

Introspection is painful and difficult because:

- Introspection brings out our weaknesses, deficiencies, and shortcomings to the surface and into our conscious level.

- Introspection compels us to recognize that we are not perfect, and it forces us to accept that we have weaknesses, shortcomings, and deficiencies.

- Introspection forces us to accept the fact that we have weaknesses, shortcomings, and deficiencies which must be resolved or eliminated.

- Introspection forces us to face these weaknesses, shortcomings, and deficiencies which we have been nonconsciously avoiding.

- Introspection prevents us from externalation and from shifting focus externally onto other-things and other-people.

- Our emotional desire is to avoid pain, to feel good, or at the minimum, to feel less-bad; hence, observing and recognizing our weaknesses, deficiencies, and shortcomings, which is uncomfortable and often painful, makes introspection a difficult task.

Theory of Self-Relativity classifies the nature of introspection binarily:

1. **Positive-Introspection:** Is self-inspection and awareness in order to identify and improve our shortcomings and deficiencies. Positive-introspection is what we do to self-improve. Positive-introspection is constructive because it looks within to improve personal-weaknesses.

2. **Negative-Introspection:** Is self-inspection and awareness which leads us to self-blame or self-criticize. Negative-introspection focuses on our deficiencies by criticizing these deficiencies, instead of using our findings to improve our shortcomings. Negative-introspection is destructive. Although negative-introspection is destructive, sometimes, self-blame is adopted as a means of creating more sense of control for the occurrence of an event that was random or by chance. For example, getting into an accident as

a result of another driver's fault. By blaming our Self and by fallaciously reasoning that had we not decided to leave the house at that time, the accident would not have happened; we attempt to create a reason for something that had no reason and was not in our control. By blaming our Self, we create fallacious meaning in order to give our Self a false sense of control so that we would not feel as stressed-out and as susceptible about something that we had no control over.

There is a fine line between positive-introspection and negative-introspection; therefore, to begin introspection, we must be open and ready to face the difficulties of accepting our weaknesses, shortcomings, and deficiencies. We must understand that introspection will be a difficult task to undertake but the end result will be transformational and it should lead us to a more balanced and stable existence.

Introspection is an integral component for mindfulness, self-reflection, and factual-thinking; therefore, introspection can surface many negative-feelings such as guilt, shame, self-blame, lack of self-worth, etc. Since emotions and mindsets such as guilt, shame, or self-criticism are difficult to face, a great deal of therapy time and effort goes into trying to minimize and resolve such emotions. However, as discussed in detail in other sections throughout Theory of Self-Relativity, guilt, shame, and self-criticism could actually be constructive as long as they are implemented as interim and transitional emotions towards improving actions. For example, if introspection makes us aware of something shameful that we have done; that shame can be used to make changes to improve or resolve the cause of our shameful feeling, hence, it can resolve the feeling of shame itself. Shame and guilt become chronic and problematic when they are buried, or when they are carried on continuously without any resolution.

According to Theory of Self-Relativity, many Self negative-emotions could become constructive if held not as finality, but as temporary pathways to resolution and improvement. A negative-feeling is the symptom of a cause, and as discussed throughout Theory of Self-Relativity, the cause of every negative-emotion is a "thought." Since negative-feelings are symptoms of a cause, as long as negative-emotions are felt temporarily and are used to identify, resolve, and eliminate the cause of the feeling; negative-emotions could be used as interim and temporary diagnostic tools to fix their underlying causal problems.

Therefore, even a negative Self demeaning emotion such as shame or guilt, if held as an "interim" state-of-mind or as an "interim" feeling, could lead us to the discovery of its cause. Once the thought which is causing the negative-emotion is discovered, the cause of that thought will be addressed by either changing, resolving, and improving the cause; or by eliminating that cause if the cause has no factual-basis. If we cannot find factual-causes associated with our thoughts that are causing our negative-feelings such as guilt or shame; then we dismiss the thought, and when the thought gets dismissed or eliminated, the resulting symptomatic negative-feeling will consequently disappear as well. Therefore, as difficult, as uncomfortable, or as painful as it might be to look into the facts associated with our weaknesses and shortcomings; by using our feelings as temporary tools to find their underlying causes, and by fixing or by eliminating their causes, we will consequently improve or eliminate our negative-feelings.

Factual-thinking enables us to see the positive buried in every negativity.

Since introspection exposes Self weaknesses and deficiencies, we should do the same with the negative-feelings that surface as a result of our introspection. Instead of being defensive or even scared to introspect, we should welcome introspection; because self-inspection helps us find weaknesses that need change and improvement. For example, self-criticism, shame, and guilt can be healthy components of introspection, as long as they are used as diagnostic tools to identify problems that must be resolved. When we self-criticize or feel guilty for something that we did or did not do; by recognizing the problem, we can resolve the issue, by turning our self-criticism into self-reflection. In-turn, our guilt and shame feelings will disappear, because we used those negative-feelings to find and fix the cause of those feelings. This is why, it is important to know that despite introspection being an uncomfortable, or even a painful task; introspection is integral in transforming the quality of our lives. We should know that there is improvement and positivity on the other side of what self-reflection and introspection expose.

Turn self-criticism into self-reflection so that you can fix what you dislike.

However, if we do not do anything to resolve these negative-feelings, because these feelings are uncomfortable to face up to; we will then constantly carry these feelings as finalities and as a part of our existence. In other words, if we do not resolve, for example, what caused us to feel guilty or shameful; we will then feel guilty and shameful forever, which will lead to a low self-esteem, an inferior self-identity, as well as, continuous self-bashing and self-criticism. Self-criticism, shame, guilt, and other negative self-attributes that surface as a result of our introspection should only be used as diagnostic tools for improvement; however,

Introspection should never be turned into a tool for self-criticism.

Introspection, when followed by fact-based action, will lead to positive-change; but if introspection is not followed by effort to make a positive-change, introspection will be ineffective. This is why, as discussed throughout Theory of Self-Relativity, mindfulness by itself is not as beneficial as mindfulness that is followed by thoughtfulness and action for change.

We can either evaluate a thought, an emotion, or a situation in a negative way and stay stuck with the negativity it represents; or we can try to understand the facts associated with what is making us feel negative by taking action to improve, resolve, or eliminate the cause of the negativity. Through practice, we can learn to implement real-time dynamic-introspection as part of our routine awareness and existence. Introspection, as an interactive-tool, alongside factual-thinking, can become our system of checks and balances. Therefore, if we have the desire to change, improve, and be fulfilled, and if we can learn to introspect knowing that introspection will open the door for quality transformation; we will then be able to truly, dynamically, and continuously self-improve.

Introspection allows us to turn our focus onto our own Self, rather than being focused onto the outside. When we learn to introspect first before we extrospect; our extrospection ability will go to new heights as we can then begin to identify other-people's deficiencies too. This, in-turn, should enable us to have better quality relationships and to surround our Self with emotionally healthy and non-defensive people, while avoiding those who are not in touch with their own Self. In order for us to relate to others and to interact with them in a healthy and constructive manner, we need to first be able to be in balance and harmony with our own Self.

Introspection allows us to:

- Turn our observation and perception cameras inward towards our own Self.
- Place our Self-first.
- Focus on our Self.
- Self-reflect in order to recognize our weaknesses and our strengths.
- Become self-aware so that we can continuously improve our Self.

Since our intangible-feelings or our emotions are caused by our thoughts, introspection helps us to identify the thoughts behind our negative-emotions. When we introspect and identify the causal-thought behind a feeling, we can then engage *"Metacognition"* to analyze and evaluate that thought.

Metacognition is defined as *"thinking about thinking,"* and it is an important tool for self-awareness and improving thinking-skills. Metacognition allows us to understand our thoughts. Metacognition and introspection combined are valuable tools for self-improvement. While introspection is our ability to inspect and become aware of our thoughts and emotions; metacognition is our ability to understand them. To effectively metacognate, we must first be able to introspect. Metaphorically speaking:

Introspection is self-inspection while metacognition is thought-inspection.

Although there are a multitude of comparisons of introspection and metacognition; Theory of Self-Relativity defines this relativity as:

"Introspection is the conscious awareness of our thoughts and feelings; while metacognition is the conscious understanding of our thoughts."

Introspection is similar to mindfulness, while metacognition is similar to thoughtfulness.

Introspection	Metacognition
• Similar to Mindfulness	• Similar to Thoughtfulness
• Self-Inspection	• Thought-Inspection
• Feelings & Thoughts	• Thoughts
• Identification & Awareness	• Analyzation & Understanding
• Observing and Recognizing Thoughts	• Thinking about Thoughts
• Information & Facts Gathering	• Information & Facts Analysis
• Precedes Metacognition	• Succeeds and/or Overlaps Introspection
• Conscious, Cognitive & Experiential	• Conscious & Cognitive +/- Experiential

Introspection is like turning our observation cameras towards our Self, while metacognition is analogous to us evaluating and understanding what the cameras see and observe. Simply stated, introspection is observing, while metacognition is understanding what is observed; therefore, introspection is a core component for metacognition because without awareness and observation of information and facts, there can be no analysis and understanding of facts.

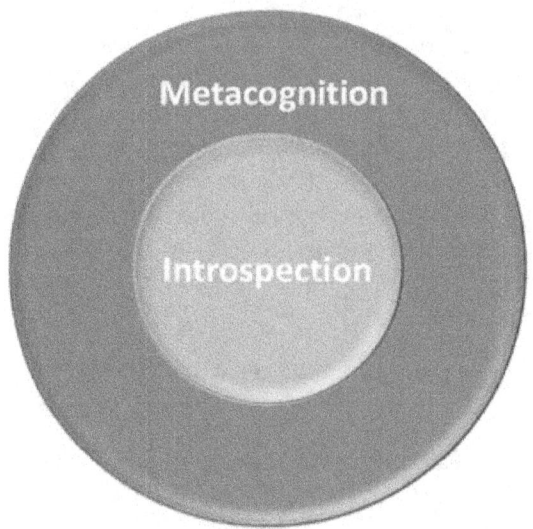

According to Theory of Self-Relativity, introspection and metacognition combined make up our *"Self-Diagnostics"* system.

Self-Diagnostics = Introspection + Metacognition

Although introspection and metacognition are necessary diagnostic tools, introspection and metacognition will not automatically create factual-thinking; because:

The human mind has a tendency to alter facts and reality to its liking.

Even though, many, might know how to introspect and even metacognate, people still twist and alter facts into ulterior meanings in order to make the facts fit to their feelings; hence why:

The biggest lies we hear are the lies we tell our Self.

One of the most common forms of altering facts to fit feelings is through interpretation. This is why, Theory of Self-Relativity advocates factual-thinking, because facts are not open to interpretation. As stated, facts are open to examination and even to replacement; however, facts are not open to interpretation. The reason the human mind has a tendency of altering facts, especially through interpretation, is because although facts are objective, facts are experienced subjectively. According to Theory of Self-Relativity:

Interpretation is the most common form of altering facts, in order to deny the dislikable reality.

Because as a self-deception tool:

Interpretation is an attempt to adapt to the absence of evidence, or an attempt to deny the contradictory evidence.

The mind has the nonconscious ability to twist and alter uncomfortable facts into likeable or more tolerable biases and even delusions. Additionally, the mind could even choose to ignore facts despite having introspected and metacognated. This is why, thought-management via factual-thinking is integral to self-improvement and to living a quality life. By first becoming aware of our thoughts through introspection, and subsequently by understanding our thoughts through meta-cognition; we can then verify, modify, or dismiss each thought based on what the facts represent, and not based on how we want to feel. By accepting, modifying, or dismissing our thoughts, we can then take action, change course of action, or abstain from taking action.

Behavior does not tell us what we are thinking; behavior tells us how our brain has responded.

Thought-management leads to creating rationally-supported feelings; and in-turn, it leads to rational behavior.

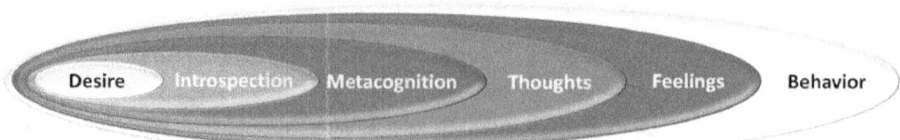

Desire — Introspection — Metacognition — Thoughts — Feelings — Behavior

The best way to think factually, feel truthfully, and behave rationally, is for us to want to change and self-improve based on how reality is, and not based on how we want reality to be; this is why, desire and introspection are the two non-negotiables for self-improvement. Therefore, the best person to help us to self-improve is our own Self. Just as we cannot pay someone else to lose weight for us, we cannot have someone else make us change or improve either. We are with our Self constantly; thus, we are the only person who can always be there for our Self.

As discussed, externalation, through distraction and preoccupation, is the major contributor for avoiding introspection. By distracting and by preoccupying our mind we enable our focus to shift away from the Self, externally, onto other-people and other-things. Distraction and preoccupation, which are the enablers of externalation, are also the common factors for procrastination. Distraction could be a momentary and short-term shift in focus, or it could be a long-term and prolonged means of avoidance. Such distractions could be simple mental or behavioral shifts intended to avoid initiating, improving, or finalizing a task; for example, checking social-networks in the middle of a task, or getting a snack before starting or completing a task. Distractions could also be more complex and involved routines such as addictions, which are intended to delay or disable a person from change and improvement.

According to Theory of Self-Relativity, the main reason people engage in addictive-behavior is introspection-avoidance; hence, the main reason people become addicted is because they want to avoid pain, they want to feel good, or at the minimum, they want to feel less-bad. In other words, people get addicted because they simply want to improve how they feel, even if it is temporary. Addictions facilitate externalation, which in-turn, disable introspection and getting in touch with one's own internal-weaknesses. As stated throughout Theory of Self-Relativity, introspection is an uncomfortable and often a painful task; therefore, addictions help shift the focus away from the Self onto other-things and other-people in order to avoid observing one's own deficiencies and shortcomings. Addictions are a form of externalation; we distract and preoccupy our Self with the addiction, in order to avoid the pain and the discomfort associated with dealing with our weaknesses, our deficiencies, and our shortcomings.

Addictions arise because we want to feel good, without addressing the causes of why we feel bad.

According to Theory of Self-Relativity, the most addictive agents are those which can most effectively distract and preoccupy the mind from introspection. The better and the longer an addiction can disable introspection, the more effective the addictive-agent will be in its addictive nature; hence, the more difficult it will be to quit the addiction. Because, once a person becomes aware of self-deficiencies and personal-shortcomings, either the person would have to live with the constant pain of facing the deficiency, or one would have to take action to change and improve the shortcoming. Most people do not want to face their deficiencies and shortcomings because most do not want to make the effort to make a change and improve; because, change, although necessary, is difficult to undertake, therefore, many would rather avoid introspection.

This is why, motivation alone does not yield results. Introspection-avoidance often involves the fallacy of "what I don't know won't hurt me," which lessens the need to get motivated. Furthermore, as much as self-improvement is a desired outcome for most who get motivated; the reason motivation often fails to lead to self-improvement is because most people do not follow-through with the effort necessary to change and improve.

The main purpose of becoming an addict is to numb, avoid, or lessen the effects of uncomfortable, dislikable, and painful personal thoughts and feelings. Introspection-avoidance, through distraction and preoccupation, enables the addict to focus on the addiction by shifting the focus away from the Self. Addictions not only distract and preoccupy the mind when engaged; but they also distract and preoccupy the mind during the "chase" of getting to the high of the addiction. This happens because addictions create an externally-derived "purpose".

It is not the "high" of the addiction that is most effective in disabling introspection; but it is the "chase" and the "withdrawal" periods that kill the most amount of time away from introspection. By preoccupying the mind for the next engagement, addictions create an external purpose and enable prolonged introspection-avoidance. This is why, according to Theory of Self-Relativity, the most effective addictions are those that can distract and preoccupy the mind away for the longest periods of "time."

It is not the high or the effect of addiction that is an addiction's primary effectiveness; but it is the addiction's ability to kill the most amount of "time" away from self-reflection and introspection that makes an addiction the most effective.

According to Theory of Self-Relativity, the most dangerous addictions are not necessarily those that produce the biggest "high" or the strongest chemical "rush." The most dangerous addictions are those that can separate a person the longest period of "time" from seeing their own internal-deficiencies. Therefore, the most dangerous and the most addictive addictions are those that can prolong the cycle of the addiction. The longer the "chase" and the longer the "withdrawal" period, the more the mind is distracted from introspection, and the less opportunity the subject would have to face one's own internal-deficiencies. Although substance overdose could kill, the most destructive addictions are not those that kill a person and put an end to one's life. According to Thery of Self-Relativity the most dangerous addictions are those that waste the most amount of a person's "lifetime."

The most destructive addictions are not those that kill a person, but are those that kill the most of a person's time.

Common examples of addictions which enable externalation in order to avoid introspection and self-improvement are, drugs, gambling, alcoholism, shopaholism, sex-addiction, social-networks, and other forms of mental and substance-based preoccupiers and distractors. Additionally, addictions do not always have to be negative in nature. Addictions could also be constructive, such as workaholism, making more money, becoming an overachiever, or the quest for gaining fame, power, and status. While success, progress, and improvement are important personal-accomplishments; achieving and acquiring such accomplishments to compensate for internal-deficiencies and shortcomings could be problematic, and even destructive; especially in the long-run. This is why, wealth and achievements cannot buy happiness. When wealth, fame, power, and even success become external agents of purpose, validation, or distraction; they simply act as external cover-ups or externalation mechanisms for lack of self-worth and internally-derived self-esteem. According to Theory of Self-Relativity:

All addictions are catalysts for engaging in externalation and avoiding introspection.

Therefore:

Addictions are agents of externalation.

By shifting the focus, by distracting, and by preoccupying the mind with the external addictive agent or cause, the pursuit of the next pleasure or high becomes the purpose that takes the mind away from the deficient and weak Self, and focuses it on other-things and other-people. Addictive substances are effective because by increasing feel-good hormones such as dopamine, they temporarily suppress the need to identify and improve self-deficiencies. Although addictions, especially substance addictions, are most effective in the short-term via their influence on hormonal activities; in order for such addictive agents to be most effective, they also need to be able to cover-up negative-feelings for the longest possible period of "time." In other words, the most addictive addictions assist the addict to avoid self-reflection and introspection by prolonging the person's externalation. The longer an addiction can take a person's mind away from having to face internal-deficiencies, by shifting the focus externally to the addiction; the more effective that addiction will be in becoming the addiction of choice. This is why, Theory of Self-Relativity considers "others" as the most dangerous word; because by preoccupying our mind with other-things or other-people, we can disengage from observing our own self-deficiencies and weaknesses that need to be resolved and improved.

To truly feel better, we must look within to resolve our internal-issues; and not to distract and preoccupy ourselves externally through other-people or via other-things.

Addictions are addicting because of our desire to avoid pain, to feel good, or at the minimum, to feel less-bad, at that moment. Just as it is much easier to self-deceive by creating false-thoughts and comforting-beliefs that support our desired-feelings; it is likewise easier to engage in an addiction in order to feel better, or to feel less-bad, in the short-term. Addictions are no different than self-deception and self-lies; they are both intended to make us avoid pain, to feel good, or at the minimum, to feel less-bad, at that moment.

It is much easier to create a quick fallacious-thought or to engage in a quick addictive-behavior to temporarily feel better and to get away from feeling bad; than it is to try to change internal-deficiencies and personal-shortcomings, because change takes time and effort. Even though we nonconsciously might know that quick-fixes are not long-term solutions; we continuously engage in such self-destructive behavior at the expense of longer-term solutions. As discussed throughout Theory of Self-Relativity, the immediate need to avoid discomfort and pain, and the need to feel good, or at the minimum, the need to feel less-bad quickly, is the overpowering reason for our inability to change and improve. Whether it is the creation of a fallacious-thought, or engaging in externalation; as long as these vehicles can create immediate gratification and temporarily minimize negativity, many, continuously participate in sacrificing long-term solutions for short-term shot-in-the-arm cover-ups. This is why, empty-motivation and positive-thinking never leads to concrete results.

Our need to feel good versus the necessity to think well is a core factor that inhibits change and blocks self-improvement.

When we feel better, or at the minimum, when we feel less-bad, regardless of how it is achieved; we allow the body to release dopamine. Dopamine is the "happy-juice;" it is a hormone that our body releases which makes us feel good and happy. As stated, in order for us to feel positive or happy, we must first minimize negativity; therefore, in order for dopamine to be released effectively, negativity must first be minimized. The only ways that we can feel good is to minimize negativity, and we do so by either resolving or eliminating the cause of the negativity; or by covering-up the negativity by taking our focus away from its cause. Since resolving or eliminating negativity requires planning, time, and effort; we often choose to ignore, avoid, or cover-up the negativity by taking our attention away from its cause.

This is why, we engage in self-deception, addictions, or other thought-altering and attention-deviating activities in order to allow our body to release dopamine and make us feel good. It is because of the short-term and temporary shot-in-the-arm effect of dopamine that we engage in placebo-thinking and in the fabrication of false-thoughts and fallacious-beliefs, in order to feel better. Beliefs and happy thoughts release short-term dopamine; however, feeling better due to any means of dopamine release does not resolve or improve our situation.

Dopamine also increases when we feel rewarded because dopamine is also a moti-vator; hence, dopamine and happiness are directly related with one another. As stated throughout Theory of Self-Relativity, happiness is not a state-of-existence, it is a state-of-experience in the form of reward; therefore, dopamine is increased when we feel rewarded and when that reward continues to be reinforced. Since reward makes us feel good and happy, dopamine reinforces the positivity asso-ciated with our reward-system; thus, we are constantly in the quest for being rewarded in order to feel positive.

Since rewards increase the level of dopamine and because rewards make us feel good, nature has created its reward-system known as the *"Primary-Reinforcers."* As a reward system, primary-reinforcers encourage humans and other animals to survive, to thrive, and to continue their species. By generating and by increasing the level of dopamine, primary-reinforcers are naturally associated with pleasure, feeling good, and even with happiness. By blackmailing humans with dopamine and pleasure associated with these primary-reinforcers, nature has conditioned humans to continuously engage with these primary-reinforcers in order to survive, to multiply, and to avoid extinction.

These primary-reinforcers which are directly associated with reward and pleasure are:

1. Food
2. Drink
3. Reproduction or Sex

Since eating, drinking, and reproduction are necessary for survival, for procreation, and for evolution; to ensure that these activities take place, nature has associated them with pleasure. Food and water are necessary agents for energy and regulation of bodily functions; therefore, if hunger and thirst would not have been associated with negative-feelings, and if eating and drinking were not associated with plea-sure, many species would die and become extinct, because they would not have pain and pleasure-based incentives to survive and thrive. This is why, hunger and thirst create negative-feelings, while eating and drinking not only eliminate the negative-feelings, but they produce positive-feelings and even happiness. Same applies to reproduction. By ensuring sex to be pleasurable, nature has incentivized humans and other animals to engage in sex actively for reproduction; therefore, it is not coincidental that we find pleasure in eating, drinking, and having sex. These primary-reinforcers are tagged as primary because they are inherently programmed and do not require learning.

Since positive-feelings, pleasure, and even happiness, which are associated with the primary-reinforcers, can only be achieved when negativity is minimized; Theory of Self-Relativity has added a few other conditions without which primary-reinforcers would not be able to exert their influence. These components, although they do not directly cause happiness and they don't directly produce dopamine, are howe-ver, necessary for humans and other animals to minimize negativity, in order for the primary-reinforcers to have their positive effect. These additional reinforcers, which minimize negativity and danger, and enable contentment, are the necessary steppingstones for the classical primary-reinforcers to exert their influence. Theory of Self-Relativity has termed these reinforcers as *"Necessary-Reinforcers."* According to Theory of Self-Relativity, without the necessary-reinforcers, the primary-rein-forcers would not be effective. These necessary-reinforcers are:

1. Shelter and Safety
2. Sleep

As discussed throughout Theory of Self-Relativity, our primitive-mind does not care if we are happy, it only cares if we are safe; therefore, in order for the classical primitive-reinforcers to make their influence, we need to minimize danger and create a neutral, stable, and content environment and state-of-existence. Shelter and other forms of safety ensure survivability, and survivability allows a species to live so that they could eat, drink, and reproduce. Shelter also provides safety, which allows for humans and animals to sleep, because sleep allows for regulation, reset, and contentment; which in-turn, allow for the pleasure oriented classical primary-reinforcers of eating, drinking, and reproduction to take place.

Therefore, according to Theory of Self-Relativity, in order for humans and for other animals to survive, thrive, and multiply; shelter and sleep, which are not directly related to pleasure and dopamine, are necessary-reinforcers for enabling the pleasure-based primary-reinforcers to be effective. Consequently, Theory of Self-Relativity has renamed the classical primary-reinforcers of eating, drinking, and reproduction as the *"Pleasure-Reinforcers;"* and thereby, it has recategorized primary-reinforcers as having two subcategories of "Necessary-Reinforcers" and "Pleasure-Reinforcers."

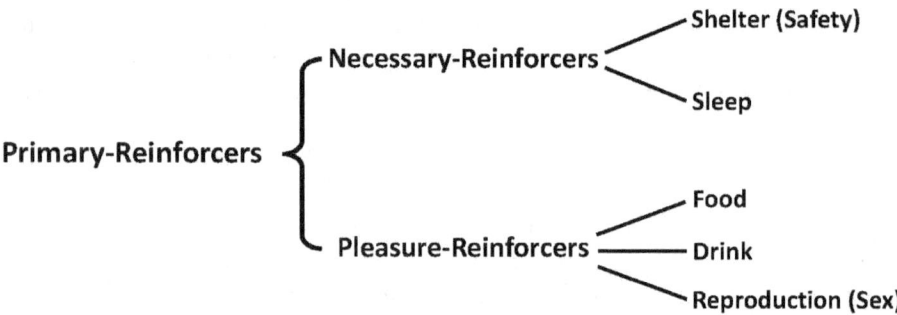

Since primary-reinforcers cause pleasure and satiety, whenever we want to feel good, or whenever we want to feel less-bad, we have learned to manipulate and enable other means of receiving even higher and more frequent doses of pleasure. For example, we do so by overeating or by having more frequent sex without the sole intention of survival or reproduction, in order to feel good. According to Theory of Self-Relativity, when pleasure-reinforcers become externalation-mechanisms for temporarily feeling good; the pleasure component of these reinforcers, which nature provided to ensure survival and procreation, become mechanisms of addiction. This is how addictions are formed; by us manipulating the ways to decrease displeasure, by increasing short-term dopamine production and pleasure.

As stated, in order for us to truly experience and increase pleasure in a consistent and stable format, we must first minimize or avoid negativity. However, to increase dopamine and pleasure, instead of directly and actively resolving the internal causes of our negativity; we often self-deceive and externalate by shifting the focus away from our own internal negativities and weaknesses, by focusing and by engaging with other-things and with other-people. Such a shift to external focus in order to receive temporary but instantaneous shots-in-the-arms of pleasure, comes in different forms of addictions. According to Theory of Self-Relativity, we are all addicted to something; the difference is, does the addiction cause more externalation and introspection-avoidance, or is the person able to introspect and improve internal-deficiencies and shortcomings, while being focused onto the external commitments. In other words, if the person is able to keep the self-equation in dynamic balance between the Self and others; then external-focus without becoming addicted will become constructive.

Having persistence and commitment to other-things and other-people is not the same as being addicted; as long as that commitment is in balance with the Self side of the self-equation, and as long as the external commitment is not engaged as a means of avoiding internal-improvement. Although addictions are not simple to treat and overcome, according to Theory of Self-Relativity, by learning to focus on one's Self and by learning to conduct introspection, one should slowly be able to tackle, resolve, or eliminate one's self-deficiencies and shortcomings which are leading to the person's addictions. This shift in focus from one thing to another is commonly known as *"Cognitive-Shifting."* This is why, self-focus and self-improvement are integral to alleviating negative and self-destructive habits such as addictions.

On rare occasions, distractions can be more beneficial than the current state of thought that a person might be experiencing; for example, in the case of addictions. As discussed, everyone has some kind of an addiction, because addictions cause short-term boost in dopamine productions and create routines; thus, addictions are generally associated with pleasure. However, getting used to short-term dopamine shot-in-the-arm due to the externalation nature of addictions could become destructive. Cognitive-shifting, when implemented constructively as a form of positive-distraction, could teach the mind to shift the focus of dopamine production from a negative external-source to a positive internal-source. In other words:

Cognitive-shifting can teach a person to learn to shift from externalation to introspection.

For example, by learning to focus on the Self and by engaging in self-improvement, we can shift our focus from others, to resolving or eliminating our internal-weaknesses. Although such cognitive-shifting and positive-distractions might be easier said than done; thought and behavior modifications that lead to self-improvement could help in achieving such goals. Therefore, to achieve longer lasting positive-feelings, a person must have the desire to put in effort to make a more stable and long-term internal-change; versus wanting to get a quick short-term shot-in-the-arm to temporarily feel good.

Self-improvement and personal-transformation is a process; not an event.

This is why:

Theory of Self-Relativity defines a "process" as "a continuum of events."

Therefore, we must learn to engage in factual-thinking, rather than living life based on how we want to feel. Factual-thinking allows us to get involved with the process and to look deep into the cause of why we are feeling less than we prefer; rather than to cover-up the cause via external distractions or preoccupation. Likewise, factual-thinking helps to prevent self-deception and fabrication of false-thoughts and fallacious-beliefs in order to support short-term desired-feelings. However, to think factually and to be able to look at our own internal-weaknesses and short-comings, we must have the desire to want to correct our internal-weaknesses and deficiencies. To learn factual-thinking and to make positive-change, we must take personal-responsibility to change on our own with minimal to no dependency on others; because dependency and reliance on others would take our self-focus away, and could place us in a position of being controlled by others.

Decisions made by others will rarely be as favorable or as desirable as the decisions you make for your Self.

IV.
Dependency & Reliance

Some of the most integral characteristics for self-improvement are independence and self-sufficiency; likewise, some of the most inhibitive characteristics for self-improvement are dependency and reliance on others. As discussed throughout Theory of Self-Relativity, "Self" is the most important word and, "others," meaning other-people and other-things, is the most dangerous word for living a fulfilled life. Although Self is the most important word, the self-equation, which is comprised of our Self on one side and others on the other side, is in its most optimal state when it is in equilibrium relative to our Self and relative to others.

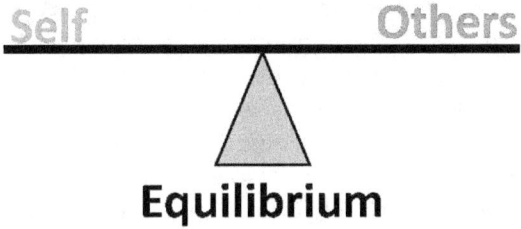

Equilibrium

This balance is best achieved when we are able to prioritize our Self over others, but not without consideration for others or at the expense of others. Furthermore, this balance is best maintained when we don't prioritize others over our Self or at the expense of our Self. However, when the focus is tilted heavily on others and when our existence becomes too dependent and reliant on others; our self-identity and self-worth become compromised. Dependency and reliance on others is the epitome of living one's life from the outside-in rather than from the inside-out; because when we are dependent on others, our fulcrum of focus and the weight of our attention is directed to the outside, rather than towards our own Self.

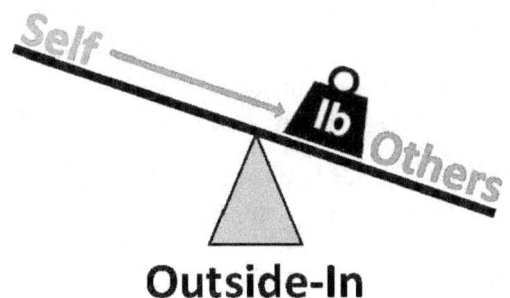

Outside-In

Theory of Self-Relativity categorizes dependency and reliance binarily:

1. **Tangible-Dependency and Reliance:** Occurs when a person is, or becomes dependent or reliant on others for monetary and material things. For example, a child's dependency on parents, or a wife's dependency on a providing husband, or on a larger scale, one's reliance on government to provide for shelter, healthcare, and other goods and services; because, one is incapable of fulfilling such monetary-based needs for one's Self. Tangible-dependency is also referred to a person's desire and need to attain and maintain tangible and material goods and services as a measure of self-validation and portrayal of self-image. This is why, Theory of Self-Relativity refers to others collectively as "other-people and other-things." People who are tangibly dependent on other-people or on other-things commonly find their self-identity and personal-validation externally reliant through other-people or through other-things. Such individuals are often incapable of living their lives happily or even contently on their own, as they are continuously focused onto the outside in order to get validation and to feel fulfilled through external entities.

2. **Intangible-Dependency and Reliance:** Occurs when a person is, or becomes reliant on others for emotional and immaterial purpose and reasons. Intangible-dependency usually involves emotional neediness; for example, the need to be loved by others as a means of self-validation, or having the need to be in a relationship because without being involved in an interpersonal-relationship one cannot be alone by one's own Self. Dependency and reliance, especially intangible-dependency, is the core reason a person becomes a people-pleaser. By continuously focusing onto others, the person tries to maintain receiving love and attention from others. It is such dependency and reliance which is one of the reasons Theory of Self-Relativity identifies others as the most dangerous word ever for self-improvement. By focusing onto others in order to get love, affection, and approval; the self-equation completely shifts externally against the welfare of the Self.

When our relationships are based on neediness rather than compatibility, such relationships could lead to dependency, reliance, lack of control, and increased uncertainties. Control and certainty are increased when we become more self-reliant and when we take matters in our own hands; and conversely, uncertainty and lack of control increase when we become dependent and reliant on other-people and on other-things. Dependency, reliance, lack of control, and uncertainty take the focus away from the Self and shift it externally onto other-people or other-things; thus, they tilt the self-equation to an externally imbalanced position.

Dependency and reliance do not have to be only relative to other-people, they could also be relative to other-things; therefore, such dependency and reliance takes away the ability to derive and improve our self-identity from within. For example, striving to make more money or buying expensive things in order to standout in society is a form of dependency and reliance on other-things. Although having money and being able to acquire and accomplish things through the power of money could make one's life easier; having more than basic amount of money does not improve one's inner self-deficiencies and self-identity.

If our self-identity is tied to and reliant on the material-things that we acquire; should something happen that we lose our material wealth, our self-identity could be severely affected. This is why, Theory of Self-Relativity has termed this form of dependency on other-things as tangible-dependency. Tangible-dependency and reliance could also coexist alongside intangible-dependency and reliance; for example, one could not only be in an emotionally difficult and dependent relationship with another person, but one could also be dependent on that person financially. Or one could be keeping and holding onto the other person in the relationship through the provision of material possessions.

Intangible-dependency and reliance occurs when we become dependent and reliant on an immaterial or emotional level. The most common forms of intangible-dependencies occur with interpersonal-relationships, especially familial and romantic personal-relationships. Intangible-dependency and reliance could be even more problematic than tangible-dependency and reliance, because such dependency is often based on emotional-neediness. Intangible-dependency, when combined with tangible-dependency, often leads to being mistreated, being controlled, and even being abused; hence, such dependency takes one's ability away from being able to have choices, and it disables the person from being able to make independent decisions that are good for the Self. Because, as stated:

Choices and decisions made by others are seldom as desirable or as favorable as the decisions we make for our own Self.

Although there are a multitude of factors coming together that lead to control and abuse; the primary reason someone gets abused is because of one's dependency, reliance, and attachment onto the abuser. This is why, children, the elderly, and pets, are often the subjects of mistreatment, control, and even abuse. Although dependent children, the elderly, or pets, do not have much choice in being dependent or controlled; these examples clearly represent how dependency and reliance create the environment for control and even abuse. It should be noted that while one could also self-abuse; Theory of Self-Relativity focuses on control and abuse by others that is directed towards the Self, because self-focused people who are looking to self-improve are generally not going to be the type of individuals who would be inclined to self-abuse, or to control and abuse others. Therefore, Theory of Self-Relativity's perspective is to focus and address on why a cognitively capable adult person who could have a choice, would be in a position to allow and tolerate control and abuse from others.

Since Theory of Self-Relativity categorizes dependency and reliance binarily, as tangible and intangible dependency and reliance; it also categorizes control and abuse binarily as:

1. **Tangible-Control and Tangible-Abuse:** Tangible-control or tangible-abuse could occur if, for example, a person is dependent on the

controller or the abuser for food, shelter, and money. Not all tangible-controls or tangible-abuses have physical symptoms; hence why, Theory of Self-Relativity does not refer to them as physical-abuse. For example, by limiting the amount of money that a dependent person receives, the dependent will often be controlled or even abused into submission to do what the controlling or the abusive provider wants; but the dependent might not necessarily display signs of physical-abuse. Regardless, Theory of Self-Relativity categorizes physical-abuse also as tangible-abuse. Although tangible-control or tangible-abuse might not always have physical symptoms, it is, however, always associated with emotional symptoms; therefore, tangible-control or tangible-abuse, just like physical-abuse, almost always leads to emotional-dysregulation and emotional-pain and trauma.

2. **Intangible-Control and Intangible-Abuse:** Intangible-control or intangible-abuse could occur if, for example, a person is dependent on the controller or the abuser for attention, affection, love, or even sex. Intangible-control or intangible-abuse could not only happen as a result of neediness and intangible-dependency of the subject on the controller or the abuser; but it often happens in addition to the tangible-dependency of the subject on the controller or the abuser. For example, if a person is being financially dependent and reliant on someone else, the subject might have no other choice but to submit to or to be placed in a position of being emotionally controlled and abused; as well as being physically controlled and abused.

While tangible-abuse might be easier to recognize, the effects of intangible-abuse could be much more difficult to identify. For example, although not in all cases, the physical symptoms of physical-abuse could heal after the abuse ends; however, the effects of emotional-abuse could last a lifetime. Abuse, especially intangible-abuse, is often associated with post-traumatic-stress-disorder or PTSD and it could even result in Complex-PTSD or CPTSD. Intangible and emotional abuse could be considered as a form of mental-torture as its effects and bruises are generally internal, rather than external. PTSD is a condition that develops in certain people who have experienced a shocking, scary, or dangerous event. CPTSD is a psychological condition that occurs as a result of repetitive and prolonged trauma involving "sustained" abuse or abandonment with an uneven power dynamic. The distinct difference between CPTSD and PTSD is that Complex-PTSD could distort the abused person's self-identity.

A bruised-consciousness and an amputated-mind could be more disabling than most physical-injuries.

Control and abuse are more prolonged and repetitive forms of mistreatment, because they usually onset as mistreatments. This is why, self-awareness and self-reliance are important personal-traits that one must have so that when mistreatment is initiated, it either is stopped, or the person is capable of walking away before mistreatment escalates to control or even abuse. Lack of self-worth, low self-esteem, and lack of personal-boundaries allow and attract abusers and abusive relationships. People-pleasing and codependency are also character-traits that could promote abusive relationships; because, they are deeply rooted in dependency, reliance, and attachment. Personal-development and self-improvement via cognitive-therapies could be effective in minimization and treatments of PTSD and CPTSD, as well as they can be instrumental in ending and preventing further abuse. Awareness and understanding of our feelings and thoughts can help us modify our thinking-system in order to help us start strengthening our self-identity and our sense of Self. Self-improvement is key to minimizing negativities and for achieving a content, fulfilled, and happy life.

There is no excuse for abuse.

To minimize control by others and to eliminate abuse, we must learn to set proper borders and boundaries; and to be able to set and enforce our borders and boundaries, we must become independent and self-reliant. When we learn to set and enforce borders and boundaries, we will also become more capable of uttering the difficult word "NO" to others; because we will not be concerned that by saying no, we might lose popularity or the fringe-benefits that we have been receiving from the relationship.

By taking-charge of our circumstances, we can begin the implementation and the strengthening of the different aspects of our life, which will lead us to independence and self-reliance; and in-turn, will enable us to be in stronger control of our relationships. It must be noted that complete independence does not mean being selfish or not dealing with others at all. Complete independence and self-reliance means to not need others; which, consequently, will put our interactions with others on a balanced, complementary, and additive basis. According to Theory of Self-Relativity:

It is not necessarily what others do to a person that makes others the most dangerous word ever; but it is how the person prioritizes others over one's own Self that shifts the focus over to others, and at the expense of one's Self.

In other words:

It is not necessarily what others do to us that makes others the most dangerous word ever; it is what we allow others to do to us at our own expense that makes others the most dangerous word ever.

Selflessness and unconditional-love for others remove personal borders and barriers and they expose the dependent person to being disrespected, controlled, and even abused. This is why, people-pleasing and approval-seeking, which go hand-in-hand with selflessness, increase the possibilities of a person entering and staying in high-conflict, toxic, and even, abusive relationships. The need to be liked and loved, which is rooted in intangible-dependency and reliance, is so strong that people-pleasers, approval-seekers, and selfless individuals place themselves in a vulnerable state of being disrespected, controlled, and even abused.

Furthermore, since externally-reliant individuals are always seeking love and approval from others; their weaknesses could be further exploited by constant criticism, belittling, and intimidation. The reason criticism, belittling, and intimidation affect externally-dependent people is because such individuals are insecure and selfless as they are dependent and reliant on external-validation. By exploiting their insecurities, others easily exercise control over the dependent; because, codependents and externally-reliant individuals will do anything to please others so that they could receive a shred of support, praise, and approval.

Instead of focusing on the inside in order to self-improve, the observation cameras of people-pleasers and externally-dependent people are constantly focused onto the outside. Although people-pleasers and codependents are generally kind and caring towards others; they are often unkind and neglecting towards their own Self. This is why, people-pleasers, approval-seekers, codependents, and as a whole, externally-dependent people, are selfless.

Although selflessness is often portrayed by society and culture as an epic noble character; the word "Selfless" actually means "having no Self." Theory of Self-Relativity considers being a people-pleaser and an externally-dependent person not just as being selfless, but, as being self-abusive; because, selflessness sacrifices the priorities and interests of the Self for others. People-pleasers are often so selfless and forgiving of others that unless they write or record the history of their selflessness, or others' mistreatment and abuse; they often will not remember those one-sided interactions. This is why, Theory of Self-Relativity considers people-pleasers and externally-dependents as being self-abusive. Because of their dependency and reliance on others, people-pleasers and externally-dependent individuals have learned to "turn the other cheek" in order to receive praise and approval from others. They do so by placing others before their own Self, and they do so by allowing and by justifying other people's mistreatment against their own Self as being acceptable.

Selflessness and self-sacrifice is not righteous; it's self-abuse.

Throughout the last millennia, and increasingly in recent times; society, culture, and religion are continuously pressuring individuals to be selfless and to become people-pleasers, by putting others before themselves. This is often accomplished through guilt, shame, and fear. Society and culture make people feel guilty and label them as selfish if they prioritize their self-first; because, we have been conditioned to believe that if we are not selfless, we are selfish.

Prioritizing and focusing on your self-first is not the same as being selfish.

This is why, Theory of Self-Relativity strongly advocates for people to learn to live a centered-self life; which means, to learn to prioritize their self-first before others, but not at the expense of others. By living a centered-self life and by prioritizing our self-first does not mean prioritizing our Self without concern for others or at the expense of someone else. Prioritizing our Self at the expense of someone else is being selfish; however, prioritizing others at the expense of our own Self is being selfless and self-abusive.

There is a big difference between being courteous and caring than being self-sacrificial.

Sacrifice or being sacrificial, which is praised in society, culture, and religion as benevolence, is an ignorantly yet intentionally designed guilt and fear based controlling mechanism which has been carried on through generations. Sacrificing or being sacrificial is an abusive act, regardless of it being directed against the Self or against others. Whether it is sacrificing animals for imaginary-beliefs, or sacrificing our own Self to get praise and approval from others; according to Theory of Self-Relativity:

Sacrifice of any kind must be considered as abuse.

Thinking or performing any acts of sacrifice takes away worth and value from the entity that is being sacrificed. Yet, being self-sacrificial has been fallaciously portrayed and accepted as a positive-characteristic, rather than a demeaning one. Self-sacrifice does not automatically make a person a "hero."

Self-sacrifice has been incorrectly synonymized as heroism.

There is a big difference between being heroic and being self-sacrificial; because heroism, unlike being selfless and self-sacrificial, is not a way of life.

Theory of Self-Relativity defines "heroism" as "a one-time act at the expense of one's own Self, in order to make a positive-change for the good of others."

Placement of guilt-feelings by portraying a self-loving person as being selfish is a form of creating submission and control; in other words, if we want to be good, we better prioritize others before our own Self, and if we don't, we are a bad person. "Good-dogs" who roll-over as demanded by their masters are rewarded, and those that are not trained and do not respond to others' commands are called a "bad-dog." The difference here is that we are not dogs; we are human-beings who could live independently of tangible and intangible dependencies from others. By learning to become self-reliant and by creating our self-worth and by recognizing our value internally, we can begin to minimize dependency, reliance, attachment, and the need for validation from others.

This balance between self-care and caring for others is best achieved by us focusing on our Self and by improving our self-first. Our Self will guide and adapt us to all external situations, once we have defined and implemented our self-standards and our personal-boundaries. Self-improvement will teach us to have self-respect, and it will cause others to be mutually giving and respectful of us, if they want to have a relationship with us. However, as we begin to minimize seeking validation from others and as we learn to self-improve and set boundaries by focusing on our Self; we should expect to lose some of the closest people around us.

If we have been a lifelong people-pleaser, others who have been conditioned to take our availability and people-pleasing nature for granted, will have a difficult time adjusting to our "new" Self. We will confront a great deal of resistance, as well as shame and guilt-based interactions from others, as they would want to preserve the one-way path of control that they have been enjoying in dealing with us for so long. As we self-improve and as we begin setting borders and boundaries, we must be prepared to accept losing relationships, even with the closest people around us; including our friends, our spouse, our parents, and even our children. We must protect our Self by *"enforcing"* a more balanced and respectful relationship with others; because when we are selfless and a people-pleaser, we are not only controlled by others, but we are quite often disrespected by them as well. Furthermore, when we allow others to disrespect us, we are actually disrespecting our own Self.

Setting borders and boundaries are integral for creating an internally derived self-identity and for being respected. Although setting and enforcing borders and boundaries with others is important; the most important borders and boundaries are those that we implement and enforce on our own Self. When we become aware of our feelings of wanting to feel good and to be liked, and when we realize that we were seeking to fulfill this need externally; we will then learn to turn the focus back onto our Self by becoming self-sufficient. By recognizing our feelings and by understanding the thoughts that generate our feelings, we will then be able to turn the focus onto our own Self and begin the path of establishing our self-identity internally.

To create our self-identity, we must first define our self-parameters.

By becoming self-aware and self-reliant and by minimizing dependency and reliance on others, we thus begin to define our self-parameters by setting our personal borders and boundaries. Understanding and acknowledging borders and boundaries leads to respect. When we *"enforce"* our borders and boundaries, we *"enforce"* respect from others; likewise, when we learn to set our own borders and boundaries, we will also respect other-people's borders and boundaries, even if they lack any personal-boundaries. By learning to internally establish self-reliance and self-worth, we not only will not allow others to control or disrespect us; but also, we will not need to control others in order to secure our position in the relationship. However:

We cannot set and enforce our borders and boundaries, if we don't have the self-sufficiency to defend them.

To effectively set and enforce our borders and boundaries, we must be self-reliant and not have any dependency and reliance on others.

Having borders and boundaries does not mean to be defensive; having borders and boundaries means to have self-parameters in order to define our self-identity, and to continuously improve our sense of Self. Similar to other personal-traits, our borders and boundaries should be dynamic and flexible, not rigid; because rigidity creates inflexibility, which in-turn, creates defensiveness. As we improve our Self, we should be able to adjust our borders and boundaries alongside our improvements. We should not only adjust the size of our borders dynamically, but we should also adjust the permeability of our boundaries. As discussed, self-improvement is not an event, it is a process; therefore, our borders and boundaries should also remain dynamic in order to adjust to how close we allow others to get to us, and how easily we allow others to interact with us.

According to Theory of Self-Relativity, our borders and boundaries should be:

1. **Adjustable:** The size of our borders should be adjustable, depending on the person and the situation that we are dealing with.
2. **Permeable:** The permissibility of our boundaries and the degree of our interactions should be malleable, depending on the individual and the situation that we are dealing with.

This is why, Theory of Self-Relativity repeatedly advocates:

Self-improvement is a dynamic-process that is best achieved by remaining unbiased and adaptable.

When the size of our borders and the permeability of our boundaries remain flexible, we will then be able to interact with others on a bilaterally respectful manner. Unlike common clichés, according to Theory of Self-Relativity, respect is not given, nor demanded, nor earned; respect must be required, and if necessary, respect must be enforced.

Enforcement does not mean instilling authority or controlling by force; enforcement means implementing and applying the respect requirements based on a defined set of parameters and values. This is best accomplished by being self-reliant and having a well-defined self-identity that is protected by strong, yet adjustable personal borders and boundaries.

Theory of Self-Relativity defines "respect" as "to acknowledge, to show interest, and to value a person's thoughts, feelings, and way of existence; even though one might not agree with it."

We cannot demand respect from others, because if our self-identity and our self-worth is dependent or reliant on others; we do not have a leg to stand on to demand respect. Likewise, respect is not earned, because to earn respect means we have to be validated and approved by others. Both demanding and earning respect are one-sidedly dependent on the need to have a relationship with others, whereby the interaction is relative to the dominance of one side. As discussed, self-equation works best and is in its most stable equilibrium when both sides of the equation are balanced. Enforcement of borders and boundaries consequently creates bilateral-balance because when we learn to enforce respect, we are maintaining the stability of the Self side of the equation; hence, we are not forcing respect onto others, we are enforcing the respect that is required for others to deal with us.

Don't earn, demand, or force respect; require and enforce respect.

When we enforce our borders and boundaries, we are enforcing respect, because we are not dependent or reliant on others. When we are not dependent or reliant on others, we do not have to be in an interaction, nor are we obligated to have a relationship with others in an unbalanced or unfair setting. When our borders and boundaries are defined because we are self-sufficient, if others do not respect us, we can continue our life without having to live with their unfair expectations or impractical demands. However, since our borders are adjustable and our boundaries are permeable, our flexibility will allow us to adjust without tilting the self-equation in other people's favor. Likewise, when others enforce respect, we will be able to evaluate their terms of interaction; therefore, we would adjust our borders accordingly. If neither side could adjust, then interaction with that particular individual or entity should be minimized or ended; but not unilaterally compromised.

By us learning to enforce our borders and boundaries, which could only be accomplished by us remaining self-sufficient and by living our life from the inside-out; we will not only be respected by others, but we will also know how to respect others. Self-sufficiency, setting borders and boundaries, and lack of dependency and reliance on others, creates a low-stress and low-anxiety personal existence which puts us not only in harmony within our own Self, but also it places us in balance and harmony with others. Enforcing respect does not create a relationship based on fear; it creates and strengthens love in a relationship. Respect, when enforced, results from lack of neediness and dependency on others; and when neediness or dependency on others is minimized or non-existent, interactions and relationships with others become symbiotic and additive. For example, in case of romantic-relationships "love" becomes harmonious rather than unfairly compromising or sacrificial. As discussed in subsequent sections, according to Theory of Self-Relativity, respect is one of the three most important characteristics for a loving relationship; because respect is one of the "*relationship-fundamentals*" for a healthy and strong relationship.

It is better to be respected than to be loved; because true love cannot exist without respect.

In order for us to be able to apply and enforce certain characteristics and requirements on others, we should first be able to do the same with our own Self. In order for us to know how to respect and therefore love others, we must first learn to respect and love our own Self. This is why, respect is best represented as another one of Theory of Self-Relativity's trilateral-relativities. "*Trilateral-Respect,*" just like other trilateral-relativities, represents "Self-Respect" as the most important form of respect.

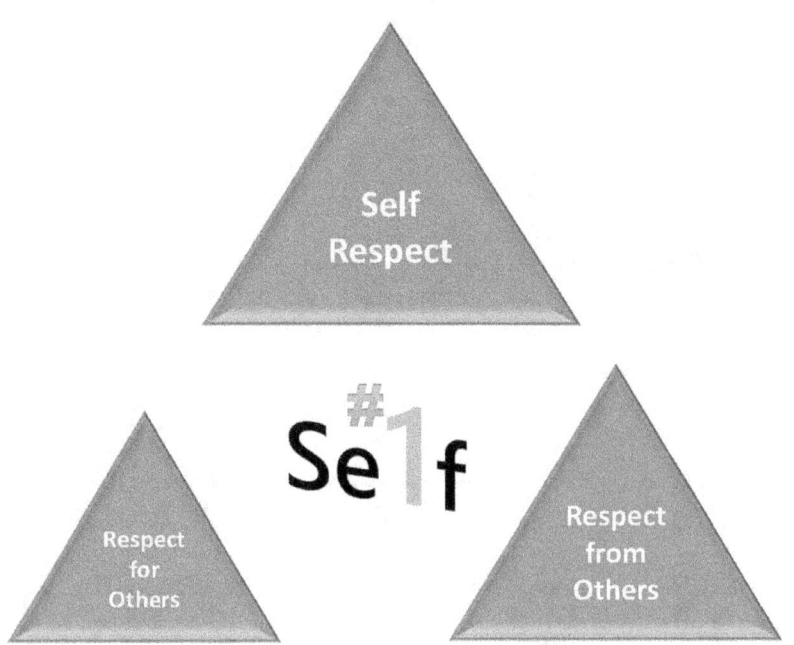

As much as it is important to have others respect us and for us to respect others; neither will be possible if we don't have self-respect. When we establish internally-derived self-identity and self-worth, which could only be achieved by minimizing dependency and reliance on others; it is only then that we can establish self-respect. And when we establish self-respect, it is only then that we will be able to have mutual-respect with others. As discussed throughout Theory of Self-Relativity, mutuality of interpersonal attributes, such as mutual-respect, is integral to keeping the self-equation between the Self and others in balance and harmony. When we learn to have self-respect and when we enforce respect from others, we will then live in a balanced self-equation. Having self-respect and being self-reliant enables us to interact with others based on our own interest and not based on our neediness; therefore, we automatically begin to respect others. When we interact with others based on interest and caring, and not based on our own neediness; respect becomes a byproduct of our mutuality.

Respect for others is a byproduct of our interest and caring for them.

According to Theory of Self-Relativity, respect is inversely-proportional to dependency and reliance on others. The more needy, the more dependent, or the more reliant we are on others, the less respect we will get from others; because, dependency and reliance disable us from setting and enforcing proper borders and boundaries.

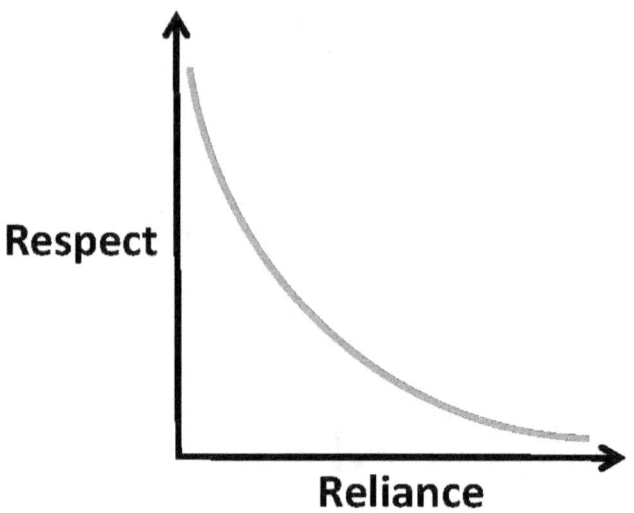

Since respect is inversely-proportional with dependency and reliance; therefore, disrespect is directly proportional to dependency and reliance; thus, when, as an adult, we become reliant on others, we open the door wide to being disrespected. Disrespect is a direct indicator of a lower perceived personal-value. When we become dependent and reliant on others, we place our Self in a position where we will be less desirable, more disposable, and more frequently disrespected. Personal-value and *"relative-personal-value"* or *RPV* is discussed in detail in subsequent sections.

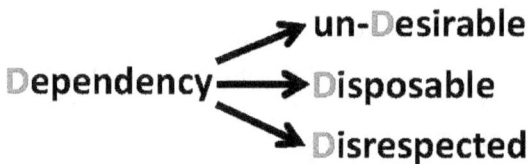

As discussed, dependency and reliance do not have to only be in the form of tangible-dependency; because intangible-dependency, such as the need to be loved and to stay in a relationship also leads to disrespect, control, and even abuse. In certain interpersonal and romantic relationships, for example, in toxic-relationships involving narcissistic and borderline high-conflict individuals; one side becomes so dependent and tolerant of the other's disrespect, whereby, one's character could be analogized to being a "doormat." Selfless individuals who have no self-esteem and who only find self-worth and validation externally, through others, are symbolically walked all over just like a doormat. This is why, if we want to be respected, we must enforce respect; and the only way that we can enforce respect, is by improving our Self so that we live a self-reliant centered-self life, without dependency and reliance on others.

People-pleasers and externally-dependent people live in someone else's Universe, rather than living in their own Universe. Although temporarily, externally-dependent individuals might feel a sense of approval when they make someone else happy; consequently, dependents constantly fear loss of control and loss of approval because their self-identity is dependent on others. Dependency and reliance on others minimizes control and increases uncertainty; and in-tun, lack of control and uncertainty creates anxiety, stress, and even fear.

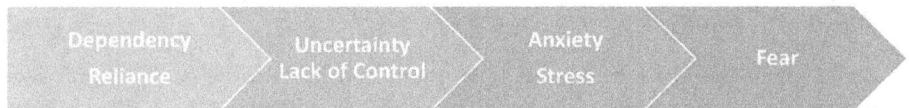

When one's existence is dependent and reliant on others, and when one lacks internally-created self-identity, one lives with attachment and the anxiety and the fear of being abandoned; because, one does not have the foundation to carry on by one's own Self. Such fear of abandonment, which is actually rooted in the fear of being alone, also causes excessive compromising; because, those who fear being alone will often go above and beyond normal limits to give-in and compromise in order to be around others.

Fear of abandonment, itself, can also be tangible or intangible. For example, tangible-dependency causes fear of abandonment because the person is not financially self-sufficient. Likewise, intangible-dependency causes fear of abandonment because the person lacks self-esteem and an independent sense of Self. According to Theory of Self-Relativity, fear of abandonment is actually a byproduct of fear of being alone and fear of feeling lonely. Hence why, in evaluating dependent-relationships, such as those involving codependents, borderlines, and narcissists; being alone is often misconstrued as abandonment.

Adults don't get abandoned; children and pets get abandoned.

This is why, the elderly, children, and pets, are often referred to as "dependents," because many are incapable of taking care of themselves; hence, they need others to assist them with their needs.

It must be noted, that asking others for help and assistance is not necessarily a sign of dependency and reliance; because a self-reliant person would also know when to seek other-people's input and assistance in order to learn something, or to accomplish a task. However, when asking for help and assistance becomes a chronic state of existence, such a relationship becomes a dependent-relationship.

To overcome dependency, we must turn the focus back onto our own Self and we must become self-reliant by learning to prioritize our Self before prioritizing others. Self-sufficiency and self-reliance are key to minimizing uncertainty and for having control. When we shift our focus onto our self-first, we end up being more in control; because we minimize uncertainties, which in-turn, helps us minimize our self-doubt and increase our self-confidence.

Having control does not mean being controlling. To have control means we are focused on our Self and we are self-reliant. Having control results from living a centered-self life and having a self-focused attitude. As discussed, living a centered-self life is not the same as being self-centered. When we are self-focused and self-reliant, we not only improve our own Self, but it is only then that we can actually help to make other people's lives better.

A strong Self knows how to cultivate strength in others, but a weak Self will always be dependent and reliant on others.

In order for us to be good to others, we must first learn to be good to our own Self. When we become self-reliant, it is only then that we will be able to have healthier relationships with others; thus, we will be able to add value to others without continuously costing our Self something.

To have a strong "we" mindset, we must first have a strong "me" mindset; and since "me" is a part of "we," we can't have a strong "we" without a strong "me."

V.
Uncertainty & Lack of Control

Dependency and reliance on others, and lack of self-reliance and self-sufficiency on our own Self, disables us from having control over our lives. Furthermore, dependency and reliance on others also allows others to control us. Additionally, when we are focused externally and when we make our Self-reliant on others, we ignore our own Self. Our inability to live a self-focused life, takes away from our ability of being in control of our own life; therefore, dependency and reliance on others is one of the major causes of us not being in control of our lives. Being in control does not mean being controlling or rigid; being in control means to have independent cognitive and decision-making abilities to make the best choices for our Self so that we can live a content, a fulfilled, and a happy life.

Theory of Self-Relativity defines "personal-control" as "the ability to independently make decision and to take actions, while remaining adaptable and unbiased to change."

Another factor which minimizes control is *"Uncertainty."* Uncertainty is caused by our inability to predict or to know the outcome of a certain situation. Additionally, uncertainty increases as the unknown or unstable variables which cause uncertainty remain, or increase. Although uncertainty minimizes control, lack of control, itself, increases uncertainty; hence why, this vicious cycle of uncertainty and lack of control are so damaging to a person's ability to change, to improve, and to live a content and fulfilled life.

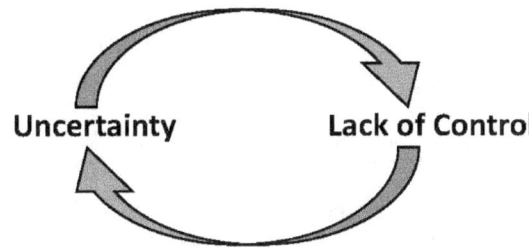

Uncertainty   **Lack of Control**

Theory of Self-Relativity defines "uncertainty" as "the inability to control, predict, or change the probability of outcomes."

Uncertainty sets in when we do not have enough facts and information to properly predict the probability of outcomes. As discussed throughout Theory of Self-Relativity, the primary role of our primitive-mind is to keep us safe, and the way that the primitive-mind tries to keep us safe is by minimizing variables;

because, variables create uncertainty, and uncertainty could expose us to danger. Additionally, variables which cause uncertainty, disable us from having control; therefore, uncertainty creates worry and anxiety. Lack of control creates the potential for something to go wrong; hence, our primitive-mind feels unsafe when we do not have certainty and control. Our primitive-mind can only begin to feel safe when we minimize variables; therefore, by having more control and by minimizing uncertainties, we minimize worry, anxiety, and stress.

When we live in uncertainty and when we do not have control, we increase our negative-feelings. Examples of such disabling negative-feelings which arise as a result of uncertainty and lack of control are anxiety, stress, doubt, and even fear and anger. When we are anxious and stressed, we increase our feelings of doubt and insecurity; thus, we live in a state of self-doubt and low self-confidence. We face negative-emotions because we do not have the facts to assess the variables and the uncertainties. When we do not have the facts, we try to assume the facts associated with the causes of the uncertainty; and in the absence of facts and information, we commonly use our emotions to make predictions and to reach conclusions. This is why, Theory of Self-Relativity advocates minimizing emotional-thinking by learning to think factually. According to Theory of Self-Relativity:

Uncertainty and lack of control are the primary causes of stress.

Although stress can be manifested as a result of a multitude of negative-feelings such as doubt, worry, anxiety, fear, and even anger; at their core, all of these feelings which lead to and which increase stress are caused by uncertainty and lack of control.

Theory of Self-Relativity characterizes "stress" as "a psychological phenomenon which manifests itself as a physiological response."

Additionally:

Theory of Self-Relativity defines "stress" as "the perception or interpretation of negative-thoughts that generate negative-emotions, which in-turn, lead to physiological manifestations and reactions."

While there are countless definitions and approaches to what stress is and how to deal with it; stress is generally initiated, increased, or even prolonged due to an underlying perceived or real thought that is triggered as a result of an uncertain or an unfavorable situation or an event. Stress is initiated, escalated, and prolonged, when we are unable to predict or to resolve the situation or the event; or as a result of the thoughts associated with that situation or event. Additionally, stress commonly lingers on and even escalates the longer we hold onto the stress-causing thought. This lack of control over the outcome of the stress-causing situation or event can not only lead to constant and continuous negative-thoughts which cause negative-emotions; but it could also lead to physical and physiological reactions in our body. Stress can not only affect our mood and memory, but stress can affect our muscles and internal organs.

As discussed, stress causing thoughts, which are rooted in uncertainty and lack of control, create negative-feelings. The only way that stress and its associated negative-feelings can be resolved or eliminated is to resolve or eliminate the uncertainty associated with the stress-causing thoughts. Resolution increases personal-control and minimizes uncertainty, because the variables that were unresolved and were causing the stress-causing thoughts get eliminated upon resolution.

According to Theory of Self-Relativity, these stress-causing thoughts can be categorized binarily in their fundamental-format:

1. **Perceived-Stress:** Occurs as a result of perceiving or interpreting that a situation or an event results in negativity or danger. Although the feelings associated with perceived-stress are valid; the causal-thoughts associated with perceived-stress might not necessarily be factual. For example, we might be stressed because we had a dream that something bad was going to happen to us or to a loved one. Although the feeling of worry and anxiety is real, the causal-thought that is creating the anxiety and stress is not factually-real. In this situation, to minimize or eliminate the stress, we must factually evaluate the causal-thought that is inducing the stress-causing negative-feelings. When we realize that we are stressed based on a dream, and as we realize that there is no factual-reason for the dream; we can then stop thinking about the dream, hence, we will eliminate the negative-feelings of worry and anxiety that caused the stress. Once we eliminated the stress-causing thought, we automatically eliminated the stress; because stress is manifested as a result of negative-emotion, and as stated throughout Theory of Self-Relativity, an emotion cannot exist on its own unless there is an underlying thought that is creating and supporting that feeling.

2. **Real-Stress:** Occurs as a result of the actual existence of a situation or an event which is resulting or which could result in a negative, unfavorable, or a dangerous outcome. Although stress is a negative state-of-existence, if stress is the result of an actual situation or an event which is causing the stress; by resolving the cause or by eliminating the cause, the stress will be resolved or eliminated. However, if the actual thing or event is not yet resulting in an unfavorable or negative-outcome, but "could" result in one; then the stress could be prolonged. Either way, by identifying the cause of the uncertainty and by resolving or by eliminating the cause; in-turn, the stress, will be minimized or eliminated. This resolution or elimination of the cause is what positive-change and improvement is about; not just thinking positive thoughts via positive-thinking.

Stress, whether perceived or real, is caused by uncertainty and lack of control; however, stress, itself, is supported by negative-feelings such as doubt, worry, anxiety, fear, and even anger. Once the causal-thoughts of these negative-feelings are resolved or eliminated; the stress begins to subside and even disappear. Therefore, because stress is supported by negative-emotions, factual-thinking will address the validity of the stress-causing negative-feelings; hence, it can lead to the resolution or elimination of the causes of these feelings, and thereby, the elimination of the stress. According to Theory of Self-Relativity, one of the main reasons that stress is prolonged is because of our inability to recognize, evaluate, and act upon the stress-causing thoughts; and the only way to do so is by addressing the factuality of the stress-causing thoughts. Prolonged stress could have damaging and irreversible effects on the body; hence why, stress, just like other negative-feelings must be dealt with via factual-thinking.

Since stress is caused by uncertainty and lack of control; therefore, stress is inversely relative to positive-change and self-improvement. And since self-improvement is best achieved through introspection, through minimization of dependency, and by increasing certainty and control; in-turn, stress is minimized as a result of self-improvement. Furthermore, since self-improvement is not an event, but it is a process of change; as long as we transform by strengthening our self-improvement skills, in due time, we will begin to minimize stress.

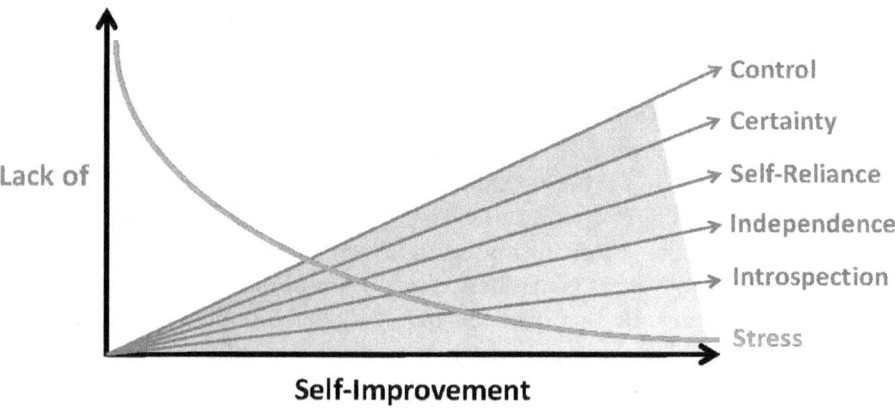

Self-Improvement

Resolving or eliminating negativities such as stress does not mean ignoring or denying these negativities, or to not think about them. Resolving or eliminating negativities means to identify these negativities and the thoughts that are causing them. For example, to minimize uncertainty, we must think factually so that we resolve or eliminate the causes of the uncertainty. Resolution or elimination requires effort and action in order to make a positive-change; therefore, to minimize or eliminate uncertainty, we must learn to self-improve. However, change and improvement, itself, creates variables, which increase uncertainties; thus, change increases the potential for something to go wrong. This potential for mishap and danger is why our mind does not like change; therefore, our mind tries to prevent us from changing so that it minimizes our exposure to new variables, uncertainties, and even danger.

Although change, itself, increases anxiety and stress in the short-term; in the long-term, positive-change actually resolves or eliminates lingering uncertainties and its associated stresses. Change might be uncomfortable or painful in the short-term; but positive-change that is based on factual-thinking, creates stability and improvement in the long-term. This is why, self-improvement, which itself is a form of positive-change, is not an overnight event; but it is an ongoing process.

Since uncertainty and lack of control create negative-feelings such as worry, anxiety and stress; uncertainty and lack of control are also the primary causes of fear, anger, and even rage.

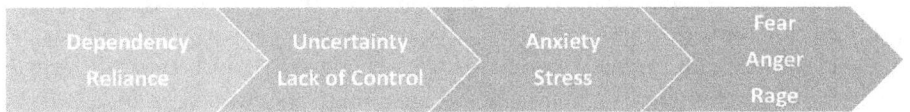

Theory of Self-Relativity defines "fear" as "a negative-emotion caused by uncertainty or a perceived threat which could result in an unfavorable, adverse, or dangerous outcome."

Fear is an uncomfortable or unpleasant negative-emotion which is associated with the perception, anticipation, or awareness of something negative occurring. Although fear is associated with the potential of something negative, dangerous, or even painful occurring; fear, itself, is caused by the lack of control and uncertainty associated with the outcome of the event. As discussed, our primitive-mind does not like uncertainty because uncertainty is caused by unknown variables. When we do not have enough information and facts about the unknown variables that cause fear, our fear lingers on and even increases as long as the variables remain unresolved. Variables and unknowns cause uncertainty, and uncertainty leads to lack of control; which in-turn, causes us to experience fear.

Theory of Self-Relativity categorizes fear binarily:

1. **Real-Fear:** Is experienced when the agent which causes the fear is identifiable or is defined. For example, fear of bungie jumping, fear of wild animals, etc.

2. **Perceived-Fear:** Is experienced when the agent which causes the fear is not identifiable, is undefined, or is imaginary. For example, fear-of-rejection, fear of the boogieman, etc.

Fear is minimized or eliminated when we gain more information and knowledge about the cause or the agent of the fear. The more information we have, the less we will be fearful, because we will be dealing with less unknowns and fewer variables; thus, the fewer unknowns and the less variables, the more certainty and control we will have. Therefore, the best way to minimize and eliminate fear is to get enough information and facts to assess the threat or the potential danger associated with the cause of the fear. By having as many facts as possible about the cause or the agent of our fear, we can then assess and analyze the factuality and applicability of the information; therefore, we can better resolve or eliminate the fear. This means, what we think, creates or adjusts our feelings accordingly; in this case, the fear feeling.

Fear, just like our other feelings, is a strong negative-emotion which results from our thoughts. The amygdala, which is a part of our brain, is best known for running our fight-or-flight responses. The amygdala's primary role is to detect danger. Since the amygdala is associated with fear, anxiety, and stress; the amygdala is also instrumental in memory, because memory and experience help to recognize danger quicker. Although the amygdala detects threats and danger, and its detections make physiological changes in our body such as increased heart rate and sweaty-palms; the amygdala does not create the feeling of fear. In order for the amygdala's message of danger to be experienced as anxiety or fear, it has to be processed by our mind; therefore, as discussed, our mind and our thoughts create our feelings; and in this case, our feeling of fear. This is also why, mindfulness, thoughtfulness, and factual-thinking are important in self-regulation; and why, medications alone are not always effective.

The amygdala detects threats and danger, the mind processes amygdala's message as fear.

Fear, just like all our other emotions, is the symptom of what our mind is processing; or more precisely, what we are thinking about. When we cannot think factually because we do not have enough information and facts about the cause of the fear; we are left to assume or imagine the cause of the fear and the potential consequences associated with the cause. Since the default-state of our primitive-mind is to keep us safe; in the absence of facts and information, and in the presence of uncertainties, which arise as a result of lack of information or insufficient data, we become fearful in order to get into a fight-or-flight mode so that we can quickly deal with the potential threat or danger that made us fearful. Fear is a necessary feeling that triggers our fight-or-flight responses in order for us to deal with threats and danger. Fear, just like other negative-feelings, is there to protect us and to signal to us that there might be a potential for threat or danger. Since our primitive-mind's primary default-state is to keep us safe; the primitive-mind initiates feelings of fear so that we can act via fight-or-flight, in order to deal with the potential threat or danger. As commonly known and as discussed, our thoughts create our feelings, and our feelings, in-turn, enable us to take action. Therefore, by our mind creating the feeling of fear, our mind enables us to take action to confront, or to run from the potential threat or danger.

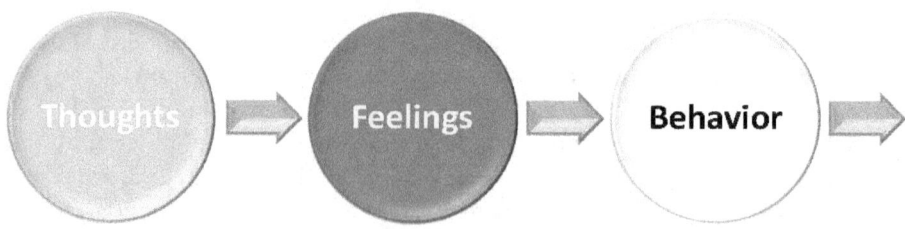

Behavior doesn't represent nor does it tell us what we are thinking; behavior tells us how the brain has responded.

If we do not have enough information, our mind assumes the worst-case scenario in order to keep us safe; because it is better for us to overreact against a potential threat or danger, even if it wasn't real, than to underreact or not react and be exposed to a real threat or danger. When we overreact and the danger was not real, and it was only assumed; our error in judgment does not have a drastic effect on us, because it simply results in a false-positive. However, if we did not overreact and the threat or the danger was real, then the threat could have drastic and potentially detrimental effects on us. Therefore, our primitive-mind, in the absence of data, information, and facts, creates the feeling of fear in order to keep us safe; and by staying safe rather than by being right, we have a better chance for survival.

The primitive-mind does not care if we are right; all it cares about is if we are safe.

Hence, as a survival mechanism, our primitive-mind's default approach is to minimize variables and uncertainties, in order to minimize our exposure to threats and danger. In other words, "it is better to be safe than sorry."

The primary role of fear is to keep us safe.

However, because of this default-state, where our mind creates fear in order to keep us safe; we often become fearful whenever we are uncertain and when we do not have enough facts about a situation, hence, the popular reference to the "fear of the unknown." Since fear, in the absence of information and facts can be disabling; therefore, in order to minimize fear and its disabling effects, we must evaluate and factually analyze the thoughts which cause our fear.

Information and facts minimize fear.

This is why, factual-thinking is integral in dealing with fear, and as a whole, in dealing with negative-emotions. As we gather more data and information about the cause of the fear, the uncertainties associated with the fear begin to diminish and disappear; thus, our fear begins to dissipate. Facts and information enable our mind to switch from assumption and imagination, to factual-thinking; which in-turn, creates more certainty and control. Since fear is as a direct result of the number of unknown variables and the level of uncertainty; as we minimize dependency and reliance, which in-turn minimizes uncertainty, we become more in control of our lives, and we experience less feelings of fear. Therefore, the less dependent and reliant we are on others and the more we have control, the more self-sufficient and self-reliant we will be; hence, we will experience less fear.

Don't be afraid of fear; just know the facts.

Factual-thinking and willingness to change and improve are key to minimizing and eliminating fear. By identifying the facts associated with our thoughts that are causing our feelings of fear, we can take proper action to resolve or eliminate the uncertainties or the threats and dangers which make us fearful. Since fear can also be perceived, assumed, or imagined; if unresolved, fear can disable us from living a productive and happy life. Unresolved fear causes worry, which in-turn, could lead to pessimism, depression, and even mental and physical exhaustion. Additionally, unresolved and prolonged fear, especially fear caused by lack of self-sufficiency and independence, could manifest itself in anger and rage.

Theory of Self-Relativity defines "anger" as "a strong dislike which manifests itself as a consequence of another predisposing negative-feeling."

According to Theory of Self-Relativity, anger is commonly associated with frustration, helplessness, fear, and other negative-emotions; therefore, anger is a secondary-emotion, thus anger is as a result of a previously manifested negative-feeling. According to Theory of Self-Relativity, the primary causes of anger are the same causes that manifest fear; namely, uncertainty and lack of control. When uncertainty and lack of control are prolonged and unresolved, anger begins to emerge; and when anger persists for a longer period of time, anger could escalate into rage.

Theory of Self-Relativity defines "rage" as "the manifestation of prolonged and unresolved anger."

Both anger and rage, just like fear, are directly related to lack of control and uncertainty. Anger and rage persist when we are unable to take action in order to resolve or eliminate the cause of the anger; or when we take incorrect, ill-thought-out, or hasty action to resolve or eliminate the primary negative-feelings, such as fear, that are causing the anger. Therefore, anger and its underlying primary negative-feelings, which cause anger, are as a result of dependency and reliance on other-people or on other-things; hence, such dependency and reliance takes away our control of the situation. As discussed, dependency, reliance, and lack of self-sufficiency are the causes of lack of control and uncertainty; and prolonged uncertainty and lack of control often lead to frustration, anger and even rage.

To eliminate anger, we must first resolve or eliminate the primary negative-feelings such as frustration, helplessness, and fear, which are causing the anger. As discussed, anger manifests itself as a result of our inability to make decisions and to take improving action; or anger emerges as a result of us making bad decisions which lead to incorrect action. Both scenarios result because of improper thinking to make proper decisions and to take proper action. For example, instead of evaluating the facts that are causing our fear which leads to our anger; we choose to directly, and often emotionally, act based on our feelings of fear. Therefore, we often make incorrect decisions, and we take improper and hasty actions, which in-turn, end up leading us to even more frustration, helplessness, and fear. This is why, when we make bad decisions, our self-induced frustration leads us to the extremes of anger, rage, and resentment.

Causes of Fear	Causes of Anger
• Dependency	• Dependency
• Reliance	• Reliance
• Uncertainty	• Uncertainty
• Lack of Control	• Lack of Control
• Anxiety	• Anxiety
• Stress	• Stress
• Frustration	• Frustration
• Helplessness	• Helplessness
	• Fear

Fear is an emotion that clearly represents how our mind creates our thoughts, and how our thoughts create our emotions; in this case, the emotion of fear. Fear is a protective emotion which arises when we face uncertainty and when we lack control. This is why, Theory of Self-Relativity categorizes "Dependency & Reliance" and "Uncertainty & Lack of Control" as two of the 10-Enemies of Self-Improvement; and this is also why, Theory of Self-Relativity categorizes "Control & Certainty" and "Independence & Self-Reliance" as two of the 10-Commandments for Self-Improvement.

When we are dependent on others or when we face uncertainties, we increase the potential for something to go wrong; because we have no control, which in-turn, increases our anxiety and stress. As the uncertainty remains unresolved, our anxiety and stress remain elevated; and consequently, prolonged anxiety and stress often lead to frustration, helplessness, fear, and even anger.

Fear is intended to make us aware of uncertainty and to force us into action in order to minimize the uncertainty; and in-turn, to minimize potential threats and danger. However, fear, especially when fear is based on perception or incorrect cognition, could also make us abstain from taking certain actions that could have changed and improved our circumstances. Fear is intended to lead us into corrective action, via fight-or-flight; however, as modern cognitive entities, and as a side-effect of our intelligence, we have introduced a third line of behavior in the form of *"freeze."* Therefore, instead of fight-or-flight, in order to eliminate or get away from uncertainty and danger; we sometimes end up freezing, which lets things be as they are. Consequently, to freeze or to do nothing could further expose us to potential danger, or it can prevent us from improving our circumstances.

Fear is not only the precursor to anger and rage; but it is also the factor that limits contentment, happiness, and success.

Fear of uncertainty and fear of lack of control are primary feelings that prevent progress and self-improvement. Some common examples of such personal fears are:

- Fear-of-failure
- Fear-of-loss
- Fear of unfavorable outcomes
- Fear-of-rejection
- Fear-of-ridicule
- Fear-of-social-interaction
- Fear-of-injury
- Fear-of-death

Although some of these fears are justified as they have inherent risks involved with them, for example, fear-of-injury or fear-of-death; the risks associated with other fears are often assumed or imagined, because they are commonly based on primary negative-emotions, which themselves, are as a result of thoughts that are dealing with uncertainty and lack of control.

Since fear is a strong negative-feeling; therefore, it is important to get-in-touch with our thoughts that are causing our fear. Awareness and understanding of the factuality and the value of our fear-causing thoughts is important in the reduction and elimination of our feelings of fear. If the facts associated with our thoughts justify our fear; we should then, based on these facts, take action to resolve or eliminate the causes of our fear. If we cannot find the facts which are associated with the cause of our fear; we should either continue looking for the facts, or we should stop assuming or perceiving an imaginary cause. By finding the facts associated with the fear causing thoughts, or by eliminating the assumptions of the causes of fear, we can then eliminate our fears.

When we take control of our thoughts by looking at the facts associated with them, and when we take action to resolve or eliminate the causes of our thoughts and feelings; we will then achieve more certainty by taking control over situations that affect us. This is why, self-sufficiency and self-reliance are important in improving our life, because they help us to minimize external-variables and they give us more internal-control, while increasing certainty.

Control and certainty are so important for self-improvement that they are designated as one of Theory of Self-Relativity's 10-Commandments for Self-Improvement. Although control is important, it is noteworthy to reiterate that control does not mean to be controlling. Control means to be in control of our decisions and actions and for us to have more say in the outcomes of things that relate to us. Likewise, although certainty is the ultimate goal; we can never reach absolute certainty, especially with regards to future events. Theory of Self-Relativity designates certainty as an important component for living a content and even happy life; however, what it refers to as certainty, is actually a state of higher probability, better predictability, or less uncertainty.

True certainty is the state of higher probability, better predictability, or less uncertainty; because no such thing as absolute-certainty could exist.

Therefore, our goal to reach certainty, should actually be our goal to increase the probability of favorable outcomes; and in order to increase such favorable probabilities, or to get as close to certainty as possible, we must first minimize uncertainty. Just as to increase positivity and happiness we must first minimize negativities; likewise, to increase control and certainty, we must first minimize uncertainty.

Fear and anger, just as other negative-feelings are intended to be protective; therefore, when dealt with them properly, fear and anger can actually lead us to minimize danger. Fear and anger, just like other feelings, such as guilt and shame, are messages to us to deal with their underlying real or perceived causes; hence, to take corrective action. As long as we deal with fear, and even anger, as intermediate messages to take control and to correct or eliminate their causes; fear and anger, just like the majority of our other negative-emotions, can become constructive steppingstones for betterment, for positive-change, and for progress.

As discussed throughout Theory of Self-Relativity, a feeling is a symptom of an underlying cause, and the cause of intangible-feelings, such as fear and anger, is always an underlying-thought. By using the message of the symptom or the-feeling to identify the cause of the symptom or the-thought, we can then take action or inaction, to resolve or eliminate the causal-thought; thereby, to resolve or eliminate our negative-emotions of fear and even anger.

Fear and anger become problematic when they linger on for long periods of time without resolution or elimination. Instead of us relying on external-factors such as other-people or other-things in order to minimize or eliminate our fears; by having more control and by minimizing uncertainty, we can instill self-agency and personal-responsibility to resolve or eliminate our fear and anger causing thoughts. Therefore, by analyzing, by resolving, or by eliminating our thoughts; we can minimize our fears and our anger, and we can even prevent our outbursts of rage and our feelings of resentment.

This is why, anger-management is best achieved via factual-thinking and self-improvement; because negative-emotions could lead us to have more control if we use the message of our negative-feelings, such as our fear and anger, to resolve or eliminate their causes, rather than to impulsively react to them.

Since uncertainty and lack of control create a slew of negative-feelings; therefore, being in control and having certainty, which means having better predictability, become important characteristics for self-improvement.

To have more certainty, we must improve the predictability of our outcomes.

In psychology, psychotherapy, and other self-help systems, control is often portrayed as a negative characteristic; because control is often viewed as being controlling. There is a big difference between being controlling and being in control. To minimize anxiety, stress, and even, fear and anger, having certainty and being in control are important conditions.

Theory of Self-Relativity categorizes control binarily:

1. **Negative-Control:** Can further be subdivided binarily as:

    a) **Being Controlled:** Is the classic form of control that is an enemy of self-improvement. Being controlled by others primarily arises as a result of neediness or dependency and reliance on others.

    b) **Being Controlling:** Although this form of control is commonly directed externally; being controlling could disable a person from having a balanced relationship with others, and even with one's own Self. Being controlling is commonly a trait that one deploys as a means of shielding personal-weaknesses and self-deficiencies by trying to control others and their variables. Likewise, being controlling could also be a means of one's primitive-mind trying to minimize variables in order for the person to feel safe.

2. **Positive-Control:** Is best described as:

    ● **Having Control or Being in Control:** Which is the proper form of control that is important for self-improvement and for living a content and happy life. When we have control, we have less variables and unknowns to deal with; hence, we have more certainty and predictability, therefore, we have better probability of favorable outcomes.

Theory of Self-Relativity defines "having control" or "being in control," also referred to as "personal-control," as "the ability to make decision and to take actions, while remaining adaptable and unbiased to change."

Since control and uncertainty are inversely relative to one another; personal-control minimizes uncertainty, which in-turn, minimizes negative-feelings such as anxiety, stress, doubt, fear, and even, anger. Therefore, personal-control minimizes emotional-reasoning and increases factual-thinking; which itself, is the precursor for discipline and self-confidence.

Theory of Self-Relativity defines "discipline" as "the consistent application of factual-thoughts to decision-making and behavior."

As discussed, control and certainty, which arise from independence and self-reliance, create discipline; thus, discipline is a predisposing factor for having confidence. Since discipline is based on consistency; therefore, consistency minimizes uncertainty and increases control, which in-turn, increases self-confidence. By learning to consistently think factually, we can minimize self-doubt, and we can create and nurture discipline, on the path to increasing our self-confidence. Since discipline and confidence are learned, hence, they can be improved. This is why, unlike popular beliefs, discipline and confidence are not simply mindsets or attitudes that are adopted via positive-thinking or through mental manifestation; they are skills that can be improved.

Discipline and confidence are not mindsets or attitudes; they are learned skills.

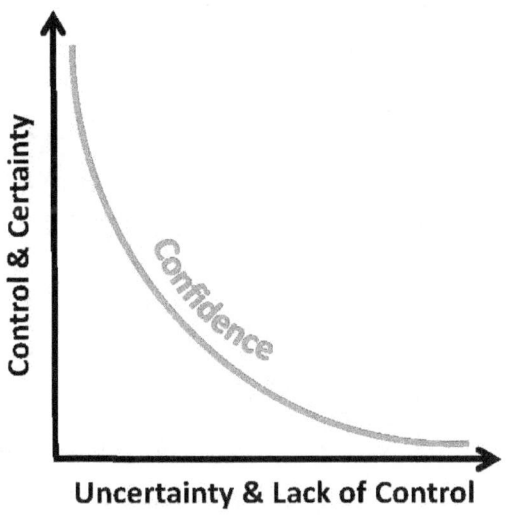

To create, to maintain, and to increase self-confidence, we must learn to become disciplined by minimizing self-doubt. Discipline could only be achieved via self-reliance and the acquisition and application of knowledge and experience, which are best achieved through factual-thinking. Discipline and self-confidence are skills that are created and improved by us, from within. Therefore, to become disciplined and self-confident, we must learn to minimize uncertainty, we must increase control, and we must minimize and eliminate our dependency and reliance on others, as we increase our independence and self-reliance.

Self-confidence arises as a result of minimizing self-doubt, by being in control, and by having personal-control. As discussed, personal-control is best achieved by having self-reliance and by living our life with minimal reliance and independent of others. Living a life independent of others requires self-agency and personal-responsibility; this is why, "Self-Agency and Personal-Responsibility" is another one of Theory of Self-Relativity's 10-Commandments for Self-Improvement. Since self-improvement requires minimizing dependency and reliance on others; similarly, self-reliance and living a centered-self life can only be achieved if we also learn to minimize self-victimization and blame-shifting onto others. To minimize self-victimization and blame-shifting, we must take on the responsibility that goes along with being in control.

Many, mistaken their ego with self-confidence; hence, egotistical people often have a false-sense of believing that they are self-confident. Confident people commonly fact-check and balance their mindset with facts and evidence to ensure that their thoughts are based on facts and evidence; so that when they make decisions and take actions, they do so based on best evidence of how reality is, and not based on false-assumptions or preferred-feelings of what they think reality is.

On the contrary, egotistical people believe they know everything and they have ample information and knowledge; hence, they abstain from fact-checking their mindset. Egotists do not like to fact-check their thoughts, because facts could prove their thoughts wrong; which in-turn, could weaken their ego. Ego is commonly defined as a person's sense of self-esteem and self-importance; therefore, one's ego could very well be flawed, if not fact-checked and verified. Ego often makes us over-estimate our own abilities and self-worth, while under-estimating the effort and skill required to achieve our goals. As discussed in subsequent sections, ego often coexists with ignorance. Therefore, it is better to create, cultivate, and rely on our self-confidence than to have an ego; and to do so properly, we must be able to stay open to feedback and contradictory evidence. As stated:

To change and improve, we must remain adaptable and unbiased.

This is why, introspection is a non-negotiable requirement for self-improvement. If we have an ego, we will have difficulty engaging in introspection, because our ego will not want to find out if we have any weaknesses and deficiencies; nor would it like to know that we are wrong. Hence why, egotists constantly rationalize and justify their perceived self-confidence.

If one is truly confident, one wouldn't need to rationalize and justify constantly.

Because, according to Theory of Self-Relativity:

Claims of confidence are a means of justifying and rationalizing doubt.

Once we commit to change and improvement by looking at our own weaknesses, we must also take personal-responsibility to accept, resolve, or eliminate our weaknesses and deficiencies. Self-reliance, independence, and being in control, which begin by focusing on our Self and by minimizing focusing onto others; come with the responsibility to take personal-agency for our own improvement. Just as we should not rely on others if we want to improve, we also should learn to not shift the responsibility that goes along with our own self-improvement onto others. This is why, self-agency and personal-responsibility are integral to becoming independent, to creating discipline, to minimizing self-doubt, and to increasing self-confidence.

Theory of Self-Relativity defines "self-agency" as "taking personal-responsibility to control one's own thoughts and actions."

By taking personal-responsibility, one not only minimizes dependency and reliance on others, but one also takes control of one's own life so that one does not need to blame-shift onto others. Once people increase personal-control and minimize blame-shifting and responsibility onto others; they will then be able to personally minimize uncertainty, and thereby, reduce anxiety and stress in their lives. Personal-responsibility and self-agency, in-turn, enable people to minimize self-doubt and increase their self-confidence; because by having personal-responsibility and self-agency, they can take-charge of their life and continued improvement. Minimization of self-doubt and increase in self-confidence could only be achieved by knowing that one can resolve and eliminate any negativity that arises in one's life. Gaining and increasing self-confidence, just like other self-improvement processes, is not an event, it is an ongoing process; thus, confidence, just like other skills, must be maintained and improved.

Building confidence, builds confidence.

Building confidence is a process, just like building a building or building muscles; therefore, it takes time to build confidence. Furthermore, anything we build, we must also maintain, if not, it will diminish and even fall apart. Therefore, as stated throughout Theory of Self-Relativity, confidence is a skill and not simply an attitude or a mindset. Since confidence is a learned skill that could improve over time; thus, confidence is the end result of other personal-developments and improvements. Because, building confidence is achieved down the line of other self-improvement processes; hence, confidence must have a solid foundation, just like a building does. This is why, those who are confident represent a solid and unshakable self-image. Therefore, self-confidence is directly related to taking personal-responsibility and having self-agency; which result from minimizing reliance on others, and by having personal-control in minimizing and resolving life's uncertainties.

Confidence is a deeper level of achievement that results from continuous positive-change and improvement; therefore, there are a multitude of factors that could prevent or destroy confidence. The following diagram represents the primary factors and conditions that disable us from building and increasing our self-confidence:

There is a big difference between having self-confidence and feelings confident. Confidence is a skill that is increased as we acquire and apply more fact-based knowledge and experience. As we realize that our skill of applying our fact-based knowledge and experience increases our confidence that we can handle any situation; we subsequently feel more confident.

Therefore:

To feel confident, we must have confidence.

Because:

Confidence is a skill. Feeling confident is a mindset that is as a result of having confidence.

To increase self-confidence, we must do it on our own; therefore, we must begin by minimizing dependency and reliance on others, and by learning to take personal-responsibility by increasing control and certainty in all aspects of our existence. Self-confidence and minimization of self-doubt is discussed in detail in the 10-Commandments for Self-Improvement section.

The more confident and independent one is, the less bad behavior one would tolerate from others.

In order for us to self-improve, we must be in control of our lives; and the only way that we can be in as much control of our lives as possible is for us to be open to change. As discussed throughout Theory of Self-Relativity, "true" change, just like other personal characteristics, is not an event, it is an ongoing process; because, in order for us to change most effectively, we must minimize and maintain the variables which cause uncertainty. As much as improvement is a necessary process, maintaining the improvements achieved is also an integral part of progress; therefore, in order to change, improve, and to maintain the improvements achieved, we must minimize uncertainty and we must maximize personal-control. By minimizing uncertainties and by maximizing personal-control, we will create the discipline and confidence required to reach success, fulfillment, and happiness.

Don't control and don't be controlled... Take control.

VI.
Denial & Ignorance

If it conflicts with what I want to be true... Then I don't want to hear it!

The main problem in self-improvement is our desire to avoid discomfort and pain, our need to feel good, or at the minimum, our attempts to feel less-bad; because facing facts is often an emotionally difficult task.

Avoiding negative-feelings is the main reason we self-deceive and why we cannot self-improve.

To avoid feeling bad, we often self-lie and self-deceive in order to abstain from dealing with negative-emotions. Avoiding undesirable feelings goes hand-in-hand with not wanting to take personal-responsibility to deal with undesirable-facts that cause these negative-feelings; because taking responsibility to make a positive-change takes time and requires effort. This lack of desire to actively deal with dislikable-facts and to change them into more favorable reality is the main problem associated with our desire to avoid pain, discomfort, and negativity.

Our need to feel good versus the necessity to think well is a core factor that inhibits change and blocks self-improvement.

This dislike and lack of desire to deal with facts is a direct consequence of us wanting to avoid painful truths, wanting to feel good, or at the minimum, wanting to feel less-bad. However, in order to change, we must face factual-reality, even if it is uncomfortable and undesirable. If we do not learn to face uncomfortable and dislikeable facts, the only other option that we have is to lie to our Self, so that we can perceive the truth the way we want it to be; rather than to engage with the truth the way it truly is. This is why:

The biggest lies we hear are the lies we tell our Self, because the easiest person to fool is our Self.

Self-deception is easier because it makes us quickly feel better without having to face the facts, and without putting in the effort to make a positive-change. Additionally, we also self-deceive indirectly by assigning purpose to external-things that do not have any purpose. We do so by concocting, by assuming, and by believing that undefined external-agents, especially intentional-agents, will somehow change dislikeable facts in our favor, because we are special. These externally concocted agencies are often relative to chance, or they are based on supernatural-beliefs. We commonly do so by creating, by imagining, or by believing in higher powers, external-purpose, and through beliefs in magical and miraculous occurrences, so that we can shift the responsibility of change to some other-person or to some other-thing. Through familial, cultural, and personal beliefs, we create false-hope and logical-fallacies, to avoid dealing with uncomfortable-facts, and to ignore and deny the dislikable-reality. Instead of fixing the cause of the negativity, we reason and rationalize through fallacies as to why reality is "not" the dislikable and uncomfortable situation that we are dealing with.

Statements such as:

- "Everything happens for a reason"
- "It was meant to be"
- "Everything will be fine"
- "Think positive and good things will happen"
- "Time will solve everything"
- "God works in mysterious ways"

are all examples of us assigning purpose onto other unproven or nonfactual agents, in order for us to avoid becoming the necessary "agent" in dealing with the unpleasant facts associated with our life. Concocting, believing, and assigning responsibility to an external-agency is comforting; because it gives us a sense of purpose and belonging.

As human-beings, we do not like to know that we exist without any purpose, because existing without purpose and without anyone else watching over us could be very lonely and frightening. Thus, we choose to lie to our Self in dealing with the dislikable and uncomfortable facts in one of two following ways:

1. **Avoidance:** We avoid dealing with facts, so that we see facts as we want them to be, rather than to see them as how they are. We do so via:
    a. **Denying** facts and evidence.
    b. **Ignoring** facts and evidence.

2. **Shifting:** By "passing-on" the responsibility of dealing with the facts, we take the burden of dealing with the facts and the necessary effort required to change the facts away from our Self, and we pass that burden onto someone-else or onto something-else. We pass-on this responsibility via the mindsets of:
    a. **Faith**
    b. **Hope**
    c. **Beliefs**

    And we do so:
    i.   By believing, by hoping, and by having faith that the uncomfortable or the undesirable facts will "somehow" be changed, resolved,

or eliminated on their own, and in our favor. For example, by leaving it up to chance.

ii. By believing, by hoping, and by having faith that some other agent will change, resolve, or eliminate the uncomfortable or undesirable facts in our favor. For example, God will change things for the better.

When attempting to avoid the facts, denial becomes a powerful defense-mechanism that many deploy in uncomfortable or undesired situations. Denial is commonly deployed in situations when the truth, especially if proven factually, could make the denier feel negatively. Denial is often associated with ignoring the cause, even when the cause is identified. In denial, the truth hurts; therefore, the denier does not want to consider the truth. Denial is rooted in our desire to feel better than we would have felt otherwise if we considered the facts and the truth. Denial, just like ignorance, is one of the primary quick means of how we avoid dealing with the uncomfortable reality, and how we self-deceive.

Ignoring facts, just like denying them, is another defense-mechanism that one deploys in order to overlook information and knowledge about the facts, or to abstain from wanting to know the facts. Ignorance can not only be a defense-mechanism in order to avoid facing facts, but if carried on for a lengthy period of time and as a way of life; ignorance could lead the person to become ignorant. Being ignorant is a restrictive trait for progress and improvement because ignorant people are actively, yet often nonconsciously, trying to avoid gaining knowledge, so they avoid feeling negative. By avoiding facts and knowledge, ignorant people actively but often unintentionally try to remain less-informed by trying to avoid negative-emotions that are brought on by the uncomfortable facts that contradict their preferred mindset.

Ignorant people are one of the most difficult people to have interactions and relationships with; because they simply do not care about the facts, and they try to avoid facts because facts make them feel uncomfortable. Thus, ignorant people often react outwardly and angrily if one tries to confront them with facts. Ignorant people will use any divergent technique to avoid facts, as they often engage in techniques such as gaslighting and mind-games in order to alter the facts. Ignorance and denial often go hand-in-hand; therefore, ignorant people commonly deny, and often, delusionally alter facts. The way that many, but especially ignorant people, alter the facts is by convincing themselves via self-deception that things are the way they want them to be; rather than by recognizing the way that things really are. Hence, ignorant people actively avoid learning about facts, because facts make them feel bad; but most importantly, because facts prove them wrong. Theory of Self-Relativity's direct quote about ignorant people states:

It is better to be stupid than ignorant, because stupid people can become less-stupid by learning, but ignorant people are too stupid to learn of their own ignorance.

Ignorant people are some of the most difficult people to deal with as they are not open to getting information and gaining knowledge; because, facts, information, and knowledge could prove them wrong. To be proven wrong is detrimental for ignorant people; because being corrected or being proven wrong is viewed by the ignorant as being inferior and not being good enough. Since most ignorant people have a low self-esteem and a fragile sense of Self that is commonly covered-up by a false and grandiose façade of superiority and being a know-it-all; ignorant people will fight tooth and nail in disagreements in order to not be proven wrong. Instead of learning and correcting their incorrect position, hence improving themselves; ignorant people would rather deny, ignore, or twist the truth so that they can abstain from accepting their mistake. This is why, Theory of Self-Relativity states:

Ignorant people don't debate to learn; ignorant people argue to not be wrong.

Furthermore, deniers and ignorant people not only try to not be proven wrong, but they create a false sense of competition in an attempt to prove others wrong; because, in order for them to hold onto their preferred reality, deniers and ignorant people falsely convince themselves to be right if they could prove someone else to be wrong. Therefore:

Ignorant people argue to see who loses first.

This is in contrast to how healthy people consider and deal with lack of information or knowledge. A healthy person would consider being wrong as an opportunity to learn and improve; hence why, Theory of Self-Relativity states:

Disagreements are good for learning; debate to learn, don't debate to not be wrong.

By not gaining information and knowledge, ignorant people end up having a limited and often incorrect perspective on people, on situations, and as a whole, they are generally wrong about the facts. However, since ignorant people often have a false and grandiose sense of Self, they also commonly insert themselves into conversations and interactions in order to represent their grandiose but false sense of knowledge, intelligence, and importance. Ignorant people often make fools of themselves, and when confronted with contradictory facts, they either rabbit-hole the conversation away from the subject matter that proved them wrong; or they falsely convince themselves that they were right, but the information was wrong. Ignorance is one of the biggest self-inflicted wounds; this is why, according to Theory of Self-Relativity:

The words of an ignorant person are his worst enemy.

Furthermore, ignorant people, due to their false sense of superiority, are commonly bullies; because, they are nonconsciously trying to protect their false façade. However, when they are confronted with facts and reason, and as they realize their ignorance is being exposed; ignorant people, just like other bullies, often resort to self-victimization and blame-shifting. Although not dealing with ignorant people is the correct choice; if we are forced to be in contact with ignorant people, such as at work or in family settings, we should confront ignorant people with facts and reason so that they realize they cannot bully us into silence.

The main difference between denial and ignorance is that in denial, the awareness and knowledge about the facts is often identified but the person choses to ignore them; however, in ignorance, the person overlooks or abstains from having any awareness and knowledge about the facts. Furthermore, denial is considered a more active and engaged form of ignorance; because, in denial, one generally has some knowledge of the facts but one chooses to ignore or suppress that information. On the other hand, ignorance is more passive, as one tries to find comfort in not knowing the facts; in other words, "what I don't know won't hurt me."

In both denial and ignorance, a person wants to feel not as bad as how they would have felt if they had to consider the facts; therefore, by not acknowledging or by not knowing the facts, they try to feel better than if they would have felt had they known the facts. Although in the long run, facts will catch up with the denier; in order to kick the can of undesired-feelings down the road, deniers will deny and ignore evidence and facts so that they continue to feel better.

Denial and ignorance are often associated with avoidance and defensiveness; because the people who are denying and ignoring the truth are subconsciously trying to avoid acknowledging and facing the facts. Defensiveness allows people to block themselves from facing the uncomfortable facts.

Additionally, denial can be such a powerful and nonconscious defense-mechanism, whereby, the denier, for example, a high-conflict or a personality-disordered individual, will consider the facts that they are actively denying, as threats or lies. When presented with facts, the denier will claim the evidence to be a lie and the presenter to be a liar, so that the denier could avoid the dislikeable feeling associated with the facts. Altering reality and facts, or rewriting history in order to deny the factual-truth, is in-fact a means of self-lying and self-deception. Denial not only leads to lying to one's own Self, but it is also a form of projection of one's own lies onto others; hence, deniers lie to themselves, and they also lie to others. Deniers must lie in order to avoid facing the facts, and thus, facing reality, so that they can abstain from feeling bad.

Deniers live in lies because deniers are liars.

According to Theory of Self-Relativity, another defense-mechanism or coping-mechanism that is often rooted in denial and ignorance is sarcasm. Although sarcasm, when used sporadically could be a means of enlivening a situation; when sarcasm is used as a defense-mechanism, it becomes a means of denying and ignoring the uncomfortable facts that someone or something is conveying to the sarcastic-person. In simple terms, sarcasm is used when sarcastic-people do not like how others are making them feel.

Sarcasm could become a deflecting-mechanism, as a form of externalation, in order to deny the external-truth; but more importantly, yet more subtly, sarcasm is also a means of avoiding introspection. Therefore, sarcasm is often initiated without cause or trigger, because the insecure or the dishonest sarcastic-person engages in sarcasm due to feeling anxious, stressed, and even scared. This fear and anxiety is commonly caused by the sarcastic-person's inability to adapt to something, or due to the person feeling inferior or challenged by others; without provocation.

Theory of Self-relativity defines "sarcasm" as "the defense-mechanism of an insecure or dishonest person who feels challenged without provocation."

Sarcasm, when overused, is intended to be a passive-aggressive behavior in the form of personal-attacks on others; which indicates that the sarcastic-person does not have the knowledge, the experience, or the confidence to confront the dislikable, but often, the true comments that another person made to the sarcastic-person.

The following points best summarize the characteristics associated with sarcasm:

- Defense-mechanism intended to deny or ignore an uncomfortable truth.
- Passive-aggressive behavior.
- Commonly associated with insecurity and dishonesty.
- A means of externalation and avoiding introspection.
- A means of projection.
- Generally triggered without provocation.

Those who have denial and ignorance tendencies cannot achieve self-improvement, because they are not open to accepting the facts and the truth. Accepting the facts and the truth means accepting reality that makes them uncomfortable, because reality is not to the way that they want it to be. This is why, it is difficult to engage a denier or an ignorant person in a debate that could prove them wrong. Although many do not like being proven wrong, and most people's initial reaction to being proven wrong could be defensive or argumentative; this holds even truer with those who actively engage in self-deception via denial and ignorance.

Most people don't debate to learn the truth; most people argue to not be wrong.

The reason factual-reality makes these individuals uncomfortable is because facts often directly represent their self-deficiencies. Denial and ignorance generally go hand-in-hand, and are interchanged as defense-mechanisms in people who do not want to see the facts; because they cannot handle the factual-truth. People who engage in denial of facts also tend to pass on the responsibility of facing facts onto other entities. They do so by either believing that things will work out favorably on their own, or that some other agent will change facts in their favor. This mindset is commonly undertaken in the form of having faith, hope, and beliefs. As discussed throughout Theory of Self-Relativity:

A belief is simply a thought that hasn't been proven with facts. When a belief is proven with facts, it is no more a belief; it is knowledge.

We can either deal with reality as reality is so that we can begin the process of changing difficulties in our favor; or we can continue to kick the can of denying reality down the road via empty-faith, false-hope, and comforting-beliefs, just so that we can temporarily feel good. We can use the double-edged-sword of our intelligence to make positive-change, by changing our circumstances for the better; or we can use our intelligence to create false-hope and fallacious-beliefs so that our fragile feelings will not get hurt.

It takes intelligence to manipulate intelligence.

This is why, Theory of Self-Relativity is founded upon the principle of factual-thinking, so that we can use our intelligence to deal with reality as reality is, rather than dealing with reality as how we want reality to be.

VII.
Faith, Hope & Beliefs

Theory of Self-Relativity defines "faith" as "having trust or confidence in something or someone without any facts or reason."

Theory of Self-Relativity defines "hope" as "an expectation or a wish for something desired to happen."

Theory of Self-Relativity defines a "belief" as "a thought, an opinion, or an idea that is assumed but unproven with facts and evidence."

According to Theory of Self-Relativity, faith, hope, and beliefs can also be described as *"thinking without evidence;"* therefore, faith, hope, and beliefs are unreliable.

Faith can be personal or learned from family, culture, and society. Faith is often associated with hope and beliefs. Faith, is a belief in something desired or comforting; hence, faith, just like hope, does not require factual proof or evidence in order for it to be effective. As discussed, because facing facts is often an emotionally difficult task, and because of our inherent and impulsive desire to avoid pain, to feel good, or at the minimum, to feel less-bad; we engage in having faith in order to improve our feelings. Faith and hope can easily offer that comforting-feeling indefinitely and without requiring any effort; because all we have to do is to create a faith-based belief, hence, convince our Self our faith-based thoughts, at some point, will deliver favorable results. Faith and hope make us feel good by making us believe in a better or in a less-than-bad reality; without any factually supportive evidence.

Faith, hope, and beliefs are mindsets that are closely associated with comforting feelings.

According to Theory of Self-Relativity:

Faith is a means of supporting a desired conclusion, not a path to discovering the truth.

Although unreliable, Theory of Self-Relativity does not reject faith, hope, and beliefs, as long as these mindsets are held temporarily and as short-term and intermediate mindsets; until they are proven with facts, or unless they are dismissed because of lack of supporting facts and evidence. Faith, hope, and beliefs require facts for validation, and they require effort and action for them to become reality. Therefore, faith, hope, and beliefs should only be held temporarily until supportive facts are found; because when faith, hope, and belief are proven factually, they become knowledge. If faith, hope, and beliefs cannot be proven factually, they must then be discarded and replaced with other forms of thought that are factual, or that could eventually be proven factually so they become knowledge.

Hope could be a good short-term mindset only if it follows an action that we took, and not as a standalone wishful-thought that makes us feel good.

This is why, Theory of Self-Relativity maintains that faith, hope, and belief should not be held long-term without proving their underlying validity and factual-value. Once the facts associated with our faith, hope, and beliefs are proven and they morph into knowledge; we can then take action based on that knowledge. For example, simply having faith and hope that someday we will become wealthy, famous, or that we will meet our dream partner, will not make these wishes come true. The only way for faith, hope, and beliefs to have a chance of becoming reality is for us to take action that would turn them into reality. By getting educated, through businesses, or by meeting the right people, we can increase the chances of our faithful and hopeful beliefs of becoming rich, famous, or meeting the partner of our dreams into becoming a reality. However, by just sitting there and hoping without taking action, the chances of any of the aforementioned exampled-events coming true would be minimal to none.

Many, simply hold faith and hope without taking any action; this is why, most hopes are shattered and turned into disappointments. Although faith and hope can give us temporary positive-feelings and even motivation; in the long run, faith and hope can actually create stronger negative-feelings of disappointment, hopelessness, and withdrawal.

Losing faith or hope is a harder fall than never having hoped for something.

Because:

It is easier to not have something, than to have it and then lose it.

Since Theory of Self-Relativity defines "faith" as *"having trust or confidence in some-thing or someone without any facts or evidence;"* therefore, faith creates a sense of confidence that is based on emotions rather than facts. A false sense of confidence could create a false sense of security and a false sense of reality; hence, unfounded faith, which itself is unreliable, could lead to shattered dreams and irreversible negative outcomes. As discussed throughout Theory of Self-Relativity, confidence is not a wish, an attitude, or something that we manifest overnight. Confidence is the byproduct of knowledge and experience; therefore, it takes time to develop and strengthen confidence. When we know that our thoughts are based on facts, we can then have the confidence to take action that could lead us to better outcomes; because we relied on knowledge and facts. However, if we do not have the knowledge, our confidence would be based on our feelings rather than based on our knowledge; hence, our faith could mislead us into a situation whereby the results would be unfavorable against the false-sense of confidence that faith created for us. This is further example of faith's unreliability.

Faith, hope, and beliefs are assumptive, speculative, and often imaginary forms of thought, because they have no factual-basis for their existence, unless proven otherwise. Therefor faith, hope, and unfounded-beliefs are not a formula for certainty; consequently, they should not be relied upon as a foundation for action. As stated:

Theory of Self-Relativity defines "hope" as "an expectation or a wish for something desired to happen."

Although faith, hope, and beliefs are not factual-thoughts; this does not mean that we should never have faith, hope, and beliefs. Faith, hope, and beliefs are motivational forms of thought that could be helpful with initiating action, in order to change and improve. However, just like other motivational mindsets, faith, hope, and beliefs, if not followed through with action, will lose their motivational intent and will become long-term nonfactual forms of thought that disable us from taking action; as we await in the faithful, hopeful, and believing stage for change and improvement to happen on its own.

Faith and hope could be good short-term motivators, but they are terrible long-term strategies.

Theory of Self-Relativity categorizes hope binarily:

1. **Positive-Hope or a Wish:** Is the type of hope that we associate with a well-wish or a positive-expectation; for example, hoping to win the lottery. Another well-known example of positive-hope is "wishful-thinking." Theory of Self-Relativity refers to positive-hope as a categorical definition of classic-hope, whereby the wish or the hope is associated with some kind of an expected, or more so, some kind of a desired positive outcome. While positive-hope can be directed to others; positive-hope is generally self-serving. Although positive-hope, or as referred to from now on as simply "hope," is a good moral boost; positive-hope, if not followed through with action in order to yield positive results could lead to disappointments. Since hope is founded on the basis of "expectations," this is why, Theory of Self-Relativity strongly recommends minimizing expectations; because, *"unmet expectations often lead to disappointments."* Instead of expectations, we should be more focused on creating purpose and setting achievable goals. Purpose, meaning, and goals are discussed in detail in subsequent sections.

2. **Negative-Hope or an Ill-Wish:** Is the type of hope which is normally directed externally, away from the Self; because negative-hope commonly involves others. For example, hoping something bad happens to a competitor, an enemy, or an ex. Negative-hope or an ill-wish is often the result of a low self-esteem and lack of self-confidence projected outwardly; and some of the most common emotions that negative-hope is associated with are jealousy, envy and resentment. Negative-hope or an ill-wish usually happens when one is incapable of self-improvement; thus, one would rather see others brought down to one's own level.

Since faith and hope are forward-looking, assumptive, and unreliable mindsets; therefore, they do not create certainty. In order for humans to feel safe, certainty and control are needed; this is why, faith and hope, when implemented, should only be used as short-term motivators. As discussed throughout Theory of Self-Relativity, motivation alone cannot create positive-change; motivation must be followed through with implementation and action in order to create positive-change.

True motivation shouldn't be empty-faith or a wishful-hope. True motivation should be an achievable roadmap followed by implementation.

Neither hope nor faith can create change, if the person having hope or faith does not take action. This is why, having empty-faith or false-hope can lead to severe hopelessness and withdrawal; because faith and hope are not a strategy to improve life, they are simply interim-stages of thought that must be followed with constructive-action.

There's no worse feeling than a shattered false-hope.

When hope and faith, just like a belief, are held long-term without follow-through action; the motivation of hope and faith subsides and uncertainty emerges. As discussed throughout Theory of Self-Relativity, lack of control and uncertainty, which often result in instability, are the root causes of anxiety and stress. Hence, when the expectations associated with unsupported hope and faith do not materialize, the fall-off often results in disappointment, anxiety, and even stress.

Faith, hope, and beliefs should only be held as short-term motivational states of mind, and not as long-term thinking strategies.

Faith, hope, and beliefs are intended to be comforting but they are not based on facts and evidence. Faith, hope, and beliefs are forms of placebo-thinking if they are held without follow through constructive-action. This is why, faith, hope, and beliefs should only be used as short-term motivators in order for them to lead us into taking action. However, the reason faith, hope, and beliefs create long-term drawbacks is because majority of people who hold these mindsets for the long-term and without factual verification; end up wasting a great deal of valuable time when these thought-processes fail without positive-outcomes.

A faith, a hope, or a belief, which is held but not evaluated for its validity; is simply a state-of-mind which is not factual or based on reality. A hope or a belief that is not factually verifiable cannot lead to transformation; and any followed through action based on such unverified mindsets could have unfavorable outcomes. If a hope or a belief cannot be factually verified and proven, that hope or belief is simply a false-hope or a fallacious-belief. Conversely, when a hope or a belief is verified with facts; that hope or belief becomes knowledge.

False-hopes and fallacious-beliefs, which are often associated with denial, are some of the most destructive forms of self-deception. In an attempt to feel good or to feel less-bad, we engage in creating false-hopes and fallacious-beliefs so that we can ignore and deny a dislikeable reality. Having baseless-faith, false-hopes, and fallacious-beliefs, are coping-mechanisms to create false-facts in order to fit them to our feelings. Theory of Self-Relativity classifies faith, hope, and beliefs as placebo-thoughts. Placebo-thinking, which Theory of Self-Relativity defines as "a form of rationalization through emotional-reasoning," is the creation of nonfactual-thoughts in order to feel better. Placebo-thoughts are created with the intent to support and justify how we want to feel, even though how we want to feel is contrary to how we should feel.

Hope and beliefs are the most common forms of placebo-thinking, because they are rationalizations that we create in order to feel good.

Faith, Hope & Beliefs Common Characteristics

- Placebo-Mindsets
- Thinking without Evidence
- Thinking with Feelings
- Comforting Feelings-Based
  - Motivational
    - Assumed
    - Convinced
  - False-Confidence
    - Unreliable
    - Uncertain
    - Unstable
    - Unproven
  - Forward Looking
  - Expectation-Based
    - Subjective

Theory of Self-Relativity considers faith, hope, and beliefs as good short-term motivators, only if they are followed through with constructive action. For example, we can hope that we would pass a class that we took if we properly attended the class, if we put in the effort to learn the material, and if we participated in taking all the exams associated with that class. However, if we did not attend the class or if we did not study for the exams, hoping to pass the class will simply be a false-hope and wishful-thinking. In order for faith, hope, and beliefs to produce favorable results, they have to be verified with facts, and they must be followed through with action. Although hope is generally more personal; a belief can be a more broadly based mindset that is not only personal, but also, it is a cultural, societal, and traditional mindset.

Theory of Self-Relativity defines a "belief" as "a thought, an opinion, or an idea that is assumed but unproven with facts and evidence."

The key words to focus on in the definition of belief are "assumed" and "unproven," because a belief is simply a form of thought that has not been factually verified; therefore, a belief, just like faith and hope, is unreliable. Thus, a belief should only be held as an interim or temporary state-of-mind, until it is proven to factually be true; or until it is discarded or dismissed, because it could not be proven to be factually true. In other words, a belief should be discarded when, after a certain period of fact-seeking, supportive facts and evidence for that belief could not be found. Therefore, we do not have to prove a belief to be false; we simply have to consider it as untrue, if after some time, supportive evidence for that belief cannot be found.

This is why, majority of "long-term" beliefs, just like false-hope and baseless-faith, are simply fallacies; because they are personally or socially constructed placebo-mindsets. Although beliefs are supposed to be comforting and motivational, beliefs should only be held as comforting or motivational in the short-term. However, because unfounded or unproven beliefs are not compatible with factual-reality; nonfactual-beliefs, just like long-term faith and hope, when held as long-term strategies, could be damaging and even destructive to one's life's outcomes. When faith, hope, and beliefs are verified and supported by facts and evidence, they will no longer be faith, hope, and beliefs; they will become knowledge. Therefore, faith, hope, and beliefs should be temporary mindsets until verified with facts and turned into knowledge; or until they are dismissed due to lack of supportive facts and evidence.

When you believe, you assume that you know; but you don't know that you know.

Although most thoughts are initially assumed, we must learn to move from the assumption stage to verification stage; if not, our assumed thoughts will turn into beliefs, instead of becoming knowledge. This is why, Theory of Self-Relativity defines a "belief" as:

A thought, an opinion, or an idea, that is assumed but unproven with facts and evidence.

When we have a thought, an idea, or an opinion, and when we assume the thought, the idea, or the opinion has merit; we turn that thought, idea, or opinion into a belief. Once we turn a thought, an idea, or an opinion into a belief, we should then seek to find the supportive facts to that belief so that we turn that belief into knowledge. If after a certain time we cannot find the supportive facts to that belief, we should consequently dismiss that belief as being nonfactual.

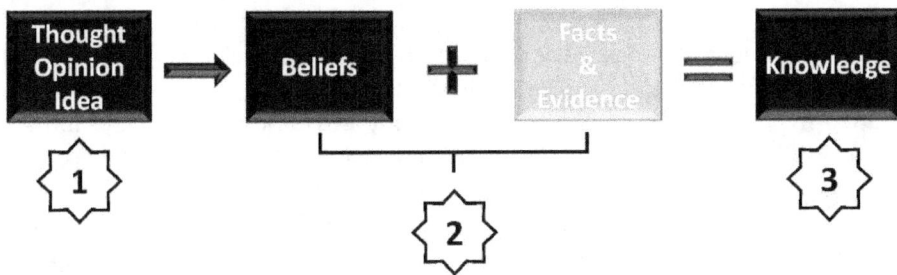

The word "belief" is a derivative of the word "believe," which is commonly defined as "a subjective opinion that is accepted as truth;" however:

"Accepted" as truth is not the same as "proven" as truth.

Likewise, subjective means based on, or influenced by, personal or cultural opinions; therefore:

A belief is subjective and unproven, as compared to knowledge, which is objective and proven.

Thus:

A belief is an assumed thought, but knowledge is an affirmed thought.

Opinions are thoughts that can be factual or perceived; therefore, beliefs could also be factual or perceived, and even fictitious. Beliefs could also become more acceptable when repeated over time and believed broadly by more people; however, broad acceptability, such as social-beliefs, often masks the falsity of fallacious-beliefs. A belief could become main-stream by being passed on from one person to another and from one generation to another generation without verification of its factuality; this is how, many myths and logical-fallacies are created. Many, confuse beliefs as being synonymous with facts without verifying the factuality of those beliefs; hence, they adopt their beliefs as the basis for their thinking. Beliefs are thoughts, opinions, or ideas that could "feel" valid, but they might not necessarily have factual-value; therefore, our beliefs, just like our individual-thoughts, must be evaluated for their factuality.

When a belief proves to be factual, that belief will simply cease to exist as a belief, and it will become knowledge. If a belief cannot be proven with facts and turned into knowledge, that belief should not carry as much weight as a knowledge should. If supportive-facts for a belief could not be found, then "time" should become the decisive factor for holding or for dismissing a belief. The longer a belief is held without supportive facts being found for that belief, the less value and influence that belief should have in our life. If after a sufficient amount of time no supportive evidence for a belief is found; we should thus, dismiss or eliminate that belief.

In the absence of facts, time is the best validator.

A belief must be dealt with similar to a scientific hypothesis. A scientific hypothesis is a thought or an idea that a scientist has which the scientist believes could be true. Neither the scientist, nor companies, nor the government begin relying on that hypothesis, until and unless that hypothesis is proven factually; and the hypothesis becomes knowledge. When a hypothesis is proven factually, it becomes knowledge, and it is only then adopted into our way of life. More importantly, and more commonly in science, when a hypothesis cannot be disproven factually, it becomes a valid and reliable theory that is as close to knowledge as possible.

Additionally, and more commonly, other scientists also try to replicate or disprove the hypothesis or the theory by doing more experiments and facts searching. If what was thought to be factual is proven to be nonfactual, or if the hypothesis can be falsified; that hypothesis is then modified, replaced, or discarded, and therefore, it is not treated as knowledge. However, if the hypothesis, the theory, or the knowledge cannot be falsified by other scientists, the hypothesis or the theory stands, and it is thus treated as knowledge.

This is why, science is not absolute and it is always changing and progressing. Since science is not absolute, Theory of Self-Relativity refers to science and scientific theories as:

The best explanation of the observed facts.

We should treat our thoughts, our ideas, our opinions, and ultimately, our beliefs, in similar fashion; by trying to falsify them. Regardless of the source of our belief, be it personal, cultural, or societal; we should always seek the factual-value of that belief. If a belief is held for a long time and no facts or evidence have been discovered about that belief; then that belief should not be treated as knowledge, and we should not make decisions nor should we take action based on that belief. On the contrary, we should put less value and reliance on any belief that has been held for a lengthy period of time without factual verification. Therefore, it is safe to conclude that prolonged lack of evidence for a belief, most probably means no evidence exists.

Although absence of evidence does not necessarily mean evidence of absence; prolonged absence of evidence indicates a high probability of evidence of absence.

The word believe itself is a forward-looking verb which represents uncertainty; for example, we believe that an asset will rise in value, hence, we invest in it; or we buy that asset with the hope or belief of it appreciating in value. When many people believe in the value of that asset, the asset price rises because of a widely held sentiment or belief. As indicated by "consumer sentiment," should sentiment begin to shift and the number of believers rise or diminish, the value of that asset tends to follow the sentiment; however, in the long run, the value of an asset will ultimately be proven by the facts and the evidence that supports that value. Biotech companies are a good example of such beliefs versus knowledge.

A biotech company could lose money for a long time, but its stock could continue to rise based on the belief of the potential for the drug or vaccine that the company is developing. After multiple phases of experiments and trials, the results of the drug's efficacy begin to show. If the results are positive and the drug shows to factually be effective for what it is intended for, the value of the stock will be justified or will even rise further. However, should the results of the trials not be as favorable to support the claims for the drug, the sentiment and belief in the drug will be shaken, and the stock price will fall. Although in the short-term, a rising or falling stock price may be reliant on faith, hope, and beliefs; in the long-run, it gets proven via the verification of facts associated with the underlying company and its fundamentals that are being represented by the stock. Either the drug gets accepted, and the stock price gets verified; or the drug is not accepted, or it is abandoned, hence, the stock price drops to reflect the value accordingly.

Therefore:

Short-term sentiment is either verified or challenged by long-term evidence.

Similar scenarios could be applied to business forecasts, politics, religion, and other personal-matters, including emotions and relationships. Since beliefs and believing in something is more sentiment related and subjective, than it is factual and objective; such beliefs could create behavior that is not based on solid factual foundation, but one that is based on emotions. Beliefs and other nonfactual-thoughts such as faith and hope are commonly created or adopted by a person in order to make the individual feel good; but it does not mean that these thoughts and beliefs necessarily set a forward path for positive accomplishments. Therefore, to value such beliefs, these beliefs must be verified with facts and turned into knowledge, so that they would become reliable mindsets for further action.

Theory of Self-Relativity does not strictly recommend for us to not take action based on a belief; because sometimes, for example, in urgent situations, we must act in the absence of evidence. However, we must be cognizant that the level and the frequency of action that we take based on a belief should not be as frequent or as significant as the level of action that we would take based on knowledge. As discussed, beliefs are unproven and assumptive; therefore, to solely act on a belief would be more of a speculation than a knowledge-based action. For instance, the aforementioned example of financial-assumptions and consumer-sentiment are partially based on assumptions, expectations, and sentiment. This is why, investing, trading, and gambling, all carry forward-looking statements of risk; and they are categorized under the philosophy of "Behavioral-Economics."

Religion and Politics are two other segments of our existence that are personifications of beliefs. The reason religion and politics can both be controversial, and are always debated, is because they are often based on personal beliefs and biases; and they are based on subjective-interpretations. Spirituality, which could be religious, new-age, or metaphysical, is also an example of similar attributes. This is why, science and knowledge, which are fact-based, often come into conflicts with religious, political, spiritual, and personal beliefs and biases.

For example, although atheism claims it is not a belief-system because atheism does not claim a belief in the non-existence of God; some atheists who argue the non-existence of God based on the absence of factual-evidence, do hold a belief that God does not exist. Conventional atheism claims it cannot prove the non-existence of God, because one cannot prove a negative; however, the absence of evidence for the existence of God or the supernatural serves as the reason the God hypothesis or supernaturalism should not be relied upon. Atheists should be open to accepting the existence of God or other supernatural entities if facts and evidence emerge that prove the existence of God or the supernatural; and in the same manner, theists should also consider the role and the influence of their religious-beliefs in guiding their life, because there has been no direct or empirical evidence for the existence of God or the supernatural.

As uncomfortable as it may be for believers reading this; since, in lieu of millennia of beliefs, there has not been any factual evidence for the existence of supernatural-entities, according to Theory of Self-Relativity, which is founded upon the principle of factual-thinking, it is more prudent to consider the non-existence of supernatural-entities than, to believe in their existence. Therefore, since there has been no direct and empirical evidence of the existence of the supernatural; one must base one's life and the rules one follows on only factual-knowledge, and not based on presumed or assumed beliefs. However, one should remain adaptable and unbiased should new contradictory facts emerge. This lack of evidence for the existence of the supernatural is discussed further in subsequent sections of Theory of Self-Relativity.

Whether we believe or not, we should allow the weight of the evidence and facts to guide that decision for us. When we turn beliefs into knowledge, we can then base our decisions and actions on that knowledge. Our beliefs could be and are often biased and subjective; therefore, it is important for us to evaluate the objectivity of our beliefs and thoughts in order to live a balanced life in an effective and realistic manner. This is why, it is important for us to adapt to change in order to improve; and we must do so by seeking the facts, by examining the facts, and by making decisions based on the facts. Since only one form of fact exists for every situation, and because facts, unlike beliefs, are not open to interpretation; in order to self-improve, we must learn to be cognizant of our thoughts and beliefs, hence, we should be able to quickly and cleverly evaluate our thoughts and beliefs based on facts and evidence. Factual-thinking increases objectivity, while minimizing subjective-preferences and biases.

Factual-thinking proves or disproves our assumptions, our perceptions, and our beliefs.

Objectivity performs best when we can manage biases and thoughts cognitively and factually. It is this cognitive evaluation of the quality of our thoughts and beliefs that forms the basis of our true intellectual-existence; not just what we feel or believe in. When we manage our thoughts, our feelings adjust accordingly to the underlying thought; hence, our actions become more based on factual-reality rather than just based on preferred and perceived-reality. As long as we understand that objectivity and factual evaluation of our thoughts and beliefs could require us to make changes in the way we think, or in what we believe in; we can then find the best balance between objectivity of factual-reality, versus the subjectivity of how our beliefs make us feel. As stated throughout Theory of Self-Relativity:

Facts can be experienced subjectively but must be dealt with objectively.

Therefore, factual-thinking does not mean to not have subjective views and perspectives; on the contrary, our subjective-perspective and personal-experiences aid to tailor our preferences within that factual-reality. Theory of Self-Relativity recommends that our primary analytical approach should be objective, and our secondary or supportive approach can be subjective. Objectivity is like the foundation of a building, and subjectivity is the design and the details of the building. Once we establish objectivity, we can then add our personal and subjective touches to build upon that solid and factual-foundation of our objective thinking.

Theory of Self-Relativity defines "objectivity" as "one's ability to consider values and facts that are external to one's Self; and are independent of one's perceptions, beliefs, or feelings."

Although objectivity, which deals with external-factors, is not dependent on a person; objectivity is relative to that person. However, unlike objectivity or an objective-value, which is better defined and more quantifiable; subjectivity or a subjective-value, which is personal, is not always well-defined and it is not necessarily fact-based. Subjectivity is based on individual-perceptions, personal-experiences, and adopted-beliefs; and it is influenced by the individual's thoughts, feelings, and experiences. An example of subjectivity versus objectivity is "perfection;" as what one thinks is perfect, might not be considered as perfect by others.

Although one might put a great deal of value in achieving or attaining perfection, others might not see any increase in value based on one's perception of perfection. This is why, we must evaluate and analyze things objectively before adding our subjective preferences to it; however, once we have begun subjective experiences and contributions, we must regularly evaluate the value and the factuality of our subjective-interpretations and subjective-experiences relative to the objective-value of the overall situation.

Objectivity enables us to observe and understand reality as it is, while subjectivity enables us to experience reality relative to our Self.

Objectivity is closer to reality because it is fact-based; however, subjectivity is influenced by personal-perspectives which are often feelings-based. Hence why, Theory of Self-Relativity advocates factual-thinking and recommends objectivity to be the core of how we think and how we analyze things and events. Although subjectivity creates individual uniqueness and it cultivates revolutionary and innovative creativity; to solely depend on subjectivity, we run the risk of not being able to check and balance our thoughts and actions objectively and factually. Objectivity is generally considered to be more rational and fact-based, while subjectivity is more influenced by emotions, interpretations, and experiences. Subjectivity injects personal-variables into a situation that could be factual; or as they often are, they could be emotional.

Objectivity is considered to be more rational because objectivity is influenced more broadly from multiple inputs and from different perspectives; thus, objectivity is considered to be more factual and reason-based. Although objectivity keeps checks and balances on subjectivity; subjectivity, in certain situations, could actually bring rationality to long held objective-beliefs and perspectives which themselves originated subjectively from a single source. Subjectivity can give a personal-perspective on a broadly held objective-value, which itself, could be nonfactual and based on long-times of unverified beliefs and practices that originated from a subjective origin. Religions, rituals, and dogmas, are examples of such ancient traditions and beliefs which are widely held without verification of the factuality of their origin, and without demonstration of the supportive evidence for their claims. They are so widely held and believed for so long, that their subjective origin is morphed by their nonfactual perception of objectivity. This is why, factual-thinking on a personal-level should run checks and balances on all aspects of our life's dealings; including such widely held "perceived-objective-values" that we often adopt as traditions and cultural values.

We create comforting-beliefs and nonfactual-thoughts to feel good, and we do so by thinking likeable-thoughts, rather than by taking action to improve dislikable situations. To improve, we must take action, and to take proper action, we must be able to think factually. Factual-reality is not necessarily likeable; however, creation of nonfactual comforting-beliefs is destined to clash with factual-reality, regardless, if the source of such beliefs is personal, societal, cultural, or traditional. This is why, science clashes with other belief-based doctrines such as religion and supernatural fallacies and myths; because science evaluates facts, evidence, and data, without preemptively deducing a preferred conclusion, and then trying to support the conclusion via rationalizations or feelings.

While science and religion could create conflicts, especially on the extreme ends; we should choose and adapt our beliefs based on facts and evidence. Religion should not have absolute rigid control over our thoughts and beliefs; and neither should science. Only knowledge, which is based on facts and evidence, should guide our actions. This balance could only be achieved by us learning to evaluate our thoughts and beliefs objectively. Although others could agree with, or might criticize our beliefs; we should be able to evaluate, adapt, or modify our beliefs based on supportive facts and evidence. This is how revolutionary thinkers are able to dethrone widely held comforting-beliefs and replace them with evolutionary knowledge.

If beliefs cannot be consistent with factual-reality, factual-reality will always win; because factual-reality is dictated by how reality is relative to our Self and to our existence. Beliefs can be helpful in establishing and maintaining our values, but beliefs will fall apart if they are not supported by facts. As stated, beliefs are a more mature form of thoughts, opinions, and ideas; therefore, fallacious-beliefs, such as blind-faith and false-hope, will fail in the long-term, if they do not transform into knowledge.

Shattered-hopes and failed-beliefs are some of the most painful emotional experiences.

When we say we believe in something, it is not because we know that something to be factually true; but it is because we want that something to be true, or we feel it to be true, thus, we convince our Self of that truth. To truly feel the power or the potential danger of nonfactual-beliefs, the next time we state a sentence which includes the word "I believe," we should replace the word "believe" with the word "know," and see how it will immediately stop us in our tracks to evaluate the factual-value of our belief. The instance we replace "I believe" with "I know," we can then realize how much we really do not know and how we convince and fool our Self into thinking that our nonfactual-beliefs are actually knowledge.

When one has some knowledge, that's when one knows how much one doesn't know.

Unlike knowledge, faith, hope, and beliefs are commonly associated with feelings; therefore, if we replace "I believe" with "I feel" we get the same comforting result.

What we feel or believe is not necessarily what is true.

For example, some of us believe that we will one day win the lottery and that belief gives us a purpose to keep going; hence, we state, "I believe, or I feel that I'm going to win the lottery someday." The instant we change "I believe, or I feel" with "I know," as "I know that I'm going to win the lottery someday," we then realizes that our belief is nothing but a comforting mindset, rather than actual reality; because there is no way for us to know that we are going to win the lottery. Since we don't "know" that we will win the lottery, we are simply hoping that despite the odds, we will win the lottery. By hanging onto false-hope, this is how people waste precious time waiting for something good to happen, instead of themselves making the change.

Stop chasing an exception and start building a foundation.

Same could be true about other beliefs, such as a belief in God; however, in such instances, many have already replaced "I believe" with "I know" without even realizing their own definitive statement of knowing has not been factually proven. If we state "I know that God exists and he's watching over me;" we have actually provided no factual, tangible, or measurable evidence that this belief, which we are mistakenly assuming to be knowledge, has ever been proven. We should realize what we "think, feel, or believe" to be knowledge to us, is just a strong sentimental or emotional mindset, and not an actual fact. In strong beliefs, especially those that are believed by a large number of people and have been traditionally passed on from generation-to-generation without verification of their underlying facts; the emotional strength and the vast acceptability of the belief often makes believers deceptively convince themselves what they "feel or believe" is actually "knowle-dge." As discussed, such mindset of beliefs are described as logical-fallacies; and in this particular example, we are dealing with the logical-fallacies of appeal-to-tradition and appeal-to-popularity.

To get to the facts, we must question everything.

Just because a large number of the population believes in something, such a widely held belief does not actually equate to be knowledge. The only way to validate a belief to be potentially true is for us to seek and verify the belief with facts. People have a tendency of conforming to culture, society, and tradition, and such conformity could often feed on itself to strengthen a nonfactual-belief. Add to that, the long time that a belief might have been held and passed on from generation-to-generation, and that belief could fallaciously be accepted as knowledge.

Furthermore, there is more neuroscientific evidence emerging that beliefs increase the levels of the hormone dopamine, which is known as the feel-good hormone or the happy-juice. Hence why, it is difficult for people to change their beliefs or to get rid of their beliefs. This is also further reason we continuously create new beliefs, or we want to enforce our existing comforting-beliefs. This increase in dopamine that is associated with beliefs is further evidence that supports Theory of Self-Relativity's observation that we engage in self-deception in order to avoid pain, to feel good, or at the minimum, to feel less-bad. This association of dopamine with beliefs is further evidence why human-beings gravitate towards religion; because religious-beliefs tend to be comforting. Consequently, beliefs are closely associated with emotions.

Our need to feel good versus the necessity to think well is a core factor that inhibits change and blocks self-improvement.

A truly self-improved and transformed person must remain skeptical and must always ask questions and seek the facts for a belief; be it for a religious-belief or a scientific-hypothesis, regardless of how that concept originated and how long it has been believed. For example, for centuries, it was believed that the Sun rotated around the Earth. Had that belief not been challenged and factually corrected, true knowledge could not have been established. Without the proper establishment of true knowledge about the Sun and the Earth, other technological and human advancements would not have been possible. Therefore, all forms of thoughts, beliefs, and even, knowledge, must always be open to questioning.

This is why, Theory of Self-Relativity insists on seeking, acquiring, and using facts to support our thoughts. By searching for facts and by verifying the factuality of our thoughts and beliefs, we can prevent precious time and precious lifetime from being wasted on falsities. Factual-thinking is the only form of thinking that can align us realistically with reality and with The-Universe. Through cognitive-practices, we will learn that what we believe, is not necessarily what we know; it is only then that we will begin to distinguish between the value of beliefs versus the value of knowledge so that we will make a habit of always seeking and verifying our thoughts and beliefs with facts. When we lessen unfounded-beliefs and as we seek facts and evidence to turn our beliefs into knowledge, we will then begin to make better decisions and we will act constructively. To progress, to succeed, and to transform, our thoughts and our beliefs must lead us to make positive-change by taking constructive-action. We cannot indefinitely just stay stuck in the feel-good and comforting transitional-stage of our preferred but unsubstantiated beliefs.

Since feelings are the transitional-stage between our thoughts and our behavior, and since beliefs are a transitional-stage between our thoughts and knowledge; both of these transitional stages must reach a final destination. It is also because of this transitional intermediate nature of feelings and beliefs, that beliefs are closely associated with feelings; hence why, beliefs are intended to make us feel good. Therefore, in order to get out of transition and into a final destination, we must look for facts to support our beliefs that are closely interconnected with our feelings. Once our beliefs are accepted as knowledge or are dismissed because they were nonfactual, we can then proceed to taking action or inaction based on the facts and knowledge that we have gained about our underlying beliefs.

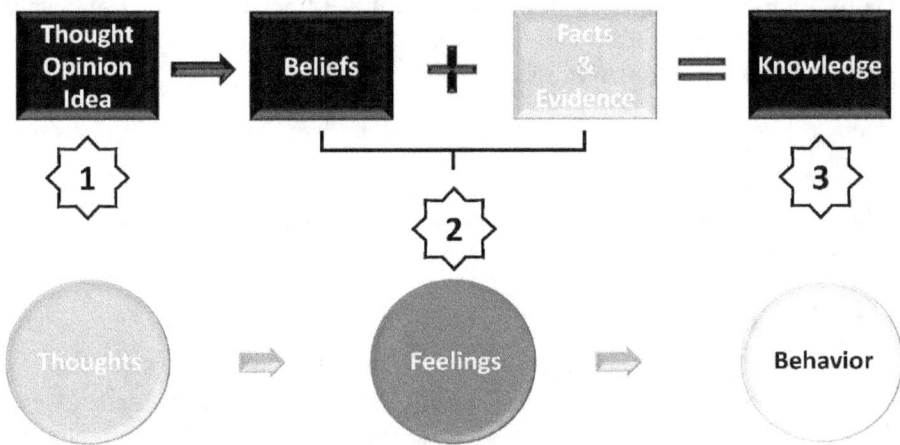

Having a belief, or believing in something, should not be a perpetual state-of-mind; it should only be a transitional mindset until facts and evidence are found to support that belief, in order to turn the belief into knowledge.

If facts and evidence could not be found to support believing in something, that belief must be dismissed and discarded; especially if that belief has been held for an unreasonably long period of time.

The only thing you should believe is believing in your Self that you will always seek facts in order to improve your circumstances.

Unlike a belief, when we know something, we would not have to continuously affirm our knowledge through interpretation, rationalization, or justifications. It is only when we are not sure of the factual value of a comforting-belief that we continuously try to find ways of confirming, justifying, and rationalizing those desired beliefs so that we can hold onto the beliefs that are making us feel good.

When you are truly comfortable with the facts of a thought, you wouldn't believe in it; you would know it.

To best achieve self-improvement, we must learn to not hold beliefs for too long; we must either turn our beliefs into knowledge, by treating beliefs as interim-states to gaining knowledge; or we must discard our beliefs if no supportive evidence could be found. Therefore, our actions must be based on knowledge, and not based on beliefs. Every time we say I believe in something, we should always ask the following question: "do we believe in that thing because we are looking to find the supportive facts; or do we believe in that thing because believing in that thing makes us feel good?"

Don't believe for comfort…Know for a fact.

Facts and evidence are the only things that validate reality. Although human intellectual evolution has been constructive for our progress; consequently, we are also a victim of our advanced intelligence. We have learned to rationalize, justify, and manipulate our mind in order to feel good; even though that manipulation is contrary to what facts indicate about our reality. Other animals do not change their understanding of reality in order to feel good; because other species are not capable of rationalization as humans are.

Theory of Self-Relativity defines "rationalization" as "using intelligence for deceptive reasoning."

Other species deal with reality as reality is, because that is the only way that they can stay safe and survive.

It takes intelligence, to manipulate intelligence.

Since humans, due to their intelligence, can and do manipulate their mind in order to self-deceive; therefore, we must learn to use these intellectual and cognitive abilities to become aware of, to understand, and to abstain from altering our perception of reality.

When we learn to base our thinking and actions on facts and not act based on how we want to feel, we will then be able to create positive-feelings and happiness that are more stable. Instead of creating thoughts to make us feel the way we want to feel temporarily; we will only deal with thoughts based on factuality, so that our eventual positive-feelings will have longer-lasting effects. When thoughts are factual, they create knowledge; and knowledge is what keeps us safe and in harmony with The-Universe. Although initially, facing facts might be an emotionally difficult challenge; once we learn to think factually and get the continuum of factual-thinking going, factual-thinking, and living based on facts and knowledge will become an intuitive part of our existence.

Therefore, we must learn to get over the initial hump of the discomfort of facing facts. The sooner we learn to deal with undesired and uncomfortable facts, and the sooner we resolve, change, or eliminate their negative causes; the sooner we will reach a point where only favorable and desired facts will remain in our lives. It is only then that we will begin to observe and experience reality as reality is, instead of perceiving reality as we want it to be. Facts and knowledge of facts is what should guide our existence. Albert Einstein famously stated:

"A man should look for what is, not what he thinks should be."

This is why, "Knowledge is Power."

Theory of Self-Relativity defines "knowledge" as "a thought, an idea, or a belief which is supported with facts."

Belief = Thought − Facts

vs

Knowledge = Thought + Facts

In contrast:

Theory of Self-Relativity defines a "belief" as "a thought, an opinion, or an idea that is assumed but unproven with facts and evidence."

Simply stated:

A belief is a thought that has not been proven with facts.

However, in the absence of facts, "time," is the second most important verifier or disqualifier of a belief. If after a while, no supportive evidence is found to turn a belief into knowledge; we should then strongly consider that the belief we hold is potentially wrong or nonfactual.

Time is the second worst enemy of unfounded beliefs.

The main difference and the single most important distinguishing factor between belief and knowledge is fact or evidence. In due time, we should either find the facts and the evidence to turn our belief into knowledge; or we should discard our belief because no supportive fact or evidence could be found. Therefore:

Until supportive facts for a belief are found, that belief remains unreliable.

Opinion

Thought　　**Belief**　　Knowledge　　Facts

Idea

Knowledge exists when a thought, an idea, or a belief, is verified and supported with fact and evidence. Knowledge remains true as long as all supportive facts verify that particular knowledge; or until and unless new, different, or additional facts emerge that disprove or modify that knowledge. Therefore, "true" knowledge is always open to change. If in lieu of differing or new evidence, knowledge is not open to change; then that is not knowledge, it is a belief or a dogma. If despite contradictory and conflicting facts and evidence one refuses to abandon one's belief; that is when emotional-thinking overrides factual-thinking.

Knowledge, unlike beliefs, is not influenced by emotions.

Although knowledge is often mistaken to only be associated with science; knowledge as a whole, is a collection of supportive factual information that is used to apply to all aspects of our thinking, understanding, and existence. This includes science, religion, and politics, as well as social and personal interactions. For example, through the evolution and advancement of knowledge and the discovery of new facts we are able to prolong our life expectancy by treating and curing diseases. Likewise, through gaining knowledge, we are able to create new rules and amend existing laws and regulations in business, in government, and in society. Additionally, knowledge has allowed for human technological advancements.

As a whole, it is the discovery and evolution associated with knowledge that has allowed for human advancements. The ability to place facts at the core of the truth allows us to stay objective and factual with our sense of the truth and reality. By focusing on facts, we can create our strongest sense, our best understanding, and our competent knowledge of reality. This is why, scientists and knowledge-based individuals are open to modify or disprove their knowledge, if and when new facts and evidence emerge.

Knowledge evolves continuously as new information and facts emerge; however, beliefs, especially those which are not open to questioning or to factual-evaluation, do not evolve, and are closed-off from factual verification. This is especially true of feel-good and comforting-beliefs, especially those beliefs which have been carried on for long periods of time and have stayed resistant to change and evolution. Fact-based information, such as knowledge, are always open to questioning, but they are not open to selective-interpretation or intentional-manipulation. However, unlike knowledge, unfounded-beliefs or dogma are rigid and not open to questioning; because the questioning and examination of a long-held unfounded belief will most likely disprove that belief. This is why, beliefs, especially authoritarian and dogmatic beliefs, are forcefully or guilt-riddenly guarded against questioning and scrutiny. For example, the labeling of something as being sacred or negatively-consequential to inquiry, is a way of protecting unfounded-beliefs from dismantling.

The flexibility and progress of knowledge is only possible because of its ability to unbiasedly adapt to new information that is based on the most recent and the strongest collection of evidence and facts. Knowledge and science could not progress if scientists and innovators were rigid or biased with their thoughts, ideas, or beliefs; and if they were not open to change and improvement.

To improve, question everything so that you know the facts.

Knowledge is a factually proven belief, and knowledge is open to change if new facts emerge; however, unfounded, comforting, and nonfactual-beliefs are not open to change, because facts would invalidate nonfactual-thoughts and fallacious-beliefs. Therefore, in order to maintain a comforting-belief, one has to self-deceive by ignoring and by denying the evidence; or one has to make the belief resistant to fact-based challenges. In order to prevent a belief from factual-challenge and to maintain such unsupported claims; people and societies often proclaim beliefs to be unchallengeable or even sacred. This is the basis of dogma and dogmatic-principle. However, nothing should be closed to questioning, skepticism, or factual-analysis. Hence why, Theory of Self-Relativity repeatedly states that in order to self-improve, we must remain unbiased and adaptable so that we can evaluate our thoughts and our beliefs factually. Thus:

Until supportive facts are recognized, a particular belief must not be considered as true.

Likewise:

Until and unless current facts change; a particular knowledge is considered to be true.

Factual-thinking unclutters our mind from unnecessary and ruminating thoughts; and it filters out emotional-reasoning and the holding of unsubstantiated and nonfactual-beliefs. Likewise, since beliefs are not verified with facts and evidence, beliefs increase uncertainty and anxiety; whereas, knowledge minimizes-uncertainty, hence, in the long-term, knowledge minimizes negative-emotions. Knowing the facts associated with a mindset or a situation minimizes uncertainty and anxiety; therefore, knowledge increases certainty and confidence.

No matter how much a person believes in something, to not know the facts about that something increases uncertainty, which in-turn, increases stress and anxiety. To minimize anxiety and stress associated with the instability of an unproven-belief, one must seek facts in order to turn that belief into knowledge. Having knowledge and facts about a thing increases confidence and predictability, while minimizing uncertainty; which in-turn, minimizes negative-feelings such as worry, anxiety, and even, stress and fear.

This is why, many scholars state that "knowledge is power," because knowledge minimizes uncertainty and unpredictability, while it increases certainty and predictability. Knowledge allows for better understanding of a thing or a situation and its causes. Knowledge is achieved via learning; and learning creates awareness and understanding to gain further knowledge. Although gaining knowledge creates more certainty and predictability, just learning and gaining knowledge is not enough to transform our Self into a self-improved person. It is true that knowledge is power; however, in order to take advantage of the power of knowledge, that power must be put to use. Hence why, Theory of Self-Relativity states:

Knowledge is power, when applied.

Awareness and understanding of our thoughts are important steps to the organization and improvement of our thinking-process. An easy thinking-process improves our state-of-mind; hence, it eases and improves our feelings. A strong and fact-based thinking mind can reduce clutter, increase focus, and enable us to make decisions quickly and cleverly, and to take proper action. Such a state-of-mind creates continuous and consistent self-fulfilling change.

Most mindfulness-techniques, such as meditation, recommend slowing down our thinking-system, by focusing on basic distractions, such as our breathing, in order to clear our thoughts and our mind. While mediation and some other mindfulness-techniques have been helpful in stress-reduction and in calming inner commotions; most mindfulness-techniques do not give us the thoughtfulness skills to actually resolve or eliminate conflicting and nonfactual-thoughts. Current mindfulness-techniques, such as meditation, try to calm our mind so that we can hopefully try to minimize the effects of our negative, cluttering, and ruminating thoughts; yet, after a meditation session or any other mindfulness practice ends, and as we enter back into our normal day, the problematic-thoughts and the lingering problems creep back into our mind and into our lives. Although mindfulness, as described by Theory of Self-Relativity, helps to identify thoughts; mindfulness alone does not and cannot resolve or eliminate problematic thoughts.

Furthermore, just like the myths of meditation, the popular belief that we only use 10% of our brain is untrue; as it is a sensationalistic way of making us believe in our "supposedly" hidden cognitive-potentials that we are not efficiently cultivating. It is an effective selling point to commit us to programs which "could" enable us to use more of our brain. Even if we were only using 10% of our brain, such systems and their claims of increasing brain usage potential are immeasurable and unquantifiable. Regardless, contrary to the aforementioned claims, we are always using 100% of our brain, all of the time.

The problem is not the fact that we are not using the complete potential of our brain; the real problem is that despite the fact that we are operating 100% of our brain all of the time, we are only conscious and aware of only 10% of the operations of our brain. This means, we are only aware of and in touch with 10% of what we are thinking about; therefore, 90% of what we think, and feel are nonconscious.

We use 100% of our brain all of the time; but we are only aware of 10% of our thoughts.

Thus, to train our mind properly, we must increase the awareness of our thoughts; and in order for us to get in touch with our thoughts, we need to bring our mind and our mental-activities into our consciousness. The best way to do this is to become mindful and to learn to identify our thoughts through our feelings. Theory of Self-Relativity's Cognitive-Cognition-Technique is exactly such a tool. The Cognitive-Cognition-Technique streamlines and programs our thought-awareness to become an integral part of our daily activities and our existence. A valuable self-improvement and mindfulness system must not only enable us to search for and to recognize mental clutter and negativity; but more importantly, it must teach us to apply solutions to the awareness that we have achieved. Awareness of our thoughts is an important first step; however, achieving awareness without knowing what to do with it, is like knowing that a train is approaching but to remain frozen in the path of the oncoming train. Awareness of our thoughts and the application of factual-thinking by evaluating the factualities of those thoughts, is what The Cognitive-Cognition-Technique teaches us.

The Cognitive-Cognition-Technique exercises our mind, by developing, by increasing, and by enhancing our brain's neural-pathways. By filtering out nonfactual-thoughts, our neural-pathways develop only in the direction of factuality. Increasing fact-based neural-pathways creates more efficiency and effectiveness of thinking, and it could even increase the level of our intelligence.

Theory of Self-Relativity defines "intelligence" as "the ability to acquire, process, and apply information and knowledge."

Knowledge is best acquired, not through memorization, but through awareness and understanding of its supportive information. Knowledge and intellect are power; but knowledge and intelligence are powerless if not applied. Therefore, just like knowledge:

Intelligence is useless if not applied.

Efficiency is a mechanism to streamline output with, or especially, without increasing the size of the hardware; and when it comes to the mind, the efficiency of thinking, which could only be achieved through the quicker application of facts and knowledge, leads to an increase in learning and intelligence. This is why, Theory of Self-Relativity refers to The Cognitive-Cognition-Technique as our mental-algorithm; because The Cognitive-Cognition-Technique teaches us how to apply emotional-intelligence and thought-management in a quick and repeatable format to all of our thinking activities, decision-making, and behavior.

Intelligence is increased via knowledge, and knowledge can only be attained by learning. Likewise, true learning can only be achieved via factual-thinking. Intelligence could actually be increased, not necessarily by increasing the measurement of intelligence; but through the efficient application of learned-knowledge. Continuous application of knowledge through problem-solving is effective in streamlining the efficient application of intelligence; hence, it manifests itself as increased intelligence.

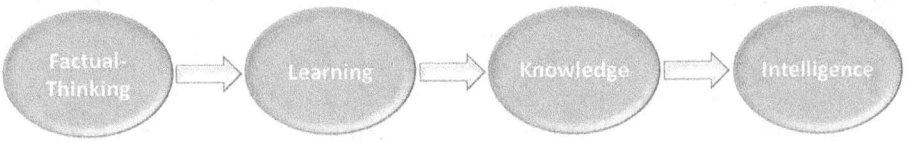

Same applies to information, IQ, and even wittiness; yet, there are many smart individuals who do dumb things and continue wasting their intellect because they do not know how to cultivate their intelligence, and how to put their knowledge to use. Although awareness of our thoughts is a core component for change and self-improvement; application of our awareness, which increases and improves our wisdom, is even more important.

Theory of Self-Relativity further defines "wisdom" as "the effective application of constantly evolving knowledge and experience, which is not contingent to subjective-interpretations."

Things cannot improve, and results cannot be achieved, if knowledge and wisdom are not applied. Application of awareness and knowledge enforces and enhances change and improvement. While most people have difficulty in becoming aware of their thoughts, many, who actually learn to become aware of their thoughts either deny these uncomfortable-thoughts, or they do not use their wisdom to understand these dislikable-thoughts in order to resolve or eliminate them.

Information and intelligence are most valuable when applied.

Wisdom is not just the acquisition of knowledge and experience, but wisdom is the effective application and sharing of such knowledge and experience through factual-thinking and via reason-based analysis. True wisdom is constantly evolving and it is not influenced by subjective-interpretation and comforting-feelings. A wise-person does not reason with emotions; a wise person reasons with facts and proven experience.

A wise person observes and absorbs reality as reality is, and not as he/she wants reality to be.

Although knowing the facts is an important first step in self-improvement; simply knowing the facts, but not using them, is similar to having bullets in a gun but the gun jamming in a life-threatening situation.

Don't just know…Apply!

This is why, behavior-modification is an integral part of the application of knowledge and intelligence. Because, as stated:

Our behavior does not represent how we are thinking; it only represents how we are responding.

Awareness and consciousness must be applied, and it must be followed by action, in order to make a positive-change. Thus, knowledge can be gained, and intelligence can be enhanced through the gained knowledge. As discussed, to gain knowledge, we must be willing to learn. Likewise, learning could only happen if we have the facts, and if we use the facts, as dislikable as facts might be, in order to make positive-change. Although factual-thinking must be the core of our existence, the knowledge gained through factual-thinking will be useless if we choose to ignore or deny the facts, because the facts make us feel bad, or because the facts do not make us feel as good as we want to.

True learning can only take place via factual-thinking.

VIII.
Patterns, Biases & Purpose

Patterns, biases, and purpose create familiarity, and familiarity creates comfort.

Seeking and recognizing patterns is integral for our safety and survival.

Theory of Self-Relativity describes "pattern-seeking" and "pattern-recognition" as "human and animal attributes which are based on sensory and environmental inputs that the brain processes for awareness, for understanding, and for potential action."

The process of pattern-recognition uses knowledge, memory, and experience to match and understand the information received. The internal attributes of knowledge, memory, and experience are matched with the external information and input (sensory-stimuli) received, in order to make sense of a pattern. Pattern-recognition is also associated and enhanced with repetition of these experiences.

Pattern-Recognition = (External) Stimulus + (Internal) Memory

Pattern-recognition is important for survival because it allows humans and animals to use patterns, for example, to locate food and shelter for survival and safety. Theory of Self-Relativity considers pattern-seeking and pattern-recognition crucial protective-mechanisms that are used to increase one's chances of survival, because recognizing patterns allows us to minimize uncertainty by predicting and by anticipating a future event. However, in contrast to other animals, the intelligent and emotionally sophisticated human-beings have learned to seek and recognize false-patterns, to deceptively make themselves feel better. Pattern-seeking, and especially pattern-recognition, attempt to create familiarity and understanding, while attempting to minimize uncertainty; therefore, pattern-seeking and pattern-recognition could act as comforting-skills. Uncertainty and lack-of-predictability are some of the common causes of worry, anxiety, stress, and even fear. Pattern-seeking and pattern-recognition help to create predictability, which in-turn, helps to minimize uncertainty and other negative-feelings; even if the patterns are falsely recognized. Thus, familiarity, minimizes anxiety, and creates comfort.

True pattern-recognition is not only helpful, but it is crucial to human and animal safety and survival. As discussed throughout Theory of Self-Relativity, in order for us to feel good and to experience positivity, we must first minimize negativity and danger. After minimization of negativities, our primitive-mind calms down and stops worrying about our safety; thus, we can then proceed to enjoy positivities. Since the intelligent modern-human does not commonly confront many of the primitive-dangers for safety and for survival, and since the primitive-mind in the modern-times is less-defensive than it would have been in the primitive-times; the modern-human has transformed the safety and survival attributes of pattern-recognition, into creating false-patterns as comforting tools. Deceptive human pattern-recognition is one of the main causes of self-imposed faulty-thinking habits, and it is regularly engaged because it is intended to make us feel good.

Regardless of the primitive safety need or the modern comforting need, pattern-seeking and pattern-recognition is intended to minimize variables and uncertainties; which in-turn, result in less negativity, hence, they result in improved feelings.

Pattern-Seeking and Pattern-Recognition:

- Reduce variables and uncertainties
- Increase familiarity
- Therefore, it is comforting

Since deceptive human pattern-recognition is a faulty-thinking habit that is engaged "only" by humans in order to feel better; such false, fallacious, and faulty-thinking habits associated with false pattern-recognition are some of the causes of self-deception and one's inability to improve difficulties. Furthermore, since such fabrications are intended to be comforting; pattern-seeking and pattern-recognition are also closely associated with faith, hope, and beliefs. The reason humans are the only entities that engage in purpose-based false pattern-recognition is because of their intelligence and reasoning. Although mistakenly, other animals could engage in false pattern-recognition; other animals instinctively engage in pattern-recognition for purely safety and survival reasons. However, the modern-human intentionally engages in false pattern-recognition in order to feel better. False pattern-seeking and pattern-recognition is another byproduct of the double-edged sword of human intelligence; because:

It takes intelligence to manipulate intelligence.

Faith, hope, and beliefs, alongside intentional false pattern-seeking and pattern-recognition are intended to be comforting by making a person feel good, or at the minimum, to make the person feel less-bad. These mental processes are commonly undertaken in situations where facts, evidence, and information are unavailable; or where facts, evidence, and information are denied and ignored. Such fallacious forms of thinking usually occurs when there is a gap of facts, information, and knowledge present. Instead of seeking and recognizing true facts, evidence, and patterns; many, often fill these gaps of information and knowledge with concocted-patterns, comforting-reasons, and even, with non-existent purpose and agency.

According to Theory of Self-Relativity, people believe and engage in comforting yet nonfactual gap-fillers in order to make themselves feel good. For example, one of the most common gap-fillers is the insertion of a supernatural agency into the gap of information. Whenever information is lacking, or more commonly when convenient, we convince our Self to believe that an event or a thing occurred because "it was meant to be" or because "God did it." Many choose to assign agency to God or other supernatural or pseudoscientific gap-fillers, than to actually seek, find, and recognize the factual reason and cause of that thing or that event. It is often preferred to fill an open gap with a nonfactual-agent or with a fallacious-belief; because factual-truth is often dislikable or even painful. Additionally, gap-filling is a form of laziness and passing responsibility onto other-things or other-agencies. By assigning purpose and agency to undiscovered, non-existent, or intentionally concocted agents; personal-responsibility gets passed on. This is why, as discussed, personal-responsibility is integral to living a fulfilled life.

Although God and religion are the most common forms of gap-fillers; other gap-fillers, especially purpose-based events, and agencies, are also commonly assigned and implemented. Some examples of other common gap-fillers are:

- **Everything will be fine:** Things left on their own would generally not be fine, unless we actively seek and identify the cause of the negativity, and until we put in effort to make an improving change. If something occurs favorably for us without us having properly positioned our Self for that event, then such an event primarily occurred because of chance and probability. However, to increase the potential of positive-events and to minimize the potential of negativities, we must put in active-effort.

Theory of Self-Relativity defines "chance" as "the possibility or probability of something happening."

- **Everything happens for a reason:** Though everything has a cause and often a reason, things do not need to happen for a reason. Many, confuse reason with purpose; thus, those who believe in this statement want to convey that everything has a purpose, hence, it was meant to be. Although everything has a cause as to how it happened; everything does not need to have a reason, and more importantly, everything does not need to have a purpose or a meaning as to why it happened. Since everything does not happen for a purpose; therefore, not every occurrence needs to have a meaning either.

Things have a cause; however, things don't need to have a reason, a purpose, or a meaning.

- **It was meant to be:** Not everything is meant to be. There does not need to be a purpose or a meaning, in order for events to occur or for things to exist. Although things and events occur because something natural caused it, we often tend to feel better as we create a sense of belonging when we assign an intentional supernatural-agent to the cause; rather than to simply accept the natural cause as the reason for the occurrence of the event. Everything has a cause; however, everything does not need to have a reason, a purpose, a meaning, or an intentional-agent. Things happen because they always have a cause, but the cause does not need to have a reason, a purpose, or a meaning; therefore, everything does not need to have a purpose or a meaning. Things happen naturally and as a result of physical laws; although, in our personal-matters, the cause or the reason of why something good or bad happens to us is usually as a result of our positioning, our thinking, our decision-making, and our actions or inactions.

Things happen to us when our decisions, actions, or inactions, meet probability and chance.

- **It was luck:** According to Theory of Self-Relativity, there is no such thing as luck. Everything that is categorized as luck, when examined in detail, will have a cause. Luck is not the same thing as chance; and in order for chance to materialize, one has to be in the path of crossing the chance which is often as a result of one's intent, action, and positioning. This applies to good and bad luck. Although luck could be good-luck or bad-luck; in order for us to experience good-luck, we must take action. A positive-outcome or what we sometimes refer to as luck does not occur passively by itself. Positive-outcomes can have best chances of occurrence when we put in effort to make positive-change. Positive-change occurs best via consistency and persistence of action that is based on factual-thinking. For example, to win the lottery requires us putting in active-effort to buy at least a ticket; and the more consistently we buy, the better the probability of us winning could be. However, if we do not put in effort to buy the ticket, we can wait for luck till eternity and we will not have any chance of winning the lottery. In order for chance to have the probability to result in a positive-outcome, we must put in effort; however, if we do not put in effort and if leave things to chance, they often result in negative or less than favorable outcomes. Therefore:

Theory of Self-Relativity defines "luck" as "when determination and action create opportunity."

- **Time heals all wounds:** *Time does not heal anything; people do.* Things either change on their own without our input and control, or we can influence change to become more favorable for us if we put in effort and we take action. By leaving things to time, we are passively sitting back and leaving things to chance, and not to time. As discussed, due to the nature of The-Universe, when things are left alone, there are more ways for things to go wrong than for them to go right; therefore, when things are left to chance, especially at our personal-level, the probability of unfavorable outcomes increases in comparison to the probability of favorable ones. Since Theory of Self-Relativity defines *"chance" as "the probability or possibility of something happening;"* when left to chance, things will more often result in unfavorable outcomes for us. Therefore, nothing or no one would or could make as many favorable outcomes for us as we could.

Choices and decisions made by others are seldom as favorable or as desirable as the decisions we make for our own Self.

- **Think Positive, or Positive-Energy:** Positive-thinking, or believing in positive-energy, is nothing but self-deception via the creation of fallacious-beliefs in order to feel good. Such nonfactual and sensationalistic motivational statements are simply peptalks that are intended to make us feel good, by giving us hope and purpose without any supportive facts, reason, or evidence; thus, empty positive-thinking should actually be termed as *"positive-feeling."* Rather than positive-thinking, having a positive-attitude could be helpful, if it is followed by effort to make a positive-change; however, by just thinking positive, positive-things don't happen. Positive-thinking is simply a short-term shot-in-the-arm for the purpose of increasing our dopamine levels for motivation. Dopamine is a hormone that the body produces which motivates us and makes us feel good; therefore, positive-thinking has short-term effects, hence why, these effects disappear quickly. As a result, to get another shot-in-the-arm, we will have to waste more time, and think more positive-thoughts, hoping something good would happen.

Positive-thinking or positive-energy are like drugs; they make you feel good temporarily, without making any positive impact in your life.

A common myth is the notion that humans have positive-energies and negative-energies. These are nothing but fallacies created by people in order to feel good; or they are fallacies marketed by those who want to benefit at the expense of people who are looking to improve their lives. Energy, as described in physics, simply means, "the capacity to do work." While many, might think of work, as, for example, working at a job; work, in physics, means to move something. Thus, energy is the capacity to do work, or to move something. Energy is not a thing; energy is simply a property of a system. And since energy, in science and physics, can be categorized as positive-energy or as negative-energy; pseudoscience has tried twisting this scientific principle by referencing personal-energy as "good-energy" or as "bad-energy." No such thing as personal-energy exists, as it is a myth; hence, no such thing as personal good-energy and personal bad-energy exist either. Personal-energy simply means nothing.

Same applies to the myth of personal-frequency and vibration. No such thing as personal-frequency or vibration exists. Frequency and vibration, just like the misleading categorizations and uses of energy, are intended to represent these physical references as magic. Frequency is simply a physical-phenomenon that is defined as "the number of complete wave-cycles per unit time; or per second." Therefore, high-frequency or low-frequency, simply refers to the number of cycles measured. For example, wavelength is a measure of frequency; thus, some properties have longer wavelength, which means they have lower frequency, and some properties have shorter wavelength, which means they have higher frequency. However, in modern-age-pseudoscience, it has been misrepresented that humans have frequencies. Just like positive-energy and negative-energy have been manipulated to represent non-existent human good-energy and bad-energy; pseudoscience and myths have misrepresented the concept of high-frequency and low-frequency, as if humans have "good-frequencies" and "bad-frequencies." No such things exist.

Additionally, many, mistaken positive-thinking with optimism. Optimism is good; however, as discussed, baseless and unfounded positive-thinking is not good. The difference between optimism and positive-thinking is that optimism is based on an anticipation of a future positive occurrence, as a result of an action that a person took; whereas, positive-thinking is simply expecting something positive to happen passively, without any plan or action.

Theory of Self-Relativity defines "optimism" as "a positive mindset with the anticipation of a positive outcome, in lieu of an action taken."

Therefore, relative to non-existent personal-attributes, designations of good and bad, as well as designations of positive and negative, are intended to be comforting and to improve how we feel. This is why, pattern-seeking and pattern-recognition, as well as gap-fillers, are overused and abused by the modern-human in order to feel better, without addressing the cause. Although at their core, pattern-seeking and pattern-recognition are intended to be for safety and for survival; since pattern-recognition minimizes uncertainty, and therefore, it minimizes negativity, humans tend to over-engage in pattern-seeking and pattern-recognition for comfort. Instead of facing dislikable truths, many of us, consciously or nonconsciously, engage in false pattern-seeking and pattern-recognition, in order to create an alternate likable reality.

Theory of Self-Relativity classifies the nature of patterns binarily:

1. **Real-Patterns (or Factual-Patterns):** Are patterns that match facts and data; hence, no gap-filling of information via interpretation or via confirmation-bias is needed to recognize the pattern. Some examples of real-patterns are:

   ● A square has four sides.

   ● Birth ends with death.

   ● Traffic lights turn yellow before turning red.

2. **Perceived-Patterns (or False-Patterns):** Are patterns that are perceived to be real, but are not necessarily supported with facts or data. Perceived-patterns are often associated with feelings, beliefs, and other personal or cultural biases. Although pattern-seeking and pattern-recognition are originally intended for safety and for protection; in the modern-times, we over-engage and overuse pattern-seeking and pattern-recognition as a form of placebo-thinking, in order to alter the perception of reality to our liking, or to fill the information-gap with comforting-thoughts and preferred-agents. Furthermore, sometimes, despite the fact that a favorable outcome was as a result of chance, or as a result of an action that the pattern-seeker took; the pattern-seeker incorrectly connects or relates the favorable outcome to a perceived-pattern, and to a perceived-agent. For example, a gambler who won, connects the winning to a phone call he received prior to the game from a friend whom he had not spoken to for a

long time. Additionally, perceived-patterns get ignored and dismissed more often, if favorable results do not materialize. For example, in the aforementioned example, same gambler would not connect his loss to a phone call from a long-lost friend. Simply stated, pattern-seekers have a tendency of selectively remembering their few hits and connecting them to unrelated but perceived-patterns; while ignoring and not remembering their many misses with perceived-patterns, unless they want to blame-shift their loss or a negativity to a perceived-pattern or to a perceived intentional-agent.

Some common examples of perceived-patterns are:

- **Magical-thinking:** Is believing that something or an event happens as a result of another unrelated thing or event, without there being any supportive evidence for this relationship. For example, because they were playing my favorite song as I walked into the store; therefore, I will get an "A" on my upcoming exam.

- **Delusion:** Is a belief or an impression that one holds despite there being contradictory-evidence for that belief or impression. Delusions are often associated with neutral or insignificant things or events as having special meaning; for example, a pattern resembling a sacred figure on a burnt-toast or on a wet window gets recognized as a sign of the existence of that supernatural entity, and as a sign that there is a hidden message in that pattern that is intended for the good of the observer.

- **Superstition:** Is a nonfactual and unsupported supernatural-belief often leading to taking certain actions based on such beliefs. For example, knocking on wood to gain good fortune or to ward off bad luck.

- **Apophenia:** Is the human tendency to see patterns that do not actually exist. For example, the face of a man on the moon, the shape of a cloud resembling an animal, or a burnt-toast resembling a sacred-figure. Apophenia is a neutral or insignificant event or impression, as long as it is not fallaciously believed in or incorrectly acted upon. As long as apophenia does not result in reliance or action based on its falsely assumed nature; apophenia is usually harmless. Apophenia or false-patterns become problematic when they are relied on or if they are acted upon.

- **Conspiracy-Theory:** Is another common mindset of concocting, recognizing, and engaging in perceived-patterns. According to Theory of Self-Relativity, conspiracy-theories are a form of externalation. A conspiracy-theory is a belief or a mindset that tries to explain that an event or a situation is the result of a covert or secretive operation by powerful and influential entities. Since conspiracy-theories are assumed or believed, they often lack significant supportive evidence; however, due to their sensationalistic nature, conspiracy-theories commonly find a great deal of support from those who are seeking to find confirmation for their desired comforting-beliefs. By fabricating or by joining in a conspiracy-theory, people shift the focus away from reality that is unfavorable or contradictory to their position; by believing that the reason the truth or reality is not to their liking or in their favor is because an intentional-agent is trying to deceive them. Although conspiracy-theories can sometimes be proven to be true; often, many conspiracy-theories, on a personal level, are engaged in as a means of externalation in order to avoid dislikable personal truths, by preoccupying and by distracting one's mind externally.

A perceived-pattern, just like a belief, should only be dealt with temporarily until facts and evidence confirm that perceived-pattern as a factual or real-pattern. If supportive evidence is not found for the perceived-pattern; subsequently, any meaning, purpose, and reliance relative to that pattern must be eliminated, so that one would not rely on, nor would one take action based on that perceived-pattern. Perceived-patterns are commonly feeling and belief based, which further confirms the association of beliefs with the desire to feel better. Since beliefs are simply unsupported and nonfactual-thoughts, beliefs are easy to fabricate in order to support and rationalize a comforting-pattern; and vice versa, patterns are concocted to support comforting-beliefs. Hence why, beliefs are strongly correlated with personal-emotions. This fabrication and false pattern-recognition in order to fit them into one's desired-feelings or comforting-beliefs, is referred to as a *"Confirmation-Bias."*

Theory of Self-Relativity defines a "confirmation-bias" as "interpretation of something as confirmation of an existing conclusion or belief."

By fabricating supportive reasoning, we choose to engage in confirmation-bias in order to justify our thoughts and beliefs; and we do so mainly via "interpretation" to our liking. Instead of using facts and evidence to reach a conclusion; we establish a desired conclusion and then work backwards to support the conclusion by any means possible. Confirmation-bias is closely associated with another cognitive phenomenon known as *"Motivated-Reasoning,"* which uses emotionally biased reasoning to produce justifications or to make decisions that are most desired, rather than those that accurately reflect the evidence. In other words, motivated-reasoning is the tendency to find arguments in favor of conclusions we want to believe, than to find arguments for conclusions we do not want to believe.

Theory of Self-Relativity categorizes motivated-reasoning binarily:

1. **Positive-Motivated-Reasoning:** Is the type of rationalization that one engages in when one wants to justify decisions and conclusions that deal with an additive action that one is taking. For example, justifying why we need to buy more material-things, or why an asset we own would go up in value, or why we should get deeper involved in a relationship. Positive-motivated-reasoning is emotionally easier to engage in than negative-motivated-reasoning; because positive-motivated-reasoning often involves adding something.

2. **Negative-Motivated-Reasoning:** Is the type of rationalization that one engages in when one wants to justify decisions and conclusions that deal with a deductive action that one does not want to take. For example, not wanting to part with material-things or hanging on to material-things when one cannot afford them, or not wanting to sell a depreciating asset and taking a loss, or not wanting to end an unhealthy relationship. This is why, negative-motivated-reasoning is more difficult to engage in than positive-motivated-reasoning, because negative-motivated-reasoning often involves losing something; hence, such rationalization attempts to abstain from making difficult decisions.

According to Theory of Self-Relativity, confirmation-bias and motivated-reasoning are always rooted in placebo-thinking; because:

Confirmation-bias fits facts to thoughts rather than fitting thoughts to facts.

The key word to pay attention to in recognizing when we are engaging in confirmation-bias or when we are appealing to perceived-patterns, is "interpretation;" instead of "affirmation" or "validation." In confirmation-bias, confirmation is not intended to confirm factuality; on the contrary, confirmation is intended to confirm a comforting-desire or a preferred existing-belief, often without any interest or care about the evidence. The intent in confirmation-bias is to confirm a desired-belief in order to rationalize a comforting-feeling, but not to confirm the factuality of the belief itself. This is why, emotional-thinking, emotional-reasoning, and comforting-beliefs, are almost always associated with interpretation.

Confirmation-bias is reliant on interpretation, because it is often associated with emotional-thinking or emotional-reasoning.

Confirmation-bias relies on interpretation; because, interpretation enables manipulation of the information to one's liking. Confirmation-bias is an attempt to fit the square-peg of feelings and preferences into the round-hole of facts. Since confirmation-bias is reliant on interpretation rather than on factual-evaluation; confirmation-bias "selectively" enables us to see things how we want to see them, rather than to see things how they really are. Additionally, even in the presence of facts and evidence that contradict our beliefs; in the longer-term, we selectively forget when facts and evidence proved our thoughts, our beliefs, or our predictions to be wrong; yet, we "selectively" choose to only remember the few chance-based and coincidental times when our thoughts, our beliefs, or our predictions matched with facts and evidence. In other words, by interpreting facts to be otherwise when they do not confirm our thoughts, our beliefs, or our predications, and by confirming them when facts happen to match our thoughts, our beliefs, or our predictions; we selectively confirm and remember our "hits," yet, we selectively dismiss and forget our "misses."

Interpretation is associated with selective-acceptability or selective-rejection of information.

This is why, Theory of Self-relativity states:

Interpretation enables manipulation.

According to Theory of Self-Relativity, since facts are not open to interpretation; therefore, facts are not open to manipulation. This is why, Theory of Self-Relativity persists on factual-thinking, rather than thinking without evidence or thinking based on subjective or selective-interpretation. Factual-thinking does not require interpretation; because, if facts exist, facts always turn a thought or a belief into knowledge. When there are no facts or when facts are intentionally ignored or denied because facts contradict our desired-feelings, that is when interpretation kicks in. To keep holding onto our belief, we often choose to selectively interpret a situation in a manner that supports our desire-feeling, so that we can justify and hold on to that comforting-thought.

Interpretation opens the door for manipulation and deception.

For example, a woman who suspects her 9 to 5 working salaried husband of cheating, despite having seen texts from another woman and despite not being able to communicate with him after regular work hours; chooses to believe, interpret, and accept his excuse of after-work meetings as the reason for him not coming home after work hours. To accept the fact that the husband is cheating will be painful, and instead of accepting the uncomfortable and painful fact of recognizing that the husband is cheating; the woman instead, chooses to ignore the facts, as she accepts an alternative interpretation as a reason for the late evenings. Another example of a widely held and accepted mindset deeply associated with interpretation is faith; especially faith that is associated with religion. In order to justify holding on to a faith or a comforting-belief; a common practice is the interpretation of a phrase from a holy book, to have a completely unrelated meaning than what it was originally written for.

Since recognizing patterns is associated with thinking and recalling memory; a proper thinking-system is required to deal with true pattern-recognition, and to block or eliminate the need for creating or recognizing false-patterns. As discussed throughout Theory of Self-Relativity, facts are not open to interpretation; thus, factual-thinking minimizes and prevents interpretation-based thinking processes such as emotional-thinking, pattern-recognition, and motivated-reasoning.

If something is open to interpretation, it will also be open to manipulation.

An incidental pattern-recognition, such as the figure of a saint on a burnt-toast, could be harmless or even amusing; however, to make decisions and to take action on an unrelated matter based on this chance appearance of a pattern on a burnt-toast, would be unwise and irrational. Likewise, believing or interpreting that getting a salary-raise on the day of seeing the toast pattern had something to do with the pattern's appearance, would be a form of confirmation-bias.

Confirmation-biases are rooted in active and intentional pattern-recognition. Confirmation-biases contribute to overconfidence in personal-beliefs, and can maintain or even strengthen false-beliefs in the face of contrary evidence. Beliefs are unproven-thoughts. Instead of believing via false pattern-recognition and base-less confirmation-biases; the way to strengthen beliefs is to find their supportive facts so that we could turn those beliefs into knowledge. But if, we cannot find the supportive facts to that belief, then the belief should not be relied upon.

As discussed, despite the factual or perceived nature of patterns; pattern-recognition in humans and in animals is instinctualized for "safety" and for "survival." As further discussed, safety and being safe reduces negative-feelings; therefore, feeling safe is desired and comforting. However, as primitive-dangers in the modern-era diminished, the need to be safe has changed to the need for "comfort". Since safety and survival are associated with negative-feelings, especially feelings of anxiety and fear; dangerous pattern-recognition caused primitive humans to feel fear in order to take action to survive. Pattern-recognition forced action to minimize threats and danger, thereby it minimized fear and other negative-feelings associated with the recognized pattern. This decrease of fear and other negative-feelings via recognition of patterns, enabled humans to realize that by seeking and by recognizing patterns, they could minimize negative-feelings; therefore, pattern-seeking and pattern-recognition improved how they felt. As primitive-humans slowly transformed into modern-humans and began to advance in civilizations by minimizing primitive-dangers; they continued practicing pattern-seeking and pattern-recognition not for safety, but to sustain their comforting-feelings.

This is how, supernatural-beliefs began taking shape. Via false pattern-seeking and false pattern-recognition, and by creating comforting yet fallacious-beliefs, humans began to learn to deceptively manipulate themselves to feel better. As stated, self-deception is one of the main enemies of self-improvement; thus, we self-deceive, in order to feel better, or at the minimum, to not to feel as bad. And, one of the most common ways that we engage in self-deception is through pattern-recognition, confirmation-bias, and motivated-reasoning.

By holding onto nonfactual and unsupported, yet, comforting-beliefs; people seek, and even, concoct nonfactual-patterns in order to confirm and maintain their comforting-feelings. This is also how emotional-thinking and emotional-reasoning operate. Emotional-thinking makes people attempt to fit facts to their feelings, rather than fitting their feelings to facts. Likewise, emotional-thinking makes people fit false or perceived-patterns to their feelings, rather than fitting their feelings to factual-patterns. Emotional-thinking, just like positive-thinking, is actually an oxymoron; because we think with our minds, we should not be thinking with our emotions. According to Theory of Self-Relativity, just as positive-thinking should be renamed positive-feeling, emotional-thinking should also be renamed emotional-feeling.

Feelings are for feeling, not for thinking.

Emotions, which are a collection of intangible-feelings, are only as rational as their underlying causal-thoughts; therefore, emotions that are generated as a result of fallacious-beliefs or false-patterns are also irrational. Yet, we often make decisions and we take action based on what we feel, without understanding the rational-value of our feelings. This is why, emotional-thinking or emotional-reasoning is also commonly the cause of our incorrect actions and impulsive reactions.

Placebo-thinking, as termed and defined by Theory of Self-Relativity, is the creation of preferred feel-good-thoughts that have no factual-basis, and it is a form of rationalization through emotional-reasoning. Placebo-thinking often goes hand-in-hand with pattern-recognition, confirmation-bias, hindsight-bias, as well as, nonfactual-thinking and logical-fallacies. Emotional-reasoning, through confirmation-bias, makes us selectively extract information that we like, and it causes us to ignore dislikeable facts and information, in order to not refute our comforting-beliefs and preferred-thoughts. This is all done with the goal of making us feel better so that we could avoid uncomfortable and dislikable-feelings. Through emotional-thinking, we seek to find patterns that do not exist. We subsequently confirm these patterns via confirmation-biases, just so that we can continue feeling good; or just so that we can feel less-bad.

Furthermore, we not only extract selective-information, but we also interpret such information to the way we want that information to mean, rather than to objectively evaluate what the information is truly indicating. This is how, old-beliefs and traditional-practices, which are based on ancient-understandings and nonfactual-information, try to adapt and show their relevance to newly discovered facts and knowledge. For example, in religion, certain statements are now proven to be false; because, our knowledge and our understanding of The-Universe has changed and advanced. However, in order to continuously make these false-claims relevant, and to not undermine the misinformation associated with the religion; believers either selectively ignore these falsities and pick and choose the verses that might apply, or they interpret the meaning of the verses and statements to their liking, in an attempt to match current knowledge to their false-beliefs. If all else fails, instead of dropping their false-beliefs, believers will choose to explain that such beliefs and statements are not meant to actually apply to reality; they are simply metaphors.

As stated throughout Theory of Self-Relativity, facts are open to examination, but facts are not open to interpretation; hence, facts are not open to manipulation. Metaphors and examples can be valuable in trying to understand a complex subject; but not in trying to prevent refuting the factuality of a subject, or in trying to misrepresent facts about the subject. Metaphors should be used as references and not as proofs for beliefs.

While science would simply toss away or replace a previously accepted hypothesis when new or contradictory evidence is found; in ideologies and in other belief-based practices, throwing away statements and hypothesis would disprove that ideology and its teachings. Therefore, to maintain religious, or even, personal and cultural beliefs; believers selectively interpret facts to adapt to their beliefs, rather than change their beliefs and thoughts to adapt to the newly discovered facts. Likewise, by claiming certain beliefs and ideologies as dogmatic or sacred;

such ideologies and doctrines prevent the questioning and challenging of their claims.

Creating nonfactual-beliefs could result in negative-outcomes because they are not based on factual-reality. Instead of trying to verify unsupported-beliefs via nonexistent relationships with other unrelated things or events; we should seek facts, rather than seek patterns, to validate or challenge our beliefs. When we dismiss nonfactual-beliefs and only hold on to fact supported knowledge; we will then think and live based on factual-reality. As discussed, there is no such thing as a "factual-belief." Beliefs are believed because they are assumed thoughts that have not been supported with facts. Once a belief is verified with facts, it then becomes knowledge.

To truly get in touch with reality, you must learn to factually-validate things, instead of selectively-interpreting them.

In other words:

Objective-evaluation instead of subjective-interpretation.

Although real pattern-recognition increases certainty and predictability; percei-ved-pattern recognition can create instability and even chaos. Some certainty and predictability associated with pattern-seeking and pattern-recognition is intended to keep us safe, by minimizing threats and danger; hence, as a result of safety, pattern-seeking and pattern-recognition minimize negativity, which in-turn, crea-tes neutral or even positive feelings. However, to constantly seek patterns and to engage in false pattern-recognition in order to feel good, not only defeats the intended purpose of pattern-seeking and pattern-recognition, but it creates a false-reality.

As discussed, pattern-seeking, at the primitive-mind's level, is intended to be protective for survival. The safety and protective aspects of pattern-seeking are not only innate, but they are mostly instinctive; because, our mind is programmed to seek dangerous patterns in order to keep us safe. For example, a loud popping noise in a calm place, or the movement or rustling sound of tree branches in the woods alerts us to be on the lookout for potential danger. Therefore, pattern-see-king and pattern-recognition should be engaged for fight-or-flight responses and for problem-solving; and not for supporting and rationalizing desired-feelings.

As further discussed throughout Theory of Self-Relativity, the primary and primi-tive role of our mind is to keep us safe. Since our mind is defaulted to recognize potentially dangerous patterns, our mind instinctively reacts to these potentially dangerous patterns in order to keep us safe; rather than to not react by assuming that the potential pattern is not dangerous. Our mind will warn us to react and become alert rather than to not react and passively "hope" or "assume" that there is no danger. Therefore:

The primitive-mind, unlike the intelligent-mind, doesn't hope or assume; it reacts.

If no danger exists, a false-positive will not endanger or kill us; but if the threat is real, we would have time to proactively increase the chances of our safety, and even, our survival. Quick, clever, and alert life forms increase the chances of their survival by becoming cognitively fitter and reaction-wise quicker; thus, quick and cleverer thinking, and faster reacting animals have a better chance of surviving and passing on their genes to the next generation.

Such primitive and evolutionary pattern-seeking characteristics are easily observed, for example, with birds, as they are always jittery and on the lookout for danger. Even a hungry bird feeding on seeds will fly away at the onset of unusual movement or noise. When birds are feeding in a group, the first bird that suddenly stops eating and flies away will automatically cause other birds in the flock to fly away impulsively. They will rely on the quickest collective reaction of the group rather than to take a chance against potential danger. If the perceived danger was a false-positive, they can always return back to finish their feeding; however, if the potential threat was real, they just succeeded to live another day by reacting quickly, and by not waiting to get more data and information on the potential threat.

Safety-first, is a natural instinct among humans and animals. Safety-first is generally triggered by our primitive-mind through pattern-recognition, and it is implemented to minimize danger and to ensure survival. Once the danger is subsided or eliminated, our primitive-mind will relax and it will then allow our intelligent-mind to seek positivity.

When our primitive-mind feels safe, we consequently feel less-bad.

It is this inherent reduction of negativity and the increase in feeling good, or in feeling less-bad, that causes us to create beliefs, to look for false-patterns, and to deny dislikeable-truths. Via the manipulation of our intelligent-mind, we try to fool our primitive-mind to calm-down so that we could feel better. We look for, we try to recognize, and even sometimes, we create false-patterns, or we assign non-existent purpose to something, in order to calm-down and relax our primitive-mind. Since, in the modern-times, we are faced with less primitive-dangers, instead of looking for and reacting to danger, we use pattern-seeking and pattern-recognition to make ourselves feel better. Therefore, instead of safety reasons, we more commonly engage in pattern-seeking and pattern-recognition for instant-gratification, and for improving our feelings; regardless of the factual or nonfactual basis for these patterns. As stated:

It takes intelligence to manipulate intelligence.

When pattern-seeking, pattern-recognition, faith, hope, beliefs, biases, logical-fallacies, and even purpose and meaning are created by the mind to make us avoid pain, to feel good, or at the minimum, for us to feel less-bad; we are engaging in rationalization through emotional-reasoning and placebo-thinking. To minimize emotional-reasoning and placebo-thinking, one of the most important factors for self-improvement is to not only be conscious and aware of our feelings, but to be mindful of our thoughts and our tendency to rationalize our feelings. However, just being mindful is not enough; we must also be thoughtful, which means we must understand our thoughts so that we can act based on thoughtfulness.

Theory of Self-Relativity teaches how to use our feelings to identify the thoughts which are causing our feelings. To change our feelings for the better, we must change our thoughts; not create new supporting fallacious-thoughts to feel better. By factually evaluating our thoughts, we can then make a decision whether to keep the thought or to dismiss the thought. Our feelings should lead us to our thoughts, but our thoughts must create our feelings.

Your feelings should not change your thoughts; your thoughts must change your feelings.

Dealing with facts can be a difficult and uncomfortable process; however, in order for us to sync our Self with factual-reality, we must learn to seek, find, and deal with facts so that we can live in balance and in harmony with reality. We should not seek, concoct, or interpret patterns in order to justify an uncomfortable fact; for example, we should not fabricate false-beliefs or false-patterns to justify non-existent purpose and meaning. It is the discomfort of facing facts that triggers most people into changing their thoughts, so they can quickly feel better. Instant-gratification, and more importantly, the need for quick minimization of negative-feelings, is one of the main obstacles in self-improvement. This is the distinguishing factor between emotional-thinking and critical-thinking; and this is why, awareness and control of the need for instant-gratification is important in self-transformation. Additionally, the need for instant-gratification is also a significant underlying cause of impulsivity and addictive-behaviors.

Theory of Self-Relativity defines "emotional-thinking" as "thinking based on how we want to feel."

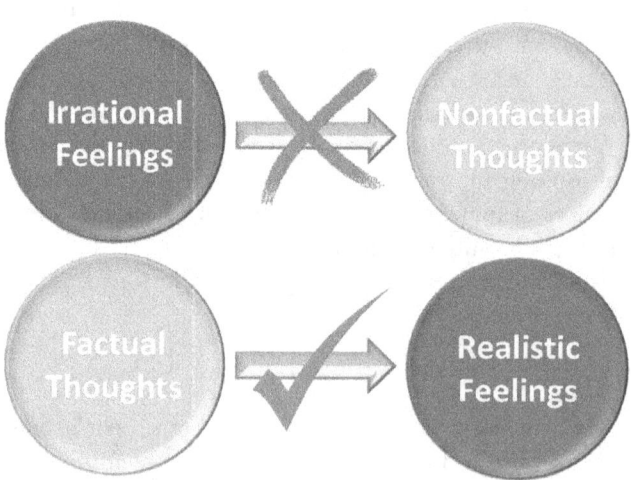

As discussed throughout Theory of Self-Relativity, our need to feel good versus the necessity to think well, is the main culprit against our ability to change and improve. By allowing our feelings to influence our thoughts, and therefore, our actions; we end up living in disharmony with how reality and The-Universe actually operate. And we commonly do so by seeking and by fabricating false-patterns in order to concoct a purpose and meaning for a dislikeable event.

As pattern-seeking animals, we are conditioned to make the meaningless have meaning.

We simply do so in order to feel better; or as a first step, we do so to feel less-bad. This backwardation or reversal of the correct order of thinking to feelings could have devastating and long-lasting negative effects on the quality of our decisions, and our existence. Self-improvement via factual-thinking is the only means of combatting, reversing, and eliminating, our irrational, deceptive, and false pattern-seeking and pattern-recognition practices.

Because:

We often tend to see patterns where none exist.

By learning to dismiss and eliminate non-factual thoughts, we can learn to eliminate the need for false pattern-seeking and false pattern-recognition. Instead of allowing our irrational-feelings to make us look for comforting and perceived-patterns in order to rationalize those feelings; we should guide our mind to only recognize factual-patterns, if they truly exist. We cannot force the identification of patterns; patterns should only be recognized and identified if they truly exist.

We should observe patterns, not imagine them.

The human mind is innately programmed to constantly seek and recognize patterns. We not only seek patterns, but we also live with established-patterns. Time related measurements such as hours, days, and years are a prime example of not only pattern-seeking, but the manmade creation of patterns. In reality, no such thing as hours, days or years exists, because time is linear not cyclical; however, by creating repeatable cycles based on patterns, we enable our Self to create repetition in order to have higher predictability and more certainty in our lives.

Creating patterns, such as time, is beneficial in living our life with better predictability. Pattern-creation is not wrong if creating patterns helps to scale and streamline reality in a repeatable and predictable format. However, concocting patterns with the intent to feel good or to support comforting-beliefs, is self-deceptive and delusive. As stated, pattern-seeking and pattern-recognition is intended for improving our predictability of what is coming; which means, we will be taking action based on our identification, recognition, and evaluation of the patterns. However, if patterns that we rely on are imagined in order to support our desired-feelings, our evaluation and understanding of these patterns could be faulty; hence, we could make mistakes, or worse, we might expose our Self to risks, threats, and even danger.

By using pattern references from the past and by repetition through pattern-recognition, the mind seeks dynamic-patterns based on past events in order to forecast and predict future outcomes. For example, financial technical-analysis is a field which deals with patterns to make predictions. Using financial data and performance parameters from similar past situations allows humans to make cal-culated predictions for the future. Although technical-analysis is an actual field of practice, technical-analysis itself relies on probabilities, possibilities, and chance. Technical-analysis allows us to make calculated, though not guaranteed, predica-tions of what a stock or an asset-class could do based on its past performance and based on reactions of other stocks or assets in similar past situations. However, technical-analysis, just like many other forms of pattern-recognition and pat-tern-seeking, could, and often does become biased.

The major drawback and disadvantage of pattern-seeking is the creation of biases; especially confirmation-bias where one begins to see patterns the way one wants to see them, rather than to see what those patterns, if any, are actually indicating. For example, we could be holding a stock, and because we bought the stock with the hopes of the stock going up, we might force our Self into believing that the chart is showing the stock should be moving up. Since we have a bias for the stock to go up, even if the stock is not moving up as we hoped it would, or if the stock is going down; despite our continuous losses, we might fallaciously convince our Self that the stock will eventually go up, or that the stock decline is due to some imagined nefarious activity.

In this scenario, just as in other biased situations, we see what we want to see, rather than seeing what should see. We are using our mind to create future patterns that are not necessarily true, or for which we do not have any control over. Since selling a stock and taking a loss is emotionally difficult to do; we create patterns, we form beliefs, and we engage in confirmation-bias in order to convince our Self that things will get better. Furthermore, we might choose to ignore the facts and indicators of a stock's lack of performance, and instead of recognizing that the stock is not performing properly and that we are constantly losing money; instead, we choose to become believers in the company. This is why, in behavio-ral-economics it is implied to:

Never let a bad-trade become a loved-investment.

Therefore, in life:

Never let a bad-decision become a loved-mindset.

By convincing our Self, without evidence, that the stock will perform, we are fallaciously trying to make our Self feel good with the hope, but not with the knowledge, that the stock will rise in value. Since selling a stock at a loss is emotio-nally difficult, we concoct false-patterns to enable our Self into placebo-thinking, so that we would feel better at that moment; or so that we would not feel as bad at that moment. Although this false-hope and false pattern-recognition might make us avoid reality or might make us feel better in the short-term; such a state-of-mind could have potentially damaging implications in the longer timeframe.

Likewise, confirmation-bias causes us to create a pattern after we take an action; as in this example, instead of seeing the pattern in advance, which is impossible, our mind tries to create confirmation-bias after multiple event-points. If the stock that we own goes up, our confirmation-bias will be strengthened as would our confidence; because we would believe that we knew in advance this was going to happen. We might even seek a similar situation for the next stock, only to be completely surprised as to why the next stock did not go up; hence, the following familiar disclosure associated with financial investments:

Past performance does not guarantee future results.

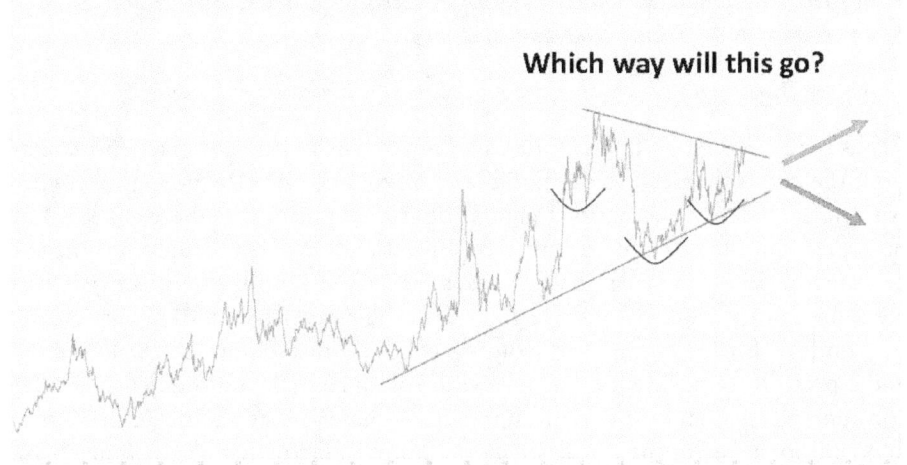

Which way will this go?

Conversely, if the stock goes down, our mind will commonly slip into *"Hindsight-Bias"* to convince us that the pattern existed before, but we chose to ignore it; despite the fact that no predictable pattern existed. This is why, hindsight-bias is sometimes referred to as the "I knew it all along effect." In this example of behavioral-finance, confirmation-bias and hindsight-bias limit our abilities to make objective-decisions; because:

Confirmation-bias tends to make people pay closer attention to information that confirms their belief, and to ignore information that contradicts it.

In such situations, bias, and perceived pattern-recognition causes us to ignore facts in order to remain with our unfounded comforting-beliefs; because our beliefs make us feel good, and more importantly, they help us justify not taking an uncomfortable action, since taking a loss is difficult to do. The reason selling a stock, especially at a loss, is often difficult to do is because we tend to view taking a loss as failure and as a reflection of our low self-image. We often also speculate, assume, and even believe that right after we sell the stock, the stock will go up and we would feel even more stupid. This is why, money and finance are closely associated with human emotions; and when dealing with money, especially with speculative investments, one must have the discipline and the understanding to deal with the risks and the consequences.

Theory of Self-Relativity defines a "bias" as "a belief or an action for or against a thing or a person in an unequal or preferential manner."

According to Theory of Self-Relativity, a bias is conceived, adopted, or acted upon, based on subjective-perspectives and personal-beliefs, in order to influence how the biased-person feels. Although a bias is a mental-state, biases are guided by emotions, and they are consciously or nonconsciously conceived or adopted to support and justify a person's desired-feelings; therefore, all biases are a form of placebo-thinking. Since biases are commonly focused externally towards other-people or other-things, biases are often deployed as a means of externalation, in order to cover-up one's own personal-weaknesses and self-deficiencies; hence why, biases are associated with emotional-reasoning, because they are intended to be convincing without facts and evidence.

Biases are irrational because they are rooted in and fueled by emotions.

Biases tend to often go hand-in-hand with pattern-seeking and pattern-recognition; therefore, the need to develop biases originated with the need to recognize patterns for safety. In situations such as fight-or-flight, where there is a need for quick reaction; biases and pattern-recognition are intended to prevent a negative-outcome. Biases are created to address a person's or a group's perspectives which are rooted in their beliefs, their feelings, and their experiences. Biases are created for comfort, for belonging, for avoiding pain and discomfort, for feeling good; and especially, for feeling less-bad. Biases are often factually unfounded as they are commonly broad and stereotypical; therefore, biases are as a result of perception and emotional-reasoning, rather than as a result of factual-thinking. Since biases are closely associated with pattern-seeking and pattern-recognition; biases are also associated with a person's memories and experiences.

Although a multitude of different biases exist, Theory of Self-Relativity considers confirmation-bias and hindsight-bias as the most frequently engaged biases which regularly influence our feelings and our thoughts, as well as our sense of Self.

- **Confirmation-Bias:** Theory of Self-Relativity considers confirmation-bias as one of the most commonly held and practiced forms of biases. Theory of Self-Relativity describes *"confirmation-bias"* as *"the tendency to interpret new information or evidence as a confirmation of one's existing thoughts or beliefs."*

Confirmation-bias is a form of incorrect or unfounded cognitive-reasoning.

According to Theory of Self-Relativity, a confirmation-bias is often associated with pattern-seeking and it commonly uses imaginary or perceived pattern-recognition. A confirmation-bias occurs when one's thoughts are influenced by establishing unrelated-relationships between new-evidence or a future-event, with a preexisting thought or a belief; often in the form of images, patterns, and actions. By thinking and by believing about a preexisting belief, a biased mind seeks or creates non-existent patterns and false-facts at a future time, in order to relate these unrelated or unreal patterns and facts to the previously held preferred, but not necessarily factual, thought or belief. The primary purpose of engaging in confirmation-bias is to confirm an already preferred or desired conclusion by any means possible.

A confirmation-bias is sometimes implemented against contradictory evidence with the intent to abstain from changing or eliminating a preexisting incorrect, but comforting, thought or belief. Since these incorrect mindsets are comforting, hence, a confirmation-bias is also intended to be comforting.

In a confirmation-bias, instead of changing one's thoughts or beliefs based on the evidence at hand; one chooses to interpret the evidence differently, or one chooses to seek or fabricate other patterns, in order to justify, support, and rationalize one's previously held thought or belief. Similarly, contradictory, or discrediting evidence regarding the previously held thought or belief gets ignored, denied, or dismissed; in order to not weaken the previously held desired-thought or belief. For example, if we like cannabis, we choose to only do web searches on the benefits of cannabis, rather than to search for both its benefits and disadvantages. By limiting research and knowledge to the benefits of cannabis, we create selective-confirmation of our desired characteristics and conclusions; in this case, the positives associated with cannabis. Furthermore, by selectively-ignoring the negatives of using cannabis, we confirm our desired conclusion by ignoring the contradictory negativities associated with cannabis. According to Theory of Self-Relativity, confirmation-biases coexist and are closely associated with ignorance.

- **Hindsight-Bias:** Also known as the "knew-it-all-along effect," is a form of cognitive-positioning that is implemented at a later time relative to a preexisting event. Hindsight-bias is hallmarked by denial and with an irrational attempt to justify the past. Hindsight-bias is commonly associated with placebo-thinking, and it often involves nonfactual-thinking. Hindsight-bias is also often associated with *"Rumination"* and with *"Regret."*

Theory of Self-Relativity defines "hindsight-bias" as "a previously unknown or undefined future event which post-occurrence is now perceived to have been known or predictable then."

Hindsight-bias takes shape by convincing one's Self that the occurrence of a past event was predictable, when in fact, prior to the event, the person had no idea that the event would occur, or what the outcome of the event would have been. This is why, hindsight-bias is often associated with self-directed negative-feelings such as regret, remorse, or self-criticism. To minimize these negative-emotions, the subject engages in hindsight-bias, in order to justify or to ditch responsibility for the unfavorable or for the less than favorable outcome. Although hindsight-bias is often associated with regret, remorse, and self-criticism, because the thinker thinks "I should've known better;" hindsight-bias creates emotionally rationalizing, although ineffective and nonfactual-thoughts. Hindsight-bias is often associated with "regret" because post outcome of the event, one begins to affirmatively, although falsely, believe that the outcome of the event was obvious, yet one chose to ignore all signs associated with it.

A variation of hindsight-bias is known as "recency-bias," where more recent things, information, and events are remembered better or are assigned stronger significance and value than things, information, and events from further past. For example, as discussed in other sections, the effects of a recent relationship breakup feels much stronger than the effects of a past breakup of similar or even stronger magnitude.

The primary difference between confirmation-bias and hindsight-bias is that in confirmation-bias, the subject holds a belief or a mindset and looks for patterns and other confirming agents in order to justify the belief or the mindset; however, in hindsight-bias, the subject changes the belief or the mindset from the past, after the belief or the mindset is proven to have been wrong. In confirmation-bias a person does not accept being wrong; but in hindsight-bias, the person admits to being wrong with an excuse from the past. This is why, hindsight-bias is commonly associated with blame-shifting, self-victimization, and an inability to take personal-responsibility. Both confirmation-bias and hindsight-bias can create a false sense of overconfidence in a person's abilities to predict the future; this is why, Theory of Self-Relativity insists on factual-thinking, because factual-thinking will not allow us to create such fallacies about our predictive-abilities.

Confirmation-Bias	Hindsight-Bias
• Confirms the mindset with selective information	• Changes the mindset to match new information
• Does not accept being wrong	• Accepts being wrong with an excuse
• Creates false sense of overconfidence	• Creates false sense of overconfidence
• Leads to ignorance	• Leads to ignorance

Ignorance often goes hand-in-hand with biases because in order to preserve a bias, biased-people often disregard facts, by abstaining from seeking information and knowledge; or by denying contradictory-evidence. By having less information about an event or a person, biased-people simplify more complex situations and box themselves into a corner. Getting boxed into a corner prevents a person from changing and improving; however, since their nonconscious philosophy is "what I don't know, won't hurt me," such ignorance and denial allows them to temporarily feel good until reality catches up with them. Biased-people are generally emotion-driven because they try to maintain a state of ignorance to protect their preferred mindset in order to feel good, or at the minimum, in order to feel less-bad. Any time that an argument or evidence of facts is presented to them, biased-people generally act defensively in order to block the communication and consideration of the uncomfortable-evidence. Because of this defensiveness, which is a reflection of their insecurity, biased-people also often resort to personal-attacks against people who contradict their biases with facts.

If the message conflicts with what I want to be true; I must attack the messenger.

"Ignorance is bliss" is a phrase which clearly describes such cognitive-biases. By not having enough knowledge and experience, or by choosing to ignore facts; a biased and ignorant person forms opinions, makes comments, and even presents losing arguments against facts, evidence, and reason. By denying facts about a bias, the biased person chooses to ignore such information, and argues from a limited knowledge perspective. By nonconsciously or by actively limiting and minimizing information and knowledge gathering to prevent from being proven wrong; a biased person tries to hold on to the bias in order to feel good, or more commonly, in order to feel less-bad.

Holding a bias through limited knowledge and experience, or through ignorance causes biased people to experience:

1. **Ignorance is bliss:** Biased-people ignore, deny, and cover-up facts and evidence which are contrary to their biased-perspective, in order to preserve their desired-feelings.

2. **What I don't know won't hurt me:** Biased-people abstain from seeking further facts, information, and knowledge, in order to maintain their bias; so that they can hold on to their comforting-feelings.

3. **A little knowledge is more dangerous than none:** Also known as the *"Dunning-Kruger Effect,"* which Theory of Self-Relativity considers as *"the middle ground between lack of information and ignorance of information;"* is a typical mindset associated with biased and ignorant people.

The "Dunning-Kruger Effect" is a cognitive-bias whereby one believes to be smarter and more intelligent than one really is. This is a form of fallacious-bias because one cannot comparatively evaluate one's cognitive-abilities versus the rest of the population. The Dunning-Kruger effect is often associated with a false-sense of overconfidence which arises as a result of a person's lack of or ignorance of information, knowledge, and facts. By nonconsciously staying ignorant, ignorant people can make themselves feel good by thinking what they know is all there is to know regarding a person, a subject, or a situation. To truly become an expert in a subject or a situation, normally, a person would do so by gaining more information, knowledge, and experience about the subject or the situation; but people with a false sense of Self believe they are experts without sufficient knowledge or experience about that subject or the situation.

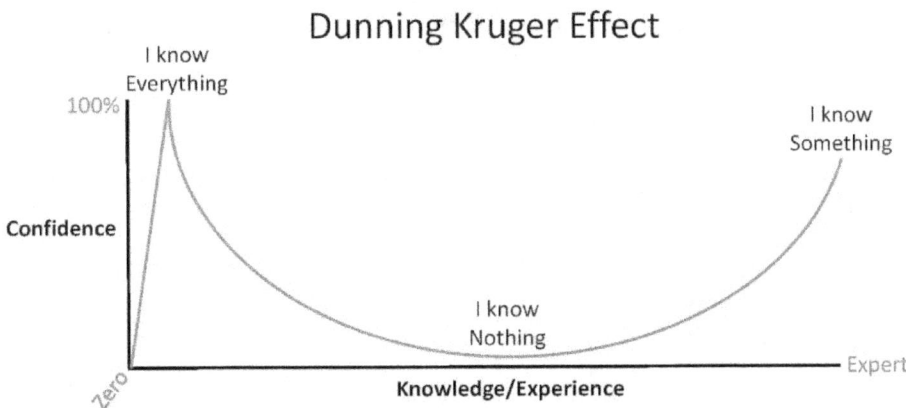

Due to the false overconfidence associated with the Dunning-Kruger effect, Theory of Self-Relativity proverbs The Dunning Kruger Effect as:

By not knowing much, one thinks one knows a whole bunch.

Therefore, as stated by Theory of Self-Relativity:

The words of an ignorant person are his worst enemy.

Delusions of grandeur and false sense of superiority are characteristics that are often associated with biased people as represented by The Dunning Kruger Effect. Ignorance, avoidance, denial, and deflection of information and knowledge keeps these individuals in a false state of feeling superior. Such delusions and denial of facts are also especially common in fragile and high-conflict personality-disordered individuals, such as narcissists and sociopaths. Consequently, prolonged ignorance of dislikeable factual-evidence could lead to incorrect decision-making and incorrect actions. According to Theory of Self-Relativity:

Biases affect and corrupt one's perception of reality.

Instead of holding biases, instead of seeking and creating false-patterns, and instead of trying to find purpose and meaning to things that do not have any purpose or meaning; one should learn to seek and recognize facts without biases, and without giving much emphasis to the need for purpose or meaning. By seeking and by recognizing facts, one can then live one's life objectively and based on factual-reality. This is why, self-improvement via factual-thinking is the only means of harmonizing one's thoughts, one's feelings, and one's actions with reality. Baseless and deep-seated comforting-beliefs could only be changed or eliminated when one learns to look at the facts and the evidence of factuality, rather than by trying to interpret reality to one's liking. Biases, beliefs, and the need for recognizing patterns and purpose could severely affect and even corrupt a person's perception of reality; therefore, it could also have devastating effects on others that the person deals with.

Biases, especially hindsight-bias, are a major cause of our mind getting stuck in the past and not being able to move forward with time. Additionally, rumination and regret are also other common mindsets which keep our mind stuck in the past. As discussed throughout Theory of Self-Relativity:

The only thing that could go back in time and remain in the past, is our mind.

According to Theory of Self-Relativity, the main causes of our mind going back in time and getting stuck in the past are:

1. Hindsight-Bias
2. Rumination and Dwelling
3. Regret and Remorse

When our mind gets stuck in the past or when it is unable to move forward with time, it does so by remembering. Although remembering is based on recalling memories and experiences; we remember things, including the past, with our emotions rather than with actual thoughts. Despite the fact that we do have positive-memories from the past, it is our negative-memories and their influences that prevent us from letting go of the past and from being able to move forward in time.

We remember with feelings rather than with thoughts.

As discussed throughout Theory of Self-Relativity, and in detail in subsequent chapters, time only moves in forward direction; and this forward direction of time is known as the *"arrow-of-time."* Hence, because of the arrow-of-time, the laws-of-physics do not allow for anything to go back in time; yet, the mind is the only entity that could go back in time and stay back in time. The reason the mind can do so is because our mind is an immaterial-byproduct of our physical-brain's activities. Our mind is an immaterial-process, hence, it can incorrectly keep itself stuck in the past, because immaterial cognitive-processes do not interact with anything. Although our mind does not directly abide by the laws-of-physics because it is a property of our brain; however, our physical-brain, which creates our mind, does abide by the laws-of-physics. When our immaterial-mind, which creates our immaterial-thoughts, falls out of sync with reality; our "material" existence ends up paying the price for our mind's incorrect thinking and for its inability to unstuck itself from the past.

Thus, in order for us to stop engaging in hindsight-bias, rumination, regret, or other counterfactual-thoughts that keep our mind stuck in the past; our mind must get back to the present-moment and learn to rationally deal with reality. The only way to minimize and eliminate the causes of our mind getting stuck in the past and to enable it to move forward with time, is for us to learn to address our thoughts factually and not emotionally, so that we can once and for all either resolve or eliminate these thoughts accordingly. By becoming aware of our thoughts, we can evaluate them factually to see how we could move forward from the events of the past; instead of letting our mind keep travelling to the past, in order to try to change the past.

Continuous unresolved thoughts don't just waste time; they steal time.

Although we remember things with our emotions; we must learn to deal with recurring thoughts such as hindsight-bias, rumination, and regret, with facts and reason, rather than with emotions. To prevent our mind from getting stuck in the past, we should not try to avoid thinking of the past; but we should try to resolve or eliminate the causes of the thoughts that keep dragging our mind into the past. The reason these thoughts are so powerful is because such thoughts that are associated with memory are emotionally-tagged thoughts; and the thoughts that are tagged with stronger emotions overpower the thoughts that are not associated with such emotional intensity.

As discussed, we remember the past with our emotions, because we assign emotions to thoughts and memories that are important to us so that we can quickly retrieve them from the storage spaces of our mind. By assigning emotions to our thoughts, we assign importance to them. Although we can only remember by thinking, it is the negative-emotions that are associated with our unresolved-thoughts that keep dragging us into remembering the past and not being able to let go. Our unresolved negatively-tagged memories overpower our positively-tagged memories; hence why, we dwell more on past negativity than we do with positivity from the past. Since we remember the past with our feelings:

To let go of the past, we must think of the past; not live in the past.

Although feelings enable us to remember the past, once our feelings enable us to recall a memory, we must switch from feelings to thinking in order to analyze that memory with our thoughts, and not with our feelings. Because, as discussed, feelings are irrational. Emotionally-tagged memories, especially those that deal with a negativity or a trauma, not only keep us stuck in the past, but they trap us into regurgitating the same thoughts over and over again in trying to change the past.

Since our mind can go back to the past, and since the memory of the past that troubles us is often associated with a negative-emotion; instead of resolving or eliminating these thoughts, our mind wants to keep thinking about ways that it could change the past, based on current information, so that our present feelings would improve. This is contrary to the laws-of-physics, because we cannot change the past; hence why, we keep ruminating, as our mind is trying to fight nature. As discussed, *"Rumination"* is another form of incorrect counterfactual-thinking that prevents our mind from moving forward with time.

Theory of Self-Relativity defines "rumination" as "one's tendency to repetitively think about and reanalyze the circumstances of a past personal-experience, without reaching any resolution."

One of the most destructive mental-attributes blocking self-improvement is our inability to change the past and our inability to resolve or eliminate our thoughts associated with the past, therefore, our inability to move-forward with time. Dwelling on the same thoughts and getting stuck in time, especially in the past, are hallmarks of remembering with emotions rather than remembering with thoughts; this is why, rumination and dwelling are the hallmarks of a mind that is stuck in time. While rumination and dwelling often go hand-in-hand, Theory of Self-Relativity distinguishes rumination from dwelling as:

Rumination is repetitively thinking over and over again about something without resolution; while dwelling is getting stuck as a result of rumination.

The reason rumination has such negative effects and could be destructive is because rumination keeps us stuck in constant repetitive analysis of "cause and consequence," without allowing us to resolve and break-free from the cycle of overthinking. Rumination is an overthinking process commonly associated with the results or consequences of an event, which led to a negative or less than desired outcome.

Rumination and dwelling are commonly associated with hindsight-bias, nonfactual-thinking, and placebo-thinking; thus, rumination and dwelling are common factors in the majority of overthinking processes that deal with memory and experiences. Ruminating and dwelling on the results and consequences of an event disallows us from making decisions to move forward. To be able to move forward from an undesired, negative, or a traumatic event; we must learn to resolve or eliminate the thoughts which are causing us to ruminate.

Theory of Self-Relativity refers to rumination as "the whirlwind of the mind."

Rumination is rooted in thinking things over and over again and it is a clear indication of remembering based on feelings and not based on resolved-thoughts. Rumination is a prime example of why emotional-thinking is problematic and how it could have negative consequences in our life. While many associate ruminations with depression, Theory of Self-Relativity recognizes that rumination is much broader and more prevalent than a more involved depressive psychological mindset. Rumination and dwelling are experienced routinely throughout all mental-states, including non-depressed individuals; because when we ruminate, we remember and ruminate with our feelings rather than through the proper resolution of our thoughts.

Another reason rumination is so addicting is because rumination, according to Theory of Self-Relativity, is a form of externalation. By keeping our focus on an event from the past, we create a rationalized and justified reason to not attend to our current weaknesses or problems that require resolution and improvement. For example, by making a big deal about something that someone said or something that someone did; we keep our mind distracted and preoccupied externally about that event, and we dwell in the past about what happened or what was said, so that we justifiably create an excuse for abstaining from introspection that is required to fix or improve other current and real-time dislikable or deficient personal-weaknesses.

As discussed throughout Theory of Self-Relativity, introspection, which is the ability to observe and inspect one's Self, is a non-negotiable condition for self-improvement. Externalation, which in this case is in the form of rumination, is a common contributor to blocking introspection and self-awareness. Since rumination is also often deployed nonconsciously as a form of externalation; rumination keeps our mind focused on something or someone else, away from our own fragile Self. This is why, those who have a tendency to constantly ruminate, often create drama and chaos. Drama and chaos preoccupy the mind so that the mind does not have the time or the ability to think about the weak sense of Self. Externalation, drama, and chaos are all attributes that are antagonistic to introspection; therefore, they are defense-mechanisms that keep our mind and attention focused to the outside, rather than bringing the focus back onto the Self.

With the need for instant-gratification, human-beings instinctually prefer making a decision that would prevent them from feeling bad at that moment, rather than to face uncomfortable-facts and to take corrective-action which could actually have long-term benefits. Our default program is to avoid pain, to feel good, or at the minimum, to feel less-bad; even if we have to fabricate nonfactual-thoughts in order to support our desired-feelings. Rumination, in combination with other thought-processes such as confirmation-bias, hindsight-bias, nonfactual-thinking, and rationalization through placebo-thinking, are some of the common coping-mechanisms we deploy to keep our mind distracted and preoccupied so that we can avoid discomfort and we can feel better; or at the minimum, we can feel less-bad.

Due to this externalation aspect of rumination, both rumination and dwelling could become compulsive and addicting; especially if there are other underlying conditions such as depression, Obsessive-Compulsive-Disorder (OCD), or other addictions.

Since rumination is repetitive; repetition, even if unhealthy or ritualistic, gives a sense of familiarity and safety to those who are afraid of change. This is why, cognitive-approaches and factual-thinking are key to breaking the habits of rumination and dwelling. By thinking factually and by bringing the focus to self-improvement, the focus shifts to the Self and away from the thoughts which cause rumination. By bringing the focus to the Self and by evaluating our memories factually; we should be able to resolve, improve, or eliminate the causes of our rumination, hence, we will have better ability to minimize and eliminate our ruminating and dwelling tendencies.

To distract the mind from rumination, certain therapies suggest focusing onto the outside and to get involved in mind and time occupying social activities. While distraction on a momentary or short-term basis could be an effective tool in disrupting unhealthy repetitive mental-processes; distraction is a defense-mechanism which only delays the inevitable. Distraction will eventually cause a person to ruminate about the unresolved and dwelling thoughts, again, at a later time. Distracting our Self in order to stop ruminating, is like kicking the mental-can of unresolved dwelling-thoughts down the road of denial. Corrective-thinking requires resolution or elimination of thoughts, not avoiding or covering-up of thoughts. While distraction might be a good short-term bandage; distraction is not a solution, it is a coping-mechanism. The solution to ending rumination and other unhealthy mental-activities is to become aware of and to understand the causal-thoughts of these mindsets.

Although rumination could occur with future events which have not yet happened; rumination, relative to past events, is a nonfactual wishful-thinking type mindset that keeps taking us back in time because of our desire to want to fix a wrong from the past, or to change the past. Despite the fact that we know we cannot change the past, we continue ruminating about the past event by wishing that we could've changed what happened. By trying to change the past, we continue wasting more time in the present-moment, instead of moving forward with time towards a better future.

Rumination steals time.

While rumination and dwelling could also happen regarding future events and with things that have not happened yet; such continuous thinking about future events tends to create more feelings of worry and anxiety, than feelings of regret, blame, guilt and self-criticism. Since the consequences of future events have not happened yet; adjusting or abstaining from making incorrect decisions associated with the future event would give us the ability to change or correct our course of thinking and action.

We can influence the future, but we cannot change the past.

Hence, Theory of Self-Relativity focuses more on rumination and dwelling associated with the past and with events which have already occurred, because they are unchangeable. This is also true regarding other negative past events such as unfavorable outcomes or "failure;" and it is also true regarding a negative future feeling due to a past event, such as "regret" or "remorse."

Failure is a prime example of an event which is commonly associated with hindsight-bias, constant-rumination, and obsessive-dwelling. By allowing a failed event to become the final occurrence in a chain of events, and by not allowing the failure to become a steppingstone for continuation and improvement of the process; failure causes constant rumination and regret. Failure causes us to continuously relive an unfavorable past event in our mind without any resolution; this is why, failure is closely associated with rumination and dwelling. The more a person relives a negative past-experience, the more time gets wasted, and the farther time will move away from the failed-event that is causing the person's mind to stay stuck in the past.

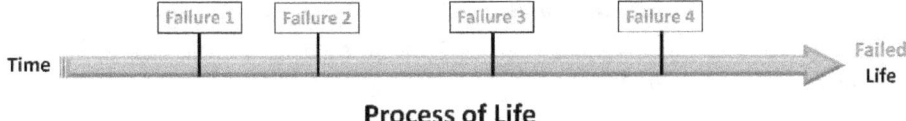

Process of Life

This is why, instead of allowing an unfavorable-outcome, also known as failure, to disable us, we should take failure as an event in the process of improvement; hence, we should use that event to course-correct by making changes in the continuum of the process. According to Theory of Self-Relativity, there should be no such a thing as failure; because:

Mistakes and failures are simply events in the timeline of progress and success.

Therefore:

Theory of Self-Relativity classically defines "failure" as "an unsuccessful event."

However:

Theory of Self-Relativity, in the context of self-improvement, specifically defines "failure" as "an unfavorable event within the continuum of the success-process."

Failure only materializes when we accept a negative or an unfavorable outcome as finality. However, when we consider failure as a failed-attempt or an unfavorable-event in the timeline of success-process; such failed-attempt or unfavorable-event simply becomes a marker or a steppingstone in the continued timeline of progress.

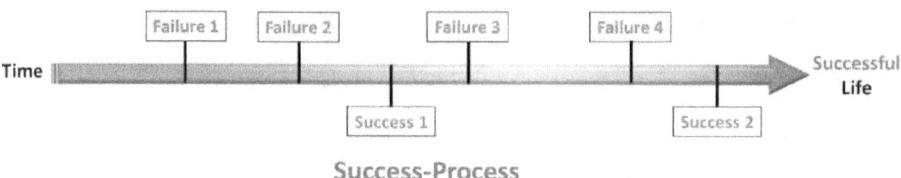

Success-Process

Failure is simply a steppingstone in the success-process.

Therefore:

Failure and success are simply steppingstone events in the process of life.

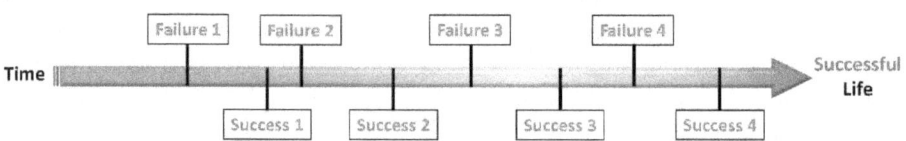

Failed-Events = Success-Process = Process of Life

What one might perceive as a failure, should be considered as simply a bump on the road to success. Human progress, scientific success, and medical breakthroughs are all as a result of years and decades of trials and failures; until the correct path was identified and success was achieved. Without failure, the true value of success would not be appreciated.

Failure is what makes success memorable.

When we take any mishap or negative-outcome as simply a steppingstone in the path to success; we will never experience failure. We will only experience failure when we accept the unfavorable-outcome or the negative-event as finality.

If you've never failed, it means you've never tried; and without trying, you will never succeed.

When we make change and improvement as a natural part of our life, neither failure nor success will be final-events; because we will keep on improving upon them. When we do not accept failure and when we learn to take negative-events as part of the process to progress and success; we will then learn to become persistent. Likewise, when we learn how to become persistent, we will become more inclined to achieve favorable results; hence, we will have a higher degree of resolve. According to Theory of Self-Relativity:

Results come from persistent-resolve.

It must be noted that persistence is not synonymous with being stubborn. Persistence should be based on data, information, and facts, and persistence should be open to change; however, stubbornness is not open to change, regardless of the facts and data. Furthermore, persistent-resolve does not mean only working hard; but it means gaining knowledge and applying experience persistently, to achieve favorable outcomes. Therefore, since results come from persistent-resolve, this means there should be no reliance on nonfactual-mindsets such as empty-hope, wishful-thinking, or even luck; because luck is a matter of action-based persistent-resolve and determination creating a favorable-opportunity.

Theory of Self-Relativity defines "luck" as "when determination and action create opportunity."

This is why, those who believe in luck or those who claim to be unlucky, are the type of people who do not commit to long-term persistence and action in order to create favorable change for themselves. Such individuals commonly call themselves unlucky, and they regularly engage in self-victimization and blame-shifting their misfortunes onto something or someone else.

Those who claim to be unlucky, aren't unlucky; they simply blame-shift by not taking personal-responsibility to make a positive-change.

According to Theory of Self-Relativity, no such a thing as luck exists. Although luck is often described as "when preparation meets opportunity;" opportunity is not out there for us to stumble upon, and neither will it come knocking on our door as we sit and wait. The opportunity that preparation or persistence must meet is something we must create. Furthermore, opportunity, only looks like an opportunity in hindsight; because, we only label something as an opportunity if we took action and the action resulted in a positive-outcome, or if we did not take action and the situation proved that it could have had favorable results for us had we acted. However, if a situation we took action leads to an unfavorable-outcome, we do not call it an opportunity; likewise, if we did not take action in the past and if what we did not do, didn't transpire into a positive-outcome, we would not consider it a missed-opportunity. Therefore, an opportunity only looks like an opportunity if one takes action in the past to achieve future results; hence, an opportunity must be based on an action one takes to create a favorable-outcome. This why, there is no such a thing as luck, and this is why:

Opportunities are created by the opportunist.

Similar to an opportunity, since failure is an event in the past, the longer we obsess about it, the less we will be able to move forward; therefore, instead of obsessing over a negative-outcome, we must have the resolve to create an opportunity out of that unfavorable-event. Failure keeps us stuck in the past. By recognizing what we call failure, to be a negative-experience or an undesired-outcome, and by learning from it; we can move forward by taking a negative-event from our past and by changing it to something positive towards our future.

Although we can't change the past, we can use the past to influence the future.

By learning the weaknesses associated with a negative-outcome from the past; we can use that knowledge and experience to pivot our path towards a more favorable future outcome.

You can learn from failure, or you can fail to learn.

Success is not an event; it is the process of the continuum of many failed and many successful events leading us on the path of further success. When we make change and improvement as a normal part of our life, neither failure nor success will become final-events.

Success is not a destination, it is a never-ending process; because the minute the process stops, success stops.

To be successful, we must continue to progress and improve while maintaining the results achieved. This is why, we cannot simply achieve success and stop; we must, at the minimum, maintain our success and our achievements. Success is not an event or a destination; success is a process.

You can't succeed just once; you must continue to succeed.

According to Theory of Self-Relativity, success is best achieved when success becomes part of our purpose, our goals, and our dreams; because:

True success is measured by the level of our fulfillment.

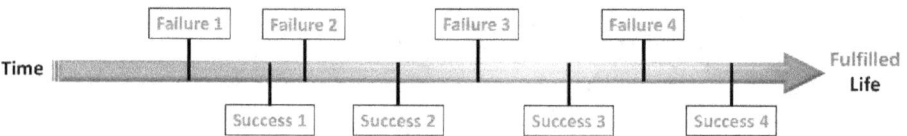

Failed-Events = Success-Process = **Process of Life** = Fulfillment

Success that creates fulfillment is an achievement that makes us feel a sense of satisfaction; as we fulfill our self-created purpose, and as we reach our personal-goals.

Theory of Self-Relativity further defines "success" as "fulfilling a purpose by accomplishing the next goal."

True success could only be measured by how fulfilled and truly satisfied we feel; because as stated throughout Theory of Self-Relativity:

Wealth, fame, and power are simply byproducts of success. True success is measured by the level of your fulfillment.

Success does not necessarily mean achieving financial wealth or material abundance. Success is fulfilling and strengthening our self-created purpose by achieving our next goal. This goal could be as simple as walking after a disabling accident; or quitting smoking, or finishing a book we have always wanted to read. If our purpose, our goals, and our dreams are genuinely important for our Self, and if they bring us contentment and fulfillment; that should be the yardstick that we measure our success with. Although monetary success is important for living a comfortable life, as money is the medium that we use in exchange for goods and services; measuring success purely by financial achievements will not create fulfillment, which is a necessary mindset for experiencing longer lasting frequencies of happiness.

Money can save you lots of misery, but money cannot buy you lasting happiness.

Despite the fact that success is often measured by accomplishments, by achieving status, and by making money; true success is best measured by our evolving sense of satisfaction, contentment, and fulfillment.

Theory of Self-Relativity defines "fulfillment" as "an evolving satisfactory state-of-mind that is built upon a stable foundation of contentment."

Fulfillment, especially self-fulfillment, is discussed in detail in many other sections of the Theory of Self-Relativity. The reason Theory of Self-Relativity signifies success with the level of fulfillment is because the feeling of success results from a personal-mindset that is primarily subjective, and secondarily relative to others. Thus, the mindset and the feeling of success varies from person-to-person; hence, it's subjective, and therefore, it is relative.

Since true success should be measured by self-fulfillment, and not by the amount of money and status one achieves; therefore, true success should also not be measured against others, it should be measured against our own self-created purpose and goals.

The reason many successful people, especially overachievers end-up unhappy, is because they consider their success as failure against someone else's comparable success level. Self-improvement, through self-focus, allows us to measure success within our own parameters, regardless of what others might be doing. Although learning from and being competitive with others is an important way of increasing motivation to reach success; however, we must remain realistic with our purpose and goals for progress and success.

True success is measured by fulfillment, and fulfillment is personal.

As discussed, although success is often remembered by events, true success should not be defined by achievement timestamps; because true success is an ongoing process. True success is measured by fulfillment, which simply stated, is how satisfied we are with our state-of-existence. As long as we are improving today over yesterday, and as long as we are fulfilling our internally created purpose by getting closer to our next goal and our next dreams; we are achieving success. Therefore, as discussed throughout Theory of Self-Relativity, if we do not accept a negative-experience or a setback as a final-event of failure; we will never experience failure.

The only true failure is death, and the only true success is living our life to its fullest.

Until death comes upon us, we should not consider anything else in our life as failure; we must enjoy our "life" as a road to continuous success.

Failure will only become a reality if you stop trying; therefore, failure is the pre-requisite for success.

Likewise, regret, which is closely associated with failure and rumination, is due to continuously living with a past unfavorable or a past unsuccessful event. We feel regret as a result of our behavior, because we did or we did not take an action in the past which could have resulted in a favorable outcome; or which could have prevented an unfavorable-outcome.

Theory of Self-Relativity defines "regret" as "a future feeling one experiences as a result of past action or inaction."

Regret is an archetype indicator of how our feelings are directly associated with our thoughts and behavior. We regret something because we are constantly thinking about an event, and we constantly wish we would have dealt with it differently; therefore, regret is a strong emotion that is also associated with self-criticism. Additionally, regret is closely associated with hindsight-bias, because regret arises from thinking about a previous less than optimal behavior that cannot be changed; consequently, regret commonly arises as a result of a negative, or a less than optimum outcome.

Regret is generally associated with a wish, a want, or a desire for a different past outcome. Regret is not necessarily negative like shame and guilt are, because regret indicates that we have evaluated a situation or an action that we were responsible for, or that we had a part in. Above all, regret is often associated with remorse because regret deals with something from the past. Regret is similar to failure because despite the fact that we cannot change the past; we can use the past to influence and improve our future. Regret, just like failure and other similar leftover-negativities from the past, could be used to influence the future positively.

Leftover-negativities from the past should be used to influence the future positively.

Regret can either have a negative strangle hold on us or it can be a positive learning experience; therefore, Theory of Self-Relativity categorizes regret binarily:

1. **Positive-Regret (What we did or didn't do):** Positive-regret is our openness and ability to look back at our decisions and actions and to evaluate them as to how they could have been handled differently, and how we could have achieved more favorable-outcomes. Positive-regret allows us to consider past actions in order to change and improve our future behavior in a similar situation. Positive-regret can become part of self-reflection. Positive-regret creates experience which can be used for future improvement.

2. **Negative-Regret (What we could've, should've, or would've done):** Negative-regret, or classic-regret, also referred to as regret, keeps us stuck in

the past primarily via rumination, dwelling, counterfactual-thinking, and hindsight-bias. Negative-regret prevents us from moving forward by not allowing us to distance our Self from something that has already happened and which could not be changed. When regret associates itself with blame, shame, and guilt; that is when we crossover to the negative-regret zone. By turning negative-regret into positive-regret, we can shift from blaming our Self to improving our Self.

Regret is another indicator of how the human mind thinks about safety rather than happiness; therefore, the regret of not committing to an opportunity is easier to overcome than the regret of having committed and achieved unfavorable-results. For example, it is easier to have missed-out on the potential gains of a business opportunity, than to take a loss in it; likewise, it is easier to not have committed to an incorrect relationship, than to have experienced the difficulties of a prolonged incompatibility by staying in a bad relationship. As discussed, when of equal value, negativity has more influence on us than does positivity.

Since our primitive-mind does not care if we are happy, and all it cares about is if we are safe; by keeping us safe through minimizing variables and uncertainties, our mind tries to minimize danger and negativity. But in order to progress and to improve, we must change; yet, change, itself, creates variables and uncertainty. Change, especially positive-change, requires decisions and actions which could create uncertainties and unfavorable outcomes. Our primitive-mind wants to prevent these uncertainties by not allowing us to change, because it is defaulted to consider that change could jeopardize our safety. This is why, we experience regret; because:

It is easier to say maybe I should've, than to say I wish I wouldn't have.

To minimize regret and to use regret as a positive influence, it is important to create a strong sense of Self via self-improvement and growing self-confidence. When we self-improve, we can use past events and learned experiences to influence and improve our future. Regret, just like failure, is associated with an event in the timeline of a process; therefore, instead of being regretful by continuously engaging in counterfactual-thinking, we can utilize our sense of regret to create an opportunity from what we are regretful about.

Opportunities are created by the opportunist.

Another feeling closely associated with regret that keeps looking into the past is *"remorse."* Remorse is also often rooted in guilt and shame. As described throughout Theory of Self-Relativity, regret, guilt, shame, failure, and even remorse are caused by leaving an unfavorable-outcome or a negative-experience as a final-event in the past. By learning that although life is experienced as events, it should not be determined by events, and by understanding that events are simply components of the continuum of the process; we will then know that we can use every unfavorable outcome to change that event into a new future positive-outcome.

Life is experienced as events; but it should not be determined by events.

Once we learn to address negativities as steppingstones in the foundation of building positivities; we will rarely experience long-term guilt, shame, regret, remorse, or even failure. Instead of feeling remorseful about something that we did or did not do, we must take that experience and build upon it just as we would with failure. Remorse, if felt temporarily, could be constructive; because it can be used to improve a past event. However, just like other negative personal emotions such as guilt, shame, and regret, remorse becomes problematic if it is held as a finality relative to a past unfavorable-outcome or a past negative-experience.

Being able to feel remorse is a good trait, as long as the feeling of remorse is used to increase awareness of our decisions and actions not only relative to our own Self, but also relative to others. Instead of submerging in chronic-remorse, when we use our feeling of remorse to evaluate the thoughts that are causing us to feel remorse; we will consequently begin to increase our sense of accountability and responsibility. By being able to feel remorse, we will be able to become cognizant of alternative perspectives; hence, we will minimize the chances of becoming selfish. Self-centered people do not feel guilt, shame, and remorse; because by blocking those feelings, they are able to continue their self-serving agendas. However, when we feel remorse, or when we feel guilt and shame, we are then able to evaluate the cause of those feelings by repairing, by improving, or by changing those causes.

Regardless of how our mind gets stuck in the past, we should not be afraid of negative-feelings associated with past events. When experienced temporarily, rumination and hindsight-bias, which cause negative-feelings of guilt, shame, regret, and remorse; could be constructive for our awareness of how we interact with our self and with others. When rumination is used as an evaluation tool rather than as a criticism tool; rumination and evaluation of past events can become constructive in the long-term.

Awareness and understanding the factualities of our thoughts will help us to comprehend and objectively evaluate them. When we become aware of and as we begin to understand the causal-thoughts of our rumination and dwelling, we can then resolve or eliminate these thoughts from our memory, and in-turn, we can abstain from self-criticism; hence, we can minimize and eliminate our feelings of regret, remorse, and failure.

Use the awareness of your negative-feelings as an evaluation tool, not as a self-criticism tool.

Rumination, which Theory of Self-Relativity refers to as "the whirlwind of our mind," is metaphorically circular in nature and it keeps our mind behind in time; while time, like an arrow, continues to linearly move forward. Self-improvement, via mindfulness and factual-thoughtfulness, will enable us to break the cycle of rumination and will help us align our thoughts forwardly and in sync with the arrow-of-time. This is why, hindsight-bias, rumination, and regret, which are all mental processes that commonly deal with already occurred events, often overlap with one another.

Regardless of hindsight-bias, rumination, or regret; getting stuck in overthinking, especially regarding events which have already occurred, does nothing but waste time and prevent us from moving forward in life. Overthinking, especially about events which have already occurred, causes what is sometimes known as "paralysis by analysis." By thinking about the same thing over and over again in a ruminative fashion and without reaching any resolution, we are trying to change something that cannot be changed. Despite the fact that we know that by thinking about the same thing over and over again nothing would change; we still engage in repetitive thinking and behavior because moving on to a new change is emotionally difficult. Additionally, despite our inability to change the past, we tend to ruminate, because the negativity of the past is comfortably more familiar than the uncertainty of a future change.

The correct way to not only minimize, but to eliminate such repetitive thinking, is for us to evaluate the thoughts that are causing us to think this way. As explained, the reason we create these thoughts and the reason we get stuck on them is because identifying the cause of a dislikeable or a regretful event through introspection is difficult and even painful. We create these thoughts, and we engage in such repetitive and overthinking styles in order to avoid pain, to feel good, or at the minimum, to feel less-bad. The correct way of addressing these thoughts is by bringing the focus onto our Self and by examining events factually. When we factually evaluate our thoughts, we can then either resolve or eliminate the cause of these thoughts, or we can learn from the experiences associated with the event; and therefore, we can move on from that past event.

As further discussed, patterns are as a result of relationships between things and events, and they affect our thinking-system by influencing our thoughts, our biases, and our sense of reality. Thus, it is common that when we cannot resolve our feelings of regret, remorse, or even failure; we then engage in pattern-seeking, pattern-recognition, confirmation-bias, and even, motivated-reasoning, in order to justify why we feel such emotions. We do so because the mind feels most comfortable when it can establish cause, effect, and relativity between things.

Our mind continuously seeks to find relativity between things.

Although at the basic animal instinctive level, pattern-seeking and pattern-recognition are necessary protective characteristics; pattern-seeking and pattern-recognition could become inhibitive and even destructive when created and practiced for comforting purposes.

When a cause, a reason, a purpose, or a meaning for something or for an event is not readily known; the natural tendency of the human mind is to fill-in this knowledge-gap with something or with some agency, often a comforting one; even if that thing or that agent would have to be imagined and concocted.

Our mind continuously seeks to find cause, effect, purpose, meaning, and relativity between things.

Consequently, pattern-seeking and pattern-recognition often involves assumptions, speculations, and non-existent relationships between two or more unrelated entities; because it is believed that finding a relationship between things or events leads to finding the cause, the reason, the purpose, or the meaning for those things. Although finding the cause or reason for something is important in filling the knowledge-gap, the human mind is conditioned to feel more comfortable by knowing the purpose and the meaning for something; because not knowing the purpose and meaning for something causes uncertainty. Despite the facts that people react negatively for not knowing the purpose, the meaning, and the reason for something; purpose, meaning, and even, reason, are not as important as is the cause of something.

Although things in nature have a cause, they don't necessarily have to have a reason, a purpose, or a meaning.

When people believe that they are searching for the reason for something, because it is popularly, yet fallaciously believed that "everything happens for a reason;" people are more commonly searching for a purpose and a meaning, and not necessarily for the reason of that thing. For example, magical-thinking, fortune-telling, and even astrology, are nonfactual pattern-seeking and pattern-recognition mindsets that are fabricated and imagined in order to make sense of something that does not exist or does not make sense. Such beliefs and rituals are undertaken because creating, assuming, and believing in non-factual patterns, and assigning purpose and meaning to them, makes us feel good. These practices have a protective and comforting intent to create purpose and meaning for us. Likewise, our mind will fabricate false-patterns with the nonconscious excuse of trying to keep us safe; although it is actually doing so in order to make us feel good, or more commonly, it is doing so, in order to make us feel less-bad. This is why, logical-fallacies use rationalization to justify a comforting mindset.

Logical-fallacies are intended to make sense of the nonsense.

This is how delusions begin. A common example of such fallacious-thinking is the assignment of the unexplainable onto something else. For example, if an event is unpleasant and if we cannot find a cause or a reason for it; our mind often tries to assign an unrealistic or an imaginary agent to the event in order to fill-in the gap of purpose and agency. Some examples of popular purpose and meaning gap-fillers are "it was meant to be" or "it was God's will."

It should be noted, that although many animals, including humans, engage in pattern-seeking for safety and for survival; engaging in intentionally false, perceived, and fabricated pattern-seeking, is only a human trait. This is the drawback of human intelligence; because humans have an analytical-mind that is inclined to not only find patterns, but it is also evolved to find cause, reason, purpose, and even meaning for something. Other animals look for patterns, animals do not look for cause, reason, purpose, or meaning; therefore, therefore, other animals do not intentionally create false-patterns in order to convince and comfort themselves. However, in contrast, and as a result of human intelligence, humans do so, because cognitively finding a cause, a reason, and even, a purpose for something has been the main reason for the human species' survival and advancements.

Although finding cause, reason, purpose, and meaning is unique to humans, because humans are intellectually-advanced; such intelligence also becomes inhibiting for us because we fail to accept that some things just do not have a purpose or a meaning. Because of our intelligence and the comfort associated with finding a purpose and knowing a meaning, we are continuously seeking to find purpose and meaning for things, because purpose and meaning give us hope and a sense of belonging; and also, because purpose and meaning help demonstrate intentional-agency associated with an event or an outcome. Without reason, purpose, and meaning, the human mind is uncomfortable to simply accept the cause; therefore, in the absence of reason, purpose, or meaning, humans tend to fabricate a reason, a purpose, and even, a meaning, in order to fill-in the knowledge-gap for something that does not have a reason, a purpose, or a meaning, thus, we fabricate intentional-agency with a purpose for the occurrence.

Reason and purpose give meaning to humans, and without meaning, humans have a difficult time accepting reality as it is; because purpose and meaning make us feel good, make us feel safe, and most importantly, purpose and meaning make us feel special by making us believe that an intentional-agent caused an event for the purpose of having our best interest in mind.

Where no purpose exists, fabricating a purpose gives people a sense of belonging and a sense of an intentional-agent watching over them. Furthermore, such fabricated agents are often characterized as caring and as having an interest for our safety and protection. Our intelligent-mind can, and often does, purposely fabricate false-patterns in order to create a false-reason and a non-existent purpose; with the intent to make us feel good and special. Intentional pattern-seeking, false pattern-recognition, and confirmation-biases, in the name of comfort and purpose, are defense-mechanisms that we deploy to support our comforting-beliefs. This false, protective, and safe feeling is not only comforting; but it unfortunately enables us to ditch personal-responsibility away from our Self, by passing on the obligation of change and improvement to an external-agency.

Many mistaken The-Universe's natural order of cause and effect, with purpose and meaning.

Because of The Big-Bang, all things have a cause and many things have a reason; but not all things need to have a purpose or a meaning. Purpose and meaning are intent-based, which means an intentional-agent is the cause of a thing or an event; and this agent has a purpose or a meaning for that thing or event. Hence, the quote "for all intents and purposes."

The Big-Bang and entropy, which are discussed in detail throughout Theory of Self-Relativity and in length in subsequent sections, are responsible for the order of cause-and-effect; therefore, to have an effect or a result, there needs to be a cause. Because of this forward arrow caused by The Big-Bang and entropy, which are also responsible for the arrow-of-time; while some causes could be the effect of a previous cause or a prior outcome, all effects or outcomes require a previous cause. The principle of "Causality" is the influence by which an event, a process, a state, or an object contributes to the production of another event, process, state, or object; whereby, the cause is all or partly responsible for the effect, and the effect is all or partly dependent on that cause, or on the confluence of prior causes.

As stated, many things have a reason, and all reasons have a cause, but the cause does not have to directly create the reason. For example, people with peanut-allergy break-out in hives; therefore, in a person with peanut-allergy, peanuts are the cause of the hives, and peanuts create the reason for the hives. The reason for the hives is the body's allergic response to peanuts; therefore, in order for a reason to exist, there always needs to be a cause. Although peanuts could cause hives, peanuts are not the reason for the hives; the body's allergic response is the reason for the hives. If peanuts were the reason for hives, then everyone eating peanuts would get rashes and hives. Hence, peanuts are the cause, the body's allergic response is the reason, and the hives are the effect of the peanut allergy. Although the peanut allergy has a cause, a reason, and an effect; there is no purpose or meaning for the hives or for the allergic response to peanuts.

Therefore, things that have a reason also always have a cause. Although a reason "could" also have a purpose; however, the reason for something "does not" necessarily need to have a purpose. In other words, while something might have a reason and that reason had a cause; this does not mean that thing has a purpose or a meaning. When people say, "everything happens for a reason," although they are right that everything happens "because of a cause;" however, not everything happens "for a reason." The need to find purpose is why, many mistaken cause or reason with purpose; thus, their intention for this statement is meant to be that "everything has a purpose." People mistakenly confuse looking for a purpose with searching for a cause or a reason. A reason is not synonymous with purpose.

Reason ≠ Purpose

Humans have a tendency to incorrectly assume that a reason for something automatically means that thing has a purpose. For example, just because The-Universe, the laws-of-physics, and our existence are caused by something, and that cause led to a reason for this existence; this reason does not mean that our existence has a purpose, or that it has a meaning given by someone or by something else. Reason for something is not the same as purpose and meaning.

Reason ≠ Purpose & Meaning

Furthermore, many humans tend to incorrectly think that The-Universe; the laws-of-physics, and human existence have a purpose and meaning. Contrary to what many believe, although The-Universe exists because of a reason and that reason had a cause; the cause of The-Universe's existence does not mean its existence has or needs to have a purpose or a meaning.

Cause ⟶ Reason ≠ Purpose & Meaning

The-Universe was not created for the purpose of human existence; humans simply exist because The-Universe exists. The-Universe and humans exist without any purpose or meaning.

In this example, the current understanding of the reason for the existence of The-Universe is known to be The Big-Bang; however, the cause of The Big-Bang is still under investigation. Just because the cause of the formation of The-Universe is unknown at this time, this does not mean that we should fill-in this knowledge-gap for the cause with a supernatural intentional-agent in order to assign purpose and meaning for our existence. Just as the reason for the existence of The-Universe, which is now known to be The Big-Bang, was not known a century ago, and scientists did not stop looking for the reason by accepting the God theory; we also should not fill the knowledge-gap of not knowing the cause of The-Universe with an assumed or imaginary purpose-based supernatural intentional-agent. Therefore, in order for something to have purpose and meaning, that thing must have an agent with consciousness and intent to give it purpose and meaning. However, cause or reason do not require consciousness or intent.

In order for something to have purpose or meaning, that thing must have a conscious agent.

Since things happen, everything that happens or exists is the "effect" of, or as a result of a cause. Humans are therefore inherently conditioned to look for the cause of something. A thing or an event always has a cause and an effect; however, the existence of a cause and effect does not necessitate the need for a reason, a purpose, or a meaning. In contrast, purpose and meaning always have a cause and a reason; however, as stated before, the cause for something does not necessarily need to have a reason, a purpose, or a meaning.

Although cause and reason do not need to have a purpose or a meaning; purpose and meaning must always have a cause and a reason that is intended by "an agent." However, cause and reason by themselves, do not need to have an agent, because cause and reason do not necessarily have to have purpose and meaning.

Purpose and meaning are therefore created or assigned by an intentional-agent who caused something to result in an effect or in an outcome that was desired or intended by the agent. Hence, for an intentional-agent to cause something, the agent must have a purpose or a goal for doing so; and commonly, causing or doing something with a purpose, is also done with intent. Additionally, an intentional-agent with a purpose could also give the goal or the outcome of the purpose a meaning. Therefore, intentional-agents who have a purpose, must be alive, must be conscious, or at the minimum, must be able to interact with The-Universe; and, such agents must have some cognitive-ability to desire or intent a certain outcome.

Since cause-and-effect are fundamental, and because effect is the result of a cause, in the diagram below, effect is placed before reason; although if reason exists, reason usually precedes effect. Therefore, if a reason exists, both reason and effect are as a result of a cause. As discussed, The Big-Bang and entropy are the pre-requisite and the grand-cause for the following order.

Big-Bang & Entropy	Cause	Effect	Reason	Agent	Purpose & Meaning	
Cause	▉	X	X	X	X	
Effect	✓	▉	X	X	X	Order
Reason	✓	✓	▉	X	X	
Purpose & Meaning	✓	✓	✓	✓	▉	

Prerequisites

Things that happen naturally have a cause and "could" also have a reason, a purpose, and a meaning. Furthermore, things that have a purpose or meaning always have a "natural" agent with an "intent" that caused it; hence, intent creates the purpose, which in-turn, could also give it a meaning. Furthermore, for something to have meaning, it not only requires an intentional-agent with a purpose, but the agent must also be conscious and cognitive. For example:

- A predator killing a prey.
- Reproduction.
- Sleep.

Likewise, things that happen naturally have a cause but do not necessarily need to have a reason, a purpose, or a meaning. Therefore, when things happen without a reason, a purpose, or a meaning; an "intentional" agent is not necessary for the cause. For example:

- The formation of The-Universe.
- Solar eclipses.
- Earthquakes.

The conflict of purpose and meaning with cause and reason arises when humans insist on assigning purpose and meaning to things that do not have a purpose; and especially to things that do not have a meaning. Since things that do not have a purpose or a meaning do not have an agent either; to give these things purpose and meaning, humans fallaciously concoct agency, and we commonly do so by assigning "supernatural" and or "imaginary" agencies, where no natural-agent exists, or where one could not be identified. For example:

- God created The-Universe.
- Solar eclipses happened because the gods were angry.
- Earthquakes were caused by restless giant creatures or slumbering gods sleep beneath the Earth.

Additionally, agents, be it natural or supernatural, who cause something for a purpose, always have an intent; hence, the reference to these agents as "intentional-agents." Therefore, purpose and meaning require a conscious and cognitive intentional-agent. For example:

- A predator, who is a natural-agent, attacks the prey with the intent to kill the prey, and for the purpose of eating it.
- People, who are natural-agents, have sex for the intent of pleasure or reproduction; and such desire could mean that they are in love together.
- God, who is a supernatural-agent, created The-Universe with the intent for humans to exist; and for the purpose is for God to have a relationship with humans.

As stated throughout Theory of Self-Relativity, everything has a cause, but everything does not need to have a reason, a purpose, or a meaning. Most people incorrectly search for the purpose of something, where instead, they should be looking for the cause for that thing. They do so because purpose allows for explaining why something happened, and because purpose gives meaning to that things. Humans want to assign meaning to something because without meaning, people have difficulty navigating through life. Since humans are intentional-agents, which means we are agents with desire, intent, and purpose for whatever we do; we tend to think that everything else that occurs must also have a purpose, and therefore, it must also have an "intentional" agent behind it.

Intentional-agency requires "consciousness" because to have an intention means to be able to have cognition, or at the minimum, to have awareness.

For example, to "know" that we exist by chance and for no apparent purpose is a difficult perspective for most people; this is why, many choose to "believe" in the purpose and meaning of something, instead of choosing to "know" the cause of that thing. When we choose to believe in a purpose, we then need to find or create an intentional-agent who intended that purpose. Because of our intelligence, humans are the only species who engage in such fallacious-mindsets; however, unlike humans, other animals do not care for the purpose or for the meaning of something, they just live with the cause and the effect of it. For example, humans thought that thunder and lightning were caused by angry gods. However, other animals simply seek safety and protection when lightning and thunder occur; they do not think about who or what caused it, and more so, they don't think as to why it happened.

For most humans, it feels scary and lonely to know that the most important and the most integral events that ever happened, and which continue to happen in their life, did so without a meaning or purpose. For example, the existence of The-Universe, our own existence, and our own death. Not having a purpose for our existence makes us feel insignificant and uncertain with our own Self; because we want to believe that there is a purpose and a meaning to our existence, and that some caring and purposeful powerful-entity caused it. We do so, because, by believing in a more powerful agency causing our existence, we can, in-turn, believe that such intentional-agent would be watching over us and will protect us with our best interest in mind.

Humans are instinctively programmed to assume agency in order to stay safe and to feel better; because belief of agency, minimizes uncertainty.

Purpose, meaning, and intentional-agency minimize uncertainties of the unknowns; hence, they comfort us by leading us to identifying a reason. Since the cause or the reason for something could not always be known; in order to create certainty, we fabricate agents with a purpose as gap-fillers for the unknown reason, so that we can give that thing a meaning. It is this comforting need to find purpose and meaning which is one of the main contributors to our flawed-thinking and our inability to self-improve. Purpose and meaning, although commonly confused with cause or reason, tend to create certainty; thus, this feeling of certainty causes us to feel safe, to feel good, or at the minimum, it causes us to not feel as bad as we would have felt if we did not have a purpose and if we did not associate a meaning with something. This is why, placebo-thoughts, such as faith, hope, and beliefs, which are not based on facts, are comforting. Therefore, we choose to believe in purpose and meaning, by fabricating purpose and meaning causing intentional-agents, in order to feel good; or at the minimum, in order to not feel as bad. And because intention requires consciousness; thus, our imaginary intentional-agents are also assumed to have consciousness, intelligence, and even, morality.

However, just because purpose, meaning, and more importantly, intentional-agency is comforting; this does not mean that we have to fabricate false and imaginary agents in order to justify assumed and believed purpose and meaning. Furthermore, if we cannot understand, or if we do not know the cause for something, we should not assume an intentional-agent with a purpose that caused it; because that is how we create false-beliefs, myths, and superstitions.

As defined by Theory of Self-Relativity:

A "belief" is "a thought, an opinion, or an idea that is assumed but unproven with facts and evidence."

Therefore, if we cannot understand or know the cause of something, it simply means we do not have enough information to understand the cause of that thing or that event. But to assign a purpose, such as, "it was meant to be," or "it was God's will," in order give it a meaning so that we can feel better; is self-deceiving and irrational. Since feelings are irrational, believing in something that is nonfactual in order to support that comforting irrational-feeling; is itself, just as irrational. This is why, Theory of Self-Relativity insists on our fact-based rational-thoughts to create our feelings; and not our irrational-feelings creating irrational-thoughts.

The way to bring rationality into our thinking is to ensure that our thoughts are verified with facts; in other words, we must verify that our thoughts are parallel with reality and with the truth. A thought, just like a claim, could either be true or false; this is why, Theory of Self-Relativity advocates factual-thinking, because either a fact for a thought or a claim exists, or it does not. However, facts are not always immediately available and they often require discovery; thus, according to Theory of Self-Relativity, all mindsets, except knowledge, must only be held as interim states-of-mind, until the supportive facts for those mindsets are found. Therefore, faith, hope, and beliefs, which are thoughts and mindsets that are not based on facts, should only be held as temporary mindsets, until supportive evidence is found, and thus, turns them into knowledge. This is the basis for skepticism, which is simply questioning the validity of a thought or a claim; unless or until supportive facts and evidence are identified.

A claim could be true, not-true, or false; and a thought could be factual or non-factual. However, the possible positions of thought that we could take on the path of discovering the supportive facts, or lack thereof, could be:

1. To believe for the thought or claim to be true.
2. To believe for the thought or claim to not be true; but also not necessarily false.
3. To not know either way if a thought or a claim is true or false, until supportive facts for the thought or claim are found. In other words, to have an "I don't know" mindset.

The reason Theory of Self-Relativity does not recommend proving falsehood is because:

a) One cannot prove a negative; therefore, one should not place one's Self in the position of trying to prove a negative.
b) The burden of proving a claim or a thought should be on the person making the claim or thinking the thought; not on others to prove the falsity of the claim or the thought.

This is why, in legal matters, the court does not pass judgment as "guilty" or "innocent;" the verdict is as "guilty" or "not-guilty." Verdicts are guilty or not-guilty because someone could actually be guilty but there might not have been enough evidence to render a guilty judgment, hence, the verdict was not-guilty, but it was not innocent.

"I don't know" is one of the most difficult mindsets for humans to carry; because, according to Theory of Self-Relativity, binary choices, and certainty, minimize mental anxiety and stress. Therefore, we continuously try to take a quick position of true or false regarding a proposition, a claim, or a thought, so that we can create certainty; and we often do so without having proper information and knowledge about the proposition, the claim, or the thought. In the absence of facts, we commonly do so, by using our feelings, because as discussed, emotional-thinking can provide a quicker comforting-mindset than the interim stage of not knowing, which requires time and effort to find the supportive facts. Therefore, unless the supportive facts to a mindset are known, it is best to not act or react to an unproven-claim, to an unsupported-thought, or to an unverified-proposition; until supportive facts are found or presented. This includes claims made by others, or thoughts of our own.

By nature, human-beings have difficulty in not knowing something, because not knowing creates uncertainty. This why, it is commonly difficult for people to simply say "I don't know." By speculating, by assuming, and by even falsely creating beliefs which are misrepresented as knowledge; people will come up with any explanation, in order to fill-in the knowledge-gap. And, while they are assuming or fabricating a cause or a reason for something, they will take that assumption and fabrication a step further, by filling the knowledge-gap through rationalization with false-beliefs, flawed-reasoning, and non-existent agents.

Additionally, by saying "I don't know," and by admitting lack of knowledge, many, due to their own low self-esteem, equate saying "I don't know" with "I'm stupid." They not only believe that by saying "I don't know" they would come across to others as being stupid; but their own weak sense of Self also believes that if they don't know, that means they are stupid. Such individuals are generally defensive in nature and lack introspection because to them "I don't know" is synonymous with "I'm an idiot," "I'm not good enough," and especially in personality-disordered people such as narcissists and borderlines, "I don't know" means "I am bad." This fear-of-the-unknown is another reason that causes many to concoct answers and opinions to fill-in the knowledge-gap; because to them, not knowing, is a reflection of a weak self-image and demonstration of their low self-worth.

I don't know means I don't know now; but by learning I might know later.

Many, because of their own personal-weaknesses and insecurities, think that not knowing or saying "I don't know" is a negative reflection of their Self. They do not consider that "I don't know" means "I don't know now;" but it could also mean that by learning, "I might know later." This is how we gain knowledge; by gaining information and by learning the facts about something we did not know before.

To not know is not shameful or wrong; therefore, we do not have to speculate or concoct an assumptive cause, a comforting reason, or an imaginary agent for our lack of knowledge. We do not have to fill the gap of not knowing by creating a nonsensical or nonfactual made-up answer. Even in legal settings, if we make up an answer, what we say could be used against us; thus, it is better to just say "I don't know," than to have to give an answer. Many do not realize that in a legal setting, making up something, even if it is innocently done to not look stupid, is actually lying. However, by saying "I don't know," they are actually being truthful.

When examined, in the absence of facts regarding a claim, the majority of mindsets should be in the form of interim fact-discovery state of "I don't know;" than as a state of fact-less "belief," assumed as knowledge. When the facts are discovered, the "I don't know" will turn to knowledge; and if after a while, no facts could be found, then the thought or the claim is most probably nonfactual, and should be re-examined or abandoned. There is nothing wrong with not knowing, because in order to know, we must first form a thought to verify it with facts. But, to simply remain in an unresolved assumptive mindset of belief, it is self-deceptive and lazy.

Assignment of purpose is also a cup-out for ditching responsibility. To bypass personal-responsibility onto other-agents, assigning purpose is a means of putting meaning on things and events in order to feel better. Instead of taking personal-responsibility by evaluating an unfavorable-outcome, and instead of taking action to change or improve the result; we accept unfavorable-outcomes as finality with the justification that something or someone else with a purpose caused it. Hence, we rationalize, that we could not control, nor could we improve that outcome; and we do so, for example, by stating, "God works in mysterious ways."

Purpose and meaning provide a sense of certainty, and certainty makes us feel safer.

To live without purpose and meaning is a scary proposition for many; this is why, we often look to explain purpose and meaning for things that do not have any purpose or meaning. This need to find an agent and to assign a purpose and meaning to everything is one of the main contributors to our faulty-thinking. By taking the easy path of assigning purpose and meaning externally, we are deviating away from finding the actual cause for that thing or event; because, the cause, as often is the case, is an uncomfortable or dislikable personal-attribute which does not have any externally ambiguous reason, purpose, or meaning.

As stated, everything has a cause, and commonly, everything has a reason; however, everything or every event does not need to have a purpose or a meaning. It is completely alright for things to not have purpose and meaning, because certain things just happen naturally without any purpose and meaning. If we want to improve our life and our existence, we do not need to know the purpose and meaning of something; but we should always try to find its cause. The-Universe, earthquakes, tsunamis, floods, or plagues did not occur because there was a purpose or a meaning behind them; they simply occurred as natural phenomenon obeying the laws-of-physics. Although there were causes, and commonly reasons behind these natural occurrences; however, there did not need to be a purpose or meaning behind them, nor was there a need for an intentional-agent with an desire or a purpose to cause these events.

Due to human knowledge or intellectual limitations, the cause or the reason behind certain things or certain events might not be obvious, or may never be discovered. If we cannot identify a cause or a reason, this does not mean we have to assign a nonfactual or a comforting reason in order for us to falsely support our need for purpose and meaning. To assign a perceived purpose and meaning, such as "God did it," or that it happened because "it was meant to be," is a form of logical-fallacy, flawed-reasoning, and nonfactual-thinking. Unless we can factually pinpoint to a cause, we should not concoct purpose and meaning, nor should we assign agency to it. It is alright for something to not have an intentional-agent that created a purpose and a meaning for it; just as it is alright for us to not know of the purpose or the meaning of something, even if one exists.

Cause and reason happen with or without an agent; but purpose and meaning require an intentional-agent.

We should try to "know" the cause and the reason for something, or for an event; but we must not base our existence on the unproven "belief" for its cause and reason. More importantly, we should not create a reason or an agent to support a nonfactual-belief for a non-existent purpose and meaning. This is why, it is important to look for the facts of the cause for a thing, rather than to look for the reason, the purpose, or the meaning for it. Once we find the facts for a cause, we can then look to see if there is a reason, a purpose, or a meaning behind it. We should find the reason for the purpose and the meaning by identifying the cause, not the other way around; we should not concoct a non-existent reason by assigning a purpose and meaning to it.

Purpose is personal; meaning is relative.

Since purpose and meaning are personal and relative to one's Self, we should not be looking to find purpose and meaning externally from other-people, or from other-things; we must create our own purpose and meaning in our life.

Purpose is neither found nor given; purpose is created from within.

Thinking factually and evaluating everything with reason will enable us to create the most favorable purpose and meaning for our own Self and for everyone else around us. While we might not always have control over the cause or the reason for something; however, we can try to influence the resulting effect of that thing. This could only happen if we look at the cause and the reason factually, and if we act based on what the evidence shows us. By looking at the facts of the cause, or even the reason for something, and by making changes to improve that thing; we can then create our own purpose and meaning for that thing.

No one and nothing can give us purpose and meaning, because we must create, cultivate, and grow our own purpose and meaning. The continuous need to externally find purpose and meaning for our life is itself a means of externalation. We externalate because creating a purpose and meaning in our own life requires us to take personal-responsibility by becoming the agent for our own change and improvement. Change and improvement not only require effort, but to know what we need to change and improve, we must self-reflect and introspect so that we can identify our weaknesses. As discussed, we externalate because self-reflection and introspection are generally uncomfortable and could even be painful; hence, instead of taking the responsibility to create our own purpose and meaning, we choose to look externally to give our life purpose and meaning through other-people or through other-things, while preoccupying and distracting our mind away from our own weaknesses and shortcomings.

However, by minimizing externalation and by increasing introspection, we will be able to identify our weaknesses that need improvement. Consequently, by taking action to change and improve our Self, we can, in-turn, create and improve the purpose and the meaning of our existence. Through introspection and self-improvement, we will learn to create our own purpose and meaning of life without needing someone else or something else to give us purpose and meaning. Purpose and meaning must be derived internally; not externally. We must not look for purpose and meaning; we must also create our own purpose and meaning.

You must become the creator of your own purpose and meaning.

Although we continuously strive to find purpose and meaning, which is commonly done by asking "why;" we should, instead, focus on finding the cause of something, which is done by asking "how." Regardless, we should always question everything, because that is the way to gain knowledge. The way to minimize the desire to find purpose and meaning is to learn to think factually; because factual-thinking prevents the mind from false pattern-seeking and incorrect pattern-recognition, in order to create a comforting-purpose for something.

You don't find your purpose; you create your purpose.

We must create our own purpose from within. Purpose, meaning, and goals, just like ambitions and dreams are ours to create; they are not out there for us to find. Purpose, meaning, and goals are not given to us by someone else or by something else; we give our Self purpose, and we must set our own goals in order for us to live a meaningful life. Although other-people and other-things can be motivational and could add to the quality of our life; getting motivated does not mean for us to look to find purpose from other-people or from other-things. Despite the fact that motivation could come from other sources:

a) We should not be looking for someone else to give us purpose; for example, a relationship-partner, a mentor, or a hero.

b) We should not be looking for something else to give us purpose; for example, nature, The-Universe, or material-possessions.

c) We should not be looking for the unproven, the paranormal, or the supernatural to give us purpose; for example, God, imaginary-patterns, or the afterlife.

Things such as nature and The-Universe exist because of natural and physical-laws; therefore, things in our lives happen because of natural and physical laws interacting with our Self and with everything else. Things such as natural-events happen because of a natural-cause and sometimes for a natural-reason, but they don't necessarily happen for any purpose or meaning; and especially not for a purpose or meaning solely intended for humans. The-Universe exists because of the laws-of-physics, and we exist because The-Universe and the laws-of-physics exist. Neither The-Universe nor nature exist nor were created for the purpose of our existence.

Humans exist without a purpose; however, we should live for our own self-created purpose.

Since The-Universe was not created for human-beings; therefore, human-beings are not special to The-Universe. The-Universe cannot and does not care about anything, nor does it care about us; it simply exists without a care and without a purpose or a meaning. Although The-Universe does not care any differently about us than it does about a rock on Mars, and although we are not special to The-Universe; we must remain special for our own Self. Despite the fact that we are not special to The-Universe, we can make Our-Universe special by creating our own purpose and meaning in our life. And when we learn to fulfill our own life, we can then give our Self the purpose to fulfill other-people's lives. We will do so not by giving others purpose and meaning, but by helping them create their own purpose and meaning in life. This is why:

Purpose is personal, meaning is relative.

To set our own purpose for a fulfilled and happy life, we must learn to look at things factually rather than emotionally. We must realize that it is alright for The-Universe to not have any purpose, and it is alright for our existence to not have any external meaning. When we recognize these facts, which at first, could be uncomfortable; we can then learn to give Our-Universe our own purpose and meaning, and we can teach others how to give Their-Universe their own purpose and meaning. To live a fulfilling life, we must create our own purpose, and we must set our own goals; because purpose and goals give us reasons to commit to change and improvement. Purpose and goals can be anything; from being successful, to being healthy, or by becoming a volunteer to charities, or to simply being content with our own Self. Because, the meaning of our life must come from our own self-created purpose and goals.

Purpose and goal are not found nor are they given; they are self-created.

When we seek to find purpose externally, we engage in externalation; which means, we shift our focus externally in order to avoid observing and recognizing our own personal weaknesses and deficiencies. This is why, Theory of Self-Relativity insists on self-focus, and on creating our own purpose in life from within. When we become the responsible agent to create our own purpose, we will then be able to recognize our weaknesses that require improvement.

An internally-derived purpose coincides with an improving Self.

As described throughout Theory of Self-Relativity, desire is one of the two non-negotiables for self-improvement. The other non-negotiable is introspection, which is our ability to self-inspect and to recognize our weaknesses. Therefore, if we do not have the desire to improve and to live a fulfilled life; no peptalk nor any other chest-pounding motivational system could help us.

As discussed, purpose must come from within, and purpose is not found from the outside nor is it given to us by others. We must create our own purpose, because fulfilling our purpose will make our dreams come true. When we desire to improve, we must create a purpose, we must set a goal, and we should dream a dream; because our purpose will lead us to our goal, and our goal will lead us to our dream.

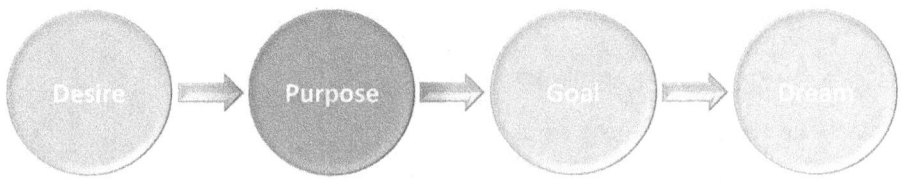

As long as we have a purpose, we can set a goal, and we can even dream a dream. As we reach our goal, this newly achieved goal gets added to our purpose, and our purpose becomes bigger. Subsequently, our initial dream becomes our next goal, and we move to dream a new dream. As our dreams become our next goals and as we fulfill each goal, our life's purpose gets bigger, and our life's meaning becomes richer. Goals and dreams are the best way to create, replenish, and increase our purpose, as we move forward in time, and as we go through life.

As we make our purpose in life bigger; the meaning of our life becomes richer.

Therefore:

To be fulfilled, don't just dream big; make your purpose bigger.

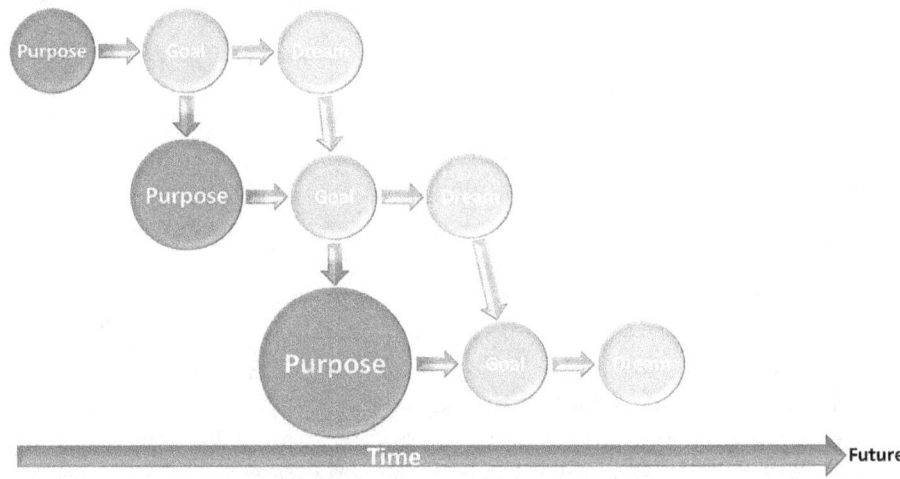

Dreams are in the Future...Purpose is in the Present

This is why, to continuously evolve our process of self-improvement:

1. We must create a purpose
2. We must set a goal
3. We must dream a dream

Hence, as we move forward in our life "time":

1. We accomplish our purpose
2. We achieve our goals
3. We reach our dreams

Creating our own purpose, by setting and by reaching our goals and dreams, gives our life meaning.

To give your life meaning, create your purpose, set your goals, and reach your dreams.

We must always have something to look forward to, such as a purpose or a goal, because purpose and goals give our life meaning. This could only be set and achieved by us, and not by others. While others can help to motivate us, personal-drive, and motivation, could only come from within. This is why, constant change and improvement are integral to living a fulfilled life.

Change or you'll be changed!

Theory of Self-Relativity, via its Cognitive-Cognition-Technique, teaches us how to bring the focus onto our own Self, and to live the most realistic and the strongest self-focused life possible. But to do so, we must first learn to control our feelings. Therefore, instead of thinking emotionally, we must learn to think factually. Factual-thinking enables us to set realistic purpose, with achievable goals, and attainable dreams. It is only then that our goals and dreams will not be based on fabricated comforting-beliefs; but they will be based on factual-reality.

Theory of Self-Relativity gives us the tools to identify our cluttered-thoughts that are disabling us from moving forward. By identifying our thoughts and by uncluttering our thinking-system, we can cultivate our action-skills as we bring the focus to our productive and constructive thoughts. When our purpose in life is based on how reality is and not based on how we want reality to be; we can then set goals that are realistically attainable, and we can set our Self on the path of experiencing less setbacks and more favorable outcomes.

To be fulfilled, deal with reality as is and not as you want it to be.

When we deal with reality as reality is, we will then be able to create and guide our purpose and meaning in life in syn with reality; therefore, we will be able to achieve our goals and dreams with a higher probability.

The ultimate formula for succeeding in our achievements is to start with a desire and by taking the initiative to create our own purpose. Once we create our purpose, we can then follow through to reach our goals, and continue persisting to see our dreams come true. This is how we give meaning to our life.

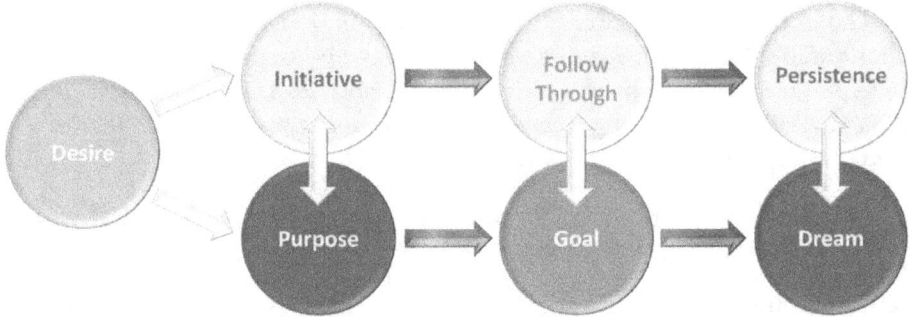

Your dreams don't have to be imaginary; your dreams can become your purpose in life.

IX.
Cognitive-Dissonance & Procrastination

The need to feel good versus the necessity to think well is a core factor that inhibits change and blocks self-improvement.

As discussed throughout Theory of Self-Relativity, emotional-rationalization, and especially, placebo-thinking causes us to create false-patterns, fallacious-thoughts, and flawed-reasonings that are not based on how things are but they are based on how we want things to be. Instead of adapting our feelings to facts, we continuously try to adapt facts to our feelings so that we can avoid pain, we can feel good, or at the minimum, we can feel less-bad at any given moment. Since creating false-thoughts and flawed-reasoning goes against factual-reality; our mind is continuously battling to maintain our fallacious-thoughts and flawed-reasoning in lieu of conflicting and even contradictory evidence. This mental-state of holding at least two conflicting or contradictory thoughts or beliefs simultaneously is known as *"Cognitive-Dissonance."*

Theory of Self-Relativity defines "cognitive-dissonance" as "the mental-state of holding two or more conflicting-thoughts simultaneously."

Cognitive-dissonance is hallmarked by confusion, over-analysis, constant-justification, rationalization, and by trying to make sense of something that just does not seem to make sense. Cognitive-dissonance occurs when we either do not have the facts and evidence; or more commonly, when we choose to deny, and especially, ignore the facts and evidence which are conflicting with or are contradictory to our comforting and preferred nonfactual-thoughts and false-beliefs.

The primary cause of cognitive-dissonance is when we allow our emotional-thinking to conflict with our factual-thinking.

Cognitive-dissonance is associated with nonfactual-thinking and emotional-reasoning, and it results from our desire to want to avoid pain, to feel good, or at the minimum, to feel less-bad; instead of facing and accepting the uncomfortable truth. Cognitive-dissonance occurs when we consciously or nonconsciously try to convince our Self that things are how we want them to be, rather than accepting how things really are. We do so by ignoring or by explaining away conflicting or contradictory evidence which are clearly against our feel-good thoughts and comforting-beliefs. Cognitive-dissonance could also occur when, through avoidance, ignorance, or denial, we choose to abstain from seeking facts and evidence; or when we choose to explain away the dislikable evidence so that we can continue to hold on to our fallacious but comforting-thoughts and beliefs.

Simply stated:

Cognitive-dissonance occurs when our mind clashes with reality.

The more and the longer we are invested in something, the harder it is for us to give it up, even in the face of contradictory facts and evidence. This is even more applicable when we know that giving up our feel-good thoughts or comforting-beliefs is going to affect us negatively. Hence, cognitive-dissonance occurs when our likable-thoughts and comforting-beliefs are contradictory to the evidence of how reality is relative to those thoughts and belief. Thus, cognitive-dissonance often creates anxiety and even stress if held for a long time, because our comforting-thoughts and beliefs are clashing with factual-reality. Cognitive-dissonance is commonly associated with misinformation, lack of information, and often with lies and deceptions. Such lies could be deceptions by others or deceptions caused by our own Self. Theory of Self-Relativity recognizes lack of self-awareness, inability to introspect, and emotional-rationalization through placebo-thinking, as primary causes of cognitive-dissonance.

Causes of Cognitive-Dissonance

- Misinformation
- Lack of Information
- Lies & Deception
- Lack of Self-Awareness
- Lack of Introspection
- Emotional-Rationalization (Placebo-Thinking)

Theory of Self-Relativity categorizes cognitive-dissonance binarily:

1. **Internal-Dissonance:** Occurs when we choose to ignore facts or when we choose to convince, justify, or lie to our own Self of how we want reality to be, rather than accepting how reality actually is. For example, we suspect that our partner is cheating on us; yet, we choose to not pursue further discovery of facts, or we choose to ignore the facts which indicate our partner is being unfaithful. In other words, we would rather ignore the facts or abstain from further discovery of facts so that we do not have to face the painful truth of realizing that our partner is being unfaithful. Such a situation will create cognitive-dissonance, because what we want to believe, is not how things really are. This is why, Theory of Self-Relativity emphasizes that "Self-Deception" is one of the 10-Enemies of Self-Improvement.

2. **External-Dissonance:** Occurs when others convince, justify, or lie to us of how they want us to believe reality is, rather than how reality actually is. Often, the reality which others try to convince us of, is a self-serving reality for them. For example, we suspect that our partner is cheating on us and we also have probable cause to believe that they are doing so. However, when confronting our partner, we would rather believe the lies that they tell us about not being a cheater, rather than us concluding that they are cheating; even when the evidence clearly indicates that they are being unfaithful.

In the aforementioned examples, cognitive-dissonance could occur, because in our mind, we suspect or know that our partner is cheating on us; however, accepting the fact that we are being cheated on is painfully difficult. Therefore, we choose to convince our Self to the contrary, by denying or by ignoring any such evidence. Our mind, by recognizing the signs and evidence, wants to constantly protect us by thinking about the potential of our partner cheating on us; however, because being cheated on by someone that we love is often a painful reality to accept, we try to justify to our Self that maybe our partner is not cheating on us. We do so, because we want to hold onto the comfort of the relationship; but most importantly, we do so, because we want to avoid the discomfort of having to make a difficult change. As stated throughout Theory of Self-Relativity:

We often think things and we do things not because they are good for us; but because they make us feel good.

Cognitive-dissonance is caused by lack of understanding or by denying of facts, and it is commonly associated with lies and misinformation. Since the factual-truth is often painful to accept; we sometimes choose to ignore the facts and evidence by either believing the lies that make us feel better, or by choosing to fabricate mistruths so that we can hold onto our preferred false-thoughts and comforting-beliefs.

Feelings are not facts, and in trying to fabricate alternative-facts based on our preferred feelings, we are creating a false-reality which clashes with factual-reality in the form of cognitive-dissonance. Since cognitive-dissonance occurs as a result of us holding two or more conflicting or contradictory thoughts; therefore, at least one or all of our dissonant-thoughts are wrong. Cognitive-dissonance is most especially present in self-deception; this means we experience cognitive-dissonance when we lie to our own Self by ignoring and by denying reality, or by creating fallacious-thoughts in order to fit our thoughts to our desired-feelings, through rationalization and justification. Cognitive-dissonance is also quite prevalent in interpersonal-relationships, especially romantic-relationships. This is why, cognitive-dissonance is almost always present in difficult, high-conflict, and deceptive-relationships.

A common symptom of cognitive-dissonance is constant-justification and over-analysis. Constant-justification enables people to continue carrying their comforting but conflicting thoughts, by denying the inconvenient or uncomfortable evidence. Cognitive-dissonance is central to wishful-thinking and it is associated with situations where the urge to "want things to be a certain way" overrides the consideration of "how things actually are." Anytime we feel confused, or when we feel that we are over-analyzing or justifying too much; that is usually a sign of a problem associated with contradictory or conflicting thoughts. Confusion, constant-justification, and over-analysis are signs of contradictory and conflicting thoughts associated with deception; either in the form of self-deception or deception by others. Because, as discussed throughout Theory of Self-Relativity:

Lies and deceptions, regardless of the source of the deception, are rooted in persuading the deceived.

Constant-justification and over-analysis are the result of confusion and incompatibility of thoughts. They are also a sign of us trying to reason why some things are not the way we want them to be. Constant-justification and over-analysis are often associated with emotional-thinking and with our inability to make a decision to change or eliminate a belief or a thought. Constant-justification and over-analysis are also associated with our inability to end a conflicting-relationship. Constant-justification and over-analysis are like trying to force the square-peg of feelings into the round-hole of facts.

When despite contrary evidence, we try to constantly convince our Self that something is the way we want it to be; we are deceiving our Self by changing the facts, by ignoring the facts, or by creating new false-facts in order to keep our desired-feelings in place. Constant-justification and over-analysis are often signs of dissonance, because our fallacious-thoughts are clashing with factual-reality. However, as difficult as it may be to accept factual-reality, we can minimize the necessity for constant-justification and over-analysis by seeking facts and by thinking factually. When we seek facts or when we think and make decisions based on facts; constant-justification and over-analysis will become unnecessary, because we would then know the facts and we will accept them as they are. When we accept the facts, we will not need to constantly justify how things are, because as stated; facts are not open to interpretation or manipulation.

As discussed throughout Theory of Self-Relativity, our primitive-mind, whose primary role is to keep us safe, reacts quickly and impulsively in order to minimize danger and negativity; therefore, majority of our quick and hasty actions are taken without being able to verify their underlying facts. This is why, we use pattern-seeking, pattern-recognition, and other quick-thinking strategies to quickly get away from potential danger; hence, the reason we often make mistakes in recognizing and responding to reality. For primitive-humans, getting away from danger was more important than being right; because if they got away from danger, they lived another day, but if they tried to verify the facts, they could have become a prey.

However, in the modern times, we do not face the same primitive-dangers; yet our primitive-mind reacts to negativity in the same way in order to keep us safe. Since in the modern-times, our primitive-mind does not have primitive-dangers to react to; it still reacts to other negativity and discomfort just as strongly, because pain and negativity are commonly associated with threats and danger. Since negativity feels undesirable and uncomfortable; by acting quickly to get away from negativity, we react to our strongest undesirable-negativities the same way that we would have reacted to primitive-dangers. In other words, we react to modern-negativities similarly as we would have reacted to primitive-dangers. Consequently, we often react to the strongest non-threatening dislikable-realities more severely than we should.

In the absence of primitive-dangers, our primitive-mind reacts to the strongest of our modern-negativities as if they were primitive-dangers.

This is why, for example, negativities that are troubling a wealthy person, which would be a non-issue for the poor; are as troubling and as emotionally-negative to the wealthy, as it would be for the poor to not have the next meal to eat. Although the troubles of the wealthy might seem petty compared to the real problems that poor people face; in the absence of primitive-dangers, if one is not self-aware, the primitive-mind could treat the most negative-emotions of the person as if they were life-threatening dangers. This is why, people who live more comfortable lifestyles tend to have more drama associated with their lives.

We try to get away from modern-negativity and dislikeable-reality in one of two ways:

1. **Fight-or-Flight:** In order to resolve or to distance our Self from negativity quickly, we impulsively react to negativity as if it were a primitive-danger.
2. **Freeze or Procrastination:** We try to not react to negativity, by ignoring or by denying it.

If we don't react to a negativities as if they were primitive-dangers, we react to dislikeable and uncomfortable truths by ignoring or by justification that the cause of our negativity is not what it really is. We change what is to what we want it to be, in order to avoid that negativity, so that we will not feel as bad. In other words, we change our thinking so that we can improve how we feel. Therefore, by trying to fit facts to our feelings instead of fitting our feelings to facts, we induce and prolong our state of cognitive-dissonance.

By changing our perception of reality, or by denying and by ignoring the reality from what it is to what we want it to be; we in-turn, abstain from having to face the dislike of dealing with the uncomfortable or painful reality. Despite the fact that we know that the square-peg of feelings will not fit into the round-hole of facts; we continue to justify that maybe if we try hard enough, and if we give it enough time, we will at a later time find a way to fit the square-peg of feelings into the round-hole of facts. Through justification and rationalization, we try to buy ourselves time to postpone facing the inevitable reality that the square-peg of feelings will never fit into the round-hole of facts; hence, we prolong our state of cognitive-dissonance.

We ignore and deny facts, often by giving our Self false-hope and unsubstantiated-faith, in order to feel good at that moment; because dealing with facts and taking action to change them is uncomfortable, and it requires effort and dedication of time. We try to achieve instant-gratification, even when we know deep inside, that the negativity which we are avoiding will catch up with us at a later time. Our desire for gratification is instant; however, not facing the inconvenient reality is a delay defense-mechanism. By constantly justifying to our Self that things are not as bad, we go as far as creating hope, faith, and beliefs, to convince our Self that the square-peg of feelings is or will be compatible with the round-hole of facts.

Cognitive-dissonance, which is the state of holding two or more conflicting or contradictory thoughts at a given time, arises when we try to convince and justify to our Self that reality is not what it is, but reality is what we want it to be. When we change our perception of reality by convincing and by justifying to our Self that the truth is different than the uncomfortable-truth or the dislikable-reality that we are facing; our mind goes into cognitive-dissonance. Likewise, we cause cognitive-dissonance when we ignore or deny the dislikable-facts and evidence associated with reality, in order to abstain from having to take difficult actions to change the reality. Furthermore, even when we are forced to accept reality the way it is; we often delay and postpone taking action to change it so that we can abstain from committing to the undesirable process of change. Altogether, instead of facing and resolving the uncomfortable causes of our cognitive-dissonance, we often choose to not experience cognitive-dissonance by convincing, justifying, ignoring, denying, or by procrastinating dealing with the causes of our dissonance.

Procrastination is a means of avoiding cognitive-dissonance without resolving the causes of the dissonance.

The dissonance and confusion which are generated from our desire to feel good versus evaluating what the facts are showing us, arise from our false and deceptive longing for the square-peg of our feelings to fit into the round-hole of facts. Since the square-peg will never fit the round-hole, we constantly try to give ourselves hope, by justifying that the peg will eventually fit into the hole. We try to convince our Self that we will eventually find a way to fit the square-peg into the round-hole, because that is how we want things to be. We do so all in the name of avoiding and not facing the fact that how we want to feel, is incompatible with how we should feel. In other words, we go through these self-deceptive tactics to perceive reality to be the way we want it to be, rather than to accept reality the way it really is, in order to justify and hold on to our comforting-feelings.

This is how faith, hope, and beliefs are created. They are created as a result of people wanting for something to be a certain way because it makes them feel good; rather than to accept the way certain things are regardless of how it makes them feel. For example, the belief that there is life after death is comforting despite the fact that there has been no evidence of such possibility. Although it makes many feel good to believe existence continues after death because that is how many want things to be; there is no scientific evidence for the afterlife. On the contrary, all facts and evidence indicate no such thing is possible. The square-peg of wanting life to continue after death is obviously not going to fit into the round-hole of facts that indicate our existence is as a result of our physical-body's functions. Once the physical-body stops functioning; life ceases to exist. This is why, we have survival-instincts, not dying-instincts; because instinctually we know we must survive life, however, intellectually we manipulate our Self into believing in comforting manmade beliefs. No matter how we try to rationalize, and no matter what justifications, false-reasonings, and fallacious-beliefs we concoct; all evidence and facts point to life ending at the time of death.

Faith, hope, and beliefs are some of the most common causes of cognitive-dissonance.

Despite realizing that the square-peg of our feelings of believing in afterlife is not going to fit the round-hole of the facts that the afterlife is highly unlikely; by believing in nonfactual-things in order to feel better, we therefore create dissonance in our mind. If there is an afterlife, then why do we cry when someone dies; we should be happy for them that they have embarked into their eternal-life. Likewise, if there is an afterlife, why are we scared of dying? The reason for being sad of someone's passing or for being scared of dying is because we know that the facts indicate there is no afterlife; however, we choose to believe that there is life after death because it is comforting, hence, it makes us feel good to believe.

In the absence of facts, we can fit any belief into our feelings.

When a false-belief such as the afterlife clashes with factual-thoughts, we experience cognitive-dissonance; because a belief unlike knowledge is a thought that has no supportive evidence. Believing that there is afterlife, which makes us feel good, is a form of rationalization through placebo-thinking. By believing in afterlife, we use our intellect to concoct fallacies, in order to comfort our feelings. Humans are the only animals that are aware of their mortality and that is because of our higher intelligence. However, the same intelligence double-edged sword that we use to understand and prolong our mortality; we use it to concoct false-thoughts and fallacious-beliefs so that the dislikable-truth would be more to our liking.

Cognitive-dissonance is as a result of the conflicting applications of our intellect.

Cognitive-dissonance caused by our placebo-thinking is not only the underlying cause of constant-justification and over-analysis, but it is also the cause of our procrastination. Instead of facing the reality that the square-peg of feelings and the round-hole of facts are incompatible; we not only justify why they should be compatible, but more commonly, we choose to postpone evaluating and dealing with this incompatibility to a later time. By falsely reasoning, justifying, and convincing our Self that we will resolve the issue at a later time; we procrastinate facing and resolving the dislikable truth that is before us. This procrastination helps us to hang on to our comforting false-belief by avoiding dealing with the factual-reality that the square-peg and the round-hole are incompatible. Procrastination causes us to continue our cognitive-dissonance without resolving the causes of the dissonance.

Procrastination is a means of avoiding cognitive-dissonance without resolving the causes of the dissonance.

We procrastinate tasks that are disliked and undesirable, because if we do not procrastinate, we would have to face the dislikable-truth. Procrastination allows us to fallaciously buy our Self time from dealing with the dislikable-truth. Procrastination allows us to bury our cognitive-dissonance by delaying the inevitable. This is why, we rarely procrastinate a gratifying or pleasant task, but we would procrastinate a dislikable-task, in order to avoid feeling dislike, discomfort, or negativity.

We rarely procrastinate the likable; we only procrastinate the dislikable.

Doing something requires a person to make a change, and changing something requires self-reflection and introspection to face facts. Facing facts is often an emotionally difficult task because facts that require change are often uncomfortable to deal with; hence, it is easier to fool our Self by thinking about changing at a later time, than it is to actually commit to change at that moment. By postponing dealing with the issue to a later time and by leaving the unresolved matter open; we avoid feeling bad at that moment. By postponing dealing with the dislikable and uncomfortable facts, we make our Self avoid pain, we try to feel better, or at the minimum, we attempt to make our Self feel not as bad as we would have felt had we faced the issue at hand. Regardless, no matter how we ignore, deny, or delay dealing with the dislikable-realty; the cognitive-dissonance will remain unresolved.

Our need to feel good versus the necessity to think well is a core factor that inhibits change and blocks self-improvement.

Procrastination is a form of "reverse" instant-gratification, and it is done so to delay dealing with undesirable facts; instead of quickly feeling better. In other words, procrastination is a disguised form of externalation that is engaged via placebo-thinking and motivated-reasoning.

Procrastination is reverse-gratification; because procrastination delays feeling bad, instead of quickly feeling better.

According to Theory of Self-Relativity, procrastination is as a result of place-bo-thinking; because we choose to deal with unpleasant factual-thoughts at a later time, in order to maintain our false but comforting-thoughts and beliefs momentarily. Although procrastination temporarily softens the stressful effects of cognitive-dissonance; in the long-term, procrastination keeps cognitive-dissonance alive.

As defined throughout Theory of Self-Relativity, "placebo-thinking" is "creating comforting thoughts, reasons, and rationalizations, in order to avoid pain, to feel good, or at the minimum, to feel less-bad."

By thinking emotionally, by reasoning fallaciously, and by falsely justifying to our Self that we will revisit an unresolved matter at a later time; we try to avoid the dislike or the pain of facing and accepting a dislikable reality. To delay dealing with dislikable reality, we even go as far as concocting beliefs such as "time will solve everything" or "everything will be fine;" in order to shift the responsibility away from us, because we are unwilling to commit to difficult action to change things. When we abstain or refuse from seeing reality the way reality is, we then surrender being in control of our life; therefore, we make our existence dependent and reliant on others or on chance. When we lose control over our life's matters, by lessening our ability to make decisions for our own Self, we become more dependent and reliant on other-people or on other-things; including allowing chance, to dictate how our life will move forward.

Decisions and resolutions made by others or left to chance; are not going to be as favorable as decisions and actions you make for your Self.

This is why, procrastination will often lead to results that are unfavorable to the way we would have wanted an outcome to be. The continuous clash of knowing things are not the way we want them to be but refusing to make a change to create more favorable results, is how cognitive-dissonance lingers on and how we engage in procrastination. Cognitive-dissonance is as a result of us wanting to hang on to false-thoughts and fallacious-beliefs in order to feel good; and procrastination enables us to prolong staying with these false-thoughts and fallacious-beliefs so that we can continue feeling better temporarily, via the rationalization of our incorrect thoughts that support our desired-feelings.

Theory of Self-Relativity defines "procrastination" as "postponing or delaying something, to avoid the dislikeable feelings of dealing with that thing."

Cognitive-dissonance and procrastination are rooted in confusion, constant-justification, and over-analysis. Cognitive-dissonance and procrastination are different means of achieving the same result of trying to avoid pain, to feel good, or at the minimum, to feel less-bad at a given moment. While cognitive-dissonance is often less-conscious, procrastination is generally higher up on the consciousness level. Cognitive-dissonance is associated more with lack of awareness, denial, and ignorance, which may never lead to action; while, procrastination is associated with delay of action. Cognitive-dissonance uses rationalization through justification to maintain the comforting placebo-thoughts; whereas, procrastination uses reasoning to delay the undesired action which is required to resolve or eliminate these thoughts.

Cognitive-dissonance results from not wanting to face facts, while procrastination results from not wanting to deal with facts.

Cognitive-Dissonance	Procrastination
Self-Deception	Self-Deception
Avoidance-Mindset	Delay-Mindset
Denying & Ignoring Facts	Delay Dealing with Facts
Leads to Procrastination	Prolongs Cognitive-Dissonance
Less Conscious	Higher-up in Consciousness
Maintains False-Thoughts	Prolongs False-Thoughts
Cognitive & Emotional	Cognitive, Emotional & Behavioral
Inaction	Inaction or Delay of Action
Placebo-Thinking	Placebo-Thinking
Confusion	Rationalization
Constant-Justification	Reasoning
Over-Analysis	Delay of Resolution

Therefore, according to Theory of Self-Relativity, cognitive-dissonance is as a result of avoidance-mechanism; while procrastination, which prolongs cognitive-dissonance, is as a result of delay-mechanism. Cognitive-dissonance and procrastination are mental-states which are associated with self-deception. By maintaining desired and comfortable placebo-thoughts, in lieu of conflicting and contradictory facts and evidence, and by delaying course of action in resolving or eliminating these comforting yet fallacious-thoughts; we self-deceive so that we can avoid or delay feeling bad.

Cognitive-dissonance is caused by avoiding negativity, while procrastination tries to delay negativity.

When we procrastinate, we often know what needs to be corrected; therefore, some awareness and introspection has gone into it. However, despite having faced the uncomfortable or even painful reality of what needs to be improved, we still choose to delay the action because facing and dealing with the negativity is undesired, dislikable, and even, painful. Until and unless we put in the effort to change what needs to be changed, we will continuously have to live with the negative-feelings associated with it; hence, by procrastinating, we choose to delay and distract our Self from feeling the discomfort and pain of having to deal with the dislikable or difficult thing that needs to be changed.

Even if we manage to minimize procrastination, we still find another way of delaying change, in the name of "perfection." According to Theory of Self-Relativity, perfection is a deceptively fancy way of procrastination. We commonly engage in setting and achieving perfection, to once again, avoid or delay facing the uncomfortable process of change. Hence, according to Theory of Self-Relativity, perfection, itself, is the tail-end of procrastination. In the name of perfection, we often choose to set unachievable milestones which give us the excuse to avoid dealing with the uncomfortable or painful responsibility that the change brings about. By chasing unachievable perfection, we nonconsciously try to delay taking the responsibility that finalization of change brings about. Since change is difficult, we engage in procrastination and perfection in order to avoid dealing with the uncomfortable and painful process of change. Perfection, just like procrastination, delays resolution of cognitive-dissonance.

Furthermore, procrastination and perfection are not only rooted in trying to avoid dealing with uncomfortable issues that need to be changed; but procrastination and perfection are also associated with the fear-of-failure. By procrastinating and by setting unending perfection parameters, we avoid finalization of change, because the result of change could be unfavorable or unpopular. By fearing failure, we choose to procrastinate and set ever-changing perfection parameters so that we will not have to possibly deal with failure. In addition to not wanting to face uncomfortable facts, fear-of-failure is a common contributory factor to procrastination and perfection.

Procrastination and perfection are rooted in the fear of rejection, fear of not being good enough, or fear of failure.

Perfectionists and procrastinators have difficulty initiating, adapting, and evolving with situations and with the times, because they like to stay within their comfort-zone. This is why, perfectionists and procrastinators are often biased with their thoughts and perspectives as they are resistant to change. Perfectionists and procrastinators try to change as an event, rather than improve within the process; because, an event minimizes their exposure to variables. Therefore, perfectionists and procrastinators are usually black-and-white thinkers, and they approach people and situations in an all-or-none format. However, to minimize procrastination and perfection, we must learn to think factually, and we must understand that change and evolution are normal processes of our ongoing-existence.

Instead of trying to achieve perfection with a final-event, continuously improve the outcomes within the ongoing-process.

Procrastination and perfection diminish as we learn to strengthen our inner-self. When we learn to adapt and be unbiased, that is when we can implement the best format of change; however, to do so, we must learn to observe our own Self and our relativity with everything and with everyone else based on facts, and not based on how we want reality to be.

To change, you must remain unbiased and adaptable.

Confusion, constant-justification, and rationalization are discussed throughout Theory of Self-Relativity in variety of situations, especially relative to interpersonal-relationships. Confusion, justification, rationalization, placebo-thinking, and as a whole, cognitive-dissonance, are all hallmarks of relationships; especially personal-relationships and romantic-relationships with high-conflict and Cluster-B personality-disordered individuals such as those involving narcissists and borderline-personality-disordered partners. The main reason for confusion, justification, and cognitive-dissonance being present in relationships involving narcissists and borderlines is because such relationships almost always include some kind of deception; either self-created by one's own Self, or deployed by the partner in the relationship.

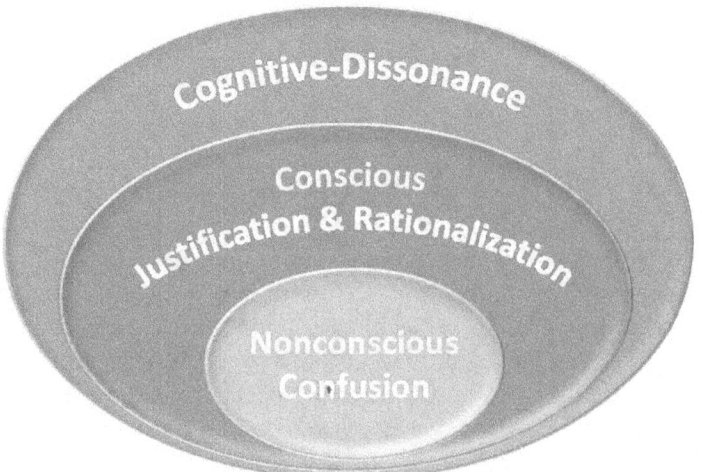

Confusion happens on a nonconscious level; however, justification and rationalization occur at higher levels of consciousness. It is this unrealized connection between the nonconscious and the conscious levels of our consciousness that contributes to our inability to recognize the incorrect and conflicting thoughts that we commonly engage in. It is this unrealized connection of holding contradictory or conflicting thoughts at different levels of our consciousness that causes our cognitive-dissonance.

Cognitive-dissonance is a symptom of our placebo-thoughts clashing with factual-reality.

This is why, recognizing and eliminating cognitive-dissonance is integral to self-improvement. Confusion, constant-justification, and over-analysis through rationalization, are hallmarks of cognitive-dissonance; and they are the precursors for procrastination, perfection, and other delay-mechanisms.

Therefore, instead of ignoring and avoiding the causes of our dissonance, we should try to become aware that we are engaging in such mindsets. When we self-reflect and become aware, we will then be able to examine the facts associated with our dissonance; hence, we will be able to resolve or eliminate these causes. We must learn to become aware of and to recognize our dissonance in order for us to realize that the square-peg of our desired-feelings is not fitting into the round-hole of factual-reality; not-even, through our relentless attempts of rationalization and self-deception. If we do not do anything about our placebo-thinking and its resulting dissonance, or if we push too hard to live in denial and ignorance; the square-peg of comforting cover-ups will eventually break in our attempts of trying to fit it into the incompatible round hole of factual-reality.

Additionally, cognitive-dissonance is also commonly associated with confirmation-bias, motivated-reasoning, and even with rumination. When we are in a state of cognitive-dissonance, rather than adapting our thoughts and beliefs to the evidence, we engage in confirmation-bias and motivated-reasoning, in order to justify our false-thoughts and comforting-beliefs. Instead of using facts and evidence to reach a conclusion; we establish a desired conclusion and then work backwards to support the conclusion by any means possible.

Confirmation-bias fits facts to thoughts, rather than fitting thoughts to facts.

To Summarize:

Placebo-thinking fits facts to feelings; confirmation-bias fits facts to thoughts.

Confirmation-bias and cognitive-dissonance result from other cognitive defense-mechanisms that we create in order to make us observe things the way we want them to be, rather than to observe and deal with them the way they really are. Cognitive-dissonance occurs when emotional-thinking, especially placebo-thinking, which is affiliated with cognitive-biases, clashes with facts. Our mind creates confirmation-biases to rationalize our desired-feelings so that we can feel good; however, this, almost always, leads to cognitive-dissonance and confusion.

Confusion is a hallmark of cognitive-dissonance.

Confusion is one of the most common side-effects of cognitive-dissonance, especially when implemented intentionally by someone else. As discussed, quite commonly in interpersonal-relationships, especially those involving personality-disordered individuals such as narcissists, borderlines, and psychopaths; cognitive-dissonance creates inconsistency and confusion for the victim and could have profound long-term psychological effects. In such instances, cognitive-dissonance is commonly associated with deceptive and often intentionally misleading behaviors such as gaslighting and crazy-making. As is often the case, it is difficult to abstain from self-deception; therefore, awareness and understanding of how we think is critically important for our self-improvement. It becomes even more difficult to be aware of and to stop deceptive behavior when dealing with high-conflict and manipulative people; hence why, in our interactions with high-conflict people, we will almost always experience cognitive-dissonance.

High-conflict individuals do not like facts, because facts shatter their false sense of Self and the false reality that they live in and portray to others. Additionally, facts and evidence prove them wrong, and in order for them to have the upper hand in a relationship, they must be in control; which means they cannot be wrong. Such control is often instilled through lies and deceptions, and the creation of cognitive-dissonance on their partner, in order to prevent the exposure of the false-reality that these high-conflicts are portraying. Cognitive-dissonance creates confusion, and confusion creates doubt, which puts the victim in a low self-esteemed and submissive position. This is why, interacting with a high-conflict person is often referred to as "crazy-making;" because, the confusion and self-doubt created by cognitive-dissonance distorts the victim's sense of reality.

High-conflict individuals, such as narcissists and sociopaths, are not only masters of deception, but they are also masters of self-deception; because their default-state-of-mind is to deny facts. They not only deny facts and reality that is not to their benefit, but they also deny other-people's facts and realities in lieu of overwhelming evidence. When someone is involved with a high-conflict person, and especially if that person is a people-pleaser or a codependent, which is often the case for high-conflict partners; the individual's tendency and goal is to make the relationship work smoothly. By being determined to keep the relationship peaceful, those involved with high-conflicts often suffer from cognitive-dissonance, because high-conflict individuals are not interested in facts. High-conflicts deny facts and reality via gaslighting and other deceptive tactics, by making the target doubt one's sense of reality. High-conflicts commonly do so by changing history, by rewriting history, and by deviating away from the subject of the conflict; in order to send the target after a wild goose chase.

Theory of Self-Relativity defines "gaslighting" also known as "crazy-making" as "an intentional behavior to manipulate someone into questioning one's own memory, perception, and even, one's own sanity."

Gaslighting uses persistent-denial, misdirection, contradiction, and lying, in order to destabilize the target and delegitimize the target's memory and sense of reality. Gaslighting and crazy-making are predatory tactics commonly used by personality-disordered individuals such as narcissistic-personality-disordered (NPD) individuals, borderline personality-disordered (BPD) individuals; as well as by sociopaths. Gaslighting is an intentionally abusive behavior because it affects a victim negatively for the personal agenda of the manipulator. Gaslighting is intended to gain control over the victim by making the victim question their own reality and to doubt their own sanity.

Gaslighting causes confusion and cognitive-dissonance by creating inconsistencies for the victim, and it has profound long-term psychological effects on the gaslighted person. As exampled before, one catches one's partner cheating with another person but the partner tries to convince the cheated that the cheating did not actually happen. From the cheated partner's perspective, because accepting that being cheated on is painful, the cheated becomes more open to accepting the lies of the cheating partner. In this example, despite the fact that the gaslighting victim is aware of being cheated on; the cheated tries as hard as possible to ignore the facts, in order to avoid making the painful choice of having to walk out of the relationship. Thereby, the gaslighting victim constantly overthinks, justifies, and ruminates over the events and actions of the cheater, hoping to find a conciliatory medium to keep the status-quo going. The desire to ignore and deny reality in order to avoid feeling pain is so strong, that despite the victim's own observation of reality, the cheated chooses to second-guess what is real and what is not.

Gaslighting and crazy-making is a form of abuse.

Gaslighting and crazy-making are intentional acts with the intent to create cognitive-dissonance for the victim; because cognitive-dissonance creates confusion, which in-turn, enables the subject to be controlled.

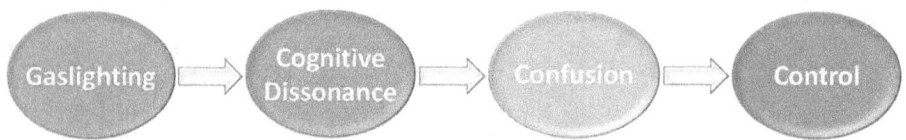

Self-improvement and self-reliance are integral in minimizing dependency and control by a manipulative abuser. Minimizing dependency in such relationships could only be achieved through self-awareness and by distancing one's Self from the abuser. The abuser is rendered helpless when the victim stops listening to and dealing with the abuser; and instead, the victim seeks for facts in order to confirm one's own sense of reality.

Since tactics such as gaslighting are subtle and are implemented over a long period of time; self-awareness through factual-thinking is important in breaking this cycle. To eliminate the potential for abuse, one must self-improve; hence, one must minimize dependency and reliance on others by becoming self-sufficient and by setting and enforcing borders and boundaries.

Cognitive-dissonance, whether it is caused by others or it is self-inflicted, could be eliminated when one learns to think factually. By fact-checking our thoughts and our interactions with others; we will not only be able to minimize confusion, but we will also be able to eliminate cognitive-dissonance, and in-turn, we will abstain from getting involved in controlling and abusive relationships.

Factual-thinking is not just about ensuring that our thoughts are fact-based. Factual-thinking also enables us to ensure that what others are thinking and portraying is also based on facts and evidence. Whether others think nonfactually without awareness because they want to fool themselves in order to hold on to their own comforting beliefs, or whether others lie and deceive with falsities in order to manipulate and control us; factual-thinking enables us to minimize cognitive-dissonance so that we will have less conflicts with our thought relative to factual-reality.

As discussed, cognitive-dissonance occurs when we hold two or more conflicting thoughts or beliefs; and these thoughts are generally engaged because one or more of these thoughts or beliefs are comforting. Therefore, cognitive-dissonance occurs when our thoughts and mindsets are directed by our emotions rather than by facts and the truth. This is why, Theory of Self-Relativity designates placebo-thinking and confirmation-bias as enemies of self-improvement; because they both influence our thinking based on how we want to feel, rather than based on how reality is. This is also why, Theory of Self-Relativity advocates and teaches factual-thinking, so that we will deal with reality as reality is, and not as we want reality to be.

Placebo-thinking fits facts to feelings, confirmation-bias fits facts to thoughts; however, factual-thinking fits feelings and thoughts to facts.

When we deal with our own thoughts and with others' thoughts and beliefs based on facts, we will thus prevent our feelings from influencing our thoughts; hence, we will have better chance of minimizing and resolving cognitive-dissonances. By making us aware of our thoughts and feelings, factual-thinking enables us to quickly become aware of and identify conflicting thoughts by recognizing our symptoms of confusion, constant-justification, and over-analysis. When we think factually, we can recognize the signs of confusion and dissonance; therefore, we will be able to resolve and eliminate nonfactual-thoughts that are causing these symptoms.

The following are some of the more common signs of experiencing cognitive-dissonance.

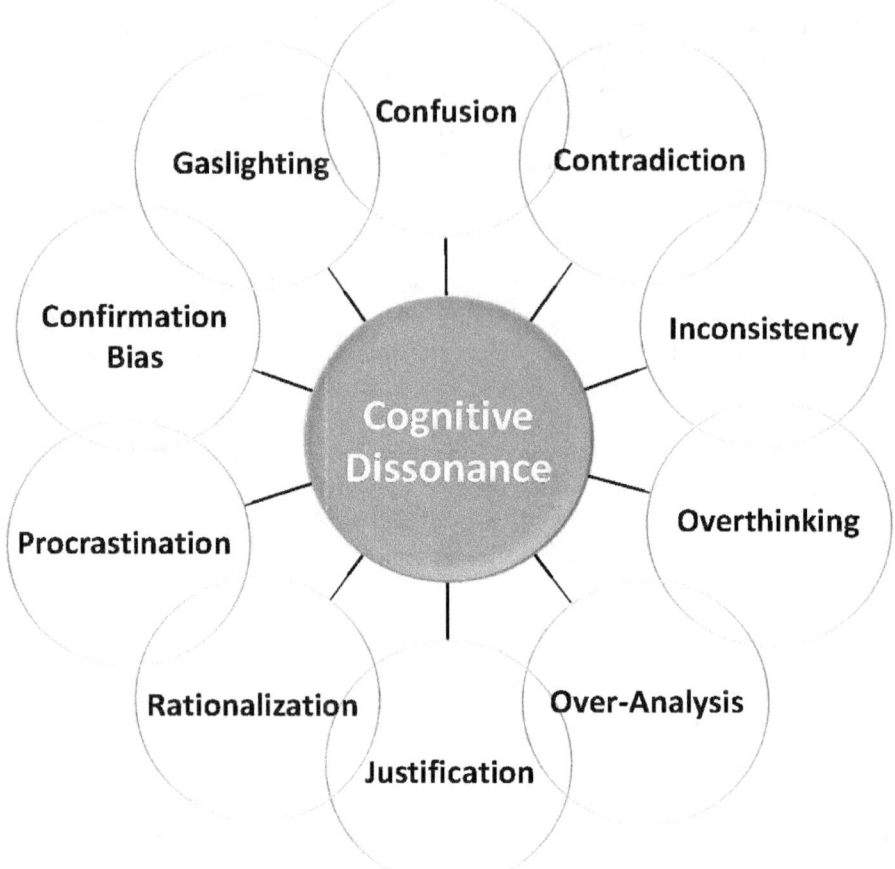

In summary, cognitive-dissonance occurs when our nonfactual-thoughts and comforting-beliefs clash with facts and reality. Cognitive-dissonance occurs when we really want to believe in something badly; therefore, we try to explain away anything that conflicts with it.

In other words:

If it conflicts with what I want to be true, therefore it must be false.

This is why, self-awareness helps us alleviate cognitive-dissonance by learning to evaluate the factualities of our thoughts and beliefs. Since our thoughts create our feelings and behavior, when we try to rationalize our desired-feelings by behaving based on nonfactual-thoughts or based on fallacious-beliefs because they make us feel good; we end up with unfavorable-outcomes in our life. To minimize dissonance, our mind and our thoughts need to stay in a state of synchronization and harmony with our feelings and with factual-reality. The only means of overcoming the disharmony of our thoughts with factual-reality is to ensure our thinking-system is based on factual-thinking.

Just as our logic and conscious-reasoning want to force us to dismiss or modify our nonfactual-thoughts and beliefs; our feelings want to force us to create and maintain thoughts that feel good, regardless of their factuality. Feelings are not rational; hence, emotional-thoughts such as placebo-thinking which through rationalization attempt to support our irrational-feelings are also nonfactual and irrational. Therefore, to bring about rationality to our feelings, we must support our feelings via rational-thoughts.

You should not create thoughts based on comforting-feelings; you should create feelings based on factual-thoughts.

If our thoughts are based on feelings and they are contrary to, or are unsupported with facts; dissonance and confusion will set in. Dissonance causes severe mental and physical stress. Dissonance, if left unresolved, could lead to sadness and even depression. Minimizing dissonance enables us to improve our focus and to increase our quick and efficient thinking abilities. Minimizing confusion and justifications associated with dissonance also minimizes procrastination. To minimize dissonance, we must undertake thought and behavior modification via awareness and self-improvement. Proper self-improvement could only take place and stay effective when we learn to seek facts and evidence, and when we learn to live our life by thinking factually.

Facts shall set you free!

X.
Living in Scarcity

Scarcity is commonly defined as something that is in limited availability or in short supply. Scarcity, in economics and in reference to commodities and things, refers to the unique value of that commodity or that thing; therefore, scarcity is relative to supply and demand. The more in demand something is and the less of it is available, the scarcer that thing would be, and the higher value it would have. Likewise, the more abundant a thing is and the more readily available that thing is relative to its demand, the lesser value it would have. Thus, scarcity and abundance are relative to supply and demand, which in-turn, sets the value for things.

Additionally, supply and demand increase or decrease based on the "desirability" of a thing. This desirability is directly related to the "perception" associated with that thing; hence, according to Theory of Self-Relativity, the most important and core characteristic for setting value, especially in the short-term, is perception; which itself is rooted in psychology, subjectivity, and emotions. Since perception, psychology, and mindsets change, the desirability associated with the value of a thing also fluctuates; therefore, value changes. Thus, according to Theory of Self-Relativity, value is perceived and price indicates that perception.

Theory of Self-Relativity defines "value" as "the perceived desirability of a thing."

This is why, especially in the shorter-term; price, which is set by the perceived-value of a thing, changes from time-to-time. Although in the longer-term, value is better defined and set by the characteristics and the attributes of a thing; in the shorter-term, value is correlated more with psychology and emotions. Thus, passage-of-time will better quantify the value of a thing, because time will allow for better discovery of the facts associated with the characteristics and the attributes of that thing. Since time will allow for better discovery of value; by improving the characteristics and qualities of a thing, the value of that thing could be increased. Therefore, by increasing and by improving the qualities and characteristics of a thing, we can improve the value of that thing. Although, many, refer to price as what you pay and value as what you get out of a thing; Theory of Self-Relativity refers to what you get out of a thing as the "return." Although return is also often perceived; return, is more quantifiable than value.

Price is what one pays, value is what one thinks it's worth, return is what one gets out of it.

Therefore,

- *Value is the perceived-desirability.*
- *Price is what one pays for the perceived-value.*
- *Return is what one takes out of the perceived-value.*

Likewise, on a personal scale, being scarce due to having special-skills and unique-attributes, increases personal-value; and conversely, not having special-skills and unique-attributes decreases personal-value. This is why, self-improvement increases personal-value; because, personal-value is also perceived, and therefore relative.

By increasing our self-worth and by improving our self-image, we become more in demand; which in-turn, leads to an increase in our personal-value. Personal-value is not necessarily a measurement of financial worth; it is a measurement of how we and others "perceive" our Self. According to Theory of Self-Relativity, personal-value is a combination of different qualities and attributes such as character, status, finances, etc.; therefore, self-improvement increases our personal-value, because it makes us scarcer and it puts us in a higher-demand level.

As discussed, since value is perceived, therefore, value is relative; hence, personal- value can be increased by remaining unbiased and adaptable to change and improvement. Theory of Self-Relativity refers to a person's perceived personal-value, which reflects the person's relative level of scarcity or abundance, as "*Relative-Personal-Value*" *or* "*RPV.*"

Theory of Self-Relativity defines "Relative-Personal-Value" or "RPV" as "a person's perceived desirability and value."

Relative-Personal-Value or RPV is based on perception, which measures value relative to different mental, personal, and social scales and standards; therefore, RPV increases as a person improves and changes for the better. Since RPV is a measure of perception, the most important aspect of RPV is how one values one's own Self. Although other people's perception is also important, especially in personal and social settings; a person's RPV will consequently be higher when the one improves and expands one's own personal qualities and attributes. However, our relative-personal-value should not be solely measured by someone else's perception or valuation of, for example, our material-possessions and accomplishments.

Since relative-personal-value represents perception of a person's value; Theory of Self-Relativity's references to personal-value and relative-personal-value is not the same as referring to a person's "human-values." Human-values consist of a person's character, beliefs, attributes, and virtues, which the person operates from, and which also guide the person's interactions with others; for example, one's empathy, ethics, biases, etc. Although human-values such as beliefs and ideologies influence a person's sense of self-worth and self-image, as well as how one is perceived by others; relative-personal-value is the perception of a person's comprehensive values, which includes human-values.

Human-Values = Characters + Beliefs + Attributes + Virtues
vs
Relative-Personal-Value (RPV) = Perceived-Value + Human-Values

Additionally, relative-personal-value or RPV is not the same as the value of a person as a human-being. According to Theory of Self-Relativity, all human-beings and all human lives have equal value, regardless of their tangible or intangible differences. Thus, RPV is based on the "perception" of a person's relative qualities and characteristics, but it is not a representation of a person's value as a human-being. Although relative-personal-value can be perceived as high or low; Theory of Self-Relativity recognizes every human life as equally valuable.

As discussed, scarcity and abundance are a reflection of a thing or a person's uniqueness or commonness; therefore, according to Theory of Self-Relativity, scarcity and abundance affect a person's RPV. Since being scarce is a measurement of higher RPV, living in scarcity is the complete opposite to being scarce; hence, living in scarcity represents a lower RPV. According to Theory of Self-Relativity, living in scarcity means not have an abundance of choices and options, because the person does not have a high RPV. Living in scarcity means having fewer choices and limited options, because when we live in scarcity, we do not have the personal-skills and unique-attributes to create and surround our Self with abundance of choices and options. Furthermore, when we live in scarcity, we are not considered to be scarce or in high demand; therefore, we are considered to be one of many abundant choices. Although scarce things usually have higher value; this should not be mistaken for living in scarcity, which represents a lower relative-personal-value.

When we have a higher RPV, we are more in demand and we have more choices and options; therefore, we live in abundance because we are scarcer. However, when we live in scarcity, we have a lower RPV, because we have less choices and fewer options. Living in scarcity is the opposite of being scarce, and living in abundance is the opposite of being abundant.

Since RPV is psychological because it is based on perception of value; RPV is directly proportional to living in abundance, and inversely-proportional to living in scarcity. The higher RPV we have, the scarcer we are, which means, the more in demand we are, and the more choices and options we have. This is why, living in scarcity is categorized by Theory of Self-Relativity as one of its 10-Enemies of Self-Improvement; and living in abundance and having choices is categorized as one of the 10-Commandments for Self-Improvement. Therefore, to live in abundance, we must increase our RPV via self-improvement, so that we can increase our choices and options in life.

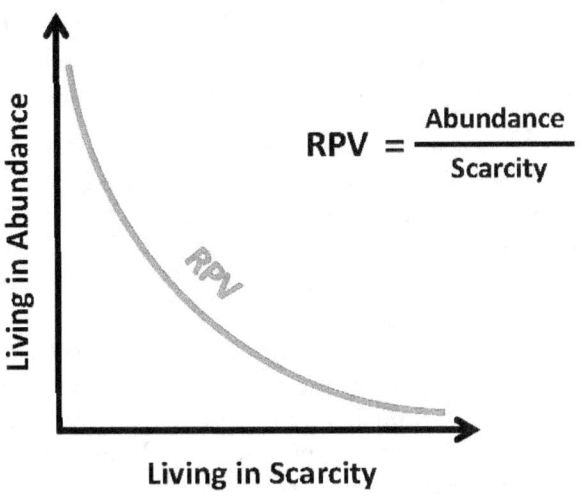

$$RPV = \frac{Abundance}{Scarcity}$$

It is important to reiterate that our perception of our own RPV must be based on facts and evidence; not based on how we feel. Although in the short-term, RPV is perceived; in the longer-term, this perception must be verified with supportive facts and evidence. In other words, we cannot peptalk our Self into believing that we have a higher RPV; because in due time, such incorrect perception of our RPV will come crashing down in value. Our perception, and most importantly our knowledge of our RPV, must be based on factual-thinking; which means we must evaluate our qualities and attributes based on supportive facts and evidence. If our perception of our RPV is not in sync with what the factual-value of our RPV; in due time, our incorrect higher perception of our RPV will adjust down. This is why, we cannot improve our self-worth or our self-image simply via peptalk and positive-thinking.

Thus, to achieve true higher RPV, we must continuously engage in change and self-improvement, so that we can maintain and increase our RPV. As we improve, we can verify the improving value of our RPV via factual-thinking; therefore, when we factually know that our RPV is elevating, so would others. When we want to increase our RPV, we must begin by believing in our Self, and we must want to self-improve; however, to strengthen and maintain our improved RPV, we must evaluate our self-belief and our personal-perception of our higher RPV via facts and evidence; and not through placebo-thoughts and comforting-beliefs.

As discussed, just as a belief is supposed to be temporary until supportive facts and evidence are found to turn that belief into knowledge; the perception of our higher RPV must also be checked and verified by supportive evidence, because factual-thinking proves or disproves our forward-looking mindsets such as our assumptions, perceptions, and beliefs, relative to reality. If our perception and belief of our higher RPV does not match what facts and evidence are indicating, we should make changes to get on the correct path of increasing our RPV. Since low RPV is caused by low self-attributes such as low self-image, low self-worth, and mediocre personal-accomplishments; therefore, a low RPV causes us to live in scarcity, which means, we have fewer-choices and limited-options in life. To increase our RPV, which in-turn, will increase our choices and options in life and will put us in the position of living in abundance; we must self-improve.

Although initially we perceive but we must fact-check to ensure and to know that our RPV is truly high; even then, regardless of our knowledge of our RPV, others might continue to perceive our RPV, for example, at a lower value, even though we might truly have a higher RPV than what others perceive. Just as in due time, our personally perceived RPV will adjust up or down based on facts and the quality of our improvements; other-people's perception of our RPV will also adjust based on the qualities and attributes that we carry to support our RPV. Therefore, self-improvement is best achieved by bringing the focus onto our Self, by not only improving our personal qualities, but also by minimizing dependency and reliance on others. Thus, in order to increase our RPV and to live in abundance so that other-people's perception of our RPV does not negatively affect our life; we must become self-reliant and self-sufficient, and we must improve from within.

As discussed, Theory of Self-Relativity considers "Dependency and Reliance" on others as one of the 10-Enemies of Self-Improvement; because dependency and reliance on others lessens personal control and increases uncertainty. Less control and higher uncertainty, in-turn, diminish our ability to have choices and options, because we remain preoccupied with the uncertainties. Fewer choices and limited options mean we are living in scarcity; therefore, we are limited in our ability to make the best decisions and to have the best outcomes for our Self. Consequently, living in scarcity, in-turn, leads us to become more dependent and more reliant on others because of the few choices and options that we have; thus, this vicious cycle repeats itself. Theory of Self-Relativity refers to this cycle as the *"Dependency-Cycle."*

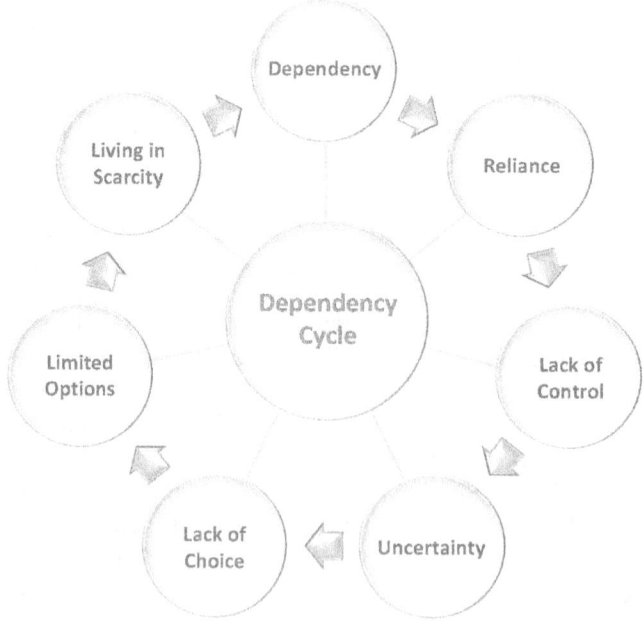

According to Theory of Self-Relativity, and as discussed in earlier chapters, the dependency-cycle and its components are also the primary causes of worry, anxiety, and stress; therefore, to minimize worry, anxiety, and stress, we must increase our RPV, by living in abundance and by not living in scarcity. This means, we must constantly change and improve.

Living in scarcity directly affects our relative-personal-value. The fewer resources, choices, and options we have in life, the lower our RPV would be; therefore, to increase our RPV, which ultimately affects our sense of self-worth, we must learn to increase our choices and options in life. The way to increase our choices and options in life is by increasing our "personal-resources," which are things, skills, or people that could improve the quality of our life.

Theory of Self-Relativity classifies personal-resources binarily:

1. **Tangible-Resources:** Are resources which are tangible or physical; or resources which could be quantified materially. For example, wealth, credit, connections, and other material-things.

2. **Intangible-Resources:** Are resources which are non-tangible or are non-physical. For example, intelligence, knowledge, empathy, and other personal attributes and skills.

Although resources commonly refer to financial and tangible commodities; according to Theory of Self-Relativity, our intangible-resources are more valuable, because without proper intangible-resources, we would not be able to increase our tangible-resources. Intangible-resources are personality-traits such as one's cognitive-intelligence and emotional-intelligence; which represent how smart a person is with regards to knowledge and reasoning, as well as how aware and stable the person is emotionally. While cognitive-intelligence and emotional-intelligence are sometimes quantified as intelligence-quotient (IQ) and emotional-quotient (EQ); Theory of Self-Relativity does not advocate valuing intangible-resources simply via quantifiable demonstrations; because, intellect, emotions, and wisdom are not static traits, they are dynamic, thus, they should constantly be evolving and improving.

Increasing our resources increases our RPV and enables us to have diversity of choices and abundance of options. Conversely, lack of resources lowers our RPV and minimizes our choices and options in life. By increasing our resources, hence, by increasing our RPV, we strengthen our ability to live in abundance; and this increase in choices and options enables us to be less inclined to *"down-compromise"* and to settle for less. As a reminder and as discussed, value is perceived, and value does not necessarily refer to price; value refers to the quality and the scarcity of tangible and intangible characteristics of a thing. Compromise, in a productive and mutual manner, is a synergic attribute; however, to down-compromise in order to settle for less, or to down-compromise due to lack of selection, is as a result of living in scarcity due to lower RPV. Compromise is discussed in detail in subsequent sections.

Therefore, in order for us to have a higher RPV and a higher sense of self-worth, we must live in abundance and not in scarcity. This means, we must not be limited with our choices and options, and we must seek to continuously change, improve, and create better and more abundant choices for our Self.

Value is perceived, hence value is relative; therefore, value can be increased by remaining unbiased and adaptable to change and improvement.

Diversity of choice and abundance of options could only be achieved via personal-change and through self-improvement. When we bring the focus onto our Self and keep our Self focused with personal-change and with self-improvement; instead of preoccupying our Self with others, we will automatically prioritize our self-first. When we self-improve, our personal-attributes such as our physical health, our financial success, and our relationships, will in-turn, have a better chance of improving. Furthermore, through our improved thinking and reasoning style, we will begin to evaluate and perceive others from an objective and factual perceptive. Instead of us seeking other-people's approval; we will be in a position where we will make our best choice of others. This means, instead of us compromising or competing to be accepted by others; others will compete to be accepted by us.

You create value for yourself, you add value to others.

Relative-personal-value and self-worth are neither given nor achieved from the outside, they are created and improved from the inside; this is why, Theory of Self-Relativity advocates living a centered-self life, from the inside-out. When we learn to improve our Self and increase our choices by increasing our resources and diversity of options; we will then be living a centered-self life, in abundance and not in scarcity. When we live in abundance, we can then choose the best of things and the best of people to deal with in our life; and, this is especially true in our personal-relationships with others. For example, instead of staying in an unhealthy romantic-relationship because we do not believe that we could have a better option; by improving our Self, we will consequently create abundance of choices and options, hence, we will not have to unilaterally compromise by staying in such a relationship. Likewise, when others know that we have choices and options and that we can move on; they will be more attentive, appreciative, and respectful of their relationship with us.

By bringing the focus onto our Self and by living our life from the inside-out, rather than from the outside-in; we can thereby focus on increasing our RPV. Instead of us focusing on others and down-compromising or unilaterally compromising to keep other-people around us; when we focus on improving our Self, we will be able to live our life based on self-sufficiency, rather than based on neediness, therefore, others will only become complementary to our existence.

When we self-improve and become a complete person on our own, our relationship with others will be on a complementary-basis, and not on a completing-basis. Therefore, others will not complete us; they will complement our existence. When others do not complete us, our relationship with them will be as an additive relationship, and not based on neediness. This, in-turn, will increase our relative-personal-value or RPV, because our self-worth will not be contingent on others; it will be coming from within our own Self. This is why, "Complementary, not Completing" is one of Theory of Self-Relativity's 10-Commandments for Self-Improvement.

Additionally, when we interact with others on a complementary basis, we will then be able to live our life from the position of having *"Nothing-to-lose."* By learning to rely on our Self and by minimizing dependency and reliance on others, we will then not have many reasons to down-compromise to our disadvantage; therefore, we will enter interactions with others from the perspective of having nothing-to-lose. When we have nothing-to-lose, we will not have the urgency to enter and stay in unfavorable-relationships; because we will be able to cut loose and change direction by moving on quickly. Furthermore, we will not seek validation externally by needing other people to validate us, or by needing to have other material-things, in order to feel worthy. When we enter every interaction from the perspective of having nothing-to-lose; everything that we gain will be additive and not based on neediness. Having nothing-to-lose does not mean being reckless; but it means to approach interactions from a solid foundation of self-sufficiency.

Neediness, which in-turn, goes hand-in-hand with dependency and reliance, is a sign of a low RPV and as a result of living in scarcity. Neediness is not only an inhibitor of improvement, but it is an extremely unattractive personal-trait; especially in interpersonal-relationships and in romantic-relationships.

Relationship neediness is similar to other forms of self-deficiencies which create dependency and reliance. Neediness could be real or perceived and it is caused by internal-deficiencies and personal-weaknesses that a person is trying to fulfil and improve from the outside. Instead of focusing on one's own Self to improve and resolve such internal-deficiencies; the needy person focuses onto others in an attempt to try to fill-in and complete these personal-weaknesses.

Inability to self-reflect and introspect to recognize one's own internal-deficiencies is a major contributor to neediness. When we are needy, instead of looking within our Self, we focus onto the outside to see how someone-else or something-else could resolve our deficiencies and weaknesses; thus, we look externally to see how other-people or other-things could make us feel complete. As discussed throughout Theory of Self-Relativity, we can only focus on one side of the self-equation; externally on others, or internally on our own Self. We can either look to the outside in order for others to complete us; or we can look to the inside, to complete our own Self. While sensationalistic movie and poetic statements such as telling a romantic partner "you complete me" may sound ideal on the surface; such beliefs and mindsets are nothing but fallacies that hinder people from having healthy relationships.

No one should complete you except your own Self.

Therefore, as stated throughout Theory of Self-Relativity:

Relationships must be complementary; not completing.

A completing relationship is based on neediness, which, itself, is based on living in scarcity; because one is depending and relying on others. Additionally, what we often think are things that we "need," are actually things that we "want." Need is something that is crucial for our survival, our existence, and for our safety. Need is what our primitive-mind needs, not what our intelligent-mind wants; however, since we live in the modern-era where primitive-dangers are minimized and our primitive-needs are mostly met, we tend to spoil ourselves by thinking what we want is actually what we need.

Things that we need are things that we cannot survive without; or they are things that not having them will undermine our safety, hence, jeopardize our existence. Things like air, water, food, and shelter are examples of things that we need. Although social and personal qualities such as getting and giving love, empathy, and even procreation are necessary requirements for living a quality and fulfilled life; without these attributes, we can still survive. Likewise, other-things such as a new car, designer-clothes, or other-people such as a model-looking girlfriend, or a wealthy husband are not things that we need; because we can survive without them. These are examples of things that we want but our intelligent-mind, in the absence of primitive-dangers, tricks our primitive-mind into thinking these are things that we need.

Things that we truly need are things that we would fight tooth and nail to attain, in order for us to survive. If we are hungry and starving, we will do anything and we would look anywhere to find food to stay alive; because if we cannot find food to eat, we will die. However, we would not die if we could not have the next pair of designer shoes, the new model car, or even the person of our dreams that we so truly believe that we cannot live without. Exceptionally, there are certain situations in life where we would need others, but these are rare situations which require us to depend and rely on others in order to survive. For example, if our kidneys are failing and we need a kidney from a donor, such neediness is a matter of life and death; hence, it is a matter of survival. We do not need someone else's love to survive; however, if both our kidneys have failed, we would need someone else's kidney to survive. Therefore, our sense of neediness must only be deployed in situations where our real suffering could be eliminated; or if our life depended on it.

Once we learn to distinguish between what we truly need and what we desire or want; we will then realize that most things that we think we need are actually things that we desire and want. Once we learn to not elevate everything that we desire and want to the level of need, we can then begin to slowly build the foundation of change; and as long as we "desire" to reach a better tomorrow than today, we will only then be truly improving our life. By learning to distinguish between things that we need versus things that we want or desire, we will then be able to keep our Self in the contentment-zone. Once we are in the contentment-zone, we can then try to reach for things that we want, without categorizing them fallaciously as being things that we need.

We cannot seek happiness from other-people or from other-things if we cannot distinguish between things that we need and things that we want. As described throughout Theory of Self-Relativity, in order for us to be happy, we must first minimize negativity so that we can elevate our Self from the negativity-zone to the contentment-zone. Once we reach the contentment-zone, we can then seek to have more frequent experiences of happiness. Likewise, in order for us to have the things and the people in our life that would make us happy; we would have to first minimize the things that we truly need in our life. Once we minimize the needs in our life, we can then seek to gain the things that we want in our life.

When we need something, we automatically want that thing and we have a desire for it; however, when we desire or want something, it does not mean we need that thing. Likewise, when we want something, we must have a desire for it; but, when we desire something, it does not mean that we want that thing, or that we need to have that thing. Therefore, we must be aware and cognizant to separate our desires, wants, and needs from one another.

Desire is by choice; need is by necessity.

As stated, due to the luxury of our modern life, we incorrectly perceive desires and wants as needs, because we do not really have as many needs that are going to affect our survival; therefore, most things that we think we need are simply desires and wants which we could live without. Once we learn to realize that we do not need other-things and other-people, and that the feeling of neediness that we experience is simply a feeling of desire or a want at best; we can then realize that attaining many things that we desire or want is easier than when we thought we needed them. Likewise, when we realize many things that we thought we needed were simply things that we desire or want; it will be easier to live our lives without those things.

When we realize that many things that we thought we needed are simply things that we desire or want, we will then begin to approach life from the inside-out; because, by minimizing neediness, we can live a more balanced and content life from within. When we reach this state of contentment, we will then be able to have a much higher sense of self-worth; as this is when we will realize that our accomplishments come from within us, rather than from other-things or from other-people. This is why, self-awareness and self-improvement are so important in living a balanced and a harmonious life. Once we minimize the constant chaos of needing things and needing people, we can then seek to have things and be with people based on our simple desires and wants. Likewise, if we do not get what we desire or want, not having it will not be the end of the world. When we are less chaotic to constantly need others, our contentment and balance will consequently enable us to have what we desire and want.

When we are less needy, we can then get what we want.

Just as we do not need another new pair of shoes or a new car to increase our self-worth; we also do not need another person to complete us or to validate us. When we improve our Self from within, we will then be able to set our borders and boundaries of how others will behave and interact with us. When others know that we are not needy of them, they will then interact with us based on our terms; which in-turn, raises our RPV. Although RPV is perceived, the higher perception of our RPV is contingent on our actual and not perceived understanding of our desires, our wants, and our needs; because as stated, what we often think we need, is simply something that we want.

Self-sufficiency increases our self-worth and our social and personal-values; there-fore, it allows us to rely on our Self without needing someone else. Although we might desire or want someone else; when we become self-sufficient, we will then realize that desiring or wanting others does not mean that we need them, or that we cannot live without them. When we learn that we do not need others, we will then learn that we can be on our own; hence, we will not feel isolated and lonely. Despite social-isolation being one of the major public-health problems in the modern-times; when we become self-sufficient, we will experience minimal to no isolation. Although we are social-animals and contact and interactivity with other human-beings is an important part of our social and cultural existence; in order for us to have healthy relationships with others, we must first learn to have a healthy relationship with our own Self.

We must learn to be alone, without feeling lonely.

When we learn to be alone without feeling lonely, we will then realize that we may desire and want others to be in our life, but we will not need them to feel complete. This is why, relationships and interactions with other-people or with other-things must be on a complementary basis; and not based on a completing need.

To be alone means to have the desire to be by your Self; to be lonely means to have the need to be with others.

Both loneliness and being-alone describe separation of the Self from others; the difference is that being lonely is based on external-need, and being alone is based on internal-contentment. However, if we do not learn to be alone by becoming self-sufficient; we could be in a room full of people, yet we would still feel lonely.

It is better to be alone for the right reason, than to be with someone else for the wrong reasons.

Same holds true if we want to be good to others. If we are capable of not needing others, we also would not force others to be with us because they might need us. Unhealthy relationships that thrive on control, operate based on the neediness of one side onto the other; because neediness opens the door for control. While others might need our help and assistance with certain aspects of their life, we should not control them; we should help to minimize their neediness by teaching them how to become independent and self-reliant. When others are not forced to be in a relationship with us because they do not need us; they will then choose to be in a relationship with us because they want to be with us. Therefore:

To add value to others, you must first create value for your Self.

In order for us to have a healthy relationship with others, we must first have a healthy relationship with our own Self; which means, we must learn to be content with our own *"Self-Time."* When we learn to be content with our self-time, we will also learn to create our own happiness from within, while we will teach others how to do the same for themselves.

What time is it? it's self-time.

Personal-Development
& Self-Improvement

Although information and knowledge about "who we are," "why we are here," and "where we are going," are important for our existence; regardless of the answers to these questions, we must try to live the best quality of life that we can at every moment of our life. We are what we are and we are where we are, because regardless of how we got here, what matters is how we can do the best with every moment of our life. To start living a quality life and to make every moment of our life be the best that it could be; we have to stop looking for answers elsewhere, and we must begin creating our own meaning by focusing on our own Self.

It is not as important where you came from, as it is important where you are going.

This is why, self-improvement must be an essential, integral, and a continuous part of our life and our existence; so that we can master the art of living a quality and fulfilled life. To live the best life and to continuously elevate the quality of our life, we must learn to adapt, change, and self-improve; however, self-improvement has been one of the most difficult things for us to master because we have not been able to understand how to self-improve. One of the main problems associated with self-improvement has been the incorrect belief that improvement and enlightenment happens suddenly. As described throughout Theory of Self-Relativity, personal-development and self-improvement is not an event; it is an ongoing process.

Change and improvement are not singular events; they are continuum of events in the process of life.

This is why:

Theory of Self-Relativity defines a "process" as "a continuum of events."

We must understand the reason self-improvement has been difficult for many, is not because there is something wrong with us; but it is because the industry has been approaching it incorrectly. Majority of self-improvement and motivational programs are not only outdated, and even ancient, but they fail to address the requirements of living in our current fast-paced and technology-based societies. Technology, information, and quicker communication methods overload our thinking-system, yet most self-help programs have not properly adapted to, nor do they properly address the modern-day requirements for self-improvement.

Current self-improvement and motivational techniques either peptalk us endlessly with motivational quotes and speeches; or they try to teach us how to slow-down our thinking-processes, in order to clear our mind. Peptalk is all talk and no action, and slowing down our mind in order to clear our thoughts is no different than using picks and shovels to build a sky-scraper; they simply do not work. This is why:

Motivation alone won't get you any results.

Complexity, confusion, and sensationalism have been the core problems with many self-improvement programs. There are thousands of self-improvement teaching methods, lectures, and even workshops; but they mostly fail to have long-term, sustainable, and easily repeatable solutions for achieving self-improvement. Likewise, our desire to have someone else or something else improve our Self, continues to sabotage, and undermine our self-improvement goals. We would rather take a pill, pay someone else, or jump from one thing to another, hoping one of these external factors will help us to improve quickly; yet we somehow seem to overlook the most obvious and closest person who should be in charge of helping us to self-improve continuously. That person is our own Self.

The reason external self-help techniques, including psychotherapy, motivational-programs, and even ancient practices such as meditation have limited success is because they are primarily reliant on other-people's help; therefore, they are often very time consuming. The churn and exhaustion rates from these programs are very high, and commitment is generally more of a chore than a pleasant experience. Most of all, these practices waste a great deal of the most important finite commodity that we have; our "time."

The reason these programs waste time and are not cost-effective, is because they require lots of preparation and time commitment to implement. Additionally, these practices are very difficult to understand, intuit, and apply, on-the-go; because many are ill-defined and lack structure. Furthermore, the initial hyped-up excitement of getting into these practices is soon followed by the commonly experienced disappointments and withdrawals as their high expectations and over promises failed to deliver. Even older self-improvement techniques such as meditation and spiritual-yoga have limited to no success and a high churn rate, because they require extreme time and discipline commitment. Trying to establish discipline without understanding why we are creating discipline is like memorizing content without understanding what the content is about; and how the context of the content could differ in different settings. Since these practices are ill-defined and impractical; many, ambiguously identify and label themselves as "spiritual" in nature. Hence why, Theory of Self-Relativity states:

True spirituality is not believing in something mystical or mythical; true spirituality is to use the awareness of our emotions, to improve our thoughts, and to strengthen our actions.

Meditation and spiritual practices were invented millenia ago when human life and societies were much simpler, and they functioned at a slower pace. Additionally, the level of knowledge and understanding of how The-Universe and things in it functioned were severely limited and were mostly based on perception rather than experimentation, understanding, and facts. To meditate, those who practiced meditation, had the time and peacefulness that meditation required to retreat, to become mindful, and to not worry about modern-day time-sensitive tasks and financial obligations they left behind. Meditation requires lengthy time-dedication, and not many, can afford to have such dedication to meditation and other time-consuming practices which offer questionable success. Time is a valuable commodity and in our modern fast-paced life, the value of time has inflated even more than before. Self-improvement should not be a luxury; it should be every person's goal to live a quality and fulfilled life.

Although mindfulness is an important component of self-improvement; ancient-mindfulness, even if it could be accomplished, does very little to resolve our emotional-problems, address our financial-obligations, or even strengthen our self-identity. Many traditional-teachings and rituals do not adapt well to our modern and scientific awareness and understanding of how The-Universe works; hence, they become ambiguous and difficult to follow. For example, the appeals-to-tradition fallacy that "it's been done this way for a long time therefore it must be true." Ancient or classic-mindfulness attempts to teach us how to slow-down our thinking and to live in the present-moment, to become aware of our thoughts, and to observe our thoughts without judgment. However, just observing our thoughts will not resolve the thoughts that trouble us and make us feel worried, anxious, and stressed. This is why, thoughtfulness, especially modern-thoughtfulness, is even more important than mindfulness.

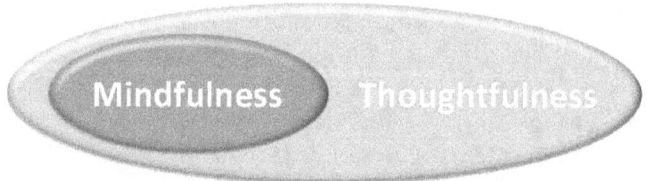

Although mindfulness is a prerequisite for thoughtfulness, mindfulness must always be followed by thoughtfulness; because without thoughtfulness, mindfulness has limited value and it is unstable. Thoughtfulness not only allows us to become aware of our thoughts, but thoughtfulness allows us to use our thought-awareness to resolve or eliminate our useless and troubling thoughts; not just to observe them or push them to the side.

Times have changed and life moves at a much faster pace, and the pace gets even faster as technology progresses; therefore, we need quicker, smarter, and on-the-go thoughtfulness techniques for self-improvement. Techniques that require slowing down, pausing, and even stopping activities to become mindful are not applicable anymore, and they often clash with our modern-life requirements. Our mind is a thinking-machine, therefore, in order for it to keep up with changing times, it must think constantly, and it must learn to think faster; not think less, or think slower. Furthermore, thoughtfulness, itself, which must always succeed mindfulness, must be succeeded by behavior in order to implement the changes that are necessary for improving the shortcomings that mindfulness and thoughtfulness revealed.

Mindfulness is awareness, thoughtfulness is understanding, and behavior is change and improvement.

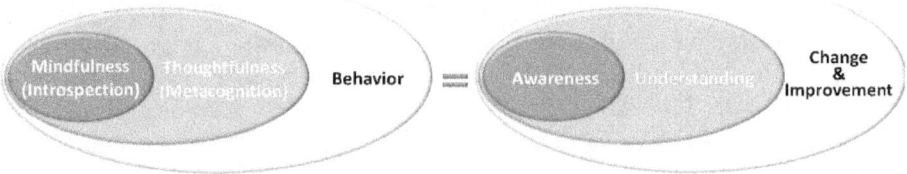

However, as stated throughout Theory of Self-Relativity, behavior must be as a result of proper thinking; which itself is based on awareness and understanding. This means, as we enter the thoughtfulness stage, which makes us evaluate and understand our thoughts for their factuality; we can then make a pragmatic conclusion if a certain thought we have is based on fact and evidence or if it is an emotionally comforting placebo-thought. If the thought has factual merit, then the behavior needed to follow-through with the thought would be an action or inaction. Behavior is action or inaction, because despite a thought being factual, we do not always have to do something. However, if the thought proves to not be factual, we should abstain from taking an action and we should wait until we find the supportive facts for that thought or mindset. If we cannot find the supportive facts, we must then dismiss the thought; therefore, we will take no action. Accepting thoughts could lead to action or inaction; however, dismissing thoughts always leads to inaction, because when we don't think of a thought, we can't feel, we can't decide, hence, we can't act. This is the basis of the absolute-order.

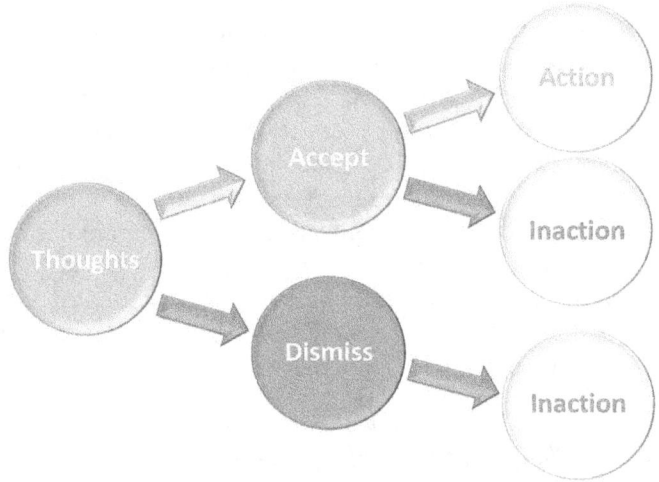

When supportive facts for a thought are missing or are not present, that thought is most-probably nonfactual; thus, at the minimum, it should be approached with caution. As stated throughout Theory of Self-Relativity, when we objectively and factually evaluate and understand our thoughts, we will then begin to realize that the majority of our thoughts, especially the problematic and cluttering ones, are nonfactual. Therefore, and especially at the beginning stages of practicing factual-thinking and The Cognitive-Cognition-Technique, we will dismiss more thoughts than we will accept; hence, we will engage in more inaction than action.

The same approach must be inherent to any applicable self-improvement system. Talk is important, but action is more important. Mindfulness, which is what many personal-development and motivational-teachings preach, is important; however, mindfulness is similar to just talking. Therefore, mindfulness is all talk but thoughtfulness leads to action. This is why, many motivational systems, especially new-age mystical-motivation, pseudoscientific-spiritual motivation, and ancient traditional motivational systems, after a while, make us feel as if we are not good enough; because, slowing down and observing our thoughts, or trying to live in the moment-of-now, do not resolve or eliminate our difficulties.

Majority of personal-development and motivational systems work off creating excitement, motivation, and feel-good peptalk; however, not many actually give us the understanding and the roadmap as to how to make the change constantly, consistently, and in a repeatable format.

True motivation shouldn't be empty peptalk. True motivation should be an achievable roadmap followed by implementation.

Additionally, many of these systems and techniques deceptively portray that everyone else succeeds with these teaching; but then we wonder why we could not do the same!

Motivation is easy; the difficult part is how to turn motivation into results.

Empty motivation without implementation of follow through action is like knowing we need to eat to stay alive, but not knowing how to find the food. A true self-improvement system should not rely on hype and peptalk to simply elevate a person by motivating them, and then letting them fall. Motivation is easy to achieve; however, to turn motivation into sustainable and consistent action requires a solid and factually understandable method. A true self-help and personal-development system must teach us how to be our own best coach, therapist, and listener. A true self-improvement system should not only teach us how to think objectively and factually, but it must also teach us that in order to feel better, to reach better stages of existence, and to live a fulfilled and happy life; we must first minimize our negativities. We cannot just cover-up our negativities with comforting-thoughts or with empty "positive-thinking."

A good self-help system shouldn't help some of the people some of the time. A good self-help system should help most of the people most of the time.

Additionally, most motivational speeches and programs show us highly accomplished business people, celebrities, and powerful figures who discuss their accomplishments; but they commonly fall short of showing us "how to" replicate similar accomplishments for our own Self. These examples of high accomplishments, while could be motivational in the short-term, are often discouraging in the long-term; because they are too large of a yardstick for comparison and too high of a bar to jump over. These motivational programs do not present the history, the advantages, or the variables these mentors had; and they certainly do not represent how exceptionally rare these types of extreme success-stories are.

No one questions the satisfaction of the final destination, but many have difficulty taking the journey.

Self-improvement is a continuing process, not an event; and especially not a task with a final prize. Many of these high-action programs become momentary shot-in-the-arm but they also have severe withdrawal effects after the effect of the pep-talk subsides and as reality sets back in. Many participants subsequently drop the program and sink back into their abyss of thinking that there must be something wrong with themselves, because others seem to have mastered self-improvement, but they are such losers that they do not even have the ability to understand how they need to take the first steps towards self-improvement.

Unrealistic peptalk is the perfect setup for failure.

The behind-the-scenes reality is the high churn and drop-off rate of the participants and subscribers of these peptalking, wealth-flashing, and celebrity-promoting programs. The new hopefuls are the only visible part of the iceberg, because the initial excitement is similar to many other high-promising novelties that people discover for themselves. What many cannot see and what is not shown, are all the fallen-off and submerged portions of the iceberg that ended up losing their excitement, that abandoned the programs, and who sunk deeper into the despair of losing whatever remaining self-worth they had. Simply stated, majority of current self-help and self-improvement programs, and majority of new-age spiritual and meditational practices, are a revolving door for new hopefuls becoming disappointed drop-offs, within the statistics of broken self-images, shattered-dreams, and hopelessness.

Dangling the carrot of rare success and wealth should not be a representation of self-improvement and motivation; instead, at the beginning of transformation, a minimally-negative and content state of life should be the primary goal for personal-development. When we begin by minimizing negativity and by experiencing contentment, we can then attempt to reach for fulfillment and happiness. We must first clean out our clutter before we can proceed to achieving bigger scales of accomplishments. Without minimizing negativities and without learning to be content and fulfilled, we will not be able to achieve bigger goals. We must learn to walk before we run. As exampled and discussed, we must first remove our body-odor before trying to smell good; we cannot just cover-up body-odor without bathing, because:

The stink of negativity cannot be covered-up; it will eventually rise-up to the surface.

Personal-development and self-improvement should be an invigorating experience and a liberating journey. It should not require blind-faith, forced-memorization, or a great deal of hard work. Likewise, self-improvement should not be based on misrepresentations of fame, fortune and celebrity. On the contrary, it is actually a known fact that many famous, wealthy, and powerful people are often unhappy. Additionally, wealthy people are actually those who can afford to seek therapy; however, if the program is ineffective and the system is unrealistic, all it takes is for a single trigger or one negative-thought to destroy years of therapy and self-help work. We have all seen, heard of, or even followed the dramatic lives of the rich and the famous, and the self-inflicted sabotage they caused. These misfortunes happen because many who did not manage to first resolve their negativities, mistakenly believed when they become wealthy, famous, or powerful, they would reach the utopia of human fulfillment and happiness.

Wealth, fame and power are simply byproducts of success. True success is measured by the level of your fulfillment.

When self-improvement programs are based on emotional-excitement rather than understanding and learning how to change; they come on with a big-bang and quickly fizzle out into the darkness of further hopelessness. Problem-solving and skill-building tools cannot be just motivational and feelings-based; they must be cognitive and thinking-based.

We shouldn't feel self-improvement; we must know self-improvement.

The proper way to address our issues and to get on the correct path of self-improvement is to recognize our feelings, and to use these feelings as the gateway to get in touch with our thoughts that are making us feel a certain way. While there are currently some cognitive-methods which require third party participation and assistance; in practice, these methods do not simplify and standardize on-the-go skills which could apply repetitively and uniformly to all aspects of our lives.

Self-improvement must be enjoyable and exciting; something to look forward to, and at some point, it must become nonconscious and intuitive, like many of our other automatic activities such as walking and driving. After initial awareness, understanding, and implementation; our self-improvement habits should become a normal part of our life, because improvement and transformation is a continuous process, and not a singular-event. Just as we learn as a child to take baby-steps before we walk, and we learn to walk before we run; as we move forward in life, walking and running become intuitive actions that we take without consciously thinking about them. Self-improvement should be no different. Personal-development and self-mastery, just like walking and running must begin with understanding, learning, and then improving, in order for it to become intuitive and nonconscious. When self-improvement becomes an understood, learned, and intuitive skill, it can then lead us to multitasking; just as we multitask other things such as talking on the phone when we walk or when we drive, without affecting our walking or our driving goals.

Self-mastery, and even, motivation, must be cognitive and not emotional. Theory of Self-Relativity, through its Cognitive-Cognition-Technique, shows how to develop our skills for personal-development and self-improvement. Theory of Self-Relativity shows how to think factually and how to live our life based on facts and evidence; instead of living life through self-deception and placebo-thinking. Although our feelings are valid, this does not mean that our feelings are rational. Feelings do not have any rationality; therefore, emotional-thinking will lead us astray. However, when we base our thinking on facts and evidence, our subsequent feelings and emotions, which are generated as a result of our factual-thinking, will not only be valid, but they will be genuine and rationality-based. The only means of having rational-feelings is for us to generate these feelings as a result of rational-thinking, so that our feelings are based on how reality is and not based on how we want reality to be.

To truly self-improve, we must let our thoughts dictate our feelings; not to let our feelings dictate our thoughts.

To properly learn how to self-improve, we must learn to understand the inner-workings of our mind by becoming aware of our thoughts and our feelings, and by learning to properly address them. Listening to someone else telling us their exceptional story of how they succeeded or self-improved is not a proper yardstick or a guarantee for our betterment. This is why, self-improvement must be understood and cognitive; not emotional and imitating. Therefore:

Self-improvement is relative, because it consists of numerous personal, time, and place variables which are specific to each person.

A proper self-improvement system should give people the understanding and the tools for them to plug-in their specific variables. An effective self-improvement system should be an inherently evolving mental-algorithm. An algorithm is a sequence of instructions telling a computer what to do, while the algorithm itself evolves and improves with repetition; hence, same should apply to our thoughts, as our thoughts should instruct and guide our personal-development and transformation.

Theory of Self-Relativity's Cognitive-Cognition-Technique is your mental algorithm.

The modern mental-algorithm for self-improvement should make us think faster and more efficiently, instead of attempting to slow-down our thinking; because, thinking is a mental process occurring in time, and time is a valuable commodity that once gone it can never be regained.

Time-efficiency must be one of the most important results of true self-improvement; because when our thinking becomes efficient, our responses become quicker.

Proper self-improvement should be cognitive and fact-based; or at the minimum, it should not hypothetically try to violate the laws-of-physics which govern how the-Universe operates. While practices such as meditation or standalone mindfulness could be good means of relaxation and retreat; these practices are not long-term effective in getting us to think efficiently, quickly, and cleverly. Meditation and pseudoscientific-mindfulness require dedication of time which is a commodity in shortage; likewise, these techniques time-related benefit-to-cost effectiveness is not efficient or practical.

Our evolving society is moving at a faster and faster pace requiring multi-tasking. To slow-down thinking or to simply sit and try to observe our thoughts is not an effective means of dealing with modern-thinking requirements. Our mind is a thinking-machine, and its job is to think continuously; just as our heart's job is to always pump blood. While slowing down our mind in certain situations could be beneficial; our mind, just like our heart, must be able to handle everyday thinking challenges without slowing down to unhealthy and dangerous levels. On the contrary, our mind should actually be able to quicken its activities on demand, so that it can handle the everyday requirements and challenges associated with living in the fast-paced modern-times.

Efficiency of time and minimization of repetitive thinking are keys to strengthening and speeding up our thinking abilities. Although psychotherapy is an effective tool in identifying our feelings and thoughts; according to Theory of Self-Relativity, long-term psychotherapy could actually be counter-productive for self-improvement. If we have to spend hours of our time to discuss a past situation that happened in a few seconds or in a few minutes; that is an inefficient process. This is why, in psychotherapy, each event that troubles us, often goes back on the frustrating table of discussion for multiple sessions; and then, we run of time without any resolution, until the next session. Psychotherapy is effective for many psychological issues as well as in personality-disorders; but according to Theory of Self-Relativity, psychotherapy is not the most practical and most efficient tool for on-the-go self-improvement.

Other more recent novelty self-improvement systems preach new-age scientific sounding theories of the mind that mishmash consciousness with quantum-mechanics or other supernatural and out of body experiences, in order to make these baseless hypotheses appear as "smart." These preachings use confusion through complication and ambiguity, to instill submission, by making people feel intimidated or stupid. They capitalize on the notion that if it sounds difficult to understand and if it is complicated and confusing, therefore, it must be really ingenious and effective. Since people looking to self-improve are often susceptible, these complicated sounding practices capitalize on people's weaknesses and susceptibilities, rather than helping them alleviate these weaknesses. Word-salading scientific sounding ambiguous jargon with mystical concepts does not make a fantastical-story legitimate, factual, or effective.

Ambiguity is not an indication of complexity.

Many think, ambiguity means complexity; hence, "it is not easy." On the contrary, ambiguity means either the subject matter is not clear; or *"Intentional-Ambiguity"* creates the opportunity to capitalize on people who are desperately yearning for awareness and self-improvement. Stringing together intelligent sounding yet ambiguous personal-opinions and claims which have no factual-basis is one of the oldest techniques used to control interactions; for example, in cults. Since people who are seeking self-improvement are already willing and open to discovering their weaknesses; and this susceptibility creates the opportunity for opportunists to instill further self-doubt in the person seeking improvement, in order to control the interaction, and to create a following. Control could be for multiple reasons, including financial and popularity gains. When a few weaker people begin to believe in what they are hearing, without understanding it; then a potential avalanche of popularity begins for something that has no factual, and more importantly, no common-sense basis. This is how, many societal-beliefs and cultural-traditions such as Santa Clause, Easter-bunny and even spirits, souls, ghosts and goblins got started. As discussed, this form of logical-fallacy is referred to as an appeal-to-popularity.

As discussed, confusion and ambiguity are hallmarks of cognitive-dissonance, which is one of Theory of Self-Relativity's 10-Enemies of Self-Improvement. Cognitive-dissonance arises when we hold two or more conflicting thoughts which constantly clash with reality. When we are susceptible and self-doubting, and when we are desperately looking for someone else to give us an answer and meanings that would help us straighten-out our life; that is when the opportunists try to implement and maintain control over us, in order for them to capitalize at our expense. This is common not only in financial matters, but it is even more common in unhealthy and high-conflict personal and romantic-relationships.

Ambiguity and confusion are hallmarks of deceptive interactions.

Furthermore, as older Eastern and other cultural relaxation methods are finding themselves into the modern-age self-improvement markets, many of these perception-based nonfactual teachings are causing further confusion for those seeking clarity. Just as massage-therapy does not fix broken bones, relaxation techniques that are centuries old do not apply to the "Self;" because they do not address or resolve improper thinking with proper cognitive-solutions. As discussed, in the appeals-to-tradition and the appeals-to-popularity sections, just because it's been done this way for a long time, doesn't mean it is true. These "unevolved" practices are simply ancient unwinding and relaxation techniques carried over from eras when human life was at a much simpler and slower pace; and when human understanding of nature, existence, and The-Universe was limited and flawed.

These practices were developed millennia ago by humans who did not have much understanding of biology, physics, and science. Ancient philosophers mostly based their philosophies on how they imagined and perceived nature was, and not based on facts and data of how nature and reality actually work. Since many of these philosophies were perceived and assumed without factual verification, these ambiguous-beliefs were carried to the present with the incorrect assumption of their unrealistic and flawed teachings. Just like humans, ideas, beliefs, and philosophies must be open to change so that they can interact properly with reality.

To improve; one must adapt, change, and evolve.

Ancient philosophies and doctrines that cannot adapt, change, or evolve, are mostly nonfactual. Factual concepts and theories adapt, change, and evolve; they do not just rely on subjective-interpretation. Facts and laws-of-physics, once discovered and understood, do not need interpretation, nor can they be manipulated; however, ancient and supernatural imaginations do require constant interpretation in order to make them applicable to modernity, and to prevent them from falling apart. Therefore, these concepts are open to manipulation.

This is why, Theory of Self-Relativity states:

Only one form of fact exists for every situation; hence, facts are facts, and facts are not open to interpretations. Since facts are not open to interpretation; therefore, facts are not open to manipulation.

Just being ancient and old does not mean being true; because despite the mythical representation of oldness as being wise, wisdom does not mean accepting ancient nonfactual-philosophies by uttering mystical sounding sentences. As discussed, true wisdom is the application of constantly evolving experience and knowledge.

Theory of Self-Relativity further defines "wisdom" as "the effective application of constantly evolving knowledge and experience, which is not contingent to subjective-interpretations."

In other words:

Wisdom is to see reality as it is; not as we want it to be.

Another intentionally-deceptive strategy, especially in modern personal-development and self-improvement, is what Theory of Self-Relativity refers to as "*Toxic-Sympathy.*"

Theory of Self-Relativity defines "Toxic-Sympathy" as "Intentionally nurturing victimhood, in order to manipulate and win over the weak and the susceptible."

Increasingly, especially in motivational and leadership teachings, as well as in politics, and in society as a whole; there have been entities and individuals who try to win over quantities of followers by engaging in what Theory of Self-Relativity has termed and defined as "toxic-sympathy." They do so through philosophies and ideologies disguised as being sympathetic and empathetic; not because they have genuine empathy for the people, but they do so for their own personal or group agenda. By appealing to people's emotions, instead of representing the truth, these entities manipulate the followers in order to persuade the masses to support their ideology and their agenda.

An appeal-to-emotion is a logical-fallacy that one deploys by manipulating the recipient's emotions; for example, one's empathy, in order to persuade or to win an argument in the absence of, or contrary to, factual-evidence. Appeal-to-emotions become stronger and wider accepted as more people get manipulated and persuaded to subscribe to and support the fallacy or the ideology. This is how, appeal-to-emotion transforms to appeal-to-popularity and appeal-to-tradition, which become the foundation for ideological-based groups such as cults, religion, politics, etc.; and the basis for their recruitment, indoctrination, and operations.

Theory of Self-Relativity further refers to such manipulative tactics of appealing to people's emotions, especially to their empathy, as the *"Empathy-Crusade."* The empathy-crusade, similar to toxic-sympathy, is intended for personal gains of the manipulator, which is derived at the expense of the followers and the believers; commonly, without the followers' or believers' awareness.

Theory of Self-Relativity defines "Empathy-Crusade" as "Appealing to the emotions of the weak and the susceptible, in order to manipulate them for personal gains."

One of the main ways that toxic-sympathy and empathy-crusades win so many people over so quickly is through nurturing victimhood and blame-shifting; by sympathizing with the intended targets that the causes of their life's mishaps and negativities are other-things or other-people. For example, these manipulators promote and persuade the fallacy that the targets' leaders, employers, or simply, the richer and the more successful people, are the causes of the person's difficulties or unhappiness in life. Toxic-sympathy and empathy-crusade promote self-victimization via blame-shifting onto other-people or onto other-things; including blaming fallacies such as bad-luck or destiny, in order to persuade and deceive the unsuspected.

Those who practice toxic-sympathy and empathy-crusade on others portray the world as being unfair; by implying that, for example, employers are unfairly and without care enjoying their success at the expense of their employees. These preaching motivational-teachers, often disguised as leadership-teachers, further portray the susceptible person as a victim who is vulnerable, yet courageous to live in such unfairness. They furthermore analogize the weak and the susceptible person's life as a suffering; while portraying leaders, business-owners, and people in-charge of others as self-centered and selfish.

By dividing people into falsely-fabricated opposing and antagonistic groups, and by working these groups against one-another; these influencers and motivational figures use appeal-to-emotions in order to create division by victimizing followers or employees, while vilifying leaders, business-owners, and higher-up organiza-tional management team-members. Such divisive practices, which are rooted in tribalism and as an us-against-them mentality; is one of the oldest tactics that ideological-groups such as cults, religion, society, politics, and other organized entities use to attract the weak and the susceptible, while demonizing the strong and the independent. Furthermore, while religious and other older and ancient organizations portray servitude as a noble characteristic; in the modern-times, especially after the invention of social-media, social-influencers, motivational-teachers, and leadership-preachers, tout and misrepresent the flawed concept of *"servant-leadership"* as a righteous and honorable character. By colluding and by manipulating the concept of providing a service with servitude, and by guilt-riddenly misrepresenting the role of a leader as a servant, and even as a minion; these ideologues create conflict and chaos so that they could benefit from bringing peace and harmony, through ambiguous and unreal concepts such as servant-leadership, to the very conflict, chaos, and division that they intentionally and connivingly created.

By appealing to such extreme human emotions, these manipulators quickly win over large numbers of followers, by helping the followers to self-deceive via toxic-sympathy. By shifting the personal- responsibility from the weak and the susceptible to other imaginary causes, or other-people who have nothing to do with the followers' life's difficulties, challenges, or setbacks; these motivational-teachers benefit handsomely at the expense of the weak and the susceptible. Improvement-seekers are easy to manipulate, because chronic-susceptibility often results in desperation to quickly want to make things better. According to Theory of Self-Relativity, this desperate need for quick-fixes and instant-gratification is the basis for gullibility.

Gullibility is the unintended consequence of susceptibility and desperation.

This is why, the weak and the susceptible are often mislabeled as gullible or naïve, because they are desperate to find quick-fixes to their problems; hence, they often fall victims to deceptive-ideologies, Ponzi schemes and other financial and quick-fix promising frauds. Therefore, the easiest and the quickest means of deceiving the susceptible from recognizing the truth, or to separate the gullible from their money, is to appeal to their emotions and to give them hope and a quick reason to feel better. Consequently:

Ideologies promote reliance on faith, instead of building confidence with facts and knowledge.

Since faith, hope, and beliefs do not require factual-verification; this is why, faith, hope, and beliefs are the primary tactics for an appeal-to-emotion. It is also for the same reasoning, those who rely on faith, hope, and beliefs, more often fall victim to misinformation, disinformation, and outright frauds. Hence why, the faithful are commonly referred to as naïve or as gullible.

Since *"gullibility is the unintended consequence of susceptibility and desperation;"* therefore:

Gullibility is the only requirement for ideology.

Thus:

- Gullibility is the only requirement for faith.
- Gullibility is the only requirement for wishful-thinking.
- Gullibility is the only requirement for empty-hope.
- Gullibility is the only requirement for false-beliefs.
- Gullibility is the only requirement for religion.
- Gullibility is the only requirement for new-age spirituality.
- Gullibility is the only requirement for cults.
- Gullibility is the only requirement for tribalism.

Those who deploy toxic-sympathy and empathy-crusades, end up causing lots of damage to susceptible-people in the long-run; because what is being fallaciously advocated in the short-term, is not how reality truly works. This is why, Theory of Self-Relativity advocates factual-thinking; because if we cannot evaluate thoughts and intents with facts, we could fall victim for ill-intent that is cleverly disguised to benefit the manipulator, at the expense of our own Self.

The right self-improvement system should simplify the process by helping us understand it, not by forcing us to try to learn something unlearnable through memorization or by subscribing to unrealistic and ambiguous ideologies. A valuable self-improvement system should also have time-efficiency so that it is not arduous. Once learned, a true self-improvement system should become efficient and should easily adapt and evolve; it should not require continuous effort to squeeze a barely noticeable result out of it. As stated throughout Theory of self-Relativity:

A true self-improvement and personal-development system should teach flexibility and adaptability.

A true "effective" Self-improvement system:

1. Must be universal.
2. Must be repeatable.
3. Must not be confusing.
4. Must be easy to understand.
5. Must be learned and not memorized.
6. Must be fact-based and not feelings-based.
7. Must evolve to quicken and become intuitive.
8. Must be applicable to all aspects of one's existence.
9. Must be mostly Self-based and not solely reliant on others.
10. Must adapt to how things are; not how one wants things to be.

Cognitive and factual-thinking enables us to not only address our own self-weaknesses factually, but it also allows us to connect to other-people and other-things in a factual and analytical format. Factual-thinking enables us to relate to everything and everyone else on an objective and factual-basis, and not on a purely desired emotional level. Theory of Self-Relativity is a personal-development and self-improvement system which is founded upon what it has termed as "the principle of factual-thinking." Only one form of fact exists for every situation. Facts are facts and facts are not open to interpretation; therefore, facts are not open to manipulation. Facts are open to examination and facts are even open to replacement should new and stronger facts emerge; however, facts are not open to interpretation. Unlike rules, laws, and agreements that are open to interpretation and amendment; facts are not open to amendment, but facts are open to replacement.

Rules and laws are amendable; but facts are not.

We can amend rules and laws, but we cannot change facts; because:

Rules and laws are established based on how we apply facts to a situation.

To change facts, we must change the circumstances associated with those facts so that the facts change in our favor. The only way that true improvement, fulfillment, and happiness could be achieved is by first minimizing negativities and uncertainties associated with the dislikable facts. Facts are the filter of our thoughts; therefore, facts can put us in control of our own virtues. Just as we cannot pay someone else to lose weight for us, we cannot expect someone else to help us improve; we must learn to do it on our own. Factual-thinking enables us to rely and depend on our own Self in order to improve, transform, and live a fulfilled life.

We must become our own BFFF "Best Factual Friend Forever."

Instead of peptalk and pure motivation, System of Self-Relativity, through its Cognitive-Cognition-Technique, which is based on factual-thinking, teaches us to approach improvement by first minimizing negativity, instead of trying to jump into happiness and positivity. Negativity minimization could only occur by first resolving or eliminating the causes of the negativity.

Contrary to popularly fallacious-beliefs, negativity cannot be eliminated simply by "positive-thinking." Theory of Self-Relativity demonstrates why positive-thinking is nothing but self-deception, because when we think positive, good things do not necessarily happen to us; and if they ever do, it was either as a matter of an action that we took, or it was as a result of chance. Furthermore, to live a happy life, we should not only minimize negativity, but we should learn to reach contentment. Theory of Self-Relativity further demonstrates that negativity is a state-of-existence; however, positivity or happiness are not states-of-existence, they are states-of-experience in the form of "incentive" or "reward." Therefore, longer-lasting positivity and happiness could only materialize in the absence of negativity and as a result of continuous effort, action, and change, in order to keep negativity under control.

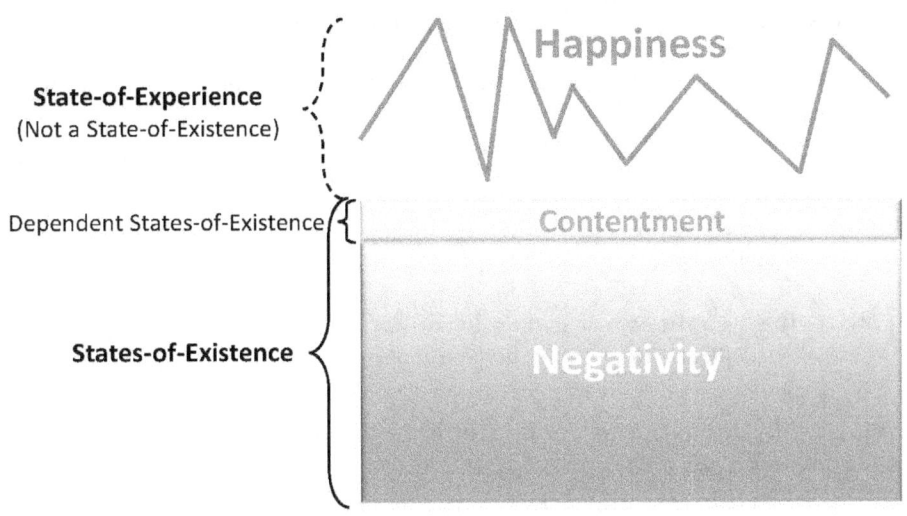

Therefore, statements such as "in pursuit of happiness" are nothing but unattainable chase-the-dragon fallacies; because happiness cannot be pursued. Positivity and happiness must be created from within the Self. According to Theory of Self-Relativity:

Happiness cannot be pursued; it must be produced.

This is why, factual-thinking is so important in preventing self-deception. It is better to realize and accept the dislikable fact that negativity is the default-state of our existence, and that happiness is only a sporadic form of reward; than to falsely believe if we think positive-thoughts or if we pray hard, good things will happen to us. When we realize that we must take the bitter pill of factuality in order to reach sustainable experiences of happiness; we will then be able to:

Live our life based on the stability of how reality works, rather than the instability of how we want reality to be.

When we take facts, as dislikable as they might be, and use them to make changes to adapt to factual-reality; many negativities that we tried to cover-up, ignore, or runaway from, will become realities that we fixed and got in-tune with. When we fix negativities, only then, we will truly be able to eliminate our negative personal-characteristics that we developed in coping with the false-realities that we were living with. For example, characteristics such as lying and jealousy are as a result of living our life based on how we want reality to be, rather than dealing with reality based on how it really is. Lying is undertaken for a multitude of reasons, but the most common reason for lying is to portray the dislikable reality in a more likable light. People lie, to misrepresent or to over-represent a certain situation or characteristic that they know is not true. People usually lie in order to represent their Self or their situation in a better light. People lie, because it is easier to lie and represent a falseness as truth, than it is to put in effort to correct and improve the shortcoming that they are lying about.

Theory of Self-Relativity categorizes targets of lies binarily:

1. **Lying to Others:** When people lie to others, they generally do so in order to:
   a. To present or convince others with a better than true representation of their own Self; for example, self-boasting.
   b. To take advantage of others by misrepresenting the truth; for example, with an intent to deceive or steal from others.

2. **Lying to Self:** When people lie to their own Self, which is known as self-deception, they usually do so in order to minimize the discomfort and pain associated with some truth or reality. They do so:
   a. By denying or by ignoring the less than optimal or even painful reality.
   b. By convincing themselves that reality is not as dislikable or as bad as it really is.

Lying is a deliberate act and it could be conscious or nonconscious. People lie for a multitude of reasons; however, Theory of Self-Relativity categorizes the reasons for lying, binarily:

1. **Intentional-Lying:** Is usually done for a self-serving purpose, which is commonly at the expense of someone else. For example, lying to others in order to gain something from them.

2. **Defensive-Lying:** Is usually protective and emotional in nature and manifests itself in the form of a defense-mechanism. Defensive-lying is commonly at the expense of the Self in the long-term, but it is undertaken in order to perceptually elevate one's own self-image in the short-term. For example, we lie to our Self in order to avoid pain, to feel good, or at the minimum, to feel less-bad, when the truth is emotionally dislikable; or we lie to others in order for them to like us.

To stop lying to our own Self and to others, we must learn to accept and face facts and reality that are not to our liking. Instead of lying to misrepresent the truth, when we accept facts as they are, regardless of how uncomfortable or how painful facts may be; we will then be able to use the facts to change the reality in our favor. When we put in effort to change the facts, and when the facts change in our favor because we put in the effort to make the change; we will then turn a potential lie into the truth. We can change uncomfortable and painful facts, not by lying and by covering-up the truth; but by changing the circumstances associated with the facts.

To stop lying, fix what you were lying about so it becomes the truth.

To accept facts in order to change, we must be able to have self-reflective and introspective ability; which according to Theory of Self-Relativity, is one of the two non-negotiables for self-improvement. No matter how painful and uncomfortable it may be, we must be able to seek and find what needs to be changed. To eliminate the need, the desire, or the habit of lying, we must first become aware of the fact that we lie; or at the minimum, we must become aware that we have a tendency to twist the truth. Self-improvement, which means to change and to progress for the better; is the only means to eliminate lying.

Fix what you are lying about, and your lie becomes the truth.

According to Theory of Self-Relativity, to truly improve, we must seek facts, as dislikable as they might be; and we must use these facts to change things in our favor so that the truth becomes more to our liking. This can only be done through factual-thinking. To think factually, we use language in order to understand the factual-values of our thoughts. Although language is used for speaking; the majority of our language is actually used for thinking. When we think of something, we think of it in language; and when we speak to someone, our speech is simply an outward expression of our thoughts. In fact, when we are thinking, we are actually having internal-dialogue with our own Self. Contrary to popular belief, the main reason that human-beings developed language was not to communicate with others; but it was to communicate with our own Self, in the form of thinking and internal-dialogue.

Our internal-dialogue or internal-monologue, also known as our self-talk, is our inner-voice which is as a result of our thoughts. Our self-talk is a reflection of our feelings, it is an expression of our thoughts, and collectively, it is a representation of our self-image and our sense of Self. This is why, self-improvement must be based on factual-thinking, because a healthy internal-dialogue is necessary for having a healthy sense of Self. Since language is primarily used to help us think; a healthy inner-voice, which is how we perceive our own Self, could only exist if our thinking-system is based on facts, and not based on feelings.

The ability to communicate is an essential characteristic of living things. Communication ability, and skills of communication increase and become more detailed and effective as the intelligence and problem-solving abilities of the living-thing increases. While communication could exist between animate and inanimate things, majority of communication which represents connection with the Self involves living-things. Communication is a direct indication of the relativity and interactions between living-things. Communication is the connection, interaction, or the exchange of things among entities.

According to Theory of Self-Relativity:

Communication creates and preserves connections, while it maintains and evolves relationships.

Language, on the other hand, is a communication method that intelligent-living-things possess; and for the time being, humans are the only animals known to be capable of communicating through language.

According to Theory of Self-Relativity:

- Language enables us to form and to understand our thoughts.
- Language enables us to communicate our thoughts with our own Self and with others.
- Language is one of the necessary contributors for the advancement of our species.
- Communication of language is our most common form of behavior.

Language is our most common behavior, and its primary purpose is the understanding and communication of our thoughts.

Since language is a form of communication of information; therefore, Theory of Self-Relativity considers communication of language as our most common form of behavior. Although language is an advanced form of communication between people; as discussed, the primary reason for development of language and the primary role of language is for thinking.

Language enables communication of thoughts with our own Self, because before we use language to communicate our thoughts with others, we first need to be able to process and understand our thoughts in a language format with our own Self. Language is essential for change, progress, and for the advancement of intelligence. Language is an advanced form of communication; however, language is not the only means of communication.

Communication is a form of exchange between two or more entities. Theory of Self-Relativity categorizes communication binarily:

1. **Intangible-Communication:** Is the most aware form of communication that we engage in, which is the exchange of information and dialogue between our Self with our Self, with other-people, or with other communication-capable living-things. For example, talking, writing, body-language, eye-contact, etc.

2. **Tangible-Communication:** Can also be physical which relies on our five senses. Although we might not often be aware that interaction through our senses is a form of communication; though, tangible communication is commonly associated with intangible-communication. For example, touch, sex, physical-altercation, etc. Tangible-communication could also be in other forms; for example, communication of disease by transferring disease causing bacteria and viruses between people or species.

Theory of Self-Relativity primarily focuses on the importance of communication through thinking, feelings, and behavior, within our own Self, as well as, between our Self and others; because intangible-communication is not only a form of exchange of content and information, but it is also a form of exchange of emotions, which is an essential component of our relationships. Hence, according to Theory of Self-Relativity:

The influence of emotions on communication often changes the context of the communication.

Communication is an action, and just like any other behavior, communication is a result of our thoughts and feelings. The majority of our "personal" communications are initiated and guided by our thoughts and feelings; therefore, it is essential for us to be mindful and aware of the causes of our thoughts and emotions that precede any form of communication.

"Think before you speak" is an old adage that represents this important observation. To be a strong and effective communicator, it is important for us to have self-regulation and self-awareness; because communication is commonly a combination of thoughts and emotions, as well as tangible and intangible skills. With the advent of new technologies such as the internet, social-media, and other forms of electronic communication; the need for quick and clever thinking, as well as emotional-regulation, which translate to the quality and effectiveness of our communication, is even more important than ever before. Misinterpretations of content or emotionally-based communication could have significant repercussions in the virtual world; hence, proper communication-skills that are based on proper thinking is an important requirement for modern-day self-improvement. Therefore:

Think before you speak; think before you click.

According to Theory of Self-Relativity, communication, and especially language in the form of speech, is one of the most important, if not the most important forms of behavior that we undertake. To speak or not to speak, is to act or not act; which results in the expression of our thoughts externally. Therefore, in order for our words and statements to have real-value and strength, our thoughts must be based on facts.

Our words and our statements represent our mindset. Although, they don't necessarily represent what we are thinking, they do represent how we are expressing our thoughts.

The less-cluttered our thinking is the more precise the expressions of our thoughts would be; therefore, the more our language and our communication abilities evolve, the more we need to learn to improve our skills of communication. Speaking, writing, and all other forms of communication are skills that we learn and develop; yet we are rarely aware that our language and communication capabilities are the main expressions of our thoughts that are represented in our behavior. When we learn and improve our skills of thinking factually, we will consequently rid our Self of unnecessary cluttering nonfactual-thoughts; and this clearer mental-state will enable us to express our thoughts quickly, cleverly, and effectively. Clarity of thinking and clarity of communication is how we create the best representation of our Self; not only from other-people's perspective, but also as our own self-identity. Therefore, since communication is the most common form of behavior, in order to learn and improve our skills of communication, we must improve the way we think.

Since communication is the most common form of personal-behavior; to improve your communication skills, you must improve how you think.

This is further reason, Theory of Self-Relativity advocates what it has termed as factual-thinking; because, factual-thinking enables us to act, react, or inact based on how reality is, and not based on how we want to believe reality is, or not based on how others want us to believe reality is. Since language is the most common form of behavior; therefore, factual-thinking enables us to think rationally, thereby, it enables us to connect, interact, and behave based on how reality is, and not based on how we want reality to be, and not based on how others want to control what our reality should be. Consequently, since language is our most common form of behavior; hence, how we speak, how we communicate, and how we express our Self, is a reflection of how we respond to our thoughts. If our thoughts are based on facts, then our expressions and behavior will be based on how reality is. However, if we cannot think factually, and if we are influenced by ideologies and dogmas fabricated by culture, society, religion, and as a whole, by other-people; subsequently, our language, our expressions, and our behavior will be influenced and controlled by other factors, instead of being supported and guided by facts.

Therefore, if our thoughts are influenced by ideologies instead of facts, and if we are taught to think and express words, sentences, and our language based on societal fabrications instead of representations of our fact-based thinking; then, our thinking, our language, and our behavior will be controlled by ideological-influences and social-constructs, instead of our language and our behavior being an expression of our independent factual-thinking.

Language should express thoughts; language should not control thoughts.

When we are told that our words and our language have other meanings and define other purpose than what they were intended to reflect and express; then, our language, which is a form of our behavior, becomes controlled by others, hence, our thoughts and our sense of Self are defined by others. When language becomes prescriptive, instead of it being descriptive; that is when we are societally and ideologically being mind-controlled.

Language should be descriptive of thoughts; not prescriptive for thinking.

When language becomes relativistic or when it becomes a social-construct; that is when we are societally, culturally, and intellectually regressing backwards to the dark-ages. Social-construct of language is no different than dogmatic oppression of thinking in the form of thought-control. When language expresses and reflects beliefs, especially dogmatic-beliefs instilled upon us by culture, society, and religion; that is when our thinking and our behavior reflect a mindset that is based on preferences, feelings, and beliefs, rather than them being based on factual-thoughts and knowledge. As discussed throughout Theory of Self-Relativity, a belief is a mindset that is not proven with facts; therefore, a belief is not knowledge. Unless beliefs are constructed as a hypothesis on the path of discovering the supportive facts for that belief, in order to turn the belief into knowledge; most beliefs are manmade fabricated mindsets intended to support a preferred or a comforting emotion. Therefore, beliefs are closely associated with feelings; and even modern neuroscientific studies demonstrate an increase in dopamine production in association with strong comforting-beliefs. It is because of language that:

Only humans believe; other animals don't.

Due to their lower intelligence, other animals are incapable of language; hence, they are incapable of self-deception through beliefs. However, humans created language so they can understand and communicate their thoughts by giving them meaning; and in doing so, humans also learned how to manipulate their thoughts through language to self-deceive and feel better.

Words have meanings; therefore, language must represent a true reflection and description of the originally intended meaning of words used in the communication of language. If words are intentionally and falsely manipulated by ideologies, dogmas, or social-construct to have other meanings; then we cannot properly express and communicate our thoughts with others, or with our own Self. This is especially true for the young, the inexperienced, the weak, and the susceptible people; because, lack of knowledge, lack of experience, and the inability for critical-thinking could influence such individuals in improperly identifying the usage and application of words and language, and thus, influence the way they think. Therefore, ill-intent, flawed-thinking, and emotional-reasoning, could alter the meaning of words and the concept of expressed language; thereby, influence, alter, and destroy proper thinking ability.

If one truly believes saying a few words alongside manmade rituals over a piece of bread and a glass of wine, turns the bread and the wine into the body and the blood of a supernatural- being, or if one is convinced that the biological fact of the fundamental binary nature of male and female sex is malleable through social-construct to indicate a countless number of personally preferred or societally constructed genders; consequently, the meaning of words that define the language that we think with and that we communicate our thoughts and behavior with others, will become corrupted. In such situations, instead of reflecting and communicating our thoughts; words and language will control our thoughts.

Language-control, thought-control, and behavior-control is how dogmas and autocracies control people. Modern-era social-constructs are no different than ancient religious-dogmas or authoritarian-rules; they create control through guilt-ridden and shame-based accusations, into self-censorship and blind adherence to the fabricated ideology. When language and words are manipulated for control, independent and critical-thinking takes a backseat to following the crowd; because, not being a follower gets depicted as being insensitive, selfish, and even evil. When people are told what to say, and when they are blamed, ridiculed, ousted, and even punished for not following ideological mindsets reflected by their words, language, and behavior; that is when cognitive-dissonance, which is one of Theory of Self-Relativity's 10-Enemies of Self-Improvement, sets in.

When language and expression of thoughts are manipulated to represent collective-guilt for something that a member of society had nothing to do with, or when it is used to represent original-sin from real or fabricated ancient dogma that a modern individual has nothing to do with; that is when words and language become a form of thought-control and mind-control instead of expressions of independent, critical, and factual-thinking, originating from individually independent minds.

Because language and communication connect the Self with the Self and with others; connections, which are commonly associated with interactions, is how we relate to our Self and to everything and everyone else. This is why, communication, especially in the form of language, is a good demonstration of how everything and everyone in The-Universe is relative to one another. Since communication is a means of exchange of information among things, and since all things are made of matter; hence, all things are made of atoms.

Since humans are made of atoms, just as everything else in The-Universe is made of atoms; consequently, the laws-of-physics which govern The-Universe apply equally to all matter, because all matter, including humans, are made of atoms. Just as the principles of general physics are always the same for all matter across The-Universe; therefore, the principles of relativity are always the same for everyone and everything in The-Universe.

Theory of Self-Relativity defines "Relativity" as "a thing's or a person's state-of-existence in relation to everything and everyone else."

Although all laws-of-physics apply equally and in the same way to all matter including humans; Einstein's Special Theory of Relativity states that these laws become "relative" to different matter when matter is in motion. To simplify, although humans and all other objects are made of atoms and the laws-of-physics apply equally to us and to all other objects; these laws become relative to us or to other-people or to other-things, when we or others are in motion.

When we are in motion, our location in space and our time of travel become relative to someone else's location and time of travel, which is measured as the speed of travel. Speed is simply a measurement of how much space is traveled in a certain amount of time; therefore, anything that moves, travels through some length of "space" and in a certain amount of "time." Since motion creates movement through space at a certain speed, and since speed is a measure of amount of distance moved in a certain amount of time; thus, motion indicates that space and time are also relative to each other. It is this observation of motion that proves space and time are intertwined and cannot be separated. This relationship of space and time is known as *"SpaceTime;"* and SpaceTime exists because everything in The-Universe is constantly in motion.

If there was no motion, there would be no space and no time; therefore, nothing would exist.

If there was no motion, nothing would exist, because without motion there would be no change. Thus, change is the natural order of The-Universe; therefore:

Change is a measure of motion, and time is a measurement of change.

As further discussed, nothing is stationary and everything is in motion. Newton's first law of motion, sometimes referred to as the Law of Inertia, states that "an object at rest stays at rest, and an object in motion stays in motion with the same speed and in the same direction unless acted upon by an unbalanced force."

Contrary to our common thinking, to move something, we do not have to push or pull it, but to make something stop, we must apply force to stop it; because, motion is the natural order of The-Universe. For example, although the chair that we are sitting on seems stationary and not moving, the only reason the chair is not moving is because forces such as gravity and friction are keeping it in place "relative" to Earth. If the chair was not affected by the Earth's gravity or by the friction between its legs and the floor, the chair would be travelling in space at the same speed that the Earth is currently travelling through space. Furthermore, although the chair is stationary relative to Earth, the chair is actually travelling through space and time as Earth travels around the Sun, as our Solar-System travels around our the Milky-Way-Galaxy, and as our Galaxy travels through the ever-expanding Universe. In summary:

Since everything in The-Universe is in motion; therefore, motion creates relativity between space, time, and everything and everyone.

The faster an object moves, the less time it will take for that object to travel through a certain distance in space; likewise, the slower an object moves, the more time it will take for that object to travel the same distance in space. This means, time for the faster moving object travels slower than time does for the slower moving object; because the same distance takes less time to travel for the faster moving object.

The fastest that an object could move in space, as allowed by the laws-of-physics, is at the speed of light, which is also known as the "cosmic-speed-limit;" and that value is about 186,000 miles per second or about 300,000 kilometers per second. If an object could move at the speed of light, time for that object would become stationary; hence, time would stop. The closer an object travels to the speed of light, the slower that object would experience the passage-of-time; conversely, the slower an object travels, the faster it will experience time passing by.

The slowest speed that a thing can travel is zero, which means that thing is (relatively) stationary. Since the faster an object travels, the slower time passes for it; therefore, objects that are at rest and not moving are experiencing the fastest passage-of-time. The fastest passage-of-time as scaled and measured by humans is one-second-per-second; thus, the fastest passage-of-time is one-second-per-second, and the slowest passage-of-time is zero seconds.

SpaceTime Relativity		
Motion (mi/sec)	**Space/Distance (mi)**	**Time (sec)**
Stationary (0 mi/sec)	0 (mi)	1 sec/sec
Light-Speed (186k mi/sec)	186,000 (mi)	0 sec/sec

Therefore, the extreme measurements of SpaceTime and motion can be considered binarily:

1. **No-Motion:** When an object is (relatively) stationary; for example, a chair:

   a) No motion exists, and no Space is travelled.

   b) Time ticks at its fastest limit of one-second-per-second.

2. **Fastest-Motion:** When an object travels at maximum possible speed:

   a) Space is travelled at its fastest pace of about 186,000 mile per second.

   b) Time does not tick, hence, time stands still; thus, time becomes stationary.

Since space and time are relative to one-another, and since everything in space and time is in motion; therefore, we, as humans, are also relative to not only everything in SpaceTime or in The-Universe, but we are also relative to one-another.

Similar constancies and relativities apply to our own Self, as described in Theory of Self-Relativity. Since humans are made of matter, the laws-of-physics, chemistry, and biology, which make up each and every person, are the same for all people; but they are relative to each person's SpaceTime. As discussed throughout Theory of Self-Relativity, everything and everyone is relative to one another; hence, just as the laws-of-physics apply uniformly to all things including humans, the principles of Self-Relativity are also uniformly applicable and relative to everyone. Although Self-Relativity is uniformly applicable to everyone, unlike the laws-of-physics, Self-Relativity is not absolute.

Theory of Self-Relativity defines "Self-Relativity" as "the interactions and relationships of the Self internally and externally with the Self and with everything and everyone else."

Theory of Self-Relativity categorizes "Self-Relativity" binarily:

1. **Tangible-Self-Relativity:** Represents our physical connectivity and interactions with our own Self, and with everything and everyone else.

2. **Intangible-Self-Relativity:** Represents our mental, emotional, and behavioral connectivity and interactions with our own Self, and with everything and everyone else.

Since everything is relative, in order to have a strong Self-Relativity, especially relative to other-people; it is important to have a well-developed *"Perspective-Taking"* ability. Theory-of-mind is the ability for us to understand our Self and other-people's mental-states such as thoughts, feelings, beliefs, etc. Theory-of-mind allows us to recognize and distinguish that others have different perspectives and that they could think, feel, and behave differently than we would in similar situations. Perspective-taking is the act of perceiving a situation, or understanding a concept, from an alternative point-of-view; such as that of another individual.

Theory of Self-Relativity defines "perspective-taking" as "one's ability to objectively exercise and engage in extrospection."

By having perspective and by recognizing and understanding these differentiating characteristics; we will be able to have more efficient, tolerant and rewarding interactions and relationships with our Self and with others. Theory-of-mind and perspective-taking are further indications of the relativities of different people's thinking, feeling, and experience to the same situation. Perspective-taking shows how, situations, thoughts, and feelings could be relative to each person's or each observer's point-of-view. For example, we might see the below figure as the number 9 while someone else from a different perspective sees it as the number 6.

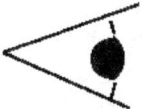  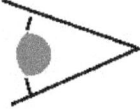

Another example could be if we and a friend are sitting across a small table in a crowded coffee shop; our experience, even in the same locality, will be different than that of our friend's. As we and our friend are having a face-to-face conversation, we could be observing the cars in the street, which are behind our friend; while our friend is observing the counter of the store which is behind us. The activity in each differing background gives each of us a different awareness, perspective, and even experience of the same environment. A yellow car in the street in our line of sight could trigger a different thought or experience in our mind than the view of a certain customer at the counter behind us would for our friend.

Although theory-of-mind, which is the ability to understand and accept that others have separate thoughts, feelings, and experiences than us, appears to be an innate potential for humans; according to Theory of Self-Relativity, theory-of-mind and perspective-taking can be cultivated into a more efficient and quicker thinking-system via self-improvement. Perspective-taking allows us to adapt and think quicker relative to others, while it enables us to realize that others think and experience things differently than we do relative to the same scenario or similar situation. By understanding that, even in similar situations, people could have different perspectives and could think differently, we will then be able to be less-judgmental; thus, we could have less-conflicting and more balanced relationships with others. Likewise, by mastering theory-of-mind and by understanding the subjectivities of people's perspectives; we will also be less critical of our Self, by realizing that other-people's perspectives are their own and those perspectives are not necessarily a reflection of our self-worth. Theory-of-mind and perspective-taking are important characteristics in relating to others and even in relating to our own Self.

Perspective-taking enables us to become less judgmental of others while being less critical of our own Self.

Perspective-taking is not only important for understanding, for having empathy, and for maintaining a balanced-relationship with others; but it is also a winning characteristic in other human interactions such as negotiations, politics, and legal proceedings. Our perspective-taking ability enhances our persuasive-speech ability. By being able to understand other-people's perspectives, we can relate to others more effectively, thus, we can become a better negotiator, a stronger deal-maker, and a more successful influencer; especially in neutral-settings or with undecided-parties. Perspective-taking can significantly increase our persuasive abilities, especially with those who need convincing to make a decision in our favor; for example, voters, lawmakers, and mediators. Perspective-taking can give us a "legitimate" ability to be a good salesperson, a strong closer, and a respected person in business and in interpersonal relationships.

A good closer doesn't need to lie or exaggerate; a good closer is one who can present a situation from other-people's perspective.

Perspective-taking can also be an important factor for team work; for example, in business and in sports. Successful outcomes are the result of not only having a good listening ability, but also as a result of our ability to see and think from other-people's perspective.

Similarly, in personal and in romantic-relationships, by being a good listener and by taking perspective, we can be more caring, more empathetic, and we can even be more tolerant in our interactions with our loved-ones.

Theory-of-mind and perspective-taking follow similar principles to personal-thoughtfulness, which as discussed, is an important attribute for self-improvement. Just as we should be mindful and thoughtful of our own thoughts and feelings, we should do the same with others. Although feelings are not rational, feelings are valid; therefore, what someone else thinks or feels, is real to them. While other-people's thoughts and feelings about a situation or an issue might not be factual; by perspective-taking, we can have better understanding of their point-of-view, hence, we can have more interest and empathy for what they are feeling.

The reverse is also true. By others being able to share our perspective, be it factual or not; they can have better understanding and more empathy for us. When people learn to take other people's perspectives, correcting the differences and adapting to each other will be a much smoother and less-defensive process.

Perspective-taking addresses the cognitive aspect of interactions, while empathy addresses the emotional aspect.

Perspective-taking, in interpersonal-relationships, increases understanding; which in-turn, increases empathy, respect, and courtesy for one another. Relationships are further discussed in detail in subsequent sections.

Perspective-taking and empathy are integral for positive interpersonal interactions and relationships.

As discussed, perspective-taking is the act of perceiving a situation or understanding a concept from an alternate point of view, such as that of another individual; therefore, self-improvement and living a quality existence also require understanding how we think, feel, and behave, relative to others and how others do so relative to us. This *"Bilateral-Perspective"* is important in balancing our self-equation by realizing that we are on one side of the equation, while others are on the other side; therefore, we see things relative to our perspective, while others see things relative to their own perspective.

Theory of Self-Relativity defines "bilateral-perspective" as "our ability to take perspective of others' thoughts and emotions, while requiring others to take perspective of our thoughts and emotions."

Bilateral-perspective is our ability to see things and situations from others' point of view, while evaluating it relative to our own perspective of things. Likewise, bilateral-perspective involves other-people's ability to see things from our point of view, and to evaluate it relative to their perspective of things. Therefore, perspective-taking must be bilateral and bidirectional; in other words, in interpersonal-relationships, perspective-taking must be a two way-street.

Bilateral-perspective establishes respect and courtesy, while creating reciprocity and mutuality.

Bilateral-Perspective

Perspective-taking and the ability to have bilateral-perspective is a core requirement for our *"Self-Relativity"* with others. However, despite the fact that perspective-taking and bilateral-perspective should become a routine part of our interactive abilities; *"Self-Relativity"* or *"Personal-Relativity"* should not be just two-dimensional. As discussed:

Theory of Self-Relativity defines "Self-Relativity" as "the interactions and relationships of the Self internally and externally with the Self and with everything and everyone else."

Therefore, although bilateral-perspective is an integral part of Self-Relativity; true Self-Relativity must be viewed from three different perspectives, better known as Theory of Self-Relativity's *"Trilateral-Relativity."* Because, just like other personal-relativities, our Self-Relativity or our Personal-Relativity is best understood and engaged when observed from three distinct perspectives.

As described:

Theory of Self-Relativity defines "Trilateral-Relativity" as "the three-sided relationships, connections and interactivities of one's Self with the Self and with others."

Trilateral-Relativity consists of:

1. **Self-to-Self Relativity:** How we relate to our own Self; and how we view, perceive, understand, feel, and value our own Self. This is the most important, yet often, the most ignored of all Self-Relativities.
2. **Self-to-Others Relativity**: How we relate to our own Self; and how we view, perceive, understand, feel, and value our Self relative to others. This is the second most important of all Self-Relativities.
3. **Others-to-Self Relativity:** How others relate to our Self; and how others view, perceive, understand, feel, and value our Self relative to their own Self. Although significant, according to Theory of Self-Relativity, other people's relativity to us takes a back seat to our own personal-perspective of our Self; because if we cannot be aware of how we relate to and how we view, perceive, understand, feel, and value our own Self, we would not be able to properly relate to how others view, perceive, understand, feel, and value us either. This is why, Theory of Self-Relativity insists on living a centered-self life, and to live our life from the inside-out.

Trilateral-Relativity enables us to have better self-awareness and stronger ability to self-reflect.

We must know our own Self so that others can better know who we are.

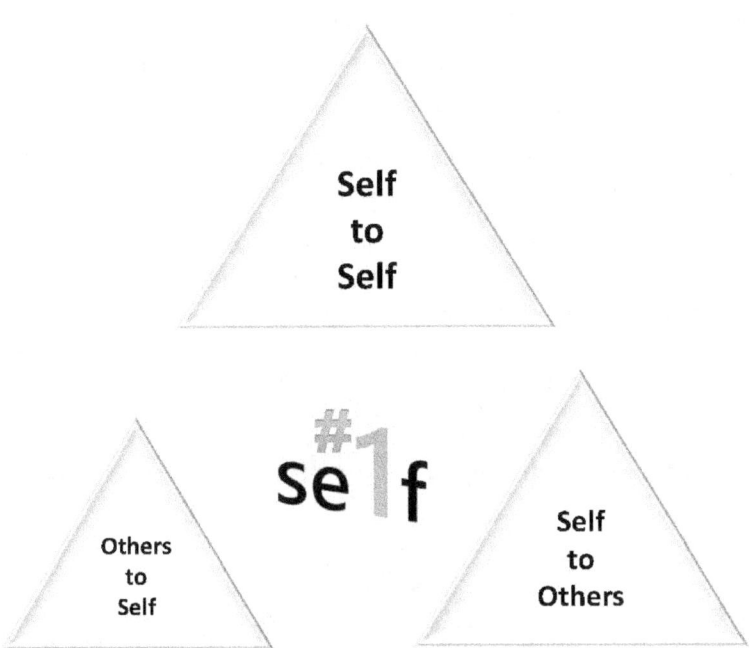

Humans are social-animals, and interactions with other-people is an important aspect of our existence; however, our interactions with others cannot be healthy if we do not know how to first prioritize our own Self, and how to have healthy interactions and relativities with our Self. This is why, we must have a healthy sense of Self before we can relate to others. As discussed throughout Theory of Self-Relativity, our Self must be the most important entity in our life. If our Self does not exist or if our Self is not healthy, nothing else matters; because we will not be able to interact with or be of value to others. Theory of Self-Relativity brings focus to the Self and to the relativities of the Self with the Self, and, with everything and everyone else. To properly be able to relate to our Self and to others, we must first establish and improve our own self-identity; and this begins by our ability to *"Self-Reflect."*

Theory of Self-Relativity defines "self-reflection" as "our ability to exercise and engage in introspection."

Therefore, self-reflection could be viewed as the reverse of perspective-taking. Self-reflection allows us to introspect and examine our own positive or negative qualities, traits, and characteristics, so that we can improve upon them. Awareness and understanding of our traits and characteristics are cognitive-processes; therefore, we must be able to evaluate our underlying thoughts that are associated with our traits and characteristics. As discussed throughout Theory of Self-Relativity, our self-identity, our self-image, and our sense of Self are all as a result of how we think; therefore:

We are our thoughts.

Our sense of Self is as a result of how and what we think, and how these thoughts manifest themselves into our feelings, behavior, and interactions within our own Self and with everything and everyone else.

Our existence and our self-identity are "relative" to how we think, how we feel, how we behave, and how we interact with our Self and with everything and everyone else.

As discussed, our mind, which is where our thinking takes place, is the metaphoric immaterial-byproduct of our material-brain's activities. Furthermore, the three main categories that make up our self-identity which are also immaterial-byproducts of our physical-brain's activities are; our thoughts, our feelings, and our behavior. Therefore, as stated by Theory of Self-Relativity:

I think...therefore I feel...therefore I am

Self-Identity

- Our thoughts are the underlying causes of our feelings; hence, our feelings are a symptom of our thoughts.
- Our feelings, which are caused by our thoughts, are the catalysts which lead to our behavior; thus, our feelings are the mediators of our behavior.
- Our behavior, is the result or the effect of how we feel; therefore, our behavior is caused by our thoughts and it reflects how we respond to our thoughts.
- In summary, how we think is responsible for how we behave.

This is why:

Our behavior does not represent how we are thinking; it only represents how we are responding.

Although our behavior, which could be in the form of an action or inaction, is as a result of how we think; however, our behavior does not represent what we are thinking, our behavior represents how have expressed our thoughts and how we have responded to them.

The primary inhibiting factor for self-improvement is that most people live their lives in response to their feelings; because feelings are readily and easily accessible as they are closer to our behavior than our thoughts are. Although feelings are real and feelings are valid, feelings do not have rationality; therefore, those feelings which tend to get us into trouble, are mostly generated as a result of nonfactual and irrational thoughts. Feelings are a symptom, and to react to a symptom without understanding its underlying cause is no different than covering up a problem without resolving its cause. To correctly *"interact"* with a situation, we must first *"understand"* the real and actual cause of the situation; and to understand something, we must first become *"aware"* of the cause of that something.

As discussed throughout Theory of Self-Relativity, the cause of an intangible-feeling or an emotion is an underlying-thought; therefore, in order to resolve or eliminate a negative-feeling, we must first become aware of the thought that is causing our feeling. Once through awareness, we identify the thought, we then move to understand the thought by evaluating it to see if the thought is factual or nonfactual. If the thought is factual, then the positive or negative feeling that we feel is also genuine; hence, we can proceed to taking an action based on our feeling. However, if the thought is nonfactual, we either abstain from taking an action until we find the factual cause of the thought; or we dismiss the thought for being nonfactual because no supportive-facts can be found. By dismissing a thought, its underlying feeling automatically disappears; which means, we take no action. When we don't think of a thought, we don't generate a feeling; therefore, no action is taken. Likewise, when we dismiss or eliminate a thought, the feeling which was generated as a result of that thought also disappears automatically.

System of Self-Relativity provides clever cognitive-tools so that we can develop our quick thinking-skills, in order to achieve awareness and understanding for effective personal-transformation. According to Theory of Self-Relativity, many self-help, and even, therapy programs solely focus incorrectly on feelings; in contrast, The Cognitive-Cognition-Technique enables us to recognize that our feelings are directly related to and are as a result of our thoughts. Our intangible-feelings or our emotions are a symptom of their underlying causes, and these causes are always our thoughts. By becoming aware of our feelings and by understanding their underlying thoughts, we can then take proper action or inaction; hence why, our thoughts must always precede our feelings. By learning to allow our thoughts to generate our feelings, and by not allowing our feelings to create false-thoughts to rationalize our desired-feelings; we can then get on the path of minimizing our emotional-thinking.

We must fit feelings to thoughts; not try to fit thoughts to feelings.

As discussed, feelings are irrational. Furthermore, feelings are unstable and cannot exist as standalone entities because a feeling is a symptom of its underlying cause; therefore, the nature of every intangible-feeling or an emotion is completely reliant on the thought which is supporting the existence of that feeling. If the thought that causes or supports a feeling goes away, that feeling will immediately disappear; thus, the real-value of a feeling is completely reliant on the real-value of the thought that is generating and supporting that feeling. If the thought is factual, then the resulting feeling will also be as a result of facts and true-reality. However, although all our feelings are valid, this does not mean all of our feelings have factual-value. When we minimize our random feelings controlling us and when we allow our factual-thoughts to direct our self-identity; we will then generate reality-based genuine-feelings and we will then take action based on our "Factual-Feelings."

Theory of Self-Relativity defines a "factual-feeling" as "an emotion which is generated and supported by an underlying factual-thought."

By allowing our factual-thoughts to control our feelings, we will enable our feelings and emotions to become better defined and to be less-chaotic and less-negative. When we learn to only keep feelings that are as a result of factual-thoughts; we will then begin to eliminate unnecessary, unfounded, and often, self-inflicted negative-emotions. Although reference to a factual-feeling, just as references to emotional-thinking, is metaphorical; such metaphor helps to visualize and perceive how we can use facts as the main filter to reach emotional-stability. By learning to think factually we will have focused and genuine-feelings, rather than a clutter of fluctuating emotions that bombard our mind and inhibit us from proper decision-making.

1. Uncluttered and focused thoughts lead to filtered and focused-thinking.
2. Uncluttered and focused thoughts lead to filtered and clear-feelings.
3. Uncluttered and focused thoughts lead to filtered and effective-behavior.

The filter of thoughts are facts; the confuser of thoughts are feelings.

The best way to unclutter our mind and to focus our thoughts is through evaluating our "individual" or "fundamental" thoughts in a binary-format. Our mind is most comfortable when it thinks binarily, which means when it views, observes, or analyses something in one of its two basic-states, or one of its two potential forms. Choosing "either or" of the choices of a situation is much easier and carries less potential for confusion or mistakes than when facing a multitude of choices. As discussed, the role of our primitive-mind is to keep us safe. During primitive-times, the way that our primitive-mind kept us safe was to make quick decisions. The quickest decisions can be made when there are only two choices to choose from. During primitive-times, quick decision-making could have been the difference between life and death. When confronted with a wild animal, our ancestors had to make quick decisions as to fight-or-flight; they did not have time to make complicated decisions by gathering more data and information.

Binary thought-processing quickens our thinking; because the quickest decisions are made when there are only two choices to choose from.

However, as humans have advanced, we have minimized primitive-dangers while increasing choices; which in-turn, have complicated how we think and how we make decisions. Consequently, this increase in choices and the resulting complexity in thinking and decision-making has preoccupied our mind and confused our feelings. Although our mind keeps wanting to deal with things in a simple and binary-format, we are forced to think of multiple choices and a multitude of issues and problems simultaneously. The more confused and the more overloaded our thinking becomes, the more confused and stressed our feelings become. Therefore, to minimize stress, to increase focus, and to quicken our thinking, we should learn to adapt our individual-thoughts with the format that our mind feels least stressed and most comfortable with; namely, the binary-approach. The binary-approach helps us to minimize confusion and it enables us to sort and organize best of two choices from the bottom-up and at the fundamental-level of our thinking; specifically, at the level of our individual-thoughts.

The human mind, the human body, the world around us, The-Universe, and everything at its simplest form of perception and fundamental state of observation is binary in nature. Even symmetry is binary; therefore, almost everything that, we as humans, deal with could be identified in a binary-format at its fundamental-level. For example:

- It either is, or it isn't.
- It either exists or it doesn't exist.
- It's either stationary or it's in motion (in relative terms).
- It's either positive or it's negative.
- It's either light or it's dark.
- It's either living or it's non-living.
- And for our thinking; it's either factual or it's nonfactual.

The binary-approach not only eases our individual-thought-processes, but it is commonly used in many of our everyday life choices. Additionally, the binary-format is inherent to many of our personal, traditional, cultural, and societal aspects of life. For example:

- We are either a male or a female.
- We are either single or married.
- We are either religious or non-religious.
- We are either employed or unemployed.
- We are either a plaintiff or a defendant.
- We either root for one sports team or the other.
- We are either alive or dead.

The binary-approach introduces speed and efficiency in problem-solving, and when faced with complex issues, if the issue could be narrowed down to its fundamental-components and dealt with in a binary-format, the result could be more precise, and it could be achieved with more speed and efficiency. As discussed, it is not a coincidence, nor is it by chance, that many human designed technologies that operate on software and that utilize algorithms are also based on binary-search or binary-logic at their fundamental operational levels. Binary-format and problem-solving creates more efficiency and speed, especially if the binary-approach could be undertaken at the fundamental-level of the issue at hand. Even at the macro-level of human existence, binary-approach such as fight-or-flight, despite its potential errors, could be the difference between life and death.

Almost everything in its simplest perspective or in its fundamental-format can be categorized and further subcategorized in a binary-format; for example, all things are either:

1. **Material-things:** Are things that are made of matter; for example, humans, animals, rocks, etc. Material-things themselves can subsequently be categorized into:

    a. **Tangible (material-things):** Are things that we can touch; for example, a person, a rock, etc. Tangible-material-things, in-turn, can be:

        i. **Animate (material-things):** Are living things that are alive due to biochemical-reactions; for example, humans, trees, etc.

        ii. **Inanimate (material-things):** Are non-living things that are not alive because they do not have any biochemical-reactions; for example, rocks, water, etc.

    b. **Intangible (material-things):** Are things that cannot be touched physically; for example, light, odors, etc.

2. **Immaterial-Things:** Are things that are not made of matter; for example, thoughts, feelings, etc. Immaterial-things can subsequently be categorized binarily into:

    a. **Factual-Immaterial-Things (also referred to as byproducts or processes):** Are things that are fact and evidence based as they are provable. Factual-immaterial-things, aka immaterial-byproducts, aka immaterial-processes, are as a result of the activities of their underlying material-things; or they are associated with material-things. For example, mathematics, knowledge, etc.

    b. **Nonfactual-Immaterial-Things:** Are things that lack evidence or things that are perceived and are unprovable. Nonfactual-immaterial-things are not as a result of underlying material-things and they are not associated with matter. For example, astrology, ghosts, the supernatural, etc.

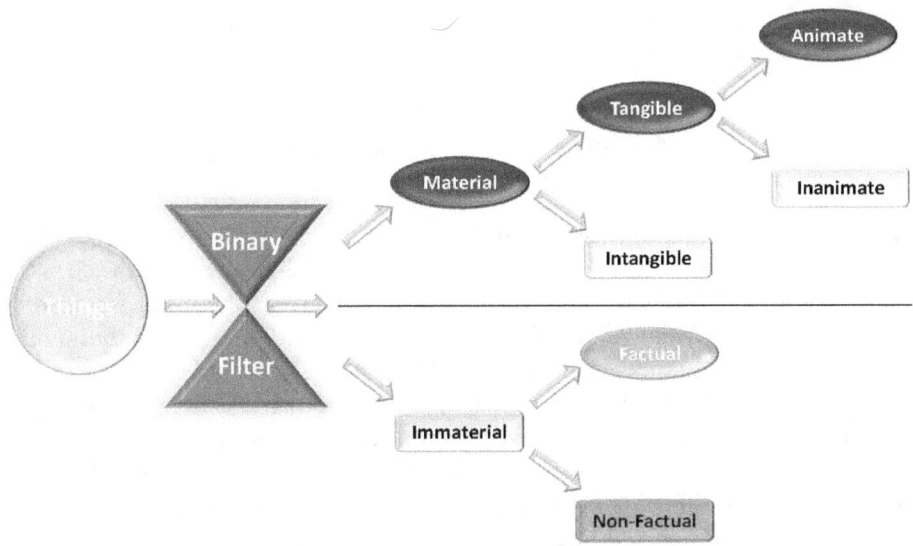

Therefore, observing, perceiving, and understanding in a binary-format at the most elementary and foundational level is not only correct, but it should be the basis for categorization, organization, and comprehension, in all aspects of our existence; including our thinking.

As discussed, binary-processing is also what machines do; however, this does not mean that we have to become like machines. When machines process logic, they do not generate feelings, hence, their processing creates an outcome; however, when we process logic in the form of thoughts, we do generate feelings which complicate the outcome or the resulting behavior. Computer-logic is analogous to an individual human thought; it either turns a single command on or off, and it generates an action; or it refrains from taking action. The resulting collection of actions become its output; or in the case of humans, it becomes our behavior. Therefore, our behavior results from the collection of our individually passed-through and processed thoughts.

Not all thoughts lead to action, but every action is as a result of an accepted thought.

Therefore, Theory of Self-Relativity recommends processing our individual-thoughts, but not our collective-thinking, in a binary-format. Just like the binary-logic used in computers, our individual-thoughts also exist in one of two possible states. In other words, our individual-thoughts are like "zero or one," "black or white," or better yet, "factual or nonfactual." Thus, Theory of Self-Relativity advocates thinking from the bottom-up rather than from the top-down. This means, to master the most stable and most effective form of thinking, we must first learn to address each individual-thought on its own merits of factuality. Although Theory of Self-Relativity considers *"Binary-Thinking"* to be an unhealthy and incorrect form of thinking; Theory of Self-Relativity recommends addressing each individual-thought in a binary-format. As discussed, Theory of Self-Relativity has termed approaching each individual-thought in a binary-format as the *"Binary-Approach"* also referred to as *"Binary-Thought-Processing."*

Theory of Self-Relativity defines "Binary-Thought-Processing" or "Binary-Approach" as "the process of observing and evaluating each individual-thought as being factual or nonfactual."

As discussed throughout Theory of Self-Relativity, our "thinking" is the collection of all of our "individual-thoughts;" hence, our individual-thoughts are the elementary, fundamental, and structural building-blocks of our total thinking. Therefore, in order for "the structure" or "the building" of our thinking to be sound and stable, its structural-foundation and its building-blocks must individually be solid and flawless. Additionally, and as discussed, our thinking-system must be in shades-of-gray and it should be able to dynamically fluctuate its grayscale within wide ranges of shades-of-grayness. However, we must think individual-thoughts in blacks or whites in order to achieve the proper thinking shade-of-gray. This is why, binary-evaluation and binary-approach must only occur at the most fundamental and basic level where only two choices exist; but not when two choices can selectively be chosen from a multitude of possibilities. Binary-analysis should only happen at the fundamental-level where there are no more than two-choices available; and at the fundamental-level of individual-thoughts, a thought could either be factual or nonfactual, because only one fact exists per situation.

Thinking is a combination of multiple individual-thoughts; therefore, thinking cannot, and should not be binary. However, individual-thoughts, which make up our collective thinking-system, could and should be evaluated in a binary-format. Contrary to popular belief, we cannot think in metaphorical shades-of-gray, because a grayscale is the resulting combination of its black and white components or pixels. Furthermore, black, or white, themselves, could actually be considered as the extreme shades-of-gray; hence, by accumulating the right number of individual-thoughts in the metaphorical shade of black and white, we can automatically reach the proper metaphorical shade-of-gray thinking. Additionally, the color gray is the result of the combination of its black and white pixels and the collective gray shade can be lightened or intensified by adjusting the number of its black and white pixels.

Same holds true for our thoughts as we should accept our factual-thoughts and we must dismiss our nonfactual ones. Our macro thinking should always be in the metaphorical shades-of-gray, which is the result of the combination of its metaphorical black and white individual-thoughts. To best understand the difference between our micro individual-thoughts and our macro thinking, consider each individual-thought as being analogous to an individual black or white pixel. Therefore, the collection of our metaphorical black and white individual-thoughts creates our proper metaphorical gray shade of thinking.

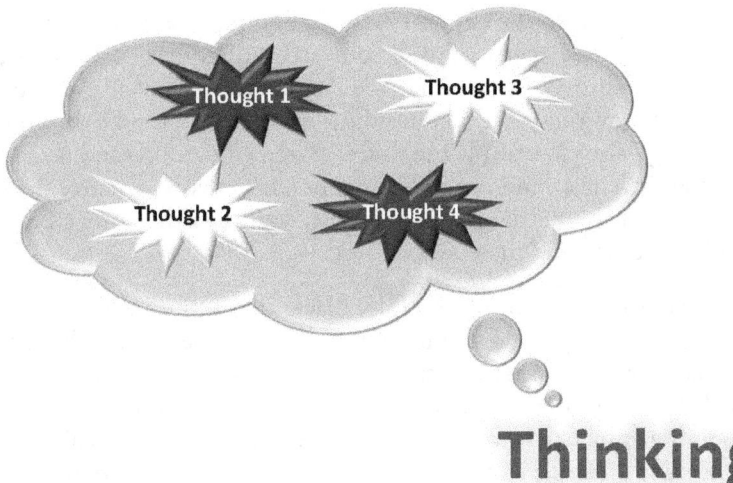

Thinking

Thinking in the shades-of-gray is a metaphorical term used in psychology in order to demonstrate that our thinking should be adaptable, flexible, and malleable; but not rigid. However, to have flexibility of thinking, we cannot approach it from the macro or collective-thinking level; we must approach it from the micro or individual-thought level. To think in the shade-of-gray means to try to think from the top down or to think from the outside in; it is impossible to think in shades-of-gray. We cannot choose the right gray shade by thinking gray; however, by learning to individually address each thought in black or white, the correct shade-of-gray thinking will automatically take shape.

Our thoughts change continuously as we think new individual-thoughts; hence, the gray shade of our thinking also changes as we keep, add, or eliminate these individual-thoughts which occupy our mind. Since our individual-thoughts appear, disappear, and change; therefore, the collective gray shade of our thinking should also adapt and change. This is why, thinking in shades-of-gray is an impossible task, because to try to think in a shade-of-gray, we will be endlessly chasing the dynamic and changing pattern of our individual-thoughts that pop into and out of existence. However, when we become mindful and thoughtful of our individual-thoughts, we can then keep or eliminate each individual-thought based on its factual-value.

A common example of binary-thinking, or black and white thinking, is when someone considers another person as all good or as all bad; or if one would suddenly classify another person one has known for a while as all good or all bad based on a single interaction or a single event. For example, romantic-relationships with high-conflict and toxic-people. In such relationships, we could be love-bombed and considered a high-value partner, or we could even be pedestalized for months and even for years; but suddenly, based on a single interaction or event, which could be real, or as often is perceived by the other person, we could be devalued and dropped from the relationship by being hated and being categorized as a bad person.

To swing quickly between the extremes of love and hate is the hallmark of relationships with Cluster-B personality-disordered individuals such as narcissists and borderlines. Instead of evaluating the single interaction or event that was not to their liking, or as is more commonly, it was perceived to be threatening to them; personality-disordered individuals feel extreme emotions and take extreme measures, often in a hasty and impulsive manner, in order to distance themselves from perceived threats and danger. This is why, cognitive-therapies are often the recommended protocol for these individuals.

As a less extreme non-romantic example, black and white thinking, or all-or-none thinking, is more prevalent among gamblers and speculators. For example, someone might own many shares of stock in a company for a long time; but based on a dislikable pattern that the person sees, or based on frustration, he sells all of his stock holding, only to witness the price of the stock rise after he sold his shares. Instead of seeking facts to verify negative developments, by liquidating all of his position instead of selling a portion, the investors acted in an all-or-none manner, which was as a result of his black and white thinking. Therefore, to abstain from black and white thinking and to think in shades-of-gray, we must evaluate the factuality of our individual-thoughts associated with an event; instead of acting emotionally and hastily to it.

The right shade-of-gray thinking, or factual-thinking, is best achieved by only keeping factual-thoughts and by eliminating the nonfactual ones; hence, our remaining thoughts will comprise our factual-thinking-system. As discussed, Theory of Self-Relativity has termed this binary way of evaluating our individual-thoughts as the "Binary-Thought-Process" or the "Binary-Approach." The binary-thought-processing enables us to address each individual-thought as metaphorically black or white, or cognitively, as factual, or nonfactual. This individual-thought-processing based on each individual-thought's factual-value enables our thinking-system to take on the right shade-of-gray and to become factual. The binary-thought-process uses the metaphorical *"Binary-Filter"* to select the black or white, aka factual, or nonfactual thoughts that we should keep or eliminate. The binary-filter itself is a metaphorical name given by Theory of Self-Relativity to our immaterial-mental-activities of analyzing and filtering out our individual-thoughts.

Since our thinking is a collection of our thoughts and our thoughts are the building-blocks of our collective-thinking; when we learn to engage in the binary-thought-process, we use our binary-filter to implement the *"process-of-elimination."* By using the binary-filter alongside the process-of-elimination, we filter our individual-thoughts that make up our collective-thinking-system. By evaluating our individual-thoughts for their factual-value, we can then use our binary-filter to filter-out and eliminate or dismiss our nonfactual-thoughts, and to filter-through and keep or accept our factual ones. By filtering through each individual-thought in a binary-format and by eliminating the unnecessary and nonfactual thoughts, we can then filter in only the necessary thoughts that really matter. These filtered-in thoughts which have not been eliminated will give us the proper final format of our collective-thinking.

The process-of-elimination is a commonly used practice in science and in problem-solving in order to filter through only the best answers, the best choices, and the best solutions for a situation. In science, the process-of-elimination is often undertaken via falsification; whereby the person with the observation, the hypothesis, or the theory, as well as other colleagues and competitors, attempt to falsify the observation, the hypothesis, or the theory. If they were able to falsify it, then the observation, the hypothesis, or the theory would be modified or discarded; however, if the observation, the hypothesis, or the theory could not be falsified, it would then remain as valid until or unless falsified at a later time. Therefore, the process-of-elimination is about retaining the best, the most qualified, and the most applicable answers; while discarding the least qualified and the least applicable ones.

The same holds true regarding applying the process-of-elimination to our thoughts. If we can falsify our thoughts or if we cannot find facts to support our thoughts, we then use the process-of-elimination to filter-out our nonfactual-thoughts and to only retain our thoughts that are based on facts and evidence. However, unlike falsification in science, we can also verify our thoughts by proving each individual-thought's factuality. Therefore, we do not have to only rely on falsification; we can also rely on verification. In summary, we should always look for facts to support our thoughts, opinions, ideas, and beliefs; and if we cannot find the supportive facts, we should then dismiss our thoughts, or at the minimum, we should not act on them until the supportive facts are discovered.

Theory of Self-Relativity defines the "Process-of-Elimination" as "a mental and logical process that allows us to keep the best-available, the best-applicable, or the most-relevant of existing choices; by removing or by eliminating all other choices."

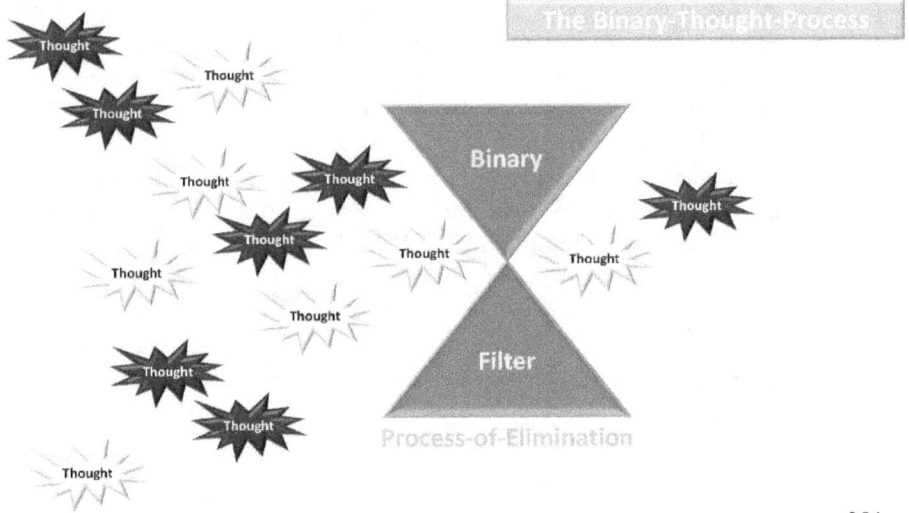

381

The process-of-elimination allows for the best applicable choices to remain and the rest to be dismissed or discarded. The same principle applies to our thoughts. The binary-thought-process uses the process-of-elimination through the binary-filter, enabling us to eliminate our cluttering and nonfactual-thoughts, and to only keep our factual-thoughts. By evaluating and by filtering out our nonfactual-thoughts, we then only keep the factual-thoughts which are based on the way reality is, and not based on how we want reality to be. When we are able to evaluate and observe our nonfactual-thoughts without accepting them; we will then be able to dismiss and eliminate many nonfactual, counter-factual, and repetitive thoughts out of our thinking-system.

As Aristotle stated: "It is the mark of an educated mind to be able to entertain a thought without accepting it."

The process-of-elimination removes and eliminates clutter by bringing the focus to only thoughts which have factual-basis. Since the process-of-elimination is a cognitive activity; therefore, the binary-thought-process, itself, requires mindfulness and thoughtfulness in order to achieve the most efficient and high-quality retention of factual-thoughts. This is why, Theory of Self-Relativity insists that mindfulness alone cannot be effective, and it must be followed by thoughtfulness. Theory of Self-Relativity refers to this combination of thoughtfulness and binary-thought-process as our *"Thought-Management"* skill.

Theory of Self-Relativity defines "Thought-Management" as "the process of eliminating nonfactual-thoughts and only retaining factual-thoughts."

Therefore, in order for thought-management to exist and to be most effective, a thinking entity must not only be conscious and have a mind, but the entity must also be able to be mindful and thoughtful. This means, the entity must be aware of its thoughts, and to be able to evaluate and understand the message of those thoughts; hence, it will have intelligence and it will be considered to be an intelligent-entity. In case of higher intelligent-entities such as humans, to properly manage our thoughts, we must also be able to have analytical-thinking and critical-thinking abilities. Analytical-thinking and critical-thinking are skills that we must develop and strengthen in order to be able to have quicker and more efficient interactions in the modern-world. The binary-thought-process streamlines our analytical-thinking and critical-thinking skills by eliminating nonfactual-thoughts and by only allowing us to keep our factual-thoughts. Therefore, to have the most efficient and most effective thought-management skills, the following components should be in place.

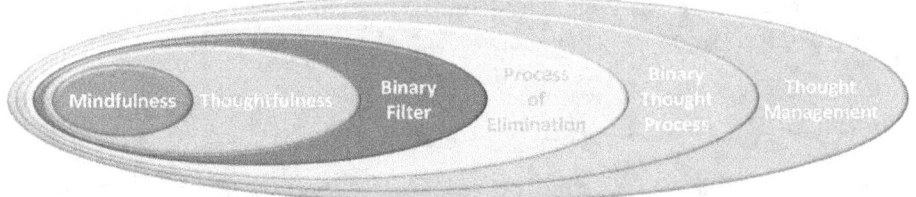

As discussed, our feelings lead to our behavior and our thoughts create our feelings; but because we are more aware of and we are more in touch with our feelings than we are with our thoughts, therefore, we often think things or we do things as a direct result of our feelings, without being aware of and without understanding what thoughts are creating those feelings. Although taking action based on feelings is the correct order, we must ensure that our feelings which are guiding our behavior are generated by underlying factual-thoughts. This awareness and understanding of feelings is often referred to as *"Emotional-Intelligence."*

Theory of Self-Relativity defines "emotional-intelligence" as "one's ability to be aware of and to understand one's own and others' emotions, and consequently, their thoughts."

Emotional-intelligence is commonly described as "a mechanism to get in touch with our own feelings and with those of others and to allow this awareness to *"guide"* our thinking and behavior." However, Theory of Self-Relativity takes issue with this definition. Although emotional-intelligence should guide our behavior, emotional-intelligence should not guide our thinking; on the contrary, our thinking should guide our emotions. According to Theory of Self-Relativity, emotional-intelligence should not "guide" our thoughts, but instead, it should use our feelings to trace back and to become aware of our thoughts that are creating our feelings.

Although feelings guide our behavior, feelings should not guide our thoughts. Since emotional-intelligence requires awareness and understanding; therefore, fact-based emotional-intelligence is a learned skill and not an innate ability. Just like any other learned skill, emotional-intelligence can improve and become quicker as we apply it more frequently. Emotional-intelligence allows us to get in touch with our feelings and to master them on-the-go. When we use our feelings to become aware of their underlying thoughts that are creating our feelings, we can then ensure that our feelings are actually created as a result of our thoughts. Simply stated:

Theory of Self-Relativity defines "true" "emotional-intelligence" as "awareness and understanding of the facts associated with the thoughts that are generating our feelings."

Theory of Self-Relativity strongly opposes the notion that emotional-intelligence should guide our thoughts. On the contrary, emotional-intelligence should be used as an awareness and understanding tool to "identify" the thoughts that cause the feelings; but the factuality of those thoughts must "guide" our life. When we use feelings-awareness to dive deeper into ours and others' thoughts, we then recognize if ours or others' thoughts are factual or not.

When we know how it is to feel something; we will then have a better understanding of how others feel about the same thing.

When we learn to master this skill of "reading" feelings, we will then become like a mind-reader. Although this reference to becoming a mind-reader is metaphorical, feelings-awareness can lead to clearly recognizing how everyone's feelings and behavior are manifested by their thought-processes. This method of using feelings to access and recognize thoughts is the core discipline behind Theory of Self-Relativity's *"Cognitive-Cognition-Technique."*

Theory of Self-Relativity defines the "Cognitive-Cognition-Technique" as "The ability to use our feelings, to access and identify our thoughts, in order to take proper action."

Theory of Self-Relativity describes the "Cognitive-Cognition-Technique" as "Our mental-algorithm for proper thinking."

Since we are more in touch with our feelings than we are with our thoughts, The Cognitive-Cognition-Technique teaches us how to use our feelings to recognize our thoughts for their factual-value. Once we recognize our individual-thoughts that are creating our individual-feelings, which collectively make up our emotions; we can then either dismiss, modify, or accept these thoughts based on their factuality. The Cognitive-Cognition-Technique teaches instead of using our emotions, especially our negative-feelings to quickly behave; we should use our negative-feelings to evaluate and understand the thoughts which are causing these emotions. Once we have verified our thoughts to be factual, we can then use our feelings to behave (to take action or inaction).

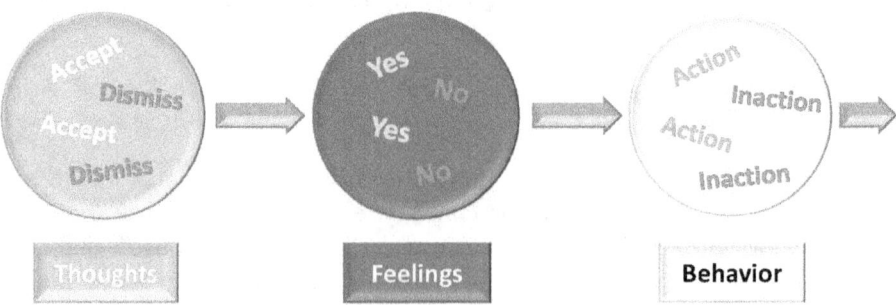

The only criteria that we use to understand and evaluate our thoughts is their factual-value. If a thought is based on facts and evidence, then that thought is what Theory of Self-Relativity defines as a *"factual-thought;"* however, if a thought cannot be supported by facts and evidence, then according to Theory of Self-Relativity, that thought is a *"nonfactual-thought."* If a thought is a factual-thought, we will then accept that thought and proceed to taking an action or we will abstain from taking action if no action is necessary. However, if the thought is a nonfactual-thought, we will then proceed to dismiss the thought, and when we dismiss the thought that is causing our feeling, our feeling will automatically disappear; therefore, we will not need to take any action based on that dismissed thought. Dismissing a thought should only occur if the thought is determined to be nonfactual; in other words, if no facts can be found to support the thought. However, dismissing a nonfactual-thought must be distinguished from ignoring or denying an uncomfortable but a potentially factual-thought.

Furthermore, sometimes, the evidence for a thought might not be readily available; therefore, we must take some time to find the facts behind our thoughts. However, if after a certain amount of time we cannot find supporting facts for a thought, we should then categorize that thought as nonfactual and proceed to dismiss it. Nonfactual-thoughts are often assumed or imagined; and more often than not, such thoughts are created in order to rationalize, support, and reinforce a desired-feeling. Feelings are not supposed to create thoughts, thoughts are supposed to create feelings; therefore, by understanding the factual-value of our thoughts, we can then sync our thinking with how reality is and not as how we want reality to be.

In summary, The Cognitive-Cognition-Technique works via:

1. Feeling-awareness
2. Thought-awareness
3. Thought-evaluation

    a. Accept factual-thoughts

    b. Dismiss nonfactual-thoughts

4. Generating correct-feelings
5. Engaging in best behavior

    a. Action

    b. Inaction

This is how Theory of Self-Relativity's Cognitive-Cognition-Technique works. Through awareness, understanding, and implementation, we learn to clear out our unnecessary and cluttering thoughts by evaluating them for their factuality; thereby, we only keep thoughts that are fact-based.

As discussed throughout Theory of Self-Relativity, majority of our feelings are negative because negative-feelings exist as a protective and preventive mechanism in order for us to stay safe, and for us to be forced to correct something that is wrong. A feeling is a symptom of an underlying cause; hence, dislikable, and uncomfortable negative-feelings commonly exist to force us into corrective-action, so that we can eliminate the cause of the negativity. The only true and long-lasting means of eliminating negativity is by correcting or by eliminating the cause of the negativity. Once the cause is corrected or eliminated, the negative-feeling will truly disappear; thus, it won't be covered-up. To do so, we must become aware of and we must understand what is causing the negativity so that we can correct or eliminate that cause. We cannot just feel a negative-feeling, and without understanding what is causing that feeling, we should not attempt to take action in order to feel better. If the cause is not identified and understood, any action we take will most probably be wrong, or it will be a temporary cover-up.

The stench of negativity always arises after the perfume of positive cover-up fades away.

The Cognitive-Cognition-Technique enables us to use our negative-feelings to look for their underlying thoughts that are making us feel negative. These thoughts could be factual, which means they are giving us a message that there is something wrong that needs to be fixed; or they can be nonfactual, which means they are based on feelings such as anxiety or fear, therefore they might not have factual-basis.

Instead of impulsively reacting to our negative-feelings, The Cognitive-Cognition-Technique allows us to use our feelings to identify their causal-thoughts. The Cognitive-Cognition-Technique enables us to slow-down our reactivity to our emotions; therefore, it enables us to control, minimize, and eventually eliminate our impulsivities and our reactive-behavior. The Cognitive-Cognition-Technique teaches us how to recognize, sustain, and increase our self-control.

As discussed, we think things and we do things in order to avoid pain, to feel good, or at the minimum, to feel less-bad at that moment; this is why, we often have the urgency to say, think, and more commonly, do something when we experience discomfort. This need to constantly intervene and take action in order to improve an uncomfortable situation or a dislikable-feeling is one of the main reasons we make so many hasty decisions and so many mistakes. Intervening and taking action gives us a sense of being in control; thus, it is this emotional-urgency that causes us to hastily intervene to act. As described, Theory of Self-Relativity has termed this need to act to immediately to feel better quickly as *"Self-Interventionism."*

Theory of Self-Relativity defines "Self-Interventionism" as "the urge to take an action in order to improve a dislikable-feeling or an uncomfortable-situation."

By practicing The Cognitive-Cognition-Technique, we can learn to take our time to become aware of our thoughts before we take action. This slowing down of reactivity is how we develop patience and self-control, and how we minimize impulsivity and instant-gratification. The Cognitive-Cognition-Technique inherently slows down our impulsivity in order for our behavior to become more methodical and fact-based, rather than it being emotional and impulsive. As we practice The Cognitive-Cognition-Technique and as we develop and improve our factual-thinking-based behavior skills, our factual-thinking abilities become more streamlined and quicker, and our feelings and behavior become more reality-based.

When we learn to address individual-thoughts binarily, and when we use the process-of-elimination to filter-out our cluttering thoughts, we can then become more focused on the remainder of our thoughts that lead to our feelings and behavior. As we filter-out our nonfactual-thoughts, we will begin to realize that dismissing unnecessary and nonfactual-thoughts, and not taking action based on nonfactual-thoughts, could actually be more constructive than continuously trying to do something to quickly feel better. The Cognitive-Cognition-Technique demonstrates that unlike the urge to take a corrective action so that we can feel better quickly; by dismissing our nonfactual-thoughts, we will more often end up not taking any action when one is not necessary. By dismissing nonfactual-thoughts, we will realize that often, the best thing to do is to do nothing; and, we can move forward to the next thought.

When uncertain, the best action is often inaction.

In other words:

When in doubt, stay out.

The Cognitive-Cognition-Technique also enables us to increase our focus in thinking, in learning, and in decision-making. In the age of modern-technology and the need to multitask, being focused and having the ability to think and act quickly without being impulsive can be of major advantage. When we resolve and eliminate our negative and nonfactual-thoughts, which according to Theory of Self-Relativity, comprise the majority of our thoughts; we will subsequently be left with only factual-thoughts that are actually applicable to our life. This uncluttering of thoughts not only takes the weight off our mind, but it also enables us to increase our attention and focus on our remaining thoughts that truly matter to us. This increased focus strengthens our ability for quicker and cleverer thinking, while helping us to become more aware and cognizant of other-people and our surrounding.

Being a quick-thinker gives us an advantage compared to others because it enables us to proactively think and behave before others do. This increased focus and awareness is not only important in effectively dealing with others, but it is also important for our safety and security. When we are not preoccupied by recurring, ruminating, and cluttering-thoughts, we can be more aware of external threats that might be coming our way. For example, we can better avoid potential accidents by being focused and aware of our surrounding conditions, or we can have better awareness of our surroundings when we are walking in the streets.

Quick and clever thinking results in strong and effective behavior.

Increased focus and elimination of unnecessary and nonfactual-thoughts can also help in multitasking which is an inherent requirement for advancement in the modern-era. Although multitasking, per se, is a fallacy, because the human mind cannot attend to more than one thought or more than one task at any given moment; what is referred to as multitasking is not actually thinking multiple thoughts or attending to multiple tasks simultaneously. Those who seem to multitask are actually able to shift their focus dynamically and quickly between multiple thoughts and multiple tasks in short intervals. Dynamic-equilibrium and dynamic-shifting between thoughts and tasks can become most effective when it is as a result of focused and uncluttered-thinking. Once we learn to initiate and continue multitasking, or as renamed by Theory of Self-Relativity as *"Dynamic-Thought-Shifting"*; the effort needed for the shifting will become more routine and intuitive.

Theory of Self-Relativity defines "Dynamic-Thought-Shifting" as "One's ability to quickly and cleverly shift between thoughts."

Additionally, focused and uncluttered-thinking leads to more efficient and effective problem-solving abilities, as it enhances our analytical-thinking skills. When we keep the influences of our emotions out of our thinking and as our thinking becomes more analytical; we increase the effectiveness of our intelligence because our thought-evaluation efforts are directed to only those thoughts that matter.

Theory of Self-Relativity defines "intelligence" as "the ability to acquire, process, and apply information and knowledge."

Therefore, by minimizing clutter and distractions in thinking, we can increase the "effectiveness" of our intelligence, which manifests itself as if we increased the quantifiable "level" of our intelligence. More effective-intelligence, in-turn, enables quicker and cleverer thinking abilities; which, consequently, effectuates the strength of our behavior.

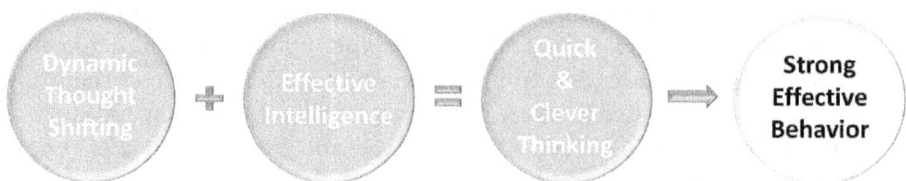

To effectuate intelligence to the highest possible level is analogous to increasing a car's performance by enhancing its internal working characteristics. By servicing the car and by consistently changing its air, oil, and fuel filters; and by redirecting air, oil, and fuel in a more direct and efficient manner, we improve the vehicle's performance. Similar thing happens to our thinking and our intelligence. We enhance our intellectual-performance by filtering out cluttering and nonfactual thoughts, and by redirecting our thinking to more focused and efficient evaluation of our thoughts. Therefore, personal-development and self-improvement are best achieved by changing and by enhancing the way we think; hence, by keeping feelings out of the way of our thinking.

Many, synonymize success as the ultimate achievement of self-improvement, while others reflect wealth, fame, popularity, or power to be the reflection of ultimate self-improvement. However, neither one of these achievements could have long-lasting effects because personal-development and self-improvement are not external-events. Personal-development and self-improvement are ongoing processes which should always be actively and dynamically changing and improving from within. Although creating purpose, setting goals, and having dreams are defined timelines and achievement parameters that could contribute to our improvement and betterment; they are not one-time solutions for permanent transformation. Transformation requires change, and change itself is an ongoing process. As stated:

Process is a continuum of events.

The key to making transformation, change, and improvement ti become an ongoing process, is to learn and practice proper thinking abilities. When factual-thinking becomes routine and intuitive, we can then apply it, on-the-go, and as needed. Just as we do not ever stop thinking, we cannot stop changing, transforming, and improving; therefore, self-improvement should become a normal part of our daily living. Although success, wealth, power and other accomplishments could be reflections of an improved Self; none of these accomplishments truly reflect an improved person if the improvement does not create *"Self-Fulfillment."*

Money and status are the byproducts of success; true success is measured by fulfillment.

Fulfillment is commonly defined as achieving something desired, hoped for, or promised. In common terms, fulfillment is more of a defined conclusion, accomplishment, or an achievement; however, envisioning fulfillment as a defined achievement makes fulfillment an event and not a process. As described throughout Theory of Self-Relativity, personal-development and self-improvement are not events, they are continuous and ongoing lifetime processes; therefore, self-fulfillment must also be an ongoing process.

As further discussed, to be able to experience more frequent and longer lasting happiness, we must first minimize negativity so that we can reach the stable zone of contentment. Similarly, self-fulfillment is also reliant on our state of contentment. Although accomplishing a purpose, achieving a goal, and reaching a dream could make us happy and elated; the feelings of happiness and elation disappear after a while. Therefore, once happiness fades-away, we should settle back down into the contentment-zone. Likewise, fulfillment is similar to contentment as it is built on the foundation of contentment; which means just like experiencing happiness, in order to experience fulfillment, we must first minimize negativities and become content. Thus, fulfillment, just like positivity, is a dependent state-of-experience; therefore, when we learn to become content, we can then create, maintain, and evolve our personal state of self-fulfillment, and proceed to experiencing more frequent and longer-lasting happiness.

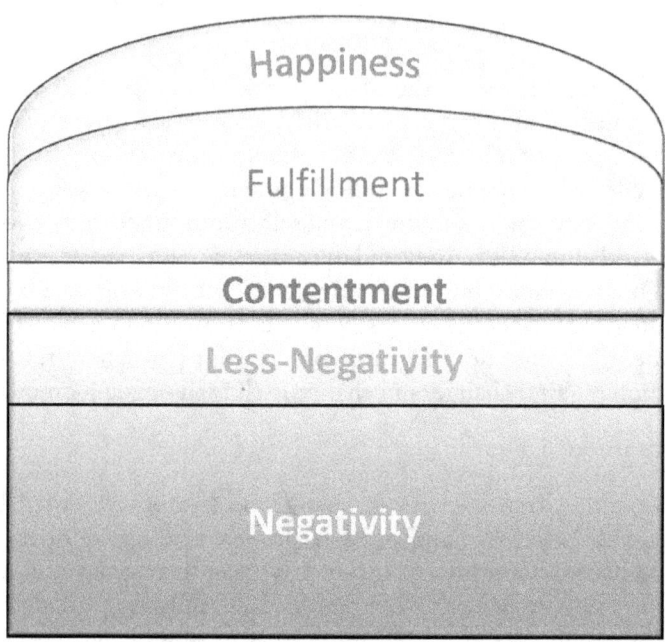

Since true and lasting happiness could only be achieved after we have reached contentment and fulfillment; therefore, achieving and maintaining happiness is a learned skill. According to Theory of Self-Relativity, although we experience happiness as an emotion; to experience happiness, we must be skillful enough to know how to reach and sustain happiness. This is why, true happiness is achieved down the line of contentment, fulfillment, and self-improvement.

Happiness is not a mindset or an attitude, happiness is a state-of-experience; therefore, true happiness is experienced by first achieving contentment and fulfillment.

Similarly, the same path of achieving fulfillment and happiness that is built upon the foundation of contentment, is also the path to establishing and increasing confidence. However, unlike happiness, which is a state-of-experience; confidence is not a mindset, a feeling, or an attitude. Confidence is purely a skill that is based on experience, but should not be experienced emotionally as happiness is experienced.

Confidence is a cognitive-skill; not an emotional-experience.

Therefore:

Confidence can increase happiness; however, happiness does not necessarily increase confidence.

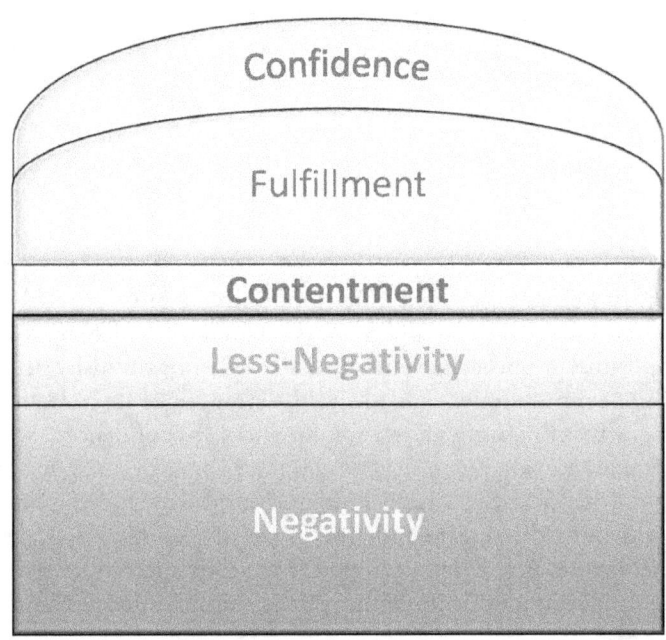

As we minimize negativity and create a solid foundation of contentment; each time we accomplish a purpose, achieve a goal, or reach a dream, instead of experiencing short-term bursts of happiness, we will dynamically build upon the foundational strength of our self-fulfillment. Thereby, when self-fulfillment is built upon a stable foundation of contentment; self-fulfillment will allow happiness and elation to last longer and to be more meaningful.

Theory of Self-Relativity defines "fulfillment" as "an evolving satisfactory state-of-mind that is built upon a stable foundation of contentment."

This is why, Theory of Self-Relativity states that not only confidence is a cognitive-skill, but, happiness, and even love, which are strong emotional-experiences, are also skills, Because, in order for us to experience more stable and longer-lasting feelings of happiness and love, we must have the ability to be content and fulfilled.

Therefore, the stability of our contentment and the growth of our self-fulfillment not only increase the frequencies and duration of our happiness, but they also grow and strengthen our sense of self-confidence.

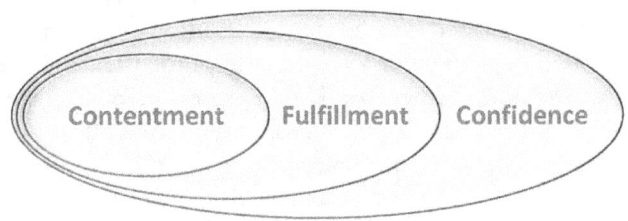

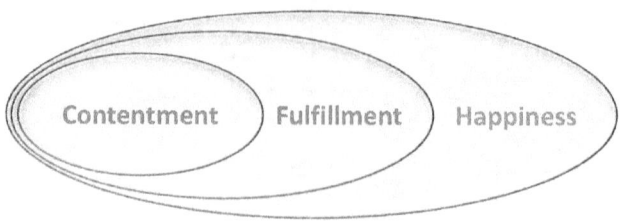

Although self-fulfillment is created by accomplishing a purpose, achieving a goal, and reaching a dream; true self-fulfillment is maintained by feeling content about each accomplishment and achievement, while it is improved by accomplishing and achieving new milestones that add to the strength of its contentment foundation. This is why, contentment, self-fulfillment, self-confidence, and as a whole, self-improvement, are ongoing processes and not sporadic events. It is the fulfilled and confident outcome of accomplishing our purpose, achieving our goals, and reaching our dreams that create and strengthen our sense of Self; and as stated throughout Theory of Self-Relativity, our self-identity, and our sense of Self, is the collective-combination of our thoughts, our feelings, and our behavior.

I think…Therefore I feel…Therefore I am

Self-Identity

Therefore, as we achieve our goals and as we reach our dreams and become fulfilled, we become more confident and happier; because we then know that we can handle and improve any situation. Such fulfillment-based confidence is how we make our purpose in life bigger.

As discussed, unlike popular-beliefs and traditional-teaching, purpose is not found nor is it given; purpose is self-created, because contrary to comforting-fallacies, we weren't born with a purpose or a meaning to our existence. We exist because The-Universe exists, and neither The-Universe nor anyone or anything else is obligated to give our life and our existence a purpose or a meaning. It is up to us to not only create a purpose in our life, but it is up to us to continuously make our life's purpose bigger and more meaningful. When we create our own life's purpose, we can then become more fulfilled and we can give our life our own meaning. Therefore, it is our responsibility to create, cultivate, and grow our own purpose from within.

As long as we have a purpose, we can set a goal, and we can even dream a dream. As we achieve our goal, this newly achieved goal gets added to our purpose, because our goal is no longer a goal, but it has now become a part of our bigger purpose. Subsequently, as we achieve our goal and as we make our purpose bigger, our initial dream becomes our next goal, and we move to dream a new dream. As our dreams become our next goals and as we fulfill each goal; our purpose in life gets bigger and our life's meaning becomes richer. Goals and dreams are the best way for us to continuously create, replenish, and increase our purpose as we move forward in time and as we go through life. The more goals we achieve, and the more dreams we reach, the bigger our purpose in life becomes.

To be fulfilled, don't just dream big; make your purpose bigger.

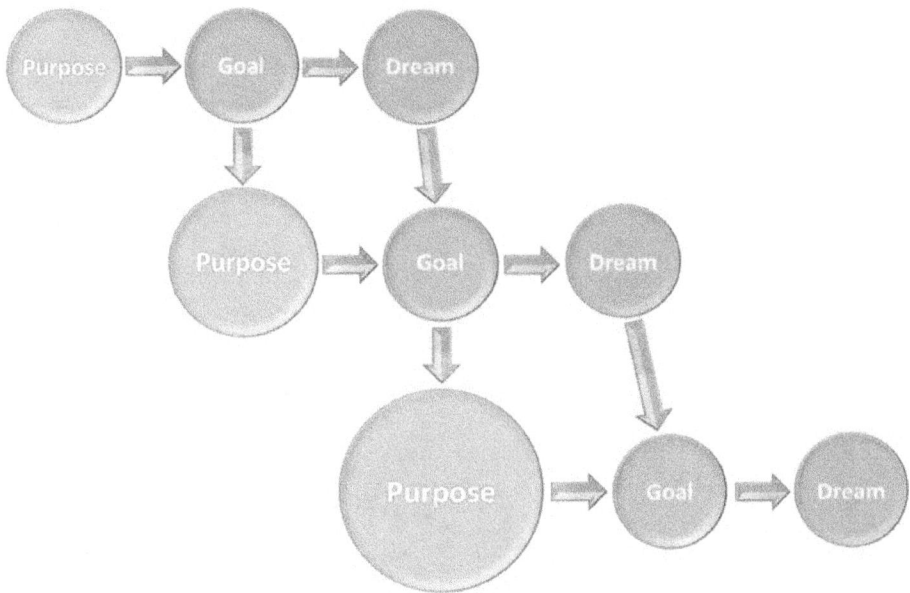

The bigger our purpose becomes, the more fulfilled we will feel and the more self-confident we will become. Consequently, the more self-confident we become, the more stable we will feel; and the more stable we feel, the more control we will have and the less uncertainties we will experience. The more self-confident we become, the more self-reliant and self-sufficient we will be, and as we become more self-sufficient, we will be less reliant on others; therefore, we will become the agent of our own happiness and we will not need others to make us happy.

The more confident and independent one is, the less bad behavior one would tolerate from others.

It is this chain of events of minimizing negativities to being content, to feeling fulfilled, and being confident, that allows us to experience more frequent and longer lasting periods of happiness.

It is not achieving a goal or reaching a dream that creates our happiness or validates our self-identity; but it is our growing purpose that fulfills our existence.

Therefore:

To be fulfilled and happy, don't just dream big; make your purpose bigger.

The 10-Commandments for Self-Improvement

To change and to improve, we must not only understand how to make the change, but we must also know what we need to change in order to improve. For things to change and improve, we must first minimize and eliminate negativities so that we can then focus on increasing positivities in our lives. The aforementioned 10-Enemies of Self-Improvement explain the negative-contributors that must be understood and addressed in order for us to be able to get on the path of change and improvement. After becoming aware and by understanding the influences of these negative-contributors on our existence, we can then begin to focus on the things that we need to pay attention to in order to get on the path of change and improvement.

Theory of Self-Relativity has termed the following necessary attributes for change and improvement as the "10-Commandments for Self-Improvement." Since change and improvement are not events but they are ongoing lifelong processes; therefore, awareness, understanding, and implementation of these 10-Commandments will help change negativities effectively, so that we can begin to experience positivity and happiness more frequently.

10 Commandments

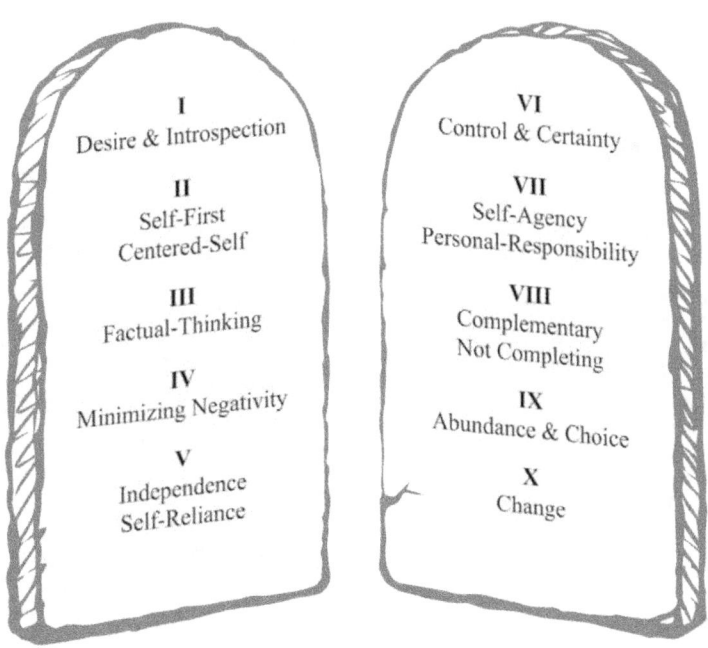

I
Desire & Introspection

II
Self-First
Centered-Self

III
Factual-Thinking

IV
Minimizing Negativity

V
Independence
Self-Reliance

VI
Control & Certainty

VII
Self-Agency
Personal-Responsibility

VIII
Complementary
Not Completing

IX
Abundance & Choice

X
Change

I. **Desire & Introspection:** Thou shalt want to improve thy weaknesses.

II. **Self-First & Centered-Self:** Thou shalt prioritize thy Self before others; but not at the expense of others.

III. **Factual-Thinking:** Thou shalt think and live factually with facts, evidence, and reason.

IV. **Minimizing Negativity:** Thou shalt minimize, resolve, and eliminate negativity, before attempting to reach positivity and happiness.

V. **Independence & Self-Reliance:** Thou shalt rely on thy Self and minimize dependency on others.

VI. **Control & Certainty:** Thou shalt create and maintain control and certainty.

VII. **Self-Agency & Personal-Responsibility:** Thou shalt take responsibility for thy Self.

VIII. **Complementary; not Completing:** Thou shalt be complete by thy Self.

IX. **Abundance & Choice:** Thou shalt live in abundance and with choice.

X. **Change:** Thou shalt change constantly, consistently, and continuously.

I.
Desire & Introspection

To change and improve, we must want to change, and we must know what we need to improve.

The reason personal change and improvement is a difficult and challenging task is because change and improvement require awareness and understanding of our weaknesses and shortcomings. However, as discussed throughout Theory of Self-Relativity, the reason some people do not change is because either they are too ignorant, too self-centered, or too defensive to want to change. In other words, they either think there is nothing to change; or they are too scared to look within their own Self to identify their deficiencies, weakness, and shortcoming that need improvement. According to Theory of Self-Relativity, at its core, even those who do not think that they need to change are covering up their fear of facing their deficiencies and shortcomings by becoming ignorant, self-centered, or defensive.

The need to feel good versus the necessity to think well is a core factor that inhibits change and blocks self-improvement.

Although our thoughts generate our emotions, as humans, we are generally not as much in touch with our thoughts as we are with our feelings. Our *"desired"* emotional-state is to avoid pain, to feel good, or at the minimum, to feel less-bad, at that moment. We simply do not like negative-feelings; however, what we desire is not what we are programmed to feel, because our *"default"* emotional-setting is to feel negative. As described throughout Theory of Self-Relativity, our primitive-mind is default-programmed to be negative because its primary role is to keep us safe. Our primitive-mind does not care if we are happy; all it cares about is if we are safe, and it does so by creating negative-emotions whenever it feels uncertain, stressed, or threatened. Uncertainty, which is often caused as a result of change, puts our primitive-mind on the edge, because uncertainty increases the potential for something to go wrong; and since the role of our primitive-mind is to minimize and eliminate anything that could potentially expose us to uncertainty and danger, hence, minimization of uncertainty is one of the main reasons we do not like change.

As described throughout Theory of Self-Relativity, our feelings are always a symptom of an underlying cause; and our emotions, which are our intangible-feelings, are always the symptom of their underlying-thoughts. Simply put, our thoughts cause our feelings, and our feelings represent our thoughts. When we feel negative, this means we are experiencing a negative-thought; and this thought could be conscious, or as is the case with our primitive-mind, the negative-thoughts that it generates are often nonconscious. When our primitive-mind generates a negative-feeling, this means our mind is signaling that there is something potentially wrong that is causing us to think and feel negative. A negative-feeling is simply a symptom or a message for us to pay attention to the cause of the negative-feeling; therefore, our primitive-mind is signaling that it is recognizing there is an uncertainty or a potential danger that is making it feel uneasy and negative. Thus, by generating the negative-feeling, our primitive-mind wants us to look at the cause of our negativity so that we can resolve or eliminate the cause of the negative-feeling. Since our primitive-mind thinks at a very basic level, it does not have the ability to recognize whether a negative-feeling is caused by a perceived-uncertainty or if it is caused by a true life-threatening danger. Our primitive-mind, simply treats the strongest of our negative-feelings that require attention as indication of something threatening or dangerous.

As discussed, since a feeling is a symptom of an underlying thought, and since a thought is generated because of an underlying cause or a trigger; in order to resolve or eliminate our negative-feelings, we must resolve or eliminate the cause of our negative-thoughts. Therefore, to calm down our primitive-mind so that it does not feel danger, we must make our primitive-mind sense that the threat that it felt is resolved or eliminated.

Furthermore, since our "desired" feelings are positive but our primitive-mind's "default" state is to look for negativity; every time that our primitive-mind makes us feel negative, we look for a quick solution to calm down the primitive-mind so that it would let go of the negativity and we could feel better quickly. We seek quick-fixes to feel better, or at the minimum, to not feel as bad, because quick reactions to negativity kept our ancestors safe against threats and dangers. The primitive-human had to react quickly to perceived or real negativity, threats, or dangers, because quick reactions saved them from predators and other natural dangers. When faced with danger and potential predators, our ancestors did not have time to gather data and information if the negativity, the threat, or the danger that they felt was real or perceived. By treating all negativities as potentially dangerous, our ancestors managed to stay safe; because misinterpreting a perceived-negativity would not have been as detrimental as misinterpreting a real threat or danger could be. This is why, we seek quick resolutions of negativities.

We resolve or eliminate negativities in one of the two ways:

1. **The lengthy but correct approach:** As described throughout Theory of Self-Relativity, our feelings are always a symptom of an underlying cause; and our emotions, which are our intangible-feelings, are always a symptom of an underlying-thought. Simply put, our thoughts cause our feelings, and our feelings represent our thoughts. When we feel negative, this means we are experiencing a negative-thought, and this thought could be conscious, or as is the case with our primitive-mind, the negative-thoughts that it generates are often nonconscious. When our primitive-mind generates a

negative-feeling, this means our mind is signaling that there is something potentially wrong that is causing us to think and feel negative. Since a negative-feeling is intended to be protective as it is a symptom of an underlying cause; therefore, the correct way of dealing with this feeling and its cause is to identify and fix the cause so that our negative-feeling improves or disappears. To fix the cause of our negative-feelings, we must look for the cause so that we can find a solution for it. When we find the cause and when we resolve or eliminate the cause of our negative-feeling; our negative-feeling automatically disappears. The reason we do not like taking this approach, which is the correct approach, is because to seek the cause of a negative-feeling is often an emotionally difficult task. Furthermore, after discovering the cause, fixing and resolving these causes takes time and effort, which means we won't be able to feel better quickly.

2. **The quick but incorrect approach:** Since getting in touch with our thoughts and the causes of our thoughts is often an emotionally difficult task because the things that cause us to feel negative are undesired or painful self-truths; instead of looking for the thoughts and the causes of our negative-feelings, we often try to trick our primitive-mind by creating false-thoughts and deceptive-beliefs so that our primitive-mind would calm down. Since our primitive-mind treats the strongest of our negative-feelings as indicators of threats and danger, it also treats all approaches that make it feel less-negative, as resolutionary to the negative-cause. In other words, our primitive-mind will calm down and minimize constant negativities if it senses or believes that the cause of the negativity has been addressed; this includes the rationalization of our feelings through the fabrication of false-thoughts and fallacious-beliefs in order to feel better. This is how self-lies and self-deception, which is one of the 10-Enemies of Self-Improvement, causes us to stay stagnant and stuck in time without being able to make any actual constructive change.

Therefore, we can feel better by either changing our circumstances for the better, which takes time and effort and facing the dislikable truth; or we can feel better by creating false-thoughts and fallacious-beliefs, and by ignoring and by denying the truth in order to convince our Self that things are not as bad, or that things will get better on their own.

As discussed, we must change in order to improve our life; however, change is difficult, because by nature, we do not like change, as change, exposes us to uncertainties and even to potential danger. Furthermore, change requires facing negativities and shortcomings in order for us to know what we need to change. Facing negativities is disliked and undesired; hence, we often choose self-deception over self-improvement in order to quickly feel better. Self-lies and self-deception have been discussed in detail throughout Theory of Self-Relativity as the #1 Enemy of Self-Improvement; therefore, to abstain from self-deception, we must learn and commit to address the causes of our negativities, instead of trying to cover them up.

According to Theory of Self-Relativity, the main way that we can abstain from self-deception is by learning to evaluate and resolve our negativities and our troubling thoughts via factual-thinking. However, to be able to think factually, we must first find out what it is that needs to be addressed, resolved, or eliminated; so that we can then factually evaluate it for proper action. This requires our willingness and desire to look for our internal and external contributors that are making us feel negative and which need to be improved. To do so, we must have *"Desire and Introspection;"* in other words, we must want to improve, and we must be able to look within our Self to see what needs improvement.

If we do not have the desire to change and improve, or if we do not think that we need to change and improve; no motivational program nor any self-improvement system can make us change. Therefore, in order for us to change and improve, we must have the desire to change and improve; and once we establish the desire to change and improve, we must then have the ability to introspect so that we can see what needs change and improvement.

Theory of Self-Relativity defines "introspection" as "one's awareness, observation, and understanding of one's own mental-processes and emotional-traits."

As described throughout Theory of Self-Relativity, introspection is simply a person's ability to "self-inspect." Although introspection does include evaluating one's positive-traits; for the purpose of learning to change and improve, Theory of Self-Relativity primarily focuses on introspection as our willingness and our ability to look within our own Self in order to identify our weaknesses, our shortcomings, and our deficiencies. By observing and by identifying our negative-traits, we can then place our focus on the traits and mindsets that need attention and improvement. However, the reason introspection is difficult to achieve is because looking at our weaknesses, which are what need to be changed and improved, is a difficult, dislikable, and often a painful undertaking. Therefore, many, instead of facing their weaknesses, they choose to deploy other evasive and avoidance mechanisms such as externalation, distraction, denial, and ignorance, in order to avoid the painful task of introspection and self-reflection.

In addition to evasive and avoidance mechanisms, many, through rationalization and justification, choose to also create false-thoughts and fallacious-beliefs in order to deceptively feel better. As discussed, Theory of Self-Relativity refers to the creation of such feel-good thoughts and comforting-beliefs as *"Placebo-Thinking."*

Theory of Self-Relativity defines "Placebo-Thinking" as "thoughts that we concoct regardless of their factuality, in order to support our desired feelings."

Introspection-avoidance, or as termed and discussed by Theory of Self-Relativity, *"Externalation,"* is implemented through mechanisms that distract us away from our own Self and place the focus onto the outside; namely onto other-people and other-things.

Externalation is one of the main reasons Theory of Self-Relativity identifies "others" as the most dangerous word; because as further discussed, when we put too much focus externally onto other-people or on other-things, the self-equation shifts and tilts to the outside, hence, this takes the focus away from our own Self. Although for proper self-improvement we must bring the focus onto our Self, we often nonconsciously try to shift the focus away from our Self so that we won't have to remain with our dislikable negative-thoughts, and we won't have to pay attention to our personal-weaknesses and shortcomings. This is why, self-awareness, self-reflection, and introspection are emotionally difficult undertakings; because they expose us to many personal weaknesses that need identification, as well as time and effort consuming corrective action.

The dilemma with self-improvement is that, on one hand we should bring the focus onto our Self to improve our weaknesses; however, on the other hand, we nonconsciously try to avoid self-inspecting our weaknesses, because self-reflection and introspection are dislikable and painful.

In mainstream psychology, such ways of dealing with discomfort and stress is commonly labeled as defense-mechanisms; which are psychological strategies that are nonconsciously used to protect a person from anxiety arising from unacceptable thoughts or feelings. However, if these defense-mechanisms are deployed constantly and continuously in order to avoid uncomfortable feelings; they then become "unhealthy" avoidance-coping-skills, which in-turn, is defined as nonconscious psychological responses that prevent us from feeling any anxiety or upset that can arise from a difficult or harmful stimulus.

To reiterate, Theory of Self-Relativity has termed the defense-mechanism to avoid and abstain from introspection as "externalation;" and when externalation is deployed and used on a regular basis in order to avoid dealing with the dislikable reality and the discovery of our personal-weaknesses, externalation becomes an unhealthy avoidance-coping-skill.

According to Theory of Self-Relativity, externalation reflects any conscious, but mostly nonconscious mental and behavioral activities that we engage in and deploy that distracts and preoccupies our mind with other-things or with other-people, in order to avoid self-reflection and introspection.

Theory of Self-relativity defines "externalation" as "one's focus and preoccupation with external things and events, in order to avoid and distract one's Self from observing and recognizing one's own deficiencies and weaknesses."

As further discussed, such defense-mechanisms and avoidance-coping-skills can evolve into personality-traits and even personality-disorders, if they are learned and deployed continuously from earlier years in life such as childhood and adolescence.

Childhood and early life skills and habits often become personality-traits as we age.

If one does not learn to develop proper self-sufficiency and self-reliance skills from early years, and instead of dealing with reality as is, one continuously avoids dealing with dislikable truths; one will intuitively resort to externalation as a means of avoiding factual-reality, or as a means of dealing with an alternate comforting fabrication of a nonfactual-reality. This is why, Theory of Self-Relativity places special emphasis on the dangerous combination of externalation and placebo-thinking; because placebo-thinking enables sustained engagement of externalation.

Externalation, as simply defined, is the antagonist of introspection. Theory of Self-Relativity more specifically views externalation as a collection of defense-mechanisms and avoidance-coping-skills which enable a person to avoid introspection, by shifting the focus to external distractions and preoccupations. The primary mode of deploying externalation is by shifting the focus away from the Self, onto others, and this focus could be in a positive way such as excessive over-caring and concern, or even altruisms, towards others; or in a negative way such as excessive gossip, anger, and even ill-wishing towards others. If and when reality puts so much pressure on one's Self where externalation becomes difficult; one, then commonly shifts and resorts to placebo-thinking, so that one can deny and ignore the dislikable and often painful truth. As long as the shift, the distraction, and the preoccupation are primarily intended to avoid introspection; any such mindsets and behavior could be classified as externalation. Externalation in every specific situation includes at least one or more of the following traits.

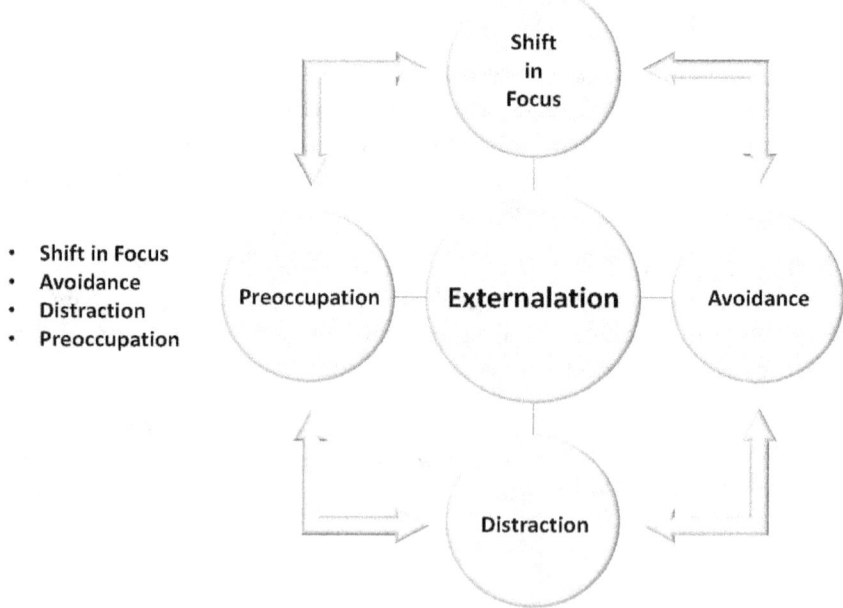

- **Shift in Focus**
- **Avoidance**
- **Distraction**
- **Preoccupation**

According to Theory of Self-Relativity, some of the most common defense-mechanisms and avoidance-coping-skills that we deploy in order to engage in externalation and to avoid introspection are best demonstrated below.

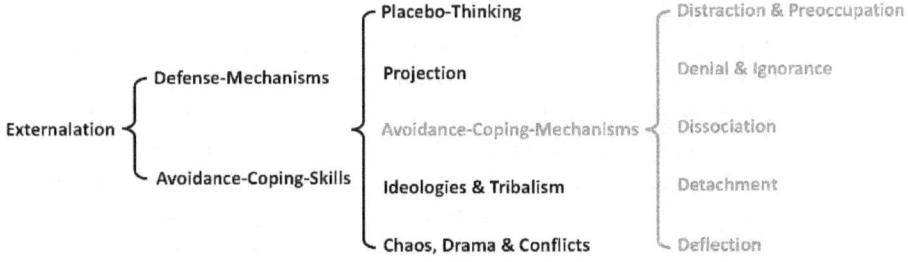

I. **Placebo-Thinking:** As discussed and termed by Theory of Self-Relativity, placebo-thinking is a mechanism that we deploy in order to create thoughts to justify and support our desired-feelings. One of the common ways that we justify and support the creation and acceptance of comforting-thoughts is through the defense-mechanism of rationalization. Rationalization is the action of attempting to explain or justify behavior, or maintain an attitude with fallacious logical-reasons, even if these reasons are not appropriate. Placebo-thinking often coexists with confirmation-bias and motivated-reasoning which is the rationalization of our biased-beliefs, because such beliefs provide purpose, meaning, and comfort for us. Placebo-thinking is most commonly used where we want to convince our Self that reality isn't as bad as it is, or when we want to rationalize that certain things we think and do, such as addictive behaviors, are justified. Placebo-Thinking is discussed in detail throughout Theory of Self-Relativity.

II. **Projection:** Is the nonconscious projection or throwing of our undesired-thoughts and beliefs and our uncomfortable-feelings and emotions onto others, instead of us admitting and dealing with them. Although projection might on the surface appear similar to externalation; they are not the same. Externalation is primarily the shifting of focus and attention onto other-people or other-things in order to avoid awareness and recognition of one's own undesired-thoughts and uncomfortable-feelings; however, projection is nonconsciously reflecting our own weaknesses and deficiencies onto others as if it were the others' negative-traits. Projection, by definition, is shifting the focus onto others and can be the reason for externalation; however, externalation, by definition, does not have to be projection of one's own feelings. Projection is a good example of why it is difficult to introspect and to realize our self-weaknesses. Theory of Self-Relativity categorizes projection binarily:

1. **Negative-Projection:** Is the projections of our negative or undesired-thoughts and uncomfortable-feelings onto others. For example, because we lie about something and we are nonconsciously aware that we lie, we blame someone else for lying about that same subject. Negative-projection is often rooted in "denial" of our own

negative-characteristics. Negative-projection is a common characteristic of ignorant and arrogant people.

Projection does wonders to expose the ignorant and the unaware.

2. **Positive-Projection:** Is projecting our constructive-thoughts and positive-feelings onto others. For example, because we never lie, we automatically assume that others do not lie either, even when the evidence clearly shows we are being lied to. Positive-projection is often rooted in the "naivety" of believing everyone else shares and practices our positive-characteristics. Positive-projection is a common trait among naive-people; because, naivety is commonly coexistence with gullibility, as both traits arise from personal-weaknesses.

Naivety is the unintended consequence of susceptibility and desperation.

III. **The 5-Ds of Avoidance-Coping-Mechanisms:** According to Theory of Self-Relativity, 5-Ds refers to the following five avoidance-copying-mechanisms that a person deploys to move away from a negative or undesired-thought, or from an uncomfortable-feeling.

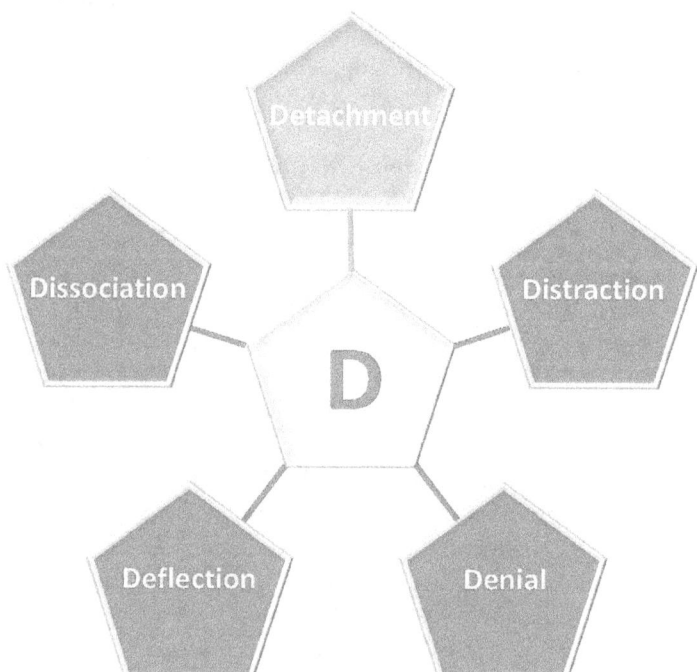

1. **Distraction and Preoccupation:** Is a defense mechanism which enables us to avoid facing factual-reality as it focuses our attention away from confronting uncomfortable-thoughts that cause our undesired-negative-feelings. Although distraction could be an effective tool to break the cycle of repetitive-thinking in the short-term; in the longer-term and as a habitual pattern, distraction can become an

unhealthy coping and avoidance-defense-mechanism. According to Theory of Self-Relativity, distraction is the most common characteristic present in externalation, and the primary role of externalation is to distract and preoccupy the mind away from the Self, in order to avoid introspection. Distraction can be caused by long-term strategies such as procrastination and perfection; or distraction and preoccupation could engage us in externalation via short-term strategies such as checking texts and emails, getting on social-media, gambling, addictions, etc. According to Theory of Self-Relativity, short-term distractions and preoccupations can cause more damage than longer-term ones, because short-term distractions rarely lead to positive-change. Compared to self-deception, which is directly cognitive, whereby we believe or create false-thoughts and fallacious-beliefs in order to support our desired-feelings; Theory of Self-Relativity considers distractions and procrastinations as behaviors that are rooted in the nonconscious desire to abstain from introspection and dealing with the dislikable. Thus, distractions are not just purely thought-based, as they could also be more engagement and behavior based.

2. **Denial and Ignorance:** Are discussed in detail as one of Theory of Self-Relativity's 10-Enemies for Self-Improvement. Denial is a powerful defense-mechanism that many deploy in uncomfortable or undesired situations. Denial is commonly deployed in situations where the truth, especially if proven factually, could make the denier feel negatively. Denial is often associated with ignoring the cause, even when the cause is identified. In denial, the truth hurts, therefore the denier does not want to consider the truth. In other words, *"if it conflicts with what I want to be true, therefore it is not true."* Ignorance or the tendency to ignore facts, just like denying facts, is another defense-mechanism that people deploy in order to overlook information and knowledge about the facts; or to abstain from wanting to know the facts. Ignorance can not only be a defense-mechanism to avoid facing facts, but if carried on for a lengthy period of time and as a way of life, it can commonly lead to the person becoming ignorant. Denial and ignorance are the epitome of personal-cover-ups.

3. **Deflection:** Is changing the direction of an uncomfortable thought, in order to avoid the negative-feelings associated with that thought. Deflection, when used as a defense-mechanism to avoid uncomfortable facts, is done with the purpose of deflecting or blocking awareness of a thought, and it is commonly used as a means of manipulative strategy to pass the blame and responsibility of the truth onto someone or onto something else. Deflection often goes hand-in-hand with blame-shifting and it is commonly engaged by people suffering from personality-disorders such as Narcissistic-Personality-Disorder (NPD) and Borderline-Personality-Disorder (BPD). These personality-disorders are discussed further in other sections.

4. **Dissociation:** Seems similar to detachment; however, in dissociation, the person nonconsciously creates a "false-reality" in order to detach from the negative-thoughts and uncomfortable-feelings. Dissociation is generally involuntary and is a result of becoming overwhelmed and unable to deal with a certain thought or a feeling; whereas detachment is often cognitive and by choice. Dissociation, unlike detachment, is an "unhealthy" avoidance-copying-mechanism. Dissociation is also commonly associated with trauma.

5. **Detachment:** Is a healthy way of dismissing one's own or other-people's thoughts by becoming disinterested and neutral. Detachment is simply separating or moving-away from a thought, from a feeling, or from a situation. The reason detachment is healthy is because the person detaching actually evaluates the thought or the situation and recognizes the nonfactuality or inapplicability of that thought or the situation relative to one's own existence. Detachment is usually deployed after some cognitive evaluation of the thought or the situation. Detachment does not resolve or eliminate the thought or the cause; detachment simply distances the person from that thought or the situation because the person recognizes that the thought or the situation has no relevance or is not a threat to one's life. Although detachment and dissociation seem similar, dissociation could be considered unhealthy-detachment. Healthy-detachment often involves separating one's Self from the thoughts, feelings, and emotions of one's own Self or that of others. The key attribute to consider when engaging in healthy-detachment is the "factuality" of the thought and the "relevancy" of the thought, the feeling, or the situation to one's own Self.

IV. **Ideologies and Tribalism:** Although tribalism is commonly defined as being organized in a group based on certain common attributes; Theory of Self-Relativity views long-term and unhealthy-tribalism as a means of strengthening ideologies and biases which create a "me versus them" mindset. By doing so, in the name of dedication to certain causes and beliefs, one rigidly shifts the focus away from one's own Self by making the common attributes and causes of one's beliefs and tribalism the center of one's focus and attention. As discussed throughout Theory of Self-Relativity, the self-equation dictates that focus can only be directed to one side of the equation at any given time; hence, by taking the focus away from the Self and by directing it to others in the form of ideologies, biases, and even hatred, one nonconsciously projects one's frustrations with one's own deficiencies and shortcomings onto others by means of beliefs, biases, and ideologies. According to Theory of Self-Relativity, the reason people can quickly take sides and become biased is because such mindset gives them the ability to excuse and justify their lack of interest and willingness to engage in introspection. People who engage heavily in justifying and fighting for their beliefs, their ideologies, and their tribalism, do so in order to cover-up and abstain from awareness and understanding of their own personal-shortcomings. Although establishing beliefs, standing up for ideologies, and tribalism are intended to be constructive in the short-term; if these are held long-term and if they are continuously deployed without attaining some kind of positive-result, they become externalation and introspection-avoidance-coping-mechanisms. This is why, long-term passionate tribalism and standing up for ideologies and beliefs could take on the form of conflict and chaos; because such individuals are externally projecting personal-frustrations as beliefs onto others. Additionally, just as in other forms of externalation, tribalism provides the means for people to try to find externally-derived purpose, instead of creating their own purpose from within. The more such individuals and groups focus on others, especially with a negative-mindset, the more they enable themselves to abstain from introspection.

Ideologies and tribalism focus on hating others and their causes, instead of loving one's own Self and one's own purpose.

In other words, many subscribe to ideologies not because they absolutely believe in the principles of the ideology and the tribe; but they do so because anyone else who is not subscribed to the ideology and the beliefs of the group, presents a potential for shifting focus away from the Self onto them, in the form of criticism and even hatred. Instead of focusing on the beliefs that the ideology and their tribe represents, ideological and biased people shift their focus onto others who do not agree with all or parts of their ideology.

Simply stated:

Tribalism isn't as much about loving the tribe, as it is about hating others.

According to Theory of Self-Relativity, since most ideologies are engaged as a means of externalation:

Ideological externalation isn't as much about loving one's Self, as it is about hating others.

Therefore, when biases, ideologies, and tribalism become a means of externalation; then:

Ideologies aren't as much about believing in a mutual-cause, as they are about hating others.

Furthermore, ideological-people signal to others that they belong and that they are "good-people;" which in-turn, gives them more reason to commit to their ideology and to ignore their own personal-weaknesses that need to be improved. This social-signaling is commonly known as "virtue-signaling." For example, many subscribe to being religious not just because religion is comforting or because they believe in higher-powers; but they do so as a means of signaling to others that because they are religious, therefore, they are good-people. Likewise, many associate themselves with scientific and technological advancements as a means of signaling that they are better-people than those who do not adhere to new technologies; for example, driving electric-vehicles or EVs. Although many adopt and drive EVs because of their claimed environmental friendliness; however, many also drive EVs because they want to signal to others that they are conscientious, hence, they are good-people. Other similar examples of science being used as an ideological virtue-signaling tool are vaccines and climate-change.

When science and technology become the means of ideological identification or virtue-signaling; that is when science and technology become another form of religion.

V. **Chaos, Drama and Conflicts:** Unlike other psychology, self-help, and self-improvement teachings, Theory of Self-Relativity considers chaos, drama, and conflicts, especially those involving others, as common tactics that are deployed in order to engage in externalation and to avoid introspection. Chaos, drama, and conflict commonly include many of the aforementioned avoidance-coping-mechanisms such as deflection, projection and blame-shifting. By creating dramatic and exaggerated conflicts, those who are unable to self-reflect, preoccupy their mind away from their own Self by shifting the focus onto others via conflicts. This is not only a common trait among ideologues and biased individuals and their groups; but also, chaos, drama, and conflicts are common characteristics of individuals suffering from personality-disorders such as narcissistic-personality-disorder, borderline-personality-disorder, histrionics, anti-socials, and those possessing sociopathic characteristics. The aforementioned personality-disordered individuals are categorized under the Diagnostics and Statistics Manual's (DSM's) classifications as Cluster-B personality-disorders. The Cluster-B disorders are also referred to as the "Dramatic-Personality-Disorders" or "High-Conflict-Disorders." Since self-improvement requires taking personal-responsibility to improve, these dramatic and high-conflict individuals do not take personal-responsibility for their actions and for their life's difficulties; therefore, blame-shifting, sense-of-entitlement, and externalation, are common traits that they deploy in their relationships.

Introspection is a difficult undertaking; because, the pain of recognizing one's own self-deficiencies is often greater than the desire to improve.

Chaos, crisis, and drama, which are often nonconsciously deployed and engaged, preoccupy the mind from introspection and from looking at one's own fragilities and weaknesses. This is why, with chaotic people, as soon as one crisis is about to end, a new crisis arises; because the high-conflicts want to keep the momentum of distraction and externalation going. Going from crisis to crisis enable self-victimization and blame-shifting, which in-turn, help to avoid introspection. Therefore, calmness and down-time makes high-conflicts uncomfortable, because calmness and down-time forces them to remain with their own thoughts. For the high-conflicts, calmness and lack of chaos is never a preferred state-of-existence; because being by themselves and staying with their own thoughts brings the awareness and focus back to their own weak Self. Chaos and crisis help to disrupt calmness, by creating distractions, hence, enabling high-conflicts from observing their own self-deficiencies and personal-weaknesses. For the high-conflict and Cluster-B personality-disordered individuals, such distractions and externalation are the primary means of avoiding introspection.

High-conflicts are also referred to as "toxic-people," and relationships involving them are referred to as "toxic-relationships;" because, when involved in a toxic-relationship, the chaos and conflicts of the relationship inherently shift the non-toxic partner's focus away from the Self and onto the chaos and conflicts of the relationship created by the high-conflict individual. This is why, being involved in a long-term toxic-relationship can affect the non-toxic partner negatively and it could leave the non-toxic person traumatized and broken. Therefore, post-traumatic-stress-disorder or PTSD is a common side-effect of toxic-relationships, especially after the relationship ends; because these relationships almost never end amicably as the high-conflict person commits one final emotionally damaging act such as infidelity, theft, or even false accusations against the non-toxic partner. Relationships with high-conflicts often end in not only destruction of the relationship, but commonly in traumatic outcomes for the non-toxic partner. High-conflicts also try to smear and defame the non-toxic partner post-relationship.

As discussed, the main reason high-conflicts like having chaos, drama, and conflict is this keeps them engaged in externalation, while avoiding introspection; and, they do so because deep- inside they are nonconsciously aware of the many shortcoming that they have covered-up. Such aggressive mask-wearing individuals are actually fragile deep within; hence why, they are usually aggressive, loud, opinionated, threatening, and tantrum-throwing. They are high-conflict because a loud and aggressive stance is the false façade and fake mask that helps protect them from their own weak, fragile, and often developmentally arrested childish inner-self. By being overwhelming, high-conflicts force others to backoff from challenging their perspectives; which in-turn, prevents the exposure of their weak, fragile, and false self-identity.

Although high-conflict and toxic-people will almost never admit to their own shortcomings, and would practically do anything to prevent others from discovering their inner-weaknesses; it is also worth noting that such individuals, themselves, often have an extremely negative and even hateful self-image. When a partner, a friend, or an associate tries to confront the high-conflict person's often baseless, false, and even imaginary stance with facts and contradictory evidence; these high-conflicts commonly go into anger and rage, or they will throw fits and tantrums in order to deny, ignore, and deflect the facts which are about to uncover their false façade, or which are about to prove them wrong. Because of their own self-hate and weak self-image, for high-conflicts to be proven wrong, means admitting that they are worthless. Furthermore, in the face of contradictory-evidence, high-conflicts also have a habit of hanging-up the phone, storming out of the room, and engaging in silent-treatment; in order to prevent others from presenting the contradictory evidence that would uncover their inner weaknesses.

The end result of long-term high-conflict relationships often leads to the regression and trauma of the non-toxic partner; instead of making positive-changes for the high-conflict and the toxic-individual. Relationships with high-conflict and personality-disordered individuals are further discussed throughout Theory of Self-Relativity.

Instead of trying to change toxic people so they would be kinder to you; fix yourself so that you would never tolerate toxicity.

Since both desire and introspection require mental and emotional engagement, and without these two traits one will not be able to change and improve; this is why, Theory of Self-Relativity classifies desire and introspection as the *"Two Non-Negotiables for Self-Improvement."* The sooner we commit to peeling away the layers of weaknesses and negativities that we have buried, the sooner we will be able to resolve or eliminate them; and the best way to do so is by evaluating every hidden weakness with factual-thoughts to see if these weaknesses are real or imagined. If our weaknesses and negativities are factual and true, we then take action to change and improve them; hence, we resolve our weaknesses. However, if they are nonfactual and untrue, and they are mostly belief-based or emotionally fabricated; we can then dismiss and eliminate them.

We have the ability and the free-will to change and improve our life and our circumstances; therefore, it is up to us to change our life and our circumstances for the better. However, to do so, we must be able to face our negativities and shortcomings. It is our self-responsibility and our self-given-right to make the best out of our life and to live the most fulfilled and the happiest life possible. To do so, we must have the desire to change, and we must initiate and continue the process of change and improvement. Since everything changes constantly, including The-Universe; therefore, we must put in the effort to make positive-change by changing along with The-Universe. Change requires our input, and since we have the free-will to make a decision to change, we must use our free-will to free our mind from its shackles of not wanting to change; because:

If we don't choose to change; The-Universe will force change upon us.

Although the concept of free-will, similar to the concept of consciousness, is a highly debated subject; Theory of Self-Relativity contends that cognitive, and especially intelligent animals, including humans, are capable of having free-will. As science and our knowledge of nature have progressed exponentially, a contentious and contested philosophical debate has grown on the topic of the existence of free-will, which directly affects self-improvement.

Theory of Self-Relativity defines "free-will" as "the ability for humans and cognitive living-things to make independent decisions, and to create choices for action."

Current leading theories of free-will fall under one of two extremes:

1. **Deterministic Free-Will:** Determinism is the philosophical theory that all events, including moral choices are completely determined by previously

existing causes. Determinism suggests that no free-will exists and what we think to be free-will is determined by a previous cause and these causes are all determined by the laws-of-physics that govern the The-Universe. Determinism claims that some of these previous causes are not only related to physics but are also determined by our past-experiences and by other determined attributes such as genetics. Many science-oriented individuals are deterministic in their beliefs.

2. **Indeterministic Free-Will:** Indeterminism is the idea that events are not caused deterministically. Indeterminism is the antagonistic view to determinism as indeterminism states that free-will exists without limitation and it is determined by chance and randomness. Metaphysical, supernatural, and non-science-oriented people, as well as our legal-system are generally indeterministic, as they contend that we have a choice with our decisions and actions.

The concept of free-will is where one's ability to remain unbiased and adaptable becomes apparent. Being strictly deterministic or strictly indeterministic becomes ideological; and as discussed, rigid and extreme ideologies create biases and inflexibility to adapt. This is why, facts, and only facts, should guide our thoughts and our actions; because our mindset could and is often influenced by biases which create rigidity. Hence why, Theory of Self-Relativity states:

To improve, we must remain unbiased and adaptable; and the only way that we can do so is by allowing facts to dictate our thinking.

Determinism and indeterminism create a dichotomy regarding free-will where people are forced to choose one or the other. Although Theory of Self-Relativity is fact-based and science-oriented, it contends that free-will cannot be explained from such extreme and limiting positions. Theory of Self-Relativity views free-will as our intents, decisions, and actions that apply to a future event; therefore, this future event may or may not be related to a past event but it is usually guided by our past-experiences. Thus, we use our free-will and we use our past-experiences to guide and influence a relative future-event; and we do so from the many and often infinite possible choices. Therefore, according to Theory of Self-Relativity, we should:

Use our past-experiences to guide our future.

According to Theory of Self-Relativity, although this future event is as a result of a past occurrence; this future event is not solely determined by what happened prior to it. Thus, our free-will enables us to use our past "experiences" and "knowledge" to "guide" and "influence" future events; therefore, we are not "determined" by our past in order to move forward into a predetermined future. While Theory of Self-Relativity is founded upon the factual and scientific principles that are governed by the laws-of-physics; according to Theory of Self-Relativity, being governed by the laws-of-physics does not mean we are slaves of the laws-of-physics.

The governance of the laws-of-physics means that we cannot violate the laws-of-physics; however, according to Theory of Self-Relativity, as long as we stay within the parameters of the laws-of-physics, we have no limitations to freely move around, make decisions, and take actions to guide and influence our future, based on the choices that are available within the parameters dictated by the laws-of-physics. For example, although gravity forces us to be grounded on the surface of the Earth, by using our free-will and intelligence, we are able to take flight by defying gravity. As long as we use the laws-of-physics to transform matter into energy, which is allowed by the laws-of-physics; we can use this energy to fly our planes and launch our spaceships, contrary to the law of gravity. According to theory of Self-Relativity:

The laws-of-physics don't determine what happens; the laws-of-physics limit what could happen.

The laws-of-physics are descriptive, not prescriptive; therefore, the laws-of-physics determine the limitations of what could happen, but they don't determine what must happen, especially when a cognitive and intelligent free-will entity is influencing and guiding the decisions and actions. As long as the decisions and actions of a cognitive-agent do not violate the laws-of-physics, there could be countless possibilities of events and outcomes that could happen. If a decision, action, or an outcome is intended to violate the laws-of-physics; that decision, action, or event will simply not be able to take place, because in order for things to materialize or happen, they must abide by the laws-of-physics.

For example, no matter how much we believe that we have free-will and if we walk-off a high-rise building nothing will happen to us; the laws-of-physics dictate that if we do so, we will fall off the building to the ground, and we will get injured or we will probably die. However, although the laws-of-physics dictate that if we walk off the high-rise building we will fall; by using a parachute, we can use the same laws-of-physics to slow-down our descend to the ground. Therefore, having free-will does not mean overcoming the laws-of-physics; having free-will means to have the ability to make decisions and to create choices from the potential possibilities within the limitations of the laws-of-physics, without violating these laws. Due to the limitations of the laws-of-physics, Theory of Self-Relativity has termed the kind of free-will that we have and that we enjoy as *"Limited Free-Will"* or *"Limited-Will."*

Theory of Self-Relativity defines "limited-free-will" as "the ability for humans and living-things to make independent decisions and to create choices for action; within the boundaries of the laws-of-physics that govern The-Universe."

Since the laws-of-physics that govern The-Universe are absolute and do not change; therefore, our free-will is limited to how the laws-of-physics allow everything and everyone to exist, function, and interact with one another, and with The-Universe.

According to Theory of Self-Relativity:

The only thing that is absolute, are the laws-of-physics that govern the Universe.

Although our free-will is limited by the laws-of-physics; for all intents and purposes, since we will never be violating the laws-of-physics, we can consider our limited-free-will to be synonymous with free-will, especially at the local-level of Our-Universe. Therefore, Theory of Self-Relativity's references to free-will is synonymous with limited-will or limited-free-will. Consequently, as long as we do not attempt to violate the governing laws-of-physics, we can often slow-down and even stop some of the influences of The-Universe on our existence, and at the local-level of Our-Universe. Therefore, Theory of Self-Relativity contends that:

Free-will is more deterministic at the macro-level of The-Universe, but more indeterministic at the local-level of Our-Universe.

Although free-will is dependent on The-Universe and the laws-of-physics, The-Universe itself does not have free-will, because free-will is considered to be a trait of living, conscious, and largely, thinking organisms. Therefore, for humans and for other thinking animals, free-will is a subjective and local-trait.

Theory of Self-Relativity considers free-will as not being totally absolute, but as it being situational with limitations which can be expanded and increased with thinking, reasoning, knowledge, and through intellectual advancements. Simply stated, free-will exists and has limitations, but these limitations can be increased locally through thinking, knowledge, and intelligence; as long as the attempts to raise these limitations do not violate the laws-of-physics. Logic, knowledge, and intelligence can expand and override limitations locally, but they cannot completely ignore the larger macro-scale deterministic forces of nature. Thus, according to Theory of Self-Relativity, free-will is subjective and its applications are more limited locally by the limitation of knowledge and experience of an individual or a group; rather than by the macro-scale limitations of the laws-of-physics.

Our physical-brain is made of matter, and it is affected, influenced, and governed by the same laws-of-physics that affect other matter such as a rock, a planet, and even The-Universe. As discussed, our matter-based physical-brain gives rise to our immaterial-functions or processes of thinking, reasoning, and intelligence. These immaterial-byproducts of our material-brain's activities give us the ability to have free-will, by evaluating and by creating choices; and by making decisions. Theory of Self-Relativity considers free-will, just like a thought, to be an immaterial-byproduct of the functions of our material-brain, which arises from our consciousness, our thinking, and our decisions.

As discussed, although mental-functions such as thinking, feeling, reasoning, etc. are commonly referred to as "states" of our mind; these states of the mind are often interchanged with what Theory of Self-Relativity refers to as the immaterial-byproducts of our material-brain's activities. Because such references inherently imply the relativities between our brain and our mental-states.

Free-will, just like thinking and consciousness, is a byproduct of the brain's activities.

The laws-of-physics that apply to matter are well known and do not vary from one form of matter to another, especially at the macro-scale. However, free-will is immaterial, therefore on the *"local"* human-scale, our free-will, just like our mind and our thoughts, can exist independently of the predetermined laws-of-physics, biology, and even genetics; as long as our physiological-brain is functioning normally. These immaterial-byproducts of our brain enable us to cheat the laws-of-nature and physics through active-effort; whereas an inanimate object or a non-cognitive entity such as a rock, which is made of similar elementary particles as we are, would not be able to do so. Although all matter is made of atoms, what distinguishes animate-matter, such as a human-being, from an inanimate-matter, such as a rock, are the biochemical-reactions that occur in animate-objects. These biochemical-reactions lead to an object being a living thing; and in more complex and evolved species such as humans, these biochemical-activities give rise to our consciousness, our intelligence, and our free-will. Hence why, in most simple terms:

Theory of Self-Relativity defines "life" as "the byproduct of biochemical reactions."

As stated, although the laws-of-physics cannot be violated, our free-will enables us to slow-down or even temporarily halt the effects of certain laws-of-physics, at the local level of Our-Universe. For example, when we decide to, we can build a skyscraper, and by locally putting in active-effort and constant input, we can maintain the building in its operating state for years, decades, and even for centuries. However, as The-Universe moves forward in time and as the macro laws-of-physics which govern The-Universe affect and change the state of our locality; at that time, our free-will and intervention will not be effective anymore. In about 5 billion years, when the Earth gets devoured by the engorging dying Sun, no matter how much free-will we have, we will not be able to remain alive nor maintain the building. Therefore, local free-will and effort have limitations relative to the longer time and larger scale of The-Universe.

As discussed in detail in other sections, although due to entropy, The-Universe is in a state of increasing disorder; influences such as our intent and free-will can minimize, or even, can temporarily halt the effects of The-Universe's disorder, locally. Such local influences also can and do create "complexity" in the face of The-Universe's inherent disorder; as long as the total macro disorder of The-Universe is not affected, and its total entropy continues to increase. Complexities such as intelligent life can arise naturally as we go from a low state of disorder or entropy to a higher state of disorder; therefore, complexity is temporary. However, as The-Universe ages, expands, and becomes more disorderly, all complexities will eventually disappear. Disorder, entropy, and complexity are discussed in detail in subsequent sections.

A functioning material-brain allows progress and improvement through its immaterial-byproducts of consciousness, intelligence, and free-will. Just because we are born with certain physiological and genetic attributes it does not mean we cannot change the present, or we cannot influence the tomorrow locally, and in the scale of Our-Universe. Although we are born with certain predisposing factors and we are made of matter which abides by the laws-of-physics that govern how matter behaves; locally, we can create change and favorable outcomes via proper manipulation of Our-Universe, using our intelligence and our free-will.

Therefore, despite the fact that The-Universe is governed by the laws-of-nature and we might be born with certain predispositions; with proper thinking and with effort-based input, we can locally and in the short-term, slow-down, modify, manipulate, and even eliminate the effects of these factors. For example, a man who is balding has predisposing genetic factors that determines he will be bald and remain bald for the rest of his life. According to and as termed by Theory of Self-Relativity, hair loss and other esthetically diminishing conditions are consi-dered to be a form of entropy dubbed as *"Cosmetic-Entropy;"* therefore, as we age, our cosmetic-entropy increases. As evidenced, once pattern-baldness commen-ces, it will not stop or improve until the baldness cycle is completed; however, when we use our free-will, we can take action and put in effort to restore our pattern-baldness via hair-transplants. Congratulations; we just locally cheated the laws-of-physics, and we just expanded the limitations placed by nature at the local-level of Our-Universe.

This example demonstrates how we can not only have free-will to slow-down the cosmetic-entropy of baldness; but we can reverse it permanently in our locality and for our lifetime. This reversal does not mean pattern-baldness will be eliminated for our son, as pattern-baldness is governed by a dominant gene in men; however, by having free-will and by using the advancement of science and modern-medi-cine, which are as a result of human thinking, intelligence, and free-will, we were able to influence disorder locally in Our-Universe.

The immaterial-byproducts and processes of the brain such as thinking and free-will, could locally influence, modify, and even eliminate the effects of the laws-of-physics.

Our free-will, intelligence, and thinking might even be able to influence but not violate the macro-scale of The-Universe. Multiple free-wills, when combined, could produce even larger effects on the limitation of natural-laws; this is how humans progress, advance, and evolve. Multiple free-wills from multiple-people overlapping and being shared together, can combine and increase the effects of individual free-wills on a larger scale, by bringing together multiple localities. When the collective free-wills, experiences, and knowledge of human technology and science reaches a certain plateau; humans might even be able to slow-down, stop, or even cheat the laws-of-nature and physics, not just locally, but on the scale of "The-Universe." For example, free-will and effort might enable the creation of wormholes to cheat the laws-of-physics and to travel faster than the speed of light. Since The-Universe does not have feelings, The-Universe does not care if it is cheated; but The-Universe will not stand to be violated.

We can cheat the laws-of-physics, but we can't violate them.

It must be noted that cheating the laws-of-physics is not the same as violating them, which could never happen. This is why, science must be open-minded, and scientists must remain open to change. Scientists pride themselves on being open to being proven wrong, because being proven wrong enables scientists to narrow down the field of possibilities through the process-of-elimination; until they reach the most reasonable and unfalsifiable theory.

Science is not absolute; science is about having reasonable confidence about the evidence.

It is because of human free-will and their ability to change that has allowed humans to advance at faster and faster pace.

If there were no free-will, human progress, knowledge, and technology would've advanced at the very slow rate that evolution and chance would dictate.

The effects of human intelligence, free-will, and progress are most apparent in the twentieth and twenty-first centuries as the advancements of technology, information, and knowledge have doubled exponentially and at a faster and faster pace. Although according to Theory of Self-Relativity, free-will is not limitless and is constrained by the laws-of-physics; however, the limits of free-will, especially on the local-level of human lifetime, could be expanded via self-improvement and through the evolution of quick and clever thinking. Additionally, the effects of free-will can further be accelerated and advanced through the collective free-wills of the individual members of a society or multiple societies.

The advancement of intelligence and thinking creates free-will, and free-will, in-turn, accelerates intellectual evolution. Consequently, the collective-free-will from multiple minds exponentially accelerates human intellectual-evolution; which in-turn, creates stronger free-will to advance individual intelligence and cognition even further. Therefore, by having free-will and by thinking intelligently, we can advance faster than we would've, had we left things to chance; and on the larger scale, had we left things to evolution or to natural determinants. Free-will, when engaged, results from consciousness and thinking, and it leads to decision-making and action. For example, our ability to love someone is a choice that we made from within our own Self and based on our own free-will; it did not happen just because nature dictated it for us as a result of past events.

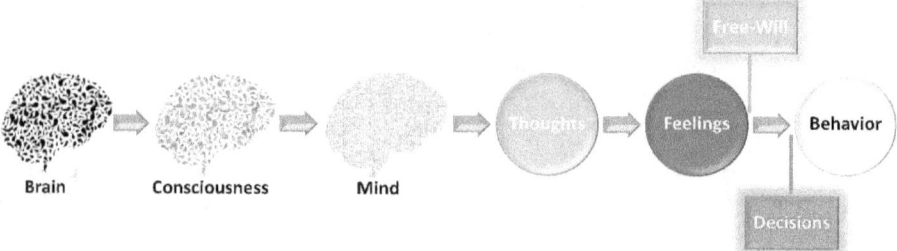

Regardless of its superficial complexities, Theory of Self-Relativity considers free-will and choice as an important aspect for self-improvement and human existence;

therefore, free-will enables us to choose to improve, and by using our free-will we can identify the traits and characteristics that we can change and improve.

Although having free-will means that we can make decisions and take actions that could guide or influence the future; this does not mean that as intelligent free-willed beings we can decide and do whatever we want. It is exactly for us having intelligence-based free-will that we have constituted social-laws so that our free-will does not violate other people's rights. Just because we have free-will and we can twist and cheat but not violate the laws-of-physics; it does not mean we can go around cheating others and committing crimes. Interestingly, the determinists claim that such unruly actions are predetermined; therefore, because of having no free-will criminals would have committed their crimes anyway. Good luck arguing that in a court of law, that criminals commit crimes because they do not have free-will; therefore, it was not their fault. Just as ignorance of the law is not an excuse in a court-of-law, neither is the deterministic concept of us having no free-will.

Theory of Self-Relativity considers the existence of our free-will to be relative to our Self and to our lifetime; therefore, Theory of Self-Relativity focuses on how we could make better decisions and how we could create better choices through self-improvement by applying our free-will at the local-level of our lifetime and Our-Universe. Theory of Self-Relativity views free-will to be a subjective and personal attribute; hence, free-will could be manipulated and strengthened to become an effective decision-making tool throughout our existence. Such well-trained, consistent, persistent, and result-oriented free-will is often referred to as "Will-Power."

Theory of Self-Relativity defines "will-power" as "a well-trained and disciplined mind-set that leads one to constructive-action."

Simply stated:

Will-power is a subjective form of free-will.

As discussed, the events of our past could influence our future choices and actions, but the events of our past do not automatically determine our future choices and actions. Therefore, our will-power, which directs our decision-making and behavior, is a more analytical and focused state of our mind; hence, Theory of Self-Relativity contends that just as we are able to think, feel, and behave by choice, our brain also gives us the ability to have free-will, and to have will-power. Just as free-will gives us the ability to choose how we want to proceed with our life; free-will and will-power also give us the personal-responsibility to change and improve our life for the better.

We must change and improve, because we have the free-will to change and improve.

Free-will, and especially will-power, is the essence behind psychology, psychotherapy, and as a whole, behavior modification. To change and improve, we must take personal-responsibility by having the desire to improve, by being able to look at the negativities that need improvement, and by taking action to change and improve. This is why, "Self-Agency and Personal-Responsibility" is designated as one of Theory of Self-Relativity's 10-Commandments for Self-Improvement.

To change and improve, we must want to change and improve, and we must know what we need to change and improve.

II.
Self-First & Centered-Self

According to Theory of Self-Relativity, the most important word is "Self," and the most dangerous word is "others;" because, in order to live a content, a fulfilled, and a happy life, we must bring the focus onto our self-first before we do so with others. If we are not healthy or if we are not the best that we could be physically, emotionally, and cognitively; we will not be able to be our best Self for others either, and we will not be able to have healthy, satisfying, and happy relationships with others.

Your-Universe

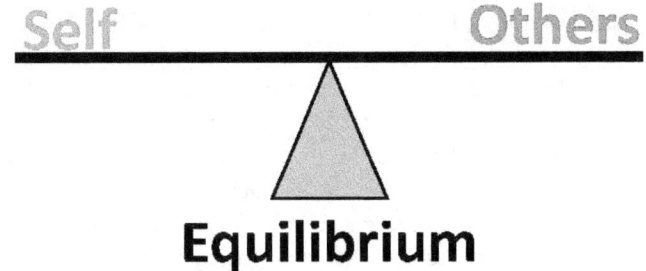

"Self-Equation"

As discussed, in Our-Universe, we are on one side of the self-equation, and other-people and other-things are on the other side. This does not mean we are antagonistic with everyone and everything else and that the self-equation is suggesting an "us versus them" stance. But, this means that in order for us to live in balance and harmony with Our-Universe, which includes other-people and other-things, we must place conscious and effort-based emphasis on both sides of the equation so that we can dynamically remain in equilibrium.

Equilibrium

For those who are having difficulty changing and improving, one of the main obstacles is the fact that they pay more attention to others rather than to their own Self. Without the Self, there will not be a relative Universe; therefore, we must make our Self the center and the balancing element of Our-Universe. As discussed, focusing on others tilts the self-equation away from the Self and could lead to selflessness; yet, focusing heavily on the Self without any regard for others, tilts the Self equation towards the Self and could lead to selfishness.

Commonly, as we go through life and as we interact with everything and everyone else, our attention begins to shift externally and we begin to focus onto others; while often ignoring, and disregarding our own Self. By focusing on other-people and other-things, we overlook and lose touch with our own Self, who is actually the only entity that is omnipresent in Our-Universe. It is because of this shifting that we need to consciously, actively, and with awareness, learn to attend to our own Self; by placing the utmost importance on our Self, before we do so with others. Theory of Self-Relativity refers to this state-of-existence as living a *"Centered-Self"* life.

Theory of Self-Relativity defines "centered-self" as "placing our Self-first before others but not at the expense of others."

As described, living a centered-self life does not mean to be self-centered; on the contrary, it is quite the opposite of self-centeredness or selfishness. Although both centered-self and self-centered prioritize the Self before others; self-centered people do so without any concern or consideration for others, and quite often they do so at the expense of others. In contrast, centered-self means to bring the focus and the attention to the Self, and to place the self-first before others; but not at the expense of others. To learn to live a centered-self life, we must not only learn to bring the focus and attention to our own self-first, but we must also live our life from the *"inside-out"* and not from the outside-in. Living from the inside-out enables us to connect to everything and everyone else; by us having core-relevancy, while maintaining outward-relativity with others. Instead of being second-in-line when living from the outside-in, we become central and first-in-line when we live from the inside-out; thus, by living a centered-self life from the inside-out, we connect to Our-Universe from a core-central position.

Centered-self does not mean to not care or to not attend to others; but it means to care for and to attend to our self-first so that we will then know how to treat others in the same manner. The problem with many who have difficulty in improving and transforming, is that some are too focused externally and onto others. Centered-self living teaches us how to remember to attend to our Self too. Since focus and distraction with others often makes us ignore our own Self; centered-self enables us to begin with the Self before we move on to others. When we learn to pay attention to and prioritize our Self before others, we will then be able to have a much better ability to perspective-take others. When we pay attention to, when we prioritize, and when we become aware of our own Self, we can then become more aware of others; therefore, we will know and understand much better how to interact with them.

If you can't be good to your own self, you won't know how to truly be good to others.

To truly become an empathetic and compassionate person, we must first learn to have empathy and compassion for our own Self. Although the bible states, "do unto other as you would have them do unto you;" Theory of Self-Relativity considers this statement just like many other social and traditional teachings to be too focused externally and onto others. According to Theory of Self-Relativity, to truly be empathetic and compassionate towards others:

Do unto others as you do unto your Self.

Since majority of human-beings do not like to hurt or harm themselves, unless they have some kind of underlying psychological and traumatic issues; by learning to pay attention to our Self and how we treat our own Self, we can then reciprocate similar attitude and behavior towards others. Our morality and values are best achieved and cultivated from within and not externally from other-people or from other-things. The best way to be empathetic, compassionate, and caring for others is for us to know how self-empathy, self-compassion, and self-love feels like. Likewise, when we learn and know what genuine empathy, compassion, and caring feels like; we will look for similar characteristics in others, and from others. We should not expect similar attributes from others, we should require and enforce these traits and characteristics to be reciprocated; and if others are incapable of reciprocating such values, we should be strong enough to minimize or cut-off our interactions with such people.

When you know how it is to feel something; you will then have a better understanding of how others feel about the same thing.

As discussed throughout Theory of Self-Relativity, we should minimize and abstain from having expectations from our Self or from others; because expectations often lead to disappointments, especially when expectations are reliant on other-people's performance. Similarly, we should not demand nor earn respect; but we should require and enforce respect. Likewise, we should not expect, demand, nor earn compassion, empathy, and caring from others; we should require and enforce it. Requiring empathy, compassion, and caring from others could only be achieved if we know what being empathetic, compassionate, and caring feels like. The way to require and enforce these qualities from others is by recognizing if others possess these characteristics; and the only way that we would know if others possess these characteristics is by us knowing what empathy and compassion feel like. If others are incapable of being empathetic or compassionate, we should not waste time hoping that they will learn. We should be realistic enough to minimize our interactions with them and we should seek relationships with people who are more in touch with their own Self, and who also know how to share and reciprocate qualities such as empathy and compassion without having to be thought or reminded to do so.

True empathy and compassion do not require reminders or effort.

Simply stated:

The only things that do not require effort are empathy and compassion.

Empathy and compassion, just like other moral-values, originate from within and are rooted in:

1. **Self-Reflection:** *Theory of Self-Relativity simply defines "self-reflection" as "one's ability to exercise and engage in introspection."*
2. **Perspective-Taking:** *Theory of Self-Relativity simply defines "perspective-taking" as "one's ability to exercise and engage in extrospection."*

Perspective-taking and empathy are integral for positive interpersonal-interactions and relationships.

This means, in order for us to be empathetic and compassionate, we must know, understand and feel how empathy and compassion truly feel like; which means, we must also be empathetic and compassionate to our own Self.

Empathy is commonly defined as "the ability to understand and feel other people's feelings;" however, by focusing on empathy as having an ability to understand other people's feelings, we often overlook self-empathy, which according to Theory of Self-Relativity, is the most important form of empathy. While empathy in popular definitions is empathy that is directed towards other-people; we must also have empathy for our own Self, atop having empathy for other humans and other living-things. Therefore, the definition of empathy by Theory of Self-Relativity includes self-empathy.

Theory of Self-Relativity defines "empathy" as "one's ability to be aware of and to understand one's own and others' feelings."

Empathy is also a prerequisite for compassion, because compassion is commonly an attempt or even an act of caring and kindness that one deploys after feeling empathetic.

Theory of Self-Relativity defines "compassion" as "one's ability to have empathy and kindness to help improve one's own or others' feelings."

Although empathy is purely feelings and emotions oriented, compassion often goes a step further by understanding, and commonly, by taking action to help improve one's own or others' feelings. Therefore, empathy and compassion are prime examples of emotional-intelligence.

If you can't be good to your own self, you won't know how to truly be good to others.

As discussed:

Theory of Self-Relativity defines "emotional-intelligence" as "one's ability to be aware of and to understand one's own and others' emotions, and consequently, their thoughts."

Empathy is integral in mature and balanced intrapersonal and interpersonal-relationships, because empathy deals with qualifying and valuing feelings. Relationships and interactions are governed by feelings; however, feelings have no rationality or logic. To achieve harmonious and minimally conflicting relationships with our Self and with others, we must cultivate and increase empathy via awareness and understanding of the underlying thoughts that generate the feelings. The reason *"Balanced-Empathy"* is difficult to achieve is because empathy requires *"understanding"* of feelings. Although what we and others feel is valid, feelings do not have logic and are not rational, because a feeling is a symptom of a causal-thought; therefore, feelings are often subjective and difficult to understand. To best achieve balanced-empathy and to understand ours and others' feelings, we must be able to understand the underlying thoughts that cause ours and others' feelings.

Theory of Self-Relativity categorizes empathy's relativity as *"Trilateral-Empathy"*:

1. **Self-Empathy:** Is empathy that we direct towards our own Self. Having empathy for our own Self is an indication of how aware and understanding we are of our own feelings and thoughts.

2. **Empathy from Others:** Is an indication of how aware and understanding others are of our feelings.

3. **Empathy for Others:** Is an indication of how aware and understanding we are of others' feelings.

Unlike other trilateral-relativities, Theory of Self-Relativity designates all three sides of trilateral-empathy to be equal in value and as important; because emotional-intelligence should be uniformly applied to all aspects of our sentient-existence.

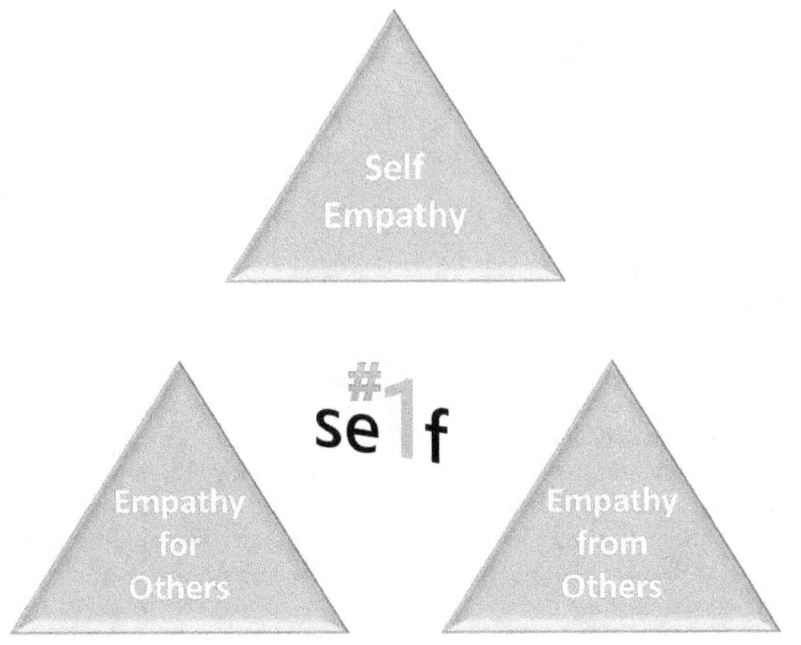

To properly validate feelings, it is best to understand how thinking causes feelings; this is why self-improvement is essential for having and developing empathy. Self-improvement teaches us to enhance and better understand our thinking-system; and in-turn, this awareness and understanding of our thoughts and our subsequent feelings enables us to have empathy for our Self and for others. By understanding the thoughts that cause feelings, we can not only become more empathetic towards our own Self and towards others, but we will also require reciprocating empathy from others. Imbalanced-empathy and lack of empathy is a significant contributor to one-sided and abusive relationships, as overly empathetic people have a tendency of giving too much empathy and not receiving reciprocal amounts back. Likewise, others who lack empathy and are in relationships with empathetic individuals, usually have a tendency of taking advantage of empathetic individuals. This imbalance is common in toxic-relationships involving Cluster-B personality disordered individuals such as narcissists and borderlines.

People who have too much empathy are often referred to as "empaths." In most cultures and societies being an empath is praised as being a moral and good person; however, empaths often have minimal to no self-love and self-empathy, because their focus is more directed towards validating other-people's feelings and wants rather than their own. This is further reason for Theory of Self-Relativity considering "others" as the most dangerous word. Family, culture, society, and religion, categorize being an empath or being concerned with the welfare of others, as a noble trait; especially if such concern and caring for others is at the expense of our own Self. However, according to Theory of Self-Relativity:

Selflessness and self-sacrifice is not righteous; it's self-abuse.

Therefore, to minimize entering into and continuing such one-sided relationships, requiring mutual-empathy just as requiring mutual-respect is absolutely essential. If someone does not value our feelings, we must either require them to change their behavior, or we must minimize or detach from having a relationship with them. By minimizing dependency and reliance on others and by developing a stronger sense of Self, we will learn to properly enforce balanced-empathy.

Empathy just like respect must be required, and if necessary, enforced.

Theory of Self-Relativity places emphasis on our Self for enforcing empathy, because individuals who have introspective-ability are usually capable of having empathy for others; however, those who are self-centered generally do not have empathy or respect for others. Although being empathetic to others is important, society already does a good job of giving us guilt-feelings to continuously have empathy for others; regardless of how others reciprocate similar characteristics. The most important aspects of empathy are strengthening self-empathy and requiring empathy from others; because if we are looking to self-improvement, we are to a degree already capable of empathizing for others. Trilateral-Empathy, just like Trilateral-Respect, demonstrates the relativity and importance of our Self in empathetic-relationships.

Although Theory of Self-Relativity considers self-empathy to be the most important form of empathy; too much self-empathy could be counter-productive and could transform into self-pity; just as too much empathy for others often leads to selflessness and *"Toxic-Altruism."*

Theory of Self-Relativity defines "toxic-altruism" as "excessive focus on kindness towards others, which is often at the expense of one's own Self."

As discussed, Theory of Self-Relativity considers toxic-altruism or excessive concern for others to be a form of externalation; whereby one attempts to cover-up and compensate for personal-weaknesses by becoming overly focused and concerned for others. Simply stated, one focuses, distracts, and preoccupies one's Self by excessively being concerned for the welfare of others, in order to abstain from introspection to identify and resolve one's own personal-weaknesses and self-deficiencies that need to be improved. Excessive concern for others becomes a means of externalation because it enables one to fallaciously reason and rationalize why one does not have the time or the urgency to attend to one's own weaknesses that need improvement.

Self-empathy, self-compassion, and self-love are important attributes for self-improvement; however, as stated, too much self-empathy or too much self-compassion could take the shape of self-sympathy and self-pity. These unhealthy transformations are further discussed throughout Theory of Self-Relativity.

Empathy, although feelings based, as a tool of emotional-intelligence gives us perspective to recognize our own thinking-patterns, as well as to recognize the thinking patterns of others. This is why, Theory of Self-Relativity considers empathy and perspective-taking as two important characteristics in successful interpersonal-relationships. By having empathy, we can become a better listener and we can have better understanding, while being less-judgmental. Unlike popular belief, being a good-listener does not mean to listen more and talk less; being a good listener means to have genuine interest to understand others.

According to Theory of Self-Relativity, to be a good-listener we must have:

1. **Empathy:** Which means, we must care to listen.
2. **Perspective-taking ability:** Which means, we must be able to observe and understand perspectives from someone else's point of view.

To be a good listener; you must have interest and you must care to understand.

Empathy teaches us to *"validate"* feelings regardless of whether we think or we consider those feelings as being irrational, wrong, or unjustified; and this includes our own feelings.

Although feelings are irrational and might not have factual-value; all feelings are valid.

By being able to validate our own feelings and those of others, we will then be able to understand the thoughts which are causing those feelings; and by understanding the thoughts that are causing the feelings, we can then be in a position of "evaluating" those feelings for their factual-value. While all feelings are valid, not all feelings have factual-value; therefore, feelings do not have rationality on their own. To value a feeling, we must value the underlying thought that is causing the feeling. If the thought is factual, we can then proceed to take action based on the feeling; however, if the thought is nonfactual, we will then dismiss the thought, hence, our feeling will automatically disappear.

Improve your thoughts, improve your feelings.

Changing our thoughts does not mean to concoct comforting-thoughts to support and rationalize our desired-feelings. Changing our thoughts means changing our circumstances so the thoughts that we think are parallel to our improved reality. Emotional-intelligence begins with understanding and addressing thoughts; and being in touch with thoughts begins with self-reflection, and it matures with perspective-taking. Empathy gives us the perspective-taking ability to relate to ours and others' thinking-system, regardless of the quality or validity of those thoughts. By understanding how others think and by viewing the world relative to their perspective, we will have better understanding of others, and we could use this understanding to have less-conflicting and more constructive interactions with them.

When we know how it is to feel something; we will then have a better understanding of how others feel about the same thing.

Having relative-perspective through empathy will also enable us to more effectively and less defensively lead others to change and adapt to our points of view. Convincing and persuading others to adapt to and accept our criteria is an important part of establishing fulfilling relationships and successful negotiations. Understanding other-people's thinking enables us to recognize whether that person will be open to improvement or whether we would have to one-sidedly compromise, in order to keep the interaction or the relationship afloat. Conflicts and abusive relationships arise from lack of empathy of at least one person in the relationship. Lack of empathy disables people from respecting and understanding one-another and it will lead to unhealthy personal-relationships, break-ups, and even failed business-relationships.

Since empathy is the ability to be aware of and to understand feelings, Theory of Self-Relativity categorizes the nature of interpersonal-empathy binarily:

1. **Positive-Empathy:** Is similar to the classic understanding of empathy, whereby one uses one's ability to feel and understand other people's feelings and to offer or give them help, support, and compassion. For example, spending time to listen and attend to a friend who just experienced a personal difficulty such as a financial loss, a relationship break-up, or a death in the family. Positive-empathy could also be in the form of help, support, and compassion for a positive situation such as spending time with and helping friends to prepare for their wedding or to launch their business.

2. **Negative-Empathy:** Is the kind of empathy whereby one uses one's ability to understand and feel other people's feelings; to manipulate, to hurt, or to take advantage of others. For example, people who enrich themselves by preying upon susceptible people who just lost their job and cannot make their mortgage payment; by scamming them into the promise of new "non-existent" programs which will assist them with their mortgage. Another common example of negative-empathy would be personal-relationships with personality-disordered individuals such as narcissists and sociopaths; whereby, these individuals take advantage of the other's feelings and emotions by lying to them and by making false-promises about their love, their caring, and about their intent in the relationship.

Balance creates stability and flexibility, and just as with many other personal attributes, balanced-empathy is important for proper relativity. However, excessive empathy can not only create dependency and reliance on others, but it can also become what Theory of Self-Relativity has termed as *"Reverse-Empathy."* Reverse-empathy is when we use our empathy for others, to abstain from introspection. Reverse-empathy is a nonconscious form of externalation and is commonly associated with excessive-altruism or with toxic-altruism.

Theory of Self-Relativity defines "reverse-empathy" as "one's nonconscious use of empathy for others as a means of externalation."

Reverse-empathy occurs when we become too interested and too concerned for other-people's feelings and affairs. Reverse-empathy can not only create a state of people-pleasing, but it is actually a form of externalation or introspection-avoidance.

As described throughout Theory of Self-Relativity, externalation and focus to the outside could become a chronic form of cover-up for abstaining from self-inspection. By distracting and by preoccupying our mind with other people's feelings and problems, or by trying to constantly do good for others while ignoring our own problems; we often unintentionally end up overlooking our own weaknesses, shortcomings, and deficiencies. This is why, Theory of Self-Relativity brings the focus back to the Self, because in order for us to be most effective and caring with others, we must first care for our own Self.

Therefore, to offer acts of compassion to others, we must first be able to have empathy for our own Self. Since empathy is a prerequisite for compassion; therefore, empathy and compassion are also prerequisites for courtesy.

Society, culture, and traditions are heavily focused on what we can do for others. However, statements such as "we before me" which are intended to represent teamwork and belonging, cannot effectively operate if each individual "me" that makes up the "we," itself, is not healthy and strong. This is why, Theory of Self-Relativity states:

To have a strong "we" mindset, we must first have a strong "me" mindset; and since "me" is a part of "we," we can't have a strong "we" without a strong "me."

Therefore, to have empathy, compassion, and courtesy for others, we must first learn to have these attributes in place for our own Self. Without us knowing how it feels to be empathetic, compassionate, and courteous, we will not be able to reciprocate such qualities onto others. Likewise, when we learn to have empathy, compassion, and courtesy for our own Self, we will only then know what it truly feels like to receive empathy, compassion, and courtesy from others. If we cannot cultivate and provide these qualities for our own Self, how do we expect others to provide them for us? To have expectations from others without knowing what it takes to fulfill those expectations is a major reason we get disappointed with others. This is why, Theory of Self-Relativity states:

Expectations often lead to disappointments, especially when reliant on others.

We should not expect anything from others, instead, we should learn to provide things for our own Self, which is the core principle of "Independence and Self-Reliance," and one of Theory of Self-Relativity's 10-Commandments for Self-Improvement. When we learn to have empathy, compassion, and courtesy for our own Self, we will not only learn how to provide such characteristics for others; but more importantly, we will also require and enforce the reciprocity of the same qualities from others. Because when we require, we place our Self in the position of control; and when we have control, we dictate the terms, we don't expect them.

True empathy and courtesy do not require many words.

In interpersonal-relationships, be it romantic, business, or otherwise; intangible-qualities such as caring, loving, and courtesy must be bilateral and balanced. Neither us nor society or culture should place us in a position of imbalance where we have to always focus on giving, but we do not focus on requiring and receiving. Emphasis; notice the absence of "expecting" to receive. If we expect to receive reciprocal treatment, we stand to be disappointed; however, when we require and enforce reciprocity, we will not only create a balanced relationship, but we will inherently create mutual-respect. Furthermore, when we require and enforce instead of expecting; as we create reciprocity based on our terms, we will know what our downside would be, therefore, we will not have any expectations that could lead us to disappointment.

We should not feel obligated nor feel guilt and shame in order to care and give; we should want to care and give without guilt, shame, or obligation. When we know how it is to care for and to love our own Self, we will then also know how it feels to receive caring and loving from others. Furthermore, a truly caring, compassionate, and well-balanced relationship, be it intrapersonal or interpersonal, should not be critical or judgmental; it should be non-judgmental and constructive. If we continuously criticize and judge our own Self or if others do so, we must be cognizant that we are dealing with lack of caring, lack of empathy, and absence of compassion. A truly empathetic, compassionate, and courteous relationship, be it intrapersonal or interpersonal, should not be guilt-ridden, criticizing, or judgmental. If we sense any such characteristics and behavior directed towards our Self, either by our own Self or by others; we must seek immediate change and improvement, or we must disengage from such interaction and behavior. This is why, Theory of Self-Relativity insists that in order for us to treat others properly and to receive proper treatment from others, we must first learn to treat our own Self accordingly.

As we learn to become more self-aware and as we recognize and understand how unaware and often selfish others could be; we will then realize how our courtesy is frequently taken as a sign of weakness, and how our courtesy is even considered to be an opportunity by others to take advantage of us. It takes a self-aware, self-compassionate, and self-caring person to have courtesy for others. Likewise, it takes an even more self-aware and self-compassionate person to not allow one's courtesy to be taken as weakness, especially by those who feel entitled; because, there is a big difference between others' sense of entitlement and one's courtesy.

Courtesy must be mutual, respectful, and without expectations.

If our courtesy confronts any of the following reactions, we should carefully evaluate and asses the value of the interaction or the relationship that we are involved in:

- **Courtesy as an Opportunity:** Is when our courteous behavior is being taken advantage of by others. This could happen as a result of an imbalance between us and others, and it is an indication of lack of reciprocity for our courtesy. When others view our courtesy as an opportunity, this is often a sign that we are dealing with a selfish and even falsely grandiose person who is not valuing us properly. Courtesy as an opportunity is a common characteristic of individuals with sociopathic traits and personality-disorders.

- **Courtesy as an Obligation:** Is when our constant courtesy is being taken for granted by others, and as others expect our continuous courtesy to be an obligation that should be the standard of the relationship. If we are dependent and reliant on others, our dependency and neediness of others commonly places us in a position where we become over-courteous, and our courtesy is viewed as our obligation to others.

- **Courtesy as a sign of weakness:** Due to their own lack of self-awareness and due to their sense-of-entitlement; others, sometimes, incorrectly judge our courtesy to be synonymous with our lack of intelligence, lack of awareness, or other personal-weaknesses. Hence why, such self-centered people tend to consider courtesy to be a sign of weakness. Individuals who continuously view courtesy as a sign of weakness tend to consciously or nonconsciously take advantage of our courtesy.

Courtesy must be reciprocal and mutual, and just like respect, courtesy must be required, and if necessary, it must be enforced. Since courtesy is commonly associated with respect; therefore, just like respect, courtesy is not a right of entitlement, as it should be a voluntary exchange.

Courtesy is not an obligation nor a right of entitlement; courtesy is an act of voluntary exchange.

One's ability to be courteous should come from the perspective of strength and strong self-esteem; therefore, courtesy, just like respect, could also be a good testing method to see the true nature of others. Selfish and narcissistic people expect courtesy from others and they utilize other-people's courtesy as an opportunity to take advantage of them. Our empathy, compassion, courtesy, and respect should come from a point of strength and not based on our neediness or based on our people-pleasing character.

Likewise, humility, which is often associated with courtesy, should also come from a point of strength, and not from the incorrect cultural cliché of subserviency. Many cultures and societies portray humility as a noble trait because they synonymize humility with being a good person. Humility does not mean being selfless or subservient, nor does it mean continuously accepting fault by agreeing with others. According to Theory of Self-Relativity, humility means to be open-minded enough to evaluate one's position with facts and not with feelings of guilt and shame, in order to be considered to be a nice person.

Theory of Self-Relativity defines "humility" as "to be able to learn when one is wrong and to be able to stand one's ground when one is right."

Humility creates a system of checks and balances; therefore, true humility, as defined by Theory of Self-Relativity, is a valuable human character for progress and improvement.

Humility enables learning while it allows knowing.

When we remain humble, we remain open to learning and gaining new knowledge, while we also remain open to supporting our knowledge against nonsense and falsehood. Humility is best achieved through self-confidence, which itself is the result of seeing reality as is and not as we would like it to be; therefore, factual-thinking is key to self-confidence and humility. This is why, self-awareness, self-compassion, and self-reliance are integral to all aspects of our interactions with others and with our own Self. Because, our morality and our moral-values, which include our empathy, compassion, and courtesy, and which often reflect as our humility and confidence; must originate and be cultivated from within, and not from external sources.

Morality, commonly refers to one's moral and psychological values; especially, things that are right and wrong, or good and bad. While morality can be subjective, certain moral-values are considered to be universal; as is the case of right and wrong, or good and bad. Morality should be a two-way street in order for it to allow reciprocal interactions between us and others. Moral-values are best established and applied through self-administration; therefore, for example, to argue that morality without religion would be purely subjective, is incorrect.

Religion or law do not need to set the standards for morality; we, as sentient human-beings, should set the standards of our moral-values from within. We don't need to become religious to be considered to be a good person, nor do we need to fear legal punishment in order to abstain from being immoral. Religion and law should only be used as guides and as supportive-systems to our internally-derived morality, but they should not be the representatives of being moral or being considered to be moral. The most genuine way to be a moral individual is for us to deal with and to treat others in the same manner that we would treat our own Self.

Do unto others as you do unto your Self.

As human-beings are evolving and advancing in intellectual capacity and knowledge, humans are becoming more moral and ethical. Humans, in contrast to less advanced animals, are moral-beings; because, they have evolved their brain to think and to be aware of the relativities between their own Self and others. For example, if a modern-human kills another human, that is immoral; but if a lion kills, it is not immoral. Through intellectual evolution and advancement of technology, humans have created and maintained a safer environment for themselves than other animals have; therefore, humans do not need to act at the expense of others in order to survive and thrive. In other words, while humans kill animals for food; humans do not have to kill in order to eliminate danger or competition so that they would be protected and safe. Thus, humans can live a centered-self life, without being self-centered to exist at any cost.

Safety minimizes the need for aggression; hence, living in a safe society increases the potential for morality.

As discussed throughout Theory of Self-Relativity, the primary concern of our primitive-mind is to keep us safe; therefore, when our mind thinks we are safe, it would then allow us to minimize the potential for immoral and unethical behavior that might have been necessary for our basic safety and survival during primitive-times. However, without safety, it would be a dog-eat-dog world out there; hence, all we would care about would be to have food and shelter at any cost, so that we could survive and be safe.

According to Theory of Self-Relativity, morality is best achieved and implemented through self-reflection, perspective-taking, and empathy; which are necessary attributes for self-improvement. This is why, true morality could not be achieved through the external controls of reward and punishment; because, morality, like other externally reflective mindsets such as courtesy and respect, must be derived from our internal values and attributes that relate and connect us to others.

Self-Reflection 〉 Perspective-Taking 〉 Empathy 〉 Morality

Although compliance might be achieved through the enforcement of fear and punishment, or even through tangible or intangible reward mechanisms; compliance is not the same thing as inherent-morality. Theory of Self-Relativity categorizes morality binarily:

1. **Internal-Morality:** Is morality that originates from within one's Self.
2. **External-Morality:** Is morality which is taught and enforced through external sources.

Morality is best achieved when it is initiated from within; however, when morality becomes conditional, that is when true long-term morality cannot be achieved. Conditionality achieves results via consequences; hence, consequential-results could only be maintained by threats, via enforcement, or through sporadic rewards. However, consequential-results could not be achieved or maintained through free-will and from self-relativity. When conditional and consequential, both internal-morality and external-morality operate via the binary format of:

1. **Reward or Positive-Consequences**
2. **Punishment or Negative-Consequences**

As stated throughout Theory of Self-Relativity, just as our morality should not be conditional, our morality and values should also not be defined by outside sources; our morality must come from within our own Self. Although as a child, when learning about the world and human-interactions, external-influencers such as parents, teachers and culture are generally considered to be good sources for guiding our morality; as we grow older, our Self should become our best guide for our moral-values. Similarly, as a child, although fear, punishment, or reward could define the parameters of our morality; as we grow more mature, our moral-values should come from within our Self and they must not be guided externally through conditionality and consequences of reward and punishment. Furthermore, our internal morality must also not be reliant on self-induced reward or punishment.

Our values and morality should arise from self-reflection and through perspective-taking abilities; and by understanding that other-people and other sentient-beings have thoughts and feelings just as we do. By recognizing this relativity that others experience happiness, sadness, and even suffering similar to the way that we do; we can then set and calibrate our morality to be guided intuitively, and not as compliance to external-conditions. Just as self-improvement and self-worth should not be externally conditional; conditionality that is based on reward and punishment does not create true morality, it creates a false moral-façade. Social-laws and other ideologies such as religion, which are external-sources, create morality through the conditionality and consequences of fear and punishment. Although social-law is necessary to keep members of a society safe against those who cannot have good moral-values; social law is most effective through bringing negative consequences and punishments if one's actions break social-laws, especially such laws that violating them could affect or harm others negatively.

Social-laws are intended to enforce morality by punishing those who violate them; however, despite its consequential and controlling nature, social-law is implemented for protecting the members of a society, especially those who already have internal-morality. Yet, just like other socially designed rules and constitutions, social-law could lose its value or could even become abusive if it crosses over from controlling immorality, to controlling people. Dictatorships and ideological governance are such examples of controlling social-law which are not intended for the creation of morality, but they are intended for creating control and submission.

Social-laws are intended to control the immoral and protect the moral; but when social-laws begin to control the moral, that is when social-laws become authoritarian.

As human knowledge and technologies advance and as populations increase; in order to effectively maintain moral-values, social-laws must be dynamic, amendable, and adaptable to change and progress. Although good social-laws would be adaptable and amendable; controlling type social-laws and most social "beliefs" are not amendable, nor are they allowed to be questioned or challenged. Even less flexible than social-laws, rigidity and lack of adaptability to change is a core characteristic of controlling social-beliefs; this is why such beliefs begin to fall apart when their rigidity and fundamentals are exposed to questioning and criticism. Such autocratic and ideological forms of beliefs tend to dismantle when exposed to facts, evidence, and reason; therefore, in order for such rigid social-laws and inflexible social-beliefs to survive, they could only exist through misguidance, via selective-interpretation, or by instilling fear via threats of negative-consequences.

Another means by which such controlling social fabrics abstain from change is by labeling their rules and ideologies as sacred, holy, and from the point of ultimate authority. By labelling a rule or doctrine as sacred or ascribed by authority; such ideologies shield themselves from challenge, change, and dismantling. Evidence, facts, and reason would severely undermine the stability of autocratic and controlling ideologies; this is why, these ideologies are aggressively shielded from questions and challenges.

Censorship or sanctity is the last refuge of a person or entity who can't handle the truth.

In the absence of evidence and reason-based critical-thinking, one of the common ways to keep the population under control is to enforce control under the gist of morality. Such enforcement of morality is accomplished effectively through punishment, and even more effectively through the fear of punishment. While social-laws dictate the terms of punishment if a member of the society violates these laws; other societal-beliefs such as religion and superstitions instill control under the disguise of morality through a forever and infinite potential for punishment. The social-belief of the afterlife concept is such an example of a manmade controlling myth. Although fear of punishment through social-laws might prevent or lessen immorality; religion and other supernatural-beliefs, through the concept of the afterlife, instill control and enforce morality by portraying the fallacy that we will continue to pay for our mortal immorality not just while we are alive; but even after we die. While the afterlife myth also has a positive aspect of eternal peace and happiness to it if we follow its instructions; the primary means of control via the concept of the afterlife is through the fear of eternal punishment and torture.

By assigning an unproven and imaginary intentional-agent who is watching and remembering every move we make, and even knowing every thought we have; religion and other forms of supernatural-beliefs can have even more control over our thoughts and behavior than social-laws could. The reason religion and superstitious-beliefs are so powerful is because religion makes us believe that not only our actions are being watched and monitored at all times, but so are our thoughts. In life, should we perform an immoral or an illegal act, we might get away from being punished by social-law if we don't get caught; however, the power of supernatural-beliefs goes a step further. While in our mortal life we might get away from punishment if we don't get caught by the law; according to religious-beliefs, there is no escaping punishment for our immoral or disapproved living acts even after we die. Because God and other supernatural-agents observe and remember everything that we do and even everything that we think; therefore, we will forever be held responsible for not just our actions, but also for our thoughts.

The power of religious conformity is so strong that unlike social-laws which would punish us for our immoral actions; religion actually instills fear in us such that we will be held responsible for even "thinking" immoral "thoughts." Religion and supernatural beliefs manage to take control not just by punishing us for our actions; but by taking control over our thoughts, our feelings, our decisions, and our behavior.

Invisible-enforcement is more powerful than physical-enforcement, because without facts and evidence our own mind and our own beliefs become our controller.

According to Theory of Self-Relativity, true moral-values must come from within one's Self. Internal-morality can be reached without the need for self-imposed or external reward and punishment systems; however, external-morality is mostly achieved through enforcement, especially enforcement with negative-consequences. Fear is a much stronger motivator for conformity than love and kindness are; hence why, there are more ways of punishing immorality than there are ways to reward morality. Reward, just like happiness is unsustainable; however, punishment, just like negativity and sadness can linger on and it could have long-lasting effects.

Unlike religion, whereby morality and control are established through reward and punishment; social-laws do not reward us for being lawful, but they would punish us if we were unlawful.

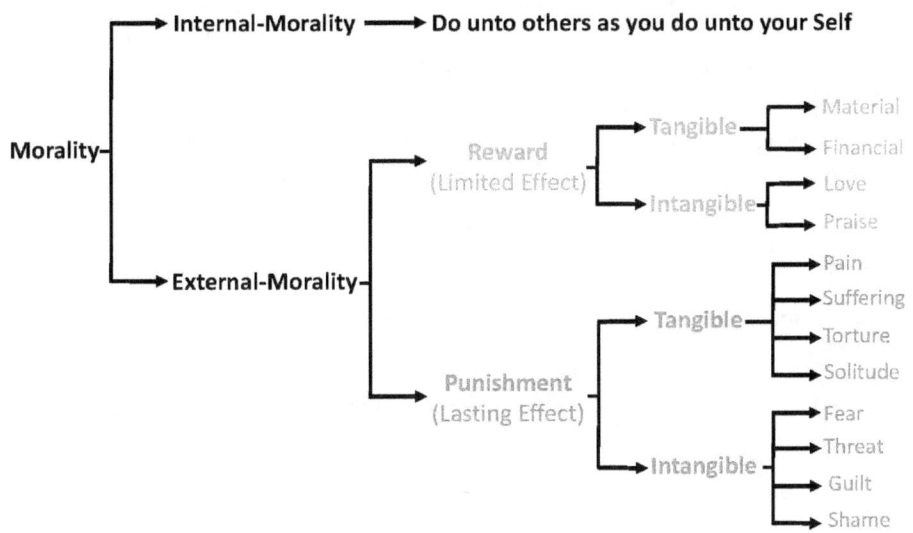

When we self-improve from within, we would not need external-enforcers such as religion or social-laws for creating value and for maintaining morality. Morality that is achieved internally is the best standard of practice for creation of personal-values. Our morality should not be prescribed by an external-authority through fear, guilt, or punishment; nor should it be bribed via the promises of reward. Our morality must be established from within our own Self and the only way that we can begin to do so is by learning and by applying factual-thinking so that we can become the controller of our own existence. As stated throughout Theory of Self-Relativity, unlike social-laws or religion, facts are not open to interpretation, therefore facts are not open to manipulation; however, facts are open to examination, and if necessary, facts are open to replacement. Thus, factual-thinking aligns us with how reality is instead of forcing us to deal with reality as others are dictating it to be.

Contrary to social-laws and religion:

Facts only rely on their evidentiary merits, and they are agnostic to reward or punishment.

Although facts are not absolute and could be examined and if necessary, replaced; as long as facts have not been falsified, we can reasonably rely on the facts to guide our thinking, our feelings, our decisions, and our existence.

Factual-thinking is about having reasonable confidence in the facts, unless or until falsified.

Law	Religion	Facts
Open to Interpretation	Open to Interpretation	Not Open to Interpretation
Open To Questioning	Not Open To Questioning	Open to Questioning
Amendable	Not Open To Change	Not Amendable
Replaceable	Not Open To Replacement	Replaceable
Punishment	Reward & Punishment	No Reward nor Punishment

This is why, living a centered-self life from the inside-out is necessary for us to not only live a life where we come first, but it enables us to live a life where we can have better understanding and empathy for others. By learning to live a centered-self life, we can become more aware of our feelings and our thoughts which are the core of our existence. Since living a centered-self life means to put our Self-first before others, but not at the expense of others; therefore, our moral-values will be reciprocal and relative to others. Consequently, true morality is best achieved from within our Self and through self-reflection and perspective-taking.

Since morality and personal-values should come from within us; thus, our moral-values and our morality should not be conditional. Although not categorized as one of Theory of Self-Relativity's 10-Enemies of Self-Improvement; conditionality, which is closely associated with validation and acceptance, is a constraint that inhibits self-improvement. Because of the broad, undefined and often invisible nature of how conditionality affects all aspects of our life; Theory of Self-Relativity sometimes refers to conditionality as the "11th Enemy" of self-improvement.

Theory of Self-Relativity defines "conditionality" as "the placement of conditions or the enforcement of consequences for acceptance or for compliance."

Theory of Self-Relativity considers conditionality as a negative attribute. Conditionality is not the same thing as setting conditions, or setting goals and achieving them. Creating a purpose and setting goals are internally set constructive conditions for self-improvement; however, conditionality is considered as a negative-constraint. Conditionality often has no predefined targets of achievement, and it is generally unrealistic, restrictive, and difficult to achieve; because it is not a real goal, it is a condition with potential consequences. Conditionality achieves results via consequences; hence, consequential results could only be maintained via reward or punishment, and not through free-will and personal-relativity.

Theory of Self-Relativity categorizes conditionality binarily:

1. **Internal-Conditionality:** Are conditions that we place on our own Self in order to allow our Self to be recognized, validated, and accepted by our own Self.

2. **External-Conditionality:** Are conditions that others place on our Self in order to allow our Self to be recognized, validated, and accepted by them.

Theory of Self-Relativity defines "validation" as "recognition, affirmation, or acceptance of a person's thoughts, feelings, and self-wroth."

According to Theory of Self-Relativity, the "value" of human life and human emotions should not be based on any form of conditionality; because every human life must have equal value and all human emotions must be considered "valid." Although emotions are individually perceived, subjective, and are often irrational; all emotions, regardless of their rationality or their factual-value, must be considered as valid, because they are truly felt by the person experiencing those feelings and emotions. Therefore, to address and improve one's feelings, feelings must always be considered as valid and without-conditionality. However, validity is not an indication of value; understanding the facts associated with that feeling affirms the value.

Although our experiences are subjective, our understanding must be objective.

As stated throughout Theory of Self-Relativity, the value of one's feelings is defined by the validity of the thoughts that are creating those feelings. Since a person's thoughts which lead to the person's feelings and behavior might not be factual, rational, or up to moral standards; therefore, by evaluating a person's factuality of thoughts that are generating those emotions, we can validate or discredit the quality and value of those thoughts. If a thought is found to not be based on facts, that thought will be considered invalid, or at the minimum, unproven until validated; hence, the value of its resulting feeling and behavior will be evaluated accordingly based on the validity of that underlying-thought.

Theory of Self-Relativity categorizes validation binarily:

1. **Internal-Validation:** Is the level of recognition, affirmation, and acceptance that we give to our own "Self" as a result of our own perspective on how our "Self" is perceived to be. Internal-validation is commonly measured by our own perceived internal and external scales of achievements and contributions to the creation of our self-worth and our self-image.

2. **External-Validation:** Is the level of recognition, affirmation, and acceptance that we get from other-people or from having other-things, which reflect on our perspective of what our Self is worth. External-validation is usually measured by other-people's perception of our achievements and contributions to the creation of our self-wroth and self-image; however, external-validation could also be measured by our own perception of how other-people or other-things add value to our self-worth. To have a

perspective that other-people and other-things can add value to us is not unhealthy; however, to perceive that other-people or other-things define or add value to our self-worth, our self-image, or our sense of Self, is an incorrect mindset.

Despite Theory of Self-Relativity categorizing validation in the internal and external binary formats; in order to be validated properly and in a healthy manner, our validation and our self-worth must come from within our own Self, and it must not be conditional to external sources. While other-people or other-things might add value to our life; other-people or other-things should not validate our self-worth or our existence. Therefore, the only way that we must look for validation is through our own perspective and understanding of facts, and not via dependency or reliance on others to validate us. While the perception of our value, especially our social-value, or as discussed, our relative-personal-value (RPV), might fluctuate; we must make sure that our personal-validation or our own sense of Self is never in doubt or in question.

Unlike value, which is perceived, validity is proven with facts; therefore, our existential attributes such as our thoughts and our emotions are valid because they exist, but they might not have perceived or factual-value.

The reason we should not look for external-validation is because external-validation often overlaps with external-conditionality, which inherently creates dependency and reliance for approval. As one of the main enemies for self-improvement, both tangible and intangible dependency and reliance could severely inhibit the creation and experience of a healthy sense of Self; because external-validation often comes with conditions of how we must think and behave, in order to feel or be validated. Relying on external-validation often turns us into selfless codependents and people-pleasers; which, consequently, forces us to place the focus of our existence externally and unto others, while ignoring our own Self.

As often is the case, if we are in a relationship where our focus is external, the goal-post of validation will continuously be shifted on us and the dangled-carrot of validation will rarely be reached. This is why, Theory of Self-Relativity states that we should "never" seek or accept external-validation as a means of validating our own Self. Furthermore, since external-validation is often conditional, external-validation is consequential; hence, it is usually based on reward or punishment, which in-turn, makes us even more reliant on others. Seeking external-validation, which is based on the fear of punishment or the hope of reward, would be similar to living our lives like a scared or obedient dog awaiting validation from others.

In the modern-era of social-media, these platforms play an even bigger role as external-sources of validation; hence, they often lead to increased levels of sadness, depression, and withdrawals for those who are looking for validation and acceptance. The reason external-validation is even more difficult through social-media is because social-media has created an increase in self-centeredness and attention-seeking personality-disorder type traits such as narcissistic, histrionic, and sociopathic tendencies. Such broad dominance of self-centeredness on social-media makes it more difficult for codependents and those seeking external-validation to navigate through. Add to this, the overabundance of fake portrayals of wealth, achievements, and happiness; and those who are unable to play the game of show-off and keeping up with the Joneses, end up having severe self-identity and self-image crisis. This is why, social-media, especially for the inexperienced and for those who have a weak internal-validation system, could be a dangerous environment to frequent regularly.

To have a healthy self-image, a strong sense of self-worth, and as a whole, to have a healthy sense of Self; we must bring the focus onto our own Self by living a centered-self life, and by accepting and by validating our own self-worth and self-image from within. This is why, self-first and centered-self, alongside independence and self-reliance, are key to developing a healthy sense of Self. Self-validation without consequential internal or external-conditionality will not only set us on the path of personally improving our own self-worth and our own sense of Self, but it will also teach us how to experience one of the most sought after and rewarding experiences of human existence; namely, loving and being loved.

Many, incorrectly, search for and seek love from the onset of getting in touch with their feelings. According to Theory of Self-Relativity, to truly love and be loved, we must not only learn to have self-love; but to learn what true self-love is, we must first define our self-image, and we must improve our sense of Self. Therefore, instead of jumping the gun of continuously searching and looking for love, we must first learn to become aware of, understand, and define our own sense of Self, which could only come from true and continuous self-improvement. Without true self-improvement, which is only possible via factual-thinking, we will not be able to experience truly fulfilling intrapersonal and interpersonal love. Just as Theory of Self-Relativity demonstrates that the primary reason we cannot achieve true-fulfillment and longer lasting happiness is because of our self-deception and our need to feel good; it is for the same reason we are unable to truly give and receive genuine love. Loving others without having self-love is like being on a ventilator to breath.

We must first learn to have self-love so that we can then love others, because we know how to love; not because we are needy for love.

In order for us to give and receive love we must not look for love externally, we must first understand what self-love feels like. Therefore, just like many other personal and interpersonal attributes, Theory of Self-Relativity represents love's relativity trilaterally, as *"Trilateral-Love."*

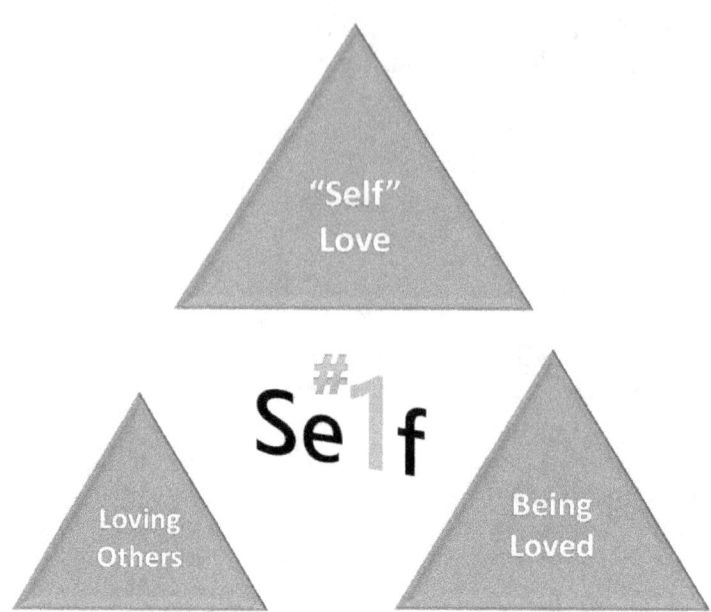

1. **Self-Love:** Is the most overlooked yet the most important form of love that could exist. If we do not know how to love our own Self, we will not know how to give or receive love properly. When we learn to love our own Self because we are secure and confident of our Self; our self-love will be unconditional and our self-worth and our sense of Self will always be validated without-conditionality.

2. **Being-Loved:** Is what we strive for, especially if we are not in touch with our own Self and if we do not have a strong self-image or a well-defined sense of Self. Although being-loved is a satisfying feeling; to truly be loved in a stable and comforting way, we must be loved based on our strengths, and not because of our neediness. We can truly be loved only when we need it the least, and that could only be achieved when we are capable of first loving our own Self. Therefore, the love that we receive should not be conditional; which means, being-loved must be without-conditions. Being loved without-conditions does not mean we cannot be criticized or be made aware of our shortcomings or our wrongdoings; but, being loved without-conditions means the love that we receive should not be conditional or consequential to our interactions and behavior. In other words, others should love us for our own Self and not based on what we can do for them or how we comply with their conditions.

3. **Loving-Others:** Can be a very satisfying state-of-mind; however, many love others because they want to be loved, or because they want to feel wanted. Unlike self-love, loving-others should not be unconditional; it must be without-conditions. This means, we should not love others unconditionally, but we could love them without-conditions. As repeatedly discussed throughout Theory of Self-Relativity, the only unconditional-love should be self-love.

Although love should not be conditional; true love must be without conditions.

Therefore:

Only self-love must be unconditional; being loved or loving others should be without conditions.

The only unconditional-love should be self-love; but, loving-others and being-loved by others must be without-conditions. Therefore, unlike popular belief, and social and cultural depictions, interpersonal-love should not be unconditional. Theory of Self-Relativity distinguishes unconditional-love from loving without-conditions as follows:

- **Unconditional-Love:** Although unconditional-love means to love with no conditions, Theory of Self-Relativity contends that the only true unconditional-love that should exist must be self-love. Having unconditional self-love does not mean to become self-centered and narcissistic; but having unconditional self-love means that if and when we make mistakes or we commit wrongdoings, we love our Self enough to allow our Self to correct-course and to get back on the path of positivity and improvement. Unconditionally loving our Self means to not dwell on self-bashing and self-criticism and to have the ability to learn and improve, while always maintaining self-empathy and self-compassion.

- **Loving without-Conditions:** Although loving without-conditions inherently exists in unconditional self-love, because we should love our self unconditionally; loving without-conditions means when we get-love or when we give-love, such love must be without-conditions. In other words, we should not choose to love others and others should not choose to love us based on meeting certain conditions, or to avoid certain consequences. Likewise, as long as the basic parameters of our relationship remains within acceptable boundaries, we should continue to love and be loved without-conditions. Of course, should conditions and circumstance that govern the relationship change from either side, the interaction and the level of loving should be reconsidered and re-evaluated for continuing the relationship. Loving and being loved without-conditions allows for true "loving emotions" to prosper without-conditions and without consequences; yet, love without-conditions also protects against unfair, controlling, or abusive relationships that are sheltered under the guise of unconditional-love.

- In summary, the primary difference between unconditional-love and loving without-conditions is to have the desire, the choice, and the flexibility to love someone without any conditions or consequences.

Loving without-conditions provides safety of love, while it protects against abuse of love.

Love, just like other feelings could not exist by itself; thus, the emotions associated with love, just like other emotions are caused and supported by their underlying thoughts. Theory of Self-Relativity considers love as not a single-feeling but as an emotion or a collection of feelings; therefore, love has a multitude of underlying causal-thoughts that create the love. Since love is a more complicated set of feelings than a standalone individual feeling is; hence, love is a more complicated and a more involved emotion to address. Furthermore, since love has a multitude of underlying causes, these causes change and fluctuate continuously, which in-turn, makes dealing with love more complicated. This is why, love can feel really good in one moment and love can hurt really bad for a long time thereafter. However, since the end result of love is an experiential positive-emotion, just like other experiential positive-emotions, such as happiness, the peak-feeling of love could not be sustained indefinitely.

Therefore, love, just like happiness and other positive-feelings, is not a state-of-existence; it is only a state-of-experience. However, because of its complexity, unlike happiness, which is a pure state-of-experience; love, like fulfillment, could sometimes be experienced as a "dependent" state-of-existence. Therefore, to get on the path of loving and being loved, we must first minimize and eliminate negativities, and we must learn to live in the contentment-zone. In other words, we must first be content on our own, before we can experience true love. The dependent state-of-existence referred to love and contentment by Theory of Self-Relativity does not mean dependency on other-people or on other-things. A dependent state-of-existence means that said dependency is dependent on the non-existence of underlying negativities. Just as deomnstrated that contentment, fulfilment, and happiness are contingent on the non-existence of underlying negativities; true-love is also dependent and contingent on the absence of negativities, and the stability of one's contentment.

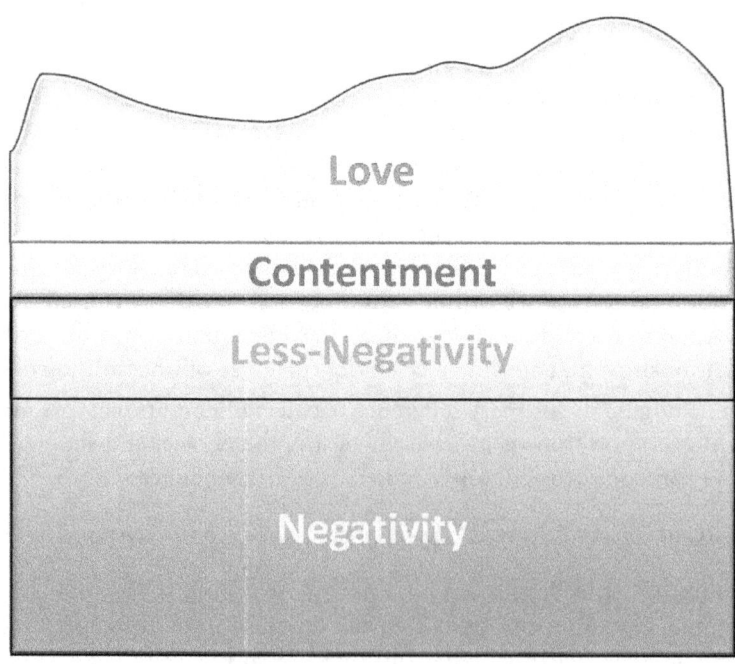

Love hurts because our approach and understanding of love has been incorrect. Love, just like purpose and meaning, cannot be "found" externally, nor could it be as a result of an "event;" because, loving and being-loved, just like success, happiness, or other continuums of human existence, is not an event, it is a process. True love does not happen in an instant; it happens over time, because love is a confluence of many emotions and experiences. Therefore:

True love doesn't happen; it grows.

Hence, there is no such thing as "love at first sight." If we fall in love with someone quickly and if we do not take the time to get to know the person; that is not love at first sight, that is love based on our neediness.

Love at first sight is a fallacy, because love is not an event; it's a process.

We can certainly feel attracted to someone and even get sexually aroused, hence we can experience lust at first sight; however, in order for true-love to exist, we must know and understand the cognitive-processes of the other person so that we can develop our deeper feelings of love for them.

Same applies to falling out of love. Falling out of love also does not happen suddenly as an event; because it takes time and a confluence of events to make us fall out of love. Just as we should not fall in love at first sight; likewise, we should not fall out of love instantly, nor should we hate a loved-one suddenly. By recognizing that falling out of love is a process, we can better understand why falling in love is also a process and not an instantaneous event. To love quickly and to fall out of love or to hate someone we loved just as quickly, is an indication of a character-flaw and, even, possibly a personality-disorder.

Black and white or binary-thinking, and dealing with people in extremes of all good or all bad, is a sign of unhealthy thought-processing. Thus, healthy relationships approach love as a process and not as an event; therefore, healthy relationships are more stable, and they have better potential for continuous growth.

Love is a dynamic process as it is a confluence of many changing thoughts and their resulting emotions.

The following table summarizes the incorrect misconceptions that we have been conditioned to believe and expect about love; and it contrasts it with the correct but sometimes misunderstood characteristics associated with true-love.

TRUE-LOVE	
✗	✓
• Is a State-of Existence	• Is a State-of Experience
• Is an Event	• Is a Dynamic Process
• Happens	• Grows
• Is Found	• Is Cultivated
• Is Unconditional	• Is Unconditional, Only in Self-Love
• Is Conditional	• Is Without Conditions
• Is Consequential	• Is Without Consequences
• Is Unpredictable	• Is Predictable, Safe & Supportive
• Happens at First-Sight	• Happens in Due Time
• Works Even If We Have Unresolved-Issues	• Is Contingent on No Personal-Negativities
• Is a Feeling	• Is a Skill, Yet a Confluence of Emotions
• Is Dependent on Others	• Is Reliant on Personal Independence
• Hurts	• Should Not Hurt

Even familial-love happens as a result of a process and not an event. When a mother gives birth to a child, prior to birth, the mother has nine months to process the love that she will have for the child. During the first few months of pregnancy, although the excitement of having a child could be intense, the feeling of love for the embryo is not the same as when the baby is born, or as the child grows up. This is because the arrow-of-time gives the parents time to go through the process of increasing and intensifying their love for their child. The more time they spend with the child, the more memories are created by timestamping a multitude of events in the continuum of the process of loving the offspring.

Same holds true for the child. The baby does not know how to love the parents when it's born, let alone when it's in the womb. Before the baby begins to feel much love, the baby becomes dependent on the parents, especially the mother, for safety and survival as the child begins bonding with them. Day-after-day, as the baby increases its bonding time with the mother and as the baby's primitive-brain begins to feel safe because of the provisions of food and shelter provided by the parents, and especially by the mother; the baby begins to develop and grow its feelings of love for the mother through bonding and dependency.

However, if the parent and the child were separated at birth and never crossed paths again until many years later; if and when they crossed paths without any knowledge about one another, they would simply not feel any special feelings nor would they feel any unique love for one another than they would have for other strangers they were crossing paths with. Because:

True-love is an emotional process, not an instantaneous feeling.

444

As the baby grows to become a child, the baby learns early on to become dependent and reliant on the parents for survival, safety, and for going through life. Unlike other animals whose young separate early-on in order to develop their own self-identity and sense of Self as survival-mechanisms; the modern-human offspring remains with parents for longer periods of time. This increase in the period of dependency is as a direct result of human's scientific, technological, and knowledge-based advancements. Since modern-humans have become more intellectual and more cognitive, in order to cultivate our intellect and technological advancements, we have created schools and other learning systems which require dedication of time for learning. This dedication of time-resources has caused the human-offspring to remain more dependent and more reliant on the parents in contrast to their ancestors. Therefore, in the modern-times, when we now identify with the word "love," we consequently include other contributory factors such as dependency, reliance, and neediness as being a part of giving and receiving love. In other words, our modern notion of love has been corrupted and has become conditional.

Due to longer periods of dependency on parents, modern-love has become conditional.

This is another reason many have difficulty with introspection and self-improvement; because we have become more and more dependent externally for everything, including exchanging love. True-love must begin from within and from the neutral contentment-zone; not from the negative-zone of neediness. To truly experience love and being-loved, just like happiness, we must first resolve and eliminate our personal-negativities; because if we do not resolve or eliminate our personal-negativities, we will be carrying our negativities into our relationships. Therefore, to make the foundation of our love solid and stable, we must build our love from a neutral-zone; and this could only be accomplished if we first minimize our personal-negativities, including our personal-weaknesses and our self-deficiencies, so that we can then begin to develop and strengthen our own self-love. This is why, to have healthy relationships, we must first improve our Self and not expect others to be the key to our improvement and happiness.

To develop self-love, we must first minimize our negativities; and as we minimize negativities, we will then elevate ourselves to and remain in the contentment-zone. As discussed, contentment, which is the neutral-zone with minimal negativity, is not only the platform that we build our happiness and love from; but contentment is also where we build and strengthen our confidence. When we feel confident, our self-identity takes shape from within and our sense of Self becomes better defined; therefore, our self-image becomes stronger. It is only then that we can confidently feel good about our own Self. When we genuinely and confidently feel good about our own Self; it is only then that we can truly have a strong self-image and develop self-love. Thus, self-love increases with personal-development and self-improvement.

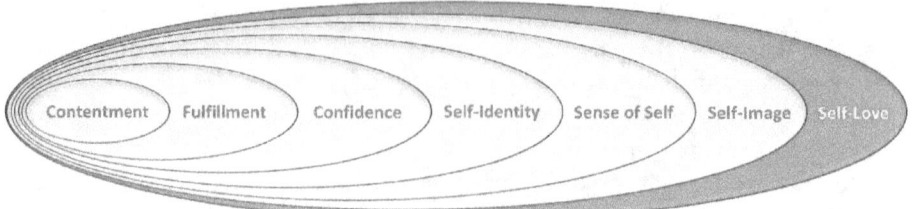

Contentment · Fulfillment · Confidence · Self-Identity · Sense of Self · Self-Image · Self-Love

Once we reach this stage of self-confidence and self-love, we will have more people who would want to love us and to be in love with us, just as we would be able to love others for the right reasons of adding value to their lives. When we learn to cultivate and reciprocate love from within; we will consider statements such as "you complete me," or "looking for love in all the wrong places," or "love-hurts," as sensationalistically incorrect, if not unrealistically-inhibiting statements. For same reasons, when love is built on the foundation of self-love, love won't hurt; because if love hurts, that's not love, it's dependency, neediness, and a lack of self-worth.

True love shouldn't hurt. If love hurts that is not true love, it's dependency and neediness.

Therefore:

As long as love is not based on neediness and conditionality, we can experience love without fear of losing the love.

When we develop self-love and when we love others because we know what love is; we can then love because we can, and not because we are needy of love. We should not love because we want to be loved; we should love because we know how to love and because we "can". When we know how to be complete on our own and when we don't look for love; being loved or loving others will become an additive value. To truly embed love in our lives, we must love for the right reasons and not for being needy. To truly love and be loved, we must learn to change and improve our own self-first; it is only then that we will know what true love is.

Love is not like a box of chocolates; because when you know what love is, you will know what you're gonna get.

Therefore, to be able to love and to be loved, we must always be changing and improving our Self so that we can have an improving self-identity and a strong sense of Self. To have a strong sense of Self and a well-defined self-identity, and in-turn, to have a positive self-image; we must learn to bring the focus onto our self-first so that we can then recognize our strengths and our weaknesses. A weak Self will not only create inner insecurities and require constant validation, but a weak Self will also lead to insecure and weak relationships with others. To strengthen our sense of Self, we must strengthen and increase our self-confidence, which could only happen by increasing control and self-reliance in our own lives.

If we do not have a clear self-identity, a defined sense of Self, and a strong self-image; we will have difficulties in having efficient relativities with our Self and with everything and everyone else. Our self-image is how we and others observe, perceive, and understand our Self; therefore, if we do not have a defined sense of Self, neither would others. It is up to us to define, adapt, and evolve our self-identity as we progress through the different stages of life and as we move forward in time. Our self-image and our sense of Self which are rooted in our self-identity must be established, defined, and maintained from within and not from the outside. Although other-people and others-things could and do reflect as part of our self-identity and our sense of Self; other-people or other-things should not dictate nor become the definer of our self-identity, our sense of Self, or our self-image.

Since our self-identity and our sense of Self are established by our cognition; therefore, our self-identity and our sense of Self are as a result of how we think, how we perceive, and how we observe our own Self. Hence, we see our Self as our perceived self-image; thus, to establish a proper and a reality-based self-image, we must base our self-identity and our sense of Self on how we actually "are," so that our perception of our Self matches factual-reality. This is why, introspection is emotionally a difficult undertaking, because it forces us to see how we really are, and not to see our Self based on how we believe or prefer our Self to be.

As discussed, a strong self-identity comes from within and if it is based on facts and self-confidence, it can strengthen our sense of Self; however, confidence could not be established and strengthened if our thinking and our sense of Self are based on feelings, beliefs, and nonfactual-thinking. If our self-identity comes from beliefs, especially familial, cultural, and social ones, and if those beliefs are not based on facts and they are based on feel-good imaginations and centuries old traditions; our self-identity would then be externally-reliant and our sense of Self would be corrupted. For example, if our self-identity is strongly tied to political or religious beliefs, we would often find our Self in the position of defending our beliefs because we are trying to defend our own self-identity. Such focus on external-things instead of internal-facts takes us away from focusing on our own Self, and it injects external-factors into the creation of our self-identity.

By basing our self-identity on external-factors, instead of placing effort to improve our Self from within; we waste a great deal of time trying to defend our position. However, a position that is based on facts does not need extensive defending, because facts are facts and facts are not open to interpretation. As discussed, the subtle and often nonconscious reason as to why we try to identify with external-things and unfounded-beliefs is because we are engaging in externalation. By focusing on external-factors and unfounded-beliefs, we distract and preoccupy our mind away from being forced to look within to improve our shortcomings. Our self-identity, just like our purpose and meaning, could either be sought externally or it can be created, cultivated, and improved internally. This is why, self-first and living a centered-self life is absolutely integral to creating a well-defined self-identity, and in maintaining and improving a strong and confident sense of Self.

A lack of internally-derived self-identity causes insecurity and creates weaknesses.

A well-defined self-identity minimizes our weaknesses because it not only brings the focus and attention to the self-first, but it helps us define, set, and enforce our borders and boundaries. Although metaphorical, a well-defined self-identity defines where our insides end and where the outside begins. Borders and boundaries are integral perceived parameters that we must set between our Self and others.

Although borders and boundaries are often used to define separation lines in interpersonal-relationships and interactions, borders and boundaries are also important in our intrapersonal-dealings. Well-defined borders and boundaries give us a clearer sense of Self and such parameters could only arise from an independent and self-reliant state of self-existence. This is why, Theory of Self-Relativity advocates living a centered-self life from the inside-out, because a centered-self position creates a defined self-identity that is properly separated from others.

We can define and enforce our borders and boundaries effortlessly by creating a strong and confident sense of Self. Borders and boundaries do not need to be rigid, as true borders and boundaries must actually be adaptable, amendable, and even permeable. Such adaptability allows for the proper flow of information and communication with others; however, adaptability and permeability must not be confused with free-flowing or diffused borders that are without enforcement.

Borders and boundaries facilitate introspection and allow us to focus on our Self without the constant influence from the outside; therefore, well-defined borders and boundaries enable self-awareness and the understanding of our own self-generated thoughts. To know who we are starts by having positive views of our own Self and by changing and by improving certain aspects of our lives that we recognize could be improved. Being aware of and being in touch with our feelings, our thoughts, and our behavior, enables us to set proper self-boundaries which are essential to having a well-defined self-identity. Borders and boundaries define the separation line between our inner-self and the outside. This, in-turn, gives definition to our parameters which enable us to establish and define our self-identity; and as discussed, our self-identity and our sense of Self define our self-image for our own Self and for others.

Therefore:

Borders and boundaries are essential in establishing and maintaining one's self-identity, one's sense of Self, and one's self-image.

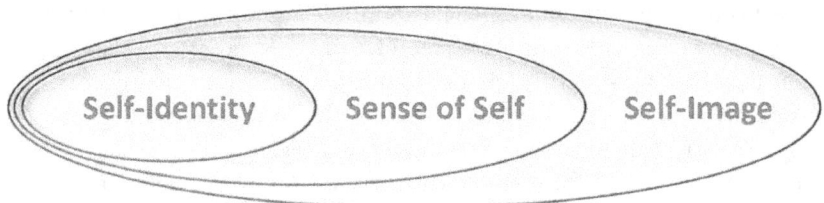

Self-Identity | Sense of Self | Self-Image

Theory of Self-Relativity categorizes self-image binarily:

1. **Internal-Self-Image:** Is how we observe and perceive our own Self.
2. **External-Self-Image:** Is how others observe and perceive our Self.

To truly have a healthy and strong external-self-image, we must first have a healthy and strong internal-self-image. Many are too focused on presenting a strong self-image externally without truly having a strong internal-self-image. One of the most common but unstable means of portraying a strong external-self-image is by affiliating one's Self with other-things or with other-people. For example, making money, buying luxury things, or socializing and affiliating with people who are famous or successful could be rooted in attempting to enhance one's self-image externally. Many, incorrectly think that having a positive self-image is achieved via reliance on external associations and accomplishments; however, if and when the external contributors of self-image diminish or disappear, such disconnect will directly affect the false self-image that was created. Although having money and being able to acquire and accomplish things through the power of money could add to one's choices and options; having more than the necessary amount of money does not make the person happier.

Money can save you lots of misery, but money can't buy you lasting happiness.

A self-image that is reliant on other-things and other-people is no different than being tangibly or intangibly dependent on other-things or other-people. This is why, Theory of Self-Relativity designates "others" as the most dangerous word. To truly have a strong, stable, and continuously improving self-image, we must learn to live a centered-self life from the inside-out. We must rely on our own Self and on our own accomplishments in order to create our own self-identity and our own defined sense of Self. This, in-turn, will eventually lead to the creation of our own internally-derived stronger self-image. This is why, we must learn to introspect so that we can see our self-deficiencies that need to be resolved and improved. To experience positivity and true self-improvement, we must first resolve or eliminate the negativities that exist from within; we cannot simply try to reach for positivities externally to improve our self-image, while still having unresolved internal-negativities. In the absence of internally cleansed and derived strong self-image, other-people and other-things will simply act as cover-up perfumes for the stench of the negativity that we carry inside.

For example, some of the internal-negativities that lead to a negative sense of Self and a negative internal-self-image are feelings of guilt and shame. Although introspection is important in awareness and understanding of our internal-weaknesses so that we can then improve these identified weaknesses; many, by introspecting, become stuck with their negativities, and instead of improving these identified negativities, they self-blame themselves for these shortcomings. As discussed, Theory of Self-Relativity refers to this as *"negative-introspection."* Whether self-inflicted or directed from the outside, blame is one the core reasons we feel guilt and shame. Blame, guilt, and shame can be severely inhibiting for change and improvement; and in trying to live a balanced, content, and fulfilled life.

Theory of Self-Relativity categorizes the origins of blame, guilt, and shame binarily:

1. **Internal or self-inflicted (Blame, Guilt, or Shame):** Self-inflicted blame, guilt, and shame can be severely disabling in moving our life forward. Self-inflicted blame, guilt, and shame are often as a result of our internally-derived perspectives, such as perceiving our Self to have a weak sense of Self or to have a negative self-image. Instead of using awareness of their self-weaknesses in order to improve them; those who self-blame and feel guilt and shame, use their personal-weaknesses to confirm their own perspective and beliefs of their lack of self-worth. Internally-inflicted blame, guilt, and shame are the predisposing factors which enables others to blame, guilt, and shame us further.

2. **External or Inflicted-by-Others (Blame, Guilt, or Shame):** Externally-inflicted blame, guilt, and shame commonly occur as a result of having weak and undefined borders and boundaries; in conjunction with a compromised self-identity and a weak sense of Self. Externally-inflicted blame, guilt, or shame are more prevalent in interpersonal-relationships where the individual is dependent and reliant on others; therefore, blame, guilt, and shame are often inflicted with the intention of creating control over the person. Usually, when interactions in a controlling relationship elevate to the levels of inflicting blame, guilt, and shame; such relationships commonly escalate from just being controlling to becoming abusive. Externally inflicted blame, guilt, and shame are almost always comorbid with a weak sense of Self and a negative internal-self-image. In other words, we must have personally weak and negative perspectives of our own Self to allow others to blame-shift us; and, to impose guilt-ridden and shameful feelings on us.

Since guilt and shame often go hand-in-hand, many have difficulty distinguishing these two negative mindsets; because as much as guilt and shame are felt as feelings, they are actually mental-states.

Guilt and shame clearly represent how our emotions are produced by our thoughts.

Theory of Self-Relativity categorizes guilt and shame binarily:

1. **"Emotional"** guilt and shame (Feelings-based):

    a. **Emotional-Guilt:** Is feeling negative or bad about what we might have thought, said, or done.

    b. **Emotional-Shame:** Is feeling negative or bad about our own Self as a result of what we might have thought, said, or done.

2. **"Cognitive"** guilt and shame (Thinking-based):

    a. **Cognitive-Guilt:** Is when we think "I thought, I said, or I did something bad."

    b. **Cognitive-Shame:** Is when we think "I am not good."

    c. **Toxic-Shame:** Is when we think "I am bad."

Blame, guilt, and shame could create or even exaggerate our weak sense of Self and our negative self-image; this is why, introspection could be a difficult and painful task. Many who have a low self-esteem or a weak sense of Self often identify their Self with how they are feeling; in other words, they become their feelings. Instead of feeling anxious, they are anxious; instead of feeling afraid, they are afraid, and instead of feeling bad, they are bad. Those who lack self-awareness and those who have a negative self-image of their own Self as being the negative-feeling that they feel, are therefore, unable to separate their Self from their feelings. This is why, those who identify their "Self" with the way that they feel, often push down their self-awareness and engage in externalation in order to abstain from introspection.

You should feel your feelings, not become your feelings.

Likewise, there is a fine-line of separation between awareness of positive Self attributes versus identifying with similar negative ones; for example, the seeming similarities between living a "centered-self" life versus being "self-centered." Living a centered-self life, just like self-centeredness means being focused on the self-first; however, unlike self-centeredness, being centered-self does not mean being selfish and inconsiderate of others.

There is similarly a big difference between self-awareness or self-check, versus self-blame; because either one could be triggered by introspection. If misunderstood or if incorrectly applied; instead of introspection leading to improvement, introspection could make us engage in self-blame, which in-turn, would make us feel guilt and shame. Thus, when we decide to introspect, we must become aware and understand that introspection is intended for the discovery of personal-traits and characteristics that we might have pushed down into our nonconscious, or that we are unaware of. Introspection is for finding our personal-weaknesses and self-deficiencies, in order to improve them; introspection is not intended for the purpose of finding these deficiencies to bash and beat our "Self" down with it. As discussed, Theory of Self-Relativity has termed this application of introspection as negative-introspection. Likewise, introspection could also result in discovering positive personal-attributes, which should then be recognized and used as credit to further improve our self-identity, our sense of Self, and our self-image. Thus, introspection is not simply intended to discover negative-traits, but it is also intended to be used to identify and strengthen positive-traits that we already have.

If untrained or misunderstood, upon discovery of their weaknesses and negativities, people who have a negative self-image and a low self-esteem could get stuck in the state of self-blame and feelings of guilt and shame. This is why, Theory of Self-Relativity insists that guilt and shame must be understood and approached as interim states-of-mind. Just as Theory of Self-Relativity describes that a belief should not be a long-held or permanent form of thought, because a belief is an unproven thought; same applies to guilt and shame. As discussed, according to Theory of Self-Relativity, a belief is supposed to be a bridge to knowledge or an interim thought until the supportive facts are found to prove the factuality of that thought. Once the fact and supportive evidence for a belief are found, that belief consequently becomes knowledge; hence, it is no longer a belief. If in due proper amount of time supportive facts and evidence could not be found, then that belief must be considered as nonfactual; therefore, it must either be discarded or it should be replaced by a new potentially factual-thought.

Same approach must be applied to guilt and shame. Guilt and shame must be treated as interim feelings, in order to resolve or eliminate the thoughts that are causing our feelings of guilt and shame. When properly applied, guilt and shame could be a bridge to improvement; or at the minimum, an interim mindset until the supportive facts for the thoughts that are making us feel guilt and shame are found. If we find the causes of the thoughts that are making us feel guilt and shame, we can then resolve or eliminate these causes; hence, our feelings of guilt and shame will either be resolved or will be eliminated. If in proper amount of time we cannot find the facts that support why we feel guilt and shame; we must then stop thinking about the nonfactual-thoughts that are making us feel guilty and shameful, thereby eliminating the causal-thoughts. As discussed throughout Theory of Self-Relativity, emotions are symptoms of their underlying-thoughts, and emotions cannot sustain themselves without their causal-thoughts; thus, once we resolve or eliminate the thoughts that are causing our feelings of guilt and shame, our feelings of guilt and shame will consequently resolve or disappear.

As difficult and painful as guilt and shame feel, when used as interim messages for personal-weaknesses that need improvement; guilt and shame, just like other protective negative-feelings could place us on the path of improvement and becoming even stronger and happier. Guilt and shame, just like beliefs or failures, become problematic only if we do not do anything about them, and if we get stuck by dwelling upon them. This is why, introspection and self-improvement are integral to improving our sense of Self and for strengthening our self-image.

When we improve our sense of Self and as we strengthen our self-image by living a centered-self life, we consequently become less-focused externally and onto others. When we become focused on improving our own Self from within, not only our feelings of guilt and shame will begin to resolve, but we will also become less-defensive and less-judgmental of our Self and of others. Furthermore, we will also minimize the potential for other negative-feelings such as jealousy, envy, and even hatred from setting in; because, we will not be externalating our feelings of guilt and shame. Consequently, when we bring the focus onto our Self and as we use our introspective abilities to correct our own personal-deficiencies and the causes of our negative-feelings such as guilt and shame; we will also become less judgmental and less hateful of not only others, but even of our own Self.

Being defensive and judgmental is often a sign of insecurity, low self-esteem, and a weak sense of Self. Defensiveness and judgmentality often coexist with other characteristics such as jealousy, hatred and vengefulness. If our first and general reaction towards others is to gossip and prejudge who and how they are; this is generally a sign of externalation to avoid, or projection to transfer our thoughts and feelings about our own Self. Externalation, as discussed throughout Theory of Self-Relativity, is a nonconscious defense-mechanism by which individuals distract and preoccupy their mind with others in order to abstain from introspection, and to avoid seeing their own weaknesses. Externalation often coexists with other defense-mechanisms such as projections, distraction, deflection and rationalization.

When we are defensive and judgmental, we are also sensitive about how others perceive and judge us; however, what we tend to overlook is that having a default mental-state of defensiveness and judgmentality is often as a result of our own hidden defensiveness and judgmentality against our own Self. This is why, Theory of Self-Relativity classifies defensiveness and judgmentality in its trilateral-relativity format as *"Trilateral-Judgmentality"*:

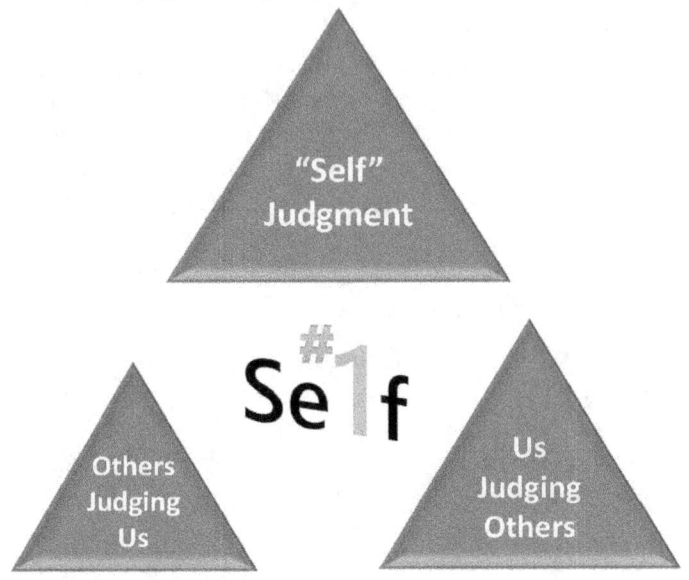

1. **Self-Judgment:** Is us judging our own Self. According to Theory of Self-Relativity, this is the most subtle yet the most powerful cause of our defensiveness and judgmentality. By continuously fault-finding with and judging our own Self negatively, we create a sense of inferiority; and often, in order to distance our Self away from such painful self-inflicted position, we project judgmentality towards others. We frequently and nonconsciously become defensive towards others, portray others in a negative image, and judge others negatively, in order to abstain from seeing our own weaknesses. We commonly engage in such mindsets by ignoring or by denying facts that would contradict our negative mindset, because facts would make it more difficult for us to maintain our preferred incorrect mindset of judging others in order to abstain from self-judgment and self-criticism.

2. **Us judging others:** As discussed in self-judgment, according to Theory of Self-Relativity, the main reason we judge others and act defensively towards them without having the facts is to engage in externalation so that we can abstain from seeing our own weaknesses. By finding faults and negativities with others; we judge, gossip, and become defensive against them, in order to cover-up and abstain from observing and recognizing our own deficiencies and weaknesses. If we were comfortable with our own sense of Self and if we had a confidence-based strong self-image, we would not be in the need of judging others; especially without having the facts or enough information about why we choose to be judgmental against them. Commonly, us judging others is a strong defense-mechanism and an avoidance-coping-mechanism in order to externalate and refrain from introspection, hence, to abstain from recognizing our own weaknesses.

3. **Others judging us:** Although this is the most conscious form of defensiveness and judgmentality that we are aware of and that we focus on; this should actually be the least important one of the three. By focusing on other people's defensiveness, judgmentality, and gossip about us; we tend to think and act negatively about their intention in trying to affect our already fragile self-image. The truth is that if we had a strong sense of Self and a positive self-image, other-people's focus on us would have been a sign of our strength and their weakness; however, by focusing on others, we give our weak Self an excuse to continue externalating. Those who truly have a strong sense of Self and a positive self-image generally do not concern themselves with gossip and judgmentality from others; or they would, at the minimum, use such controversies as opportunities to shine their positive self-image through.

Just as in other trilateral-relativities, in trilateral-judgmentality, the most important angle is how we view our own Self; therefore, our thinking, our perception, and our judgment of our Self is the most important aspect that we must be aware of and which we must try to improve. When we improve our own perception of our Self; gossip, defensiveness, and judgmentality will play no role in our life. Because, being defensive is a way of deflecting and projecting real or perceived threats, as a means of protecting our fragile self-identity and weak self-image.

Insecure and defensive people are usually quick to react to criticism; especially perceived or assumed criticism. As discussed throughout Theory of Self-Relativity, in almost all personal situations, perceiving something without evaluating the factuality of that thing could lead to an incorrect understanding of the situation; therefore, it could lead to reacting incorrectly. This is why, defensiveness is almost always followed by being judgmental; because to judge, we would first need to think to form an opinion of the situation or the person. It must be noted that being judgmental is not the same as making a judgment or judging a situation or a person. Judging is a requirement for making a decision and taking action; and, to make a sound judgment, we must have the facts associated with that person or the situation. Judging without facts is being judgmental; yet, judging based on facts is a reasonable way to make decisions and to act.

Judgment is the prerequisite for decision making. We should pass judgement, but we must not be judgmental.

Even our legal-system follows this process of facts discovery, evaluation of facts, and subsequently, passing a judgment based on the facts in order to render a decision and to take action. Judges judge by hearing the facts and by passing judgment to reach a decision, or to render a verdict. However, in modern-day motivational and leadership teachings, which are designed to appeal to the emotions of those seeking improvement; such teachings misrepresent the healthy and necessary ability to pass judgment as synonymous with being judgmental. They do so because it is easier to bring the masses into submission by falsely portraying analytical and critical-thinking as being judgmental. Thus, in order to gain control, these new-age motivational and leadership teachings intentionally encourage emotional-reasoning instead of critical-thinking. As discussed, Theory of Self-Relativity has termed this subtle manipulative tactic as "Empathy-Crusade."

Theory of Self-Relativity defines "Empathy-Crusade" as "appealing to the emotions of the weak and the susceptible, in order to manipulate them for personal gains."

As further discussed in subsequent sections, judgmentality, hence defensiveness, could be minimized and even eliminated when we learn to engage in respectful and supportive relationships. Such respect and support begins with having self-respect and support for our own thoughts, feelings, and behavior; even if our thoughts and behavior prove to be incorrect. Being less-judgmental and less self-criticizing will, in-turn, enable us to reciprocate similar respect and support for others, as well as require same from them. Instead of being judgmental, we should "evaluate" and "accept" the situation or the person so that we can pass judgment and decide to either remain with the person or the situation; or we can move on with what we evaluated to be unacceptable or wrong.

Don't judge; accept. Either accept and decide to continue, or accept and decide to move on.

When we are defensive, we have a tendency of evaluating situations and people in a negative or unfavorable way; hence, we tend to be judgmental against them.

For example, if we see a well-dressed stranger in an exotic car; instead of looking at the positive aspects of how this person might have attained his profile, we might choose to perceive or even rationalize that he attained his profile and status by illegal activities. If we had a low self-esteem; our defensiveness and projection, which causes our jealousy and envy, pushes us to bringing down someone else in order for us to temporarily feel better; or more commonly, in order for us to not feel as bad. On the other hand, if we have a healthy self-image, we might actually assume that this person attained his status as a result of hard work, higher-education, or through business-savviness. More importantly, a self-secure person will not even make any such assumptions or have the need to be judgmental without knowing the facts. A secure and healthy self-imaged person would simply accept the person and not have the need to assume or judge anything regarding this person.

We can have opinions about others, but our opinions don't always have to lead to judging them.

This is why, according to Theory of Self-Relativity, judgmental people are also cynical people; because they look to find faults with others in order to make themselves feel better. As stated:

Cynics look for faults, skeptics look for facts.

Furthermore, judgmentality, or the mindset of judging, is commonly associated with opinions, interpretations, and even cognitive and personal biases. When we judge, we form an opinion based on our personal experiences, beliefs, or knowledge. If our conclusion is based on knowledge, which means we have the facts about the situation or the person; we are not being judgmental, we are making a judgment based on the facts. When we have the knowledge to describe or categorize someone with certain characteristics, we are not being judgmental, we are being factual; regardless of how much that person might not like our description or categorization. Descriptions and categorizations allow us to compartmentalize our knowledge about reality so that we can make applied decisions, in order to take actions in our lives. When we have the facts, which means when we are knowledgeable, we are not being judgmental, we are judging or we are making a judgment based on the facts at hand; because cognitive-judgment is necessary for decision-making and for subsequent behavior. As stated:

Judgment is the prerequisite for decision making and behavior. We should pass judgement, but we must not be judgmental.

For example, referring to or categorizing a biological male as a man is not being judgmental; it is making a judgment by applying facts to the person's common characteristics discovered, categorized, and applied in biology and science. Facts are the basis of knowledge and science progresses by discovering the supportive-facts associated with a mindset or a hypothesis.

Science and scientific theories are the best explanations of observed facts.

In progressive societies, regardless of how much people might argue that a bio-logical male could and should be classified and categorized based on the gender that the person "feels" or "identifies" with; when we form opinions based on how we want to feel, or when we try to interpret facts to our liking, we are thus crea-ting a logical-fallacy and cognitive-dissonance which will ultimately clash with factual-reality. This is why, Theory of Self-Relativity states:

Facts are not open to interpretation; therefore, facts are not open to manipulation.

Even in legal settings where facts might not be readily available, judges pass judg-ment via the interpretation of the law, by issuing an opinion. This is why, rulings can be changed and even reversed; hence, legal and societal-laws can be amended. As discussed, societal and cultural rules and laws could be amended and even replaced because they are open to interpretation; however, facts could only be replaced because only one form of fact exists per situation, therefore facts are not open to interpretation. Since facts are not open to interpretation, our categori-zations, references, and most importantly, our reliance on facts allows us to have the knowledge to pass judgment, to make decisions, and to take actions based on the facts.

In the aforementioned example, where we make a reference to a biological male as a man, we are not forming an opinion nor are we being judgmental; we are making a judgment and we are taking a position by applying facts and knowledge. Having such knowledge allows us to interact with the male-subject accordingly; for example, in an emergency situation where one might have to save the person's life, the individual will be attended to as a male. By treating and by administe-ring the necessary aids in that emergency based on the person's biology, which is based on knowledge and not based on opined interpretation; one has a better chance of reversing the emergency and saving the person's life, than if the rescuer made a choice based on his own biased-opinion or based on the man's preferred categorization of his gender. Therefore, categorizing a biological-male as a man is not being judgmental nor is it biased; it is making a sound judgment by applying facts and knowledge to the person and to the situation.

This is why, Theory of Self-Relativity is based on the principle of what it has ter-med as factual-thinking; because facts minimize the need to form opinions which could be based on biases or based on interpretation. In other words, facts not only minimize deception, but facts also minimize judgmentality.

Other common coexisting characteristics with defensiveness and judgmentality are jealousy, gossip, and envy. Jealousy, similar to other defensive-characteristics, is focused externally instead of being focused on the Self. When we are jealous, we are focused on qualities and characteristics that someone else has that we are lacking. Jealousy, just like defensiveness and judgmentality is a comparative pers-pective where the jealous person perceives a weaker self-image or a lower self-worth in comparison to those that the person is jealous of. Jealousy is often accompanied by gossip and other forms of negativity that are directed at others in order to make the jealous person feel better. According to Theory of Self-Relativity:

Jealousy reflects personal-deficiencies projected outwardly.

Instead of improving one's Self, the mind of a gossiper or a jealous person tries to lower or belittle others, often by hypothetical or by assumed fault-findings, in order to make the gossiper or the jealous person feel better.

Jealousy and gossip are intended to improve one's negative-feelings temporarily, without actually improving the person's circumstances.

According to Theory of Self-Relativity:

Jealousy and gossip are forms of externalation whereby the focus is shifted away from self-deficiencies, by distracting and by preoccupying the mind with finding faults in others.

Jealousy is a strong emotion that is caused by internal-fear or external-threats which are generally associated with the inadequacy of something associated with the jealous person. Jealousy is as a direct result of low self-esteem and a negative self-image. Jealousy is a strong form of externalation because it is as a result of one's comparative focus on someone else.

Theory of Self-Relativity categorizes jealousy binarily:

1. **Negative-Jealousy:** Is the classic manifestation of jealousy that most people feel, which is a form of envy against others. Jealousy can be destructive as it can consume one's mind and existence by one continuously preoccupying one's Self with someone else's success, happiness, or achievements; while often feeling pity, sorrow, and anger against one's own Self. Negative-jealousy often coexists with self-victimization, self-pity, and blame-shifting onto others.

2. **Positive-Jealousy:** Although all jealousies are as a result of external-focus and comparative-externalation; positive-jealousy could actually be constructive. To experience positive-jealousy, we must have introspective ability. When we feel jealous of others, we can use our awareness of our envy by becoming aware of our deficiencies or weaknesses which are making us jealous. By recognizing our envy and jealousy, we can then attempt to adopt similar characteristics as those of the person we felt jealous of; therefore, by evaluating other-people's strengths against our weaknesses, we can then improve our deficiencies and shortcomings in order to improve our Self. When we improve our Self and when we use jealousy as a positive factor, we then eliminate jealousy and turn it into positive results.

To eliminate jealousy, envy, and even gossip; we must learn to bring the focus onto our own Self, rather than to stay focused externally. Once again, self-reflection and introspection is key to recognizing what we are jealous about and why we gossip. When we recognize and focus on our own deficiencies, we can then begin the process of improving our weaknesses and our personal-shortcomings; therefore, we will subsequently improve our sense of Self and our self-image to a higher level of qualities which are closer to the qualities of the person that we were jealous of, or that we were gossiping about. Furthermore, such self-focus takes the attention and the focus away from others by bringing the focus back onto our own Self; which in-turn, minimizes negative comparisons with others.

When we stop comparing our Self to others in a negative manner, we will not only minimize our feelings of jealousy, but we will begin to improve our Self by noticing the good qualities of the other person that we were jealous of. By recognizing the qualities and attributes that we were jealous of, we will then be able to work on our Self to implement and acquire those qualities for our own Self. By learning to recognize our feelings of jealousy and envy against others, we can use such awareness in a healthy manner to fix our weaknesses that are causing us to be jealous or envious of others.

Similarly, when we gossip about others, we can learn to become aware of our inclination to gossip and turn the negative-gossip into identifying our weaknesses or to identifying others' strengths that are causing us to gossip about them. When we use jealousy, envy, and gossip as an interim mindset similar to guilt, shame, and even beliefs; we will then learn to utilize our negative comparative feelings as a gateway to improving our own weaknesses and our shortcomings.

Fix what you're jealous of and others who can't fix themselves will become jealous of you.

Jealousy is a direct reflection of self-deficiency and lack of self-awareness; hence why, according to Theory of Self-Relativity, jealousy and envy are inversely-proportional to the degree of self-improvement.

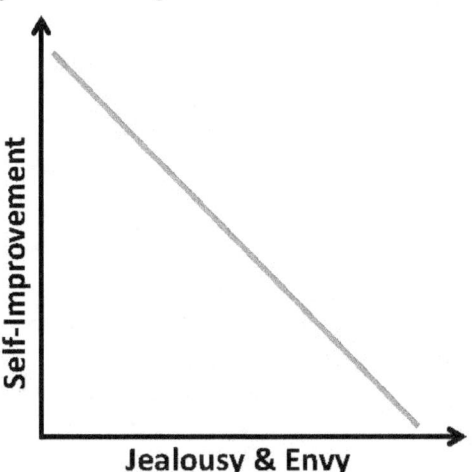

Jealousy and envy increase as our self-focus decreases and as our weaknesses remain unresolved and unimproved. Likewise, self-improvement minimizes self-deficiencies and weaknesses; therefore, it minimizes jealousy as we bring the focus back onto our Self. As we focus on our own Self and as we begin to self-improve, our mind will not have time to consume itself with others' advantages; our mind will instead begin to focus on our own improvement.

Self-improvement is crucial in minimizing and eliminating jealousy, and a good example for this is jealousy in romantic-relationships. When we are worried that our partner might leave us for someone else, this is because we do not believe or feel that we are good enough for our partner. Instead of constantly being focused and concerned on the real or perceived threat that our partner might leave us, we should turn the focus back onto our own Self to see how we can improve our Self so that we can increase our value in the relationship. For example, if we have gained weight, we should begin to focus on the fact that we have gained weight and begin a diet and exercise regimen so that we can improve our health and our appearance. Therefore, instead of focusing on others as to how much better they are than us or how much better they can do than us; by bringing the focus onto our own Self and by improving our Self, we can lessen our worries about others' superiority and we can increase our own self-worth. Thus:

As we improve by becoming more self-focused; other-people's defining role in our life diminishes in a healthy manner.

By increasing our self-worth and by improving our self-image, we subsequently increase other people's interest in wanting to be with us, rather than for them to replace us with others who have higher relative-personal-value (RPV). As discussed and defined by Theory of Self-Relativity, relative-personal-value or RPV is *"a person's perceived desirability and value;"* hence, the way to increase our RPV is to improve our Self from within so that we are reflecting our true self-worth and a strong self-image.

However, if we continue to focus onto others by ignoring our own shortcomings, we could not only feel defensive, jealous, and envious of others; but these negative-feelings could escalate even further into feelings of hatred and even the desire to take revenge. According to Theory of Self-Relativity, hatred and the need for vengeance, or to actually commit to taking revenge, are the epitomes of extreme externalation. If we hate someone or if we are thinking about taking revenge, let alone if we commit to doing so; this means we are so enamored and focused onto others that we are completely ignoring our own Self.

As described in the self-equation, we can either focus onto our own Self or we can focus onto others; therefore, hatred and vengefulness are extreme forms of focusing onto others by completely ignoring our own Self. Hatred and desire for revenge are not momentary mindsets; they require extensive periods of incorrect mental-activities such as thinking, analyzing, and escalating negative-feelings regarding others. This means that when we hate or are vengeful, we waste a great deal of valuable time thinking and feeling about someone else; thus, when we hate or when we want revenge, we are attempting to bring down someone else, instead of attempting to elevate our own Self.

According to Theory of Self-Relativity, hatred and vengefulness arise when our feelings of blame-shifting, guilt, shame, jealousy, envy, anger, and rage; as well as our mindsets of defensiveness and judgmentality go chronically unresolved. The more layers we put on to cushion our personal-weaknesses and internal-insecurities in order to abstain from introspection; the more focused we will become on externalation, and the more we will shift the focus away from improving our Self, onto trying to damage others. Such extreme focus onto others, which requires extensive amount of time investment, is commonly an indication of a low self-esteem and an almost non-existent sense of Self on the part of the vindictive person. This means, those who hate and are vengeful, often feel such severe self-hate and personal-deficiencies, that by hating others and by feeling resentful of them, they are trying with every means possible to avoid and ignore their own personal-shortcoming.

Theory of Self-Relativity defines "revenge" or "vengeance" as "to inflict emotional or physical harm on someone else, for a real or perceived wrong done to the Self."

Many also incorrectly believe that revenge will bring "closure;" because for human-beings, getting closure is a comforting mindset. By continuously focusing on wanting to take revenge or for something bad to happen to another person who perceptually or truthfully *"wronged"* us; we are actually leaving the painful wounds of our relationship open with that person. This externally directed mindset causes us to continuously focus onto others instead of focusing on our own Self. When we feel wronged or when we feel other negative-feelings which arise as a result of our interactions with others; we are actually reacting to an insecurity and weakness within our own Self, by projecting it externally. If we did not have internal-weaknesses and insecurities, others and their actions would not affect us with severe negativity; because we would not be focused onto others to such extreme, to have the need to get closure.

The need for closure is more subjective than real.

The act of revenge, and especially the need for revenge, keeps painful wounds open and does not actually allow for closure to take place; because closure is not something that is reached externally, closure must come from within. The need for revenge keeps us preoccupied by blame-shifting or by focusing on someone else in order for us to try to bring an emotional closure to a situation; rather than by resolving the situation and by moving on. Taking revenge focuses on affecting someone else negatively in order to make one's Self feel better. Instead of trying to affect someone else negatively in order for us to temporarily feel good; we should focus on improving our Self so that the other person will not play a role in our life. When we improve our Self, we will focus on affecting our Self positively, instead of trying to affect others negatively. When we bring the focus onto our Self, our attention will be shifted to our self-improvement rather than on others-people's demise.

As discussed, we not only place focus onto others as a means of externalation, but when we externalate we also live our life by being dependent and reliant on others. This is why, revenge is also intended as a means of closure; because we falsely-think that by taking revenge we can bring closure to our own personal-weaknesses. However, the need for closure, just like having purpose and meaning, is a personal state-of-mind; therefore, it is subjective. Just as purpose and meaning cannot come from external-sources and they must be cultivated and strengthened from within;

461

same applies to closure, as closure must be achieved from within. Hence, instead of spending extensive amounts of energy and wasting a great deal of valuable time by focusing onto how to take revenge on others; we should allocate those resources by shifting the focus onto our own Self so that we can address our own weaknesses.

When we self-improve from within, the need for closure disappears.

Revenge is rooted in our inability to self-improve. To minimize and to remove our Self from wishing ill for others or from wanting to take revenge on them, we must learn to improve our own Self. The phrase "success is best revenge" is rooted in this philosophy, which indicates that instead of wasting our resources of time and mind onto the downfall of others, we should focus our resources onto the rise of our own Self. However, when we truly self-improve, our focus will be so much on our own Self that we could care less about thinking of revenge.

Although success is best revenge; truly successful people do not become successful to take revenge.

Therefore, even in the face of the most heinous act that someone else might have committed against our interests; hating someone or the need to be vengeful is rooted in our own inability to change and improve. When we learn to truly self-improve, even if we initiated improvement as a result of hatred and vengeance of others; we will have no interest in other-people's rise or fall because we will then be completely focused on improving our own Self.

When we truly self-improve, instead of taking revenge, we would pity those whom we intended to take vengeance on.

A common characteristic which is often present in many of the aforementioned mindsets such as defensiveness, jealousy, hatred, and revenge, is getting *"offended"* by something that someone said or did. When someone feels offended, that is a direct indication of a self-deficiency that was triggered by the words or actions of others. For example, we got offended because someone told us that we had gained weight. If the statement reflects the truth that we have actually gained weight, we can try to diet and exercise so we lose the weight, hence we won't get offended. Or, in spite of the reality that we have gained weight, we can choose to deny the truth and become defensive to the truth of having gained weight, and have our feelings hurt. However, if the statement was not true and if the person making the statement made a mistake or intended to hurt our feelings; by having a strong sense of Self and a healthy self-image, we would know that the statement was incorrect or false, thus the statement would not get any reaction out of us, let alone for it to offend us or to hurt us.

When we self-improve through factual-thinking, we will be able to evaluate potentially offending statements for their factuality. If the statement is factual, for example, the dislikable truth of us having gained weight; we could consider the fact and make an effort to change and improve the facts by losing weight. However, if the facts are not corroborating with what the other person said, we would not need to react to the statement; therefore, no action would be necessary. Either way, by having the ability to factually evaluate any situation relative to our own Self, we can realistically assess to take an action or to abstain from taking an action; and in-turn, to resolve or to eliminate the issue.

A person who has truly learned how to think factually and to feel and behave based on the facts of a situation will not take offense to any statements or interactions by others. One could only get offended if a statement or action triggers feelings of low self-esteem and a weak sense of Self. This could only occur if the person cannot handle the truth or if the person takes falsity personally.

Fix what offended you and you won't feel offended again.

Eliminating defensiveness, jealousy, and getting offended are some examples of how, fact-based and self-focused improvement could reduce the negativities that we deal with and how it can improve the quality of our life.

Same applies to us offending others. When we are self-focused and as we deal with things factually, we will become less affected by others and we will feel less responsible for offending others, for making them jealous, or to worry about how others felt about something we said or did with good intention or without malice. When we know that our thinking and our response is based on facts, we will have the confidence to know that we are not responsible for other people's feelings and behavior; even if facts are not to their liking.

We are responsible for what we say and do; however, we can't be responsible for how others feel or react.

In summary, to properly self-improve, we must improve from the inside-out, by bringing the focus onto our own self-first. Self-improvement allows us to evaluate situations less impulsively and with a more open mind. For example, instead of impulsively judging others in a comparative and competitive manner to make our Self feel good, we will wait to get the facts before we form an opinion and before we make a judgment. Once we form an opinion and make a judgment based on facts, we will then decide to either associate with others or we will dis-engage from them. Therefore, that person or the situation will only be relative to us based on the facts we evaluated, and not based on our biased perceptions or our subjective-feelings.

Factual-thinking allows us to evaluate our thoughts realistically and not based on assumptions. By being aware of and by understanding the factual-value, instead of the perceived-value of our thoughts, we will then be able to make a judgment about others, yet be less judgmental of them. Awareness and understanding of our thoughts diffuses defensiveness and shifts the direction of our life towards a more self-focused way of existence.

Furthermore, since virtual-interactions play an increasingly important role in our modern lives, factual-thinking also holds true for what we see and perceive on social-media. By being less-defensive and less-judgmental, social-media will have more of an entertaining and informative value than a curiosity and comparative one. Our perception and value of what we see and read on social-media will shift from comparing and contrasting our self-image against others, to seeing these updates from a more factual and informational perspective. Therefore, the next time when we see someone post something that makes us feel defensive, judgmental, or even jealous; we should first consider the factuality of what they are posting, and second, its significance relative to our life. If our evaluation leads us to realize that we admire what we see from others, instead of finding fault with others or instead of lowering them in order for us to feel better; we should focus on improving our Self so that we can elevate our standards to match their qualities. This is why, skepticism and factual-thinking, in contrast to cynicism and jealousy, will enable us to improve and transform our Self continuously.

Skeptics look for facts, cynics look for faults.

Interestingly, as we truly learn to self-improve, we will not preoccupy our Self with others, as our yardstick for value and improvement will come from our own internally self-imposed purpose, goals, and dreams. This is why, people who are truly self-improving and who continue to change consistently do not concern themselves with what others are doing.

As we improve and as we become less-defensive and less-judgmental of others, we will also learn to become less-judgmental of our own Self. Instead of thinking less of our Self, we will learn to become aware of how we see and perceive our own Self. This is how, self-awareness is achieved. When we achieve self-awareness, we will then focus on and improve our Self instead of projecting our shortcomings onto others; thus, self-focus enables us to be by our own Self.

To be alone means to have the desire to be by your Self. To be lonely means to have the need to be with others.

Self-first and self-focus become fulfilling attributes that create and enable enjoyment of self-time. Hence why, Theory of Self-Relativity reminds us to always ask the following question:

What time is it? It's self-time.

Self-First and living a centered-self life is integral to properly relating to not only our own Self, but also to properly relate to everything and everyone else. According to Theory of Self-Relativity, during our lifetime, we must be the center of Our-Universe; thus, every other interaction that we engage in must emanate from a centered-self position. However, to properly engage in such interactions, we must first ensure that our Self is a solid platform from which we can relate to everything and everyone else. This is why, our self-identity, our sense of Self, and our self-image must be cultivated and grown from within. Once that is initiated and improved, we can then focus on bringing external interactions as additive-measures to our own self-identity. Therefore, external-relativities must be additive but not fundamental to our self-identity, to our sense of Self, or to our self-image.

Our self-identity is relative to how we think, how we feel, how we behave, and how we interact with our Self and with everything and everyone else.

Hence our self-identity originates in our mindset of:

I think…therefore I feel…therefore I am

Although feelings should not guide one's life, feelings are an important gateway to become aware of and to identify one's thoughts. Therefore, one must use one's feelings to feel, but not use one's feelings to think.

Feel your feelings don't become your feelings; understand your thoughts, become your thoughts.

Because:

You are what you think.

III.
Factual-Thinking

Time is not the rarest commodity anymore, common-sense is.

Although time is a rare commodity; according to Theory of Self-Relativity, reason and common-sense are becoming even more scarce.

Theory of Self-Relativity defines "reason" as "the best application of observation, knowledge, and experience, to reach a conclusion."

Thus:

Theory of Self-Relativity defines "common-sense" as "the pragmatic application of observation, knowledge, and experience."

Furthermore:

Theory of Self-Relativity defines "factual-thinking" as "thoughts that are supported by facts and reason."

Therefore, when we think factually, reason and common-sense become interchangeable with one-another.

According to Theory of Self-Relativity:

Facts are evidence in support of reality.

However, facts are not absolute. Since facts are not absolute and could be examined and if necessary, replaced; therefore:

Factual-thinking is about having reasonable confidence in the facts, unless or until falsified.

Emphasis: Factual-thinking is about having confidence in the "facts;" not having confidence in what we think, what we feel, or what we believe to be true or real.

Facts are different than the truth; because something that is not true, does not necessarily have to be false. However, unlike true or false which could also be not-true, Theory of Self-Relativity treats facts binarily, because facts are either factual or nonfactual; and if in due time we cannot identify the supportive facts, the default position must be to consider the thought to be nonfactual. When we look for facts to support a thought, our beginning mindset should be "I don't know;" however, if after a while we cannot find the facts, we should then consider the thought to be nonfactual. Unlike untrue, factual-thinking does not provide a choice for being unsure, because we must have the supportive facts in order to consider a thought as factual.

In logic, we can decide true or false if the evidence proves the argument to be true or false; however, if we cannot identify or find the evidence, we must decide not-true, but we must not decide false. We should decide not-true, which means the argument is not proven to be true, but deciding not-true does not necessarily mean that the argument is false. Therefore, in logic, if we cannot support an argument with facts, we decide the argument is untrue but not false; however, if we identify the facts that support the argument to be false, or if we disprove the argument as a logical-fallacy, we can then render the argument as false.

Our legal system also operates similarly, because the burden of proof is on the party making a claim; hence why, in criminal-law, the verdict is guilty or not-guilty, but never innocent. When insufficient evidence exists, we do not render an innocent verdict, because there might not have been enough evidence to show innocence; we render a not-guilty verdict because there also was not enough evidence to show guilt. Therefore, in legal settings, the default position is to render not-guilty instead of innocent, because the facts were insufficient to prove innocence.

Similarly, with factual-thinking, we either have the facts or we do not have the facts; hence, if we cannot identify or find the facts, we then consider a thought to be nonfactual. We do not say the thought is untrue. When we cannot find the facts, nonfactual has to be the default mindset, just as non-guilty is the default-state in legal settings. The default must be the state that was unproven, because since our feelings could influence our thinking, the burden of proof must be to show the facts to prove that what we are thinking is factual and not based on biased or comforting-feelings.

The truth is often uncomfortable and when forced to face the dislikable-truth, our emotional tendency is to deny, ignore, or deflect the truth in order to preserve and reinforce our comforting-thoughts. We ignore, deny, and even attack the truth or the messenger because the truth does not support our comforting perspective; even though that perspective might be incorrect, fallacious, and nonfactual. We often think things and we do things not because they are correct or because they are good for us; but because they help us avoid pain, they make us feel good, or at the minimum, they make us feel less-bad. In other words:

If the truth conflicts with what I want to feel; then it is not true.

We do so because:

Our need to feel good versus the necessity to think well is a core factor that inhibits change and blocks improvement.

We often take this need to feel good even a step further, by doing anything and everything that we can to abstain from facing the dislikable truth. Hence why, many engage in arguments and personal-attacks not with the intention of learning the facts; but with the intention to abstain from dismantling their false but preferred concept of the truth. Thus, for many:

If the message conflicts with how I want to feel; I must attack the messenger.

We are more in touch with our feelings than we are with our thoughts that cause our feelings; this is why, we often act or react based on our emotions, instead of acting and reacting based on our thoughts. Although what and how we feel is always valid, this does not mean our feelings always have rational-value or they are based on reality. As a matter of fact, feelings have no rationality on their own, just as emotions could not exist on their own. Emotions or intangible-feelings only exist because of their underlying causal-thoughts; hence, emotions are only as rational as the rationality of their underlying-thoughts that create them. However, if the underlying-thoughts are uncomfortable, undesirable, or painful; instead of us changing the facts that cause our dislikable-thoughts, we often attempt to create fallacious-thoughts in order to quickly improve our feelings. We do so because creating falsity is immediate, but changing things for the better takes time and effort. And when we become addicted to concocting quick fallacious and non-factual shot-in-the-arm thoughts and beliefs, we end up wasting time that could have been used to change and improve the facts and circumstances in our favor.

This is how, faith, hope, and beliefs, such as magical-thinking, superstitions, and the supernatural are created.

We attempt to rationalize our desired-feelings, by creating new fallacious-thoughts that support and reinforce those desired-feelings.

As stated, Theory of Self-Relativity has termed such emotionally-based rationalization form of thinking as placebo-thinking.

Theory of Self-Relativity defines "Placebo-Thoughts" as "thoughts that we concoct regardless of their factuality in order to support our desired feelings."

Self-deception, according to Theory of Self-Relativity, is one of the main enemies of self-improvement. The biggest lies we hear are the lies we tell our Self, because these lies make us avoid pain, make us feel good, or at the minimum, they make us feel less-bad at that moment. The lies that we tell our Self and the lies that we allow others to tell us which make us feel better is how we allow deception and falsity to take over our lives. Since the proper order of interacting with our Self and with everything else is thoughts, feelings, and then behavior; therefore, we behave based on how and what we feel, and we often do so without consideration for the rationality and the factuality of the underlying thoughts which are causing our feelings that lead to our behavior. Although this sequence is widely accepted and taught in psychology; as discussed, Theory of Self-Relativity refers to this sequence of Thoughts -> Feelings -> Behavior as the *"Absolute-Order."*

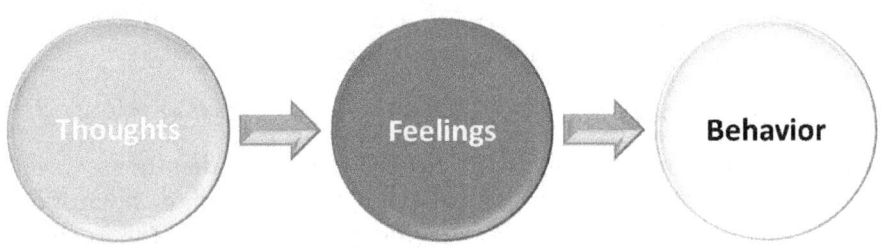

We act based on feelings, because acting on feelings is quick, and it is intended to be protective.

We feel, because feelings enable us to quickly identify, connect, and take action relative to internal and external stimuli. This quickness and impulsivity of acting on feelings is intended to be a protective mechanism for safety and survival; because in urgent situations such as in the primitive-times that our ancestors lived in, they did not have time to think if the data that they were getting was factual or not. They acted on feelings and impulse because being wrong was not as detrimental as being killed or eaten; thus, we developed more ways of feeling negative in order to stay protected and safe, because negative-feelings force us to take action so that we can resolve or eliminate the causes of those negative-feelings, hence, to get away from danger.

For example, feeling fear and running from potential danger is a negative-feeling that is intended to keep us safe. It is because of this primitive programming of our mind that we have developed more ways of feeling negative than positive, because negative-feelings notify us that there is a potential threat or danger; and since negative-feelings are unpleasant, negative-feelings force us to take quick corrective-action for safety, and in-turn, eliminate the unpleasant negative-feelings.

When we resolve or eliminate the cause of a feeling, the feeling automatically improves or disappears.

When we feel discomfort, threat, or danger, we feel negative and not positive; because undesired and uncomfortable negative-feelings force us to take action in order to resolve or eliminate the causes of our negativity. Resolving or eliminating our negativities, in-turn, eliminates our dislikable negative-feelings so that we can feel better. Nature has programmed us to get rid of the causes of our negative-feelings because those causes could be bad for us; therefore, nature has defaulted our mind with negativity so that in order to feel better, we must first minimize, resolve, or eliminate what makes us feel negative. This, in-turn, resolves the potential threat or danger that is affiliated with our negative-feeling.

Nature has not default-programmed our mind to feel good or to feel happy in the face of potential threats and danger; nature has only programmed us to feel negative because negative-emotions are dislikable, hence, they force us to take action. Furthermore, nature has only programmed our mind to minimize or eliminate negativity; nature has not programmed our mind to feel positivity. Thus, our mind doesn't care if we feel positive or if we are happy, all our mind cares about is if we feel less-negative; which means if we are in less-danger.

Our mind doesn't care if we are happy; our mind only cares if we are safe.

As discussed throughout Theory of Self-Relativity, in the modern-times, we don't face many primitive-dangers; however, the default programming of our primitive-mind still remains negative, as its intention is to keep us safe. This is why, our primitive-mind does not care if we feel good or if we are happy, it only cares if we are safe; and safety is only achieved by minimization of negativities. For this reason, our primitive-mind treats the strongest negative-feelings that we feel as if they were feelings of potential threats and danger; even if our strongest modern-time negative-feelings are simple dislikes. And because we have many times more negative-feelings than positive-feelings, our primitive-mind is constantly looking for ways to keep us safe. Therefore, the only means for us to calm down our primitive-mind so that it would let go of the negativity is for us to minimize the causes of our negativities, and to only sustain or react to those negativities that are based on facts and reality.

Since our feelings do not have rationality, and since our primitive-mind's programming is safety and danger-based; the only "true" means of minimizing negativity is to get our intelligent-mind to take the control from our primitive-mind. However, the only way that our intelligent-mind can be in control, is for our primitive-mind to sense less threats and danger. When our primitive-mind senses less-negativity, it can then take a backseat and allow the intelligent-mind to become the driver.

The intelligent-mind cannot force itself to take control; it is up to the primitive-mind to allow the intelligent-mind to be in control.

Since in the modern-times we are not normally exposed to primitive-dangers, we have the luxury of not responding to our negative-feelings as quickly as we would've had to if we were faced with real primitive-threats or primitive-dangers. Because as stated:

Our behavior does not represent how we are thinking, it only represents how we are responding.

Therefore, to minimize our negativities and to improve our feelings, we can be less reactive by becoming more aware and conscious of our negative-thoughts that are causing our negative-feelings. In the modern-times, instead of treating our negative-feelings as protective ones, which would require quick action; we can slow-down and evaluate the causal-thoughts of our negative-feelings for their factual-value. We can do so, because unlike primitive-times, we, as modern-humans, have more time to gather data and facts about the cause of our negativities; especially our lingering or our chronic-negativities.

As further discussed, all feelings are valid, but validity does not signify value; therefore, not all feelings have factual-value. To assign value to a feeling, we must assign factual-value to the underlying thought that is generating that feeling.

All feelings are valid, but not all feelings have factual-value.

In non-threatening situations, when we are able to examine our thoughts before acting directly based on our feelings, we will have a better chance of our behavior being appropriate and in sync with factual-reality. However, since negative-thoughts that require action are dislikable and undesired, and since making a change takes time and effort; instead of accepting the negative-thoughts and putting in effort to improve the circumstances associated with those negative-thoughts, we often choose to act impulsively so that we could feel better quickly. We commonly do so by either hastily taking an action to feel better, or we do so by ignoring and by denying the negative but factual-thoughts that are making us feel unpleasant. When we choose the latter approach, we do so by rationalizing our desired-feelings via the creation of new false-thoughts and fallacious-beliefs. As discussed, Theory of Self-Relativity refers to this creation of false-thoughts to support our desired-feelings as "placebo-thinking." Although placebo-thinking temporarily achieves the intended shot-in-the-arm result of feeling better; without making an actual change, all that placebo-thinking does is to cover-up the stench of suppressed negativities that we refused to confront.

As further discussed, to feel good and to eventually experience true and longer lasting frequencies of happiness, we must first resolve or eliminate our negativities; there is no other short-cut. If we do not first minimize and eventually eliminate our negativities, any other means of trying to feel good or even feel happy will be a temporary cover-up of our negativities. As analogized, negativities are like body-odor, and if we cover-up body-odor with fresheners without removing the cause of the odor; the stench of the underlying odor will resurface again quickly. In reference to body-odor, to truly achieve long-lasting freshness, we must first put in the effort to bathe and remove the odor-causing bacteria; and subsequently, we should use fresheners to smell good. We should do the same thing with our thoughts and our feelings; we should first remove the negativity before attempting to experience positivity.

Our negative-feelings are the malodors of our mind, and our negative-thoughts are the causes of our smelly negative-feelings.

Negative-thoughts are real and they exist because of real but not necessarily true causes. To clean and bathe our negative-thoughts, we cannot cover them up with feel-good positive-thinking perfumes; we must wash them out, sometimes, with irritating and dislikable mental-soap. This means, we must confront these negativities and we must either resolve or eliminate them. The only means of resolving or eliminating negative-thoughts is to understand why they are there in the first place; hence, to resolve, improve, or eliminate their causes. Therefore, the only way to truly change, improve, and feel better and happier, is to think factually. When we learn to think factually, by observing and by understanding our thoughts that are causing our negative-feelings, we can then resolve or eliminate our negative-thoughts; thus, our negative-feelings will change, improve, or be eliminated accordingly.

Theory of Self-Relativity defines "factual-thinking" as "thoughts that are supported by facts and reason."

Factual-thinking requires unbiased and unemotional analysis and reasoning, regardless of how uncomfortable, dislikable, or painful these thoughts may be; this is, why introspection is a necessary and non-negotiable requirement for self-improvement. Factual-thinking is the core principle of Theory of Self-Relativity's Cognitive-Cognition-Technique, which uses our feelings as a pathway of getting in touch with and identifying our thoughts. Since we are more aware of our feelings than we are of our thoughts, by learning to use our feelings, not to necessarily take immediate action, but to use them for identifying their underlying-thoughts; we can then become aware of our thoughts which are guiding our decisions, our actions, and our existence.

In the modern-times, we seldom face primitive-dangers; however, as discussed, our primitive-mind has a tendency of treating our strongest negative-feelings as if they were threats that were caused by primitive-dangers. When we learn to think factually, The Cognitive-Cognition-Technique will help and allow us to slow-down the impulsivity of our primitive-mind, and our need to want to act quickly to improve negativities. Since our primitive-mind is dominant, and since its primary role is our safety and not our happiness; the primitive-mind is constantly looking for negativities to help protect us, by making us react to such negativities. By thinking factually, we can thus slow-down the reactivities of our primitive-mind, and we can take our time to gather enough data, information, and facts, in order to understand whether we should react to the perceived negativity or threat; or can we delay reacting to the perceived negativity or threat. By thinking factually and by minimizing our reactivities, we can also consider dismissing a negativity completely, without the need for impulsive reaction to the negativity; if the causal-thought of the negative-feeling proved to be nonfactual.

Although in the modern-times we less often come across safety related threats or dangers; we still tend to respond to our dislikable and unwanted negative-feelings as if they were threatening or dangerous. We do so, because negativity is dislikable and unwanted; thus, we do all that we can to avoid pain, to feel good, or at the minimum, to feel less-bad, quickly. In attempting to minimize negativities, the incorrect, yet quickest and most effortless way to feel better is to rationalize our desired-feelings through the creation of false-thoughts, so that we can convince our Self that the negativity that we feel is not as dislikable or as significant. Therefore, if we ignore or deny it, the situation will improve or disappear on its own. As discussed, Theory of Self-Relativity has termed such rationalization as "placebo-thinking."

Placebo-thinking is a form of rationalization through emotional-reasoning.

For example, although we see evidence that our partner is cheating, we rationalize and convince our Self that the evidence is not true, or we nonconsciously justify to our Self that we need to find more supportive facts for this dislikable truth; hence, we try to postpone dealing with the dislikable and painful truth. Therefore, creating fallacious-thoughts to support our desired-feelings, or creating false-beliefs to avoid dealing with the undesired-truth, is one of the quickest, but incorrect means of lessening our negativities.

The other means of trying to feel better is to not just to think, but to do something to improve how we feel. We can either take an impulsive or quick action and do something as a cover-up, for example, get drunk in order to avoid the pain of recognizing our partner is cheating on us; or we can take the correct approach of accepting the dislikable truth that our partner is cheating on us and take action in order to resolve or eliminate the situation, so that in due time, our negative-feelings associated with this matter will eventually disappear and improve. Although the correct thing to do is to act by confronting the uncomfortable truth; however, the latter is the hardest, the longest, and the most dislikable means of improving our feelings. Therefore, in order to feel better quickly, we often revert back to self-deception so that we can momentarily minimize the pain and negativity that we feel; or we do something hasty to quickly improve how we feel, and end up causing even more problems for our Self by prolonging the issue.

Granted that the pain and the dislike of being cheated on is not as threatening as, for example, a lion's attack; in the absence of a lion's threat, our primitive-mind treats the pain and discomfort of being cheated with similar intensity. This intensity was instilled on us to quickly fight-or-flight the lion and to not stay with such negative-intensity for long as we resolved or eliminated the lion's threat quickly. But if our primitive-mind cannot distinguish the difference between a lion's attack or a failed-relationship; it will continue treating the strongest negativity that we feel, in this case the failed-relationship, with the same intensity as it did in reacting to a lion's attack. Dealing with a lion and surviving it could have been a ten second intense feeling; however, dealing with a broken-heart could last days, months, and even years. This is why, stress is a bigger problem in the modern-times; because we are not supposed to react to non-life-threatening situations with the same intensity as life-threatening ones.

Stress is intended to be an acute reaction; not a chronic way of life.

The reason stress is a chronic personal and public health issue is because:

Stress is inherently intended for life-threatening situations; hence, stress is supposed to have quick onset and resolution. However, in the modern-times, we continue stress for non-life-threatening situations, without any resolution.

The fight-or-flight hormones such as Adrenaline make us feel intense emotions so that we can act quickly and get away from danger. The levels of Adrenaline type hormones and the intense negative-feelings associated with fight-or-flight usually subside quickly after the threat is abated; because these hormones and these intense-feelings are like turning on the afterburners of a supersonic jet engine in order to quickly get away from danger. If engaged for too long, just as the afterburners will deplete the energy of the plane and could cause damage to the flight mechanisms; similar internal-effects could happen to our body. After a fight-or-flight situation, which is intended to last for a short period of time, we are supposed to rest and recover from the event. However, when the primitive-mind is treating ongoing negative-feelings such as the resulting emotions from a failed-relationship with the same intensity as a fight-or-flight stress situation; our internal components begin to deteriorate and fall apart, because they are not intended to operate in such high-intensity for lengthy periods of time. This is why, stress is a major contributor to diminishing health in the modern-times.

Therefore, to minimize stress and negativity, we must control our emotions by controlling their underlying causal-thoughts. Initially, factual-thinking could be dislikable; however, through learning, when factual-thinking becomes a way of life, we will develop the skills necessary to distance our Self from negativities that could linger on and become chronic, or even toxic. Since factual-thinking is a skill that develops and strengthens over time; therefore, we must become aware of our thoughts and understand their causes so that we can learn to implement factual-thinking as an intuitive part of our existence.

Theory of Self-Relativity defines "learning" as "the acquisition of information, knowledge, and skill through observation, interaction, and experience."

Although learning involves acquisition of information, knowledge, and skill; it is incumbent upon us to ensure that the information and knowledge that we are observing to learn and develop our skills with are based on facts and evidence, and not based on other nonfactual, perceived, or imagined things. Because, if we do not have certainty that the information and knowledge that we are learning and relying on is factual, we will not only learn the wrong thing and develop the wrong skills; but we could also take the wrong action. This is why, unlearning something learned is difficult, and why, modifying bad-behavior is challenging. Therefore, our observation, which bridges information and knowledge to interactions and experiences, must be fully engaged with awareness of facts and evidence.

Theory of Self-Relativity defines "observation" as "the awareness to identify and evaluate information, facts, and knowledge."

Although we gain information through our five senses, the primary ways that we observe to learn is through visual and auditory observations. Visual-observation is watching, seeing, reading, and visually evaluating a source of information; while auditory-observation is through listening in order to gather information and knowledge.

Cognitive-learning is commonly associated with both visual and auditory observations activated simultaneously; therefore, factual-thinking and The Cognitive-Cognition-Technique are best learned and implemented through visual and auditory observations, and via the application of the information and knowledge gained through our learned skills. Since observation, especially visual and auditory observation, increases our cognitive-awareness; cognitive-awareness, in-turn, enhances and increases our peripheral-awareness. Thus, by uncluttering our mind and by thinking-factually, our thinking-system not only quickens and increases its efficiency, but we also become more aware of our surrounding. Uncluttering our mind enhances our cognitive and peripheral-awareness; therefore, learning to gain information and knowledge is essential in our mental and physical connectivity and relativity with everything and everyone else. This is why, it is important for us to see and listen in order to learn.

Observe and absorb…Listen and discern.

Consequently, awareness, observation, and understanding are key to learning of knowledge and development of skills. This is why, simply being motivated or simply being mindful does not yield results; because majority of self-help and personal-development teachings are based on unstructured, ill-defined, and ambiguous claims that are opinion and tradition based, and are not based on facts and how our mind and reality actually operate. Furthermore, opportunistic teachings try to mishmash and word-salad information with pseudoscience; for example, the "observer-effect" from quantum-mechanics, in order to create even more ambiguity, by confusing suggestable and susceptible people into submission, with the intent to turn them into followers. As discussed, many personal-development and self-improvement systems use appeal-to-emotions in order to get people to sign up, by telling people what people want to hear, rather than by showing them how to improve; and one of the ways that they accomplish this is by making personal-development and self-improvement unlearnable.

According to Theory of Self-Relativity:

- Learnings is the "acquisition" of:
    o Information
    o Knowledge
    o Skill

- The most important "contributors" to learning are:
    o Observation
    o Interaction
    o Experience
        - Positive-Experiences (accomplishments and successes)
        - Negative-Experiences (setbacks and failures)

- Learning is best achieved through the "pathways" of:
    o Awareness
    o Understanding

- Learnings is best enhanced through the positive-reinforcements or "incentives" of:
    o Encouragement
    o Reward

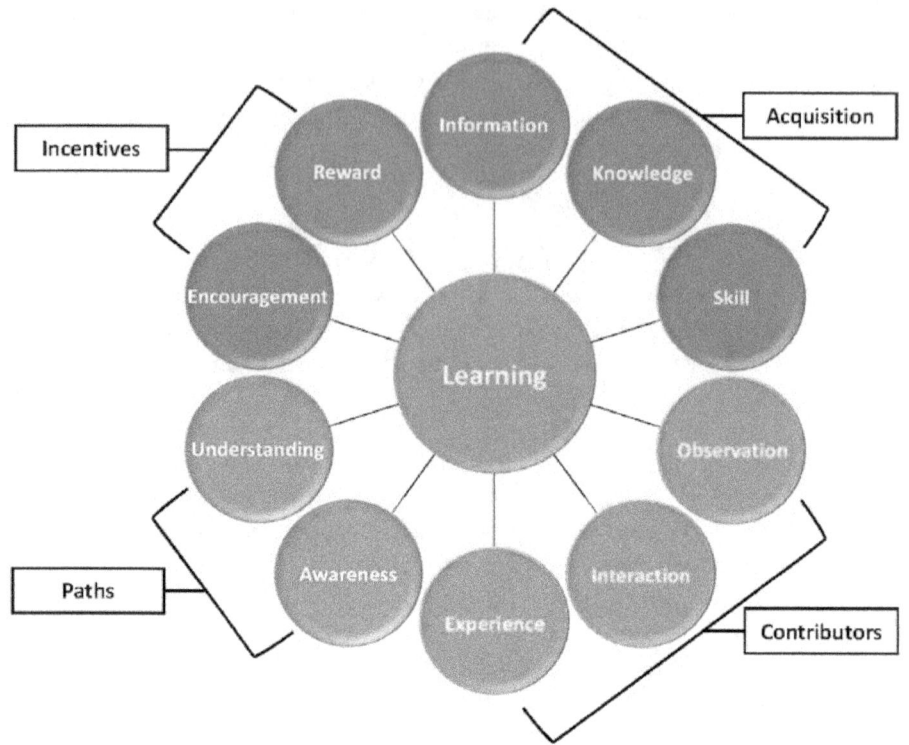

According to Theory of Self-Relativity, long-term learning is not:

- Retained through:
    - Memorization
    - Obligation

- Nor is it enhanced through negative-reinforcements of:
    - Threats
    - Punishment

Theory of Self-Relativity categorizes the nature of learning binarily:

1. **Positive-Learning:** Is the type of learning which contributes to and influences one's life in a positive and additive manner. Some examples of positive-learning are; gaining knowledge, developing skills, and self-improvement.

2. **Negative-Learning:** Is the type of learning which affects one's life negatively or destructively. Some examples of negative-learning are; low self-esteem, trauma, and addictions.

Both positive-learning and negative-learning could be rooted in and further affected by genetic and environmental factors; however, for the purpose of self-improvement, Theory of Self-Relativity focuses on our learning capabilities based on our pathways of awareness, observation, and understanding, as well as our application of information and knowledge. Therefore, in the absence of genetic, physical, or physiological negative contributors, Theory of Self-Relativity considers learning to be personal and its application to be subjective. However, subjectivity of learning is not an excuse for incorrect learning. This is why, learning must be based on information and knowledge, which means learning must be fact-based. Thus, just as in factual-thinking, learning can be learned objectively, yet it can be applied subjectively.

Learning must be objective, although learning is personal and its applications are subjective.

Our thoughts, feelings, and behavior are influenced by our experiences and how we communicate and express those experiences with our language and our behavior; therefore, learning is integral in the development of language. The primary purpose of language is to form and understand our thoughts, and secondarily, the purpose of language is to communicate our thoughts with others. As discussed, according to Theory of Self-Relativity, development of language and the ability to communicate our thoughts with our own Self and with others is the primary reason human intelligence began to flourish, and why, humans began to advance compared to other animals. The efficiency and precision in communication that language created, minimized the inefficiencies of physical and other non-language-based sights and sound-generating primitive forms of communication. This efficiency and precision in communication is the main quality of language in enabling the exponential advancement of human civilizations; and it is this advancement in knowledge and communication that improves our decision-making and behavior.

Communication is the most common form of human behavior.

According to Theory of Self-Relativity, communication, and especially speech itself, is one of the most important, if not the most important forms of human behavior. To speak or not to speak, is to take action or inaction, in order to express our thoughts externally; therefore, for our words and statements to have strength and value, our thoughts must be based on facts.

Words spoken are thoughts expressed; to speak wisely you must think factually.

Our words and our statements represent our state-of-mind and how we think. The less-cluttered our thinking is, the more precise the expression of our thoughts would be; therefore, the more our language and our communication abilities evolve, the more we need to learn to improve our communication skills. Speaking, writing, and all other forms of communication are skills that we learn and develop, yet we are rarely aware that our language and communication capabilities are the main manifestations of our behavior. When we learn and improve our skills of thinking factually, we will thus rid our Self of unnecessary, cluttering, and non-factual-thoughts, and this clearer mindset will enable us to express our thoughts quickly, effectively, and with greater precision. Clarity of thinking and clarity of communication is how we create the best perception of our Self; not only for others, but also for our own self-identity. Therefore, since communication is the most common form of behavior, to improve our communication skills, we must improve the way we think.

According to Theory of Self-Relativity:

1. Language enables us to form and to understand our thoughts.
2. Language enables us to communicate our thoughts with our own Self and with others.
3. Language communication is our most common form of behavior.
4. Language communication, as a skill, could be improved and enhanced through improving our thinking.

Our behavior, which is relative to our thoughts and our feelings, is as a result of what we have learned. Learning also leads to the development and the fine-tuning of our skills of communication and expression of our thoughts through language. Therefore:

Communication of language is our most commonly used skill.

Because:

Anything that is a form of behavior, is a skill.

Theory of Self-Relativity categorizes skill binarily:

1. **Positive-Skills:** Are skills that we learn, develop, and improve, which affect us or others positively and constructively. Some examples of positive-skills are playing musical instruments, problem-solving, or speaking different languages.
2. **Negative-Skills:** Are skills that we learn, develop, and strengthen, which affect us or others negatively or destructively. Some examples of negative-skill are stealing, pessimism, and lying.

To improve and modify our language and communication skills, or any other skills; we must learn new positive-skills, we must improve our existing positive-skills, and we must unlearn our negative-skills which are also sometimes referred to as our bad-habits.

Mistakes are something we can improve; bad-habits are mistakes we repeat.

Skills are dependent on our learning and what we have learned. What is learned can be unlearned; thus, learning to think factually and unlearning to think non-factually or emotionally is key to the improvement of our skills. By learning to think factually we will be able to nip any potential negativity in the bud as soon as the signs and evidence associated with such a situation begins to appear; therefore, by cutting-out potential negativities early on, we will not have to deal with significant chronic emotional-pain for extended periods of time. This is how we begin to minimize negativities and how we actively try to prevent adding more negativities into our life; because as negativities get minimized, our primitive-mind begins to feel safer, hence it begins to trust and allow our intelligent-mind to lead our thinking.

Since factual-thinking, especially in the learnings stages of applying The Cognitive-Cognition-Technique, would require slowing down impulsivity and reactivity to feelings; in the long-run, The Cognitive-Cognition-Technique also enables us to become a more methodical and calculated thinker in all aspects of our life. Such an approach will not only improve our ability to think cleverly and with minimal mistakes; but in due time and with practice, it will enable us to process our emotions and their causal-thoughts quicker and on-the-go. Factual-thinking, through The Cognitive-Cognition-Technique, enables us to achieve a quicker and cleverer thinking-format for continuous transformation and improvement throughout our life.

Although The Cognitive-Cognition-Technique might initially seem difficult, it actually is quite easy to streamline, because it applies consistently and uniformly to all our thoughts and emotions. Unlike other teachings, we do not have to sub-jectively-interpret or make sense of difficult instructions for each specific situation or negativity in our life; because, The Cognitive-Cognition-Technique teaches us the skills to consistently and repeatably enhance our abilities of filtering out nonfactual-thoughts and only retaining thoughts that are fact-based.

Furthermore, The Cognitive-Cognition-Technique allows us to take our time to find the facts associated with our thoughts, before we dismiss or eliminate them for their nonfactuality. The implementation and the learning of such analyti-cal-thinking skill enables us to not take action unless we can support and verify our thoughts with facts. If in due time, we cannot find supportive facts for a thought or a belief that we assumed had value, we will therefore not place too much weight on such an unsupported or unfounded-thought; hence, we won't take incorrect or hasty action on it.

As we initiate the process of The Cognitive-Cognition-Technique, we will begin to realize that we are eliminating many more thoughts than we are accepting them; because many of our negative-thoughts that we experience are often manifested as a result of internal-insecurities and personal-shortcomings that we are trying to cover-up. By eliminating many unfounded and nonfactual negative-thoughts, we will then eliminate the need to take action in order to improve things; therefore, as we practice The Cognitive-Cognition-Technique, we will further realize that we do not always need to think things or do things in order to try to feel better.

Sometimes the best thing to do, is to do nothing.

Engaging in The Cognitive-Cognition-Technique for the first time is similar to moving our place of residence. As we pack to move, we will realize how many unnecessarily cluttering-things we had stored away out of reach and out of memory. By choosing to get rid of, give-away, or sell these material-excesses, we not only resurrect some dead-value, but most importantly, we open up further room to have less-cluttered storage and a more organized living area.

The Cognitive-Cognition-Technique does similar uncluttering and organization to our thoughts and our mind. Once we reach the optimum level of unclutter by keeping only the thoughts that are factual, we can then begin to quickly and cleverly become aware of and examine our new thoughts that form in our mind. We can evaluate each new thought for its factuality and if the thought is nonfactual, inapplicable, or unnecessary, we will then dismiss it; just as we would evaluate our shopping habits if we were attempting to restart buying things that we didn't need. After a while, as we begin to look within our Self and as we begin to enjoy an organized and uncluttered mind; we would then not see the need to preoccupy our mind through unnecessary and useless thoughts. When we have only a handful of valuable-thoughts versus a collection of many useless and cluttering ones, we will then be able to utilize each valuable-thought to its full potential; just like when we have a smaller number of outfits, we will be able to get the best use out of what we have, instead of having too many outfits hanging in the closet, never worn and with the tags still on them.

When our mind is uncluttered, this organization will enable us to access our thoughts and information quicker and more precisely for implementation, similar to how a computer memory works. Therefore, the more open capacity and the more storage space, the faster the processing would be. Furthermore, uncluttering, enables us to increase focus on our relevant and remaining thoughts. Just as in an emergency or in a fight-or-flight situation, all our other thoughts and worries take a backseat and our focus becomes singular in trying to resolve the emergency by focusing on the thought associated with the urgency or the danger; we should have a similarly focused state-of-mind when dealing with our existing thoughts. While it is not recommended to live our life in a constant fight-or-flight situation in order to have focused-thinking; this example illustrates how the mind can dismiss negative-feelings in an instant by shutting down their underlying thoughts. As exampled with the emergency, the mind can become a practical and efficient vehicle of thinking about what matters at that moment and nothing else; hence, by minimizing the number of nonfactual-thoughts and by only retaining factual-thoughts, we can have more efficient ways of dealing with and navigating through our thoughts. As stated throughout Theory of Self-Relativity, mindfulness does not mean slowing down our thinking; modern-mindfulness means quickening the efficiency of our thinking-skills.

Thinking, especially critical-thinking, is a skill.

This is how we should apply our thoughts and our thinking to our everyday situations; by learning to think practically and efficiently without drama and clutter. By recognizing the fact that many of our nonfactual-thoughts are unnecessary and are based on feelings, we can filter out these cluttering-thoughts by using analytical-thinking and the process-of-elimination. The binary-filter enables us to eliminate thoughts that do not matter and to only retain and focus on thoughts that do matter and require action. By eliminating the unnecessary and non-applicable thoughts through The Cognitive-Cognition-Technique's thought-management skills, our thinking will become more succinct and more focused to what needs to be addressed and acted upon. Our thinking will become more focused and efficient because we will have less cluttered thoughts which tend to slow-down our thinking-process and our mental-performance.

As we think focused by minimizing the number of our thoughts, we become more efficient; therefore, we think less. And when we think less, especially relative to nonfactual and negative-thoughts, we therefore feel-less; hence, we experience fewer confusing and negative-feelings.

Clutter is never a good thing. A cluttered-intersection slows down traffic, cluttered-arteries slow-down blood flow and cause heart attacks and strokes, and cluttered-thinking slows down cognition and mental processing, and it diminishes competitive advantages. Cluttered-intersections make us feel angry and frustrated, cluttered-arteries make us feel tired and weak, and cluttered-thoughts make us feel negative and stressed. This is why, we must resolve our thoughts, in order to resolve our feelings, so that we can minimize our mental-clutter.

The Cognitive-Cognition-Technique can create on-the-go constant and consistent modern-mindfulness without the need for time-consuming retreats from valuable productive time in order to try to reach peace and harmony. Mindfulness is not a state-of-existence where one visits to get in touch with one's thoughts; mindfulness must be a state-of-mind that is present at all times and which recharges and improves on-the-go. It is for this reason that techniques such as meditation and hypnotherapy, which attempt to create mindfulness, are simply not cost-effective and do not provide definitive solutions for our lack of self-awareness and the inefficiencies of our thinking-system.

As stated throughout Theory of Self-Relativity, our mind is a thinking-machine and its job is to think; therefore, it is unnatural and unsustainable to try to not think, or to try to think less, or to try to slow-down our thinking. To quicken our thinking and to become cleverer, we must learn to distinguish our thoughts faster and on-the go. Life in the modern-times moves faster and the need for multitasking or for moving in between thoughts quickly is more in demand than ever before. Unlike the incorrect claims of many motivational teachings that encourage slowing down thinking; there is nothing wrong by multitasking and having multiple-thoughts if we know how to think quickly and cleverly. As a matter of fact, we must learn to think quickly and cleverly so that we can deal with the modern-life more efficiently and with less stress.

Cars and planes operate most efficiently when they are cruising at faster speeds; not when they are parked idling.

As introduced and defined previously, The Cognitive-Cognition-Technique teaches us how to use our emotional-intelligence as an awareness and understanding tool to identify the thoughts that are causing our feelings. When we use feelings-awareness to dive deeper into our own and into other-people's minds, we can then recognize if our thoughts and those of others are factual or not. When we learn to master this skill of "reading" feelings, we will then become like a mind-reader. Although this reference to becoming a mind-reader is metaphorical, feelings-awareness can lead to clearly recognizing how everyone's feelings and behavior demonstrate their thought-processes. This method of using feelings to access and recognize thoughts is the core discipline behind Theory of Self-Relativity's Cognitive-Cognition-Technique.

Theory of Self-Relativity defines the "Cognitive-Cognition-Technique" as "The ability to use our feelings, to access and identify our thoughts, in order to take proper action."

The Cognitive-Cognition-Technique not only teaches us how to learn to eliminate and filter out nonfactual-thoughts; but its consistency of application creates repetition, which is essential for creating skills. To become skillful in something, we must first learn the skill, and then, we must be able to repeat what we have learned so that we can subsequently enhance that skill. In order to learn, we must become aware of and we must understand what we are trying to learn; therefore, a true thinking-system, which should be the core of a true self-improvement system, must be easy to understand, easy to learn, easy to apply, and easy to repeat.

Repeatability validates value.

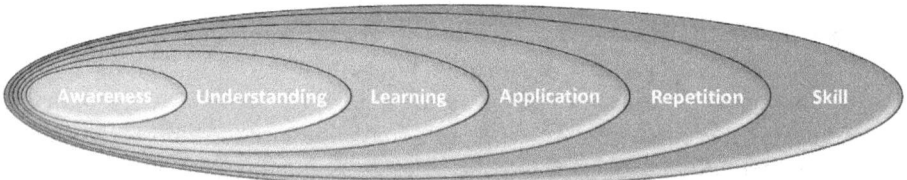

Repetition could only take place if what is being repeated can be consistently applied; therefore, the easier its application, the faster the skill will grow. Thus, in order to develop our skills in something, we must be able to consistently repeat that something.

Repetition enhances skill.

Since The Cognitive-Cognition-Technique is consistently applicable and easily repeatable; therefore, it has high intrinsic-value, because it can give us the skills that will streamline consistent self-improvement. The Cognitive-Cognition-Technique gives us the awareness and understanding tools for us to learn to develop and apply our self-improvement skills, repeatedly, and consistently. The Cognitive-Cognition-Technique is the revolutionary thinking-system that we can apply on our own, without the help of others.

The Cognitive-Cognition-Technique is our mental-algorithm.

The Cognitive-Cognition-Technique allows us to become aware of our thoughts, through the gateway of our feelings and emotions. As discussed, this awareness is often referred to as our emotional-intelligence.

Theory of Self-Relativity defines "emotional-intelligence" as "one's ability to be aware of and to understand one's own and others' emotions, and consequently, their thoughts."

Simply stated, we cultivate and evolve our emotional-intelligence so that we can support our feelings with factual-thoughts. By becoming aware of our thoughts and by correcting and improving our thinking-system, we can improve our feelings, which in-turn, should put us on the path of making better decisions and taking better actions. As we increase our emotional-intelligence and as we become more in touch with the relationship between our feelings and our thoughts, we should then become more in control of our impulsivities, our reactions, and our emotions. Our ability to exert control over our emotions is known as "Emotional-Regulation."

Theory of Self-Relativity defines "emotional-regulation" as "one's ability to manage, regulate, and control one's emotions."

Humans are constantly exposed to events and situations that trigger emotional-states and emotional-responses within them. Lack of emotional-regulation, or better known as emotional-dysregulation, could cause disruptions and even chaos in everyday life and with our intrapersonal as well as our interpersonal interactions. Emotional-dysregulation is more pronounced when dealing with negative-feelings rather than positive ones. Negative-emotions, without proper emotional-regulation, lead to impulsivity and hasty actions; therefore, impulse-control is an important attribute of achieving emotional-regulation. Emotional-intelligence and emotional-regulation are part of our self-regulation capabilities. As discussed, self-regulation means to have the ability to have awareness and understanding of our thoughts so that we can better manage our emotions. As further discussed in detail in later sections, self-regulation is integral in self-agency and personal-responsibility.

Theory of Self-Relativity defines "self-regulation" as "one's ability to manage, regulate, and control one's thoughts in order to experience better emotions and more favorable outcomes."

Self-Regulation = Emotional-Intelligence + Emotional-Regulation

Although, many experience emotional-dysregulation from time to time, and especially in situations where they do not have control over the situation or the outcome; emotional-dysregulation is more prevalent and a more consistent occurrence with high-conflict personality types. Emotional-dysregulation in such individuals who present signs of personality-disorders can sometimes be so extreme that when they are happy, they are ecstatically-happy, and when they are sad, they are depressively-sad. Individuals with emotional-dysregulation tendencies also tend to be quite dramatic and chaotic, and they act quickly and impulsively to negative-stimuli. Emotional-dysregulation generally presents a lack of cognitive-development due to childhood issues; therefore, emotional-dysregulation is often associated with the inability, or with lesser ability, to have critical-thinking skills.

Critical-thinking is commonly described as the objective analysis of facts to form a judgment. Critical-thinking is disciplined thinking that is clear, rational, open-minded, objective, and informed by reason and evidence. In critical-thinking, the thinker improves the quality of his or her thinking by skillfully analyzing, assessing, and reconstructing it; therefore, critical-thinking is self-directed.

Theory of Self-Relativity defines "critical-thinking" as "the ability to objectively, unbiasedly, and open-mindedly analyze and evaluate thoughts based on facts, and not based on feelings."

Thought-awareness and critical-thinking are key to developing and maintaining emotional-regulation, and those who do not properly develop their critical-thinking skills from childhood often have difficulty with emotional-regulation and with impulse-control in their adult years. Therefore, cognitive-development and proper thinking methods can minimize one's emotional-dysregulation. To minimize and control emotional-dysregulation and impulsivity, we must learn to have the ability to evaluate the causal-thoughts of our feelings; cognitively, and analytically. Awareness of our feelings and understanding their underlying thoughts will assist us in increasing our critical-thinking abilities, hence, it will help to increase our emotional-regulation. By being in touch with our feelings and by realizing that our feelings are caused by our thoughts, we can learn to recognize and analyze each thought behind a feeling. By taking the time to always look for and analyze the thoughts behind our feelings, we will thus begin to create impulse-control which will lead to emotional-regulation.

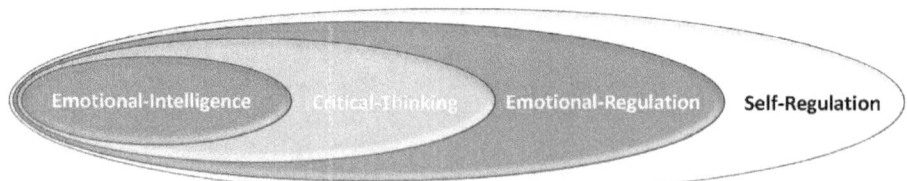

This increased emotional-regulation that is cultivated through The Cognitive-Cognition-Technique not only unclutters the mind and slows down emotional-reactivity, but it quickens our thinking and problem-solving abilities. As discussed, one of the most common forms of behavior that we undertake is communication, and one of the fastest forms that we communicate is with language; specifically, by speaking. By slowing down our impulsivities and emotional-reactivities, and by increasing our ability to become aware of and to recognize factual-thoughts quicker; The Cognitive-Cognition-Technique enables us to express our thoughts in a more concise and persuasive format. As communication formats have become faster in the modern-times, we also need to increase our communication speeds accordingly. This skill of communicating quickly and efficiently could only arise from thinking quickly and cleverly.

Words spoken are thoughts expressed; to speak wisely you must think factually.

This is why, factual-thinking is important in dealing with all aspects of our life, and especially, in our interactions with others. The way to minimize personal-conflicts and increase the effectiveness of our position in an interpersonal-relationship is to use facts and evidence as the basis for our thinking and behavior. We must become aware of our thoughts, validate them with supportive facts, and keep our emotions out so that our interactions are not based on emotions, but they are based on facts. When we use facts and evidence to base our life on, we will not only generate feelings that are based on rationality, but we will also have less interest in being right and more interest in living with the truth.

Have less interest in being right, and more interest in living with the truth.

Because:

It is better to stand corrected than to try to be right at any cost.

The Cognitive-Cognition-Technique is a critical-thinking system that uses our feelings-awareness to identify and analytically evaluate our thoughts that are creating our feelings. By using our feelings to get in touch with our thoughts and to factually evaluate them, we can then accept our factual-thoughts and dismiss our nonfactual-thoughts; hence, we can adjust or eliminate our feelings accordingly. The Cognitive-Cognition-Technique significantly improves our emotional-regulation capabilities by improving our factual-thinking abilities; therefore, the best way to control our emotions and our impulsivities is through controlling our thoughts via factual-thinking. The Cognitive-Cognition-Technique not only helps us to think rationally, but it puts rationality into our feelings. When our feelings are supported by rational and factual thoughts that are in sync with reality, our feelings become purer, more rationality-based, and better-defined as they become harmonious with factual-reality.

To feel good, we must think well.

IV.
Minimizing Negativity

If you feel negative more often than you feel positive, and if your negativities arise faster and last longer than your positivities; you are simply a normal human-being.

In the modern-times, the main reason we have not been able to reach long-lasting positivity and happiness is because we have been pursuing happiness incorrectly; we have been too focused on the desired effect of happiness without properly addressing the uncomfortable causes of our unhappiness.

The need to feel good versus the necessity to think well is a core factor that inhibits change, and blocks self-improvement.

As human-beings, we are so focused on trying to feel good that we will think of anything and we will do anything in order to avoid pain, to feel good, or at the minimum, to feel less-bad; this is why we self-deceive continuously. Motivational and self-improvement teachings, some intentionally and some unknowingly, capitalize on this human need to quickly feel good; hence, they bombard us with unrealistic and nonfactual chest-pounding and peptalking speeches, so that we would get excited and feel better. Initially, we get our hopes up by believing that the next motivational program will show us how to reach lasting happiness, only to realize a short time later that what we felt at that time was nothing but a temporary dopamine boost from a high-paced emotionally appealing sales tactic. Therefore, sensationalistic statements such as "in pursuit of happiness" are nothing but fallacies that people believe in because it makes them feel good.

We shouldn't be in pursuit of happiness; we must be in pursuit of less-negativity.

Happiness is not something that is pursued or found, happiness is something that must be created and maintained from within; because, happiness is not something that is found externally.

Happiness cannot be pursued; it must be produced.

However, we can increase the frequencies and durations of our happiness if we truly learn how to self-improve. True self-improvement begins with addressing the negative-cause of something, in this case unhappiness, before achieving the intended positive-effect.

Negativity Stinks.

Negative-feelings are disliked, uncomfortable; and, they make us feel bad. As discussed, negative-feelings are metaphorically similar to body-odor, hence, they stink; therefore, in trying to deal with them, we must treat them similarly. We cannot cover-up negativity with positivity, just as we cannot cover up body-odor with just perfumes and without bathing. Since we bathe our body in order to remove and eliminate the body-odor causing bacteria, before applying perfumes and fresheners; why is it that we don't remove or eliminate the causes of our negative-feelings before we try to feel positive? The reason is, we want to quickly feel better without addressing the cause. However, in dealing with negativity:

Don't settle for quick-fixes; reach for long-term solutions.

Removing negativity, just like bathing, is a process that takes time; we cannot just accomplish it by spraying positive-thoughts on our smelly negative-feelings. To reach positivity and to experience more frequencies of happiness, we must first minimize and remove negativities. Without removing negativities, we will not be able to experience sustainable positivities and happiness; therefore, we must learn and apply the process of bathing our thoughts so that we can ultimately reach more sustainable and longer-lasting experiences of happiness.

Bathe your thoughts…Don't cover them up!

Because:

To feel good, you must think well.

As discussed, our mind, especially our primitive-mind, which controls our basic mental-states of safety and survival, is default programmed to be negative. Our primitive-mind does not care if we feel good or if we are happy; all our primitive-mind cares about is if we are safe so that we can survive another day. Therefore, to increase our positivities and our experiences of happiness, we must first comfort our primitive-mind in feeling fewer threats and less dangers so that it could relax and allow our intelligent-mind to get into the driver's seat. The only way that we can truly accomplish this is by making good decisions and by taking correct actions which increase our cushion of safety from negativities and potentially unfavorable outcomes. However, during the process of minimizing negativity, if we make continuous mistakes that increase negativity or do not eliminate negativity; our primitive-mind loses trust in our intelligent-mind's decision-making abilities, hence, it immediately moves back into the position of control and dominance in order to keep us safe. This is why, we must think correctly in order to behave properly; because our primitive-mind must trust our intelligent-mind's reasoning and decision-making abilities, so that it will not interfere with the process of improving our feelings.

As discussed, the reason our default-state-of-existence is negative is because negativity serves as a protective mechanism. When our mind senses tangible or intangible negativity, it shuts down other operations so that it can focus on the negativity in order to resolve or eliminate the cause of the negativity. When we sense threat, danger, or any form of negativity, we generate negative-feelings and not positive ones; because negative-feelings force us to take action in order to resolve or eliminate the cause of the negativity. When we resolve or eliminate the cause of the negativity, the dislikable negative-feeling automatically disappears. Nature has programmed us with the disincentive of dislikable negative-feelings, so that we have an incentive to eliminate the causes of our negative-feelings; hence, to consequently feel better.

As exampled previously, if we have a cavity in our tooth, our tooth hurts and we experience pain; we don't experience joy or a tickle. The pain that we experience forces us to take action to fix the tooth so that our pain would go away. If we experienced a joy instead of ache, we would not take any action to minimize or remove the negative-feeling; therefore, our tooth problem would get worse and potentially lead to infection which could eventually kill us. By going to the dentist and by fixing the cavity or by removing the tooth, we fix the cause of the pain; and in-turn, our negative-feeling of pain disappears. We don't keep taking pain-pills and we don't keep thinking positive-thoughts to cover-up the pain and hoping the pain goes away. Therefore, the right thing to do would be to actually take an action and to go through the process of going to the dentist, and the dislike or even the discomfort of the dental procedure, in order to make the toothache go away.

Negativity is the default state of most things we deal with; for example, we primarily, out of necessity, engage doctors, mechanics, plumbers, and other service providers to help us resolve, improve, or eliminate a negativity or a perceived-negativity; or, to help us prevent a future negativity. Although we do selectively engage such providers for enhancements, we don't primarily engage doctors, mechanics, plumbers, or other service providers if we don't have a negativity or a perceived negativity to improve; or if we are not trying to prevent the onset of a future negativity.

It is for similar protective-reasons that we have many more negative-feelings than we have positive ones. Negativity is dislikable and it forces us to take action in order to resolve or eliminate the cause of our negativity so that we can get away from a potential threat or danger. Therefore, in order to eliminate negativity so that we can feel better, we must first try to feel less-negative by removing or by eliminating the cause of our negativity. Hence, by being defaulted to feel negative, the negativity forces us to take action in order to get away from the potential threat or danger that is making us feel negative. As we distance our Self from the threat or danger; in-turn, our negative feelings subside and disappear.

As discussed, negativity is our default-state-of-existence and positivity is only a condition of our existence. This means, positivity is contingent on the lack of existence of negativity; therefore, unlike negativity, positivity and happiness are states of "experience" and not states of "existence." Consequently, neither true positivity nor lasting happiness is possible unless we first minimize and eliminate the underlying negativity.

Furthermore, we cannot just eliminate negativity at the snap of a finger and begin to feel positivity forever. As discussed, in order to experience positivity and more frequent happiness, we must first begin the process of minimizing and even eliminating negativity, in an attempt to reach the neutral contentment-zone. Once we reach contentment and as we maintain our Self in the contentment-zone without sinking back down into negativity; it is only then that we can begin building positivities and happiness on top of our contentment.

Theory of Self-Relativity defines "contentment" as "a satisfactory state of neutral existence which is reached and maintained by minimization of negativities."

This is why, as our experiences of positivity and happiness begin to fadeaway, contentment must be our fallback buffer zone; because no matter what we do to become happy, and no matter how long our happiness lasts, our happiness will eventually fadeaway and we will end up settling back down at lower levels. We can either eliminate and maintain no negativities so that when happiness fades-away we can fallback into contentment; or, if we have not resolved our underlying negativities, we will not be able to remain in the contentment-zone, because unresolved negativities will drag us back down into the area of negativity and unhappiness.

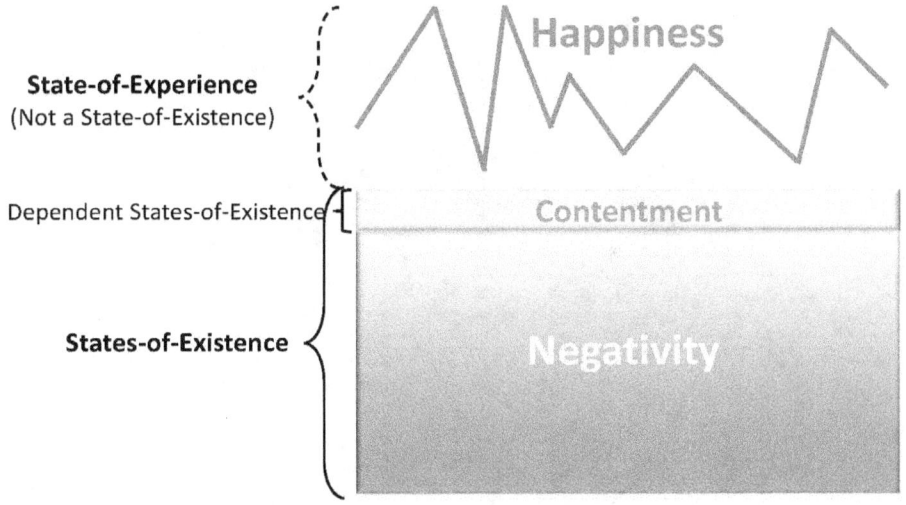

Negativity is a state-of-existence; however, positivity and happiness are states-of-experience.

Since negativity is a state-of-existence in The-Universe, and since negativity is also the default programming of our mind; this is why, if we don't do anything and if we don't constantly put in effort to make positive-change, we will sink back into negativity. Additionally, to prevent from sinking back into negativity, we must not only put in effort to make positive-change; but, we must also continue putting in effort in order to maintain the positive-change achieved. Because, as stated, due to the natural default-state of negativity:

When left alone, there are more ways for things to go wrong, than for things to go right.

Hence, the common references to negativity, unhappiness, and sadness, as having a "sinking-feeling;" because it feels like negativity has weight that pulls us down like gravity. In this metaphorical analogy, negativity effortlessly pulls us down like gravity does, because negativity is the default state of The-Universe, as well as the default state of our existence. As disheartening as this may sound, this is how nature is set up and this is how nature operates. Nature does not care if its rules are not to our liking, because nature has no care or obligations to please us. As stated:

The Universe does not exist so that we could exist; we exist because the Universe exists.

Conversely, positivity and happiness not only require effort and energy to materialize, but they also require effort and energy to maintain; because nature does not care if we prefer positivity and happiness over negativity. Nature operates without a care for how we feel, and it does so simply by adhering to the laws-of-physics that govern The-Universe. This is why, positivity, which requires effort, feels like a rocketship that must spend active energy and effort in order to escape the gravitational pull of negativity; however, negativity, just like gravity, does not require much effort or energy to pull us down. As discussed, Theory of Self-Relativity refers to this metaphoric pulling down effect of negativity as *"Negativity-Gravity."*

Since negativity-gravity pulls down and since negative-feelings give us a sinking feeling; in order to feel positive, we must first escape the pull of negativity, by minimizing and by eliminating negativity. This is why, methods such as positive-thinking and other hypothetical energy-based theories of thinking and vibrational-existence do not work; because we cannot escape the pull of nega-tivity by just trying to think or feel positive. In order to truly escape the pull of negativity, we must actually burn fuel and put in effort to make positive-change.

Negativity pulls harder than positivity.

"Negativity-Bias" is the notion that even when of equal intensity, things of negative nature, such as unpleasant thoughts, feelings, and events, have greater effect on us than do positive things. For example, losing money could have a much greater effect on us than making the same amount of money; or the effects of losing a romantic-love could be more detrimental and longer-lasting than the effects of falling in love would be.

Through evolution, the human mind is programmed to pay more attention to something negative rather than to something positive; because this negativity-bias is intended to be a protective-mechanism so that primitive-humans could recog-nize threats and dangers, in order to keep themselves safe and alive. Therefore, as a result of this instinctual conditioning, our mind recognizes and reacts to negativity more than it does to positivity; which explains why it takes more effort to cancel out the effects of a negativity, than it does to cancel out a positivity of equal value and intensity. Conversely, for same reasons, it takes less effort to feel negative than it does to feel positive.

Furthermore, because of this inherent negativity conditioning, we are more sus-ceptible to being influenced by negativity than we are with positivity; because, since negativity is intended to be protective, it attracts our attention quicker. For example, news-programs tend to be more negative than positive because negativity stands out and it captures our interest. This negative information and content makes our mind more interested and more attentive to it as negativity is intended to alert us to potential threats and danger.

This dominance of negativity is also present in our memories, because we remem-ber with our feelings. As discussed, we remember with feelings because when our mind files away the memories of past events and occurrences, our mind attaches stronger feelings to those memories that it wants to recall quickly at a future time. This is why, we tend to recall negative-memories more vividly and with more emo-tional intensity than we do positive ones; because negative-feelings have stronger influences on us than positive ones. This, in-turn, explains why we dwell more on the negative events and experiences from the past, than we do with positive ones. This negative state-of-mind is also more dominant during our sleep as we tend to remember and react to nightmares and sad dreams more often and more intensely, than we do with positive and pleasant dreams.

Although negativity is dominant relative to our cognitive functions such as our thinking and our ability to recall memories; in order to cope with this negativity, hence, to feel better, we often engage in the fallacious process that Theory of Self-Relativity refers to as *"Selective-Positivity."*

Theory of Self-Relativity defines "selective-positivity" as "one's tendency to selectively recall positive-memories, in order to improve one's feelings and to justify one's behavior."

For example, gamblers have a tendency of remembering the few big wins, but they tend to forget the many losses; because, by selectively remembering their big wins, they can override the memories of their losses, thus, they can give themselves further reason and opportunity to continue their gambling behavior. Selective-positivity is similar to placebo-thinking, where one tends to create false-thoughts and fallacious-beliefs in order to rationalize and support one's desired and comforting-feelings. Selective-positivity is also often associated with motivated-reasoning and confirmation-bias, whereby the person engaging in motivated-reasoning selectively justifies and rationalizes with reasons as to why one continues thinking or continues doing certain things. Additionally, through confirmation-bias, one looks for real or fabricated reasons or justifications that support one's desired or preferred conclusion or behavior.

It is because of selective-positivity that:

We selectively remember our hits, yet we conveniently forget our misses.

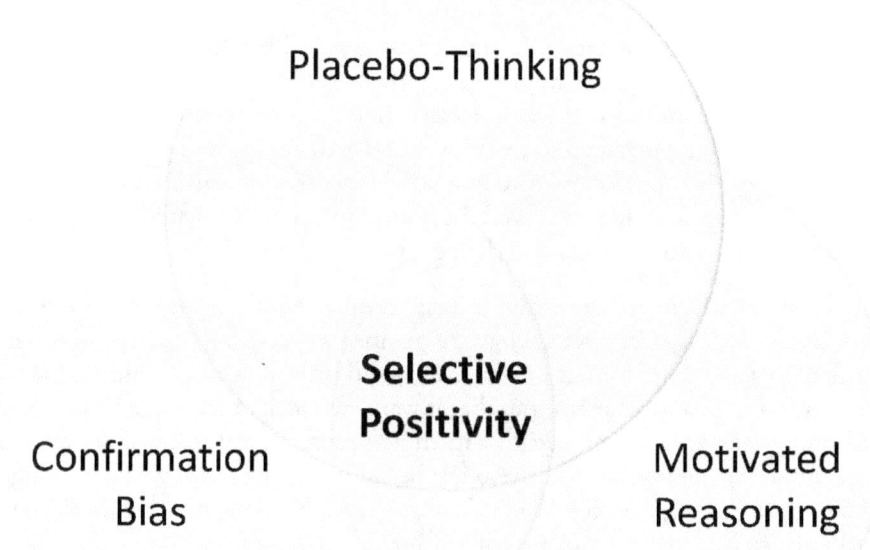

This is why, Theory of Self-Relativity considers the evolved intelligence of modern-humans to be a double-edged sword, because we tend to use our intelligence and cognitive abilities to manipulate our thoughts to fit them to the way we want to feel, rather than to feel the way we ought to feel, based on the information and data that we receive from reality.

It takes intelligence to manipulate intelligence.

Other animals feel what they should feel based on the data and information that they get from their surrounding; however, since the modern-human is not faced with many primitive-dangers, we use our intelligence to cover-up our negative-feelings in order to rationalize the way we want to feel. In other words, in the presence of negativity, we self-deceive to feel better, rather than take action in order to fix the cause of the negativity.

As discussed, we have more ways of feeling negative than we have to feel positive, because negative-feelings are intended to force us to take action so that we can resolve, eliminate, or improve the causes of those negativities. Simply stated, if we did not feel negative, we would not take action; this is why, in order to feel positive, we must put in effort to address the negativities. Likewise, since there are more ways of feeling negative; thus, in order to improve how we feel and for our positivities to last longer, we must put in effort to fix the negativities.

The following list of emotions, complied by Theory of Self-Relativity, clearly demonstrates the prevalence and the dominance of the variety of negative-feelings that we could experience, versus the few ways that we could actually feel positive.

List of Emotions

Sad	Bad	Fear	Anger	Pain	Happy
Bored	Indifferent	Hesitant	Frustrated	Confused	Content
Abandoned	Embarrassed	Worried	Disrespected	Irritated	Fulfilled
Isolated	Ashamed	Cautious	Bitter	Disappointed	Relieved
Distant	Guilty	Anxious	Critical	Deprived	Relaxed
Withdrawn	Regretful	Uncertain	Disgusted	Betrayed	Peaceful
Lonely	Inadequate	Nervous	Dismissive	Weak	Comfortable
Victimized	Insignificant	Insecure	Defensive	Powerless	Confident
Fragile	Tired	Shocked	Offended	Pressured	Trusting
Despair	Fragile	Frightened	Jealous	Shocked	Loving
Remorseful	Rejected	Scared	Judgmental	Overwhelmed	Joyful
Hopeless	Inferior	Horrified	Hate	Hurt	Elated
Grief	Worthless	Helpless	Rage	Stressed	Ecstatic
Depressed	Empty	Vulnerable	Hostile	Awful	Euphoric

According to Theory of Self-Relativity, the reason we have so many more negative-feelings than we do positive-ones is because we are defaulted to experience more negativity than we are to experience positivity; and this is as a result of us living in a constantly and consistently changing Universe. As stated throughout Theory of Self-Relativity, if left alone, there are more ways for things to go wrong than for them to go right; this is how nature operates, because negativity is the default state of our mind's existence, and disorder is the continuously increasing default existence state of The-Universe. This fact of increasing disorder in The-Universe, also known as the *"Law of Entropy,"* is discussed in detail throughout Theory of Self-Relativity, especially in the *"Change"* chapter of the 10- Commandments for Self-Improvement.

Entropy is simply the degree of disorder in a system, for example, in The-Universe; and the entropy or the disorder of The-Universe is always increasing and will continue to increase. Since The-Universe is defaulted by negative-change that is causing disorderliness, and since our primitive-mind is default programmed to be negative in order for us to detect threats, dangers, and as a whole, to detect negative-change so that we can keep our Self safe; this is why, we are constantly exposed to negativity, and why, we are continuously dealing with negative-feelings.

Negativity is the default state of the Universe, and it is the default mindset of human existence.

To summarize, the governing causes for the dominance of our negative-feelings are:

1. **Our safety-first oriented protective mindset for survival**
2. **The-Universe's entropy**

Since negativity is dominant in The-Universe, and since our negative-feelings are also dominant; therefore, we must resolve, improve, or eliminate the causes of the negativities that we deal with so that we can feel less-negative. To resolve, improve, or eliminate the causes of our negativities, we must become aware of and we must understand the causes of these negativities; and, we must put in effort to minimize or eliminate these negativities.

Regardless of their intensity and nature, since negative-feelings are there to force us to take action in order to make an improving change; therefore, negative-feelings are intended to be temporary mindsets until we resolve, improve, or eliminate their causes. When we learn to view and treat every negative feeling as a temporary mindset, we will then not fear negativity anymore; hence, we will attend to the causes of the negativity in order to resolve, improve, or eliminate these causes. Once the cause of a negative-feeling is resolved, improved, or eliminated; the negative-feeling itself will consequently be improved or eliminated.

This is why, improvement and the need to feel good and happy, cannot simply be achieved by creating false-thoughts and wishful-beliefs; or by positive-thinking or by other new-age spiritual short-term cover-ups such as meditation, prayers, and superstitious rituals. Since The-Universe is becoming more disorderly, which means it is changing more negatively, and since we are also default programmed to be negative; in order for us to reach positivity and happiness, we must first minimize and resolve negativity, so that we reach "no negativity" or neutrality.

It must be noted that once neutrality is reached, neutrality must be maintained; if not, we will sink back into negativity. Once we reach neutrality and as we put in effort to maintain neutrality; it is only then that we can try to begin to take further action to increase positivities and to begin experiencing happiness more frequently. As discussed, Theory of Self-Relativity defines this zone of neutrality as "the zone of contentment" or the "contentment-zone."

Theory of Self-Relativity defines "contentment" as "a satisfactory state of neutral existence which is reached and maintained by minimization of negativities."

Once negativity is minimized and controlled, and before attempting to experience happiness, we must first reach and stay in the contentment-zone. Happiness can be achieved easier if we learn to live in the contentment-zone and to not allow our Self to drop back into the negativity-zone. Although contentment is commonly defined as a mild form of happiness which is based on satisfaction of one's state-of-existence; Theory of Self-Relativity views contentment as a much narrower state-of-existence which is not characterized as having mild positivities, but a state which is characterized as having minimal to no negativities. Therefore, contentment, and in-turn, happiness, are contingent on the non-existence of negativity.

True contentment isn't neutral to positive; true contentment is less-negative to neutral.

Thus, to experience more frequencies of happiness:

We shouldn't be in pursuit of happiness; we should be in pursuit of less-negativity.

Therefore:

Happiness cannot be pursued; it must be produced.

Although major negativities are easier to identify so that we can try to resolve or eliminate them; what commonly holds us back from reaching contentment, and in-turn, from experiencing more frequencies of positivity and happiness, is our inability to be aware of our everyday annoying negativities that we feel. As presented, we have many more ways of feeling negative than we do with feeling positive; which means, we commonly feel more negative-feelings than we do positive-feelings. Additionally, when of equal intensity, our negative and unpleasant thoughts and feelings have a greater effect on us than do our positive ones; therefore, to minimize our negativities, we must first become aware of them so that we can identify their causes, especially the causal-thoughts that are making us feel negative.

Theory of Self-Relativity's Cognitive-Cognition-Technique teaches us how to use our feelings to identify their underlying causal-thoughts, so that we can then evaluate them for their factuality; hence, we can decide to take action or inaction in order to resolve, improve, or eliminate them. As we resolve, improve, or eliminate the causes of our negative-feelings, our feelings will adjust accordingly and they will improve. The more negativities we address and resolve, the less negativities we will experience, and the more neutral and stable our state of contentment will become. The more content we become, the better we can maintain our state of contentment, and the less our chance of slipping back into negativity will be; therefore, we will have better potential for experiencing more positivity and happiness. Since positivity and happiness are only states-of-experience and not states-of-existence; by learning to remain in the contentment-zone, we can cushion our fall when our experiences of positivity and happiness begin to fade away. Instead of sinking back into negativity, contentment will cushion our fall to its neutral platform so that we can then be better positioned for another experience of positivity and happiness.

Contentment cushions our fall from happiness.

Identification of our thoughts through awareness of our feelings is the core principle of The Cognitive-Cognition-Technique. Factual-evaluation of our thoughts helps us in dealing with all our negativities in a uniformly applicable thinking-format. Factual-thinking could even be useful in cases of PTSD (post-traumatic-stress-disorder) and depression, if one learns to focus on addressing and resolving the causal-thoughts, and not to solely and continuously focus on the resulting feelings. Furthermore, disengagement and lack of conviction, which are commonly associated with avoiding negative mindsets and difficult thoughts, are some of the main psychological reasons for depression. While neurological and genetic factors have been linked to depression, a strong psychological reason for depression is lack of purpose and conviction.

As discussed throughout Theory of Self-Relativity, the natural default programming of the human mind is to stay with the negative and with the state of least-effort. It is much easier to choose to dismiss a thought and do nothing, than to accept the thought and take action to improve. When hopelessness sets in, the "no-effort" state becomes the path of least resistance. Depressed individuals have low to no interest in anything or anyone and they disengage themselves by taking the default-state of no-effort. This is how, many succumb to the psychological effects of depression, by alienating themselves and by disengaging from activities. Although there are numerous signs and symptoms of depression, the most common ones are associated with low mood, hopelessness, and by becoming distant and disengaged. Loss of interest is the primary common factor in depression.

Additionally, PTSD is generally caused as a result of a traumatic event that happened in the past. The reliving of such event and the inability to understand and resolve the causes of the event are major contributors to the increased stress and depression associated with PTSD. Depression and PTSD are forms of stress on the brain and could be minimized and treated via mindfulness and cognitive-therapies. Awareness and understanding of the causes of our negative-feelings through mindfulness will enable us to address and resolve the causes of our negative-feelings; which as discussed, are always negative-thoughts. When we combine mindfulness and thoughtfulness together with factual-thinking, we can have a better chance of overcoming not just everyday negativities, but even more disabling conditions such as PTSD and depression. Therefore:

Change and improvement are key to overcoming any kind of trauma.

To consider negativity at an even higher level would be to reflect on "suffering." Suffering is an extreme negative state-of-existence where the only thought on one's mind would be to minimize negativity, often at any and all cost. True suffering is an actual state-of-existence in which one is enduring physical or mental pain that is beyond just negativity. Suffering is commonly associated with distress and even pain; therefore, suffering is a state-of-existence that is actually resulting in damage to the person.

Theory of Self-Relativity defines "suffering" as "the existential state of maximum negativity which is hallmarked by extreme and often prolonged pain."

Hence, suffering is an extreme feeling or perception of pain. The following diagram best demonstrates the intensity and overlap of common negative-feelings with suffering at the extreme. Suffering is the extreme feeling of pain, while pain is an intense feeling of discomfort, and discomfort is a stronger feeling of dislike, and dislike is a deeper feeling of displeasure.

Although it is theorized that all sentient-beings can experience suffering, according to Theory of Self-Relativity, human suffering was more prevalent in ancient and primitive-times than it is in the modern-times. The reasons that as modern-humans we experience less-suffering is due to the advancements in technology and medicine, and due to our better understanding and perspective-taking abilities of the human-nature and their subjective-experiences.

However, according to Theory of Self-Relativity, suffering in the modern-times, has been misused and overused by many as a victimization strategy to the point where even dislike, displeasure, or anything short of entitled euphoria are portrayed as suffering. True-suffering exists when people are dying from starvation, when they are experiencing painful terminal conditions, and when humans are being tortured. Those who claim material-losses or personal-failures as suffering are too privileged to know what suffering really is. Other than true and painful prolonged state-of-existence, majority of other references to the word "suffering" in the modern-times are overused, sensationalistic, attention-getting, sympathy-seeking, self-victimizing, and controlling practices.

From religious, cultural, and social teachings, to the dramatic statements of philosophers and preachers, to live life as a struggle or a suffering is an intentional misrepresentation and manipulation of the precious human-existence. For self-serving reasons and for the purpose of sensationalism and even control, life is often unnecessarily portrayed as a state of suffering by ideological teachings.

When referring to life, there is absolutely no reason to describe life as a prolonged process of suffering; because life is not a disaster, it is a rare and statistically improbable gift.

Life is not a suffering; it is an exceptional gift.

Working to pay for food, worrying about loved-ones, getting sick, and even dying, are all routine parts of life. Work, rent, debt, heartache, break-ups, and even aging, are not suffering; they are the routines of being alive. As modern-humans, especially those living in advanced-societies, we have entitled our Self to label any dislike or even any lack of pleasure as suffering. The quality of life for the majority of people, especially in the modern-times, is nowhere close to being labelled as suffering. Those who are truly suffering are in too much agony to even recognize that they are suffering. What primitive-civilizations, helpless-beings, and many dependent living-entities experience is a representative of suffering.

Dramatic and sensationalistic references to suffering should be banished from our daily references. Suffering is a horrific condition which is undeserving for any sentient living-entity; therefore, references to suffering should not be used loosely in order to get sympathy. Likewise, suffering, or any other form of what Theory of Self-Relativity has termed as *"Toxic-Sympathy"* should not be used by religion, society, or motivational-teachings to manipulate people into submission, via the deceptive fallacy of appeal-to emotion.

Theory of Self-Relativity defines "toxic-sympathy" as "intentionally nurturing victimhood, in order to manipulate and win over the weak and the susceptible."

Life is precious, life is short, and life is beautiful; and even with all its difficulties, there is no justification to refer to living "life" as suffering. Sometimes, unpleasant or sad, perhaps; but not suffering. Suffering should be reserved for references to torturous and tangible physical pain such as starvation and incurable physical diseases. To label life as suffering is a gross abuse of existence. We should never allow anyone or anything to ever describe our precious gift of life as suffering.

Life is not a suffering; it is an exceptional gift that we must live to its fullest possible potential.

As uncomfortable and as hurtful as physical and emotional pain could be; deep feelings of sadness and negative-emotions must not be considered as suffering, because no matter how emotionally distraught we might feel, if at that very moment a sudden accident damages or harms us physically, our emotional pain or what we perceived as suffering would immediately fadeaway in comparison to the real physical damage and pain that we are experiencing.

Therefore, we must understand that negativities and negative-emotions are a normal part of our existence, because negative-feelings are intended to be protective and to keep us safe. In order for us to experience more positivity and happiness, we must understand that unlike negativity, positivity and happiness are not states-of-existence, they are states-of-experience; hence, we must continuously put in effort to continue changing for the better, so that we can increase the frequencies and the durations of our positive experiences.

Feeling positive and experiencing happiness are not defined points in time that once reached we can then sit back and enjoy them as eternal-euphoria; because no such state-of-existence is possible. To feel positive and to experience more frequencies of happiness, we must first resolve, improve, or eliminate all of the causes of our negativities, so that we can then maintain our Self in the neutral contentment-zone. Once we reach contentment, we can then begin to take action in order to experience more positivity and more frequencies of happiness. However, even happiness is not the ultimate state of positivity that one could truly experience; the ultimate state-of-existence is the state of fulfillment. While happiness feels intense, fulfillment is the ultimate form of lasting positivity. Self-fulfillment is what gives us the ability to confidently live a productive and positive life; thus, fulfillment enables us to experience more satisfactory and longer-lasting experiences of happiness.

Theory of Self-Relativity defines "fulfillment" as "an evolving satisfactory state-of-mind that is built upon a stable foundation of contentment."

V.
Independence & Self-Reliance

Theory of Self-Relativity considers dependency and reliance as one of the significant causes of one's inability to establish a well-defined self-identity and a strong sense of Self. Dependency and reliance are also one of the most difficult enemies for self-improvement to overcome, because it is often learned and adopted since childhood or younger age. Dependency and reliance disable a person from being able to establish discipline and self-confidence, because it focuses one's attention externally rather than onto the Self. Furthermore, dependency and reliance do not allow for proper establishment of personal borders and boundaries, which in the long-term, could create the potential for being disrespected, mistreated, controlled and even abused.

Although dependency and reliance commonly refer to our interactions with other-people, dependency and reliance could also be relative to other-things. As discussed, Theory of Self-Relativity categorizes dependency and reliance binarily:

1. **Tangible-Dependency and Reliance:** Occurs when a person is or becomes dependent and reliant on others for monetary or material things. For example, a child's dependency on parents, or a wife's dependency on a providing husband, or on a larger scale, people's reliance on government to provide for shelter, healthcare, and other goods and services because they are incapable of providing such monetary-based needs for themselves. Tangible-dependency is also referred to a person's need and desire to attain and maintain tangible and material goods and services as a measure of self-validation and as a portrayal of self-worth; this is why, Theory of Self-Relativity refers to others collectively as "other-people or other-things." People who are tangibly dependent on other-people or on other-things often attempt to find and validate their self-identity externally through other-people or through other-things. These individuals are incapable of living their lives happily or even contently on their own as they are always focused on the outside for provision of goods and services, or they are focused on others for validation of their self-worth and their self-identity.

2. **Intangible-Dependency and Reliance:** Occurs when a person is or becomes reliant on others for emotional and immaterial things. For example, wanting to be loved by others as a means of feeling desired, or having the need to be in a relationship because the person cannot be alone, or having frequent sex with different partners as a means of achieving perceived higher self-worth or personal-validation. Dependency and reliance,

especially intangible-dependency, is the core reason a person becomes a people-pleaser; because people-pleasers try to receive and maintain receiving love, attention and validation from others by pleasing others, instead of receiving love and attention for their own personal qualities and attributes. Intangible-dependency and reliance is a major reason for Theory of Self-Relativity designating "others" as the most dangerous word; because, by focusing onto others in order to get love, affection, and approval, the self-equation completely shifts against the welfare of one's own Self.

Since dependency and reliance are strongly anti personal-development and anti-self-improvement; therefore, to strengthen and to improve our self-identity, our sense of Self, and our self-image, we must learn and practice independence and self-reliance. Independence and self-reliance enables us to begin relying on our Self not only in terms of improving our independent decision-making abilities; but it also enables us to cultivate our own opinions and ideas from within. No matter what self-reliance accomplishes, the most important things that independence and self-reliance allow us to achieve is self-validation; because, when we become self-reliant, we will not need others to enhance our personal qualities, others will become additive, thus, they will become complementary instead of being completing for our existence. This is why, "Complementary; not Completing" is another one of Theory of Self-Relativity's 10-Commandments for Self-Improvement.

Although external-validation is often conditional, and even, consequential to expectations and interests that others have of us; internal-validation or self-validation should not be conditional. Self-validation must come from objective evaluation of facts and evidence relevant to the characteristics that we are seeking validation for. Since validation often goes hand-in hand with self-esteem; thus, self-validation and self-reliance will help in minimizing our self-doubt. Just like other personal negativities, to self-improve, we must first minimize negativities such as dependency, reliance, and the need for external-validation. When we do so, we can then increase our positivities by becoming independent, self-reliant, and self-sufficient.

Independence and self-reliance commonly result in self-sufficiency. Self-sufficiency takes away the excessive need for external help in achieving our desires, our goals, and our dreams. Self-sufficiency enables us to create our own purpose and meaning from within, rather than seeking purpose and meaning from other-people or from other-things. Self-sufficiency enables us to become a better rounded and more complete person on our own; and self-sufficiency takes away the need for us to continuously seek others in order to feel validated and complete. When we become self-sufficient, others become an additive factor in our lives; therefore, when we become tangibly and intangibly self-sufficient, our relationships and our interactions with others becomes complementary and not completing. As stated, "Complementary, not Completing" is another one of Theory of Self-Relativity's 10-Commandments for Self-Improvement, because true self-improvement will result in us relating and interacting with others based on additive values, and not based on completing needs.

As we learn to become more independent and as we increase our self-reliance, we subsequently become more capable of being in control and we will make better decisions for our Self, by achieving more positive and more fulfilling results. As the frequencies of our better decisions and favorable results increase, our discipline and our ability to move further into transformation and improvement increases. This increase in our effective decision-making ability and discipline, in-turn, minimizes our self-doubt, and strengthens our self-confidence. As stated, our primitive-mind will only allow our intelligent-mind to take control of our decisions and actions if our primitive-mind trusts the intelligent-mind's decision-making abilities; therefore, self-confidence is established and strengthened when our primitive-mind becomes confident of our intelligent-mind's handling of our decisions and actions.

Self-confidence is one of the most desired characteristics that people who attempt to self-improve want to achieve. Although there are a multitude of perspectives on what true self-confidence is like; the ultimate representation of self-confidence is knowing that we can handle and solve any problem or difficulty that arises in our life. Self-confidence is a byproduct of self-improvement, and it is, especially, as a result of being independent and self-reliant. True self-confidence not only gives the confident person a sense of better certainty, security, and comfort; but self-confidence also exudes that very same confident self-image to others. Self-confidence represents that we have overcome self-doubt; and, that we have the information, the knowledge, and the experience to back up our self-image and how we present our Self.

Confidence exudes strength from within.

True self-confident people not only exude confidence, but they are also confident enough to know better when they don't know something. A truly self-confident person is capable of saying "I don't know" or admitting "I stand corrected;" and such a confident person is also capable of remaining unopinionated and quiet in situations where one might not have sufficient information or knowledge about the subject matter. Self-confident people are also more capable of doing things for others, and being of value to others, without having to sacrifice themselves; because self-confident people create value from within and interact with others on a complementary basis, and not from a completing or from a people-pleasing perspective.

To consider and to do for others without having to sacrifice one's Self, is the mark of a truly self-confident person.

However, unlike a self-confident person, an arrogant person is generally quite insecure and has a false and often grandiose sense of Self. Regardless of having wealth, fame, or power, arrogant people are mostly fragile and weak internally, and their arrogance is a way of covering up their internal-weaknesses and shortcomings. Arrogant people portray their self-identity externally as a reflection of their Self, rather than their self-identity exuding and emanating from within their Self; because arrogance is a façade for self-doubt and lack of self-confidence.

Arrogant people get their way with what they present, rather than as who they represent.

Arrogance often goes hand-in hand with ego, because egotistical people are mostly insecure deep within, as they try to portray arrogance as a sign of confidence. True confidence is not simply a portrayal of a characteristic; true confidence is the byproduct of internal change and improvement, therefore, confidence is a skill. Confident people do not care about how they portray themselves, because their external-image is simply a representation of their internal-strength. However, arrogant and egotistical people are focused on how they portray themselves; because the stronger the portrayal, the bigger the cover-up for their internal-weaknesses. Confident people are open to learning, because learning strengthens their confidence; however, egotists are not open to learning, because they think they already know everything. Therefore, for the egotist and the arrogant-person, learning or being corrected would be perceived as the exposure and admission of their weak and fragile inner-self.

It is because of this false façade and cover-up of internal-deficiencies that arrogant people are often ignorant of their own arrogance; and why they incorrectly project someone's else's true confidence, as arrogance.

It takes ignorance to not recognize the difference between confidence & arrogance.

According to Theory of Self-Relativity, arrogance is a sign of externalation, instead of introspection. Truly confident people do not need to prove themselves constantly by receiving attention and validation; but arrogant people do seek approval and attention continuously, especially if their wealth, fame, and power was achieved as a means of externalation. While arrogant people actively seek to get attention for validation, confident people automatically receive attention without feeding off the attention as a form of validation.

Arrogance seeks validation; confidence exudes value.

According to Theory of Self-Relativity, arrogant people have a false sense of self-confidence; thereby, arrogance is commonly associated with ignorance and grandiosity, as grandiosity, itself, is a reflection of a false sense of superiority. As a whole, arrogant people have a false sense of personal-positive-attributes, and these false-beliefs or representations are often implemented to cover-up a low self-esteem and a weak sense of Self. Therefore, to shield themselves from getting their false façade broken, arrogant people are often quite defensive. However, unlike arrogant people, confident people do what they do and say what they say without waiting for the external confirmation; thus, they are rarely on the defensive, and they are comfortable with their state of existence, because they are always open to learning more.

Arrogance attempts to reflect strength; while confidence exudes strength.

Confident people are also more open to change if facts and evidence contradicts their position, or if it can improve their position; however, arrogant people are resistant to change because they view change as an admission of their low self-wroth. This is why, in due time, arrogance will break down and the mask of arrogance will slip. Unlike confident people, arrogant people do not like to be in the long-term company of people they meet, as they are continuously concerned about their arrogant façade breaking. On the contrary, confident people flourish in long-term contacts with others as their confidence arises from their true internal substance, and not from a false façade. Since arrogant people are defensive, they also disagree, argue, and debate, not because they want to learn and improve; but they disagree, argue, and debate, in order to prevent themselves from being proven wrong.

Disagreements are good for learnings. Debate to learn, don't debate to not be wrong.

Arrogant individuals like surrounding themselves with people-pleasers, codependents, and insecure people, so that their false-façade could stay safe for a longer period of time, than if they were to surround themselves with confident and accomplished people. Truly confident and accomplished people will be able to see through an arrogant person's façade much faster than inexperienced and codependent type individuals could. Arrogance is also a common characteristic of experienced narcissists and sociopaths who not only portray a false-façade, but who are also convinced of their own false superior sense of Self. A subtle but notable physical characteristic which differentiates an arrogant person from a self-confident person is that arrogant people have a tendency of looking down with their chin up; however, confident people have an easier time holding prolonged direct and levelled eye contact.

Theory of Self-Relativity defines "narcissism" or a "narcissist" as "a weak person who lives with a false sense of grandeur."

Arrogant	Self-Confident
• Insecure	• Secure
• Ignorant	• Aware
• Lacks Knowledge, Information & Experience	• Gains/Uses Knowledge, Information & Experience
• Know it all	• Open to Learning
• Resistant to Change	• Open to Change
• Façade	• Genuine
• Externalation	• Introspection
• Active Attention-Seeker	• Automatic Attention-Getter
• Low Self-Esteemed	• Self-Esteemed
• Seeks Validation	• Represents Value
• Self-Centered	• Centered-Self
• Defensive	• Sanguine
• Self-Absorbed	• Self-Aware
• Looks Down at Others	• Looks Straight at Others

Arrogance is a false sense of self-confidence.

Arrogance is a false-façade that is built thick and heavy to cover-up internal-weaknesses; thus, arrogance is reliant on external-validation, and therefore, arrogance is as a result of externally-reliant personal-reflection. On the contrary, confidence has no false-façade because it originates from within; therefore, confidence emanates into the outside instead of reflecting the outside.

Truly self-confident people are self-aware and live a centered-self life, while arrogant people are self-absorbed and they commonly live a self-centered life. Just as there is a fine-line, but an opposite difference, between being centered-self versus self-centered; there is also a fine-line and an opposite difference between being self-aware and being self-absorbed. Self-aware people are capable of continuously checking, comparing, and balancing their personal-qualities against others and against a changing world in order to improve. However, self-absorbed people abstain from comparison and improvement because their false sense of Self is created to protect their weaknesses and deficiencies; thus, crosschecking with facts would destabilize their false sense of Self that they try to protect by their false-façade of arrogance. Such self-centeredness associated with a false-façade is a prevalent characteristic among narcissists, and in general, among personality-disordered individuals with sociopathic characteristics.

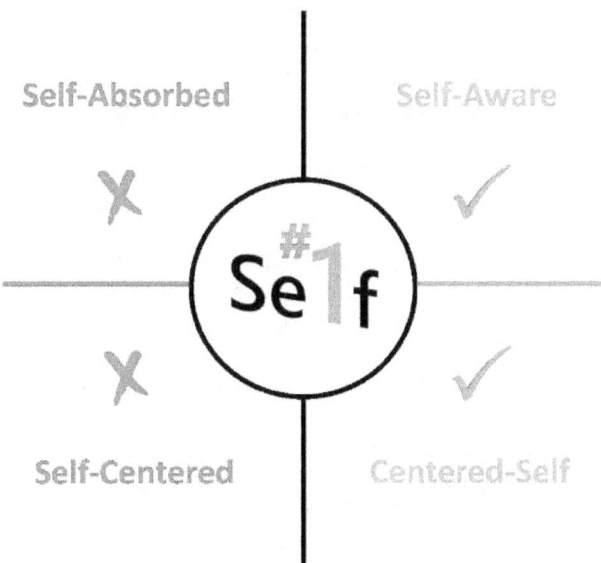

The following questions are examples that one could ask to help distinguish between people that are self-absorbed versus people that are self-aware:

- *In what way do you think you need to change?*
- *What can you improve about your Self?*
- *What do you fear the most?*
- *Do you think you're selfish?*

Insecure and self-absorbed people would become defensive, feel offended, and could even get angry for being asked the above questions because they are incapable of introspection; therefore, for them to admit that they have weaknesses or that they can change and improve is often equal to them admitting the potential self-hate and lack of self-worth that they feel in disguise. However, self-aware and self-confident people would analytically evaluate these questions and respond with potentially enlightening reactions as to how they can further improve themselves.

A significant byproduct of self-confidence is patience. Since self-confident people do not have self-doubt because they have already resolved and eliminated most of their negativities; therefore, self-confident individuals inherently know that they can find resolutions to any new negativities or problems that arise in their lives. When we establish the confidence to know that we can resolve or eliminate any new problem or negativity that arises, just as we resolved and eliminated all previous problems and negativities; we can then minimize anxiety and impulsivity by dealing with things more patiently.

Although people who lack patience want things fast; one of the most common things that most impatient individuals want is for them to quickly feel better than how they are feeling at that moment. As discussed throughout Theory of Self-Relativity, our immediate desire to not feel pain, to feel good, or at the minimum, to feel less-bad, is the main reason we think things and we do things that are not good for us. This impulsivity of needing to feel better is one of the main, if not the main reason, people are not capable of being patient.

The desire to feel good versus the necessity to think well, is one of the main reasons people can't be patient.

Many, misunderstand patience by incorrectly thinking that patience means to passively wait for something to happen. True patience, or as Theory of Self-Relativity terms it as *"Effective-Patience,"* does not mean to just wait for things to happen.

Theory of Self-Relativity defines "effective-patience" as "to methodically move things forward as one goes through the decision-making, planning, and implementation of strategy and action, to reach a favorable outcome."

Effective-patience is dynamic and requires constant input and adjustments in order to move a process forward to reach a desired or intended outcome. Effective-patience, just like optimism, should be established as a means of taking an action, by dynamically and pragmatically going through the process required to reach a goal or an outcome. Therefore, patience must be an effort-based and process-oriented mindset which could only be achieved by having internally-derived self-confidence; because *"Passive-Patience"* is nothing but wishful-thinking.

Simply waiting for favorable things to happen on their own without taking any action is not patience; that's wishful-thinking.

Passive-Patience = Wishful-Thinking

When we minimize worry, anxiety, and fear, we will then be on the road to becoming patient and methodical; because patient people do not have the anxiety or the urgency to resolve matters immediately, in order to feel better quickly. Furthermore, patient people do not have the worry and fear that they might not be able to resolve a new negativity; because patient people have the confidence to know that in due time, they will be relentless in finding ways to resolve matters in the most effective possible manner. Therefore, patience could only be achieved by having discipline, which itself is a requirement for self-confidence.

Unlike popular advice, patience is not something we can practice to gain; because, patience, like other skills, must be created from within. Self-contentment, self-improvement, and self-fulfillment, which are as a result of independence and self-reliance, allow us to trust in our Self and in our decision-making abilities; which in-turn, creates a mindset of calmness and serenity that is generally associated with patience and harmony. Independence and self-reliance give us the power to become confident in our thinking and decision-making; therefore, it removes the impulsivity that impatient people commonly feel. By becoming self-reliant and by reducing our self-doubt and uneasiness, we become confident to trust our judgment and decision-making abilities; which consequently results in having more patience to see our goals and dreams accomplished. Therefore, patience is a skill; hence, effective-patience requires awareness, understanding, and learning.

Patience is a byproduct of self-confidence, because self-confident people do not have the urgency to quickly feel better.

True self-confidence is a personal-trait; but more importantly, just like many of our other traits, true-confidence is a skill. True-confidence could only be created and improved from within, because self-confidence is a byproduct of an independent and self-reliant person. Self-confidence goes hand-in-hand with self-fulfillment, which itself, could only be achieved as a result of contentment. When we learn to achieve and maintain the state of contentment, by minimizing and by eliminating negativities, we can then be closer to achieving self-fulfillment. As discussed, self-fulfillment is not a state of elation or euphoria, but self-fulfillment is a dependent mindset where we feel content, comfortable, and satisfied with our own existence.

Theory of Self-Relativity defines "fulfillment" as "an evolving satisfactory state-of-mind that is built upon a stable foundation of contentment."

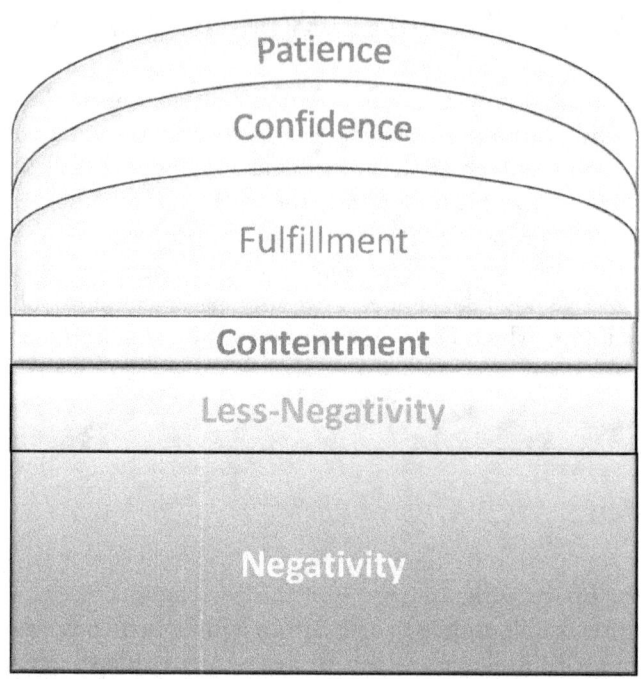

As also discussed, to create, to maintain, and to increase self-confidence, we must also learn to become disciplined. Discipline could only be achieved via self-reliance and the acquisition and application of knowledge and experience, which itself, is best achieved through factual-thinking. Discipline and self-confidence are skills that are created and improved by us, and from within. Therefore, to improve our life's discipline and to increase our self-confidence, we must learn to minimize uncertainty, we must increase control, and we must minimize and eliminate our dependency and reliance on others. When we become independent and self-reliant, we then minimize self-doubt and we gain the confidence required to handle our life's negativities; and consequently, we experience more frequent and longer lasting happiness.

To reiterate, to experience more frequencies of happiness, we must first minimize negativities so that we can reach contentment. Once we reach contentment, we can then begin our progress towards self-fulfillment; which in-turn, increases our self-confidence. As demonstrated, self-confidence is further increased by the minimization of dependency and reliance on others; which in-turn, increases our discipline, and consequently, it further increases our confidence. To simplify the final result, the more confident we become, the more fulfilled we will feel; and the more fulfilled we feel, the more confident we will become.

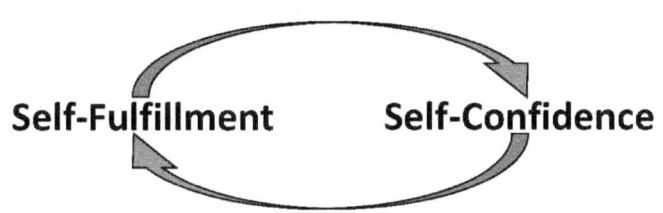

Self-Fulfillment   **Self-Confidence**

When we elevate our state-of-existence to the levels of self-fulfillment and self-confidence, it is only then that we can truly experience more frequencies of happiness; because as demonstrated:

Happiness is contingent on the non-existence of negativity.

This is why, minimizing dependency and reliance on others and becoming independent and self-reliant are important attributes to becoming a content, confident, and happy person. To truly experience more frequent and longer lasting happiness, we must cultivate and grow these attributes from within; and this could only be established by us taking control of our existence and the direction of our life. We can only become truly independent when we learn to seek and confront facts, no matter how uncomfortable facts might be. When we learn to think and live factually, it is only then that we will be able to effectively minimize and eliminate our negativities, and set our Self on the path of fulfillment and happiness.

Independence and self-reliance set us on the path of contentment and fulfillment, which in-turn, increases our self-confidence. When we become more confident, we become more reliant on our own Self; therefore, we end up having more control and certainty in our life and the direction that our life takes. This is why, "Control and Certainty" is designated as another one of Theory of Self-Relativity's 10-Commandments for Self-Improvement.

VI.
Control & Certainty

Control and certainty are interrelated with and are as a result of independence and self-reliance, because when we minimize our dependency on other-people and on other-things, and when we are capable of making-decisions and taking actions based on our evaluation of what is good and constructive for us; we can then have more control over how things affect us and we can best choose the path that we want to move forward in life.

As discussed, having control or being in control does not mean being controlling or rigid; it means to be able to make decision and to take actions on our own, while remaining adaptable and unbiased relative to others. Having control or being in control also increases certainty by minimizing uncertainty. Although in reality, absolute-certainty is unachievable; however, by increasing the probabilities of desired outcomes and by improving our predictive abilities, we can keep our Self at a higher level of certainty. Therefore, to get closer to having control and higher certainty, the best path is by minimizing uncertainty and by becoming self-reliant.

Theory of Self-Relativity defines "uncertainty" as "the inability to control, predict, or change the probability of outcomes."

Since absolute certainty is not possible nor achievable; therefore, certainty is only a state of improving our predictive-abilities of future events, by increasing the probabilities of favorable-outcomes. To achieve this intended goal of increasing the probabilities of favorable-outcomes, we must do so by first minimizing the probabilities of unfavorable-outcomes. In other words, just like to have and experience more positivity we must first minimize negativity; to get closer to certainty and better predictability, we must first minimize uncertainty.

Since certainty cannot be absolute, therefore, there always exists some level of uncertainty; thus, in order to get as close to certainty as possible, we should improve our predictive-abilities by minimizing uncertainty. Furthermore, by increasing control and by minimizing uncertainty; in-turn, we can minimize anxiety, stress, fear, and even anger, while we increase our discipline and self-confidence. Therefore, the only means of increasing control and certainty is for us to minimize the probabilities of negativities; while increasing the probabilities of positivities. This could only happen if we think, reason, and live our life based on facts and factual-reality.

There are no certainties; there are only probabilities.

To truly become independent and self-reliant, and to be in control of our lives, we must learn to think factually; which means we must not only ensure that our thoughts are based on facts, but we must also rid our Self from false-thoughts, fallacious-beliefs, and unfounded-superstitions. This is why, faith, hope, and beliefs are discussed in detail as one of Theory of Self-Relativity's 10-Enemies of Self-Improvement; because faith, hope, and beliefs are not based on facts, they are unreliable mindsets in the absence of facts. If our mindset is based on facts, we would not have to rely on faith, hope, and beliefs; we will then be relying on knowledge.

Facts are facts, and facts are not open to interpretation; therefore, facts are not open to manipulation. However, when our thinking is influenced by and becomes "dependent on" personal, societal, and cultural beliefs and ideologies that do not have any factual-basis; we then place ourselves in a position of uncertainty, because what we believe and rely on to be true, is actually assumed and not necessarily based on how reality is. When we rely on and when we are taught to accept non-factual thoughts, beliefs, and mindsets, we subsequently minimize our control and we increase our uncertainties; because our relativity with reality is not based on facts, but our relativity is based on assumed and unreliable mindsets that guide our thinking, our decision-making, and our interactions with reality.

Nonfactual-beliefs, cultural-traditions, and religious and other supernatural practices that are examples of such baseless and factually-unproven influences could affect our lives negatively; especially, when they are applied as a long-term mindset and strategy for our decision-making. Although many of these beliefs and practices are often comforting; such nonfactual-beliefs can be inhibiting and could even have destructive results when they clash with factual-reality. Furthermore, such blind-faiths, false-hopes, and fallacious-beliefs, shackle us to their rigid ideologies and biases, and they inhibit us from being able to think independently and unbiasedly in dealing with reality. When we become reliant on nonfactual-mindsets and when we don't deal with reality based on facts, we decrease our control in life and we increase our life's uncertainties; because, when we think nonfactually, we become reliant on unreliable faith, hope, beliefs, and dogmatic teachings that are not based on facts.

As discussed, dependency and reliance do not have to necessarily be tangible, as they could also be intangible. Having to adhere to, follow, and behave based on nonfactual claims and dogmas creates dependency and reliance; which in-turn, creates intended and unintended controlling mechanisms that prohibit self-improvement. A dogma is an opinion held in spite of differing opinions or evidence. A more elaborate definition of dogma is, an authoritative opinion or teaching that people are expected to or are forced to accept, believe, and act upon without any factual and evidentiary proof. Dogmas are often authoritarian or supernatural-based opinions, statements, or writings which are presented as ultimate facts and they are intended to be accepted as the final, unchallengeable, and unchangeable truth; without ever being open to questioning. Instead of evidence, the authoritarian or the supernatural characteristics associated with dogmas are the core supportive pillars of their existence. Although dogmas are generally associated with external sources; dogmas could also be self-created.

Theory of Self-Relativity defines being "dogmatic" as "to follow beliefs and ideas that are disallowed from questioning or criticism."

Therefore:

Theory of Self-Relativity defines "dogma" as "an opinion, an idea, or a belief, that is prohibited from questioning or criticism."

This addition of authoritarian or supernatural inherency ensures protection and longevity for the dogma and its authoritarian or dictatorial entity which the dogma is designed to protect. Such protection is commonly accomplished by labeling entities associated with the dogmas as "sacred" or "holy."

Theory of Self-Relativity defines "sanctity" or being "sacred" as "a condition that enables and protects the existence of a dogma."

Dogmas are also designed to protect the interests or the delusions and the non-factual-beliefs of an entity who refuses to consider contradictory facts and evidence. The moment a question, a better opinion, or new evidence arises which could undermine the dogma; instead of considering, adapting to, or amending the dogma based on the new opinion or evidence, the dogmatic-entity engages in shutting down the new opinion or evidence in order to preserve the dogma. Therefore, according to Theory of Self-Relativity, the main reason for the existence of a dogma is to control people by limiting people's critical-thinking abilities.

Theory of Self-Relativity categorizes the role of dogma and sanctity binarily:

1. **Protecting the authority or the dogmatic-entity:** By instilling fear and negative-consequences, dogmatic rules and statements are designed to protect an authoritarian-entity or a sacred-concept against challenges and questions regarding the factuality or the truth associated with the dogmatic claim. Dogmas, at their core, are unstable and would fall apart under scrutiny when questioned, when challenged, and especially, when criticized. Since dogmas are built on factually unsupported weak foundations, dogmas often associate themselves with negative-consequences or loss of positive-rewards in order to protect the authority or the concept associated with the dogma. The real or imaginary consequences, or the potential loss of rewards, associated with questioning dogmas and dogmatic-authorities are integral with all dogmatic and authoritarian claims; because fear and consequence ensures that the followers blindly believe in the dogma, and that they abstain from questioning the substance of the dogma. By claiming the dogmatic-entity as sacred; sanctity protects the dogmatic authority or belief from being undermined and dismantled.

    Censorship or Sanctity is the last refuge of a person or an entity who can't handle the truth.

2. **Controlling people:** As discussed, fear is an effective tactic to bring people under control. Even more effective, is fear which is based on claims that are not open to questions or challenges, because questioning or challenging them for factuality could expose their lack of substance. However, by instilling fear of punishment to even think about questioning their validity or factuality; dogmas place a protective shield around their claims to ensure their longevity and survival. Additionally, by promising imaginary and unproven rewards for believing, many dogmas exercise control through deception.

The chicanery of dogma and sanctity lies in their ingenious structure of making believers feel good, while maintaining control over them.

Dogmas and sacred-beliefs are easily adopted and believed by many, because believing in something that is comforting and gives hope, regardless of its factuality, is a form of placebo-thinking. Dogmas, sanctity, and as a whole, religion and other ideologies succeed because they enable people to selfishly feel good and have a sense of belonging. In other words, they enable and encourage self-deception, which is one of the main enemies of self-improvement.

However, according to Theory of Self-Relativity:

The more ideological and entitled a person or an entity becomes, the more chance of it falling on its own weight.

Religion and dogma give people the option to believe and feel good, or to not believe and face the consequences of their lack of faith and belief. When faced with two choices that are intended to yield the same result, the natural and selfish tendency is to accept the choice that on the surface is comforting and comes across as caring and positive.

Religion is selfish because it deceptively gives comfort by making people feel special.

When a belief such as religion or an ideology is broadly held and believed, it not only gives the believer rewarding feelings of acceptance by belonging to a group, which is the basis of cults; but it also gives the believer a reason to not question the false but hopeful and comforting message of the ideology or the dogma.

Dogmatic Fallacy: Since it is comforting and is believed by many, therefore it must be true.

As discussed, this logical-fallacy is often referred to as an "appeal-to-popularity." This is why, true self-improvement could only be achieved by thinking and by evaluating everything factually, and not by what others believe to be true or for how long they've been believing it. When we set our default-state-of-existence as being skeptical rather than faithfully-believing; we can then evaluate ours and others' thoughts and beliefs based on their supportive facts. By learning to think factually, we can separate our Self from the masses of believers, who like a herd of sheep, follow unfounded-beliefs. Skepticism helps to strengthen our critical-thinking abilities.

A dogma is simply smoke and mirrors that covers up the true nature of the person or the authority that is creating and enforcing the dogmatic claim. This is why, Theory of Self-Relativity designates "Self" as the most important word, because it should not matter what other-people claim and what their intent for those claims are; what matters is for us to be able to evaluate the factuality of those claims objectively. Seeking facts and thinking factually is the core of true and stable self-improvement. By seeking the facts behind any claim, including dogmatic ones, we can then set our Self on the path of bringing the focus onto our own Self. If we cannot find the facts associated with a claim or a belief, we can then dismiss the claim or the belief as being nonfactual; hence, we can abstain from acting upon it.

Beliefs and opinions which are without evidence or facts could also become the basis of many prejudices and biases. In self-dogmatism, the dogmatic person could even create a false confirmation-bias in order to self-convince that the dogma is not only real but it is factual. Dogmatism can not only hold true in religious and political settings, but it could also apply to intellectual and scientific settings. For example, scientists could have such deep desires to reach a certain scientific outcome, that they might choose to ignore the evidence in order to have their opinion or desired-outcome to be true. In this example, even though the evidence does not support the opinion or the hypothesis, scientists could take nonfactual dogmatic approaches to fit the facts to their theories, rather than fitting their theories to the facts. Therefore, a dogmatic-belief is not exclusively a religious or a supernatural mindset; but it is a manmade mindset that could be broadly applicable. Although dogmas are the hallmark of cults, religions, and authoritarian principles, dogmas can take shape in all aspects of human cognition which support a comforting and desired outcome; but ignore the factual-truth.

In order to not be influenced, controlled, and even fooled by manipulative and controlling claims, we must always seek the facts associated with that claim; especially, when an individual or a society of people is making those claims. Should we think of something that has never been thought of before, or that we have never been exposed to before; we should always seek to find the facts which support these thoughts. Likewise, should we be told or be preached a claim by someone else, we should always seek and even demand the supportive evidence, or the reason-based argument for that claim. If evidence and facts could not be presented, or if the claimant diverges by changing the subject-matter, or engages in fear mongering and blame-shifting tactics; it will be safer for us to assume that the claim does not have factual-merit, because the burden of proof is incumbent upon the claimant.

True and stable self-improvement is achieved by seeking evidence, and by factually thinking about the subject matter. If evidence could not be found, we should either continue seeking evidence before committing to believe or accept the claim;

or we should simply dismiss the claim and move on. Although thinking factually places factual-thinking on a collision course with religion, with cultural-traditions, and even with supernatural-spirituality; Theory of Self-Relativity is not antagonistic nor does it condemn the exercise of such thoughts and practices. As long as exercising, but not believing, such thoughts and practices could act as temporary relaxing and calming methods, but not as the basis of our decision-making and existence; such breaks from reality could have similar effects as watching a movie, meditating, or getting a massage-therapy.

Believing in God and being religious does not have to be absolute; because we don't have to be a fundamental-theist or a radical-atheist. As discussed throughout Theory of Self-Relativity, believing in something should only be a temporary state-of-mind until evidence is found to turn that thought or belief into knowledge. However, if facts and evidence for a belief could not be found, that belief must be discarded, or at the minimum, it should not be acted upon, until supportive facts and evidence are found.

To be in sync with reality; seek facts, and remain unbiased and adaptable.

Intuition is another difficult to define state-of-mind that enables us to make decisions. Although if approached properly, intuition could be a valuable tool for decision-making and problem-solving, people commonly and mistakenly view intuition as an inherent mystical force that is closely related to our feelings; hence, it is commonly believed that if we learn to properly tap into our intuition or our feelings, we will somehow magically be able to make the right decision and take the best action. Furthermore, because intuition is difficult to define, and because intuition is best perceived than understood; majority refer to intuition as our gut-feeling and sometimes as our instincts, therefore, they misunderstand and confuse the cognitive-basis of intuition with the emotional-experience of feelings.

Although intuition and instincts are closely related, they are not the same; because, instincts are more primitive and they are inherently deeper imbedded in our non-conscious. Intuition is also commonly referred to as the ability to acquire knowledge without proof, evidence, or conscious-reasoning; or without understanding how the knowledge was acquired. Additionally, intuition is described as immediate apprehension, direct perception of truth independent of any reasoning-process, and as having unexplained feelings that something is true, even though we have no evidence for it being true. Therefore, intuition portrays immediate knowledge that relies on senses and feelings, instead of facts and logical reasoning.

However, Theory of Self-Relativity disagrees with these notions, as for example, our younger Self would not have the same intuitions as our older Self does; because our older Self has more knowledge and experience about what we are being intuitive about. Furthermore, even in the case of our instincts, although our younger Self would inherently be preprogrammed with some basic-instincts; our older Self's instincts would be more mature and more complex than our younger Self's instincts would have been.

Unlike popular views and definitions, according to Theory of Self-Relativity, although intuition is associated with perception and feelings; intuition is primarily a cognitive-process that relies on past-experiences and previously acquired knowledge, or belief of knowledge. Even though intuition appears to be feelings and perception based, Theory of Self-Relativity views intuition as no different than our other thinking and cognitive processes and skills; except that intuition is applied quicker and more on-the-go without necessarily waiting for all facts and data to be retrieved back from memory. Therefore, Theory of Self-Relativity strongly advocates that if we could learn to think quicker and cleverer, we could consequently improve our intuitive-skills. While intuition is a quicker application of our thoughts, knowledge, and experiences; our intuitions are slower and not as instantaneous as are our instincts.

Theory of Self-Relativity defines "intuition" as "the nonconscious mental-skill of quickly applying previously gained knowledge and experience to a current situation."

Simply stated:

Theory of Self-Relativity defines "intuition" as "a quick way of accessing personal knowledge and experience."

Theory of Self-Relativity considers intuition to be a nonconsciously acquired and applied mental-skill, and since this skill is often applied without verification of facts and reasoning; our intuitions or our gut-feelings could sometimes be wrong. The key consideration when referring to intuitions and instincts is that the "knowledge" we "believe" to have, is acquired and applied "without proof or reasoning." Simply stated, our intuition could be wrong because it could be based on a belief which we are incorrectly convinced to be knowledge. True knowledge must be based on facts; thus, without facts and evidence, what we believe to be knowledge, must be treated as a nonfactual-thought or a belief, unless and until supportive facts are identified. Therefore, intuitions and gut-feelings must be treated with skepticism and not acted upon for long-term problem-solving, unless they are followed through with factual verification.

When we say we have a gut-feeling, that means we don't have all the facts; we are speculating.

Our intuition is not a mysterious internal-force, our intuition is simply a quick way of accessing personal knowledge and experience; therefore, our intuitions could actually lead us to less than optimal results, if the applied-information that we relied on was incorrect.

Intuitions could be helpful in quick and singular decision-making situations, but not for long-term problem-solving processes.

This is why, bringing nonconscious intuitions, thoughts, and beliefs into our consciousness is important for awareness and for self-improvement. Since intuition refers to quickly accessing knowledge and information without fully verifying facts or reason, this is why, intuition is commonly referred to as having a gut-feeling.

Regardless of how we define intuition or gut-feeling, intuition is better viewed as a form of "perceived" information and knowledge, rather than as "verified" information and knowledge.

Intuition should be considered as "perceived" knowledge and not acted upon as "verified" knowledge.

As stated throughout Theory of Self-Relativity, our intangible-feelings and emotions are always caused by a thought which is as a result of our brain's activities. Our physical or tangible-feelings are generally caused by systemic and sensory triggers that cause brain-activity, which subsequently produces our tangible-feelings. A feeling is a symptom not a cause; therefore, a feeling cannot be the originator of a thought or a perception. A feeling is the result of a thought or the outcome of a stimulus triggering a thought; also referred to as neural-firings.

However, a gut-feeling is actually an oxymoron in its traditional definition, by attempting to represent as if an intelligent or cognitive function is coming from our gut. A gut-feeling is simply a visceral feeling in our gut caused by a thought in our brain. This thought, itself, could be triggered by an external-stimulus such as hearing something or seeing something; or it can be caused by internal-stimuli such as hormones. Hormones, themselves, could be triggered internally or as response to external-stimuli. Since a gut-feeling is a visceral feeling in our gut caused by neural-activity in our brain; hence, it is called a gut "feeling" and not gut "thinking."

Theory of Self-Relativity categorizes gut-feelings binarily:

1. **True gut-feelings**: Come from the gut or (The Gastro Intestinal Tract; a.k.a. the GI Tract) due to responses to physical or sensory stimuli. In Theory of Self-Relativity, this type of feeling is generally referred to as a tangible-feeling because it is caused by physical stimuli, and it has a physical trigger as its origin.

   • The GI track functions are governed by an autonomic nervous system known as the Enteric Nervous System (ENS) or the Intrinsic Nervous System. The ENS is a meshwork of neurons that operate automatically to govern the functions of our stomach and GI tract. The ENS is sometimes referred to as our second-brain because it can function automatically on its own without input from The Central Nervous System (CNS) and the brain; however, automatic functioning for movement of food does not mean cognitive and reasoning ability. The ENS produces 90% of the body's Serotonin as well as 50% of the body's Dopamine which are hormones that affect our mood. While the ENS could affect our mood and emotions hormonally; the ENS, contrary to popular belief, cannot carry out cognitive, thinking, or decision-making functions. Therefore, our gut-feeling cannot actually think for us. It is the effects of the hormones associated with our mood that make us perceive that we had a thought in our gut. A gut-feeling is not a thought in the gut; it is a feeling. The hormones in our gut, which themselves are instructed by our brain, are the triggers that stimulate further thoughts and neural-activities in our brain, which in-turn, create the feelings that we feel. In recent times, some opportunists, especially in the field of motivational-teaching, have tried to capitalize on the term "second-brain" as a mysterious part of human existence which "supposedly" affects the more mysterious and confusing non-physical aspects of our existence such as our thinking and our consciousness. Theory of Self-Relativity refutes such claims as the nervous system associated with the gut has no cognitive or critical-thinking abilities. Additionally, it is also believed that the microbiome in the gut, which are simply bacteria that live in the gut, could also affect our mood because they produce neurotransmitters; however, it must be noted that unlike sensationalistic claims by certain self-help teachings, the microbiome in our gut cannot create our thoughts nor do they direct our cognitive functions. Therefore, the microbiome, because of their ability to produce neurotransmitters, could affect our mood, but not our direct thinking.

2. **Perceived gut-feelings:** Commonly referred to as our "gut-feelings," are actually emotions that are based on our brain-activities and are influenced more as a result of our mood hormones produced in the gut, because of our thoughts. Theory of Self-Relativity refers to such feelings as intangible-feelings, because they are caused by thoughts and neural-activities in the brain, and not by physical triggers and stimuli.

   ● A thought originating from the mind and the brain is an actual thought that creates intangible-feelings and emotions that do not always have to be based on physical triggers and stimuli. Therefore, a feeling in the gut is not a thought in the gut; it is a feeling in the gut that is as the result of a thought in the brain, which itself could be affected by the hormonal activities in the gut. When referring to the traditional and classical gut-feeling based on the occurrence of an event, we often state "I had a feeling this was going to happen;" we less-commonly say "I thought it was going to happen." A gut-feeling or an intuition is a metaphor for a nonconscious-thought and quite often it is as a result of hindsight-bias. Because of this hindsight-bias, gut-feelings verify themselves as knowledge when a thought, especially a nonconscious-thought, results in a future action or an event. For example, when thinking nonconsciously about something unaware and that thought materializes, we have a tendency of stating "I knew it was going to happen;" while often, we selectively-ignore the many times that our thoughts did not materialize. We retroactively treat the nonconscious-thought that manifested itself as a feeling that we had at the time of its onset; and we incorrectly categorize that feeling as prior-knowledge. As discussed in earlier sections, a hindsight-bias is a past feeling which based on current facts and knowledge presents itself as previously known knowledge. When we give credence to our gut-feeling as an intuition; it is this perceived gut-feeling closely associated with hindsight-bias that we are referencing.

We should always focus on our mind and on our brain for thinking and cognitive functions, not on our gut-feelings; because our gut can't think. As stated, our gut-feeling is metaphorically recognized as the same thing as our intuition. Although an intuition is popularly but incorrectly assimilated as a nonconscious cognitive-function that is not feelings-based; Theory of Self-Relativity considers our intuitions as cognitive-functions that are commonly feelings-based.

The difference is when we attach more emotions to a certain intuition than other intuitions, we call that particular intuition a gut-feeling. Since intuitions are cognitive-functions and thoughts that are sometimes perceived as emotional-activities or as feelings; as demonstrated by Theory of Self-Relativity, our intuitions could strengthen with more knowledge and with further experience. Consequently, since intuitions could be enhanced and improved, therefore, an intuition is a nonconscious-skill that we can improve; but to do so, we must approach intuition from a cognitive-perspective, and not from the perspective of perception or a feeling.

Our thinking comes from our mind which represents our physical-brain; thus, our thinking does not come from our gut, as there is no brain in our gut. The ENS, which is a collection of neural-networks in our gut, does not represent thinking and has no cognitive neural-pathways. For neurons to function in thinking and cognitive capacities, these neurons and their neural-pathways must be specifically developed for thinking and cognitive-functions. Although our stomach and heart could function independently of our brain, they cannot function as cognitive and thinking organs instead of our brain. We cannot have consciousness without our brain; even though our ENS, stomach, and our heart could carry their specific functions for a period of time after brain-death.

We must learn to think with our mind based on facts, and not to think with our heart based on our feelings.

Cognition, as a mental function, is different than feelings and senses. Definition of intuition is challenging because it is impossible to explain a thinking and cognitive function through feelings and emotions; especially if intuition is being referenced interchangeably with a gut-feeling.

Emotions are the resulting symptom of their underlying thoughts.

Our feelings are always valid, but our feelings and emotions, in the absence of supportive facts and reason, are irrational; therefore, our gut-feeling has no rationality. This is why, our intuitions, especially as predictive mindsets, often prove to be wrong. Hence, to qualify our feelings rationally, we must identify and verify the rationality and factuality of the thoughts that create our feelings.

We must make sure our emotions make us feel what we must feel; not make us think how we want to feel.

Although there are potential connections between diseases of the gut and their effects on the brain, as well as a relationship between micro-organisms or micro-biota in our gut and their influence on our mood; according to Theory of Self-Relativity, our instincts and our intuitions are not primarily governed to the physiology of our gut, they are primarily governed by our conscious and nonconscious thoughts coming from our brain.

Do not confuse mood, which is what we feel, with thoughts, which are what we think.

When analyzed cognitively, it is realized that our intuitions are based on knowledge and experience that we gained from our past, or from others; often without our awareness of when this knowledge or experience was acquired. Intuition, and some instincts, are learned or evolved via experience, as they are collections of thoughts, knowledge, and experience that come together for us to act upon. Therefore, as defined by Theory of Self-Relativity, intuition, just like confidence, is a skill and not a mysterious internal force. Intuition is a cognitive-process and not a pure feelings-based attribute; hence, intuition is the thought component which leads to our gut-feeling, which in-turn, leads us to our behavior. For simplicity, intuition can be recognized as a skill of applying knowledge and experience to a situation which requires quick action, but one that is not as instant and as impulsive as a situation that requires acting on instincts. Therefore, intuitions do not commonly involve critical-thinking at time of application.

Intuition is similar to our thinking, except intuition is nonconscious, and it is usually engaged without our awareness.

Instincts are embedded thoughts, knowledge, and experiences which exist even deeper in our nonconscious mind than intuitions do. Instincts are generally innate or inherited and they are usually primitive in nature; but they could also be enhanced through learning and experience. Therefore, according to Theory of Self-Relativity, instincts are also skills when repeated and strengthened through awareness, understanding and application of factual-thinking.

Intuitions and instincts come together and are implemented as a result of our experiences and learned repetitive-skills; thus, intuitions and instincts are brain-based. Unlike thoughts and conscious-thinking which could linger, ruminate, and persist; intuitions and instincts are quick, often instantaneous and even impulsive, with less associated lingering feelings.

Intuitions and instincts are not mysterious forces coming from our gut; they are cerebral and cognitive-processes.

Because we are often unaware of our intuitive and instinctive thoughts coming together nonconsciously, we tend to mistake intuitions and instincts as gut-based thinking phenomenon. Likewise, since intuitions and instincts often lead to quick or even instantaneous action after the onset of a thought; intuitions and instincts are nonconscious-thoughts that are closely associated with hormones produced in the gut.

It is because of the intimate relationship of intuitions and instincts with our gut-based hormones, that intuitions and instincts are mistakenly "felt" to originate in our gut.

Furthermore, intuitions and instincts are not chance, luck, or magic based; they are based on nonconscious-thoughts and experiences which are quick and short lasting. Intuitions and instincts commonly grow below consciousness and become more precise and effective through repetition and experience.

Intuitions and instincts are thoughts and cognitive-processes that generally happen without "conscious-reasoning;" hence the mystery associated with them.

Since intuitions and instincts are based on past-experiences and prior knowledge, intuitions and instincts have already been cognitively evaluated and reasoned at some point in the past prior to their time of application. According to Theory of Self-Relativity:

Intuitions and instincts are the nonconsciousness-thoughts that are causing our gut-feelings.

Our intuitions and instincts are necessary in making quick judgments and taking quick actions, but this association of our intuitions and instincts does not necessarily mean that our intuitions and instincts are always correct or factual. Theory of Self-Relativity considers our intuitions, and to a certain extent our instincts, to be a collection of thoughts and cognitive-processes that are below consciousness which could be influenced and improved by increasing knowledge, experience, and repetition.

Intuitions and instincts are skills; hence, they can be improved.

By becoming aware of our nonconscious-thoughts and by learning to recognize our intuitions, we can learn to have better clarity about our unaware-thoughts; and as we learn to think factually, we can begin to store our knowledge, experiences, and factual-thoughts below our consciousness where our instincts and intuitions reside. Factual-thinking strengthens our intuitions and instincts, and the more we implement factual-thinking, the more precise our intuitions and instinctual skills will become. As we learn to become more aware of our thoughts and intuitions, and as we imbed more factual-thoughts into our intuitions, we will in-turn be able to strengthen our instincts. When we incorporate factual-thinking as the skillset for our thinking-system; we will not only begin to think quicker and cleverer, but our intuitions and instincts will follow suit. We can quicken our intuitions and we can sharpen our instincts as we learn to intuit our factual-thinking skills.

Intuitions and instincts can be improved and quickened via factual-thinking and repetition.

By fine-tuning our intuitions and instincts as components of our thinking-system, we can further gain control in our life by minimizing uncertainties. When we make better, quicker, and cleverer decisions that are based on evidence and factual-reality, we can become more independent of others and we can become more self-sufficient. Hence, as we learn to improve our thinking, our intuitions, and even our instincts, we can subsequently become a more efficient and faster operating individual in all aspects of our life. Since intuitions and instincts rely on prior knowledge and past-experience; by ensuring that our knowledge is factually-verified and our experiences are based on factual-thinking, we can quicken our thinking-system to blend in with our intuitions and instincts. Such state-of-mind and thinking-system can significantly increase our ability to become independent and self-sufficient; and in-turn, become less dependent on others. It is this type of quick and clever thinking-system that will enable us to set proper borders and boundaries, and to have our relationships be based on respect and compatibility, and not based on neediness, disrespect, control, or even abuse.

When we take control of our life, we can make better and quicker decisions for our Self. In doing so, we can accept unfavorable results, should we make the wrong decision; and we can change our approach quickly if our original approach does not seem to be working. True self-improvement allows us to make better choices for our Self, and it also disallows bad outcomes from remaining stagnant with the hope of things getting better on their own. By taking-charge, self-improvement also minimizes reliance on others and their ability to make decisions for us.

Choices and decisions made by others are seldom as favorable or as desirable as the decisions we make for our own Self.

Therefore, true self-improvement must come from within and must be independent of others; hence why, it is called self-improvement, and not, others'-improvement. The only means of accomplishing internally-derived self-improvement is by becoming independent and self-reliant, and by having high levels of control and certainty in our life. This is why, "Dependency and Reliance" is designated as one of the 10-Enemies of Self-Improvement; and, "Independence and Self-Reliance" is one of the 10-Commandments for Self-Improvement.

Current popular but not necessarily evolved approaches in psychotherapy, life-coaching, and motivational and self-help programs are mostly arduous and exhausting, with often ineffective and difficult to maintain applications. Many of these programs are not only inefficient, but they are extremely frustrating. For example, motivational programs pound the table for us to stop complacency and to commit to action, meditation recommends minimizing thinking and observing thoughts, while long-term psychotherapy advocates getting in touch with our feelings; however, many of these programs are not pragmatic for our modern, technologically-oriented and fast-paced life.

While some motivational programs try to push us to become committed and less-complacent, they fail to show us a consistently repeatable and effective technique that would get us to commit and to not procrastinate. Furthermore, techniques such as meditation and mindfulness recommend us to spend countless hours to clear our mind from thinking. As discussed in detail throughout Theory of Self-Relativity, this is completely opposite of what our mind needs to do and what it is intended to do; which is to think efficiently and factually so that it can unclutter itself from unnecessary thoughts. Our mind is a thinking-machine and its job is to think continuously; therefore, it is an impossible task to get our mind to think less, or to not think at all. To try to get our mind to think less is like getting the Sun to circle the Earth. Although the Sun going around the Earth seemed logical from the perspective of our ancestors who lacked knowledge; it was similar lack of understanding of how the brain functions that made people imagine that slowing-down thinking would unclutter the mind.

Just as in ancient-times it was incorrectly thought that the Sun revolved the Earth; it's also been incorrectly thought that slowing-down thinking, improves thinking.

Centuries ago, when life was much simpler and when science and technology were not as advanced; in the absence of fast-paced modern-day mobility and the need to multitask, people could afford to take hours off to try to meditate as they didn't have much else to do. They didn't have as many fast-moving thoughts to deal with; therefore, thinking less was a natural result of simply unwinding and relaxing. Centuries ago, people had so much extra time on their hands that they not only had time to meditate and think very little, but their minds were forced to come up with fantastical thoughts in order to keep the thought-process going. This is how, many ancient rituals and nonfactual-beliefs and practices were created.

The mind is a thinking-machine and when it doesn't have real things to think about, it will begin fabricating things to think about; thus, if our mind cannot find internally originated thoughts to think about, it will wander off to the outside of our Self to find things to think about.

Furthermore, most psychotherapies suggest we get in touch with and focus on our feelings in order to try to feel better; however, as discussed, feeling better does not correspond with improving the realities of our life. Getting in touch with our feelings by becoming aware is an important step for self-improvement, but it is no different than simply observing our thoughts without thinking about them. It simply cannot be done, because simple awareness without follow through is like taking a thirsty person to the water but not letting them drink the water.

The intent of some of these teachings and practices is often to try to make us realize that awareness, as an initial first step for self-improvement is important; however, awareness, just by itself, is not going to help us improve, if awareness is not followed through with understanding and implementation. Additionally, many of these methods and practices were developed decades, if not centuries ago, when the pace and requirements of life were different. Our current fast-paced life requires awareness, understanding, and implementation to occur at a much quicker and more intuitive manner. This is why, The Cognitive-Cognition-Technique is one of the best tools available to develop, quicken, and enhance our thinking-skills. Since awareness of feelings is important, proper awareness of our feelings also leads to the awareness of our thoughts that create our feelings. By becoming aware of our thoughts, we can then evaluate our thoughts for their factuality; thus, we can choose to accept or dismiss those thoughts. As we accept or dismiss our thoughts, we can then resolve, improve, or eliminate our feelings; hence, we will be able to properly take action or we can choose inaction.

Therefore, to improve constantly and consistently, the best way to take-charge of our life is to use our feelings-awareness to get in touch with and to become aware of our thoughts. Through this mindfulness and thought-awareness, we can then evaluate our thoughts individually and choose to keep or discard them based on their factuality. The process-of-elimination and the binary-thought-processing enable us to filter-out unnecessary, nonfactual, and cluttering-thoughts, and to only keep thoughts that are factual. The Cognitive-Cognition-Technique enables us to use the symptoms of our feelings to find the causal-thoughts of our feelings. As we identify and improve the causal-thoughts, we can improve our feelings; thus, we can improve our actions, and as a whole, we can improve the quality of our life.

Independence, self-reliance, control, and certainty, could only be achieved and strengthened if we decide to take-charge of our own life, by improving our own Self. Therefore, we must stop looking externally and we must bring the focus onto our own Self from within so that we can begin to take-charge of our life. This could only be accomplished by us taking personal-responsibility to become the "agent" of our own change so that we can create and control our own destiny. Although Theory of Self-Relativity does not accept the notion of a destiny in the traditional spiritual or supernatural definition; thereby, it references destiny as the path forward that our decisions and actions take us. According to Theory of Self-Relativity, destiny is not predetermined, but it is self-created and self-influenced.

Theory of Self-Relativity defines "destiny" as "the outcome of personal action or inaction."

Independence and self-reliance, control and certainty, and personal-responsibility, are 3 important Commandments that are interrelated and will help us launch our path to a more content, fulfilled, and happier life. Therefore, in order for us to improve our life, we must become our own agent of change and improvement, by taking self-agency and personal-responsibility.

It is our self-given-right and our self-responsibility to live the best life possible.

VII.
Self-Agency & Personal-Responsibility

Dependency and reliance, which lead to an increase in lack of control and uncertainty, are some of the main factors in our inability to self-improve. Dependency on others, further gets prolonged and becomes chronic when we are incapable of taking matters in our own hands because we refuse to take charge to begin the process of change and transformation towards independence and self-reliance.

The more chronic one's dependency and reliance on others becomes, the longer and the more effort it will take for the person to change and improve. It is this negative self-fulfilling prophecy that shifts the focus of the dependent person away from the Self onto others, and commonly creates a state of blame-shifting and self-victimization. According to Theory of Self-Relativity, blame-shifting and self-victimization are classic forms of externalation, because they are rooted in shifting the focus of the self-equation externally in order to avoid introspection. Blame-shifting and self-victimization often coexist with other personality-traits such as self-pity, self-sympathy, self-doubt, hypocrisy, taking things personally, and being easily offended. In extreme externalation cases where blame-shifting and self-victimization are common traits; a sense-of-entitlement is also commonly present.

According to Theory of Self-Relativity, if unaware and uncontrolled; chronic blame-shifting and self-victimization could become a disabling defense-mechanism and a coping-skill. Those who blame-shift and self-victimize as a defense-mechanism, often do so in conjunction with other externally directed unhealthy defense-mechanisms and coping-skills such as projection, denial, deflection, and dissociation; and they do so as a means of trying to abstain from the discomfort of taking personal-responsibility for their decisions and actions. Although some lack of control and uncertainty happens without one's choice or awareness; if one wants to change one's circumstances for the better, one must have the desire and one must want to commit and personally initiate the process of self-improvement to increase control in one's life. This is why, desire and introspection are the two non-negotiables for change and for self-improvement; and why, others and externalation are the most dangerous words for self-improvement. Desire and introspection allow us to self-reflect and identify our self-deficiencies and personal-shortcomings so that we can then take charge to improve them. However, recognizing our deficiencies and shortcomings does not mean to feel self-pity, or to self-bash, and to self-denigrate because we happen to have identified our weaknesses.

Furthermore, while Theory of Self-Relativity considers self-empathy, self-compassion, and self-love as important attributes for self-awareness and for self-improvement; too much self-empathy and too much self-compassion could also be counter-productive and inhibiting. Too much self-empathy and too much self-compassion could turn into self-pity and self-sympathy, which often coexist with blame-shifting and self-victimization. Too much self-pity often leads to the creation of a victim mentality; which in-turn, shifts the personal-responsibility to improve one's circumstances away from the Self. Therefore, it is important to ensure that self-empathy and self-compassion do not deviate from self-care, into self-victimization.

Although self-victimization brings the focus to the Self; such self-focus that results in chronic self-pity, similar to the feelings of guilt and shame, is a negative-self-focus. Negative-self-focus could be as bad as lack of self-awareness, if not worst; because it could inhibit a person from accepting that they could change and improve their circumstances. Negative-self-focus such as self-pity and self-doubt creates a mental-state of hopelessness which is completely inhibiting to change and improvement, as it often defaults back to dependency and reliance on others.

Theory of Self-Relativity defines "negative-self-focus" as "when self-reflection and introspection disable a person from change and improvement."

As discussed, introspection is an integral requirement for self-improvement; however, introspection is also a difficult task to undertake, because introspection reveals many of our personal-weaknesses and self-deficiencies which could be uncomfortable and even painful to confront. Introspection becomes powerful and constructive when the personal-weaknesses and self-deficiencies that introspection reveals are used as awareness for change and improvement.

Introspection could backfire if the revelation of personal-weaknesses and self-deficiencies disable a person from moving past the negativities. By dwelling and by even becoming incapacitated in the face of these personal-shortcomings, we could begin to develop feelings of self-doubt and hopelessness, and we could consequently sink into a mental-state of self-pity. Self-doubt and hopelessness inhibit change, which in-turn, often leads to self-pity. Self-pity commonly leads to chronic self-victimization, which in-turn, creates further dependency and reliance on others; hence the cycle continues. This vicious cycle takes effect because when we are weak and hopeless, our natural tendency becomes seeking, relying on, and waiting for others to help us to feel better; or, we end up depending on others to get things done for us.

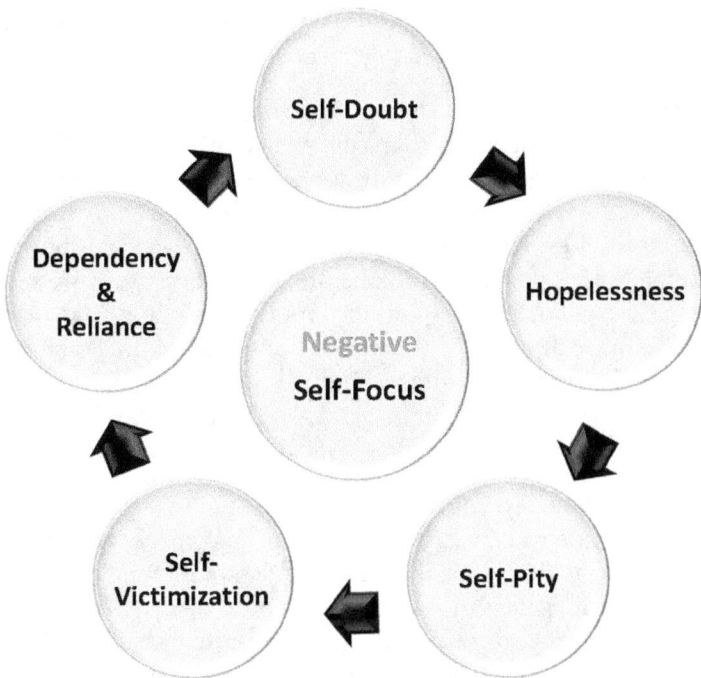

This is why, independence and self-reliance are integral for breaking the bonds of dependency on others. To become independent and self-reliant, and to have more control and certainty in our life; we must take personal-responsibility to change, improve, and transform our Self. No one or nothing could make decisions or take actions to change our circumstances for the better, as we can do for our own Self. Just as we cannot pay someone else to diet and exercise for us to lose weight; likewise, we cannot depend on or rely on other-people or on other-things to improve our lives, or to improve how we feel.

Personal-responsibility is best accomplished by us putting our Self in the middle of Our-Universe, and by learning to live a centered-self life. Although centered-self living makes us the most important entity in Our-Universe; being centered-self also makes our Self the most responsible entity for our own well-being and happiness. This means, we must become the "agent" who will be in charge of changing and improving our life.

Centered-self living not only makes us the most important person in our life; but, centered-self living also makes us the most responsible person for our own well-being and happiness.

While other-people and other-things could add value to our life and help us achieve our purpose, goals, and dreams faster; no one can replace our central position for initiating, changing, and improving our own life. Therefore, in order to take personal-responsibility, we must learn to have and to implement *"Self-Agency."*

Theory of Self-Relativity defines "self-agency" as "taking personal-responsibility to control and apply one's own thoughts, feelings, and behavior."

Self-agency gives us the ability to make our own decisions and to choose our own choices in order to take the best actions that would influence our "Self" favorably. Personal-responsibility gives us the obligation to ensure that the decisions that we make, the choices that we choose, and the actions that we take, are based on sound reasoning and solid evidence. Self-agency and personal-responsibility enable us to think before we speak and to think before we act; because, if we say or do the wrong things, we will then be responsible for our own actions and we will not be able to self-victimize or blame-shift our bad decisions and unfavorable-outcomes onto other-people or on other-things. Similarly, self-agency and personal-responsibility enable us to take credit for our good-decision and favorable-actions, and to not consider them as insignificant or as lucky.

Factual-thinking and analytical-reasoning enable us to strengthen our agency and responsibility, because when we take charge to be in control of our affairs and our life, facts and reason will give us the solid foundation to build our life on. When we learn to have self-agency and when we accept to take personal-responsibility, we will not be searching for reason or purpose externally, and neither would we try to find our destiny; we will create our own purpose and we will guide our own destiny. As discussed:

Theory of Self-Relativity defines "destiny" as "the outcome of personal action or inaction."

Although the concept of predetermined destiny is a comforting one, as if there are higher powers who for the sake of having our best interests in mind have predefined our destiny and all we have to do is to find it; according to Theory of Self-Relativity, this manmade concept of destiny is simply a form of placebo-thinking. By believing that we were given a hidden purpose and that we have a destiny, we make our Self feel better than we would have felt otherwise if we didn't have the hope and the wishful-belief of a good destiny. However, such mindset that is disconnected from reality often leads us to making decisions and taking actions that are not in sync with how factual-reality is; in other words, we end up taking action or inaction that sets us back, or even does us harm, because by believing in destiny, we choose to leave things to chance. As discussed:

When left to chance, there are more ways for things to go wrong than for things to go right.

Primitive-humans had to believe and associate everything with a reason and purpose in order for them to avoid danger, to stay safe, and to survive. Assigning agency, especially intentional-agency, is an inherent and instinctive mental process that we undertake because when our ancestors in the African savannas detected the movement of tree branches, they stayed safe by assuming that a wild animal, (who is an agent), that could eat them, (which is its purpose), caused the movement; instead of assuming that the movement of the branches was simply because of the wind. Those who assumed it was a wild animal, but it was simply the wind; they made a false-positive error which did not cause them any negative consequences. However, those who assumed it was the wind, but it was a wild-animal, they became prey. Therefore, we learned very early on in our evolution that we can be safer, hence we would feel better, when we assumed agency; even when no agent existed or was necessary. We did so because believing in an intentional-agent minimized uncertainty, even if the belief was fabricated, fallacious, and without evidence. Thus, knowing or assigning an intentional-agent, especially to difficult or dislikable situations, has a comforting effect.

Humans are instinctively programmed to assume agency, in order to stay safe, and to feel better.

As our ancestors evolved and as they realized assigning purpose and agency to things and events kept them safe and made them feel better, they began to assign external purpose and agency to things that did not have any purpose or intentional-agents. They further began assigning purpose and agency to things that did not threaten their safety; but assigning agency made them feel good and was comforting. Our ancestors used their analytical abilities as intelligent primates, and later on as ancient civilizations, to assign non-existent agency to things and events in order to experience the comforting result of feeling safe. For example, as primitive-humans advanced into ancient-civilizations, they assigned purpose and agency to the wind, thunder, lightning, and other naturally occurring phenomenon that had no purpose or agents. This is how, religion, superstitions and supernatural-beliefs began. By assuming reason and purpose, and by assigning imagined intentional-agents with reason and purpose that supposedly caused the events, humans created "beliefs" to make themselves feel safer and to feel better; hence why, beliefs, especially long-held beliefs, are closely associated with feelings.

This external assumption of reason and purpose to a cause, and the assignment of an intentional-agent with a purpose to the cause, is one of the main nonconscious reasons we have difficulty taking personal-responsibility for our own Self. Because, when we have difficulties that need improvement, it is easier to assume that there is a reason and purpose for our difficulty, and that a "caring" intentional imaginary agent is causing it; therefore, our difficulty will eventually get better on its own. It is easier to assume that there is a reason or purpose for everything, because such assumptions make us feel better in the short-term; although our troubles remain and often get worse in the longer-term. It is easier to use our intellect to fool our Self, because it is more time-consuming and more effort-based to become the responsible self-agent in charge of improving our circumstances. It is easier to concoct a fallacy to quickly but temporarily feel better, than it is to have to face the difficulties that need to be addressed and resolved. As discussed, Theory of Self-Relativity has termed this creation of false-thoughts in order to justify and rationalize our comforting-feelings and resulting behavior, as "placebo-thinking."

Theory of Self-Relativity defines "placebo-thinking" as "thoughts that we concoct regardless of their factuality in order to support our desired feelings."

Or simply stated:

Placebo-thinking is "to think based on how we want to feel."

This is why, many believe in a predetermined destiny caused by an intentional-agent; because it feels good and it takes the responsibility away from our Self, by making other-things or other-people, even if completely imaginary, as the responsible or intentional-agent for our circumstances and our existence. As discussed throughout Theory of Self-Relativity, neither our destiny nor our purpose is found nor given; they must come from within us, which means, we must become the responsible agent for the creation and guidance of our own destiny.

We must create our own purpose and we must guide our own destiny.

As long as destiny is perceived as a path of decisions and actions which move us forward in time, destiny could be a good imaginary metaphor for the forward direction of our life. Destiny must not be viewed as an autopiloted mystical road that takes us into the future; destiny must be perceived as a self-created road that we are shaping with every step that we take forward. If we do not accept the self-agency and personal-responsibility that is required for building the path of our destiny; that road will never be built on its own, and it will not lead us to any significant destination. Although Theory of Self-Relativity does not accept the notion of a destiny in the traditional spiritual or supernatural definition; it references destiny as the metaphorical path forward that our personally implemented decisions and actions take us. Unlike popular belief, and as discussed, according to Theory of Self-Relativity, destiny is not predetermined; but it is self-created, self-guided, and self-influenced. To reiterate:

Theory of Self-Relativity defines "destiny" as "the outcome of personal action or inaction."

Therefore, according to Theory of Self-Relativity, the concept of destiny is similar to the concept of luck; where neither are things that happen to us without our control or input. As discussed:

Theory of Self-relativity defines "luck" as "when determination and action create opportunity."

Hence, since destiny is also defined as an outcome that is as a result of our own "personal" action or inaction; therefore, both destiny and luck are as a result of our determination and actions yielding results, often as they cross paths with chance. As further discussed:

Theory of Self-Relativity defines "chance" as "the possibility or probability of something happening."

Therefore:

Chance is universal because it is probabilistic, but luck is personal because it is effort-based.

Since according to Theory of self-Relativity, destiny is not predetermined, and since as discussed previously, humans have the free-will to make decisions to influence their lives and their outcomes; therefore, by learning to have self-agency and by taking on personal-responsibility, we can be the best captain of our own life.

By bringing the focus onto our own Self, self-agency and personal-responsibility give us more control and allows us to become more independent and less-reliant on others. Self-agency and personal-responsibility also teach us to take matters in our own hands, to make our own choices, and to live with the results of our own decisions. Self-agency and personal-responsibility enable us to make changes and to shift directions based on our own decisions; and to not be thrown around by the decisions and actions of others.

Decisions made by others will seldom be as favorable or as desirable as the decisions we make for our own Self.

Self-agency and personal-responsibility enable us to properly evaluate our interactions with our Self and with others so that we can make the best decisions, and take the best actions in order to guide our life forward, in the most favorable path of our own "personally-designed" destiny.

To truly self-improve and continue to transform, we must bring reliance back onto our own Self, and we must become as independent as possible. Therefore, true independence could only be achieved by taking matters in our own hands; which means, we must become our own "agent" of change and transformation. As difficult as taking on personal-responsibility might be initially; in the long run, to be in control of our own decisions and to guide our own actions will enable us to have a more balanced, a more content, and a more fulfilled life. This is why, Theory of Self-Relativity insists that our purpose and our destiny must come from within; because:

To be fulfilled, don't just dream big; make your purpose bigger.

One of the main contributors to having self-agency and personal-responsibility is to learn to have self-regulation, which is best achieved via self-reflection. As discussed, awareness and introspection are key to identifying and understanding our deficiencies and shortcomings, and the most important thing that such self-reflection achieves is the awareness and understanding of our thoughts; because according to Theory of Self-Relativity:

We are our thoughts.

Although we are often unaware of our thoughts as we are more aware of our feelings and our behavior; our thoughts are what create our feelings, our behavior, and our self-identity.

Mindfulness, thoughtfulness, and thought-management, in combination with self-awareness and self-reflection, allow us to achieve self-regulation. When we learn to regulate our Self internally through cognition and via thought-management, rather than externally through assumption of purpose and agency, or through dependency and reliance on others; we can then be in more control of our own destiny, hence, we can be more in control of our own life. When we learn to self-regulate and become more in control of our life, we become less-worried and less-anxious, and we experience less feelings of fear, stress, or other negativities. The lessening of these negative-feelings, in-turn, leads us to a more balanced and calmer existence; because having control decreases uncertainty and self-doubt, which in-turn, strengthens our self-confidence.

The balance and harmony achieved through self-regulation puts us in charge of knowing that we can tackle any negativity that arises in our life, and that we can find a solution to any problem. This is how we create self-agency, and how we take on personal-responsibility to be in charge of our own life, and our own destiny.

Theory of Self-Relativity defines "self-regulation" as "one's ability to manage, regulate, and control one's thoughts, in order to experience better emotions and more favorable outcomes."

Self-regulation creates balance and harmony and puts us in charge of our life as it enables us to minimize negativities so that we can live in the contentment-zone. As discussed, to experience longer lasting positivity and more frequent happiness, we must first become content and fulfilled.

Since contentment is not only the necessary platform to reach positivity and happiness, but contentment is also the necessary platform to fall back on when our experiences of happiness begin to fadeaway; therefore, to live in the contentment-zone, we must be able to regulate our thoughts. By learning to have self-regulation via thought-management, we can subsequently access all of our preferred and desired states of experience from a much more achievable platform, namely contentment. By being self-regulated and by living in the contentment-zone, we can thus have the confidence to achieve anything that we put our mind and efforts to with greater ease, than if we were continuously sinking into the negativity-zone.

Self-regulation is best achieved and maintained via understanding and implementing Theory of Self-Relativity's 6-Cs of self-regulation.

6-Cs of Self-Regulation

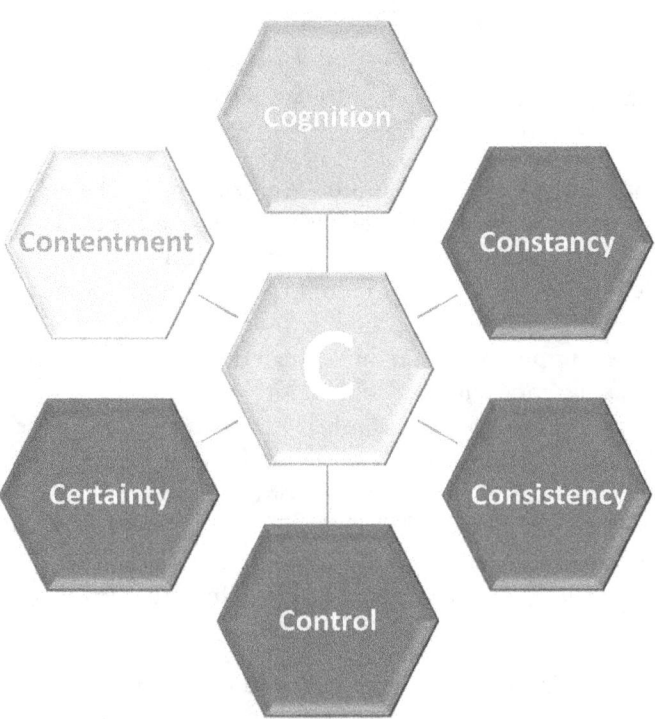

6-Cs of Self-Regulation:

1. **Cognition:** *Theory of Self-Relativity defines "cognition" as "awareness and understanding through mindfulness, thoughtfulness, and thought-management."* By becoming aware of our thoughts and by implementing The Cognitive-Cognition-Technique, we can evaluate the factualities of our thoughts so that we can manage our thoughts, our feelings, and our behavior accordingly.

2. **Constancy:** As we clear out the clutter from our thinking, and as we take control of our life by minimizing dependency and reliance on others; we can then take on self-agency and personal-responsibility to make self-improvement a constant part of our existence.

3. **Consistency:** As we filter out clutter and as we become more independent by constantly self-improving, we increase the level of consistency in our life. As we experience consistency, we experience less fluctuations and imbalances associated with worry, anxiety, and fear; hence, our existences become more balanced, stable, and content.

4. **Control:** By minimizing our dependency and reliance on others, and by increasing our self-regulation, self-agency, and personal-responsibility; we become more in control of our Self, our destiny, and as a whole, of our own life.

5. **Certainty:** When we have more control in our life, we minimize uncertainty and we increase stability; which in-turn, creates the consistency for us to live with contentment.

6. **Contentment:** *Theory of Self-Relativity defines "contentment" as "a satisfactory state of neutral existence which is reached and maintained by minimization of negativities."*

Repetition of cognitive-skills and routines in behavior can be helpful and beneficial in creating the stability and balance that self-regulation and personal-responsibility bring about. Routines not only ease implementation and application of repeatable skills, but routines also minimize uncertainty by creating a sense of familiarity and predictability. Routines play an important role in our lives as they help create structure and organization through discipline. As discussed, discipline begins with having independence and self-reliance, which itself creates control and certainty; therefore, routines can help to strengthen discipline, which ultimately leads to an increase in self-confidence. Routines, especially the daily and repetitive ones, also create comfort-zones for our existence. Routines are important, especially in more primitive settings and in earlier developmental stages of animals and humans; for example, with toddlers, with children, and even with pets, routines create a sense of familiarity, which in-turn, increases the feelings of safety, certainty, and comfort.

While routines could make life's repetitive tasks more efficient and effective, routines could also create a false sense of security and a comfort-zone which could become inhibiting to change and self-improvement. When routines lose their efficacy of creating efficiency, and when routines are practiced as imaginary and unrealistic comforting tools to influence life and personal outcomes; that is when routines turn into rituals, and even bad-habits. Rituals could actually have negative effects on our decisions, our relationships, and on our future; especially if rituals are based on nonfactual-thoughts and unsupported mindsets, or when they are based on supernatural-beliefs and magical-thinking. If not managed, routines and rituals could also lead to unhealthy thinking, obsessive behavior, and the creation of bad-habits.

Although routines and rituals are both repetitive practices and actions, they are different in their purpose. Routines are repetitive tasks that help to streamline practices necessary for maintenance; for example, brushing our teeth, taking a shower, etc. However, rituals are repetitive practices that commonly have a non-factual and unproven human-imposed purpose; for example, religious prayer, spiritual practices, etc. Unlike routines, rituals commonly require more awareness and intentional action, while routines could be deeper at the nonconscious or lower-consciousness levels. Likewise, bad-habits are learned routines that cause continued mistakes which prevent change and progress; and often create setbacks.

As Albert Einstein famously stated: *"Insanity is doing the same thing over and over again expecting different results."*

While rituals have purpose, which is often an externally imagined or supernatural-based comforting purpose; rituals could actually become inhibiting if they do not contribute to, or if they prevent progress, change, and improvement. Unlike other self-help programs, Theory of Self-Relativity recommends minimization and elimination of rituals, because rituals could not only be inhibiting, but they could also be damaging and outright dangerous. It is a fine line between routines which are intended to create efficiency and harmony in repeatable tasks without the necessary cognitive input to evaluate them constantly; and rituals, which are also deployed without deep cognition but they are only deployed because of their comforting effect rather than their actual application to streamlining repeatable tasks.

Therefore, awareness is an important factor for being able to distinguish between routines and rituals, and to ensure that rituals do not disguise themselves as routines in our lives.

Repeatability validates value, repetition enhances skill, routines create efficiency; but rituals create comfort-zones.

Routines carry less sense of belonging and dependence, hence, it is easier to break the habit of routines compared to the habit of rituals. Likewise, due to the fact that routines carry less attachment, routines could help us implement repeatable self-help techniques and practices in an intuitive manner. As long as routines do not create a comfort-zone, whereby getting out of the comfort-zone becomes uncomfortable; routines via discipline, could actually create efficiency in performing productive tasks in a nonconscious and intuitive format. Therefore, repetition, which is an inherent characteristic associated with routines, is an important enhancing and verification tool for creating efficiency and speed in the execution of our thoughts and behavior.

Routines increase discipline by increasing certainty and even predictability; however, if not careful, routines could actually prevent change when they become comforting-rituals or bad-habits. The reason humans and even other sentient-animals prefer routines and they resist change, is because routines create familiarity, comfort, and predictability; while change creates variables, discomfort, and uncertainty. This discomfort with change is often perceived rather than factual because our mind wants to minimize new variables which could expose us to danger, pain, or even death. We create routines, and even habits and rituals, because routines, habits, and rituals create familiarity, by minimizing variables and diversities. Although routines are important in creating discipline, nonconscious-routines are often implemented by our mind to keep us safe.

Routines that are based on analytical-thinking, and routines that streamline repetitive tasks into efficiency, are often used to create and increase discipline. For example, getting up every morning at 7 a.m. to be at work at 9 a.m. is a constructive-routine which creates discipline to accomplish tasks. However, when routines are based on nonfactual-thoughts, comforting-beliefs, or cultural-traditions; such routines often turn into ineffective but potentially damaging rituals.

For example, praying before an exam or a soccer-match, or rubbing a rabbit's foot before taking an action, are all examples of nonfactual and self-comforting rituals that are without any factual-basis; and are concocted and undertaken in order to make us feel good.

When routines turn into rituals, that is when we have a higher possibility of creating and adopting bad-habits. We engage in habits, because habits, similar to routines, are repetitive. However, when habits continuously cause us to make mistakes; such habits are thus bad-habits. When we create bad-habits by continuously engaging in unfavorable-routines; it is then that we begin to make mistakes. We repeat a mistake by repeating a bad-habit because our mind repeats the same faulty-thought that leads to our mistake in order to keep things familiar.

Mistakes are something we can improve; bad-habits are mistakes we repeat.

Therefore, as long as routines are based on facts and knowledge, routines could be helpful in creating good-habits, by creating stability, and by maintaining, or by even improving our circumstances. However, and as stated, if routines become too comforting to the point that routines do not allow improvement and change; routines will become inhibiting.

Routines minimize variables and uncertainty, which in-turn, increase the feelings of safety and comfort; but because of this safety derivative which is what our primitive-mind is always striving for, excessive routines could also minimize change, which is needed for improvement. Therefore, routines must be constantly evaluated, modified, and often changed, in order to keep progress and improvement going. Hence, routines must be open to evolution and improvement.

Although routines minimize change; routinely changing minimizes routines.

Theory of Self-Relativity categorizes routines binarily:

1. **Comforting-Routines:** Are those routines that are created for familiarity and comfort. These types of routines often prevent change and improvement. Habits and rituals are considered to be comforting-routines, and they are commonly rigid and unadaptable.

2. **Constructive-Routines:** Are those routines that are important in the development, maintenance, and improvement of our skills and the quality of our life. These types of routines are malleable and adaptable, and are good for self-improvement.

As long as repetition is cognitively implemented as a constructive-routine and not as a ritualistic comforting-routine; repetition could be a good indicator and verifier of the effectiveness of the routines in our life; hence why, repetition could put us in more control, by minimizing uncertainty and by increasing predictability. Repetition, especially repeated application of information and knowledge, could even improve the output of our intelligence. Although it is not proven that repeated application of information and knowledge actually increases human-intelligence-quotient or IQ; repetition of information and knowledge could make the application of intelligence more streamlined and efficient, which in-turn, improves cognitive skills.

Theory of Self-Relativity defines "intelligence" as "the ability to acquire, process, and apply information and knowledge."

Therefore, one's intelligence could be increased, not necessarily as a measurement of intelligence, but through the efficient application of information and knowledge. Continuous and repeated application of knowledge through problem-solving streamlines the efficient application of intelligence. Efficiency is a mechanism to streamline output, without increasing the size of the hardware; and when it comes to the mind, efficiency of thinking, which could only be achieved through the quicker application of facts and knowledge, is a pathway to the increase in learning and intelligence. This is why, Theory of Self-Relativity refers to The Cognitive-Cognition-Technique as our mental-algorithm; because The Cognitive-Cognition-Technique teaches us how to apply emotional-intelligence and thought-management, in a quick and repeatable format to all of our thinking activities, decision-making, and behavior.

By learning to make change and improvement a routine and repetitive part of our existence, and by taking on the self-agency and personal-responsibility to ensure that we are in charge of our own life and improvement; we can have more control and predictability in our life by setting our Self up on the path of consistent and confident self-improvement.

Stop being shackled to the outside and begin freeing your Self from within.

VIII.
Complementary; not Completing

To relate to everything and everyone else in a healthy and constructive manner, we must first learn to relate to our own Self, healthily and constructively. Just like other aspects of self-improvement, in order for us to have external-compatibility with other-people and with other-things, we must first learn to have internal-compatibility with our own Self. We not only must learn to have self-empathy, self-compassion, and self-love for our own Self before we can reflect such characteristics onto others; but in order to have such positive self-characteristics, we must first become independent, self-reliant, and self-sufficient. This is why, Theory of Self-Relativity considers "Independence and Self-Reliance" as one of its 10-Commandments for Self-Improvement. Additionally, to truly become independent and self-reliant, we must take matters in our own hands by taking on the personal-responsibility to become the agent of change and improvement for our own Self. This is also why, "Self-Agency and Personal-Responsibility" is another one of The 10-Commandments for Self-Improvement. When we reach true independence and self-reliance by becoming the agent of change and improvement, we can then have more control and less uncertainty in our lives. Therefore, "Control and Certainty" is another of Theory of Self-Relativity's 10-Commandments for Self-Improvement.

As we become independent and self-reliant and as we take the personal-responsibility of bringing the focus onto our own Self, we will naturally become less tangibly and intangibly dependent on other-people and on other-things. This minimization of dependency and reliance on others, in-turn, minimizes our neediness for other-people or other-things; and as discussed throughout Theory of Self-Relativity, when we become self-sufficient, we realize other-things and other-people that we thought we needed, were simply externally-derived desires and wants, that were not necessities. As we become independent and self-reliant by taking the personal-responsibility to provide for our own Self and to take control of our life; we will only then begin to develop our external-relationships based on compatibility, and not based on neediness. Such compatibility creates a complementary nature of existence and interactions between our Self and others, instead of it being a completing factor for our self-identity and for our existence. This is why, Theory of Self-Relativity designates "Complementary; not Completing" as another one of its 10-Commandments for Self-Improvement.

Our relativity, our relationships, and our interactions with other-people and with other-things must be on a complementary basis, and not based on a completing one. What this means is that we must be complete on our own, and other-people and other-things should be on a complementary basis to our Self and to our existence; therefore, other-people or other-things should not complete us, nor should they fill our personal-voids. When we complete our own Self, others will not only become additive to us, but we will also be additive to others. When we complete our own Self, and as others become complementary and additive to us; we will not need others because of our neediness, we will want others because of our desire.

Relationship with our Self must be a "Completing" one; relationship with others should only be a "Complementary" one.

Although human-beings are social-animals; human-beings are also capable of self-sufficiency and living on their own. While being social and living in the company of others can be beneficial and helpful for our safety and progress; to be able to live in a healthy relationship with others, we must do so based on complementarity of our relationship and not from the point of neediness. Because, if we interact with others based on neediness and from a completing perspective, we will then open the door for dependency and reliance on others. Therefore, in order for a pack, a group, or a society to be strong and healthy; each individual member of that collective must be strong and healthy on its own.

To have a strong "we" mindset, we must first have a strong "me" mindset; and since "me" is a part of "we," we can't have a strong "we" without a strong "me."

When we enter interactions and relationships with others based on complementary and not completing reasons; our relationships will not only be additive, but we will also be able to end our relationships with others quicker, should we realize that these relationships are affecting us negatively. For example, we will not have difficulty letting go of material-things if they are preventing us from improving our life, nor will we have difficulty letting go of people who are influencing us negatively. Furthermore, our ability to be complete on our own will enable us to recognize other people who are not self-reliant and who enter relationships with us based on neediness or because of self-serving reasons. Therefore, when we are complete on our own and when we interact with others based on a complementary and additive nature instead of a completing one; we can maintain and nurture compatibility and strength in our healthy relationships, just as we would be able to let go of relationships that are not compatible.

It is better to not have a relationship than to be in a relationship for the wrong reasons.

As discussed, relationships do not necessarily refer to personal or romantic ones, but they refer to all interactions we have with other-people and even with other-things. By focusing on being complete on our own, we can alleviate feelings of neediness, dependency, and reliance on others. When we become self-reliant and complete on our own, we will not be forced to have others in our life; we will choose who and what we want to be in a relationship with. Hence, when we feel content, fulfilled, and complete on our own, we will rarely experience loneliness and the negative-feelings that emerge and dwell as a result of being lonely. It is true that loneliness arises from lack of interaction with others; however, true loneliness is also often associated with one's inability to externalate and preoccupy one's mind. As discussed:

Theory of Self-Relativity defines "externalation" as "one's focus and preoccupation with external things and events, in order to avoid and distract one's Self from observing and recognizing one's own deficiencies."

Externalation, is one of the main causes of our inability to self-improve; therefore, those who are internally lonely, externalate continuously in order to avoid feeling lonely. But the minute that they get exhausted of externalation or the moment they are forced to be alone and to self-reflect, loneliness and its associated negative-feelings of sadness, fear, and depression kick in.

This is why, loneliness is a chronic modern-times personal-problem that cannot be resolved, unless we bring the focus onto our Self and begin the process of self-improvement from within. Lonely people feel lonely regardless of where they are. They can feel lonely when they are alone, and they could feel lonely if they are in a room full of people. Therefore, loneliness feels like emptiness; because no matter where we are and no matter where we go, and most importantly no matter how hard we try to externalate in order to cover up our loneliness, the minute that we are forced to be on our own, our feelings of loneliness will resurface.

Lonely people feel lonely because they do not have a fulfilled sense of completion.

This is why, for example, success that is solely directed towards the acquisition of wealth and fame does not feel completing.

Wealth, fame, and power are simply byproducts of success. True success is measured by the level of your fulfillment.

Wealthy, famous, and successful people can buy all the material things that they want, and they can interact and engage in relationships with all the people that they desire; but, in the end, if they are overachieving these attributes in order to feel a sense of accomplishment, they will always be one material-thing or one person short of feeling fulfilled. Being fulfilled does not mean living life like a monk and doing away with all material possessions or all personal desires; nor does being fulfilled mean being wealthy and famous. Being fulfilled means to be content and satisfied with one's current state-of-existence, while continuously improving one's sense of fulfillment each and every day.

Theory of Self-Relativity defines "fulfillment" as "an evolving satisfactory state-of-mind that is built upon a stable foundation of contentment."

A truly complete person who feels fulfilled will feel completeness from within and not externally. Truly complete individuals know how to experience self-time by themselves without having to occupy their time with others at all times; hence, a truly complete person knows how to be alone, without feeling lonely.

To be alone without feeling lonely is the sign of a truly fulfilled person.

There is a big difference between being lonely and being alone. Self-fulfilled and truly accomplished people can not only be alone without feeling lonely, but they often welcome their self-time alone in order to enjoy their accomplishments and to add further value to them. Thus, by sometimes spending self-time alone and in a content, productive, and satisfactory manner; truly complete people know how to elevate their sense of fulfillment.

To be alone means to have the desire to be by your Self; to be lonely means to have the need to be with others.

Most authors, painters, scientists, and even body-builders who are truly creative and fulfilled, welcome time alone so that they could get even more fulfilled by continuously adding to their accomplishments. Accomplishment is a word that is derived from the root word of "complete," as in the form of completing or fulfilling something; and since accomplishment and success go hand-in-hand, therefore, to truly feel successful, we must feel complete and fulfilled.

Theory of Self-Relativity defines "success" as "fulfilling our purpose by accomplishing our next goal."

When we feel complete on our own, we will truly feel content, fulfilled, and accomplished; hence, we will approach everyone and everything with the perspective of adding to our contentment, our accomplishment, and our fulfillment, but not with the intention of creating them through others. This is why, our relationships and interactions, and as a whole, our relativity with others must be on a complementary basis and not a completing one.

Atop alleviating neediness, "Complementary; not Completing" creates mutual-synergy rather than competitive-antagonism; thereby, making it a win-win strategy. The primary reason being complete places us in a winning strategy is because when we are complete on our own, we can approach other-people, other-things, and as a whole, we can approach every situation in life with the perspective of *"having nothing-to-lose."* When we approach interactions and relationships not from the point of neediness, but from the point of additive-value; we can then have more control over the terms of our engagement in our interactions and relationships. This positioning of having nothing-to-lose enables us to not only set and enforce proper borders and boundaries, and to establish mutual-respect parameters; but it also enables us to negotiate and enter such relationships, if not with a personal-advantage, at the minimum, without a personal-disadvantage. In other words, when we approach an interaction or when we engage in a relationship from the perspective of having nothing-to-lose; we will either engage in the best possible outcome for our Self, or we will move onto another interaction that is more favorable.

The hardest person to negotiate with is a person who has nothing-to-lose.

It must be emphasized that having nothing-to-lose does not mean being illogical, reckless, or self-centeredly stubborn. Having nothing-to-lose means to be able to enter interactions and relationships from the perspective of being complete. When we feel complete on our own, we will not need others, because those that we allow in our life will be additive and not completing to us. Therefore, negotiating from a point of strength and from the position of having nothing-to-lose will not only make the relationship be the best and most respectful relationship that it could be; but it also places others on notice that we will have no problem disengaging from the relationship, should the terms of the relationship change, or if it becomes unfavorable, controlling, or abusive. Having nothing-to-lose is a demonstration of independence and self-reliance, as it ensures that we have more control and better predictability in our relationships.

Never enter into an interaction if you're not willing to walk away from the interaction without any results.

Although compromise is necessary for interpersonal-interactions, for relationships, and even for negotiations; compromise must be fair and mutual. A healthy compromise is a skill where one is unbiased and adaptable to modification and change in order to advance a negotiation, an interaction, or a relationship. Interactions and relationships that are founded upon the principle of complementarity and not completing, are generally open to compromise, in order to engage, cultivate, and advance the relationship; because self-reliant people who are not looking to be completed by others are generally well-disciplined and self-confident people. Therefore, interactions and relationships with self-sufficient and self-complete people are often based on mutual-compromise and mutual-courtesy; because relationships involving self-complete individuals do not require unilateral-compromises, or unfair and one-sided sacrifices.

Theory of Self-Relativity defines "compromise" as "the ability to willingly and unbiasedly adapt in order to advance an agenda, an interaction, or a relationship."

Self-secure and self-confident people consider compromise as a means of progress and moving forward; however, those who are insecure and lack self-awareness generally view compromise as a sign of weakness. People who do not know how and when to compromise or be courteous tend to be rigid and they normally consider compromise as giving-in or as losing. Additionally, such individuals also consider other people's courtesy and ability to compromise as a weakness; therefore, such courtesy and compromise is viewed as potential opportunity to take advantage of others or to capitalize on such characteristics. Compromise should be made in a synergic manner in order to advance a mutual or global interest. Compromise and courtesy are wrong if they are offered unilaterally and on a regular basis in order to preserve a relationship. Theory of Self-Relativity refers to such compromise as "*down-compromise*," because down-compromise and unilateral-courtesy results from neediness to be in a relationship, rather than from a complementary position of adding to a relationship.

Never allow your compromise or courtesy to be as a result of your weakness or neediness.

It is for all the aforementioned reasons that Theory of Self-Relativity designates "Complementary; not Completing" as one of its 10-Commandments for Self-Improvement; because, without bringing the focus onto our own Self and without taking matters into our own hands so that we could have more control and better ability to guide our own life, we would not be able to have fulfilling and respectful relationships with others. Complementarity also helps us in setting borders and boundaries, because when we are not in need of others, we will then be able to choose who we allow into our lives, and how close we allow them to get to us. When we can have a choice of who we want to deal with and how closely we want to deal with them, we can then live in abundance by having choices and options in our life; rather than being forced to down-compromise by dealing with or by staying with people that are disrespectful, controlling, or even abusive towards us.

Theory of Self-Relativity defines "down-compromise" as "adapting to a situation or settling for less, because one is unwilling or unable to improve."

According to Theory of Self-Relativity, engaging in interactions and relationships on a complementary, not completing basis; strengthens the following personal-attributes:

Complementary; not Completing
Centered-Self
Independence and Self-Reliance
Control, Certainty, and Predictability
Self-Agency and Personal-Responsibility
Discipline
Self-Confidence
Ability to Set, Maintain, and Enforce, Borders and Boundaries
Ability to Disengage (walk-away)
Mutual-Respect
Mutual-Support
Mutual-Courtesy
Compromising-Skills
Negotiation-Skills
Advancement and Improvement
Contentment, Fulfilment, and Happiness

Therefore, being complete on our own is essential in having healthy interactions and relationships with other-people and with other-things. When we are complete on our own and when we are not looking for others to complete us; we will not search, seek, nor feel like we need others to validate us in order to create our self-identity and our sense of Self. Instead of looking externally, we will self-validate and we will create and cultivate our own self-identity; hence, our sense of Self will emanate from within. When we are self-reliant and complete, and when we don't need others to complete us, that is when our relationships will be based on mutually-additive value. *"Mutual-Reciprocity"* is integral to all aspects of our relationships with other-people; and the only way that we can achieve it is by us being complete on our own.

Theory of Self-Relativity defines "mutual-reciprocity" as "the fair and voluntary sharing and exchange of constructive personal attributes with others."

Mutual-reciprocity does not mean equal-mutuality, because one entity in a relationship could be better positioned for offering more to the other. Mutual-reciprocity means that there is an open and comfortable exchange of thoughts, feelings, actions, as well as information and knowledge between the parties in an interaction or in a relationship; although one entity might be able to offer more than the other.

Since a relationship, in its most simple form is defined as "the state of being connected;" therefore, in order for us to have complementary relationships with everything and with everyone else, including our own Self; we must become aware of and we must understand the relativities of our connections.

Theory of Self-Relativity categorizes relationships binarily:

1. **Tangible-Relationships:** Are the type of interactions and relationships that we have with tangible or physical-objects and beings. For example, a car, a house, a person, or any other material object creates a tangible-relationship between us and the object or the being. Tangible-relationship with an inanimate physical-object has no mutual-reciprocity, because as defined above, mutual-reciprocity is the exchange of "personal-attributes" between living-things. However, tangible-relationships, according to Theory of Self-Relativity, could also include physical-interactions between living-things. Service, business, monetary-exchange, sex, and even physical-abuse or predation between living entities is considered as a tangible-relationship.

2. **Intangible-Relationships:** Are the type of relationships that are commonly between animate or living entities. For example, emotional-exchanges such as caring, love, and even anger, are examples of interactions that represent intangible-relationships. Intangible-relationships and interactions between animate-beings includes mutual-reciprocity of emotions and behavior, although such reciprocity might not be equally-mutual. One could also have intangible-relationships with inanimate objects such as their car, clothes and other material possessions. Intangible-relationships with inanimate-objects cannot have mutual-reciprocity; thus, if inanimate-objects define one's self-identity or self-image, such intangible-relationships would

be as a result of intangible-dependency. A self-improved and complete person will not have intangible-relationship with an inanimate-object. True intangible-relationships, including emotions, must be between animate or living-things. One could have interactions with an inanimate-thing but one should not have a relationship with it.

We could have interactions with inanimate-things, but we shouldn't have emotional-relationships with them.

As discussed, it is because of our interactions, relationships, and as a whole, our relativity with everything and everyone else that Theory of Self-Relativity has implemented the self-equation. In order for the self-equation to be in balance with everything and with everyone else, we must understand our relativities with everything and everyone else; and, we must dynamically keep this relativity in the highest possible state of equilibrium.

Theory of Self-Relativity defines *"self-equation" as "the dynamic balance of the Self, relative to the Self, and to others."*

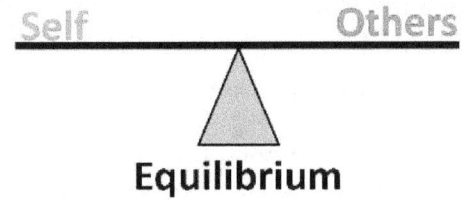

Equilibrium

By becoming aware of our relativities with other-people and with other-things, we can dynamically make changes and improvements to keep the self-equation in equilibrium. As discussed, change, improvement, and balance are not one-time events, they are ongoing processes; thus, interactions and relationships, regardless of their tangibility or intangibility, are also ongoing dynamic processes. This dynamic nature of keeping the self-equation in balance is more discernible when dealing with other animate-objects, especially with other humans; because, we also have to deal with others' personal-variables in order to keep the self-equation in equilibrium. This is why, to live the most content, fulfilled, and happy life possible, we must first improve our own Self, before we focus on others. Through self-awareness, self-reflection, and self-regulation, we can minimize our personal-variables so that we can become even more aware of other-people's variables; or, especially, their lack of self-awareness.

By doing so, we can then fairly evaluate to see if compromise and courtesy could cultivate the relationship further and bring the self-equation into equilibrium; or if others are too entitled or too unaware of their role in mutual-reciprocity for the relationship. By being self-aware and by dynamically self-reflecting, we can evaluate the realistic potential of mutual-reciprocity in a relationship; thus, we will commit realistic time and effort in trying to maintain or advance the relationship, or we would choose to walk-away from a chronically imbalanced-relationship.

A relationship, in its most simple form of definitions means "the state of being connected":

- The root word for relationship comes from the verb "to relate," which means "having a sense or a state of being related."
- The same root word of "to relate" is also the root word for "relative" which means "having a relation."
- Therefore, we have a "relation-ship" with everything and everyone else; hence, we have a sense or a state of how we "relate" to everything and everyone else.
- When we have a relationship and when we relate with everything and everyone else, we are therefore "relative" to everything and everyone else.
- And since we also relate to, have a relationship with, and we are also relative with our own Self; therefore, we have "Self-Relativity" with our own Self, and with everything and everyone else.

Theory of Self-Relativity defines "Self-Relativity" as "the interactions and relationships of the Self internally and externally with the Self, and with everything and everyone else."

Therefore, to have balance, harmony, equilibrium, and quality relationships, we must first learn to have a self-aware and quality relationship with our own Self. We cannot replace what we are missing from within us, through others; we must fill our internal-voids from within, so that we can be complete on our own. Because if we look to complete our Self externally, we will be entering relationships for the wrong reasons; and such relationships will commonly have consequences which will not be constructive or beneficial for our Self.

It is better to not be in a relationship than to be in a relationship for the wrong reason.

From the time we are conceived, to the minute that we die, we live our life in relationships. Be it in a relationship with our mother in her womb from the time of our conception, or to the relationship with the doctor or family members by our bedside at the time of our death, and all other relationships in between, we are continuously coexisting in relationships. Even when alone at night, during our sleep, or during any other form of isolation, we are in a relationship with our inner-self, and in relationship with our own thoughts and feelings. Therefore, relationships are an integral component of our "Self-Relativity" and our existence.

As stated, the word "relationship" is derived from the word "relation" which is the connection and interaction between things. Things are always in relation to other-things and being in relation means that they are relative to one another; therefore, things are directly or indirectly connected. The relativity of these relationships is not only important in the physical and proximity context; but it is even more significant at the emotional, at the thinking, and at the behavioral levels of our "Self" and our existence.

As discussed, Theory of Self-Relativity categorizes "relationships" binarily:

1. **Tangible-Relationships.**
2. **Intangible-Relationships.**

Likewise, Theory of Self-Relativity categorizes our "Self-Relativity" binarily:

1. **Intrapersonal-Relationships:** Are our interactions and relationships with our own Self, which includes our thoughts, our feelings, and our behavior.
2. **Interpersonal-Relationships:** Are our interactions and relationships with everything and everyone else. Theory of Self-Relativity further categorizes our interpersonal-relationships binarily:
   a. **Animate-Relationships:** Are our interactions and relationships with other living-things.
   b. **Inanimate-Relationships:** Are our interactions and relationships with non-living-things.

Theory of Self-Relativity further categorizes our "animate-relationships" binarily:

1. **Relationships with humans:** Are our interactions and relationships with other-humans. Our relationships with other-humans are further categorized binarily:
   a. **Relationships with loved-ones.**
   b. **Relationships with other-people.**
2. **Relationships with non-human living-things:** Are our interactions and relationships with non-human living-things. Our relationship with non-human living-things are further categorized binarily:
   a. **Relationship with pets:** Are relationships with, for example, our dogs, our cats, and other animals we consider as pets.
   b. **Relationships with other living-things:** Are relationships with, for example, wild-animals, trees, and bacteria.

Theory of Self-Relativity further categorizes "inanimate-relationships" binarily; although as discussed, we should not have emotional or intangible-relationships with inanimate-things:

1. **Personal Inanimate-Relationships:** Are our interactions and relationships with objects and things that are our own. For example, our clothes, our house, and our car.
2. **Non-Personal Inanimate-Relationships:** Are our interactions and relationships with objects and things that are not our own. For example, others-people's cars and houses.

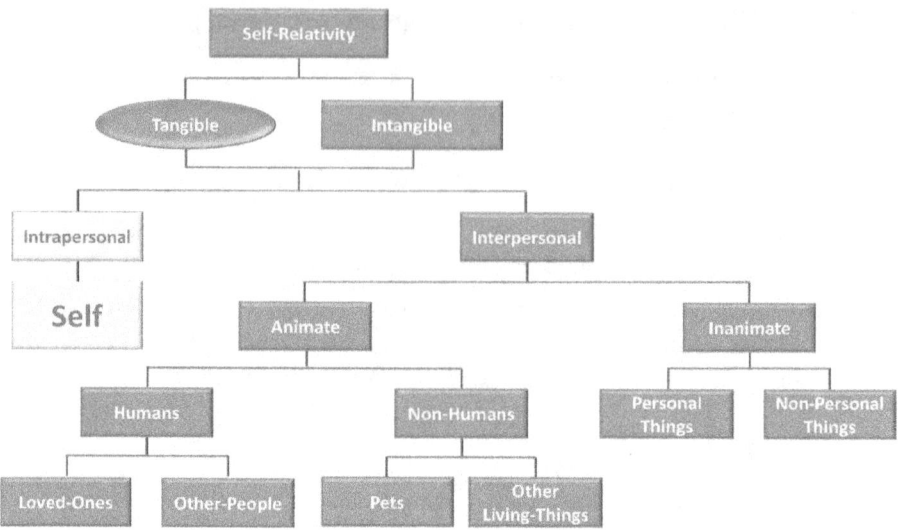

The above diagram represents the major and most closely associated categories of our Self-Relativities. These categories and sub-categories of Self-Relativity further divide into more sub-binary-groups and they cross-connect to other categories not only within Our-Universe, but also with other-people's own Self-Relativities in Their-Universe. This visualization helps us realize why relationships and self-relativities are infinitely diverse and complicated, and why it is important for us to direct all our relationships from our "centered-self" position and from the "inside-out;" rather than by working on our relationships from the outside-in and by prioritizing others before us.

Relationships with our own Self and with others are integral parts of our existence. Feelings of love, success, happiness; and even, negative-feelings of sadness, anger, and loss which can be self-directed or exchanged with others, are as a result of our own underlying triggered thoughts. These emotions are made by our brain as we need them, they are not just built-in, waiting to be deployed; hence why, we should engage in factual-thinking, because to be able to harmoniously interact with our Self and with others, we must be able to think and function based on how reality is. Humans are social-animals; therefore, being among people and interacting with others is the core of human interpersonal-existence. But to interact with others in a healthy and effective manner, we must first become content and fulfilled by having a healthy intrapersonal-relationship with our own Self that is based on facts and how reality is.

The most important relationship is our own "Self-Relationship."

We must have a healthy self-relationship in order to engage in healthy relationships with others. Interpersonal-relationships must be based on mutual-reciprocity. Reciprocity does not mean equally reciprocating, but it means having mutual-interests in relating, interacting, and maintaining relationships. True relationships are built on mutual-interests that add value; or at the minimum, that prevent loss of value from one another and from the relationship. Mutual-interest is not the same as personal-interest, because personal-interest in a relationship could exist without reciprocity; however, mutual-interest inherently carries reciprocity.

Mutual-interest inherently carries reciprocity; however, personal-interest does not necessarily carry reciprocity.

Mutual-Reciprocity
Mutual
Reciprocal
Bilateral
Balanced
Complementary; not-Completing
Additive; not-Deductive
Interest-Based; not Event-Based
Growth-Oriented
Less-Uncertain
Respectful
Supportive
More-Predictable
More-Stable

According to Theory of Self-Relativity, when relationships are established, engaged, and maintained based on mutual-reciprocity, such interactions and relationships are the most stable and predictable forms of interpersonal-relationships; hence, they are the most growth-oriented forms of relationships. Mutual-Reciprocity adds value by creating:

1. **Interest:** All relationships, whether intrapersonal, interpersonal-romantic, or interpersonal-nonromantic, must be interest-based; not event-based. Many, especially in our modern fast-paced societies, elevate the level of their personal-interest in a relationship based on an event that triggered engagement and interaction with others, and not based on mutual-interest. Relationships that are genuinely based on mutual-interest are naturally triggered, reengaged, or elevated, based on the continuous interest, and not because of social-media-notifications or because of a specific-event run-in. For example, if we get invited to a wedding by someone that we have not kept in touch with for years, such interaction is not based on an ongoing mutual-interest that they've had with us despite the event; such an

interaction is purely based on the personal-interest of the person inviting us to be present at their party, and not because of our mutual-interest. As discussed:

The primary difference between personal-interest and mutual-interest is that personal-interest is not conditional to reciprocity.

Therefore:

Relationships must be interest-based; not event-based.

1. **Stability:** When relationships are based on mutual-interest, such interest creates a system of checks and balances that complements the interests of the parties involved in the relationship. Mutual-interest is important in balancing and maintaining the self-equation's equilibrium. Stability created by mutual-interest is necessary to maintain the results achieved so that the relationship can continue to grow and flourish from a stable base.

2. **Certainty:** Achieving, maintaining, and strengthening more certainty in a relationship that is based on mutual-reciprocity, in-turn, minimizes unpredictability and elevates mutual-interests even further by improving the relationship's stability and growth potential.

3. **Growth:** As mutual-interests build and as stability and less-uncertainty stabilize and strengthen the relationship; it is only then that the relationship could begin to flourish and grow on a solid-foundation. Consequently, as the relationship grows in a stable format, the mutual-interest in the relationship grows as well. By minimizing uncertainty and by increasing predictability and certainty, such stable growth minimizes worry, anxiety, and stress that is associated with many unstable and unhealthy relationships.

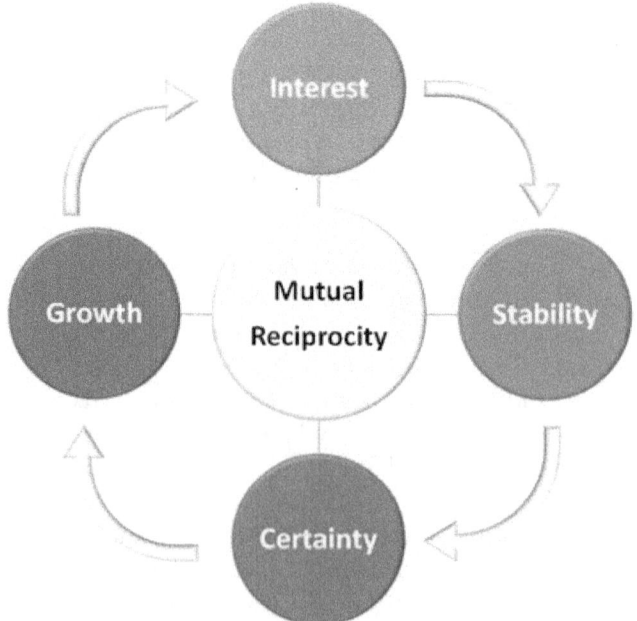

Although interest, stability, certainty, and growth are important value-adding attributes to a mutually-beneficial relationship; no relationship, not even a relationship that is based on mutual-reciprocity could fully succeed as a complementary and not completing relationship, unless it carries Theory of Self-Relativity's 3 core fundamentals requirements for a complementary-relationship. According to Theory of Self-Relativity, the 3 fundamental requirements for a complementary and not completing relationship are:

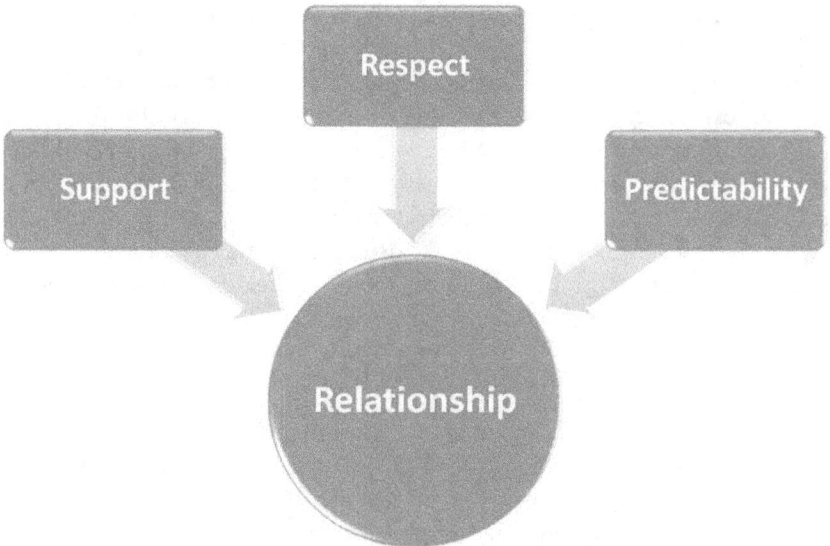

Relationship-Fundamentals

Respect, Support, and Predictability (RSP) are the necessary *"relationship-fundamentals"* for all interpersonal-relationships; as well as our own intrapersonal-relationship. To have balanced and growth-oriented relationships, and for such relationships to be based on solid-footing; RSP must be inherent. Without respect, support, and predictability, a relationship cannot sustain, strengthen, or grow; and when relationships do not sustain, strengthen, or grow, they often disengage and burn-out.

1. **Respect:** Unlike popular beliefs, and as discussed throughout Theory of Self-Relativity, respect should not be earned nor demanded; respect must be required, and if necessary, respect must be enforced. However, when respect requires enforcement, the necessity to enforce respect is a strong indicator that the underlying issues with mutual-reciprocity of the relationship are in question. Furthermore, unlike popular belief, Theory of Self-Relativity does not consider admiration or admirability as a constituent of respect; just as respect does not mean obedience or bowing down to another person as a form of authority.

Theory of Self-Relativity defines "respect" as "to acknowledge, to show interest, and to value a person's thoughts, feelings, and way of existence; even though one might not agree with it."

Therefore, to support and grow a relationship, respect must be mutual. The way that respect could best be achieved, is first, by making sure that the parties involved in an interaction or in a relationship do not disrespect each other; even in the face of disagreements. This could only begin by one learning to respect one's own self-first. As discussed, self-respect is the most important angle of Theory of Self-Relativity's trilateral-respect principle. If we do not have self-respect, and if we continuously bash our Self for our thoughts, our feelings, our actions, and for our way of existence; we will not be able to reciprocate respect for others either, and most importantly, we will not know how to enforce respect in dealing with others. When we know how to have self-respect, it is only then that we will be able to constructively engage with others; even if we are in disagreement with their thoughts, their feelings, or their way of existence. True respect minimizes defensiveness towards others and allows interactions and relationships to be unbiased and without judgmentality.

True respect inherently creates a state of non-judgmentality.

Same holds true for others interacting and engaging with us; thus, mutual-respect is integral to having a strong relationship. Mutual-respect allows for open and non-defensive exchange of thoughts and interactions; thereby, mutual-respect directs the efforts and the resources of the parties towards growth of the relationship. Mutual-respect protects and enforces personal borders and boundaries by keeping every individual as a separate and complete entity; therefore, individuals who have mutual-respect for one another become "complementary" to each other, while preserving their individual "complete" self-identity.

True respect preserves borders and boundaries.

2. **Support:** Just like respect, support inherently creates non-judgmentality between the parties in a relationship. Regardless of their agreements or disagreements, support must exist for each person's opinions, thoughts, and decisions. Support is not only instrumental in encouraging and motivating others in a relationship to innovate, flourish, and grow; but their individual improvements, in-turn, will advance and improve the relationship. Even if others are wrong in a relationship, proper support and encouragement is an essential positive reinforcement to correcting paths and for changing directions. Being supportive does not mean only doing so when one agrees with others. Being supportive is to be there for others in a relationship even though one might not agree with them. Being supportive means for others to know that despite disagreements, one will be there to support them and to help them recover, if their decisions and actions yield unfavorable results. Furthermore, support minimizes worry, anxiety, and stress in the relationship; because support creates complementarity for one another's thoughts, decisions, and goals. Mutual-support

combined with mutual-respect will create a solid-foundation to a complementary-relationship without the need for judgmentality.

3. **Predictability:** Worry, anxiety, and stress, which are commonly the result of lack of control and uncertainty, minimize our ability to make best predications of outcomes. Predictability is an important attribute that our brain uses to not only construct the best possibility of the future; but predictability is also what our brain uses to construct our understanding of the present-moment. Since everything around us is in a constant state of motion and change, and since we are relative to everything and everyone else in Our-Universe; this constant state of change creates variables that minimize our control of outcomes, therefore they affect our predictive-abilities. Therefore, while we cannot control others to our liking, we can control who we get involved with; hence, we can avoid unpredictable people.

Although the need for predictability in a relationship is more subtle than the need for respect and support; according to Theory of Self-Relativity, unpredictability could be more destructive to the foundation of a relationship than lack of respect and support would be. Instability, unpredictability, and chaos create uncertainty and lack of control; and as discussed, these are direct contributors to worry, anxiety, and stress. If one of the parties in a relationship is unpredictable, others in the relationship will constantly be on pins and needles of doubt and insecurity; therefore, navigating through such relationships is referred to as "walking on broken glass" or "walking on eggshells." As stated, unpredictability is a hallmark of relationships with high-conflict, toxic, and personality-disordered individuals; because these individuals thrive on unpredictability, as such uncertainty creates confusion and dissonance, thereby, it gives them control over others.

Personality-disorders are different than mood-disorders. Mood-disorders can be caused by a multitude of factors including, medical, mental, genetic, neurobiological, substance-use, and characterological causes. While mood-disorders such as bipolar-disorder could be manic or depressive; majority of disorders are depressive in nature, indicating once again that negativity is more prevalent than positivity. Mood-disorders associated with medical and physiological factors generally require medical and drug related interventions and assistance; however, incorrect cognitive-processes that are as a result of faulty-thinking, and which are not based on physical, physiological, chemical, or other non-cognitive causes, could effectively be improved through proper thought-management skills.

Unlike mood-disorders, personality-disorders, which also include characterological-disorders, are a common but less understood and addressed form of disorders that collectively make up a significant portion of problematic relationships. Personality-disorders are a collection of character-flaws gone haywire; and according to Theory of Self-Relativity, they comprise a significantly more than the currently recognized percentage of the population. Therefore, according to Theory of Self-Relativity, the chances of us knowing or dealing with a personality-disordered individual is substantial.

According to Theory of Self-Relativity, personality-disorders are cross-cultural and universal in nature; and they manifest themselves regardless of the person's ethnicity, religion, or race. Majority of these disorders could be dealt with and minimized cognitively, especially in case of the loved-ones and associates of the disordered-person who often end-up receiving the lash-out of the disordered person's character. However, in case of the disordered-people, the success rate could be challenging because they would first have to recognize and accept that they suffer from a disorder.

The key to dealing and interacting with toxic and disordered-people is through self-awareness and setting and enforcing borders and boundaries through self-improvement. We must learn to have self-reflection and we must become aware of and recognize why we would allow, get involved with, or continue dealing with personality-disordered people; in lieu of their continuously unpredictable and often disrespectful and even abusive behavior.

Although there are a multitude of personality-disorders, according to Theory of Self-Relativity, the most common and the most debilitating ones to be involved with are the personality-disorders which in the DSM (Diagnostic and Statistical Manual of Mental Disorders) are known as the Cluster-B disorders. The Cluster-B disordered individuals are sometimes referred to as dramatic, chaotic, or toxic individuals; and these disorders are sometimes referred to as Dramatic, Chaotic or High-Conflict disorders.

The Cluster-B disorders are:

1. Narcissistic-Personality-Disorder (NPD)
2. Unstable or Borderline-Personality-Disorder (BPD)
3. Histrionic Personality-Disorder
4. Antisocial or Sociopathic Personality-Disorder

Theory of Self-Relativity discusses these conditions as a whole and in a basic and introductory format, because they are quite complex with many personal and interpersonal variables. The reason Theory of Self-Relativity places special emphasis on Cluster-B personality-disorders is because these disorders play a significantly influential role in our modern-day technologically-oriented fast-paced interactions and relationships.

The terminology and explanation of Cluster-B disorders can be confusing, however, one general trait that these disorders have in common is that people with the disorder are often unaware of or refuse to accept their condition; thus, others who are in a relationship with these individuals commonly suffer a great deal as a result of their interactions, and especially, as a result of their relationships with these personality-disordered individuals.

There are many specifics to each personality-disordered condition which will be discussed in other Theory of Self-Relativity publications, because these conditions and dealing with these individuals requires extensive specific explanations and examples. Meanwhile, some common traits and characteristics of Cluster-B disorders are:

- Low self-esteem.
- Self-centeredness with minimal to no concern for others; and often at the expense of others.
- Attachment.
- Fear of abandonment.
- Fear of being lonely.
- Fear of being alone.
- Difficulty being alone and without external attention and without external distraction.
- Minimal to no ability to self-reflect and introspect; hence, they are often in a state of externalation in order to abstain from introspection and from seeing their own weak and fragile self-image.
- False sense of Self (and often falsely grandiose).
- Thrive on seeking attention or feeling smarter than others, even if the attention is negative; because, being recognized gives them a sense of Self and a sense of existence.
- Their self-image, their self-identity, and their sense of Self is mostly dependent externally on other-things and on other-people.
- Lack of respect for other people's borders and boundaries; therefore, their easiest targets are often people-pleasers and codependents with week personal-parameters.
- Sociopathy; as they often consider others as objects and not as living-beings.
- They are often transient and have difficulty with commitment.
- Impulsivity and lack of impulse-control.
- Pathological-lying to others and self-lying, as most believe their own lies.
- Unstable; and commonly have mentally and physically abusive personal-relationships.
- Denial and lack of accountability as it is always someone-else or something-else's fault.
- Blame-shifting.
- Self-victimization.
- Sense-of-entitlement.
- False-façade; yet insecure and self-loathing.
- Generally intelligent and often successful.
- Substance-abuse and addictive tendencies; generally, as a means of helping them with externalation.
- Charming.

Individuals living with such disorders do not generally have introspective ability and they commonly do not see anything wrong with themselves. These disordered individuals mostly suffer from a low self-esteem and a fragile sense of Self, which is often masked by positive or negative externalations. For example, some narcissists are known to be high-achievers because they continuously externalate and cover-up their inner-deficiencies by achieving wealth, fame, and even, power. Many also cover-up their weaknesses by simply pretending to be intelligent, successful, and high-achievers. Furthermore, for example, narcissists will consciously and nonconsciously protect their externally-derived false-façade, and they will fight tooth and nail to protect their image. This is why, it is known that the rage of a narcissist will surface when the cover-up mask is unveiled.

Another commonly misunderstood and misdiagnosed Cluster-B personality disorder is unstable or borderline-personality-disorder (BPD). People suffering from BPD continuously seek praise and compliments from others in order to feel validated, approved, and to even feel alive. Additionally, since Cluster-Bs have difficulty with self-reflection and have a nonconscious fear of introspection; by continuously engaging in drama, chaos, and even use of illegal substances, they manage to prevent their Self from having any downtime opportunity for self-reflection. According to Theory of Self-Relativity, Cluster-Bs engage and maintain uninterrupted externalation as they do not have the ability nor the desire for introspection. Since desire and introspection are the two non-negotiables for self-improvement; according to Theory of Self-Relativity, Cluster-Bs are the most challenging people to commit to change and improvement.

As discussed, dealing with personality-disordered people generally creates confusion and dissonance, because the way that they think and operate is purely based on what makes them feel better, and not based on how things really are. They often create a false sense of reality that supports their desired feelings, rather than facing the reality that is affecting their life and their relationships. Although most people engage in some placebo-thinking to relieve discomfort and stress temporarily; personality-disordered individuals not only engage in continuous false-rationalization and placebo-thinking; but they actually live with such false reality.

As discussed, self-deception is one of the biggest enemies of self-improvement, and almost all human-beings have some tendencies of self-deception; however, personality-disordered individuals, and especially Cluster-Bs, do not simply self-deceive or deceive other-people's perceptions, they actively try to alter the reality that they live in, and they fallaciously rewrite history. This is why, when dealing with personality-disordered individuals, especially narcissists and borderlines, the loved ones or the associates of these individuals often feel as if they are losing their mind and their sense of reality. Such gaslighting and crazy-making behavior is the main cause of cognitive-dissonance in people who deal with Cluster-Bs. Cognitive-dissonance, which as discussed, is one of Theory of Self-Relativity's 10-Enemies of Self-Improvement, is a common side-effect of being in long-term relationships with personality-disordered individuals.

Theory of Self-Relativity defines "cognitive-dissonance" as "the mental-state of holding two or more conflicting-thoughts simultaneously."

Deception is the primary coping-mechanisms that personality-disordered individuals deploy; and if they would deceive and lie to their own Self in order to avoid seeing their own weaknesses, they would have no problems deceiving and lying to others to get what they are looking for. Cluster-Bs often enter into a relationship, especially personal-relationships, with great charm that hooks others into the relationship. Once they have given a good but fake sampling of how tasty a relationship with them would be; they then tighten the grips of control. In order to continue the relationship, instead of them being complete and becoming complementary to the other person; Cluster-Bs often engage in destroying the other person's good qualities and achievements in order to get what they want and to maintain their control over others. This is why, relationships with Cluster-Bs are commonly described as parasitic-relationships; because they hook themselves onto others in order to use and to take advantage of others. Once Cluster-Bs have used-up the other and have gained control, they then proceed to devalue the person and begin the process of creating dissonance, crazy-making, gaslighting, silent-treatment, and *"Discommunication;"* which are all forms of mental-abuse.

Theory of Self-Relativity defines "discommunication" as "the punitive act of disconti-nuing communication with someone, in order to signal disapproval and to maintain control."

Discommunication, as coined and termed by Theory of Self-Relativity, is the one-sided cutting-off of communication or interactions with others, as a means of protecting, yet validating one's own weak or non-existent self-identity; while portraying and maintaining a self-soothing but a false sense of grandiosity. Discommunication is often undertaken as a punitive measure by insecure, low self-esteemed, and arrogant individuals; and as a means of proving a point, instead of addressing disagreements with others for proper resolution. Discommunication is commonly deployed by a controlling discommunicator, without the discommu-nicator having any interest in hearing the other person's perspective, and without having any intention of resolving the disagreement. Discommunicators do so because they consciously or nonconsciously, know that in the presence of facts and evidence they will be proven wrong. Hence, by closing off communication and by avoiding factual dialogue, discommunicators try to maintain authority and control over others, while preserving their own false sense of grandiosity from being proven wrong, and from being challenged and exposed.

When discommunication is deployed as a means of controlling a dependent or an empath, discommunication would then inherently include silent-treatment. Silent-treatment is the refusal to communicate verbally with someone. Although silent-treatment could be a means of avoiding the communication of one's own weaknesses and pain with others; when silent-treatment is deployed as a punitive measure, it then becomes a form of abuse. Therefore, when discommunication is engaged as a means of controlling someone else who is dependent and reliant on the discommunicator; the discommunicator uses silent-treatment alongside other evading tactics to punish the dependent, so that the dependent would be forced to succumb to the discommunicators control, rule, and authority. As stated, although discommunication could be a sulking form of avoiding others; the primary reason personality-disordered and controlling individuals engage in discommunication is as a punitive and controlling measure.

Discommunication, similar to silent-treatment, is a passive-aggressive behavior, and it is intended to protect the discommunicator's false-image while maintaining control over someone else. Discommunicators are usually individuals who have a weak sense of Self and a negative self-image; thus, for them to stand corrected is self-perceived as being inferior and unworthy. Instead of discussing and resolving disagreements; personality-disordered individuals argue disagreements so that they will not be proven wrong. As a result, especially in the modern-era of social-media, we see more displays of disinterest in learning the truth and an increase in preserving preferred mindset regardless of contradictory facts.

Most people don't debate to learn the truth; most people argue to not be wrong.

This is why high-conflict individuals would be the last people to ever adhere to the following Theory of Self Relativity's original quote about disagreements and debates; because they are not interested in learning or in being corrected.

Disagreements are good for learning; debate to learn, don't debate to not be wrong.

Due to their false sense of importance, toxic-people who engage in discommunication and silent-treatment do so because in their mind, interactions and relationships are a "race" or a "competition" to win. Therefore, if in their mind they cannot win an argument by proving someone else wrong, toxic-people will shut down dialogue, to prevent losing. Dealing with toxic-people feels like a race with no reward, because the only thing that matters in a toxic-relationship is for toxic-people to "feel" that they succeeded in making someone else lose.

Toxic-people engage in ego-race to see who loses first, since there is no winning in an ego-race.

Theory of Self-Relativity categorizes discommunication binarily:

1. **Avoidance-Discommunication:** Is the act of cutting-off communication, interaction, and engagement to enable the discommunicator avoid hearing, seeing, or acknowledging information or evidence that could expose the discommunicator's own self-deficiencies and weaknesses. According to Theory of Self-Relativity, avoidance-discommunication is a form of coping-mechanism which helps discommunicators ignore and deny reality, by abstaining from introspection, in an attempt to preserve their false-image and desired-feelings. Avoidance-discommunication is self-directed in order to protect personal-weaknesses and fragilities, and to avoid facing uncomfortable truths. Unlike silent-treatment, which could be used to avoid communicating one's own pain with others;

avoidance-discommunication is intended to prevent the person from becoming aware of one's own weaknesses and shortcomings, or to avoid being proven wrong. Therefore, while silent-treatment is directed between the Self and against others; discommunication could also be engaged to avoid getting in touch with personal-weaknesses, by forcing others to abstain from communicating the dislikable-truth.

Although silent-treatment is intended to punish others; discommunication is often engaged to protect the fragile Self.

2. **Punitive-Discommunication:** Is cutting-off communication, interaction, and engagement to enable the discommunicators to elevate their own sense of importance, and to egotistically create or maintain their false self-image. Punitive-discommunication is also commonly engaged as a means of exercising control over others; especially for controlling those who are dependent on the discommunicator. Punitive-discommunication, unlike avoidance-discommunication, is not self-directed for the protection of one's own fragile Self. Punitive-discommunication is directed externally as a means of validation of the discommunicator's sense of self-importance and control. Additionally, punitive-discommunication, especially in relationships where one party is dependent and reliant on the discommunicator, creates a power play for the discommunicator, in order to exert or increase control over the dependent. As discussed, punitive-discommunication often includes some sort of silent-treatment that is intended to exert control through cognitive-dissonance, confusion, crazy-making, gaslighting, and other forms of mental-abuse.

Discommunicators are often self-victimizing and blame-shifting people who stop communicating and speaking with others because they don't like to hear what others have to say. They do so because if what others say or present is factually true, such evidence could expose their inner-weaknesses and could threaten or undermine their authority and control; and in-turn, facts and evidence could threaten their false-reality. To a discommunicator, the truth or other-people's contrary opinion is highly undesired or too painful to consider. Dealing with Cluster-B individuals, and as a whole, dealing with discommunicators and other insecure or controlling people, is usually self-destructive and costly; because in order to preserve and maintain the relationship, a great deal of energy, time, and unilateral-compromise must be committed. When a relationship requires one-sided compromise to the point where one feels like one is sacrificing one's time, energy, and other resources just to stay in the relationship; that relationship is unhealthy and detrimental for the person who is unilaterally compromising, or who is sacrificing one's Self in order to maintain the relationship.

Sacrifice, according to Theory of Self-Relativity, is one of the most detrimental and destructive manmade delusional forms of behavior. Whether in its traditionally ritualistic format of actually sacrificing humans and animals for delusionary and imaginary gods, or in the more common societal and cultural forms of giving up something personal for others; sacrificial mindset and behavior induce control, by taking something away from the Self. If we have to give up something in order to preserve or add value to someone or something else; that itself becomes an extreme form of externalation, because we ignore our Self and we completely shift our focus onto others. Sacrifice reverses and completely takes away the ability of a person to self-focus and to be self-complete. As discussed, to have healthy and constructive relationships with others, we must first be healthy and strong on our own; which means, we have to live a centered-self life. If we must give up something essential for our existence to add value to someone else; we are then undermining or even destroying our existence and any future contributions that we could offer to others, past our last act.

Self-care is not the same thing as being selfish; however, self-sacrifice is being self-abusive.

According to Theory of Self-Relativity, to sacrifice means to give away a part, or even, all of our Self for others. Complete people will not sacrifice themselves, because there is no reason to sacrifice and break apart our completeness in order to add value to others; hence why, relationships must be complementary and not completing. Since completing relationships are costly for at least one party; to sacrifice, means being in a relationship that is not good for us.

According to Theory of Self-Relativity, instead of sacrificing and giving up things for others at the expense of our own Self; it is better to compromise. When we compromise, instead of deducting from our Self or instead of sacrificing our Self; we are thus substituting by maintaining our completeness, while enhancing our compatibility and complementary additive value with others. When substitutional-compromise accomplishes a similar outcome that a sacrifice would; this means, that the relationship is a complementary one. For example, instead of sacrificing monthly rent by going on a vacation that we cannot afford; we can plan an enjoyable night-out on the town while preserving our ability to pay the rent. Or instead of sacrificing going out with friends because our romantic-partner also wanted to go out with us; we can substitute by making plans which includes our friends and our partner. This way, our individual completeness and the complementary nature of our relationship is mutually-preserved without any sacrifice or unilateral-compromise that could endanger the stability of our romantic-relationship, or that could weaken our financial situation.

Don't sacrifice; substitute.

Unlike sacrifice, which is unilateral and personal, substitution creates balance without having to resort to unilateral-compromise, down-compromise, or sacrifice. This is why, mutual-compromise, unlike unilateral-compromise, is helpful in maintaining and growing complementary-relationships. However, unlike many psychology, self-help, and social recommendations, Theory of Self-Relativity does not consider unilateral-compromise as a necessary component for complementarity; on the contrary, it considers unilateral-compromise, especially chronic unilateral-compromise, as a negative attempt in maintaining an unbalanced relationship. Hence why, Theory of Self-Relativity favors substitutional-compromise instead of unilateral-compromise. Substitution enables replacement while maintaining complementarity, and without value deduction; however, chronic unilateral-compromise attempts to maintain value at the expense of one or more parties.

If compromise is needed to maintain and grow complementarity, such compromise must be mutual; however, when substitution is used to maintain and grow complementarity, substitutional-compromise could create complementarity while adding value without the need for mutual-participation. When each party in a relationship is complete, each individual could make personal substitutions, adjustments, and contributions unilaterally; which in-turn, would add value, or at the minimum, would maintain value without any disruption or necessity for prolonged unilateral-compromise. Such individual completeness of each and every complementary member of a relationship is how, further growth in a relationship is achieved.

Individual practicality creates mass efficiency.

If and when a compromise is needed and substitution is not an option, mutual-compromise should be the main form of compromise for the relationship. Unilateral-compromise and down-compromise, especially in the longer-term, are deductive attributes for maintaining and preserving a relationship; hence, they are costly to the compromising person. Therefore, in a complementary-relationship, mutual-compromise is the best solution and unilateral-compromise should only happen if the compromising person can do so without any loss.

When we learn to truly become self-sufficient, and when our self-identity and our sense of Self are established from within; it is only then that we could contribute our Self to a relationship as a complete-individual and on a complementary basis. When we are complete on our own and when we don't tangibly or intangibly rely on others, our relationships will become complementary and not completing. Therefore, our footing in the relationship will be from the point of strength and with the perspective of nothing-to-lose; rather than from position of neediness, having to unfairly compromise or sacrifice. Furthermore, complementary-relationships make people more resilient to difficulties and they make people more open to substitution and change; because complementary-relationships are created by complete-individuals who are inherently resilient to difficulties, as they are adaptable to change. Resilience does not mean rigidity or tolerance; on the contrary, according to Theory of Self-Relativity, resilience means to have the strength to recognize, confront, and resolve difficulties.

Theory of Self-Relativity defines "resilience" as "the ability to identify, confront, and resolve difficulties and negativities."

Theory of Self-Relativity categorizes resilience binarily:

1. **Positive-Resilience:** Is the form of resilience that enables us to confront and resolve or eliminate personal, relationship, and life's difficulties and negativities. Positive-resilience is constructive and additive to our existence

as it is a skill that we can develop to strengthen our personal-resolve, our discipline, and our self-confidence. Just like confidence, positive-resilience will strengthen as we gain more experience and knowledge based on how reality is, and not based on how we want reality to be. Positive-resilience, just like other positive personal-characteristics can be strengthened as we improve critical-thinking and factual-thinking skills.

2. **Negative-Resilience:** Is the form of resilience that is severely disabling to personal-development and self-improvement. Negative-resilience is the lack of ability and skill to confront, let alone to resolve or eliminate difficulties and negativities. Negative-resilience causes a person to accept and allow personal, relationship, and life's difficulties to persist and continue. Negative-resilience is common in externally dependent and reliant people such as codependents and people-pleasers, because in order to carry on or to even survive, they have to develop negative-resilience to tolerate difficulties. When negative-resilience persists and continues, it turns into *"tolerance,"* and those who are too tolerant, also tend to be selfless and self-sacrificial; which means, they prioritize others over their own Self. Although tolerance as a temporary overflow of resilience could be beneficial; endless tolerance is destructive. Unlike positive-resilience, which is progressive; negative-resilience is intended to be protective.

While, in interactions and in relationships, positive-resilience is a constructive attribute; according to Theory of Self-Relativity, a negative-resilience of equal value and intensity will cause more damage and setback to a person, than a positive-resilience of same magnitude would. Positive-resilience develops slowly and increases through knowledge, experience, and implementation; conversely, negative-resilience increases in the absence of change and improvement, and almost always becomes chronic as it evolves into tolerance.

Although traditional, cultural, societal, religious, spiritual, and even, psychology teachings advocate tolerance, especially in interactions and relationships; Theory of Self-Relativity considers tolerance, and especially long-term and chronic-tolerance to be detrimental for the Self. Negative-resilience, tolerance, and sacrifice are extreme manifestations of externalation and living an externally-focused life, while completely ignoring one's own Self. Negative-resilience, tolerance, and sacrifice, lead to being dependent and controlled; and these are often advocated by others such as culture and society, in order to control people. By taking advantage of human empathy, as well as via shame and guilt feelings; through manmade stories and doctrines, tolerance and sacrifice are incorrectly and manipulatively portrayed as moral human attributes.

The boiling-frog-syndrome is a good example of how chronic negative-resilience often turns into tolerance. This example is based on the premise that if a frog is suddenly put in boiling water, the frog will jump out; however, if the frog is put in a room temperature water and the water temperature is slowly brought up to a boil, the frog will not recognize or perceive the danger, and will eventually boil to death. This example clearly indicates how chronic negative-resilience leads to tolerance, and how tolerance could have severe consequences.

When we enter relationships on a completing but not a complementary basis, we enter such interactions or relationships like the exampled frog. In due time, we will be forced to unilaterally-compromise, be controlled, and potentially be forced to tolerate abuse, in order to maintain the relationship. As stated, unilateral-compromise, tolerance, and sacrifice are not value-additive to a relationship; the best they could do is to postpone the demise of the relationship. Being tolerant and sacrificial means allowing interactions in relationships to penetrate personal-boundaries and to go beyond personal-limits. Tolerance, as a short-term and one-time act could be helpful; however, tolerance as a whole, must be avoided because tolerance is always at the expense of the tolerant person.

When relationships are complementary and not based on unilateral-compromise, tolerance, and sacrifice; such relationships will grow based on mutual-reciprocity. This is especially true of personal and romantic-relationships. Although all characteristics and aspects of interactivities in relationships that are discussed by Theory of Self-Relativity apply to personal as well as business and social interactions; in this publication, more references and examples are presented with implied personal and romantic-relationships, because generally, what applies to personal and romantic-relationships, also applies to other interactions and relationships. Furthermore, personal and romantic-relationships are easier referenced and understood because almost everyone has experienced such interactions and relationships.

Another important quality in a relationship is trust, which could only be properly established and maintained if one has self-trust. Trust is a byproduct of self-confidence, and as discussed, self-confidence itself is a byproduct of personal-development; therefore, trust, just like self-confidence, is not simply an attitude, but it is a skill. Hence, trust, just life self-confidence, increases as we increase our knowledge and experience and as we decrease self-doubt.

Trust is not a feeling, a mindset, or an attitude. Trust is a skill that is the result of self-confidence.

Unlike popular teachings, we should not focus on trusting others, but we should focus on trusting our own Self; because, when we trust that we are complete on our own and we can handle any situation that arises, we will then not be concerned about trusting others. Trusting others is irrelevant because basing trust on others without trusting our own Self keeps us in a position of dependency on others; and this, in-turn, destabilizes our self-equation. When we develop self-trust, we will inherently approach interactions and relationships with others with the benefit-of-the-doubt; because we will always be able to walk away from the interaction or the relationship, if others prove to be distrusting.

To trust others, begins by having self-confidence and self-trust in knowing that we can always protect our interests.

Trusting others, and as a whole, trust in relationships, goes hand-in-hand with being self-trusting, self-confident, and self-complete. As discussed, Theory of Self-Relativity places utmost importance in the role of our Self in our interactions and relationships; because contrary to popular teachings which focus on what we can do for others, we should first learn to have a healthy and strong self-relationship.

Do unto others as you do unto your Self.

Although personal-strength and completeness is important in having a well-balanced and complementary-relationship; yet, interactions and relationships are heavily influenced by feelings and emotions. When we interact with others and as we establish and evolve through interactions and relationships with them; we initially connect with people through feelings and emotions. For example, although in social-settings, physical appearance is often an instant attraction, other traits such as self-confidence are also quickly perceived as a positive attribute; because, in interactions, even our cognitive and personal characteristics, just like our physical-characteristics, are received by others emotionally. As a matter of fact, we remember the past, we remember events, and we remember people with our emotions; therefore, our memories are often faulty. Hence why, Theory of Self-Relativity's Cognitive-Cognition-Technique emphasizes on emotional-awareness combined with cognitive-understanding.

Because:

We remember with emotions.

It should be noted that despite our memories being stored cognitively; our memories are filed away and recalled emotionally. In other words, we file away and we recall our memories as thoughts by accessing them via our emotions that we attached to these memories when we filed them away. Since we remember things emotionally because our emotions are the indexing system used for filing our memories away; likewise, we remember people by how they made us feel.

People connect with people and remember them emotionally.

Our thoughts create our feelings and emotions, but our feelings and emotions help us recall our memories and perceptions. Since our feelings influence how we perceive and how we remember things, events, and people; to have successful relationships, we should also be able to connect with others emotionally. Once we master the cognitive and factual-thinking aspect of our Self, we can then learn to flourish our emotional state, which itself, must be based on a strong cognitive personal core.

To connect to others emotionally, we must first allow our Self to experience these emotions personally; hence, to generate and experience the correct emotions, we must learn to think factually.

For example, to have empathy for others, we must first learn to have self-empathy for our own Self. Furthermore, and as discussed earlier, perspective-taking, which is our ability to perceive and feel things from another person's point of view, is another important mental skill that we should have to be able to successfully relate to and connect with others. According to Theory of Self-Relativity, the most stable and successful relationships that are complementary, are based on the completeness of each individual member of the relationship and their emotional-interconnectivities with one another.

If you can't be good to your own self, you won't know how to truly be good to others.

Even in business-relationships and in sales-interactions, to successfully "persuade" someone else in committing to our perspective or to what we are selling, we must successfully convince others that we are confident in our position and mastery of the subject-matter. Although in modern western cultures the power of persuasion is viewed as a strong and positive skill in interpersonal-relationships; Theory of Self-Relativity considers persuasion as a unilaterally dominating and potentially controlling attribute in relationships. According to Theory of Self-Relativity, interactivity and connection, rather than one-sided persuasive abilities, should be the driving form of interactions among the parties of a relationship. To properly interact and communicate our perspective and our preferences to others, empathy and perspective-taking abilities will win people over without the need for persuasion; because when we connect to and relate with others on an emotional and understanding basis, we won't need to persuade them.

Don't try to persuade others, win them over with your empathy and understanding.

However, empathy and understanding does not mean to blindly agree with and allow nonfactual and emotional positions of others to influence our interactions with them. Empathy and perspective-taking are valuable tools in interacting with others instead of persuading them, only if the basis of the interaction is based on understanding of the facts associated with the situation; and not based on protecting the feelings and emotions of those that we are being empathetic with. Perspective-taking and empathy create awareness and understanding; which in-turn, are best achieved by observing and by listening to our own Self, and to others.

Because:

Awareness and understanding are the most important attributes in dealing with reality.

Hence why:

Theory of Self-Relativity defines "cognition" as "awareness and understanding through mindfulness, thoughtfulness, and thought-management."

When we learn to become self-aware and to clearly observe, listen, and understand our own Self; we will then be able to deploy the same skills relative to others. It is only then that we will have lesser need to constantly express our Self for validation, and we will have more interest in observing and listening to others. When we know our Self and when we feel complete on our own, we will have less self-doubt and we will increase our self-confidence; therefore, we will not need to use others as convincing sounding-boards, or as echo-chambers for validation. When we are self-aware and cognizant of our own Self, our interactions and relationships with others will develop and strengthen based on our "interest" in understanding them.

To be a good listener; you must have interest, and you must care to understand.

Regardless of whether we are a leader, an interrogator, a father or a mother, a husband or a wife; as long as we are human, we cannot pretend nor can we memorize how to listen. To be an effective listener, irrespective of our position in an interaction or in a relationship, we must have an "interest" to listen, and most importantly, we must want to "understand" what others are telling us; regardless of our short-term opinion of the context of the communication. Thus, when we have an interest to understand; we then "care" to listen. Therefore, to be interested and to care to listen and understand, we must have:

1. **Empathy:** To care to listen.
2. **Perspective-taking ability:** To understand and to see things from someone else's perspective.

Empathy and perspective-taking is our interactive-bridge to others.

When we are complete on our own, we will become better observers and better listeners relative to others; and when others feel and sense that we relate to them, we will be able to have a smoother and more balanced relationship in return. Be it in sales, in business, or in personal-relationships, others want to be heard and understood; and when they feel heard and understood, they will be more open to accepting our perspective over their own. When people feel accepted and understood, they become less-defensive and more open to suggestions and recommendations.

Observe and absorb…Listen and discern.

Regardless of the nature of the interaction or the relationship, be it business, personal or romantic; when we interact with others, we are presenting, or even, we are "selling" our "Self" to them. Therefore, we must ensure that we actually know and understand what we are selling, and we must make sure what we are selling is of high quality. When we sell high-quality to others, we will not have to convince or persuade them to buy what we are selling; the value will naturally be recognized and accepted by others. Therefore, to have successful interactions with others, we don't need to persuade them; we should instead, present the value of what we are selling, thus, we should relate that value to them by understanding their perspective.

However, there will be times that others will not be able to recognize and understand the value of what we are selling; hence, by being self-secure and by knowing and understanding the value-proposition that we bring to the table, we will be able to walk-away and move on to other interactions without needing to persuade those who don't see our value, and without feeling inferior or rejected because others couldn't perceive or recognize our value proposition.

This is why, being open and unbiased is an important characteristic for living a quality life; because, when we are open to using facts to evaluate our characteristics, we can either use other people's lack of interest as an indication for self-reflection and for self-improvement, or, we can recognize that we are providing high-quality value but others are not able to recognize the value. When we can factually recognize our weaknesses or our strengths, we will then use other-people's reactions to either improve our Self, or as a means to verify our value. Being open and unbiased, based on facts, will enable us to recognize that someone else's disinterest to interact with us is not necessarily a representation of our lower personal-quality. Either way, by objectively evaluating someone else's disinterest, we will either improve our weaknesses, or if others cannot see our value proposition, we will disengage; but, we will not feel rejected.

Feeling rejected is similar to being offended; because rejection is felt as a result of some kind of internal-deficiency or weakness that is triggered or brought onto our consciousness due to our interactions with others. Rejection is commonly triggered as a result of lack of interest or as a result of exclusion in interpersonal-relationships or in social settings. According to Theory of Self-Relativity, rejection is a self-deficiency feeling that we feel when we seek external-validation. We can only feel rejected if we attach our self-identity and our self-worth externally based on other-people's reactions, or by being dependent on others. When we seek to improve externally and when we do not receive approval, acceptance, or validation from others; that is when we feel rejected. However, as described by Theory of Self-relativity, despite rejection being a strong negative personal-feeling that is triggered by others; rejection is actually subjective and personal irrespective of its triggering cause.

The degree and intensity of rejection that one feels, is directly related to one's internal-weaknesses and external-dependencies.

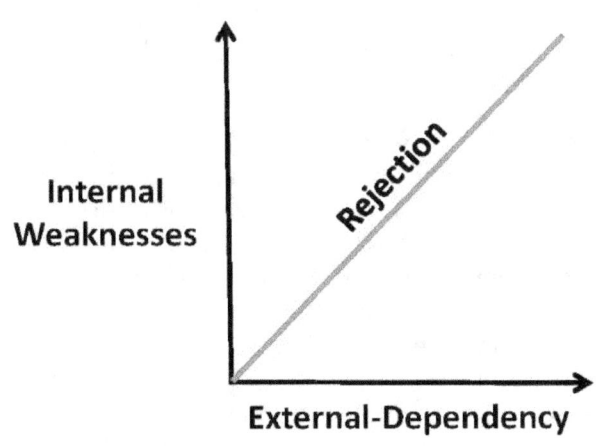

567

Although rejection feels deductive and even sometimes catastrophic:

When we feel rejected, we don't actually lose anything; we simply don't gain what we were looking for.

Therefore, one's reaction to rejection is usually exaggerated because of one's own subjective perception, and because of one's own insecurities. Since rejection is personal and subjective, there is no scale to measure the degree of rejection; this is why, rejection is subjectively-perceived rather than objectively-measured. Hence, it is not rejection that is scary, but it is the fear and anticipation of the potential rejection that is inhibiting.

It is not rejection itself that is demeaning; it is the fear-of-rejection that is debilitating.

The main problem and the consequence associated with rejection is not the actual event of being or feeling rejected; but it is the "fear-of-rejection." As discussed, fear makes us fight-or-flight, and sometimes even freeze; however, fear-of-rejection almost always causes us to flight or freeze. It is because of this fear-of-rejection that rejection is not a deductive event; but rejection prevents improvement. In the modern-times, fight-or-flight often turns into fight-or-flight-or-freeze as our fear of making decisions sometimes not only leads to negative consequences; but our indecisiveness and fear prevents us from improving. Although fear can prevent unfavorable outcomes; fear can also prevent potentially favorable outcomes.

Fear is not only the precursor to anger and rage; but fear is also the factor that limits contentment, happiness, and success.

In summary:

Although being or feeling rejected feels like we lost something, rejection itself does not cause us to lose anything; rejection simply prevents us from gaining something.

Therefore, our reactions to rejection are subjective and relative to our own weaknesses and our own insecurities. Since feeling rejected is a subjective personal-feeling; the anticipation or the potential of being rejected is what prevents us from trying new things and taking actions that could in fact be constructive and improving for our Self.

As discussed throughout Theory of Self-Relativity, worry, anxiety, and fear are directly associated with lack of control and uncertainty; therefore, when faced with a future event, we must make best predictions to minimize uncertainty so that we can improve the chances of our desired outcomes. Since rejection is directly related to our interactions with others, and because we cannot with high certainty predict the outcome of other-people's reactions towards our initiations and approaches; this uncertainty combined with prior memories of rejection, creates and intensifies our fear-of-rejection. According to Theory of Self-Relativity, since rejection is a "subjective" feeling that is as a result of a "personal" mindset; therefore, the intensity of the fear-of-rejection is directly proportional to our insecurities, and it is inversely-proportional to our level of self-confidence.

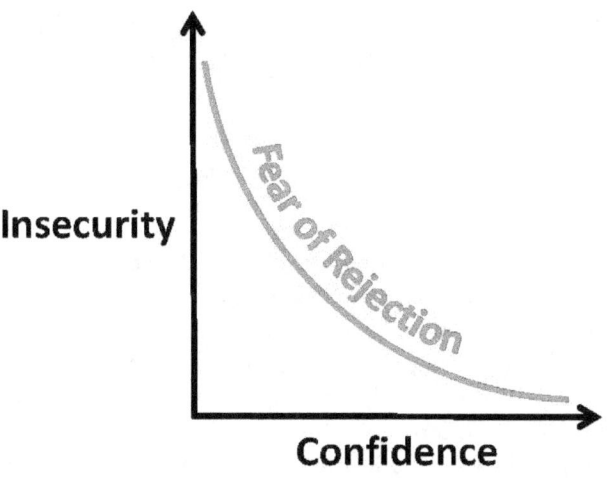

Insecurity

Fear of Rejection

Confidence

The less confident we are and the more insecure we feel, the stronger our fear-of-rejection will be, and the less potential we will have to do something that could be beneficial for us. Conversely, the more secure we feel and the less we exaggerate our fear-of-rejection, the more potential we will have to gain something positive in our quest for improvement. Fear-of-rejection is another good example of why self-improvement and personal-development must be cultivated and improved internally; and why, it should not be reliant on external sources.

Fearing rejection is no different than fearing failure. When we fear rejection or when we fear failure, despite the fact that neither rejection nor failure have actually happened; we often abstain from taking action because we fear the potential for being rejected or for failing. If we don't proceed with an action, we will never succeed; however, if we proceed with an action, although there is a possibility that we might not succeed, there is also a probability that we might actually succeed with our intended outcome.

The fear of unfavorable outcomes, guarantees lack of favorable outcomes.

When we learn to factually evaluate the underlying thoughts that are causing our fear-of-rejection or our fear-of-failure; we can then realize that such fear that we feel is often regarding a feature event that has not yet occurred. This inability to foresee a future event is what causes our uncertainty and our inability to control outcomes. Since the probability of a favorable personal outcome is minimal to zero in the absence of action; therefore, taking an action, in lieu of a potential rejection, is generally a good approach. Although rejection or failure in some situations have parallels with each other; failure, however, could sometimes cause a deductive result. Therefore, the potential for failure must be more diligently evaluated than the potential for rejection. Rejection is simply a disinterest from someone else; and since rejection is as a result of the subjectivity of another person's perspective, rejection should not have long-term negative consequences if we learn to distinguish the difference between rejection and failure.

If fear-of-rejection prevents you from trying, you are guaranteeing a "NO" answer; however, if you try, there is a potential for a "YES" answer.

Therefore:

There is a big difference between rejection and failure, if we don't treat rejections as failures.

When we learn to become aware of our feelings and when we use this awareness to factually evaluate the thoughts that are causing our feelings, we can then take proper action or inaction to improve our Self. By understanding that fear-of-rejection is a subjective-feeling and that rejection, itself, has no negative consequences; we can then minimize self-doubt and increase our self-confidence in our interactions with others and in our interpersonal-relationships. When we treat fear-of-rejection as simply disinterest from others; our self-doubt in dealing with others will decrease. As discussed throughout Theory of Self-Relativity, we should be complete on our own and we should approach others in a complimentary format and from the perspective of having nothing-to-lose. When we have nothing-to-lose, we can only gain something; therefore, if someone displays disinterest to us we can simply move on instead of taking that person's disinterest personally, by feeling rejected or by incorrectly feeling as if we failed.

Rejection is a self-made hoax.

Fear-of-rejection is common in personal and romantic-relationships; and it is especially prevalent in first meetings. Many who are attracted to another person or want to impress and be approved by others, think and evaluate too much about being rejected; hence, the potential opportunity closes after a while. For example, if a single man is at a social-setting and he finds a particular female attractive; if he doesn't approach and initiate interaction with the female to create the opportunity, at some point, other men might take the opportunity away from him, or the woman will eventually leave. In this example, regardless of how the woman's availability closed up, the fear-of-rejection guaranteed the man not meeting the woman; however, had the man approached the woman, there would've been the probability for them to meet, interact, and even create a relationship.

Therefore:

Unlike failure, which cannot be guaranteed to not happen even if we take action; rejection will be guaranteed to happen if we take no action.

Furthermore, if the man in the aforementioned example approached the woman from a position of himself being complete but she was not interested, he could have simply moved on to others; because when one is complete, one approaches interactions with the perspective of having nothing-to-lose. When one approaches situations from a default state of nothing-to-lose; one would never experience rejection. Having nothing-to-lose does not mean being reckless, or being like a psychopath without care or concern for others. Having nothing-to-lose means to have enough self-confidence to know that other-people's subjective-disinterest does not necessarily mean a personal-deficiency. This is why, self-confidence is not an attitude but it is a skill; and to have self-confidence, one must first minimize self-doubt.

However, should the man in this example realize that such disinterest is continuously happening to him with the same approach, he should then recognize and evaluate this information objectively, by considering that there might be a personal-attribute or a personal-deficiency that is causing the consistency of unfavorable outcomes. Therefore, he should evaluate to identify and improve those deficiencies. Whether it is his approach that is incorrect or whether it is a personal or physical attribute that he recognizes is causing the disinterests; by being able to introspect via self-awareness, rather than by being defensive or by making himself a victim, he can then take action to improve his personal-attributes and shortcomings, hence increase his chances of favorable outcomes. Rejection, just like failure, is only final if we make it final and if we don't use the feeling of rejection as a steppingstone event to build upon it. However, rejection, unlike failure, does not have to be deductive; because when approached with confidence and a nothing-to-lose position, other-people's rejection will not be a loss.

Fix what made you feel rejected, and you won't feel rejected again.

One of the main consequences of rejection, especially in romantic-relationships, is the feeling of inferiority and less-desirability. Romantic-relationships and dating are associated with rejection and feelings of insecurity because these relationships are the predisposing attributes for sex; which itself is a pleasure-reinforcer. The pleasures involved with dating and sex are rooted in procreation to ensure survival and continuation of the species. Sex, love, and mating are generally associated with good feelings and dopamine production because they are pleasure-based primary-reinforcers. These primary pleasure-reinforcers drive us to seek that rewarding pleasure of sex, so that we can fulfill our inherent purpose of procreation. As discussed, nature has programed us to experience pleasure and positive-feelings when we engage in behaviors that increase our chances of safety and survival; for example, eating and sex. This is why, being accepted by a potential mate is pleasant, yet not being accepted feels as rejection. However, while safety and survival enhancing behavior increase dopamine and make us feel good; nature has also programmed us to experience displeasure and negative-feelings when our safety or survival is compromised or could be in danger.

Just as pleasure rewards us to engage in behaviors that increase our safety and survival; displeasure and negative-feelings force us to engage in behaviors that minimize threats and danger. As exampled previously, a toothache is unpleasant and painful, therefore the negative-feeling of pain forces us to take action in order to resolve the potential danger of tooth-infection; which if unresolved, could result in other complications and even death. However, as humans have progressed and have become more intelligent; in many instances, instead of resolving the cause to alleviate the negative-symptom, humans have learned to manipulate and abuse ways of experiencing better feelings by engaging in dopamine producing thinking and behavior, without resolving the cause of the negative-feeling. This is how dependency and addictions are formed.

It takes intelligence to manipulate intelligence.

Since sex is closely linked with pleasure, hence, similar to other things associated with pleasure; dating and sex could also lose their intended outcome if abused as a trigger to continuously produce pleasure, or as a means of gaining external-validation. Therefore, continuous pleasure-seeking could lead to addiction, which is an unhealthy state-of-mind and behavior intended to improve positive-feelings based on external-stimuli. In case of sex, the constant chase and the incorrect hope of another person completing one's internal-weaknesses, is one of the main problems associated with failed romantic-relationships and marriages. When people engage in mating and even matrimony as a compromise for completing reasons, rather than as an additive to a complementary-relationship; such relationships often fail and lead to cheating and infidelity, which commonly result in difficult separations and painful divorces.

Theory of Self-Relativity categorizes the causes of cheating and infidelity binarily:

1. **Externalation:** Just like other forms of addiction, the more a pleasure inducer is utilized, the less its resulting level of pleasure becomes; therefore, the more of it becomes necessary to try to catch the illusive pleasure-dragon that the addict experienced the first time. Addictions, as discussed, are often developed as a form of externalation in order to abstain from the unpleasant and painful task of introspection. Same could apply to dating and sex. By continuously distracting and preoccupying the mind with others, either by engaging in dating apps or other organic means of meeting partners; those who engage in excessive dating and sexual activities often do so with the nonconscious intent to abstain from introspection and from self-improvement.

2. **Validation:** Those who are not content, fulfilled, and happy on their own or in their romantic-relationship or marriage, could look for acceptance and validation externally by meeting and by becoming intimate with other partners. The novelty of meeting someone new and their interest in one-another creates a temporary sense of validation. Instead of correcting self-deficiencies and personal-shortcomings to validate one's own Self; those who cheat, do so in an attempt to fill the internal-voids of their life that they are unwilling to personally resolve. Those who continuously seek dating and sexual partners could be doing so as a means of external-focus, by hoping the next new partner will make them feel complete, or will be the answer to their insufficiencies.

It must be noted that the concept of cheating and infidelity is a manmade, cultural, societal, and religious one. In consideration of the mammalian and animal aspects of the human-species, there is nothing that dictates having multiple mating partners is wrong. As a matter of fact, nature dictates the more partners an animal has, the better chances are for the individual to pass its genes to the next generation. However, based on cultural-beliefs and social-values, many consider cheating and infidelity or having multiple-partners as wrong; because our modern mutual understanding in romantic-relationships is defaulted in fidelity, unless otherwise agreed upon and understood between the partners. Hence, cheating and infidelity are acts against currently preferred personal, cultural, and social standards; and when cheating or infidelity occurs, they are considered as a breach of trust between the parties involved in an interaction or a relationship.

Therefore, in lieu of such commitments and understandings, Theory of Self-Relativity considers cheating and infidelity as self-serving forms of *"betrayal-of-trust"* behavior; because they are commonly associated with deception and lying that is directed against others. Although betrayal-of-trust is the core component of cheating and infidelity in romantic-relationships; betrayal-of-trust is also the core component of other violations in interpersonal-relationships such as stealing, lying, and deception. While betrayal-of-trust is most popularly perceived in love and in romantic-relationships; betrayal-of-trust also occurs as violations of understandings or agreements in other interpersonal-interactions and relationships such as in business and in politics.

Theory of Self-Relativity categorizes cheaters binarily:

1. **The Cheater:** Is the person that deceives others in order to gain an advantage against them, commonly without others' knowledge or consent. Cheaters cheat because they want to gain an advantage that otherwise they would not have been able to achieve, if the person being cheated knew of the cheater's intents and actions. *Hence why cheaters lie.*

2. **The Cheated:** Is the person being deceived or kept uninformed by the cheater, commonly through lies and misrepresentations. The cheated is cheated through deception because the cheater knows that if the cheated knew about the cheater's intentions and actions, the cheated would not have consented or agreed to the interaction. *Hence why cheaters lie.*

Cheaters must lie because without deception cheaters wouldn't be able to achieve their goals.

Cheating, infidelity, and as a whole, all forms of betrayal-of-trust are as a result of dishonesty and lack of transparency. Similar to lying, those who cheat and betray trust do so because they want to hide personal-deficiencies, or because they want to represent a better image of their own Self, in order to gain something that they would not have been able to gain without betrayal. Furthermore, the cheated, often enables and tolerates being cheated because the cheated lacks the self-confidence to not accept the comforting lies and misrepresentations; hence, to disengage from the dishonest relationship.

Additionally, betrayal-of-trust, especially relative to cheating in romantic-relationships, is often riddled with blame-shifting and excuses as to why cheating occurred. For example, one of the most common excuses of cheating in a romantic-relationship is that the cheater cheated because the cheater was not happy in the relationship. In other words, the cheater cheated because the other person could not make the cheater happy, or because the other person made the cheater do it. Such mindsets and statements are prime examples of incomplete people entering relationships in order to feel complete.

Similarly, the cheated often justifies and stays in a relationship with a cheater because of one's own weaknesses and incompleteness. For example, the cheated will stay in a relationship with a self-victimization excuse of loving the cheater too much, or for the common excuse of staying for the kids. If the relationship default is loyalty, a complete and self-secure person will not cheat, nor would one tolerate cheating. Regardless, instead of cheating to feel complete, or to replace one partner with another, a complete person would simply choose to walk-away without the need or the necessity to be in a replacement-relationship. A complete person does not need to be in a relationship to feel complete, because a complete person enters interactions and relationships on an additive and complementary-basis; not for completing reasons.

It is better to not be in a relationship, than to be in a relationship for the wrong reason.

Likewise, complete people would not tolerate being betrayed or cheated on because complete people would not be in a relationship based on the need of someone else completing their deficiencies. This is why, it is important for our interactions and relationships to be complementary and not completing, so that we enter them from a point of strength and from the position of having nothing-to-lose. When we enter interactions and relationships as a self-sufficient and complete person by having nothing-to-lose, our relationships will inherently be based on mutual-reciprocity and based on the previously discussed relationship-fundamentals of respect, support, and predictability (RSP). Because when we interact with others for additive reason and not completing ones, lack of a relationship with others won't be deductive to our life; therefore, if such relationships don't work out, we can easily move onto relationships with others who can add value to us and to the relationship.

Furthermore, when relationships are complementary and not completing, RSP consequently increases; therefore, the need for apology and forgiveness diminishes. A complete person would not need apology from someone else to feel better; neither would one need to forgive others for similar reasons. This is why, Theory of Self-Relativity insists that an apology should not be given in order to be forgiven. In a truly complementary and non-egotistical relationship, an apology should only be given in-lieu of a wrongdoing to represent that the apologizer values the other person and the relationship. Thus, apologies should only be given if the apologizer acted in a factually incorrect manner; however, apologies should not be given as a means of one-sidedly preserving the relationship, just because the other person felt hurt or disrespected.

We are responsible for what we say and do; we can't be responsible for how others feel or react.

According to Theory of self-Relativity, apologies are hypocritically over-popularized and over-utilized in society as a means of prioritizing others over one's Self. Apologies should not be handed out like candy just to make someone else who is in the wrong feel good; or to preserve a relationship unilaterally. An apology must only be offered as a means of valuing the other person enough to acknowledge one's own mistake.

Only apologize because you know you negatively impacted another person; not because you hurt someone's feelings.

Many apologize as a means of trying to keep the peace, and more commonly, in order to protect someone else's feelings. Since feelings are subjective and not factual, this is why, Theory of Self-Relativity advocates factual-thinking; thus, when we think factually, we can consequently distinguish the necessity of giving or receiving an apology. Therefore, if facts indicate that there is no need for an apology, no apology should be given in order to protect or sooth someone else's feelings because facts were dislikable or uncomfortable to that person.

We can't be responsible for other people's feelings, nor can we control their misunderstandings. However, we can help clarify their misunderstanding, only if they are interested in doing so.

When someone apologizes to us, we shouldn't take that as a confirmation of our self-worth or as a sign of victory; we should consider that the person apologizing, values and respects us. Self-secure and complete people won't have expectations nor will they have the need for someone to apologize to them; therefore, such individuals would not have the need nor the necessity to forgive someone else either. This is even truer where an apology was never given. One can acknowledge and accept an apology; however, one should not be in a self-serving or an authoritarian position to forgive someone else. If we were apologized to and the relationship continues, that is already an indication of acceptance; hence, there is no need for forgiveness. However, if we were not apologized to and we chose to unilaterally forgive someone who we believed hurt us or did something wrong to us; then unlike popular belief, such forgiveness is actually more self-serving than righteous.

Forgiveness is self-serving. We forgive because it makes us feel good; not because it adds value to someone else.

In most cultures and societies, especially those that are founded upon the principles of prioritizing others over one's Self; apology and forgiveness towards others are advocated to be acts of righteousness. According to Theory of Self-Relativity, excessive apology and a default attitude of forgiveness are actually guilt-ridden forms of externalation; because, focusing on others gives people an excuse to abstain from introspection. Many traditions, cultures, and even religions, praise apology and forgiveness just like they praise and advocate selflessness and self-sacrifice; as if prioritizing others over the Self is a representation of high moral-values. As discussed throughout Theory of Self-Relativity:

We cannot do our best for others if we cannot be the best for our own Self.

Similar to apology, forgiveness has been incorrectly portrayed as a supreme act of righteousness. According to Theory of Self-Relativity, forgiveness is an unnecessary mindset and attitude that serves a binary "self-antagonistic" purpose; because:

1. Forgiveness allows others to get away with wrongdoing at the expense of one's Self.
2. Forgiveness allows the forgiver to feel good, often without the care or knowledge of the forgiven.

The obsession with apology and forgiveness causes us to preoccupy our mind with others while we ignore our own Self. As stated, apology should only be given when we understand and know that we did or said something wrong which affected someone else negatively, or when our words and actions were at the expense of someone else. Thereby, such acknowledgment and apology indicates that we value that person. However, unlike apology, Theory of Self-Relativity recognizes no reason for forgiveness. If someone did or said something wrong against us and if they apologized to us, that should represent that they value us; therefore, there is no reason for us to forgive them if we choose to continue our relationship with them. We can accept the apology, but we should not have any need to forgive because no human-being should be autocratic to forgive another person.

Forgiveness is self-serving; acceptance is liberating.

Furthermore, unlike religious, societal, or most motivational-teachings, acceptance does not mean tolerance; because tolerance encourages selflessness, which goes hand-in-hand with forgiveness and other unilateral closure mechanisms that are intended to be self-soothing. According to Theory of Self-Relativity, the traditional act of forgiveness, which is taught through culture, religion, and spirituality, is a form of placebo-thinking intended to make the "forgiver" feel good. Forgiveness is the process or action of being forgiving or being forgiven. Since the active role of forgiveness is initiated by the forgiver; therefore, forgiveness is primarily a soothing mindset for the forgiver, that gives the forgiver a false sense of being in control.

Forgiveness is a self-soothing power-trip.

Many times, the person being forgiven doesn't even know or care about being forgiven. According to Theory of Self-Relativity, the most common reason people forgive is so that they can bring one-sided closure to a situation. Unilateral-forgiveness does not resolve anything; it simply sooths the forgiver.

Forgiveness is a self-soothing attempt for closure, where closure is unavailable.

Another characteristic similar to forgiveness that keeps us stuck is *"Gratitude."* Gratitude, in culture and religion, is encouraged as a positive-attribute or a constructive-trait for improving feelings and emotions. Gratitude is commonly defined as the quality of being thankful. Although some level of recognition, appreciation, and thankfulness is important in building a positive self-esteem and establishing constructive relationships; according to Theory of Self-Relativity, gratitude is overutilized in many cultures.

Gratitude, especially when deployed in the wrong circumstances, is intended to be a comforting mechanism to justify a negativity, or to abstain from facing to improve the negativity. For example, being thankful that we have our health when we just lost our job is such form of comforting gratitude; and just like forgiveness, gratitude is intended to make the grateful person feel better, often, in lieu of something dislikable that requires difficult decision and action. Therefore, gratitude is also a form of placebo-thinking mindset.

Being appreciative is different than being grateful because truly improving people wouldn't have time to continuously stop and pay gratitude for their circumstances and accomplishments. Those who are not improving are more prone to excessive-gratitude because gratitude helps them justify their inability or lack of willingness to improve.

Excessive-gratitude prevents improvement, because it deceptively creates a sense of contentment.

Many who engage in excessive-gratitude become grateful for minor things which do not need such continuous conscious recognition and praise. Instead of focusing on improvement and progress, those who engage in excessive-gratitude, give themselves an excuse to abstain from change and improvement by being grateful for the things they already have; or by being grateful for their life's circumstances not being as bad as it could've been.

Many mistakenly confuse gratitude with contentment.

Gratitude is simply a placebo-thinking mindset; however, contentment is a state-of-existence that is reached as a result of effort and action that is directed to minimizing negativity.

Being grateful is not the same as being content or fulfilled.

In the face of difficulties or shortcomings that need to be recognized and corrected, overutilization of gratitude, just like other forms of motivation and positive-thinking, becomes a form of placebo-thinking and externalation which is intended to make us feel better. When we replace difficult decisions and actions to correct a negativity in our life with gratitude and excessive thankfulness; we are engaging in externalation. This is why, Theory of Self-Relativity considers untimely, excessive, and continuous gratitude as a negative-trait and not as a positive one; because, in order to abstain from dealing with uncomfortable-thoughts that represent difficult realities that we must correct, we overutilize gratitude as a form of placebo-thinking. Too much gratitude could become inhibiting to further improvement, when gratitude becomes a cover-up for abstaining from self-reflection and introspection. Elevating the basics of life to the level of gratitude could become a cover-up from confronting and recognizing the negativities that need improvement. Excessive-gratitude could actually become a form of coping-me-chanism as a means of covering-up personal-deficiencies that need improvement.

Excessive-gratitude is prohibitive to improvement because it creates a false sense of contentment.

If one is constantly improving, one would not have the time or the need to stop and pay gratitude. Gratitude, in many instances, is culturally, traditionally, and religiously tagged as righteous in order to keep people in a minimalist mindset, and as a means of controlling people. Autocratic-people and controlling-cultures elevate gratitude as a moral and good mindset because the comforting nature of gratitude inherently controls and prohibits the advancement and independence of the people, without individual awareness.

Acknowledgement and appreciation of positivity is different than excessive-gratitude.

Improving people acknowledge and appreciate what they have and what they have accomplished; thus, they do not continuously give gratitude to fallaciously justify their lack of progress and their inability to improve. It is more important to feel content and fulfilled than to continuously feel grateful, because many, incorrectly use gratitude as a means of validation for having reached a state of accomplishment that does not need further improvement.

By continuously feeling gratitude for basic things, we could take away the drive to further our goals and achievements.

For example, many constantly and continuously are grateful that they have a job. Although it is good to acknowledge that one has a job as that is a good thing; by being too grateful about something that should become part of one's everyday contentment, one could actually abstain from improvement. In this case, by being too grateful, one could abstain from looking for a better job, or one could abstain from starting a business of one's own; therefore, too much gratitude could actually be negative and preventive for personal progress and improvement.

Be grateful for the good you have, but don't be overly grateful to stop improving.

Just like forgiveness, excessive-gratitude is a self-serving defense-mechanism which is intended to give unilateral-closure to the grateful person, by replacing a situation that needs improvement, with an unrelated positive or neutral personal-trait or circumstance.

According to Theory of Self-Relativity, closure is a psychological need that is generally associated with a sense of resolution and finality; however, in life, and especially in interpersonal-relationships, closure is not always possible, achievable, or necessary. The need for closure is similar to the need for trying to find mea-ning and purpose to things. Although the need for closure is strong and could be obsessive and even debilitating; according to Theory of Self-Relativity, not having closure makes no real difference in many aspects of our existence. While closure might give a sense of completion and may attempt to provide an answer for a personal-deficiency; lack of closure is one of the main culprits that keeps people stuck in the past. According to Theory of Self-Relativity, the need to seek closure and the inability to move forward when closure is unavailable or when closure is denied, is a direct reflection of one's personal-shortcomings that often coexist with dependency and reliance on others.

The need for closure is more subjective than real.

Lack of closure is particularly difficult in interpersonal-relationships, and it is especially painful and even debilitating in romantic-relationships. When a person enters an interaction or a relationship based on dependency and reliance and based on the need to be completed by others; such relationships often cause self-doubt and cognitive-dissonance. Since closure is often dependent on someone else satisfying a need or an unanswered question, and since others are unavailable or will not cooperate in giving an answer, a purpose, or a reason for the open question; lack of closure keeps the mind stuck in rehashing and ruminating the events associated with the interaction or the relationship in order to come up with a finality.

While lack of closure might seem detrimental to our need to move forward; in many cases, when evaluated objectively and not emotionally, it becomes obvious that the situation does not need or require closure in order for us to move forward. Since closure is a personal "need" as it is subjective; as discussed, what we often think we need are simply desires and wants that we elevate to the level of a need. Therefore, this self-created crippling need becomes a form of externalation for us to avoid taking personal-responsibility of resolving our own personal-weaknesses which have become reliant on someone else's acceptance or their cooperation.

Furthermore, even if at some point others gave us a reason and a direct answer so that we could reach closure; if the answer does not satisfy our internal-weakness, or if the answer is not to our liking, we will continue seeking more answers in order to reach some kind of closure that is comforting and to our liking. Closure is simply an excuse to find external purpose, reason, and solutions to our inner personal-deficiencies; hence, closure is a self-made mindset intended to prevent us from facing our inner-weakness that caused us the dependency on others. Since lack of closure makes us feel incomplete, and because closure is externally derived; it is for this subjective reason that we feel closure as being a strong personal "need."

The need for closure is self-serving; acceptance is liberating.

Just as not everything has to have a purpose or a meaning; likewise, not everything or every situation needs to have closure and finality. Self-improvement and minimization of reliance on others will enable us to achieve closure unilaterally, without the need for someone else's cooperation. Self-improvements and self-reliance also enable us to move on from an event or a situation without the need for closure and finality. As stated, the need for closure is an excuse for self-victimization, for blame-shifting, and for our unwillingness to take personal-responsibility to self-improve. The desire, especially the obsessive need for closure, is a form of externalation and a direct reflection of our lack of introspective abilities. By continuously obsessing over the need for finality and closure, we place focus externally by relying on others to make a decision for us; rather than by us taking control of our own weaknesses.

To move forward in life, resolution is not the only outcome associated with closure and finality; many times, walking-away and not caring to close a situation is the correct solution. However, to be able to walk-away, we must be self-reliant and not dependent on others; because a walk-away does not necessarily indicate failure, but often it indicates personal-strength.

We don't need to find answers in the past; we can create new opportunities in the future.

As long as a walk-away is not abandonment of a difficult situation that requires actual resolution; walking-away from a situation or a relationship could create new opportunities.

You don't need others to allow you to exist.

Interactions and relationships must be complementary and not completing; therefore, our participation in an interaction or a relationship must be based on our personally created self-identity. Our self-identity must be created, cultivated, and improved from within, and it must not be reliant externally on other-people or on other-things. Such internally derived self-identity could only be stable and growing if it is based on how reality is and not based on how we want reality to be. The only means of living in harmony with realty is to think and to evaluate everything factually. In the absence of facts, we must remain skeptical and we must seek to find supportive facts for what we see, hear, and think. We cannot rely on unverified comforting information because bad data will disable us from progressing in life independently.

We must not only become aware of our own tendencies to create false-thoughts and fallacious-beliefs that make us feel good; but we must especially be aware and skeptical of thoughts, beliefs, and information that others give us, particularly, if they cannot provide supportive facts for such information. As discussed, knowledge could only be achieved when thoughts, beliefs and information are supported by facts; therefore, factual-thinking is key to living the best quality of life possible. Getting involved with others based on neediness to feel complete or based on fallacies that make us feel good, will result in failed relationships, and wasted time. As pattern-seeking animals, we are always looking for patterns and answers externally in order to make sense of our life and our existence; and we go especially easy on patterns that might not have any purpose, meaning, or factuality, as long as such patterns are comforting. This is how superstitious and supernatural-beliefs are created and spread throughout cultures and societies; because we want to believe in things that give us closure and make us feel good.

Faith, hope, beliefs, as well as patterns-seeking and biases are discussed in detail as enemies of self-improvement. Such nonfactual and fallacious forms of thought and reasoning not only hinder our own personal-development and transformation, but they become problematic when we base our interpersonal-interactions and romantic-relationships on them. Some examples of such baseless and nonfactual-fallacies that are especially common among relationships are astrology, personality-types, and other forms of pseudoscientific and paranormal-claims.

The Barnum-effect, also known as the Forer-effect, is a common psychological phenomenon whereby individuals give high accuracy ratings to descriptions of their personality that supposedly are tailored specifically to them; but that are in fact, vague and general enough to apply to a wide range of people. This effect is best represented by astrology, paranormal-beliefs and practices, fortune-telling, aura-readings, and even personality-tests. However, none of these practices could ever be true, because in order for them to be true, they would have to violate the laws-of-physics. No star can influence our birthplace and our life, just as no aura exists that could be measured. Laws-of-physics and nature simply do not allow such occurrences; because humans, just like everything else in The-Universe are made of matter.

Personality-types and personality-tests are similar pseudoscientific fabrications as are astrology and miracles. They are intended to represent positive attributes such as purpose, meaning, and closure, in order to make us feel good; but they rarely make negative predictions or suggestions, unless if the pitch could capitalize on our fear. Personal-existence is more subjective and more dynamic than generalizations that could apply to a wide members of a population or a species; however, self-improvement does not need to be custom-made to any personality-type, just as it does not vary depending on what month of the year we were born, because the calendar itself is manmade. The reason these practices exist is because, as pattern-seeking animals, human-beings are continuously searching to find the answers to the questions "Who am I" and "Why am I here?" We do so because we incorrectly believe that if we could find the answer to these questions, we would finally find the grand purpose and meaning for our existence.

As pattern-seeking animals, we are hardwired to make the meaningless have meaning.

These practices are popular because they give people "false-sense" of purpose, meaning, and hope. These practices capitalize on the human need to feel good, by externalating purpose and meaning and by helping to prevent the uncomfortable task of self-reflection and introspection. These fallacies help one see reality the way one wants reality to be, rather than to see reality the way it truly is. Short of categorizing many of these practices and suggestions as deceptive; they have no individually-relevant factual-basis as they broadly apply to most people. These practices thrive on coincidences; and the more we expose our Self to these practices, the higher the possibility of one or some of these generalities coincidentally coming true. Such coincidences consequently confirm our false-beliefs and they become a self-fulfilling prophecy. Because, similar to other superstitions and magical-thinkings; people have a tendency of disregarding the many times that the practice or the prediction didn't come true, but remembering the few times that it coincidentally did. Because of confirmation-biases, we have a tendency of confirming and remembering the hits, but ignoring and dismissing the misses.

We selectively remember our hits, yet we conveniently forget our misses.

In the name of deceptive-comfort and avoiding the dislikable:

We want to believe the impossible and we want to act on the improbable; because it feels good.

Whether it is the effects of a distant star on our birth, or the colors of the aura that our body emanates, or the personality characteristics which categorize us in a certain group; none of these events have ever been supported by any fact and evidence, or through any repeatable and unbiased scientific experiments. These mystical claims and practices are expressions of imaginations and sensationalisms that are intended to make us feel good, by justifying our desired biases. These practices are the examples of how we prefer adapting reality to our irrational-feelings, rather than adapting our feelings to factual-reality. Therefore, basing our existence, our actions, and our relationships on such nonfactual generalizations and unproven practices could have unfavorable and even dangerous outcomes.

Common claims in mysticism and deception present reality in a mystical and immaterial format. As discussed throughout Theory of Self-Relativity, we are made of atoms and everything in The-Universe is made of atoms as well; hence, it is the interaction between the atoms of everything, including ourselves, that enables us to know of the existence of all that there is. Therefore, when self-help and motivational systems base their claims and philosophies on standalone "immaterial" components of existence; it is safe to consider these claims, practices, and ideologies as false or deceptive.

For example, references to energy in science is not the same as the personal-energy claims that alternative and pseudoscientific teachers and claimants make. Energy is referred to and defined by science as "the ability to do work;" and "work," in the definition means to "get something moving." Therefore, energy is the ability to move things; and as referenced throughout Theory of Self-Relativity, motion is associated with entropy, time, and space. Energy in a resting or non-moving object is called *"Potential-Energy,"* which means it has the potential to do work or to get something moving; and energy in a moving object is called *"Kinetic-Energy,"* which is the energy that the object has because of its motion.

Pseudoscientific claims and practices, often intentionally, or sometimes unintentionally, yet ignorantly, twist real scientific facts and principles into nonscientific false claims with the intent to deceive susceptible people; because, it feels good to believe in the comforting-impossible.

These imposters do so by claiming mysticism as the hidden secret that will change difficulties and negativities into eternal-happiness and euphoria; only if people would learn to believe and implement these secrets. It is safe to consider that any mystic or sensationalistic claim that twists science, technology, and the laws-of-physics into pseudoscientific applications, is false; and is intentionally fraudulent with the intent to deceive. Word-salad claims of vibrations, frequencies, souls, energy, auras, chakras, quantum-healing and other "quantum" claims in reference to the mind and existence must be considered as nonsense, false, and deceptive; and they must be dismissed without further waste of time. Furthermore, claims of certain substances such as ayahuasca and other mind-altering drugs that are supposed to take our minds to another dimension and state of consciousness, are simply snake-oil salesmanship tactics that are intended to profit the charlatans at the expense of the susceptible and suggestable people who are looking to improve their life.

When it comes to self-help and motivation:

Be skeptical of anyone who claims to know the mystical secret to something that will change your life for the better.

This is why, skepticism, factual-thinking, and knowledge are integral for living our life based on how reality is, and not based on how we want reality to be. Factual-thinking minimizes the effects of such practices on us and it enables us to disregard and ignore nonsensical and illusionary practices. Factual-thinking and critical-thinking minimize and eliminate the need to find purpose, meaning, and comfort through emotional-thinking and placebo-thinking; as they enable us to live our life based on how reality truly is.

As discussed, self-deception and externalation are two of the main enemies for self-improvement, because they make us feel good without making any actual positive-changes in our life. It is for same reason that self-reflection and introspection, as uncomfortable and as painful as they might be, are integral for recognizing our weaknesses and for improving them. Our self-identity and our sense of Self should not come from external-sources or from other-people; it should come from within us. This is why, we must think factually so that we can be self-reliant and complete on our own. When we are self-reliant and complete on our own, we can then enter interactions and relationships with others based on complementary reasons, and not based on completing neediness.

When we are complete on our own and when we enter interactions and relationships with others based on complementarity; it is only then that we will begin recognizing that the many fallacious, dramatic, and incorrect teachings that we have been exposed to in leadership-teaching, in motivational-teachings, and even, in cultural and societal teachings, have been nothing but manipulative tactics to win us over into the tribe, the cult, or the group.

When we are self-complete and self-reliant we will then have independent thinking ability and we will not be easily persuaded by others to follow their self-serving agendas. Instead of blindly and without thinking following others like a sheep; we will learn to lead our own lives by thinking factually and by disallowing our emotions to become a gateway of manipulation by others for their own personal gains. If we are to follow other-people's lead, we should not follow the lead of those who tell us what we want to hear; but we should follow those who show us how to improve, regardless of how difficult such change might be. Likewise, we should do the same with others who are looking at us to lead and guide them; however, as discussed throughout Theory of Self-Relativity, to lead and guide others properly, we must first learn to lead our own life accordingly. Therefore, to lead or to follow others, we must understand how to lead, and we must understand whom to follow in order to add value to our own life and to the lives of others. This is why, Theory of Self-Relativity insists that improvement must be based on awareness and understanding of what it is that needs improvement, and how to properly improve it.

It's leadership, not leadersheep. Sheep follow, people shouldn't. True leaders should teach people to think for themselves; not to tell people what they want to hear.

Because:

Leadership is not an ideology and leaders are not disciples to follow. Sheep follow, people shouldn't; people should think for themselves.

Therefore, even leadership and mentoring, just like other interpersonal-relationships must be complementary, not completing; because, true leaders teach others how to lead their own lives independently, instead of taking advantage of others for their own self-serving benefit. Sadly, most modern-day leadership and motivational-teachings don't teach independent critical-thinking, as they operate via appeal-to-emotions for their own self-serving agenda.

To be able to distinguish between manipulative and useless motivational and leadership practices, versus true leadership teachings that lead to self-improvement, we must learn to think factually and we must become complete on our own. True leadership will teach us to become our own coach and our own life's leader; because, motivation, self-improvement, and leading our life, should not be eternally dependent on one more additional expensive seminar, another repeat online video, or endless sessions with a coach or a therapist.

When we are self-complete and self-reliant, dramatic movie quotes such as "you complete me," or ideological-fallacies such as "servant-leadership" will be easily recognized as sensationalism with no factual-value; and in many cases, we will see through the deceptive intent of such ideologies and manipulative-teachings in their attempt to appeal to our emotions. This is why, Theory of Self-Relativity refers to such manipulative and deceptive teaching as "Toxic-Sympathy."

Theory of Self-Relativity defines "Toxic-Sympathy" as "intentionally nurturing victimhood, in order to manipulate and win over the weak and the susceptible."

When we are self-complete and self-reliant, we will not be manipulated by others in looking to gain our self-identity and our sense of Self externally through their manipulative ideological validation-tactics that are commonly used by groups such as cults, religions, and even governments. When we are self-complete and self-reliant, we will use "facts" to validate our thoughts, our values, and our sense of Self; and we will likewise use "facts" to validate the thoughts and the values of what others are representing. When we are self-complete, we will use facts, knowledge, and experience to lead our life, and to also help to lead others without fallacious-motivations and without appeals-to-emotion.

Leadership does not require a manuscript of morality; and neither does it require a dogmatic philosophy.

When we are self-complete and self-reliant, it is only then that we will know, in order to make a marriage stronger, to make a family stronger, to make a team and a group stronger, and to make a society stronger; each individual member of the collective must be stronger on their own. When members of a group are stronger individually and when each member is capable of leading one's own life independently and with minimal reliance on others; then, the collective of the group, the team, or the relationship will become exponentially stronger than if the relationship, the group, or the team operated around an ideology, a dogma, or an authoritarian practice founded upon the concept of control and dependency of its members on the leaders.

To have a strong "we" mindset, we must first have a strong "me" mindset; and since "me" is a part of "we," we can't have a strong "we" without a strong "me."

This is why, Theory of Self-Relativity states:

True leadership is encouragement, guidance and inclusion.

When we are self-complete and self-reliant, and when we enter interactions and relationships as complete individuals, but not based on the need to have others complete us; it is only then that our relationships become complementary and not completing. Such complementary relationships enable us to enter interactions and relationships from a point of strength and from the position of having nothing-to-lose. Whether it is a business relationship or a romantic one, as long as the interaction or the relationship is additive and not completing; that relationship will be mutually-constructive for all. Likewise, as long as we maintain our individual completeness, should an interaction or relationship become chronically deductive or damaging, we will then be able to pivot and walk away from the interaction or the relationship; because we did not originally enter the relationship with the need for completion. When we become independent and self-reliant and when we feel self-complete on our own, our self-confidence will grow and our strong sense of Self will enable us to have an abundance of choices and options in life; because:

A self-confident and self-complete person lives with abundance of choices and options.

And when we have abundance of choices and options, we will take control and we will lead our life to where we want it to go; therefore, we will create and control our own destiny.

Be the leader that stirs the ship of leadership. Don't be a sheep that follows the heard of leadersheep.

IX.
Abundance & Choice

The more accomplished we are, the more choices we have.

As discussed, the word accomplished is derived from the root word "complete;" therefore, we must be complete on our own and we must live our life without dependency and reliance on others. When we are complete and when we are independent and self-reliant, we then have the ability to move onto bigger and better things, and we are capable of accomplishing more. Accomplishments can only be achieved by building on the improvements that we have already undertaken; hence, accomplishments become self-fulfilling and improve on our completeness. When we are complete on our own, we minimize dependency and reliance on others, and we enter interactions and relationships with other-people and with other-things on a complementary and not on a completing basis. Such freedom and flexibility allows us to adapt and adjust more fluidly to different people and a variety of situations; thereby, we are able to create choices and options for our own Self.

Choices and options enable us to live in abundance.

The more complete we are the less dependent we will be and the more choices we will have in life; and the more choices we have in life the more abundant the quality of our life will be. Living in abundance and having choice does not mean to be greedy or materialistic. On the contrary, to live in abundance means to have the ability to choose from the best available choices in life. Living in abundance and having choice, in-turn, allows us to create more choices and it enables us to continue living in abundance. Living in abundance and having choices minimizes our biases, which in-turn, enables us to adapt quickly and to change more effectively.

To live in abundance and to have choices and options, we must remain unbiased and adaptable.

When we remain unbiased and adaptable, the abundance of our choices increases, which means we become more in demand; therefore, we have higher value. The more in demand something is, the higher its perceived value would be; because, according to Theory of Self-Relativity, value is perceived.

Theory of Self-Relativity defines "value" as "the perceived desirability of a thing."

The more desirable and the more in demand a thing or a person is, the higher value it would have; because more people want that thing, or because more people want to be associated with that thing or with that person. As discussed in the 10-Enemies of Self-Improvement, the higher value something has the scarcer that thing would be; therefore, the more in demand it would be. Same applies to people. The more complete and the more accomplished a person is, the more others would want to associate themselves with that person; hence, the higher value that person would have. Higher desirability creates more choice, and more choice is associated with abundance.

Since value is perceived, therefore value is relative; and since a person's value is also perceived, hence a desirable, a successful, or a popular person has a higher *"Relative-Personal-Value" or (RPV)*.

Theory of Self-Relativity defines "Relative-Personal-Value" or "RPV" as "a person's perceived desirability and value."

Relative-Personal-Value or RPV is based on perception, which measures value relative to different mental, personal, and social scales and standards; therefore, RPV increases as a person improves and changes for the better. Since RPV is a measure of perception, the most important aspect of RPV is how one values one's own Self. Although other-people's perception of a person's RPV is also important, especially in personal and social settings and interactions; a person's RPV will consequently be higher when one improves and expands one's own personal qualities and attributes.

Since value is perceived, hence value is relative; therefore, value is increased by improving the inherent qualities and attributes of a thing or a person.

As discussed, scarcity and abundance are a reflection of a thing's or a person's uniqueness or commonness. Therefore, according to Theory of Self-Relativity, scarcity and abundance affect a person's RPV. Since being scarce is a measurement of higher RPV, living in scarcity is the opposite to being scarce, and it reflects a lower RPV. According to Theory of Self-Relativity, living in scarcity means to not have abundance of choices and options because the person does not have a high RPV. Living in scarcity means having fewer choices and limited options because when one lives in scarcity, one does not have the personal-skills and unique-attributes to create and surround one's Self with abundance of choices and options. Likewise, when one lives in scarcity, one is not considered to be scarce or in high demand; one is considered to be one of many abundant choices. Although scarce things usually have higher value; this should not be mistaken with living in scarcity which represents a lower RPV.

When we have higher RPV, we are more in demand and we have more choices and options; therefore, we live in abundance. However, when we live in scarcity, we have lower RPV because we have less choices and fewer options. Living in scarcity is the opposite of being scarce and living in abundance is the opposite of being abundant. Since RPV is sociopsychological because it is based on perception of value; RPV is directly proportional to living in abundance, and inversely-proportional to living in scarcity. The higher RPV we have, the scarcer we are, which means the more in demand we are, and the more choices and options we have. Hence why "Living in Scarcity" is categorized by Theory of Self-Relativity as one of its 10-Enemies of Self-Improvement; and living in "Abundance and Choice" is categorized as one of the 10-Commandments for Self-improvement. Therefore, in order to live in abundance, we must increase our RPV via self-improvement, so that we can increase our choices and options in life.

The higher our relative-personal-value, the more choices and options we have in life.

This direct correlation of higher RPV relative to living in abundance and lower RPV relative to living in scarcity is demonstrated in the following diagram.

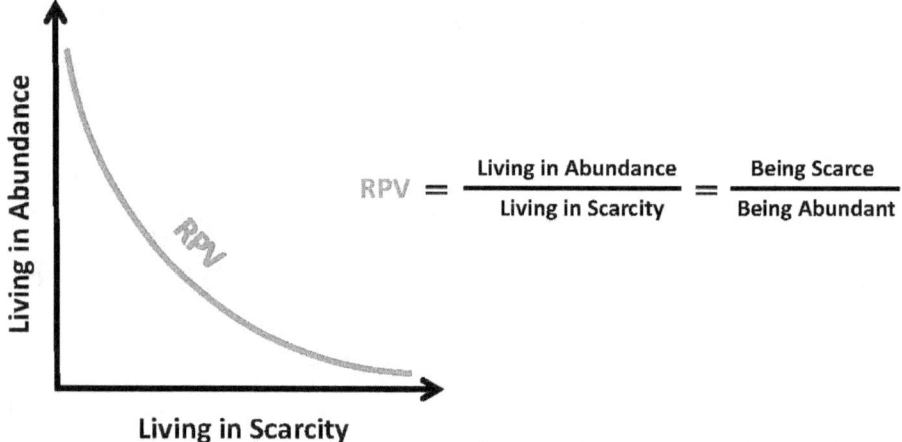

It is important to reiterate that our perception of our own RPV must be based on facts, not based on how we feel. Although in the short-term RPV is perceived; in the longer-term, this perception must be verified with supportive facts and evidence. In other words, we cannot peptalk our Self into believing that we have a higher RPV; because in due time, such incorrect perception of our RPV will come crashing down in value. Our perception, and most importantly our knowledge of our RPV must be based on factual-thinking, which means, we must evaluate our qualities and attributes based on supportive facts and evidence. If the perception of our RPV is not in synch with what the factual-value of our RPV's contributing factors are; in due time, we will realize that our incorrect higher perception of our RPV adjusts down. This is why, we cannot improve our self-worth or our self-image, simply, via peptalk and positive-thinking.

Thus, to achieve true higher RPV, we must continuously engage in change and self-improvement so that we can maintain and increase the quality of the contributors to our RPV. As we improve, we can verify the improving value of our RPV via factual-thinking; therefore, when we factually know that our RPV is increasing, so would others. When we want to increase our RPV, we must begin by believing in our Self and we must want to self-improve. However, in order to strengthen and maintain our improved RPV, we must evaluate our belief and perception of our higher RPV via facts and evidence, and not through comforting-thoughts.

Just as a belief is supposed to be temporary until supportive facts and evidence are found to turn that belief into knowledge; the perceived-value of our RPV must also be checked and verified by supportive evidence. If our perception and belief of our higher RPV does not match what facts and evidence are indicating, we should make changes so that we can get on the correct path of increasing our RPV. This is parallel with Theory of Self-Relativity's explanation of how we should turn our beliefs into knowledge, and how we should change and self-improve by thinking factually. Factual-thinking proves or disproves our forward-looking mindsets such as assumptions, perceptions, and beliefs, relative to reality.

Since low RPV is caused by low self-attributes such as low self-image, low sense of self-worth, and mediocre personal accomplishments; therefore, a low RPV causes us to live in scarcity, which means we have fewer choices and limited options in life. Furthermore, a low RPV often causes us to settle for less, which means we are not approaching interactions and relationships from a position of strength and from the perspective of having nothing-to-lose. To increase our RPV, which in-turn, will increase our choices and options in life, we must continuously change and improve. Since RPV is a personal-value that is directly proportional to self-improvement, this is why, Theory of Self-Relativity insists that we must bring the focus onto our self-first. Because, when we are focused onto others instead of being focused on our Self; we cannot increase our RPV.

Instead of changing others, improve your Self, so that you can have more choices and better options in life.

As discussed, self-improvement is not an event, but it is an ongoing process; and the more we self-focus and the more we adapt, change, and improve, the higher our RPV would be, and the more choices and options we will have in life. This is why, motivation alone does not lead to change and improvement. Motivation is easy, however, proper and efficient improvement requires awareness, understanding, and implementation of action; hence why, most motivational-teachings seldom result in long-lasting changes. It is easy to temporarily feel good, by dreaming a big dream; but to make our dreams a reality, we must create our own purpose and we must accomplish our own achievable goals.

Dreamers are abundant; achievers are scarce.

Self-improvement requires making changes, because change creates choices and options. In order for us to change, we must base our actions of change on proper thinking. If our thinking and reasoning is flawed, then our actions will be wrong, which means the changes that we make will not be improving. This is why, many continuously make mistakes and cannot get themselves out of their own way. The primary reason people think incorrectly is because they want to think based on what makes them feel good, and not based on how reality truly is.

To stop thinking incorrectly, we must learn to think factually, regardless of how uncomfortable facts make us feel.

To become a self-sufficient and self-complete person, we must deal with reality the way reality is, and not the way we want reality to be; and the only way that we can keep our Self in check with reality, is for us to look at everything and to think about everything factually. When we think factually, regardless of how uncomfortable facts may be, we can then take action to change and improve what is uncomfortable. The more we change, the less discomfort we will experience, and the better we will feel about our own Self. And the better that we feel about our own Self and the more self-confident we become, the more choices and options we will create for our own Self.

Change, improvement, and success, are not overnight events; they are lifetime processes.

To dream is a great attribute; however, dreams are only achievable if we first create our purpose and if we set our goals. Every time we reach our goal, we bring forward our dream, and we make our dream our next goal, and we dream a new dream. As we move forward in time by reaching our goals, our purpose in life gets bigger and more of our dreams become reality.

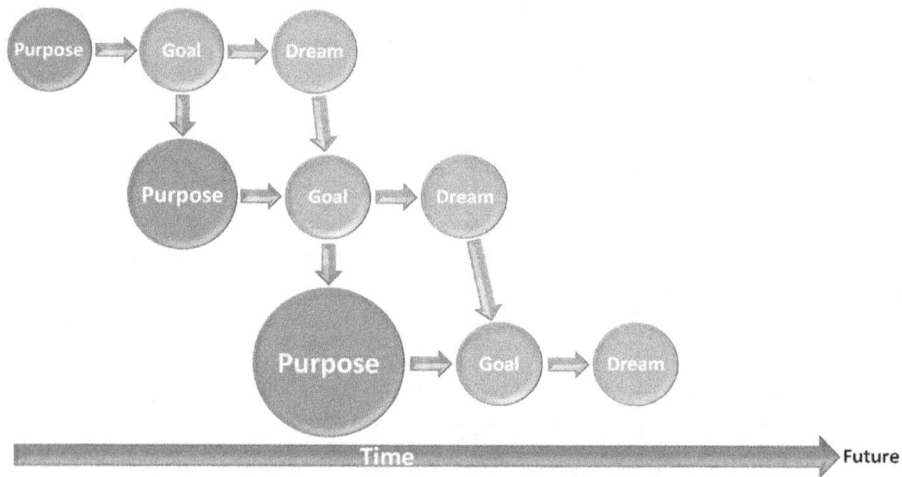

Dreams are in the Future...Purpose is in the Present

We cannot just dream, and then make our dream come true the next day; because, we must first walk the walk of purpose to goal to dream. This is why, change and improvement are not motivational overnight-events; but they are lifetime-processes.

Dreamers see success as an event, achievers experience success as a process.

The more we improve, the bigger our purpose in life becomes, the higher our RPV grows, and the more we will live in abundance. However, improvement could only happen as a result of changing, and this change must be self-focused and not focused externally.

Everything changes constantly and consistently. The-Universe and time change constantly and continuously. As everything changes, everything moves forward with time. We are born, we get older, and we eventually die, because we change; therefore, we must learn to change constantly and consistently. However, the only thing that resists change is our mind; hence, for us to be able to change in-sync with time and parallel with The-Universe, we must train our mind to change constantly and consistently with time. Change is inevitable and if we want to live the best quality of life possible, we must learn to change, so that we can improve every day.

The most effective personal-change must come from within; this is why, we must live a centered-self life, from the inside-out, and as a self-complete individual. The more self-complete we become, the more we will be in control of the changes that we make, and the better our potential will be for strengthening our personal-attributes and for increasing our RPV.

When we become self-complete, we will be in charge of our own personal-change, we will be the captain of our own self-improvement, and we will be in control of our own life. When we change based on our own completeness, it is only then that we will be able to have an abundance of choices and options that we can choose from, in order to live a more fulfilled and happier life.

X.
Change

Change happens... Change or you'll be changed.

The-Universe and everything around us changes continuously. Time changes constantly and continuously. Our physical body and brain change continuously as time moves forward. Yet, when it comes to the kind of personal-change which requires mental-input, we tend to resist such change.

According to Theory of Self-Relativity, there are two main reasons we don't like to change:

1. **Introspection:** Self-reflection and introspection means to look within our Self to identify our personal weaknesses, our shortcomings and our other attributes that need improvement. As discussed, for many, self-reflection and introspection is an emotionally difficult undertaking because introspection makes us aware of our dislikable and often painful covered-up personal-shortcomings. However, to change and to improve, we must identify what needs change and improvement; hence why, facing our weaknesses and shortcomings is an uncomfortable and often painful task. Introspection requires us to become conscious of our weaknesses, our shortcomings, and even our deficiencies, by bringing them up to the surface from our nonconscious state into our higher levels of consciousness.

2. **Primitive-Mind:** As discussed throughout Theory of Self-Relativity, our primitive-mind, which is always on the lookout for negativity and danger, is the default-state of our mind. Our primitive-mind does not care if we are happy; all it cares about is if we are safe. Therefore, the primary role of our primitive-mind is to keep us safe, and it tries to do so by lessening our variables and uncertainties in order to minimize our exposure to things that could go wrong. Change, by-nature, creates variables and uncertainties, which in-turn, could lead to something going wrong; therefore, change, itself, could increase our exposure to threats and dangers. This, in-turn, makes our primitive-mind get worried, anxious, and even fearful; hence, it kicks into action in order to minimize and prevent any change. Change is inherently contradictory to how our primitive-mind likes for things to be; because our primitive-mind is inherently programmed to seek constancy and predictability. This is how, our primitive-mind creates comfort-zones. By staying within our comfort-zone, our primitive-mind limits and prevents us from change, in an attempt to keep us safe.

Theory of Self-Relativity defines "change" as "The shift in the state of a thing from one moment to another."

Change happens, regardless of our preference for change. Although change happens, random and passive-change itself is existentially mostly unfavorable; hence, in order to make change favorable, we must first seek to change, and second, we must put in effort to improve the thing that needs to change so that change becomes more in our control and more favorable for us.

Therefore:

- *"Improvement" simply means favorable change.*

Since improvement is synonymous with favorable-change; consequently:

- *"Self-Improvement" is favorable self-change.*

And since self-improvement means favorable self-change:

- *Theory of Self-Relativity defines "self-improvement" as "changing for the better as one ages."*

Improvement means changing for the better, and self-improvement means changing our Self for the better; therefore, change is a necessary process for self-improvement. Since self-improvement means to change for the better throughout our lifetime; therefore, change is not an event, but it is an ongoing process.

As discussed, change is difficult, and our mind inherently does not like to change. Most people prefer things as they are because change creates unfamiliarity and uncertainty, and change also requires input and effort. This is why, change is difficult; therefore, we resist change. However, since everything changes, we must learn to change in order to improve; regardless of whether we like to change or because change is difficult.

As discussed, according Theory of Self-Relativity, the two non-negotiables for personal-change and for self-improvement are "Desire and Introspection;" therefore, in order to change, we must want to change, and, we must know what needs to change.

1. **Desire:** We must want to change.
2. **Introspection:** We must know what needs to change.

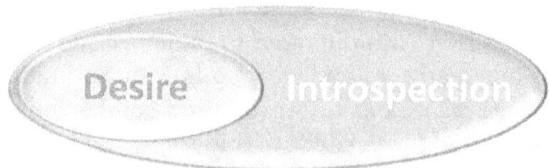

Introspection, simply defined, is self-inspection. Introspection enables us to self-reflect and become aware of and observe our weaknesses and our shortcomings in order to improve them. When we decide that we want to improve for the better, and as we recognize what it is that we need to improve; we can then motivate our Self to take constructive action to change and improve.

Personal-Change = Motivation + Action

Although it is true that personal-change or self-improvement requires motivation in order to create the desire to change; however, just being motivated does not cause change. Motivation is a commonly focused attribute for self-improvement, but unless we follow-through motivation with some kind of action, motivation by itself will not make change happen. Getting people motivated is not difficult; the problem is that since motivation is an emotional-response, motivation often subsides and dies out before it leads to any action. Empty-motivation without proper cognitive understanding of what we need to change and how to change it, will not lead to positive-change and improvement. This is why, the effects of motivational-teachings quickly fizzle out, often without yielding any results.

Motivation alone doesn't lead to results because "motivation" is an "emotional-response."

As many who have soughed to self-improve have realized, most motivational programs do not effectively result in improvement, especially long-term improvement, unless they lead to constant and consistent change. To make constant and consistent change, constant and consistent effort is needed, and constant and consistent action must be undertaken. Wanting to change without understanding what needs change and without knowing how to change is why motivation dies out. Therefore, Theory of Self-Relativity shows how changing our thinking-system through factual-thinking is the key to making favorable, constant and consistent change.

Just as breathing is essential for our survival, constant change is essential for our existence.

As discussed, change, just like other personal transformational attributes is not an event; it is an ongoing-process. Since most people seek instant-gratification in order to avoid pain, to feel good, or at the minimum, to feel less-bad, and since change is an ongoing-process; people often give up on initiating and continuing the process of change and improvement because positive-change and improvement requires effort and time commitment. Positive-change and improvement do create positive-feelings but that usually takes time; and since most people want to feel better quickly, they fail to commit to change as they look for easier ways of creating comforting-feelings. Therefore, since change is not an overnight-event and rather it is an ongoing-process; most who seek to change and improve, abandon the effort required as they revert back to their previous ways of thinking and doing things to quickly feel better.

Change requires effort, and effort is the action that leads to behavior that makes change happen. Our behavior is dependent on our way of thinking, and if we do not learn to think factually by understanding what needs to be changed and how to change it; we will not be able to change. The reason most behavior modification and motivational programs do not lead to constant, consistent, and long-lasting change, is because having to continuously put in effort to change becomes an arduous and tiring proposition. In order for transformation and self-improvement to become constant and effortless, an easy to implement universal thinking-technique is necessary. Theory of Self-Relativity's Cognitive-Cognition-Technique provides the thinking-tools to streamline our improvement-skills; constantly, and consistently. Theory of Self-Relativity demonstrates that awareness, understanding, and modification of our thinking-system to a fact and evidence-based format, is the key to our ability to change and improve.

Since everything changes constantly; without change, nothing would exist. The-Universe is changing constantly, our physical body has been changing since we were conceived, "time," itself, exists because The-Universe changes constantly; hence why, time changes constantly and consistently. Since change is inherent to and necessary for the existence of everything; therefore, positive-change is necessary for self-improvement and for living a better quality life.

Theory of Self-Relativity categorizes the "nature" of change binarily:

1. **Passive-Change:** Is the type of change that occurs without a conscious, intentional, or active-effort to cause the change. Aging, deterioration of things, and naturally occurring changes such as climate or the explosion of stars are examples of passive-change.

2. **Active-Change:** Is the type of change that requires conscious, intentional, and active-effort and input to cause the change to happen. Technological-advancements, gaining or losing weight, manmade destruction and rebuilding, and even personal-improvement are examples of active-change.

Theory of Self-Relativity further classifies the "quality" of change binarily:

1. **Positive-Change:** Occurs when change leads to a positive-outcome. Positive-change generally occurs as a result of active-change. Although positive-change could occur passively or by chance; majority of positive-changes, especially personal positive-changes, occur as a result of active-change. For example, self-improvement, which is a positive-change, requires intentional-input and active-effort.

   - A rare example of passive-change causing a positive-change is the formation of life on earth and its subsequent evolution; however, as stated, positive-change without active and intentional input occurs infrequently. This is especially true of passive personal-change at the local level of our lifetime and in Our-Universe. Hence why, positive-change requires active-effort and energy-input.

2. **Negative-Change:** Occurs when change leads to a negative-outcome. Negative-change could occur because of either passive-change or active-change. Aging and weight-loss are some examples of negative-change

which occurs passively or actively. In order to slow-down, minimize, or reverse negative-change; active-effort, or more broadly stated, energy-input is required.

- Another example of negative-change, on a personal-level, is delusional, magical, or emotional-thinking; because not dealing with reality as reality is, will lead to unfavorable outcomes. Such unfounded and nonfactual-beliefs often lead to negative-change, unless by chance, a positive-change occurs. Thus, if things are left alone and allowed to change passively, the resulting change would frequently lead to negative-change. This is especially true on the larger scale of The-Universe, because disorder occurs as a result of passive-change; as there is no conscious-agent, no intentional-input, and no active-effort behind it. This negative-change or disorder occurs because of entropy, and the only means of slowing down entropy is to input energy.

In nature, disorder, disease, and death are normal; harmony, health and happiness are not normal.

Most change, especially in nature, is passive-change and negative-change. Change, if left alone, occurs with negative-consequences, because The-Universe is in a constant and increasing state of *"disorder."* Because of this default nature of The-Universe, in order to minimize negativity and to increase positivity, we must consciously and consistently put in active-effort to slow-down disorder and to increase balance and harmony around us and in our lives. Although we cannot positively affect the macro disorder of The-Universe; but as discussed, we can affect, control, and sometimes temporarily halt *"local-disorder"* in Our-Universe.

When left alone, there are more ways for things to go wrong than to go right; therefore, if things are left to chance without active-input, negative-change will be more prevalent than positive-change.

In other words:

Change Happens!

If left alone, even at the minuscule scale of human lifetime, change will frequently lead to increased disorder; therefore, change will result in negativity. This phenomenon of increasing disorder is known as the *"Second Law of Thermodynamics"* or *"The Law of Entropy."* Entropy is the primary cause of change.

Theory of Self-Relativity categorizes the main causes of natural change as:

1. **Entropy**
2. **Motion**
3. **Time**

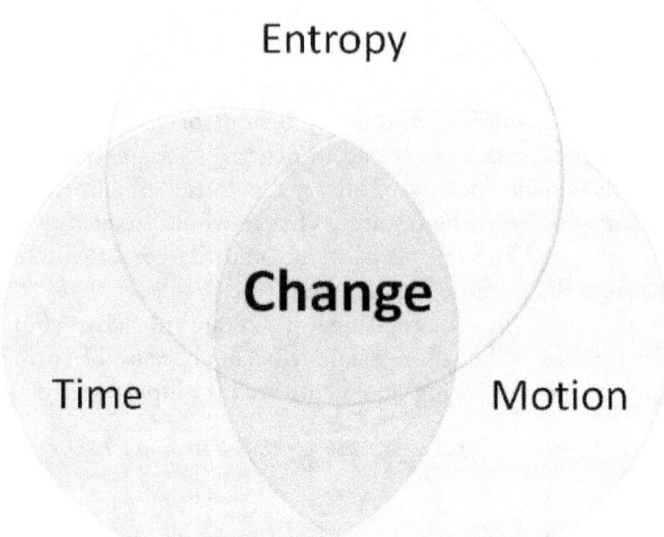

1. Entropy:

Entropy is the tendency for things to move around, or the tendency of energy to spread out. Entropy is the measure of disorder and predictability of randomness in a system. Simply stated, entropy is a "lack-of-order" or it is an increasing state of "disorder." Entropy is associated with the amount of disorderliness, or chaos in a system; which in-turn, represents the degree of change. Without entropy, things stay in equilibrium and remain orderly; therefore, without entropy things will not change. Entropy causes change by creating disorder and motion.

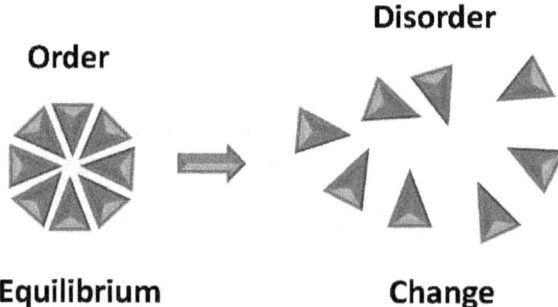

The law of entropy states that the entropy or disorder of a (closed) system always increases, and it never decreases when left on its own. The best example of entropy is the expansion of The-Universe. Since the Big-Bang, The-Universe has been in a constant state of increasing entropy; which means, things in The-Universe are becoming more disorderly. Therefore, The-Universe will continue to expand. At the time of the Big-Bang, despite the inflation of The-Universe following the

Big-Bang, The-Universe was in a state of lesser-entropy; because the baby Universe was more orderly compared to the current state of The-Universe.

Entropy always increases, unless energy or intentional-effort, which itself requires energy, is added to the system in order to control or minimize the entropy.

Because entropy causes things to be disorderly rather than orderly, if left alone, there are more ways for things to change than for things to stay constant; thus, there are more ways for things to go wrong than for things to go right. For example, if we gather all the air molecules in a room and compress them in the corner of the room, the natural tendency of these molecules would be to disburse throughout the room, and to continue to bounce and move around throughout the room in a random fashion.

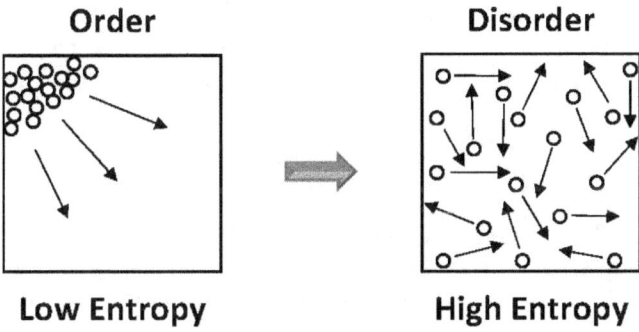

Order	Disorder
Low Entropy	High Entropy

However, it would be extremely rare for all the molecules in the room to once again aggregate in the corner of the room in an orderly state. Although the molecules gathering in the corner of the room in an orderly state is one of the many possible configurations; due to the law of entropy, when left alone, the potential of such an orderly configuration occurring on its own would be highly improbable.

Because entropy naturally causes uncontrolled disorder and change in The-Universe; such uncontrolled change could have negative consequences at the local-level of Our-Universe. For example, to build a building and to maintain it, intentional-input, active-effort, and energy must go into it; however, if left alone on its own and not upkept, the building will begin to deteriorate and eventually collapse and get destroyed. When left alone, a building will deteriorate and eventually collapse; however, when left alone, a building will not be created by itself.

Entropy is the underlying cause of why it is easier to destroy than to build.

Although the laws-of-physics, such as entropy, that govern The-Universe cannot be violated; intervention, especially by a free-willed intentional-agent could slow-down, or even temporarily halt the effects of certain laws-of-physics, at the local level of Our-Universe. For example, when we decide to, we can build a skyscraper; thus, by locally putting in active-effort and constant input, we can build and continue to maintain the building in its operating state for years, decades, and even centuries. However, as The-Universe moves forward in time and as the macro laws-of-physics which govern The-Universe affect and change the state of our locality; then, our free-will and intervention will not be effective anymore. In about 5 billion years, when the Earth gets devoured by the engorging dying Sun, no matter how much free-will humans have, humans will not be able to remain alive on Earth, nor would they be able to maintain the building.

Therefore, local free-will, effort, and input have limitations relative to the longer-time periods and the larger scale of The-Universe. As discussed, although The-Universe is in a state of increasing disorder; local influences such as our intent and our free-will could minimize or could temporarily halt the effects of The-Universe's disorder locally. Furthermore, such local influences can and do create "complexity" in the face of disorder; as long as the total macro disorder of The-Universe is not affected and continues to increase. Complexities such as stars, planets, and the occurrence of intelligent life could arise naturally as we go from a low state of disorder or entropy to a higher state of disorder; therefore, complexity is temporary. However, as The-Universe ages, expands, and becomes more disorderly, all complexities such as stars, planets, and life-forms will eventually disappear.

2. Motion:

Another law of physics affiliated with change that affects negativity is Newton's "First Law of Motion," which simply states that "all objects in motion will stay in motion and all objects at rest will stay at rest unless acted upon by a force." The First law of Motion, also known as the "Law of Inertia," states, "An object at rest stays at rest and an object in motion stays in motion with the same speed and in the same direction unless acted upon by an unbalanced force."

The "Law of Conservation of Momentum," which is a part of this First Law of Motion, has actually demonstrated that the nature of all things is to always stay in motion. The only reason something comes to rest is because an external-force such as friction or air-resistance causes it to come to rest; therefore, the natural tendency of "things" in The-Universe, regardless of size, is for things to stay in motion.

Many, incorrectly think that things around us are in a state of rest and to get them moving we must push or pull them. On the contrary, because of entropy, The-Universe and everything in it are in a constant state of motion; hence, to stop an object from moving, we actually need to exert force, or we must put an effort into it. For example, even when we are sitting down in our chair, we are in motion, because the Earth is in motion around the Sun, the Sun is in motion with the Solar-System in our Milky-Way-Galaxy, and the Galaxy itself is in motion relative to other Galaxies in The-Universe; and finally, The-Universe itself is constantly expanding. The only reason that we feel stationary in our chair is because gravity and friction are keeping us in our "local" place; however, in reality, we are in motion with the Earth relative to the rest of the objects in The-Universe. Although sitting down, we might feel stationary; motion is constant, yet relative to us. Therefore, even when something seems to be stationary "locally;" that thing is actually in a state of motion at a larger-scale, and relative to other things.

The reason motion exists is because of the increasing disorderliness of The-Universe. This is why, all objects are constantly in motion and not at rest. Consequently:

Motion exists because of entropy.

This means, because of the Big-Bang and because of entropy, everything in The-Universe is in a constant state of motion and change. This change occurs naturally and constantly as time goes by; therefore, time, itself, occurs as a result of the change that the Big-Bang and entropy bring about.

3. Time:

Time exists because of the Big-Bang and entropy, and it is entropy which causes the past to be different from the present and from the future. If there were no entropy and no motion, nothing would change; hence, there would be no time. Therefore, according to Theory of Self-Relativity, time is an emergent-property of the Big-Bang and entropy; thus, time is an emergent-property of the change that entropy creates. As stated:

Theory of Self-Relativity defines "change" as "The shift in the state of a thing from one moment to another."

Therefore:

Change occurs in time; and time is a measurement of change.

Since entropy deals with the degree of disorder of "matter" in The-Universe, and since everything in The-Universe including humans are made of matter, which means everything is made of atoms; therefore, everything in The-Universe must change. Furthermore, since we live in time, and time, itself, which is a measurement of change, exists as a result of entropy which governs the expansion of The-Universe; therefore, we, as humans, are bound by the laws-of-physics. This means, at the human local-scale, we are connected to The-Universe via our material and physical existence that is governed by the laws-of-physics. In other words, we are relative to everything in The-Universe through our material, molecular, and atomic existence; and since science has shown with certainty that everything in The-Universe is made of matter, hence, all matter, including humans, are relative to one another by obeying the laws-of-physics.

Everything in the Universe is made of matter and all matter obey the laws-of-physics.

Consequently, immaterial, metaphysical, or supernatural "things" cannot exist in The-Universe; because if they did, they could not or would not have to obey the laws-of-physics that govern the matter-based Universe. New-age spirituality, personal energy, mental vibrations, frequencies, souls, ghosts, auras, chakras, and other claims of supernaturalism have never been able to factually describe our relativities to The-Universe. For anything supernatural to exist, this means that the supernatural thing would have to violate the natural laws-of-physics. The reason there has never been any proof of the supernatural is because the laws-of-physics would not allow the existence of the supernatural. If and when any supernatural or spiritual entity is factually proven to exist, the claimed supernatural thing or phenomenon will become natural; because, in order for us to detect or to know of its existence, it would have to interact with matter. Since immaterial-things or the supernatural are claimed to not be made of matter; therefore, these immaterial-things, even if they existed, could not interact with the material Universe. This means, even if the supernatural or the metaphysical existed, we would not know of them, because they would not interact with matter for us to detect or to observe them; hence, we could not be influenced by them either. Thus, in order for something to exist in time and for it to be relative to us, that thing would be natural as it would be made of atoms.

In order for us to know about something, that thing must be able to interact with matter.

The reason humans have ideas, opinions, and beliefs on supernaturalism and the existence of immaterial-things is because such mindsets are developed as thoughts, and thoughts can either be based on observation or they can be based on imagination or even hallucination. As described, ideas, thoughts, and beliefs are immaterial-byproducts of our material-brain's activities; therefore, ideas, thoughts, and beliefs must be verifiable with facts and evidence. When we find the facts associated with an idea, a thought, or a belief; that idea, thought, or belief becomes knowledge. If after a certain period of "time" supportive facts for an idea, a thought, or a belief could not be found; that idea, thought, or belief is probably wrong and nonfactual. Therefore, everything is relative to time, and everything is made of matter, or in case of certain immaterial-processes such as our consciousness or our mind; they are simply the immaterial-byproducts of their underlying matter's activities. Consequently, immaterial-processes such as our consciousness and our mind are also bound by the laws-of-physics.

The only reason nonfactual thoughts, beliefs, and mindsets such as the supernatural persist for generations, and even for millennia, is because these mindsets are comforting; therefore, we choose to continue believing in these thoughts without seeking to find their supportive facts and evidence. For example, ideologies such as dualism which believe in a person having a material-body and an immaterial-soul are simply carried forward traditions emanating from imaginations of ancient people who did not properly understand science and the physical Universe. The only way that we can realistically understand our connection and relativity to The-Universe is by understanding how "we," as material-entities, function, relate to, and interact with other matter, within the laws-of-physics.

This is why, Theory of Self-Relativity is founded upon the principle of factual-thinking. Factual-thinking is based on facts, and facts abide by the natural laws-of-physics which govern The-Universe. When we learn to train our mind to always seek evidence for every thought that we have; we will then base our thinking and our existence on facts and knowledge, rather than basing it on imaginary "feel-good" traditions and comforting-beliefs. Even change, which is the core requirement for self-improvement, occurs because of the laws-of-physics; therefore, we, as individuals, have no choice but to change. Thus, to understand how to change parallel with time and in sync with reality, we must learn to identify the facts that guide our relativity with The-Universe. As stated, change is an ongoing-process; therefore, change happens, and change will continue to happen in The-Universe regardless of how we feel.

Change, or you'll be changed.

The sooner we accept that we must change, and the sooner we take control of change in order to make change favorable for our Self, the sooner our life will become a more fulfilling and happier existence.

Theory of Self-Relativity is not only advocating that change is a necessary requirement for living a better-quality life; but it is also demonstrating why change is an inherent part of everything that exists. The laws of entropy and motion describe how The-Universe works and how it is in a constant and never-ending state of change. Entropy and motion create time, because entropy and motion create change, and time is a measurement of change. Change occurs as time changes, yet time changes because change occurs. Although change would not be possible if time did not change in a forward direction; time, itself, would not exist if change was not an inherent and constant outcome of entropy.

Change is a measure of motion, and time is a measurement of change.

Entropy ⟶ Motion ⟶ Change ⟶ Time

Therefore:

Theory of Self-Relativity describes "Entropy" as "the motion for change."

For ease of remembering the relativity of entropy, motion, and change, we can analogize this relativity to Einstein's Special Theory of Relativity formula, E=mc2; which states that energy and mass (pr matter) are interchangeable, and that they are different forms of the same thing.

$$E=mc^2$$

Note: The following is only an analogy and not an actual mathematical formula; whereby, Theory of Self-Relativity demonstrates the interchangeability of entropy, motion, and change in an acronymic representation to that of E=mc2.

$$E=mc$$

E=Entropy
M=motion
C=change

In summary, entropy, motion, and time are interrelated and relative to each other and they are the fundamentals for change and existence.

- Entropy creates motion.
- Entropy creates time.
- Entropy creates change.
- Motion creates change.
- Time measures change.

Change is inherent to all that exists.

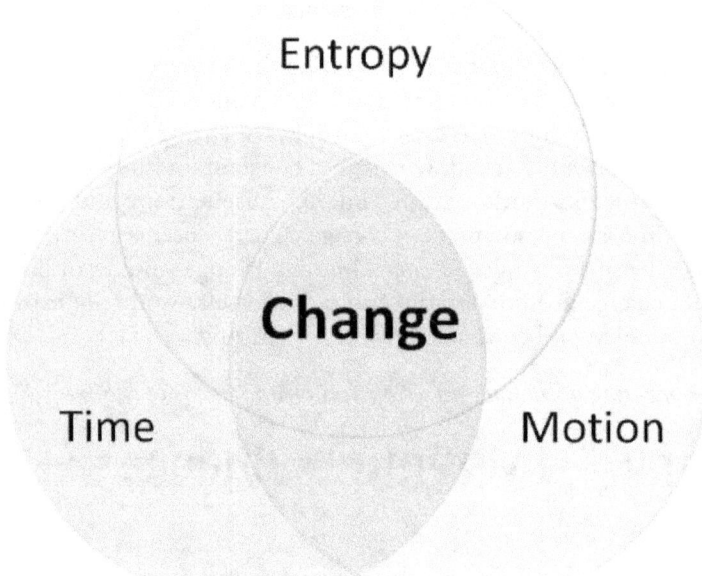

Due to entropy and motion, The-Universe has been expanding continuously since its formation at the Big-bang. The Big-Bang signifies the beginning of our understanding of the observable Universe and the beginning of our understanding of time. The Big-Bang gave rise to the baby Universe which was a low entropy and an orderly state; however, since the Big-Bang, the entropy and the disorderliness of The-Universe has been increasing. This expansion and increase in the entropy of The-Universe is causing The-Universe to "change" constantly and continuously. Simply stated, The-Universe and everything in it:

- Have always been in motion.
- Have continuously and constantly been changing.
- Will continue to constantly change into the future.
- Therefore "change" is a constant and a normal part of everything that exists.

Through this knowledge, we now have a better understanding of how we relate to The-Universe. By factually understanding how nature exists, we can now better understand how we exist in nature. Science describes that the entropy or disorderliness of The-Universe always approaches maximum; indicating that The-Universe, and therefore everything in The-Universe, is becoming more disorderly as it changes and expands continuously through time. This means, The-Universe and everything in it is constantly changing as time goes-by; thus:

Time is a measurement of change.

This forward change in time is known as *"The arrow-of-time."* The arrow-of-time indicates that time changes constantly and consistently, and time only travels in one direction; forwardly. The arrow-of-time also represents that as a system advances through time, it will become more disordered because of increasing entropy. The arrow-of-time, entropy, and motion represent that things change constantly as time itself changes consistently into the future.

The arrow-of-time causes things to change with time, and time itself changes as it moves in a forward direction. It is the arrow-of-time that differentiates the past from the present, and the present from the future. The reason the arrow-of-time only moves forward, hence why time could not move backward, is because of the increasing entropy of The-Universe. This forward only change of time is commonly referred to as *"the passage-of-time."* Since the passage-of-time only moves forward, so does change; therefore, change can only move forward. This is why, things change into the future but the past cannot be changed; because as we move forward in time, disorder increases, unless energy is put into the system. For example, we can peel a banana, but we cannot unpeel a banana to how it was before we peeled it; or we can break a glass, but we cannot unbreak a glass to its original unbroken shape. Likewise, we can mix sugar in water, but we cannot unmix sugar from water; unless we apply energy and boil the water in order to separate the sugar from water.

This irreversibility in nature is because of entropy and the arrow-of-time. Therefore:

We could influence the future, but we cannot change the past.

It is also because of entropy and the arrow-of-time as to why we remember the past, but we cannot remember the future. Time emerges as a result of entropy and motion; therefore, time, itself, represents change. Time is the sequence of different slices of moments stitched together in continuation. Reality, time, and our lives, are connected moments similar to the film slides in a movie reel. When each slide and each moment is played consecutively, we get the awareness and the sensation of changing time. Hence, time could only move forward, and consequently, everything only moves forward in time; which means, we are all "time-dependent."

The only "thing" that could manage to cheat the laws-of-physics and stay stagnant or even go back in time would be an "immaterial-thing" such as the supernatural. As discussed, an immaterial-thing is something that is not made of matter; thus, it would have to exist outside the laws-of-physics. Science has proven that no immaterial-thing could exist, or at the minimum, if it did, we would not know about it as it would not be able to interact with the physical Universe that we live in. Therefore, no "material-thing" could ever stay stagnant or go back in time.

However, there is only one entity associated with matter that could actually go-back, or stay-back, in time; and that is our "mind." Although our mind is "immaterial," as discussed, our mind is not an "immaterial-thing" that could exist independently on its own, without obeying the laws-of-physics. Our mind is an "immaterial-byproduct" or an "immaterial-process" of our material-brain's activities; therefore, our immaterial-mind only exists because our material-brain is actually producing it. Despite our mind being reliant on our brain, since our mind is an immaterial-process, it is this ability of the mind to go-back and stay-back in time that is one of the main causes of why we have difficulty changing and improving.

While time, our body, The-Universe, and everything in it change and move forward in time; our mind, when dealing with unresolved, cluttering, and non-factual-thoughts that are associated with difficult memories and emotions, could actually go-back or stay-back in time and fall out of sync with the present-moment. When our material-existence moves forward with the passage-of-time but our immaterial-mind stays-back in time; that is when we fall out of sync or we get disconnected from reality as we experience conflicting-thoughts and difficult-feelings.

The reason our mind wants to go-back in time or wants to stay-back in time is because we have unresolved-thoughts and negativities from the past that are causing our present discomfort and negativities. Since Theory of Self-Relativity, metaphorically, divides the mind into the primitive-mind and the intelligent-mind, and since the primitive-mind, whose purpose is to keep us safe, is our default mental-state; our primitive-mind wants to distance us from current negativities by going back in time in order to fix unresolved issues. When negativities remain unresolved, they cause uncertainty, and as discussed, uncertainty is a major contributor to more negative-feelings such as anxiety, sadness, stress, anger, and even fear.

Since the past is now known, therefore, things that were uncertain in the past are now certain. But since the current certainties are not to our liking, instead of taking action to change the present-moment and improve the future, our primitive-mind wants to go back to the certainty of the past, to change the past that resulted in the dislikable present-moment. Even though we could make change in the present-moment to improve our future, since the results of the change that we make now will still remain uncertain for the future, our primitive-mind finds more comfort and safety in attempting to change the known past so that the present-moment would magically become favorable. As discussed, regret and remorse are prime examples of how our mind wants to change the past in order to make the present-moment more favorable; instead of changing in the present-moment to make the future more favorable.

Although our intelligent-mind knows and wants us to resolve the present negativities; when we have unresolved negativities or unfavorable outcomes from the past, our primitive-mind, which is dominant, tries to go back in time to resolve the present negativity in the past, so that we would feel better in the present-moment. Our primitive-mind goes back in time and stays back in time because we previously refused to change things that needed to be changed. Since we cannot change the past, and since making a change in the present-moment requires dislikable introspection and time-consuming effort; we routinely choose to do the next easiest thing by thinking comforting-thoughts instead of dealing with the dislikable-facts that require change. Through positive-thinking and emotional-reasoning, we choose to make ourselves feel good at the present-moment, without putting in the effort to make positive-change; thus, our past negativities continue in the present-moment and into the future without resolution.

Thereby, instead of facing the dislikable present-moment and instead of making changes in the present-moment in order to make the future favorable for us; we chose to overlook the troubling facts associated with the present-moment as we move forward into the future. When issues and difficulties are carried forward and are not resolved or eliminated; neither would their underlying causes. It is these leftover problems that create many of our negative-feelings; because by creating negative-feelings, our mind is trying to send us a message that we must face our leftover and unresolved issues. Since feelings are symptoms of underlying causes, by being shackled to past unresolved problems, our mind prevents us from moving forward with changing time. Negative-emotions are signaling us that we must change or eliminate these unresolved situations that are causing these feelings and their associated ruminating-thoughts, so that we can finally let go of the past and move forward in sync with time.

By understanding the laws-of-physics and by realizing that our immaterial-mind could not exist separately from our physical-existence and its relativities with The-Universe; we can then objectively understand why, change, especially changing our thinking-system, is critical to our existence. Our mental-state is directly relative to our physical and material-existence, and although our mind cannot exist independently of our physical existence; by staying behind in time and by not moving forward in sync with the passage-of-time, our mind actually disables our material "Self" from constructively moving forward in life and with time.

Our mind and our thoughts are the main reason we can't change and improve.

Since entropy, which is an ever-increasing degree of disorder, causes The-Universe and everything in it, including our Self, to change constantly; we must also train our mind to change parallel with time and with The-Universe. When our mind changes along with time, it can then learn to problem-solve in the present-moment, and it can plan for the future, so that when the future becomes the present-moment-of-now, the now would be the most favorable personal present-moment possible.

It is not as important where you came from as it is important where you are going.

However, and as discussed, our mind does not like change because change creates uncertainty, which in-turn, makes our mind feel unsafe; therefore, our mind does everything that it can to minimize uncertainty, while increasing certainty and predictability. The primary way that our mind tries to minimize uncertainty is by it preventing us from change; yet as discussed, entropy, which is the increasing disorder of The-Universe, inherently causes everything to change. Since entropy represents the degree of disorder of a system; therefore, change, itself, is as a result of disorder, imbalance, and instability.

On one hand, entropy and disorder are necessary for things to change, especially at the macro-scale; yet, at the local-scale of our lifetime, order and balance are preferred so that we could live in harmony and safety. Since change occurs naturally in The-Universe, and since change is necessary for us to live in dynamic-harmony with The-Universe; therefore, in order for us to improve and to live a fulfilled and quality life, we must also learn to change. As uncomfortable as it is for our mind to accept change, and as dislikable as it is for us to face the negativities that we need to change; change is essential for living a content, fulfilled, and happy life.

As discussed, personal-change is mainly difficult because of the two following reasons:

1. **Primitive-Mind:** Our primitive-mind does not like to change because change introduces variables and uncertainty which could compromise our safety and even our survival, by exposing us to potential danger.
2. **Introspection:** Or self-inspection, is a time and effort consuming, dislikable task necessary for identifying our negativities that need change and improvement.

To change properly, we must change with The-Universe which is causing disorder; but, we must change in such a way that changing along with the disorder of The-Universe does not make Our-Universe more disorderly and uncertain. This could only happen by us putting in effort to make positive-change; but in the meantime, to actively minimize our local-disorder by dynamically creating balance and stability throughout our lifetime. This means, we have to continuously change our Self by adapting to our circumstances and our surroundings in order to minimize our local-disorder. Therefore, we not only have to change along with The-Universe because everything changes; but we must proactively change things in order to stay ahead of the change that The-Universe is going to naturally bring about. This could only happen by us proactively putting in effort to change something which is eventually going to change; but to actively change it in our favor, because as stated, passive-change is commonly not favorable for us. Hence, by making change favorable for our Self, we are actually improving our Self.

Theory of Self-Relativity defines "improvement" as "favorable change," or as "changing for the better."

Hence:

Theory of Self-Relativity defines "Self-Improvement" as "Changing for the better as one ages."

In summary:

- Improvement = Favorable-change
- Self-Improvement = Favorable self-change

Although the entropy of The-Universe always increases, at the local-level of Our-Universe, our *"Local-Entropy,"* or our local-disorderliness, could be temporarily slowed down, halted, and even reversed; as long as the macro entropy of The-Universe continues to increase. Theory of Self-Relativity also refers to local-entropy interchangeably as *"Personal-Entropy."*

Theory of Self-Relativity defines "personal-entropy" or "local-entropy" as "negativity, disorder, and chaos that influences our existence during our lifetime."

As discussed, entropy always increases, unless energy is added to the system. Although we cannot slow-down the entropy of The-Universe; however, by putting in effort and energy, we can slow-down, and even temporarily halt, the local-entropy of Our-Universe. Our local-entropy could be slowed down, minimized, and maintained if we learn to proactively change, and continue changing; which means, if we continuously put in effort and energy. By proactively and intuitively changing, we can change in an orderly manner at our local-level, in contrast to the disorderliness that exists otherwise. This is why, balance, which is an active form of equilibrium, could be achieved and maintained on the smaller and local-scale of Our-Universe. When we put in effort to change, for example when we work out, we are slowing down the entropy of our body by inputting energy; hence, as we burn calories, we are putting heat back into our surrounding, thus, we are increasing the entropy of The-Universe. Nothing and no one can influence changing The-Universe, but we can influence and change things in a more balanced and orderly manner at the local-level of Our-Universe; during our lifetime.

In another example, we can make air-conditioning units that consume energy and cool our rooms; but as a result, the air-conditioning gives off heat externally, which actually adds to the overall entropy of The-Universe. In other words, we are locally minimizing entropy and even reversing it by cooling our room; but on the macro level, we are adding to the increasing entropy of The-Universe in the form of heat that the air conditioning unit generates to cool the room, thereby, we are not violating the law-of-entropy. Similarly, we can keep food refrigerated; but to refrigerate food, the refrigerator consumes energy and gives off heat to its surrounding from its coils and condensers. This is why, we cannot cool the room with a refrigerator; because if we leave the refrigerator door open, the refrigerator will consume more energy in order to keep cooling, thus, it will consume more energy and it will produce more heat which would actually increase the room's temperature.

Increasing entropy is also the reason for the rise of complexity. For example, in the face of the increasing entropy of The-Universe, in pockets of lower to no local-entropy, complex structures such as stars, planets, and even life can form and exist for a certain period of time. As long as the creation of complexity and local-equilibrium does not interfere with the total increase in the entropy of The-Universe, such local-opportunities for complexity and equilibrium could take place. Since in-lieu of increasing entropy in The-Universe, larger pockets of equilibrium could form stars, planets, and even life; therefore, in the local-scale of Our-Universe, we can also create local-equilibrium in order to minimize, or even, temporarily halt local-entropy that affects our existence negatively.

Since the Big-Bang was low entropy and the future is going to be high entropy; we are currently in a transitional state of increasing from low to high entropy, and this transitional stage, which could take billions of years, does allow for the emergence of complexity. Therefore, complexities such as stars, galaxies, and even life-forms such as human-beings are all temporary natural results of moving from low entropy to high entropy. Consequently, complexity is an emergent-property that arises in an increasing state of disorder, but will cease to exist, in due time, as disorder further increases towards maximum. Because, as entropy increases, this increase in disorder will prevent complexity from existing; and increasing disorder will eventually destroy even matter and its fundamental components.

For ease of understanding complexity, we can evaluate the mixing of coffee and cream together. Coffee and cream, individually, are lower entropy-states, than is the final coffee and cream mixture, which is a higher entropy-state. As exampled by the movement of the air molecules in a room, if all the molecules are gathered in the corner of the room, this configuration is a low entropy-state because the molecules are more orderly. However, as the air molecules disperse and begin bouncing around in the room, the disorder of the molecules increases; hence, their entropy increases. Same holds true when coffee and cream are mixed.

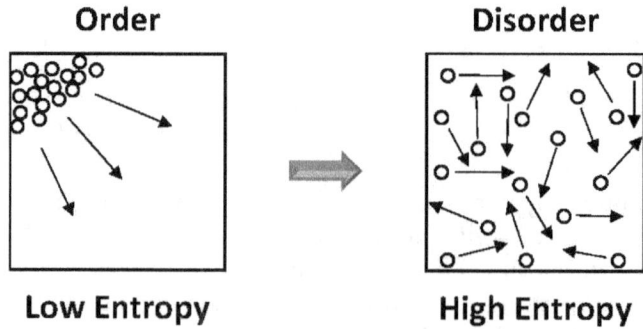

Order   **Disorder**

Low Entropy   **High Entropy**

Coffee and cream demonstrate an increase in entropy, just as the aforementioned air molecules do; because, coffee, by itself, and cream, by itself, have lower entropy, thus, they are less disorderly than when coffee and cream are fully mixed. The coffee and cream molecules on their own are more homogeneous and less disorderly than when coffee and cream are fully mixed together and the molecules of coffee and cream intertwine. Therefore, when we mix coffee and cream together, the final mixture is more disordered and has a higher entropy than the coffee and cream did before they were mixed. This is why, just as we cannot unpeel a banana once it is peeled, just as we cannot unbreak a glass once it is broken, just as we cannot revert an omelet back to its original egg form; we also cannot unmix the coffee and cream mixture back to their pre-mixed original individual states. These examples of irreversibility are because of the Big-Bang and its resulting increasing entropy which causes the forward direction of the arrow-of-time.

However, when we mix coffee and cream, and as we take them from a lower entropy-state of individual coffee and cream to a higher entropy-state of completely mixed coffee and cream; in the interim, as the coffee and cream are mixing and flowing through, we can observe the intermediate period of the formation of complexity. When coffee and cream are poured together, we can observe complex shapes and patterns emerge as they are mixed together; and as the mixture has more time to mix, the complexity of the patterns increases, but after a plateau of complexity has reached, complexity subsides and disappears as the entropy of the fully mixed coffee and cream reaches towards maximum. This analogy demonstrates how complexities such as stars, galaxies, and, even life, can emerge from the increasing entropy caused by the Big-Bang; and how, at some point into the future, when The-Universe becomes more disorderly as its entropy increases, these complexities will begin to disappear.

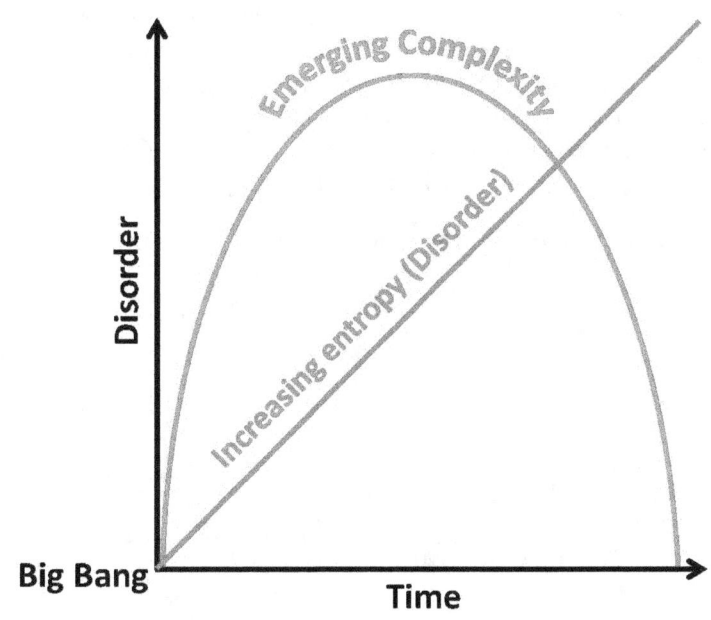

Therefore, disorder and negativity are the default-states of The-Universe, the default-state of Our-Universe, and as discussed, negativity is the default-state of our mind. Since Entropy is always increasing in The-Universe and since we are a part of The-Universe; therefore, the entropy of Our-Universe is also always increasing. Similar to the birth and transformation of The-Universe, our life at birth starts from lower entropy and moves to higher entropy as we get older and as we approach death.

Death is the ultimate personal-entropy.

The fact that we are first born, and then live, and eventually die, is an indication of how entropy and the arrow-of-time work at the human-scale and at the local-level of our lifetime. Time and entropy move us forward towards aging and death. It is because of the arrow-of-time that we die and it is because of the arrow-of-time why we cannot be resurrected from death and move backward to becoming a young adult or an infant again. Although we can try to minimize and slow-down life's local-entropy at the local-level of Our-Universe, we cannot completely eliminate entropy and disorder; hence why, we all die eventually. Being born, living life, and dying, are all indications of the movement of our lifetime through the arrow-of-time.

In nature, disorder, disease, and death are normal; but harmony, health and happiness are not normal.

Since the arrow-of-time indicates that time could only travel in one direction, which is forward; Theory of Self-Relativity refers to the stages of our life moving through the arrow-of-time as the *"Arrow-of-Lifetime."* Life, death, and time are as a result of change which are brought about by entropy, motion, and the arrow-of-time. Likewise, time exists because of entropy and motion, which means our lifetime exists because of entropy and motion; therefore, our arrow-of-lifetime exists because of entropy and motion, and as a result of the Big-Bang. Since entropy, motion, and the arrow-of-time dictate our lifetime, and since these are the same components that dictate change; therefore, we change throughout our lifetime, and in order for us to live the best possible lifetime, we must learn to change alongside time and throughout our lifetime.

To change is natural...to not change is unnatural.

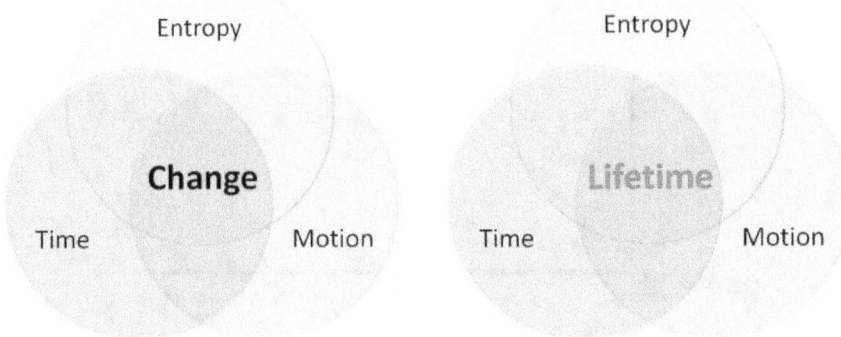

Change is the only consistent-constant.

According to Theory of Self-Relativity, space, time, our lifetime, and our existence, are all emergent-properties of The Big-Bang and entropy; because if there were no Big-Bang and no entropy, there would be no change, hence, there would be no space, no time, no lifetime, thus, there would be no existence.

If there were no entropy and no motion, nothing would change, and there would be no passage-of-time. Since we live in time; therefore, we are bound by the laws-of-physics. Entropy and motion create time, time changes consistently, and change is constant. Therefore, time and change are interchangeable because time is a measurement of change; and change is shift in the state of a thing from moment to moment. Since time changes consistently and change is constant; therefore, "Time" and "Change" are intertwined. Theory of Self-Relativity describes this inseparable relativity of "Time" and "Change" as the constant of *"ChangeTime."*

ChangeTime

Entropy and Motion create Time

Time is not constant

Time changes constantly

Time changes consistently

Time measures Change

Change is constant

Change is consistent

Time & Change are intertwined

Time & Change are interchangeable

Everything Changes constantly

Everything Changes consistently

Change is the only consistent-constant

Change is unavoidable

Everything is in a constant state of change; and change, itself, since the beginning of time, is the only *"Consistent-Constant."*

Change is unavoidable; therefore, change or you will be changed.

Although time, itself, is continuous; as an emergent-property, time does not have physical attributes. It is only humans who have arbitrarily created a scale for measuring of time, so that the passage-of-time could be quantified for reference, for planning, and for coordination. Not only modern human-beings coordinate their life and their existence by referencing time in a measured scale; but, even animals that are not cognizant of time in a scaled format are aware of the passage-of-time on a less detailed and more general "perceived" level. For example, birds go to sleep as the sun goes down and they wake up and chirp as the sun rises. Since birds use external signals such as sunlight and sundown to wake up and to sleep; they wake up and sleep at different perceived-times as the seasons change. Animals wake up earlier and go to sleep at later perceived-times of the day during the summertime, and they wake up later and go to sleep earlier during the winter times. Although animals do not have an understanding of measured-time; via changes in the external-stimuli such as sunlight, they still have a sensation and perception of different days as they adapt their life's activities to this passage-of-time. This phenomenon is often referred to as the Circadian-Clock or the Circadian-Rhythm.

When an organism uses external-stimuli, it is differentiating time in a perceived-form rather than as a measured-form. According to Theory of Self-Relativity, most living things, including humans, perceive time relative to Their-Universe; unless an organism is intelligent enough to be able to measure time relative to an arbitrarily self-created scale. For example, birds living on a planet that takes 48 hours to rotate around its axis would have a different sense of perceived-time than those living on Earth; therefore, unless time is scaled and measured by an intelligent-being, time is relative, and it is also perceived differently at any given moment by living entities.

Although time is consistent; time is relative to all things animate or inanimate. Theory of Self-Relativity contextualizes animate *"Time-Relativity"* binarily:

1. **Measured-Time:** Is real-time that is scaled which can be measured and referenced in fractions and multiples of moments. Measured-time is our classic understanding of dated time which is referenced to indicate the past, the present, and the future. Measured-time is what clocks, lifetime, and history represent. Measured-time enables us to recognize and to quantify time on a standardized scale. This scale is a manmade earth-based universal measure of time, which is only applicable and understood by humans. Measured-time is an arbitrarily created and accepted constant that is measured at a rate of one-second-per-second.

   - Although time measured in seconds is a constant, different observers could actually experience a second of time at different rates, relative to their observation position and relative their speed of motion. For example, the faster we move, the slower our time will pass relative to other stationary or slower moving entities. This means the faster moving person's time passes slower compared to the stationary or slower person's time; however, each person experiences time at one-second-per-second, in their own position. Therefore, a person who travels extremely fast, at or close to the speed of light, will actually age much slower relative to a stationary or slower moving person; however, each person will experience time at one-second-per-second in their own environment. This time-relativity, also known as time-dilation, is one of the major principles of Einstein's Special Theory of Relativity.

2. **Perceived-Time:** Is "individual" or "personal" and it is time as perceived or as experienced by different beings or different people at different times, and in different locations or in different circumstances. Perceived-time, as described by Theory of Self-Relativity, is subjectively-relative to each person; this means perceived-time is relative to how our "mind" subjectively perceives and experiences the passage-of-time. Although perceived-time could be influenced by external-stimuli such as Circadian-Rhythms; Theory of Self-Relativity focuses on perceived-time relative to humans and how our thoughts and our feelings influence our subjective perception of time.

- Based on the relative-sensations and relative-perceptions of an individual, perceived-time could subjectively be slower or faster than measured-time, regardless of the person's speed of motion. The reason, locally, speed is not a factor in the human perceived-time is because perceived-time for humans occurs on Earth or relative to it. Thus, for humans, the speed of our movement or motion in our everyday life cannot be so fast where it becomes a significant percentage of the speed of light, in order for it to make a difference in our time-relativity. Unlike measured-time, perceived-time is not an actual phenomenon which could be measured. Perceived-time is subjective as it is sensation and feeling based; hence, due to its subjectivity, perceived-time is often distorted and incorrect when compared to measured-time. In order to authenticate perceived-time, we must use a measurement instrument such as a clock to validate or invalidate our sensation of our perceived-time. Measured-time is quantifiable; while perceived-time is subjective and often distorted.

Time-Relativity

Measured-Time	Perceived-Time
Quantifiable	Sentience-Based
Objective	Subjective
Constant	Variable
Repeatable	Unrepeatable
Predictable	Unpredictable
Universally-Relative	Personally-Relative

Despite the fact that we have scaled and measured-time, time itself is inherently immeasurable, because time is a continuum. The human scale of time measurement, which is one-second-per-second, is based on an arbitrary scale chosen as a result of the Earth's rotation around its axis, at an estimated 24 hours per day, or 86,400 seconds per day. Although time, itself, is considered to be eternal; when time began or when time ends does not really matter, because the only time-relativity that matters, is its relativity to each of us during our life "time."

Furthermore, time cannot exist without Space. Since time is as a result of entropy and the motion caused by entropy; motion and change could only occur in a space and at a location. Thus, space, itself, is an emergent-property of The Big-Bang and entropy. Time and space are therefore interwoven and inseparable. In Physics, and as termed by Albert Einstein, this intertwining of space and time is known as the fabric of *"SpaceTime."* Therefore, The Big-Bang and entropy not only created time, but also created space. Since entropy creates SpaceTime and SpaceTime causes change; consequently, change always happens in a particular location in space and at a specific time. Therefore, ChangeTime, inherently includes a location in space where the change occurs; thus, SpaceTime causes The-Universe and everything in it to change.

Time, space, and change coexist, and neither could exist without the other; therefore, change is an inherent and constant part of everything that exists in The-Universe.

Change
Entropy creates Motion
Entropy creates Time
Entropy creates Space
Motion causes Change
Time and Change are intertwined
Space and Change are intertwined
SpaceTime and Change are Intertwined
Entropy, Motion and SpaceTime are relative to Change
Change is:
Continuous
Consistent
Constant
Non-Stop
Always
Everywhere
Inherent to Existence

Since change is inherent to everything and since change is required for The-Universe to exist; therefore, we must also learn to change in order to be in harmony with The-Universe. Although physicists rightly argue, that, in The-Universe, time cannot exist without space; for personal references and for our daily lives, we often refer to time separately while we implicitly assume the presence of space. Furthermore, at the local-level of Our-Universe, space is often referred to as "place;" hence, the designation of *"PlaceTime"* by Theory of Self-Relativity instead of SpaceTime when referring to our personal-existence in Our-Universe.

The-Universe	Our-Universe
SpaceTime	PlaceTime

As discussed, due to the Big-Bang, entropy, and the arrow-of-time, time only moves in forward direction; therefore, the Big-Bang is the grand cause of the order of "cause and effect." It is because of the Big-Bang why we must first have a cause in order to have an effect. Furthermore, since the arrow-of-time only moves forward; hence, time never moves backward. Likewise, time cannot stop, because due to entropy and motion, The-Universe is constantly changing and expanding; thus, time continues indefinitely. Since time does not stop and since The-Universe is constantly changing and expanding; therefore, space is constantly changing and expanding, because space and time are intertwined. Consequently, if time would stop; no space would exist, because time would not exist.

Although space and time are intertwined, time only has direction but no location. Contrary to time, space or place has a 3-dimensional location, but unlike time it has no direction. While living on Earth many mistakenly believe that space has direction; in reality and on the larger scale of The-Universe, space does not have a direction. In space, there is no North, East, West, or South, as these directional designations are simply manmade coordinates for travelling within our local places. Space, whether at the macro scale of The-Universe or at the micro-scale of atoms, has three dimensions of X, Y and Z, but it has no direction. However, at the local-level of Our-Universe; humans have created arbitrary location and direction coordinates based on the Earth's axis, to be able to reference a specific place. In summary, space has no direction, but place, as created by humans for local-referencing, has directional-references.

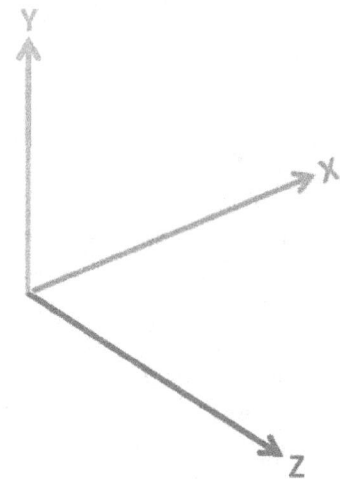

Just as a second-of-time is a manmade measurement of time; North, East, West, South are also arbitrary manmade coordinates for referencing a location or a place. These manmade measurements of time and location coordinates enable us to reference our existence relative to everything and everyone else in Our-Universe. In our everyday life, we live life by constantly referencing to PlaceTime for our existence and interactions; for example, we make a date with someone to meet them at a certain time and at a specific place. Although place is an inherent component of time; throughout our everyday "local" life, we implicitly assume an event happening in a certain place, often without mentioning the place initially. Therefore, at the local-level of our lifetime; time has priority over place because it is more important for us to know what time a certain interaction or event will take place than where it would be.

For example, we make sure to wake up every morning at 7 a.m. so that we could be at work by 9 a.m. We automatically assume we will be waking up in our bedroom and we will be going to work at our regular workplace. When we set our alarm to wake-up, we only care about the time, because the place is automatically assumed. We set our alarm to wake-up at 7a.m. but we don't additionally set our alarm to wake-up in our bedroom; hence, we don't mention or think of the place of reference when we think of the wake-up time. Therefore, despite the fact that a place could be assumed or referenced for an event; time is almost always referenced.

Another reason that at the local-level of Our-Universe time has higher priority than space is because our lifetime has defined time periods of past, present, and future. Time is a more significant component of our memories, experiences, and existence, than place is. We remember things because they happened in the past; we are experiencing things because they are happening in the present, and we anticipate things to happen in the future. Likewise, we celebrate a date, such as a birthday, every year, because birthdays are directional and they are time related; however, we don't celebrate a location every time we go there, because in reality, place has no direction. Therefore, we celebrate time because time has direction, but place or space does not have a direction; place or space only has a location.

Humans celebrate direction, they don't celebrate location.

To locate or reference something or someone, regardless of it being in the past, the present, or in the future; we must make reference to 2 coordinates, time, and place, (or when and where). The coordinate of place or space has 3 dimensions of X, Y, Z; and time, itself, has one-directional dimension, which is sometimes referred to as the 4th dimension.

As discussed, according to Einstein's Special Theory of Relativity, time, and space are absolute and interwoven, as one cannot exist without the other; hence, the designation of SpaceTime. Since, in The-Universe, SpaceTime is absolute but relative to the observer; therefore, locally, in Our-Universe and in our lifetime, PlaceTime is absolute but relative to each of us. Thus, a personal-experience or an event always occurs at a specific time and in a specific place relative to each person. This is why, subjective-experience can vary from how reality is, because as we perceive time and as we experience a location, our personal-experience could be distorted compared to reality. Furthermore, our personal-experience could not only be distorted compared to factual-reality, but our experience could be different, relative to someone else's personal-experience of the same situation or a similar event. This is why, personal-experience or subjective-experience must always be verified with objective facts and evidence.

PlaceTime	
Place	**Time**
Relative	Relative
3-Dimensional	Linear
3 Dimensions of X,Y,Z	The 4th Dimension
Location-Based	Direction-Based
Has No Direction	Has Direction
Has Location	Has No Location
Referenced or Assumed	Referenced, rarely Assumed

Although time could travel at different speeds relative to a person; at the local-level of Our-Universe and our lifetime, the differential experience of time due to the speeds of travel on Earth is insignificant; because our speeds of travel on Earth is a miniscule percentage of the speed of light. The speed differential for experiencing time differently would've been significant if one person moved at super high-speeds compared to another person. Such speeds of travel could not currently take place on Earth; hence, the relativities of experiencing time differently between people due to difference of speed of travel is miniscule, and therefore can be ignored. While, at the local-level, the difference in experiencing measured-time by different people is negligible; the experience of perceived-time, which is subjective and not relative to the speed of travel, could be quite different. Simply put, at the local-level of our lifetime, change in measured-time is same for everyone; however, different people experience time differently based on their subjective-experiences of perceived-time.

For example, since being on vacation is a fun event; for someone that is on vacation, time seems to go by faster for the vacationer than for another person who is at work during the same time-period. In reality, the arrow-of-time moves forward at one-second-per-second for both the vacationer and the working person; however, each person perceives the passage-of-time differently relative to their individual mental and emotional experience. Consequently, since perceived-time is more subjective and often based on sentience, it is important to become aware of our subjective mental and emotional states which could influence our personal and our subjective-experience of time; therefore, which could influence our life.

This is why, factual-thinking is integral to living a quality life based on how reality is and not based on how we perceive or prefer reality to be. When unsure about the passage-of-time, we can simply check our watch to confirm passage of measured-time versus our sensation of perceived-time. Likewise, when unsure of our perceived-thoughts, we should check our thoughts for their factuality, to ensure that our perceptions and assumptions are based on how reality is, and not based on how we want reality to be.

Since time and place are interwoven, and because time is relative to each person; therefore, place is also relative to each person. For example, location "here" which is where we are, is location "there" from another person's perspective. As discussed, because time changes constantly, this change occurs in a place or in a location; therefore, when time changes, so does place. Even when we are sitting down and we think our location stays constant, our location remains constant relative to our local-place; however, our location on Earth changes continuously in space relative to the Sun, relative to the Milky-Way galaxy, and relative to The-Universe. This is why, we can perceive reality to be very different than how reality actually is; hence, the only means of bringing our perceptions and our thoughts in sync with what is real and what is not, is for us to always check and verify our perceptions and our thoughts with facts and evidence.

Additionally, we not only perceive reality differently because of our physical and our relative-existence; but, we also perceive reality differently because we intentionally, but often nonconsciously, alter our thinking in order to perceive a dislikable-reality more favorably. In other words, we incorrectly perceive and interact with reality:

1. Because of our subjective-perception of our relative-existence with PlaceTime.
2. Because of our intentional alteration of perceived-reality to our liking.

It is because of these relativities of our existence and our thinking that in order to stop our mind from distorting reality and from ignoring facts, we must learn to think factually so that our perception is always based on how reality is, and not based on how we want reality to be.

Thinking must dictate feelings; feelings should not dictate thinking.

When we don't like how the present is, instead of evaluating the facts and changing them to make the new present-moment-of-now favorable for us; we often, nonconsciously, distort, ignore, or deny the dislikable facts in order to make our perception of the "now" become more to our liking. This is how we self-deceive. When we distort or change our perception and our thoughts about how things are, our mind is not able to move forward with time and reality. Our mind gets stuck in the past, because what we think is different than how reality is. Instead of changing the dislikable facts and circumstances to make reality favorable for us, we commonly choose to distort our perception of reality and we ignore the evidence in order to improve how we feel. We do so because it is easier to self-deceive by creating false-thoughts, than it is to face the dislikable facts and to have to put in the necessary and often time-consuming effort to change reality to our favor.

Since truly changing things to feel good and happy requires more effort and input than simply creating false-thoughts for quick gratification; therefore, we choose to not change, because change is not fun, change takes time and effort, and change usually requires facing dislikable-facts. Hence why, self-reflection and introspection, which enables us to become aware of these dislikable-facts, is a difficult process. Since facing dislikable-facts that we have denied or ignored for a long time is a painful and difficult task; this is why, Theory of Self-Relativity categorizes introspection as one of the two non-negotiables for self-improvement.

As discussed, introspection, which is defined as one's ability to look within one's Self, is often a difficult and painful task; because in order to resolve or eliminate these issues, self-reflection and introspection force us to face personal realities that we don't like. Therefore, and as discussed, the main reasons we do not like to change are:

1. **Primitive-mind:** Our primitive-mind does not like change because change introduces variables and uncertainties; thus, change could compromise our safety or even our survival.

2. **Introspection and Effort:** Change takes time and effort; and change requires facing dislikable personal-shortcomings, in order to resolve and improve these shortcomings.

When we resist changing to improve because change is difficult, and when we instead choose to create false-realities, or we ignore dislikable facts and evidence; our mind gets stuck in the past while time moves forward. As discussed, time moves forward constantly and consistently, yet, the only thing that often stays back in time and does not move forward with the arrow-of-time is our mind; therefore, our mind, which creates our thoughts, and which forms our self-identity and our sense of Self, disables us from moving forward with the arrow-of-time and in sync with The-Universe. Although our physical-existence moves forward with time, thus it changes and ages with everything else in Our-Universe; our mind, which is synonymous with our sense of Self, gets stuck in the past and gets left behind. It is this disconnect of our sense of "Self" and our physical "Self" from Our-Universe that causes us to rehash difficult thoughts over and over again; and to have feelings of remorse and regret by getting stuck in hindsight-biases with the "could've, would've, should've" repetitive-thoughts. This is how, our mind gets stuck in the past; because instead of resolving the issues left behind which are causing these repetitive-thoughts, our mind keeps going back in time by attempting to fix the past so that the present instantly and magically becomes better.

By lacking the ability to resolve or move-on from past events, our mind keeps rehashing and regurgitating these events, especially the negative and traumatic ones, in order to try to alter the already occurred outcome. Instead of looking at the current facts and making changes in the present-time; our mind nonconsciously keeps going back in time to alter the now known past, based on newly available current information. By engaging in counterfactual-thinking, namely, alternate thoughts than what actually happened, or by ignoring and by denying current facts, our mind constantly goes through the events of the past because it wants to change the past, with the intent to change and improve our present-moment. Thus, our mind gets stuck in the past by keeping our thoughts trapped in the past. While our thoughts are stuck in the past; time continuously moves forward, further and further away from those past events, and leaves us more and more distanced from how reality is. The longer this goes on, the more cumbersome the process of change, which is needed to bring us forward in time, becomes.

This is how, our primitive-mind clashes with our intelligent-mind. Although our intelligent-mind should be in control because our intelligent-mind is the one that can problem-solve and make changes; as discussed, when we feel discomfort or when we sense danger, our primitive-mind, which only cares about our safety, immediately kicks into action in order to distance us from potential threat, danger, or discomfort, even if that discomfort is perceived and nonfactual.

Since our primitive-mind acts quickly and instinctively, the primitive-mind acts and reacts immediately on the negative or uncomfortable feelings that we feel. In the modern-times, we rarely come across primitive-dangers that require our primitive-mind to kick in quickly and instinctively in order to minimize the danger that it senses; however, our primitive-mind, in the absence of primitive-dangers, treats the strongest of our modern negative-feelings as if they were in response to primitive-dangers. In the modern-era and in the absence of primitive-dangers, our primitive-mind treats the strongest of our negative-feelings as if they are emotions caused by a threat or a dangerous situation which could jeopardize our safety; hence, our primitive-mind causes us to act quickly in response to these feelings. Whatever causes us the most negative-feeling at that moment gets considered by our primitive-mind as a threat or danger; and the only way that our primitive-mind knows how to deal with something negative is to fight-or-flight instinctively and quickly. This is why, in the modern-times, chaos, drama, and overreactions to negative-feelings are common towards things that do not directly lead to immediate existential-harm. In other words, in the modern-times, we tend to treat the strongest of our small negativities as if they represent a potentially life-threatening situation.

Furthermore, since in the modern-times, our intelligent-mind makes more decisions than our primitive-mind did in the primitive-times; when our intelligent-mind makes a bad decision, this causes our primitive-mind to get anxious and fearful, and to lose confidence in our intelligent-mind's decision-making abilities. Therefore, our primitive-mind jumps in to take control back from the intelligent-mind, so that it can keep us safe. As discussed, the way that our primitive-mind tries to keep us safe is by forcing us to lockdown and to not make any changes, because change inherently increases variables and uncertainties which could lead to something going wrong. Since our primitive-mind locks our intelligent-mind from further decision-making based on an unfavorable event that happened in the past, the only way that our primitive-mind knows how to correct the event that led to the negativity is for it to try to go back in time, and try to relive the past, in order to change the current outcome, by changing the now known past.

This vicious and unhealthy cycle occurs because the intelligent-mind made unfavorable or bad decisions by ignoring facts and by going with nonfactual considerations. This is why, we must learn to strengthen our intelligent-mind so that our primitive-mind can gain back its confidence in the intelligent-mind's decision-making and problem-solving abilities. The only way that our primitive-mind could begin to trust our intelligent-mind is for our primitive-mind to recognize that our intelligent-mind is making sound decisions. This can only be accomplished when we begin to think factually and when we make our decisions based on facts, and not based on emotions. However, as long as we keep making mistakes, the only way that the primitive-mind knows how to resolve a negativity is for it to shut down the intelligent-mind and for the primitive-mind to get down and dirty into the situation to quickly resolve or eliminate the cause of what it perceives to be threatening or dangerous.

The way the primitive-mind senses a reduction in threat or danger is by it sensing lesser degrees of negative-feelings; however, as long as we have unresolved issues from the past, our primitive-mind remains active, and it will not allow our intelligent-mind to take over. This is why, despite the fact that in many cases the event or the cause of our negativity that is being carried forward from the past is no longer active; since we still feel negative based on that event, our primitive-mind treats such negativity as a current threat. Since we feel the negativity in the present-moment because we were unable to resolve or eliminate the thoughts associated with the negativity of our past; our primitive-mind thinks the cause of the negativity still exists in the present-moment. When our primitive-mind feels a negativity or senses a threat, it cannot distinguish if the negativity is caused by an actual cause from the present or by a thought from the past; therefore, it kicks into action to quickly resolve the situation. In this reference, since the cause of why we feel negative is from the past and not from the present, and since the only way that our primitive-mind knows how to deal with a threat or negativity is to go directly to the cause; therefore, our mind keeps going back to the past and gets stuck in the past. Consequently, our mind is trying to deal with a past event as if it were a current issue.

When our primitive-mind stays in control in order to keep us safe, and as it gets stuck in the past to try to fix or eliminate a cause from the past; our intelligent-mind cannot step-in to resolve or eliminate the thoughts that are kicking the primitive-mind into action. This is why, Theory of Self-Relativity insists that to be able to change, improve, and to become happy, we must first resolve our negativities. Time moves forward and our body and Our-Universe also move forward with time; but when our mind refuses to let go of the past and does not move forward with time, that is how we disable from change and improvement.

Our mind refuses to let go of the past because it is trying to alter a dislikeable event in the past so that we would feel better in the present-moment. After numerous attempts of rethinking and reliving the past, our mind realizes that the past could not be changed; therefore, in order for us to feel good, instead of beginning the lengthier process of changing the present-moment, we often, intuitively, choose the simpler approach of creating false-thoughts and comforting-beliefs in order to minimize the negativity that we feel at that moment. Since, to our primitive-mind, minimization of negativity, either by resolving the negativity or by creating comforting-thoughts, feels the same in the short-term; this reduction in negative-feelings calms down our primitive-mind, hence, it allows us to feel better temporarily. We feel better, because, this reduction in negative-feelings, regardless of how it was achieved, takes away the pressure of the dislikable and undesired feelings from our mind.

However, since creating false and nonfactual-thoughts to feel good does not actually resolve the cause from the past that is making us feel negative; as soon as the shot-in-the-arm effect of our comforting but false cover-up thoughts fades away, we sink right back into the same cycle of going back into the past, in trying to alter the past, in order for us to feel better at the present-moment. Yet, when that fails again, we once more try to create another comforting-thought so that we can try to improve how we feel at that moment.

Instead of getting stuck in this unhealthy cycle of reliving the past by falsely hoping to change the past so that we feel better at the present moment, and instead of trying to create comforting-thoughts to feel good; what we must do is to bite the bullet and decide that we are going to attack the causes of our negative-feelings by changing the present circumstance of the past causes, so that we can finally move forward parallel with time and in sync with reality.

As discussed, Our-Universe is a part of The-Universe which constantly increases in entropy and changes continuously. Since The-Universe changes constantly and the arrow-of-time moves forward through the present into the future; the past is set, and nothing could go back in time to change it. Additionally, due to the laws-of-physics and how they govern everything in The-Universe, nothing could past-travel because everything in The-Universe is matter-based; which means everything is made of atoms. If nothing could past-travel, this means we can't go back in time either, and neither should our mind. However, because our mind is an immaterial-byproduct of our material-brain's activities; our mind tries to defy the laws-of-physics by going back in time. The mind going back in time, or mind-travel, is a metaphor as our mind is simply a collection of our thoughts; thus, some of our thoughts, due to our intellectual and cognitive abilities, are capable of continuously thinking about the past, but they do not really separate and go back in time.

It is due to the human cognitive-ability of our mind and our thoughts going back in time, or due to our ability to think about the past, that our nonfactual and troubling thoughts and feelings ultimately clash with the present reality. Unlike other animals who do not have the intellectual ability to send their mind and their thoughts back in time; humans, due to their intelligence and their ability to distinguish the past from the present and from the future, are capable of manipulating their thoughts to go back in time, or to remain back in time. As discussed, human intelligence could sometimes act like a double-edged sword. While the ability to evaluate the past enables humans to use their knowledge and experiences to advance in life by improving their future; the same capability could also be used to hinder personal-progress.

It takes intelligence to manipulate intelligence.

Since our mind is immaterial, our thoughts could independently mind-travel to the past and stay back in time by separating from the present reality. Our mind past-travels, against how The-Universe operates, in order to make us feel better at the present-moment. By trying to separate from reality and by going back in time, our mind continuously attempts to rewrite the dislikeable past so that we would quickly feel better in the present-moment. It is this cognitive ability of our immaterial-mind to separate itself from the material world around it, that often prevents us from progress and improvement. Our mind, because of its immaterial nature, acts as if it is like a soul or a spirit; which means it attempts to violate the laws-of-physics. Since the laws-of-physics cannot be violated; therefore, our mind's attempts to go back in time and to relive the past negativities clashes with our current reality. As discussed, although our mind's ability to think of the past and to use its experiences to improve our future is an advantage of our intelligence; our mind's desire to past-travel and dwell on what happened, or to change what happened via counterfactual-thinking, is also a hinderance to our self-improvement.

We must remember that despite being an immaterial-byproduct, our mind is not an immaterial-thing; this means, the immaterial nature of our mind, our thoughts, and our feelings could not exist independently from their underlying material-brain. Therefore, when our immaterial-mind tries to violate the laws-of-physics by mind-travelling to the past, our material-existence pays the price for it.

Since our immaterial-mind only exists because of our material-brain's activities; via thought-awareness and thought-management, we can minimize the instinctive involvement of our primitive-mind while increasing the effective involvement of our intelligent-mind. When we learn to think factually, we will then make better decisions that are in sync with reality, and we will make less mistakes; thus, our primitive-mind will gain back its trust in our intelligent-mind, therefore it will let our intelligent-mind to make decisions as we move forward in time.

The role of the mind is to think, and part of its thinking ability is to examine events of the past by using these experiences to make changes for the future. Although this is a positive attribute of using experience, knowledge, and facts to guide the future; instinctually, our primitive-mind often goes astray by mind-travelling to the past, in order to change the past, so that we would feel better in the present-moment. While the right thing to do is to allow our intelligent-mind to use the past to influence the future favorably; the primitive-mind, due to its impulsivity and need for immediate-gratification, tries to go back in time to change the past, with the intent to make the present be more favorable.

To make the present-moment as favorable as possible, the correct approach would be for our mind to use the experiences of the past to anticipate and influence the future; hence, our mind should not mind-travel to the past by rehashing events of the past, in an attempt to change the past so that we feel better in the present-moment. Our mind should use the past to initiate change in the present-moment so that the future present-moments are more favorable. However, since randomness, chance, and our positioning influence the future; thus, it is difficult to predict the future. This is why, we have to use probabilities and possibilities, alongside guessing, assumptions, and predictions, as well as knowledge and experience, to make best assessments of what the future could be like. Therefore, if we use our knowledge and our past experiences to put in effort and to take action to make positive-change in the present-moment; we can, to a degree, influence the future that will become the new present-moment-of-now.

We can't change the past, but we can influence the future.

Our primitive-mind wants to mind-travel to the past because the past is now known and certain, but the future is not. As discussed, by minimizing uncertainties and variables, our primitive-mind wants to keep us safe, and this is why, we don't like to change, and why change is difficult. We don't like to change because change increases variables, therefore it increases uncertainties; and when uncertainties are increased, our primitive-mind begins to feel unsafe. In contrast, since the past is now known, thus, for our primitive-mind, dealing with the past feels safe. This is why, our primitive-mind wants to mind-travel to the safety of the known past in order to secure the present-moment-of-now.

As illogical as this sounds, our primitive-mind, which in the face of negativity and uncertainty takes control to keep us safe; reactively tries to go back in time in order to alter the past, based on the information that we now have in the present-moment. However, reality does not work that way, because we cannot change the past. What we need to change is our thinking in the present-moment-of-now, so that our thoughts are changing parallel with the arrow-of-time. Additionally, for most effective form of change, our mind must not only change with the passage-of-time, but our mind must learn to proactively take measures to make a change before change itself occurs. Therefore, in the modern-times, where primitive-dangers are rarely present, we must train our intelligent-mind to make better decisions so that it can control our thoughts, our feelings, and our behavior; and consequently, for it to minimize the engagement of the primitive-mind.

Although our mind is an immaterial-byproduct and not a standalone immaterial-thing; it is because of our mind's independent ability to mind-travel to the past while our material-existence moves forward in time, that has created fallacies such as *"Dualism."* It is this perceived, but nonfactual, separation of the immaterial-mind that has given rise to the fantastical perceptions of a person having a material-body and an immaterial-soul. Dualism, which believes that a living-thing has a material-body and an immaterial-soul, came into existence because of our immaterial-mind's ability to think independently of the material-body's interactions. However, thinking independently does not mean that we have a natural-body and a supernatural-soul or a supernatural-mind that is independent of our natural-body.

As discussed throughout Theory of Self-Relativity, our thoughts and our emotions are immaterial-byproducts or immaterial-processes of our material-brain's activities; but this does not mean that they are independent immaterial-things or supernatural-phenomenon separate from our material-brain. Our thoughts, which create our emotions, are as a result of our material-brain's neural activities; therefore, our thoughts and our mind are completely reliant on the activities of our brain. If our brain is damaged or if our brain stops functioning properly, such a change would directly affect our thoughts, our emotions, and our existence.

Our mind, our thoughts, our emotions, and as a whole, our "Self," is similar to the "wind" which is an immaterial-byproduct of atmospheric activities. Just because the wind is immaterial, it does not mean the wind is supernatural. Unlike ancient-beliefs, the wind is not caused by supernatural gods. Science, knowledge, and facts have explained that the wind is a naturally occurring immaterial-process which is produced as a result of the movement of hot and cold air molecules in the atmosphere. The atmosphere and its air molecules that create the wind are similar to our brain and its neural-firings which create our mind, our thoughts, our feelings, and our sense of Self. When the temperature of the air molecules eventually reaches equilibrium, the molecules slow-down their movement; and this decrease in activity dissipates the wind, or as commonly said, the wind "dies-out." Similar thing happens to our mind, our thoughts, our feelings, our Self, and our existence. When our brain's activities stop, our "Self" dies.

Just because the wind can move around independently does not mean the wind could sustain itself independently in the absence of the gas molecules which make up the atmosphere; hence why, there is no wind on the surface of the Moon, because the Moon does not have an atmosphere. Likewise, just because the mind can think independently or go back in time does not mean the mind could exist on its own without the brain's neural-activities. This is why, we can only be aware of our own thoughts and not someone else's thoughts; because someone else's mind and thoughts cannot separate and move around independently from that person.

Therefore, fallacies such as mind-reading, telepathy, or other mystical claims of accessing immaterial-things, are self-comforting fallacies, or they are deceptions intended to deceive the believer in thinking the truth is more to their liking than it actually is. This is why, factual-thinking and understanding the facts about our existence is important in filtering-out nonsense and fallacious-beliefs out of our thinking-system, so that we can begin improving based on how nature and reality truly are, rather than based on how we want them to be.

Since the arrow-of-time forces us to move forward with time, and since time itself and everything that is associated with time changes; thus, we should learn to make change a natural and normal part of our existence. Instead of pretending that we are changing the present-moment by sending our mind to the past, or instead of creating comforting nonfactual-thoughts to feel good; we should use the past to not try to change the past, but to influence the future. By using knowledge and experience, and through proper anticipation, we can actually influence and guide future events so that when the future arrives as the new present-moment-of-now, that new now would already be more favorable for us. Namely, instead of changing the past to correct the present; we should use the past to influence the future so that when the future arrives as the new present-moment-of-now, that new now is already favorable for us.

It is not as important where you came from as it is important where you are going.

For example, we cannot go back and change a failed personal-relationship, no matter how hard we tried. We can either stall by keeping our mind stuck in the past and by continuously rehashing what happened and what we could've changed; or we can use the past-experience to evaluate what we ignored or what we were thinking then, so that we can handle a similar situation differently in the future. We can either remain stuck with counterfactual-thinking, or we can move forward via factual-thinking. By recognizing and by understanding how we ignored or overlooked the facts, we can not only eliminate any further thoughts from our past-experience about the exampled relationship scenario; but we can use this past-experience to not make the same mistake again in the future with new relationships.

This is how we learn!

We learn by factually evaluating what we did wrong and what thoughts caused us to make a mistake. Instead of making the same mistake again, the next time we come across facts that point to similar circumstances, we can then choose to not engage in a similar relationship; no matter how good it might feel in the short-term, or how painful it feels to walk-away.

Mistakes are things we can improve; bad-habits are mistakes we repeat.

Since we cannot travel to the past and since we cannot change the past; therefore, there is no reason for our mind to keep our thoughts stuck in the past. We must learn to deal with and to overcome personal adversities, failures, and other losses, so that we can get back up to speed and in-sync with time. When our mind gets stuck in the past, we clash with the order of The-Universe; because time never stops, and everything else in The-Universe continues in motion.

Time is dynamic, time changes consistently, and time moves forward conti-nuously. To truly achieve stable and lasting self-improvement, we must learn to move our mind forward with time, and we must learn to change along with the changing arrow-of-time. Since everything changes constantly and consistently;

hence, variables and uncertainties are a natural part of our existence. Thus, there is no way that we can eliminate all variables and uncertainties in order to live in complete certainty. This is why, we must learn to change as we accept some uncertainty, because that is how The-Universe works.

The only certainty is the past and the past cannot be changed because it is certain.

This is why, training our intelligent-mind to think factually instead of nonfactually will minimize the effects of our primitive-mind from kicking in by default to seek certainty. The need for our primitive-mind to feel safe via certainty, keeps dominating our mental-state by continuously pushing us back in time in order to change the past, so that the present would be certain. However, when our intelligent-mind learns to make sound decisions and it learns to change by using facts so that it minimizes uncertainty; our primitive-mind will then begin to relax and allow our intelligent-mind to lead our thoughts, our feelings, our decisions, and our behavior.

Awareness and understanding of how our feelings influence our thoughts is integral in moving our mind forward with time, so that our mind does not keep getting stuck in the past. When we teach our mind to proactively change ahead of future events, our mind will not get stuck in the past; but it will actually look forward to influence the future based on our past-experiences. When we use our past and our present-moment to influence our future to our advantage, as the future becomes the new present-moment-of-now, this new now would be much closer to the way we would want our present-moment to be. Furthermore, when this new now becomes the past, we will not have the mental need to want go back to the past and change the past; because we already experienced a favorable present-moment-of-now that was more aligned with reality. By learning to change continuously and by planning and by influencing the future; no past-experience, not even failure, will become a finality.

Failure and success are simply steppingstone events in the process of life.

An experience or an event is only a finality if we do not continue that experience or event into the future. For example, what we call failure, will only be a failure, if we leave it as such. However, if we continue on that negative-experience or unfavorable-event and we make positive-changes, that experience or event becomes a part of the bigger process of continuous improvement. As stated throughout Theory of Self-Relativity:

A process is a continuum of events.

To change consistently and continuously, we must resolve our negative past-experiences in the present-moment; or we must discard the past-experiences and events which could not be changed presently. The way to change an unfavorable past-event that could not be changed presently, is to redirect the past-event to a new future-goal that could be influenced in the present-moment. This is how, experience evolves. This is how, we should use experience to build upon the favorable-past, or to pivot from an unfavorable past-experience. Experience helps us change, and experience helps to create a more advantageous future so that when that future becomes the present-moment-of-now, we get to truly live a fulfilled life in our new now.

Experience builds on past-success, and it redirects past-failure.

Time is a continuum and it never stops; and so is our life's events and experiences. Therefore, our life's events and experiences are a continuum and should never stop; but they should evolve. For example, when we make money or when we laugh, we don't stop making more money or we don't stop laughing again because we already made money or because we already laughed. We continue our life by making more money and we look forward to the next time that we will laugh again. We should treat negative-experiences with the same continuum. When we experience a failure, just like making money or laughter, we should not stop at that failure. We should take that failure and continue it to the next improved event in order to experience a better result. This way, there will not be any failures; all failures would simply be negative experiences and events in the process of achieving better results.

Resolving or eliminating thoughts from the past does not mean to ignore what happened. On the contrary, it means to evaluate the events based on the evidence and facts of what happened, rather than to live with the emotional-effects of the experience or the event. If the experience or the event had a justified and factual reason, we must identify and understand it, and we should take action to modify or correct it. However, if the experience or the event was emotional rather than factual, we should learn to dismiss that experience and to move on.

To let go of the past, we must learn to resolve or eliminate thoughts that we carry forward from our past. Resolving or discarding thoughts from the past does not mean denying facts and evidence. On the contrary, it means to objectively evaluate facts and evidence to resolve or dismiss lingering thoughts. Thoughts from the past are like carrying weight on our shoulders; therefore, to move forward, we must offload the extra weight so that we can move forward lighter and faster with changing time. Time is never constant, time is consistently in motion, and since time is not constant and time changes continuously; we should not stay constant either, and we must also change continuously.

The less mental-weight we carry, the faster we can change and move forward.

Since personal-change could only happen as a result of improving our thinking and behavior; true personal-change could only happen by changing, by resolving, or by eliminating our inapplicable and nonfactual-thoughts. The only way to truly resolve or eliminate our thoughts is to evaluate them for their factuality. Dwelling on thoughts without resolution prevents change and keeps our mind stuck in the past. To bring our mind forward and to keep it in the present-moment, we must resolve or eliminate our cluttering-thoughts. Change requires time and time is constantly changing; therefore, in order for us to transform and to self-improve, we must also change with time.

Time encompasses everything and time is associated with everything. Time affects everything including The-Universe, Our-Universe, and our existence. Once we learn to allow our Self to change with time and to allow our transformation to be based on factual-thinking; change will become intuitive and it will provide us with a solid thinking foundation for a fulfilled, high-quality, and confident living.

We live in time; therefore, we are bound by the laws-of-physics and nature. Time can be our worst enemy or our best friend; it is up to us to utilize our precious-time efficiently and effectively. Since we live in time and with time, we cannot change the past; but we can use the past to influence, and to even change our future. To live the best present-moment, we must learn to use the past to influence our future, so that when the future becomes the new present-moment-of-now; that new now is as favorable as we planned it to be.

Time moves forward; this time will never come back. Our location or place in time also changes, which means when we return back to that same location; we will not experience that location the same way we did the last time, because we are experiencing a changed location in a changed time. Even when we sit in a location for a few minutes, time goes by, but so does our place; because, in reality, the relativities of our location changes continuously. For example, while we were sitting for one-minute, ten people, and twenty cars passed by our location, and three birds flew from the left tree to the right tree. Therefore, as time moves forward, all our external factors and influencers also change relative to our Self.

Things are in motion not only as a result of natural physical laws, but things also move locally as our local-variables change. For example, cars driving by, birds flying across, and leaves falling are all dynamic changes that are occurring in Our-Universe and relative to one another, and relative to our Self. Time and motion create constant change; therefore, SpaceTime or PlaceTime also changes constantly relative to our Self, and relative to everything and everyone else. Additionally, during this exampled minute of change, not only our external-factors changed, but also our personal and our internal-factors changed. For example, within the aforementioned one-minute example; we lost 30,000 cells from our skin, we became one minute older, and now, we have one less minute to live our life. Therefore, since everything changes; we must also change.

Whether we like it or not, our physical-existence changes constantly; therefore, we must learn to constantly change our mental-state as well. We should not resist change just because we don't like to change, or because change makes us feel uncomfortable. We should learn to welcome change so that we can improve, because change is the natural state of The-Universe and everything in it. As stated, due to entropy, The-Universe and everything in it is in a constant state of disorderly change; yet, this change occurs in contrast to the fact that as human-beings with the need for safety and certainty, we seek orderliness and stability, hence why, we don't like to change. Our natural comfort-zone and inherent need for safety does not like change; thus, our inherent dislike of change is instinctually programmed in us, contrary to how The-Universe is set up for change.

Despite our preferences for staying safe and not wanting to change, since The-Universe changes and we cannot do anything about it; therefore, if we want to create local-order in our life, we must learn to put in effort to make positive-change. Because, if we don't put in active-effort to make positive-change, The-Universe will make us change through passive-change; which as stated, will often not be as favorable as the change that we make for our own Self.

Change, or you'll be changed!

Hence, to minimize local-disorder and to get closer to local-order, we must input active-effort and we must take proper action to make positive-change. Positive-change requires effort, because without effort, and if left alone on its own, the natural tendency of change is to become more disorderly, thus, more unfavorable for us. Similar results will happen if instead of putting in effort to make positive-change, we choose to become reliant on chance, faith, hope, beliefs, or other forms of magical-thinking and manmade supernatural-interventions.

When things are left on their own, there are more ways for things to go wrong than for things to go right.

Another way to explain entropy relative to our existence is to recognize it as a constant fighting state between balance or equilibrium, and chaos or disorder. Since entropy is inherently associated with disorder or a lack-of-order; balance and equilibrium in science are actually described as "perfect-disorder." In science, the reference point is how disorderly things are, not how orderly things are; therefore, the yardstick of how things are is measured as a reference to the "level of disorder," and not to the "level of order" or equilibrium. Although one would think balance or equilibrium is good; a balanced state would actually represent a state of no change. If everything is in equilibrium and nothing changes; time could not exist, which means neither us nor The-Universe would exist. Therefore, in order for things to exist, there should be disorder or lack of order, so that there could be change.

Things exist because everything changes.

At the scale of The-Universe, disorder and chaos is good for the creation and evolution of time, for the existence of life, and for everything associated with The-Universe. However, on the personal and local-scale of Our-Universe, the opposite is true; balance is good, and chaos and disorder are not good. Therefore, in order for us to create balance and stability in Our-Universe, we must not only change with The-Universe, but we must also take action to counter local-disorder by creating local-equilibrium. Although at the scale of The-Universe, no human effort could affect or influence its disorder and its motion; in our personal and local-scale of Our-Universe, we could minimize, improve, and even halt disorder to a certain extent.

Since we live in The-Universe, something or someone always influences our existence by creating disorder or chaos in our life. This does not mean that something or someone is always the cause or the reason of our problems or unhappiness; this simply means that we are influenced by external-factors; because we are relative to everything and everyone.

Due to entropy, increasing disorder is the default-state of our surroundings; however, balance and harmony are necessary for us to live a good quality life. Not considering chaotic and high-conflict personalities who create chaos and conflict in order to deflect from their own deficiencies and problems; the optimum external and internal environment for us to be able to live the best quality and the happiest life possible is a peaceful, balanced, and non-chaotic environment. By learning to change and to self-improve, and by minimizing the effects of external-disorders, be it other-people or other-things; we can learn to maximize the harmony and the quality of our own existence. This is why, self-awareness and dynamic self-improvement are integral to increasing the quality of our life.

Equilibrium is not good for The-Universe because lack of change due to equilibrium means time and everything else would cease to exist. However, local-equilibrium is good for Our-Universe; therefore, active-effort and input are required to create and maintain equilibrium and stability throughout our lifetime. Contrary to The-Universe, we can achieve and maintain equilibrium locally in Our-Universe if we learn to change and improve. By changing and by improving our thinking-system, we can adapt our thinking to become based on the factual-realities around us. Although we cannot influence the variables of The-Universe; via factual-thinking, we can influence the local variables of Our-Universe to a certain degree. We can mostly and easily influence the immaterial-byproducts of Our-Universe, namely our mind and our thinking, because just as our mind and our nonfactual-thoughts could create disorder in our lives; by learning to think factually and by dealing with Our-Universe based on facts and evidence, we can influence our thoughts, our feelings, and our behavior with more balance and positivity.

When we learn to change based on facts and based on how reality is, and not based on how we want reality to be; we can then begin to minimize-negativities by resolving their actual causes. As negativity is minimized, so is local-disorder and uncertainty; hence, we increase predictability, stability, and equilibrium. When we reach and maintain such state of stable balance and equilibrium, we can then begin to experience more frequent positivity and happiness.

Since everything in The-Universe, including time, is in motion and is constantly changing; therefore, we must also change along with time and with The-Universe. Since the default state of change in The-Universe is disorder and negativity, we can either become more disordered and negative by not taking any action and by allowing passive-change to negatively affect us; or we can proactively change for the better, by slowing down local-disorder, while increasing local-order and personal-stability. Because entropy, motion, and time are consistently changing

The-Universe, we must learn to actively intervene in order to slow-down negative-changes affecting us, so that we can experience more positivity in Our-Universe. This could only happen via factual-thinking and by taking action to create stability and positive-change. Facts enable us to see reality the way it is no matter how dislikable it might be. By recognizing the true nature of the reality that we are dealing with, we can then put in effort to minimize and eliminate the negativities associated with that reality, hence, we can set our Self up on the path of achieving more positivity and happiness.

By understanding how nature works and how the laws-of-physics relate to us, we can put in active-effort to locally manipulate Our-Universe into a more favorable condition for our daily life. Although no such interventions could be achieved at the macro-level of The-Universe; such interventions could be implemented at the local-level of Our-Universe. Therefore, how nature operates at the macro-level of The-Universe, could become less influential at the local level of Our-Universe and in our life. While it is important to understand that all matter and the laws-of-physics that we interact with are relative to us; it is also the same level of understanding that enables us to realize that we can manipulate our local-environment in order to make the best of our lifetime. To have the best quality of life, what works best for us locally, is not necessarily what nature's default system is. Despite the fact that we cannot reverse disorder at the grand scale of The-Universe; however, locally, by using our intellect and our knowledge, we can influence our circumstances in order to achieve more certainty, better predictability, and more stability.

As discussed, according to Theory of Self-Relativity, we as humans have free-will; or as described, we have "limited" but broad free-will to make decisions and to take actions in order to improve our circumstances. According to Theory of Self-Relativity, as long as this free-will does not attempt to violate the laws-of-physics, our free-will can influence Our-Universe locally, in order for us to create positive-change in our lifetime. Although what we create and accomplish will return back into the increasing disorder of The-Universe after we die; we can still create complexity, order, and improvements locally, in Our-Universe, while we are alive, and for many generations to benefit from our contributions.

To live a balanced and harmonious existence, we must control disorder, by locally minimizing uncertainty. This could only be achieved via factual-thinking, because the most important disorders to minimize are the imbalances and negativities associated with our mind and with our thinking-system. By thinking factually and by taking action based on facts and evidence, we can not only influence Our-Universe positively, but we can maintain and protect the successes and accomplishments that we have achieved. However, if we don't learn to think with facts and if we abstain from implementing change as a way of life; we run the potential for losing what we have, and we could sink deeper into the increasing disorder that is inherent to nature. This is why, we must think and act based on facts and knowledge, and not based on assumptions and beliefs.

When you believe, you assume that you know; but you don't know that you know.

When beliefs are formed, such beliefs must be verified with evidence so that these beliefs will turn into knowledge. Carrying beliefs for long periods of time and without supportive facts to turn them into knowledge could have negative effects, and even destructive consequences. Atop holding nonfactual-beliefs, it would be even more damaging and destructive to actually act based on these fallacies. For example, believing that having faith could prevent one's Self from dying of poisonous snakebites is a fallacious mindset that could result in negative-consequences and even death. Likewise, believing in the unproven afterlife rewards and wasting one's mortal-life for such a fallacy would be a waste of one's precious life.

If we don't deal with nature based on how nature is; nature will take its toll on us, and in due time, nature will make unfavorable-changes for us. This is why, we must think factually so that we can evaluate our life and Our-Universe with facts. Whenever we have a thought or a belief, we must become aware of that thought or belief to ensure that the thought or the belief is generated with factual-basis and not as a result of comforting-beliefs and preferred-emotions. As discussed throughout Theory of Self-Relativity, to feel good, we can either put in effort to change things in our favor; or we can take the easy way out by fabricating comforting nonfactual-thoughts and fallacious-beliefs. Fact-checking our thoughts will not only assist us in understanding the true value of our thoughts and beliefs; but most importantly, it will prevent us from holding onto our false-beliefs and nonfactual-thoughts, or acting on them.

Only one form of fact exists for every situation; hence, facts are facts, and facts are not open to interpretations. Since facts are not open to interpretation; therefore, facts are not open to manipulation.

As further stated:

Although facts are not absolute and could be examined and if necessary, replaced; factual-thinking is about having reasonable confidence in the facts, unless or until falsified.

Therefore, instead of fabricating nonfactual-thoughts and false-beliefs, we must learn to put in effort to change facts and circumstances in our favor, so that we can then live in a more favorable factual-reality. To make proper change, we must learn to change based on knowledge, and not based on beliefs; because, if our thoughts are not based on facts, then our actions will not be based on facts either. When we take the wrong action to change because our thoughts were faulty, or if we choose to not change; nature and The-Universe will make that change for us, and such change will often not be in our best interest. Likewise, if we don't make the effort to change an unfavorable reality, and when we allow others to decide or to make a change for us; what they decide or choose for us would rarely be as favorable as what we would've decided and chosen for our own Self.

Choices and decisions made by others are seldom as favorable or as desirable as the decisions we make for our own Self.

For example, most people want to be healthy, look and be fit, and live a long life; however, such change and improvement will not happen by just sitting and thinking positive-thoughts and wishing for the change to take place. If we choose to not move around and workout, we will not only gain weight, but we will begin to experience muscle atrophy and we will lose our musculoskeletal health quicker than those who actively exercise and slow-down their physical-entropy. This is why, at the local-level of our lifetime, we cannot just sit there and do nothing; because the inherent entropy and disorder of The-Universe is going to age our body. If we self-deceive by ignoring and by denying the facts, or if we self-deceive via positive-thinking that we are not getting older; we will be allowing the natural disorder of The-Universe to age us at its own natural pace.

However, by accepting the dislikable truth that we are getting older, and by factually understanding how muscles work and how exercise helps in lowering weight and minimizing musculoskeletal degeneration; we can put in active-effort to change for the better by slowing down our local-entropy, thereby slow-down our aging process. Although, eventually, the entropy and the disorder of The-Universe will cause us to get older and die, as it has done so to every human-being and to every living thing who has ever lived; however, we can slow-down the effects of The-Universe, at the local-level of Our-Universe, by taking proper action and by making positive-change in order to prolong our health and extend our life.

Entropy always increases, unless energy is added to the system; therefore, by making effort to take action, we can slow-down, and even temporarily halt the local-entropy of Our-Universe.

The same principles apply to our mental, cognitive, and thinking processes. If we do not actively engage in critical-thinking and problem-solving to maintain our cognitive-processes, our mind will deteriorate at a faster pace. When our mind diminishes quickly, so will our body and the quality of our life.

Thus, by continuously putting in effort and energy, by intervening, by tweaking, and by balancing nature's imbalances, we can slow-down the laws of entropy and motion at the local-level of Our-Universe. To keep something balanced, effort is needed; however, with awareness, understanding, and practice, the effort required to change will diminish, and change will become easier and more intuitive. By learning to think quickly, cleverly, and factually, we can make the needed changes at the local-level of our lifetime and Our-Universe. Change does not have to be an arduous and dislikeable process, because change can actually be fun and rewarding. Once we learn how to change; with practice, our change and transformational abilities will become more routine, intuitive, and even more rewarding as we age and travel further into our lifespan. When change is cognitive and through awareness and understanding of facts and how reality is, change will become more intuitive as we age; because, we will be using our fact-based knowledge and experience to apply to change.

When it comes to aging; it is the mind that matters, not the manmade concept of age.

This is why, Theory of Self-Relativity's Cognitive-Cognition-Technique advocates and teaches factual-thinking, because when change is understood and implemented cognitively; change, improvement, and transformation will be guided and advanced based on awareness and understanding of the facts and reality, and not based on incorrect-perceptions or comforting-beliefs. When we learn to deal with our life as a process of continuum of events that is guided by the arrow-of-time, and not as singular events referenced by manmade scaled-time; we will then be able to live our life as a continuum parallel with reality and in-sync with the passage-of-time, not based on the manmade concept of age.

We must learn to think in terms of time; not in terms of age.

As discussed, The-Universe, nature, and the laws-of-physics are defaulted to increase in disorder because they are continuously in motion. Disorder is contrary to our personal-preferences because disorder creates change and uncertainty; which in-turn, makes our primitive-mind worried and stressed. Atop the natural disorder of The-Universe, our primitive-mind, itself, is default programmed to be negative, because this default negativity is intended to keep us safe from threats and danger. Therefore, our primitive-mind does not want us to change so that it can keep variables to a minimum. In contrast, in order for us to live the best quality of life, we must change, so that we can be in sync with the changing Universe.

It is this clash of The-Universe requiring us to change and our primitive-mind preventing us from change, that makes change a difficult task. To live the best quality of life, on one hand and contrary to how The-Universe is, we must minimize local-disorder so that our primitive-mind is at ease; yet, on the other hand, to be in sync with The-Universe and to move forward parallel with time, we must continuously change, which is contrary to our primitive-mind's preference. This means, to change and improve, we must actively go against the way The-Universe operates, while we also go against how our primitive-mind wants to keep us safe.

This is why, self-improvement is a dynamic process; because we must continuously balance our existence with how The-Universe is, yet we must exist with how our primitive-mind is most comfortable. Therefore, awareness, understanding, and active-change via self-improvement are key for living the most fulfilling life; and the only way that we can learn to change with how The-Universe changes while keeping our primitive-mind at bay, is for us to learn to think factually. When we think factually and we deal with reality the way reality is, we will align our Self in sync with factual-reality, and we will gain the confidence of our primitive-mind by making better decisions and by taking constructive actions.

Nature's Default	Human Preference
Disorder	Order
Change	Minimal to No Change
Negativity	Positivity

Just as lack-of-order and negativity are part of The-Universe; uncertainty, anxiety, and negativity are an inherent part of Our-Universe. As discussed, humans and their brains are made of matter, and all matter is made of atoms. The laws-of-physics that govern nature apply equally to all matter, including the atoms that make up our brains. The laws-of-physics cannot distinguish between the atoms in a rock or the atoms in our brain. To The-Universe, we are nothing special, because we are a collection of atoms just like anything else. Therefore, contrary to many cultural and traditional beliefs, we are not special to The-Universe; because The-Universe does not care about our atoms any differently than it does about the atoms of a rock on Mars. Consequently, unlike our comforting-beliefs, The-Universe was not created for the purpose of human existence; we exist because The-Universe was already in existence.

The-Universe does not exist so that we could exist; we exist because The-Universe exists.

Since we are not special to The-Universe; therefore, it is up to us to make Our-Universe special for our own Self. Although this factual perspective that we are not special to The-Universe could make us feel insignificant; by being in control and by constantly changing, we can make our own existence as well as other-people's existence special and significant. To The-Universe, we are not special, but in Our-Universe, we should be the most special entity; thus, to be the most special entity in Our-Universe, we must take on the personal-responsibility to change our circumstances for the better. This is why, factual-thinking and the awareness and understanding of how everything interacts with us, based on facts and not based on our comforting or preferred feelings, is key to living a quality and a more fulfilling, happier life.

Due to the laws-of-physics and the way that disorder increases in The-Universe, we, as humans, are naturally and inherently exposed to the risks of change. We are susceptible to things going wrong because without active-effort and if left alone, more things could go wrong than could go right in our lives. However, if we commit to put in active-effort to make positive-changes, we will subsequently be able to minimize negativity and we will even slow-down local-disorder. When we learn to make positive-change and therefore minimize negativity as an inherent part of our existence; we will then experience a more stable state of contentment, a higher level of fulfillment, and more frequencies of happiness.

Effort is to minimizing personal-negativity, as energy is to slowing down entropy.

On one hand, we must learn to change so that we keep up with the changing time and with the changing Universe; but, on the other hand, our primitive-mind keeps intervening to prevent us from changing, because change introduces variables and uncertainties that increase the potential for threats and danger, thus, change increases the potential for things to go wrong. As discussed, we not only have to deal with the disorder and the chaos that The-Universe keeps throwing at us, but we also have to continuously deal with our primitive-mind kicking in to protect us from dangers and negativities. Our primitive-mind is innately programmed to focus on negativity so that it can foresee threats and dangers in order to keep us safe; hence why, our primitive-mind doesn't care, nor does it know how to focus on positivity in order to create happiness. Creating happiness is the role of our intelligent-mind, and that could only happen if our primitive-mind allows our intelligent-mind to take charge.

Creating happiness is the role of our intelligent-mind.

Our intelligent-mind could only take charge if it makes correct decisions and takes constructive actions. When our intelligent-mind makes sound decisions and takes improving actions, it is only then that our primitive-mind will take a backseat and stop intervening. To make the best decisions and to take constructive actions, our intelligent-mind must think factually so that its decisions and actions are based on how reality is. Unless our intelligent-mind can demonstrate to our primitive-mind that it can make sound decision and take constructive action, our primitive-mind will not take a backseat nor will it allow our intelligent-mind to be in control. This is why, when we make mistakes, our primitive-mind kicks in to take control away from our intelligent-mind; because the primitive-mind wants to minimize the effects of the mistake.

For example, our primitive-mind, similar to many other animals, is programmed to lookout for dangers associated with a predator. To make our primitive-mind feel safe, we must put in effort to minimize uncertainties associated with the potential predator; for example, we must find shelter. By finding a cave in the primitive-times, or by working and paying for rent or mortgage in the modern-times, we put in active-effort to minimize our exposure to the threats and dangers of not having a shelter. This active-effort and action minimizes our local-disorder and increases our local-equilibrium; which in-turn, calms down our primitive-mind and allows for our intelligent-mind to further takeover our decisions and our actions. Therefore, by putting in effort and by taking action to change and improve, we minimize our primitive-mind's negativity, uncertainty, worry, and anxiety; thereby, allowing us to experience more contentment and positivity. Making such improving changes could only happen via factual-thinking and not by creating placebo-thoughts or nonfactual-beliefs. Because, no matter how much we believed that we would have been safe if we stayed out at night in the wilderness or in the middle of downtown; our primitive-mind would not be able to calm-down and relax, regardless of how strongly we believed we were safe. In this example, our primitive-mind would only calm-down and take a backseat when it knows that we have put in active-effort to provide and maintain a shelter for our Self and for our loved ones in order to minimize our exposure to dangers, by increasing our safety.

When our primitive-mind is active, this means we are dealing with local-disorder, and we are exposed to uncertainty and potential instability. This activity of our primitive-mind occurs because our primitive-mind is programmed to sense that by being exposed, we could be in danger. In other words, when our primitive-mind is active, we are dealing with increased local-entropy and the potential for threats or danger. However, when our intelligent-mind decides to put in effort and begins to provide us with safety; our primitive-mind can then begin to trust that our intelligent-mind is making sound decisions which would not only minimize threats, dangers, and negativity, but which could lead to progress and positivity. When we think factually, and in-turn, as we minimize setbacks and negativities; our primitive-mind begins to recognize that danger is minimized, thus, our safety is increased. It is only then that our primitive-mind can begin to trust the judgment and decision-making abilities of our intelligent-mind; hence, it can then take a backseat. As discussed, the primitive-mind is "protective," while the intelligent-mind is "progressive;" therefore, protection must precede progress.

Therefore, the key to change and improvement is by changing our thinking-system to factual-thinking. Factual-thinking allows our intelligent-mind to take the lead for decision-making and actions which are based on facts and how reality is. This, in-turn, calms down our trigger-happy primitive-mind and allows it to take a backseat to our intelligent-mind's leadership. When the primitive-mind takes a backseat and as the intelligent-mind takes control; this minimizes our mental-negativity, hence, it allows for more productive thoughts and positivity to emerge. Therefore, to change and improve, we must first minimize our "personal-entropy," aka "local-entropy," so that we can, in-turn, minimize the intrusions of our primitive-mind. As discussed:

Theory of Self-Relativity defines "personal-entropy" or "local-entropy" as "negativity, disorder, and chaos that influences our existence during our lifetime."

Our personal or local-entropy refers to everything and everyone that causes or influences us negatively, including our own Self, during our lifetime. Although The-Universe is affected by entropy and motion, the macro effects of entropy and motion of The-Universe are not as significant on us during our lifetime as are the effects of our personal-entropy in Our-Universe. For example, The-Universe is constantly expanding, and it is expanding at faster and faster pace; however, this expansion of The-Universe does not affect us during our lifetime and at the local-level of Our-Universe. But an earthquake, a hurricane, or a pandemic, could create disorder and negativity at the local-level of Our-Universe. Likewise, losing a loved one, losing a job, or breaking up with a partner, could also significantly increase negativity, disorder, and even chaos in our life; while driving drunk, losing money, or doing physical self-harm, which are self-inflicted and directly as a result of our own personal-choices and decisions, could also have significant repercussions and negative-outcomes in our life.

By understanding how, personal or local-entropy affects our day-to-day living and our overall life, we can then learn to implement different approaches of minimizing, halting, and sometimes, even, temporarily reversing these personal-entropies. Just as adding energy to a system could minimize, halt, and even reverse entropy and disorder temporarily; adding energy and effort locally to our personal-entropies could also minimize, halt, and reverse naturally occurring entropies in Our-Universe.

By using our awareness, intelligence, and technological advancements, we can affect our personal-entropy in such ways that we could improve the physical and mental qualities of our life; regardless of our age. Making such changes and improvements will significantly improve the quality of our life, especially in comparison to those who in similar circumstances choose to passively go through life, by allowing nature's passive-change to make changes for them.

Therefore, when we think factually and as we deal with reality as reality is and not as we want reality to be, regardless of how dislikable the facts may be; we can then make decision and take actions that change reality to become more favorable for us. When we deal with reality as reality is and when we seek to find the facts that need change, we will then recognize the local-entropy that is influencing our life negatively; thus, we will make decisions and take actions to minimize, resolve, or eliminate these negativities, by reducing our personal-entropy. These negativities, which increase our local or personal-entropy, could be caused by internal-factors such as our material-body or our immaterial-mind; or they could be caused by external-factors such as other-people or other-things. This is why, we must think factually so that we can pinpoint the factors that are contributing to our personal-entropy and our life's difficulties.

Factual-thinking gets the primitive-mind to trust the intelligent-mind.

Although our personal-entropy could be affected by non-personal external factors; Theory of Self-Relativity focuses primarily on our internal-factors, especially our thinking-system, and how we think and react to negativities in dealing with our local or personal-entropy.

To feel good, you must think well.

Theory of Self-Relativity categorizes personal-entropy or local-entropy binarily:

1. **External-Entropy:** Are factors that are external to our Self which create disorder, instability, or change in our life. For example, earthquakes or interactions with others.

2. **Internal-Entropy:** Are factors that are internal to our Self which create disorder, instability, or change in our life. Theory of Self-Relativity further categorizes internal-entropy binarily:

    1. **Material-Internal-Entropy (Physical-Entropy):** Are internal-factors that cause disorder and change relative to our material or physical body. For example, physical-aging which represents material-changes in our body and our brain.

    2. **Immaterial-Internal-Entropy (Mental-Entropy):** Are internal-factors that cause disorder and change relative to our immaterial-byproducts or the immaterial-processes produced by our body and brain. For example, our mental-capacity, or changes in our thinking, reasoning, or cognition.

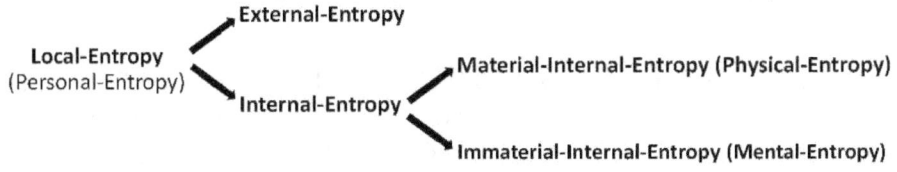

Although external-entropy could also be "material" or "immaterial," Theory of Self-Relativity recognizes internal-entropy, especially immaterial-internal-entropy or mental-entropy, as the primary local-entropy that must be addressed and minimized in order to make positive-change. While entropy refers to the degree of disorder; Theory of Self-Relativity does not refer to mental-entropy as a physical or physiological anomaly associated with the brain. Theory of Self-Relativity refers to mental-entropy as lack of order and organization in a person's thinking, reasoning, and cognition; which are generally as a result of nonfactual, counterfactual, or emotional-thinking, and not because of physical deterioration in the brain. In normal cognitive functioning people, and in the absence of physical, biological, or medical anomalies, both physical-entropy and mental-entropy could be interrupted and slowed down via proper awareness, understanding, and active-input. In the absence of physiological disorders:

Theory of Self-Relativity defines "mental-entropy" as "a faulty or disorganized thinking-system."

Because of material-tangibility, addressing entropy of the body or material-entropy is easier than addressing entropy of the mind or mental-entropy. Addressing mental-entropy is intangible and requires a different kind of awareness and understanding, and this is best achieved via changes in our thinking-system such as mindfulness and thoughtfulness; but most importantly via the adoption of factual-thinking. When we begin basing our thoughts on facts and evidence rather than on perceptions and emotions, we can then take corrective action to locally stabilize disorder in Our-Universe. By reducing disorder and by increasing fact-based balance and equilibrium in Our-Universe, we can then focus on improving and strengthening our remaining relevant thoughts, while creating newer and more productive ones.

Although without entropy everything will be in equilibrium, which means there will be no change; reaching equilibrium locally will not stop change. On the contrary, achieving "dynamic" but not "permanent" balance and equilibrium locally, will stabilize Our-Universe so that we can make change occur mostly under our influence and control. Entropy causes change; however, controlling local-entropy creates more selective and controlled change. Theory of Self-Relativity defines this controlled equilibrium as *"Personal-Equilibrium" or "Local-Equilibrium."*

Theory of Self-Relativity defines "personal-equilibrium" or "local-equilibrium" as "minimization of personal negativities and disorder by increasing personal balance and control."

Theory of Self-Relativity categorizes personal-equilibrium or local-equilibrium, binarily:

1. **Active-Personal-Equilibrium:** Refers to balance and control that is reached via active-input by a person. Active-Equilibrium offers more control, stability, and certainty for the person to make positive-change. For example, vacuuming the floors, refrigerating food after use, etc.

2. **Passive-Personal-Equilibrium:** Refers to balance but not necessarily control that is reached without a person's active input. Passive-Equilibrium does not always offer control, stability, or certainty for the person. For example, garbage collection and hauling, access to food in stores and in restaurants, etc.

The-Universe is in an increasing state of entropy or disorder, which means, we live in The-Universe which changes continuously; hence, it is becoming less balanced. As discussed, everything exists because noting stays the same; which means, nothing stays in equilibrium. In a permanent-equilibrium, nothing would exist because nothing would change. A permanent-equilibrium means no entropy and no change, which means, no existence of time; thus, in science, equilibrium is sometimes referred to as the perfect-disorder. Permanent-equilibrium could not be achieved because The-Universe is in an increasing state of entropy and change. Despite the fact that everything in The-Universe changes and there could be no permanent-equilibrium; local-equilibrium and stability are necessary for an optimum and balanced state of human existence. Therefore, in our lifetime and at the local level of Our-Universe, it really does not matter what happens at the larger scale of The-Universe; unless for example, a supernova explodes in close proximity of our Solar-System, or an asteroid impacts the Earth.

This is why, Theory of Self-Relativity focuses on our "Self" as the most important factor in our lifetime, and why we must live our life from the inside-out; locally, and relative to Our-Universe. This is also why, change is necessary for living a balanced and harmonious life. This necessary change could only be favorable if we take the initiative to want to change, and if we identify what needs to change. Contrary to the existence of The-Universe, for our personal existence, active-personal-equilibrium or active-local-equilibrium are of utmost importance. Constant and consistent change via active-input is what keeps our local-equilibrium dynamically in place. When we actively achieve personal-equilibrium and as we actively maintain our local-equilibrium, that is how our self-equation gets closer to dynamic-balance between our Self and everything and everyone else. This is why, Theory of Self-Relativity persists that change is not an overnight event, but it is a lifetime dynamic-process.

A balanced self-equation is an indication of personal-equilibrium.

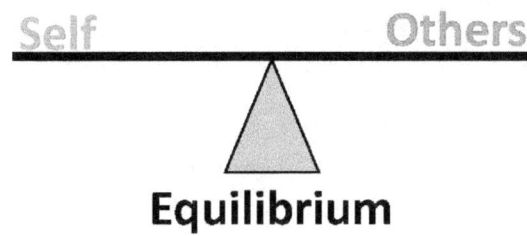

Equilibrium

Therefore, personal-change and personal-equilibrium must be dynamic and must be maintained through constant and continuous effort and input; hence why, Theory of Self-Relativity states:

Change and improvement are not singular events; they are continuum of events in the process of life.

Since the default nature of The-Universe is to be disorderly and out of equilibrium, and since contrary to the nature of The-Universe, the preferred state of our existence is to be less-disorderly and more in balance and harmony; we are constantly struggling against the forces of nature to stay in equilibrium. This is why, we need to constantly and dynamically change and improve with the ever-changing Universe; but in the meantime, we must also maintain the improved-changes by "actively" maintaining our local-equilibrium. If we don't maintain the improvement changes and the equilibrium achieved, the improved-changes and the local-equilibrium will begin to dissipate into disorder and even chaos. The only means of maintaining improvement is to ensure balance and harmony in the form of a stable personal or local-equilibrium. Change, especially proactive and constant change, improves the Self and creates dynamic local-equilibrium and stability for the Self. Personal or local-equilibrium, which is a state of balance that exists on the smaller local-scale of Our-Universe, is best achieved and maintained via active-input and through positive-change. As discussed:

Entropy always increases, unless energy or intentional-effort, which itself requires energy, is added to the system.

Since equilibrium is unstable, so is personal-equilibrium, because things are always changing; therefore, personal or local-equilibrium must actively and dynamically be maintained. Local-equilibrium could best be achieved and maintained via proper thinking and decision-making abilities which lead to improving action. This is why, factual-thinking is important for improvement, for change, and for maintaining personal-equilibrium. When we think factually, we can make changes based on facts and evidence, and based on how Our-Universe operates. When we change based on facts and evidence, our behavior leading us to change will be as a result of solid-thinking; and in-turn, the resulting change will be positive and stable, because it will directly address how Our-Universe is operating.

Therefore, local-Equilibrium is best achieved and maintained via active-effort and constant active-change that is based on factual-thinking. For achieving self-improvement, it is not just change that is important, but it is also maintenance of the improved change that is necessary to initiate and accomplish the next higher level of improvement.

Change ⟹ Improve... ∞

Change ⟹ Improvement ⟹ Maintenance

Change ⟹ Improvement ⟹ Maintenance

Therefore, to further improve to a higher level of existence, we need to change from the current level of improvement that we've achieved. This is why, self-improvement is not an event, but it is a process and a way of life. Change and improvement must be proactive and ongoing, and must become inherent to our existence. Hence, to minimize local-entropy and to achieve the best state of personal-equilibrium, we must adopt and engage with the "active-good," by minimizing and abstaining from engaging with the "passive-bad," that is listed below.

The "Active-Good"	The "Passive-Bad"
Positive-Change	Negative-Change
Active-Change	Passive-Change
Active-Equilibrium	Passive-Disorder
Local-Equilibrium	Local-Entropy
Maintaining-Equilibrium	Allowing-Disorder

The above table summarizes why we need to change, and why we need to implement change as an inherent and dynamic part of our existence. It also represents why we need to fight the forces of nature by putting in effort and energy to create local-equilibrium and balance. As we cognitively and analytically begin to understand why we prefer balance and equilibrium locally, but in the meantime, why we should change along with The-Universe; such understanding via analytical-thinking will enable us to make change a normal and intuitive part of our existence.

Change happens; but if left alone, passive-change will be unfavorable for us. To make change favorable, we must put in active-effort to make positive-change, while dynamically keeping local-equilibrium as stable as possible. It is the difficulty of balancing these two opposite forces of existence that makes personal-equilibrium and stability difficult to achieve and maintain. However, when we learn to initiate active-change and create personal-equilibrium, we can then maintain and improve upon such stability by continuing to make further changes. Once we get the momentum of change going, further change should become easier, and it will require less conscious effort. This is how the process of change becomes routine and intuitive for us.

Dynamically changing while creating and maintaining local-equilibrium is the most stable form of self-improvement.

Since entropy causes change and everything including time changes constantly; we also change with time as we age. Therefore, if everything changes because of entropy and time, and because our physical-existence also changes with time; then why is it that we, as humans, mentally resist change so much? The reason is change creates variables of unfamiliarity and uncertainty; which in-turn, create discomfort, anxiety, and even fear. As discussed, variables of unfamiliarity and uncertainty, which are the natural side-effects of change, are contrary to our primitive-mind's default orientation for safety. It is the fear of these side-effects of change that makes us resistant to change. While change, itself, requires motivation and action, getting motivated to act and change creates unfamiliarity and uncertainty; and this, in-turn, creates anxiety and fear, which tends to prevent change.

Personal-Change = Motivation + Action

Side-Effects of Personal-Change = Unfamiliarity + Uncertainty $\Longrightarrow$ Anxiety + Fear

It is this contradictory nature of change against our primitive-mind's need for safety that makes it difficult to be motivated to change. Since our primitive-mind's primary and primitive function is to keep us safe; the less we change and the less variables we encounter, the safer our primitive-mind feels. Our primitive-mind tries to keep us safe by minimizing variables and uncertainties; yet, change, inherently creates variables and uncertainty. To the primitive-mind, getting motivated to change feels as strongly as getting motivated to sky-dive for the first time; however, just like any other learned skill, practice and repetition will streamline the skill.

Although inherently and in the short-term the role of our primitive-mind is to keep us safe; by resisting change in order to stay safe, we are actually trying to fight the effects of The-Universe and the laws-of-physics. As we often realize, if we resist change, other factors such as time and The-Universe will force change upon us. As stated, change initiated by other-things or other-people will seldom be as favorable as change that we undertake for our own Self. Since change is going to happen regardless of how hard we resist it; instead of allowing other-things, other-people, or chance to dictate how change happens, we should learn to proactively guide change so that change will be favorable for us.

Change in The-Universe occurs passively and naturally without any intelligent input; however, changing our thoughts and our behavior, which is necessary for active-change, requires active-input from us. This is why, we need to learn to influence our primitive-mind, via our intelligent-mind, by proactively seeking change and by allowing change to happen. By minimizing local-entropy and by creating and maintaining local-equilibrium, we can allow our primitive-mind to feel safe and to stop triggering fear and anxiety. The process starts by first consciously making attempts to change; and with practice, change will become more routine and intuitive. Actually, change could become so inherent to our existence that any disruption in our routine for change would result in what Theory of Self-Relativity describes as *"Change-Withdrawal."*

Theory of Self-Relativity defines "change-withdrawal" as "the undesired effects that one experiences when one stops changing."

When we consciously and actively seek change, our mind will become more comfortable in knowing that we have more control over change. By evaluating what needs to change and by taking action to make that change, we can then be more in control of the outcome of the change. Control increases certainty, which in-turn, makes the mind feel more comfortable to accept change; thus, in order to increase control and certainty, we must evaluate the facts of a situation that needs to change. Once we factually recognize and understand what needs to change and improve, we will then change based on knowledge, and not just by feelings.

When our primitive-mind begins to trust that our intelligent-mind is making decisions and taking actions that are based on facts; our primitive-mind will then back-off and allow our intelligent-mind to take the decision-making lead. Since there is only one form of fact for every situation; hence, the actions that we take via factual-thinking will be based on factual-reality, which in-turn, will minimize uncertainty, and thereby, increase the potential for favorable outcomes.

Furthermore, things have best chance of changing in our favor if we place active-effort into it. Positive personal-change comes from actual, factual, and active-input. However, since humans are inherently resistant to change, but are forced to change; passive, flawed, and effortless mindsets such as faith, hope, and wishful-thinking will not necessarily change things in our favor. Change, without our personal examination of facts, without our active-input, and without our involved-guidance will generally not lead to favorable outcomes for us. Factless and effortless change is dependent on chance or on other causes or on other entities than our own Self. The negative consequences of such reliance and dependency on chance or on others has been discussed extensively throughout Theory of Self-Relativity. Chance and others do not provide certainty and control for us; hence, they will not necessarily result in favorable outcomes for us either.

Faith, hope, wishful-thinking, and long-term held beliefs rely on chance and *"Perceived-Agency."* Chance or perceived-agency are not based on active-input and factual-thought processing. Chance and perceived-agency, also referred to by Theory of Self-Relativity as *"Assigned-Agency,"* which are also the core of superstition and other supernatural-beliefs, do not lead to controlled and favorable change for us.

Theory of Self-Relativity defines "perceived-agency" or "assigned-agency" as "one's creation or assumption of non-existent agency for a thing or an event that does not necessitate agency."

As discussed, since not everything in The-Universe has a purpose and a meaning; as agency-seeking and reason-pursuing entities, humans continuously want to find reason, purpose, and meaning for naturally occurring things that do not necessarily have any reason, purpose, or meaning. We do so, because as intentional-agents we want to assign agency to the purpose or meaning of something that is believed or perceived to be true, but is not necessarily true.

As pattern-seeking animals, we are hardwired to make the meaningless have meaning.

Humans are pattern-seeking animals because during primitive-times, assuming that the movement in the tree branches was caused by a predator instead of the wind had a higher chance of keeping our ancestors safe and alive. If the cause of the movement was the wind, instead of an animal, our ancestors simply made a false-positive error in cognition, but they did not get hurt; however, if the cause of the movement of the tree branches was an animal, they managed to stay safe by proactively acting upon it. Therefore, we are the offspring of those who made an error in judgment by assuming agency with everything; including false-agency, because by assuming agency and intent, our ancestors managed to stay safe and alive.

Safety and minimization of uncertainty lessens anxiety and brings comfort; therefore, intuitively assigning agency is hardwired in humans because it is intended to be protective, thus, it is comforting. However, in the modern-times and in the absence of primitive-dangers, we tend to assign agency not for the purpose of being safe; but we do so in order to give dislikable-facts and difficult-realities comforting-purpose and special-meaning. It is this instinctual and intuitive need for pattern-seeking and agency-designation that is the basis of many superstitions and self-deceptions. We do so because we want to assign a "preferred" and "comforting" purpose and meaning to something that has no purpose or meaning. We give things and events purpose and meaning by assigning an intentional-agent to that thing or event, so that we can further justify the nonexistent but comforting purpose and meaning of a thing or an event.

In the modern-times, where safety is not as urgent as it was during primitive-times; comforting fallacious mindsets such as unnecessary agency-designation, or seeking needless purpose and meaning, will fail in the long run, because they have no factual-foundations. Therefore, positive-change could have best chance of fruition if it is based on factual cause analysis. To increase the possibility of positive-change and favorable outcomes, we must learn to take control of our life and to not allow other-things or other-people control or influence it for us. Active-effort not only creates local-equilibrium and personal-stability, but it also guides change to the direction that will be most favorable for us. Active-effort and intentional-input gives us the ability to direct change to the best path-forward; while allowing us to minimize the natural-effects of universal-disorder, at the local-level of Our-Universe.

Despite the fact that order, local-equilibrium, and personal-stability is what keeps us in balance; our surrounding and The-Universe constantly try to disorder our local-equilibrium. Although our mind wants minimal activities and prefers equilibrium, our surrounding and The-Universe are constantly changing and disrupting our local-equilibrium. To gain and maintain local-equilibrium and personal-balance, we must actively keep our mind in equilibrium by dynamically adapting and changing with Our-Universe.

Additionally, despite the constant interventions of our primitive-mind which wants to keep us safe, our intelligent-mind can override the effects of the primitive-mind in order to change for the better. An applicable analogy is flight. Human-beings are not meant to fly; however, with the change and progress of human knowledge, we have learned to cheat the environment and take flight by inventing the airplane. By constantly changing, we have advanced airplanes through the implementation of improved technologies to the point where via active-input from onboard computers, airplanes can now fly themselves better than they would've been able to if they solely relied on the active-inputs of the pilot. Without the constant and active-input of computers, modern airplanes such as the stealth-fighter would not be able to fly; because its stealth design makes balanced-flight inherently difficult. Therefore, to compensate for its unfriendly design intended for radar invisibility, onboard computers constantly and dynamically use information and data to act in order to keep the plane stable and in balanced-flight.

For the stealth-fighter, in order to change from a traditional plane to an almost radar-invisible one; the shape and flight controls had to change to allow for such transformational design. Same principle applies to our life. In order for us to operate like a modern stealth-fighter, we must change our thinking-system which is analogous to the plane's input-system, so that we could make our life more advanced, yet better balanced and harmonious with Our-Universe.

Despite its ability to maintain balanced-flight; without the aid of computers, the stealth-fighter would crash. It is the dynamic actions of the onboard computers of the stealth-fighter that actually make it a balanced airplane capable of flying. The stealth-fighter can fly better and almost invisible because its onboard computers are constantly and dynamically implementing data-based active-input to make instantaneous positive-changes. Our intelligent-mind is no different than the advanced computers of the stealth-fighter. Once our mind learns to keep balance and equilibrium via facts and active-input; change will become inherent for our mind. Change will become intuitive, and our mind will learn to inherently check and balance every step of change to ensure that we maintain the most optimum state of stability and equilibrium.

To create local-balance and personal-equilibrium and to minimize mental-entropy, we need to adopt thought-awareness and thought-control via quick and clever thinking-processes. This could only be achieved if we open our Self up to self-improvement, and if we are willing to change and improve our thinking-processes. By recognizing, by resolving, and by eliminating negative and nonfactual-thoughts, we can filter our thinking process to only concentrate on factual-thoughts that truly matter. Minimizing clutter of our thoughts enables us to have a more balanced and more relaxed mental-state; which in-turn, minimizes and slows down our mental-entropy, local-disorder, and personal-anxiety.

As stated, The-Universe affects us as material-objects, just as it does with all other matter. Once we understand and appreciate that there is no purpose or meaning in The-Universe, and that there are no hidden or supernatural entities or agents that run our lives, and once we accept that we are no special to The-Universe than the chair we are sitting on; we can then appreciate the fact that The-Universe wasn't made with a special purpose for our existence. We, as humans, have now gathered enough knowledge to understand how The-Universe affects us materially; not in mystical-energy forms, not in immaterial-spiritual manner, and not in the form of supernatural-influences. We now understand that in order for us to live the best quality of life in The-Universe, we shouldn't wait for The-Universe to give us a sign; we should take action to adapt and improve with Our-Universe.

The-Universe does not exist for us to exist; we exist because The-Universe exists.

It is only via factual-thinking that we can understand how The-Universe and everything around us works and influences us. Once we learn to evaluate things factually, we can then begin to focus our mind to guide us via factual-thinking, rather than through unfounded-beliefs which are as a result of myths and imaginary mental fabrications.

As discussed, since the default nature of our existence is negativity, we can either choose to sit-back and allow passive-change to change things for us negatively; or we can take control by creating positive-change through active-effort and input. Therefore, in order to increase positivity, we must first minimize negativity, then create a balanced and levelled field of stability and contentment; and finally, we should attempt to increase positivity. Minimizing negativity and increasing positivity requires awareness and understanding of the facts associated with reality, and it requires our conscious and intentional input and follow through to improve reality in our favor.

However, after reaching positivity, if left alone and not maintained, positive-change will once again begin to fade into negativity, disorder, and even destruction. Thus, it is important to understand why we need to change and how to change constantly and consistently, in order to maintain the results achieved.

Awareness and Understanding are the most important attributes in dealing with reality.

Whether we like it or not, this is how The-Universe is set up; and as a collection of atoms that are governed by the laws-of-physics, we are an insignificant part of The-Universe. In order to become significant, we must change alongside The-Universe via self-improvement, by putting in active-effort to change for the better. We not only must change alongside The-Universe, but we must make the change to be favorable to our existence. Since natural-change in The-Universe is negative and disorderly, we can either change alongside The-Universe passively and deal with constant negativity and disorder; or we can put in effort to make the change that The-Universe will eventually bring upon us, more favorable to our life and to our existence.

As discussed, negativity and disorder are the two natural default-states that we are born into; because just as negativity is the default nature of our existence, disorder is the default nature of the-Universe. The negativity associated with our existence is intended to be protective by creating safety on a personal-level; and the disorder in nature which is caused by entropy, creates change which inherently affects us negatively.

Negativity and disorder are the two essentials for us to exist; yet negativity and disorder are also the two personal-inhibitors of change.

Because negativity and disorder are a normal part of our existence; this is why, Theory of Self-Relativity states:

If you feel negative more often than you feel positive, and if your negativities arise faster and last longer than your positivities; you are simply a normal human being.

Therefore, our existence is associated with:

1. **Negativity:** We are inherently default programmed with negativity in order to stay safe; yet, in order for us to live a quality and fulfilled life, we must minimize negativity.
2. **Disorder:** Change happens naturally because of increasing disorder; yet, in order for us to change constructively, we must minimize disorder by increasing our personal or local-equilibrium.

Our Existence

	Default-State	Preferred-State
Internal	Negative	Less-Negative
External	Disorder	Equilibrium

Although negativity is intended to keep us safe; in order to live a quality life, we must actually minimize negativity. Likewise, although disorder causes change; in order for us to change and improve, we must change in an orderly manner. Our inherent default programming to stay safe is completely antagonistic to the need for us to change.

The need for safety is antagonistic to the necessity for change.

Similarly, the disorder in The-Universe which causes change, is completely antagonistic to how we must change in an orderly manner. This is why, change, especially consistent change, has been difficult to achieve; because simply being motivated to change does not get us to change. True and transformational change can only happen when we understand what forces prevent us from changing and how these forces affect us. When we understand our relativity to everything in The-Universe, we can then change based on how reality actually is, rather than dealing with reality as we wish it to be.

Motivation alone does not work, because to make positive-change, we must put in active-effort to minimize our inherent default-state-of-negativity; while minimizing the Universe's inherent default-state-of-disorder.

According to Theory of Self-Relativity, at the personal-level, negativity is the stronger of these two natural-forces that make change a difficult process; because personal-negativity affects us more acutely and on a shorter time-scale, while disorder affects us more chronically and on a longer-term time-scale. Therefore, personal-negativity, which springs into existence from within our own Self, prevents personal-change more than local-disorder in Our-Universe does. Our primitive-mind's negativity has quicker onsets, and it has a more immediate and acute ability to shut down our motivation; because its effects can be uninterrupted and continuous. In contrast, our local-disorder has a slower, subtler, yet more chronic influence on blocking our change, because it affects us less-continuously and more-intermittently. Additionally, local-disorder could be interrupted and even controlled as it generally requires a longer process for it to take effect. In contrast, the negativity that is inherently associated with our primitive-mind is triggered easily, it is continuous, and it could at best be subdued; but rarely eliminated.

Therefore, our mental-entropy and our inherent mental-negativity is more influential on us than is our local-entropy or local-disorder. This is why, modification of our thinking-system is of utmost necessity for self-improvement; hence, to change and improve quickly and effectively, we must do so from within. Therefore, personal-change must be from inside-out.

Internal (Personal-Negativity)	External (Local-Disorder)
Default	Background
Dominant	Auxiliary
Prominent	Subtle
Immediate	Gradual
Quick-Onset	Slow-Onset
Acute	Chronic
Continuous	Intermittent
Must be Subdued	Could be Interrupted or Controlled
Triggered by an "Event"	Influenced by a "Process"

By learning and by applying the benefits of science, knowledge, and technology via factual-thinking; we can minimize personal-negativity and local-disorder in order to live a fulfilled and happy life. This means, we can learn to change by understanding how to minimize, counteract, and even eliminate personal-negativity and local-disorder. As discussed, factual-thinking enables our intelligent-mind to make sound-decisions; hence, it puts our primitive-mind at ease. Likewise, by using facts and by thinking factually, we can takeover change by choice, and we can actively guide change to the way we would want it to take effect; rather than by becoming complacent and by allowing passive-change to dictate how we will change.

Change enables evolution.

Without change, evolution would not be possible. Change enabled the emergence of the modern-human, and change will continue to evolve humans into the future. The species that adapts the quickest to change, has the best potential for survival and continuation of its lineage into future generations. Similarly, those humans who embrace and adapt to change, have the best chance of passing their genes on to future generations. It is such evolutionary-adaptation which chooses the fittest to move on and it is this survival-of-the-fittest which leads to intellectual-evolution and scientific-advancements. In-turn, intellectual-evolution and scientific-advancements allow for further exponential improvements to take place; therefore, evolutionary-adaptations ensure survivability and allow for intellectual-complexity to flourish.

However, in the modern-times, it is active *"Intellectual-Selection,"* as termed by Theory of Self-Relativity, that can override passive "Natural-Selection."

Theory of Self-Relativity defines "intellectual-selection" as "the accelerated progress of a species through intelligence, knowledge and technological advancements."

As intelligent creatures, the complexity of our intelligence, in combination with the advancements in science and technology, have given us an edge to separate ourselves from the passive forces of natural-selection. By allowing our intellectual-selection instead of only natural-selection to guide our evolution, our intelligence enables us to overcome the obstacles of local-entropy.

Intellectual-selection actively overrides passive natural-selection.

When we learn to think factually and minimize our personal-negativities, we consequently allow for our intelligent-mind to take over from our primitive-mind; thus, we guide our existence based on how reality is and not based on what we fear reality could do to us. Instead of allowing natural-selection to "passively" guide our future; by using intellectual-selection, we take control and we "actively" guide our evolution through the most suitable path that increases the chances of us not only surviving, but thriving.

Change enables evolution; inability to change leads to extinction.

Change is the process needed to move forward with time. Since time is never constant and it consistently changes by moving forward; we must also learn to change constantly and consistently parallel with time. It is adaptation, change, and evolution that keep us moving forward in time and with time. Although passive-change occurs without our control; by implementing active-change, we can minimize and influence the effects of our naturally occurring passive-changes. However, by not changing actively, we stay back in time while time itself moves forward, as we allow passive-change to dictate our existence.

Change is natural; but our resistance to change is unnatural.

Everything changes and everything moves forward with time; however, as discussed:

- Due to uncertainty associated with change; our mind tries to resist change.
- Change is also difficult because change requires active-input based on how reality is.
- Change, especially cognitive-change, requires awareness and understanding of the facts associated with reality that need to change.
- Mental or cognitive-change requires conscious and cognitive active-effort, which is based on facts, and not based on what we "feel" or "believe" that needs to change.
- Mental-change also requires the proper thinking tools and skills to change.
- Therefore, to change properly; we should change our thinking-system so that it is in sync with factual-reality.

Mental-change is different than physical-change. Our body and our brain go through physical-changes just like other material-based objects do. Although we can slow-down our-physical change by exercising and through healthy living; our physical-body and brain will change regardless. Changing our physical-body and slowing down the process of aging requires significant effort and behavior modification; regardless, no matter how hard we try to slow-down aging, entropy will cause aging and deterioration to happen.

In contrast, we can have more control over our mental-change. Mental-change not only requires less physical effort; but mental-change, unlike continuous physical-change, could actually improve as we age. Our mental-change could have additive effects on our intelligence, reasoning, and problem-solving abilities; because as we age, we gather more knowledge and experience. It is this mental-change, combined with experience that is referred to as wisdom; hence why, wise-men are often portrayed as older individuals. Wisdom does not mean making sentences out of mystical sounding words. True wisdom is experience and knowledge that constantly evolves as we acquire more information, knowledge, and experience.

Theory of Self-Relativity further defines "wisdom" as "the effective application of constantly evolving knowledge and experience, which is not contingent to subjective-interpretations."

Wisdom is not just the acquisition of knowledge and experience; but it is the effective application and sharing of such knowledge and experience through factual-thinking and reason-based analysis. True wisdom is constantly evolving and it is not influenced by subjective-interpretation and comforting-feelings. A wise-person does not reason with emotions; a wise person reasons with facts and proven experience.

Wisdom is to see reality as it is and not as we want it to be.

Since wisdom is continuously evolving and it is not contingent on subjective-interpretation; therefore, true wisdom is based on factual-thinking. Thus, to become wiser, we must improve our thinking-system by engaging in factual-thinking. Facts never lie because only one form of a fact exists per situation; hence, facts do not require interpretation or assumptions. Factual-thinking leads us to live our life based on factual-reality; therefore, factual-thinking allows us to adapt our existence to facts. Factual-thinking enables our mind to adapt, change, and improve based on factual-reality, and not based on what feels good to us at a given moment.

Although our physical-body cannot completely resist change; our mind inherently dislikes and resists change. However, change is ongoing, and change is inevitable; because everything changes. Self-improvement is accomplished by training our mind to not only accept change, but for it to proactively and inherently seek to change. By teaching our mind to change based on facts, we can even change our physical-body and Our-Universe to a certain degree.

Proactive mental-change creates an unending cycle of improvements relative to all aspects of our existence. For example, even though our physical-body ages, by having a strong and adaptive mind, we can actually learn to abstain from food and activities that promote aging, while engaging in healthy living practices that slow-down aging. Our mind can push us to eat healthy and to go workout to not only look and feel younger, but to have a better chance of living a longer healthier life. Without a healthy and change-oriented mind we will not be able to implement a healthy physical existence. Factual-thinking also increases motivation and discipline by reducing procrastination. Most who procrastinate do so by wishing and hoping that passive-change would change things favorably for them; however, in order to change most favorably, we must do so via active-change and personal-effort.

Similarly, we can negatively affect our thinking and mental health by not being in touch with our thoughts and by being only in touch with our feelings. Emotional-thinking, instead of rational and factual-thinking, is what causes and prolongs stress. The key to living a high-quality life is to learn to change and improve our Self by changing and improving our thinking-system. This could only be achieved by learning to think factually and to live our life through evidence-based reality; not through perceived or preferred reality.

As described throughout Theory of Self-Relativity, we are more in touch with our feelings than we are with our thoughts, and we often base our actions on our feelings in order to improve how we feel. Since feelings are always caused by underlying-thoughts; when we feel bad, instead of making our feelings be generated as a result of factual-thoughts, we often feel something and then try to create a thought in order to rationalize and support our desired-feeling. It is this subconscious backwardation of trying to fit facts to feelings rather than fitting feelings to facts that is one of the main problems with people's inability to change and improve.

To truly be able to change and improve, instead of taking a feeling and going back to try to create a comforting-thought to justify that feeling; we must learn to use that feeling to evaluate the factuality of the feeling's triggering causal-thought. Emotional-regulation leads to impulse-control, which in-turn, allows us to evaluate and regulate our thoughts. Emotional-regulation is best achieved via factual-thinking. Although feelings are not rational, a feeling is as rational as the rationality of the underlying-thought which is generating that feeling. When we learn to think not based on feelings but based on facts, we will then generate feelings that are based on factual-thoughts, and not simply based on how we want to feel. Factual-thoughts based feelings are the basis for Theory of Self-Relativity's Cognitive-Cognition-Technique.

To feel good... We must think well.

This is why, Theory of Self-Relativity advocates using our feelings to identify our thoughts which are generating our feelings. Feelings are a symptom of our thoughts; however, feelings, especially negative-emotions, cannot be improved or resolved without awareness and understanding of their underlying-thoughts.

Our feelings are the gateway to our thoughts.

We should use our feelings to identify their underlying causal-thoughts, because by recognizing, observing, and analyzing our thoughts, we can then evaluate our thoughts for their factuality. Once we evaluate the factuality of our thoughts, we can then accept or dismiss our individual-thoughts. If we accept a particular thought, we then act upon it; yet if we dismiss the thought, we take no action. Therefore:

Change your thinking by recognizing your feelings; don't change your thinking by rationalizing your feelings.

Repetition through understanding of facts will help us learn how to filter-out unnecessary thoughts and feelings quickly; and in-turn, it will help us improve our critical-thinking skills. When we quicken our critical-thinking skills, we will then be able to streamline our thinking-process; therefore, we will become a quicker and faster thinker. By recognizing, by resolving, and by eliminating inhibiting nonfactual-thoughts, we can eliminate old habits and we can initiate new fact-based behavior. By implementing facts as we move forward in time, we can improve our thinking-skills; hence, we will improve our behavior and the overall quality of our life. Using facts to change with time is Theory of Self-Relativity's formula for self-improvement.

Use facts to change with time

$$S\!\! \int = \frac{F\!\!\sqrt{} + \Delta}{t}$$

$S\!\!\int$ - Self-Improvement

$F\!\!\sqrt{}$ - Facts

Δ - Change

t - Time

This self-improvement formula represents that the more we learn to change and the more facts we use to support our change, the more we will improve as we move forward in life. In other words, as we change, we will continuously add to our improvement by becoming more knowledgeable and better experienced; thus, our self-confidence and our collective state-of-existence improves as we age. As we change continuously and as we change based on factual-thinking; our sense of Self and our value of existence will improve with time.

Changing with time does not mean changing in the present-moment. Contrary to many motivational and self-improvement teachings, the present-moment or the now is not the most important time. The now or the present-moment is actually the least important period of time, because it is the least stable of all times. As soon as we think about the now, the now becomes the past and we cannot do anything about it. This is why, the future is more important than the now, because the future at some point becomes the new present-moment-of-now.

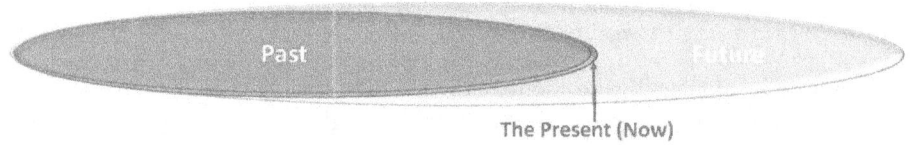

Past | Future

The Present (Now)

The now or the present-moment is only a snapshot of an unsustainable moment. By the time we think of the now, the now becomes the recent-past, and the immediate future becomes the new now. Just like the now, our lifetime is a continuum of unsustainable successive-nows. Although our lifetime is also a continuum of many nows; however, the number of nows in our lifetime is finite and will eventually end.

Since time is a continuum; therefore, living in the moment of now is nothing but a fallacy.

Even Einstein stated that time and space are continuous, which means so is our lifetime. To consider time properly, we cannot think of a snapshot of the present-moment-of-now; because time is constantly in motion, and so is our lifetime. Neither time nor our lifetime stop at a certain present-moment-of-now for us to observe that moment or to make the best out of it. The continuum of time, and therefore, the continuum of our lifetime, does not allow us to be in the present-moment-of-now. Just as discussed that we cannot stop or slow-down our mind from thinking; similarly, we cannot stop time from moving forward in order for us to live in the present-moment-of-now.

The now would be better referred to as a moment when our thoughts and feelings are active; because as conscious-entities, it is our thoughts that make us comprehend the present-moment-of-now, and it is our feelings that make us experience the now.

Our thoughts make us understand the present-moment, while our feelings make us experience the present-moment.

Because:

Thoughts are cognitive, but feelings are experiential.

Thoughts and feelings are present at the moment-of-now; yet, these thoughts and feelings are activated by an event that happened in the past, or by the anticipation of an event to happen in the future. What is important is to understand how we can control the way we think and feel in the present-moment-of-now by understanding what past events triggered our current thoughts and feelings, or what is triggering our thoughts and feelings about a future event. For example, trauma or an unfavorable event from the past, or worry and anxiety about a future event, could make our sense of the present-moment become more negative. Likewise, a fun or favorable experience such as a date we had last night, or the anticipation of a future experience such as an exciting date that is coming up, could make our present-moment-of-now be more positive.

Although in recent years, there have been a slew of baseless and nonfactual mystical motivational teachings which claim that we need to be in touch with and to live in "the moment-of-now;" such claims are nothing but fallacious sensationalism. Claims of living in the present-moment-of-now is like trying to catch a beam of light.

We cannot compartmentalize time because time is a continuum.

This is why, most people who try to follow such teachings of "living in the moment" end up either abandoning these programs, or end up feeling as if there is something wrong with themselves, because they are unable to learn to "live in the moment-of-now." Just as meditation is difficult, because meditation as a philosophy of slowing-down our thinking process is an impossibility; slowing-down our mind in order to live in the moment-of-now is also an impossibility, because it is not in harmony with factual-reality. Such supposed "mindful" practices could be undertaken as a relaxation or retreat method, just as a massage-therapy, a hot-bath, or a nap, would be soothing. However, such impossible philosophies that are completely out of touch with how reality works are pure social-construct sensationalisms that are being sold to susceptible people who are seeking to improve their lives. The reason such unrealistic philosophies were somehow effective in the ancient-times is because people then had more time and not much else to worry about; hence, they inherently lived a simpler life which did not require processing so many thoughts and so much information, so quickly.

Actually, there is nothing wrong with us if we cannot understand how to "live in the moment-of-now," or why we cannot slow-down our thinking; just as there is nothing wrong with us if we have more negative-emotions than positive ones. Because, as explained throughout Theory of Self-Relativity, these are the factual-realities of how we exist and how we relate to everything and everyone else. As a human-being, it is only natural and protective that we have more negative-feelings than positive ones; and due to the laws-of-physics and the arrow-of-time, it is also natural that we simply cannot live in the moment-of-now. Our negativity is caused by our primitive-mind's default protective programming which is intended to keep us safe; and our inability to live in the moment-of-now is caused by the Big-Bang and the nature of time being a continuum. Although our negativity is as a result of nature, our inability to live in the moment-of-now is as a result of our inability to adhere to someone else's fantastical delusions and fallacious claims. Because, in order to live in the present-moment-of-now, we would need to do the impossible; which is to violate the governing laws-of-physics.

The present-moment is an instant and the only way to understand the now is to consider it as a period ongoing from the past and continuing into the future. The now cannot be measured, therefore, unless we learn to identify and understand how the present-moment becomes the past and how the future becomes the now; the now, by itself, is insignificant, undefinable, and unsustainable. By the time we consider, we think about, or we try to not think about the present-moment-of-now, or to try to live in the present-moment-of-now; the now is history, and the future has become the now. For practical purposes and for true self-improvement, the benefit-to-cost ratio of trying to live in the moment-of-now, or the cost to benefit ratio of meditation, are uneconomical and impractical; if not impossible.

Although relaxation and calm-mindedness periods are important for our health; such retreat techniques do not in any way resolve or eliminate our problems or our negative-thoughts. Such teachings and practices simply distract and disengage our mind from our present difficulties in order for us to revisit them with a relaxed and fresher mindset at a "future" time. Other things and activities such as working-out, massage-therapy, reading, napping, or even, addictions can accomplish similar distractive, disengaging, or relaxation outcomes.

Additionally, although this approach of living in the present-moment-of-now through mindfulness sounds interesting in concept; such a practice is not just difficult, but it is impossible to execute on a realistic and consistently repeatable manner. Because, such a claim is not factual, as it is gimmick and sensationalism.

Repetition and efficiencies of repetition are important inherent qualities of a fact-based and realistic hypothesis or formula; because:

Repeatability validates applicability and practicality.

And because:

Gimmicks and scams are not repeatable.

As discussed in earlier sections:

Repeatability validates value, and repetition enhances skill.

Mystical and ancient mindfulness teachings are highly inefficient and difficult to repeat; therefore, they are not practical. The simple fact is that we cannot live in the present-moment-of-now because no such moment exists. The present-moment is unstable, and it becomes the past as soon as we try to recognize it. Many who have tried practicing meditation or living in the moment-of-now, have spent hours of their precious present-moment-of-nows by attempting to find out what it means to live in the moment-of-now. When understanding and implementing mediation or living in the moment-of-now fails; people feel even more disimproved than when they began the practice. The impossibility and lack of necessity of living in the moment-of-now, just like many other peptalking motivational programs, does nothing but to leave frustrated, confused, and even more unmotivated people behind.

Unrealistic motivation is the perfect setup for hopelessness and failure.

Such unrealistic programs and teachings are simply opportunistic, unnecessary, and unpragmatic. If it takes us hours to meditate or if it takes us weeks to try to understand what it means to simply live in the moment-of-now; then we are not learning how to live in the moment-of-now, we are simply wasting our time. As Albert Einstein properly stated:

If you can't explain it simply, you don't understand it well enough.

Likewise, if a claimant or a system cannot simply teach us how to "live in the moment-of-now;" therefore, there is nothing of substance for someone to learn. The frustration associated with meditation and with trying to live in the moment-of-now follows another one of Einstein's famous quotes describing *"insanity."*

Definition of insanity is doing the same thing over and over again, expecting different results.

Since the turnover rate of meditation or living in the moment-of-now, just like many other motivational programs is so high; doing them over and over again expecting different results can be metaphorically categorized as insanity. This is why, frustrated subjects feel almost insane after failing to adhere to and benefit from meditation or from living in the moment-of-now. No matter how relaxing meditation and living in the moment-of-now might feel; they do not resolve any of our problems, nor do they have additive effects in self-improvement as we move forward in time. Methods such as mediation and living in the moment-of-now are a time and financial luxury which many of us cannot afford.

Similar frustration also applies to other life-coaching and motivational teachings because they are not based on reality and factuality of how the human mind operates. Majority of motivational teachings are based on long, twisting, and confusing string of incomprehensible ideas which have no substance or evidence as to their claims. Change should not be a lengthy and expensive luxury with limited benefits; just as change and self-improvement should not be an arduous task that makes people quit in disappointment. Self-improvement must be repeatable, additive, and it must become more efficient with practice. Furthermore, the process of self-improvement should be enjoyable, practical, and pragmatic in nature. Therefore, a true self-improvement system should not just tell us "*what*" we need to do, but it should teach us "*how*" to do it. This is why:

Factual-thinking teaches you how to think; not what to think.

Certain ancient philosophies, meditation, and some new-age techniques of living in the moment-of-now, capitalize on convincing people to focus on nothingness; by thinking about nothing and by trying to slow-down time. These unrealistic and sensational recommendations are not only impractical, but they are impossible to implement. We cannot slow-down time, we cannot focus on nothingness, and we certainly cannot think about nothing; just as we cannot simply observe our thoughts. Therefore, to achieve the highest quality self-improvement, our thinking must be intertwined with time, and not by fallaciously trying to slow-down time.

Time is a continuum and any change in the speed of time is nothing but our perception of time. As discussed, perception is not necessarily fact, and our perception is often flawed and biased; unless it is verified with facts. Thus, instead of trying to slow-down time, or instead of trying to think of nothing; we must do the opposite, by learning to think based on facts so that we can begin to think quickly, cleverly, and efficiently.

Quick, clever, and efficient thinking maximizes utilization of time and minimizes stress on the mind.

Our mind is a thinking-machine and its job is to think. We cannot force our mind to not think, or to think about nothing. We must teach our mind to learn to look for facts and evidence and to resolve our thoughts if facts are contrary to what we are thinking; or to eliminate them if supportive-facts and evidence cannot be found. Therefore, if the evidence is contradictory to our thoughts, ideas, or beliefs; we should learn to alter our thoughts to match the evidence.

Since our mind is a thinking-machine and its job is to think, the only way that we can minimize or abstain from thinking is through unhealthy defense-mechanisms such as dissociation, distraction, and deflection, which are all coping-mechanisms used by those who are attempting to avoid unpleasant facts; thereby, avoiding change and improvement. Other than simply a relaxation or retreat method, according to Theory of Self-Relativity, to try to not think, or to try to slow-down thinking in order to live in the moment-of-now, is at best a distraction and an avoidance-mechanisms. Such soothing and calming effects could also be achieved through other practices such as playing sports, getting massage-therapy, or by napping and sleeping.

The present-moment always arrives from the future and it always becomes the past; therefore, to truly experience a quality present-moment-of-now, we should not focus on the now, we must focus on the future. When we anticipate the future, we can then try to influence the future so that when the future becomes the present-moment-of-now, the new now is more favorable and aligned with how we want the now to be.

Theory of Self-Relativity defines "anticipation" as "preparation for the future through evaluation of current facts and the application of past-experiences."

It must be noted that anticipation is awareness, understanding, and implemen-tation of actions to influence the future; therefore, anticipation, unlike popular terminology, does not mean worry and anxiety about the future. Since anti-cipation is a personal mindset that is implemented as a result of evaluation of currently known facts and information while applying past experiences; this is why, Theory of Self-Relativity recommends minimizing expectations, and ins-tead, to implement anticipation. Worry and anxiety are generally associated with expectation rather than anticipation, because expectations commonly lead to disappointments, especially when expectations are reliant on someone else's performance. Furthermore, expectations often lead to disappointments because an expectation is generally a positive mindset that is based on hope, rather than it being a realistic anticipatory mindset that is reliant on our own actions that we took at a previous time, awaiting certain outcomes.

Since the anticipation of a future event is reliant on personally applying knowle-dge and experience in the present-moment-of-now; therefore, the future is what is changeable, not the now, and certainly not the past. And since the future will become the now at some point; thus, we can only improve the now by influencing the future.

The now could only be improved by changing the future.

This is best accomplished via awareness and understanding of our active thoughts, and by using our past-experiences and knowledge to anticipate and influence our future. To have a stable and high-quality present-moment-of-now, we must use our "past" experiences and we must be aware of our "present" feelings and their causal-thoughts. We must further use this awareness of our "present" feelings and the understanding of their causal-thoughts to anticipate and influence our "future," so that when our future becomes the new present-moment-of-now; the new now would be the most favorable "present-moment-of-now" possible.

When we use our present feelings, we can then identify our thoughts that are generating our feeling; hence, we can either implement proper action based on our thoughts if our thoughts are proven to be factual, or we can dismiss our thoughts, therefore abstain from taking action and not anticipating a future outcome. When we don't anticipate a future outcome because our thoughts were nonfactual; we will then not expect a future event either. When we don't take an unnecessary action and when we don't anticipate a future event, this lack of anticipation will automatically minimize the potential for disappointments. However, when we take an action because the action was taken based on a factual-thought; we will then anticipate a certain possibility of an outcome but we won't be expecting a result that is reliant on chance or one that is dependent on someone else's performance.

The past defines the present and the future, as the future becomes the present and the past.

The function of the past is to define the nature of the present-moment, and the function of the present-moment is to define the nature of the future.

- The past defines the present.
- The present defines the future.
- The past and the present define the future.
- The future becomes the present.
- The present becomes the past.
- The future and the present become the past.

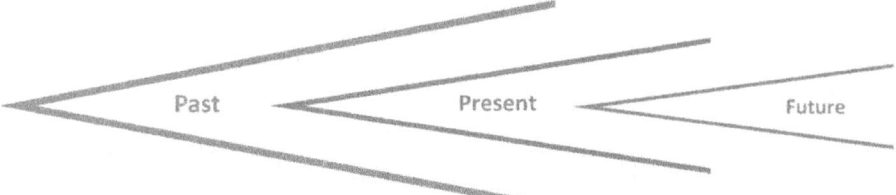

Therefore:

- The past cannot become the present or the future.
  - The future can become the present or the past.
- The future or the present cannot define the past.
  - The past can define the present or the future.

In summary, the only change that we can make relative to time is to use the knowledge and experiences of the past, to implement a fact-based change in the present-moment, in order to influence the future; so that when the future becomes the present-moment, the new present-moment-of-now would be a favorable present-moment. Therefore, instead of focusing on the past or the present, and instead of trying to live in the present-moment-of-now; the focus should be onto the future.

As discussed, we cannot change the past because the arrow-of-time only moves in the forward direction; hence, we cannot go back in time. Due to increasing entropy of The-Universe, going back in time would require reversing the disorderliness of The-Universe. Even if we were to assume that we could travel to the past, since traveling to the past would actually be a next-event; then such an event, itself, would be a future event. Additionally, per Einstein's Special Theory of Relativity, since space and time are interwoven and could not be separated; relativity dictates that the past is defined and cannot be changed, and the present is simply a frame in continuity from the past moving forward into the future.

Therefore, since time-travel is impossible and because we cannot travel to the past, the only choice we have is to use the past and the present to influence our future so that when the future arrives as our present-moment-of-now; our new now would be the best possible present-moment.

Thus, unlike the claims of many motivational-teachings, the present-moment-of-now is not as significant as is the future that will become the new present-moment. In order to experience a sequence of favorable present-moments, we should try to anticipate and influence the future, so that when the future becomes the now, the new now would be tailored to be the way we want the present-moment to be. To live fulfilled and stress-free nows, we should not try to live in the moment-of-now; on the contrary, we should take action in the moment-of-now to influence the future, so that when the future becomes the new moment-of-now, this new now would be the best possible present-moment. By presently using the knowledge and experiences gained in the past to influence the future; we can thus create more certain and more preferable future-moments-of-now.

Don't live in the present-moment…Let the future come to you.

Our decisions and actions are relative to the way we think in the "unstable" moment-of-now. This is why, it is important for us to learn to think quickly and cleverly so that we can utilize the moment-of-now efficiently. Therefore, to try to not think and just observe our thoughts in the moment-of-now is completely opposite to how time moves forward and how our mind operates; because as stated:

Our mind is a thinking-machine and its function is to think continuously.

The reasons living in the present-moment-of-now is impossible and contrary to what we should do is because of:

1. **Time:** Due to the arrow-of-time, time changes constantly and moves forward continuously; therefore, we cannot live in the moment-of-now as time does not allow the "now" to remain constant. We cannot stop time, and the only way to stop or slow-down time is to trick our mind into perceiving the passage-of-time at a different rate than the actual

measured-time. Incorrect time perception, itself, causes disharmony with reality, and such disconnect from factual-reality causes our mind and our thoughts to stay back in time, while time itself moves forward.

2. **Mind:** Our mind is a thinking-machine and its job is to think. We cannot slow-down our mind nor can we force it into not thinking; just as we cannot simply observe our thoughts without addressing them. Therefore, simply observing our thoughts or trying not to think isn't a realistic way of slowing down time. In order for our mind to use time most efficiently, we must learn to think quickly and cleverly so that we can process, resolve, or eliminate troubling thoughts faster, make decision more efficiently, and engage in most effective behavior. Once we change our thinking-system by learning how to resolve or eliminate negative and troubling thoughts; we will then not have many unresolved thoughts from the past to continuously think about them without resolution. Hence, we will be able to truly live in the present-moment-of-now without drifting back to relive troubling memories and unresolved thoughts.

Although we think and feel that we live in the present-moment-of-now, we actually don't; because by the time we sense, comprehend, and become aware of the now, we are actually experiencing the immediate past. Therefore, our brain is more inclined to perceive time rather than to measure time, because our brain has a *"delay;"* hence why, our perception of time could distort the reality of time. Our brain is programmed to compensate for this delay-shortcoming by stitching snapshots or fragments of the present-moment in order to anticipate the immediate future so that we could observe, comprehend, and experience this change in time. Our brain tries to compensate for its delay by anticipating the immediate-future as best as it can by using instincts, knowledge, and experience so that we can experience the present-moment as realistically as possible.

This delay in our brain is as the result of:

1. Fragmentation of the present-moment.
2. The delay associated with our brain in analyzing this fragmented information.

Our brain's actual delay, in combination with our mind's variable perception of time, distorts our sense of the present-moment-of-now. For example, if we are about to get involved in a rear-end collision, our brain signals to us that we will be hitting the car in front of us; therefore, we must press on the brake and hold tight on the steering wheel. But because our brain has a delay, and our mind is perceiving time differently; our reaction-time and our eventual accident could be affected not only because of our actual speed of travel, but also by our perception of time. Since our brain is anticipating the potential of us getting involved in an accident; our brain signals us to brake in order to prepare for or to try to prevent the accident. Because of our past-experiences, our brain tries to estimate where our car will be in the next few seconds and milliseconds, and it tries to use the past to anticipate our future location by making us react before that future PlaceTime arrives.

Even at the quickness of our brain, by the time our brain reacts, it is already reacting to something from the past; and since the present-moment-of-now is passingly-unstable, even the quickness of our brain is often unable to prevent us from getting into an accident. Due to this delay, by the time our brain processes something, it is actually processing something from the past, and not processing information at the present-moment-of-now.

Therefore, to compensate for the motion and instability of the present-moment, we are taught to drive slower and we learn to keep more distance with the car in front of us, so that our brain can properly anticipate the future, which is going to become the present-moment of the accident. By compensating for the motion and fragmentation of time, alongside our brain's delay in processing the present-moment-of-now; our brain has learned to anticipate the future by constructing the present-moment. In this example, our brain anticipates the future so that when the future becomes the present-moment-of-now, we have a better chance of avoiding the accident. Our brain not only predicts the immediate-future in order for us to experience the present-moment; but by anticipating and by predicting the near future, our brain tries to make the new moment-of-now that this future becomes to be more favorable.

We are never in the present-moment; we are always in the immediate-future.

The reason our brain has a delay in processing the actual fragments of the present-moment-of-now is because:

1. Although the speed of light is very fast, it still takes some time for light to get from the source to our eye.
2. Although signals travel fast through our neurons, it still takes some time for these signals to travel from our eye or other organs to our brain and back to the organ that should act to the information received.
3. The present-moment-of-now is unstable because by the time our brain processes the present-moment, our brain is actually processing something in the past.

Therefore, in order for our brain to process the present-moment-of-now properly, it has to guess, anticipate, and predict how the immediate-future is going to be; so that by the time this information is processed and this immediate-future becomes the present-moment-of-now, we have processed and prepared for it with the best probability-of-outcomes.

In other words, by anticipating the immediate-future based on past-experience, our brain tries to make the best guess as to how the present-moment will be. However, in other situations where our brain could not anticipate properly, the end result might not be as predictable or as favorable for us as we anticipated the present-moment-of-now to become. For example, when trying to hit a fly in midair or when trying to avoid a squirrel on the road, we often miss or hit the animals when the opposite was intended. Since our brain cannot anticipate where the fly or the squirrel will go next, we might end up missing the fly or sadly end up hitting the squirrel. The reason we hit or miss is because our brain cannot precisely know the immediate-future, nor could it react to the present-moment in time; because the present-moment is passingly-unstable and our perception of the present-moment is not immediate, hence, our perception is not always accurate.

This inability to perceive the present-moment and the fact that our brain cannot always predict the immediate-future, gets even more complicated when such perception and prediction is further reliant on external-variables such as another thinking or reactionary life form like the fly or the squirrel in the aforementioned example.

In summary, our brain actually recognizes that there is no such thing as the moment-of-now; hence, it tries to compensate for the present-moment by guessing, by predicting, and by anticipating the immediate future by using data, information, knowledge and past experiences.

Therefore, even by nature, our brain cannot live in the present-moment-of-now because it does not have enough data gathered to comprehend the present-moment. Everything our brain sees as the present-moment-of-now is actually a fraction of a second in the past; in other words, our brain operates by making best guesses and predictions. Thus, the only way that our brain could act and react at the present-moment-of-now is by our brain using past-experiences to anticipate what the next frame of the immediate-future that becomes the new now would be. Our brain does so by stitching the many present-moments via past-experiences and future anticipation. Our brain uses past-experiences to anticipate and predict where and how the next moment-of-now will arrive from the future. If it anticipates correctly, we miss an accident; if it doesn't, we miss the fly or we hit the squirrel. Although this is done at a miniscule fraction of time; in order to make our present-moment-of-now to be the best that it could be, our intelligent-mind needs to operate the same way and at a broader time-scale.

Since our brain and our primitive-mind are nonconsciously aware of this delay and they compensate for it; therefore, our conscious intelligent-mind, which is the byproduct of our brain's activities, must also learn to compensate by anticipating and by preparing for the future. Although our brain's and our primitive-mind's nonconscious or instinctive responses are for shorter and more instantaneous time fragments; our intelligent-mind should apply similar principles to the longer time periods associated with our existence. Fortunately, our intelligent-mind, which creates our analytical-thoughts, can have longer periods of time to prepare and anticipate for the future than the sudden and impulsive reactions that are necessary for our primitive-mind. Therefore, by learning to become aware and by understanding the facts that cause our thoughts, we can learn to more analytically, and eventually more intuitively, manage our thoughts by understanding their underlying-facts. By learning to think factually, our intelligent-mind can stitch "past-experiences" with "present-facts" to "anticipate the future;" so that when the future becomes the new present-moment-of-now, the new now will be as relevant and as real as its underlying facts and evidence are.

$$\text{The-Now} = \frac{\text{Past}}{\text{Experiences}} + \frac{\text{Present}}{\text{Facts}} + \frac{\text{Future}}{\text{Anticipation}}$$

This is why, thought-modification and thought-management are crucial to living a quality and happy life; because we must be fully aware of how reality works so that we can best adapt our existence to reality. As it is, due to our brain's physiological-design, our brain has to compensate by guessing and by predicting how things are in order to have as close of a sense of reality as possible. Add to this physiological shortcoming the irrational and nonfactual-thoughts that our mind commonly creates, or that others such as society and culture teach; and we could be significantly out of touch and out of sync with how factual-reality is. Therefore, it is important for us to learn to think factually so that we can deal with reality as reality is.

Since we cannot change our brain's physiology and how our brain operates; therefore, we should compensate for the natural delays of our brain by using our experiences and knowledge of facts to make our present-moment-of-now to be as close to reality as possible. Furthermore, since our current thoughts, decisions, and actions affect our future which will eventually become our new present-moment-of-now; once we learn how to manage our thoughts via factual-thinking, our future-nows will consequently arrive as being less uncertain and more favorable. By enhancing and by cultivating our thinking, decision-making, and problem-solving abilities, we can influence and change our future; thereby, we can experience more favorable present-moments-of-now.

Thought-awareness and thought-management does not mean to not-think or to slow-down thinking. True thought-awareness and thought-management means to think based on facts so that we can unclutter our mind by eliminating non-factual and emotionally triggered thoughts. As discussed throughout Theory of Self-Relativity, the way to achieve clear and uncluttered thinking is by resolving or by eliminating stagnant, repetitive, and nonfactual-thoughts. When we manage, resolve, or eliminate nonfactual-thoughts; we will then have a less-cluttered and a less-crowded mind. By its ability to resolve or eliminate nonfactual-thoughts, a less-cluttered mind can focus better on only factual-thoughts,

As described throughout Theory of Self-Relativity, our mind is an immaterial-byproduct of our brain. While our body and brain, as material objects, age and move forward in time; our mind should also learn to move forward in time. Actually, our mind must learn to not only move forward in time and with time, but our mind should lead our body to change with time. Mind-over-matter is an important attribute for self-improvement; however, Theory of Self-Relativity does not refer to this concept in the dualistic spiritual-sense. Although mind-over-matter is intended to demonstrate that our mind is a powerful tool to guide our physical-existence; as discussed, our mind is not a separate entity from our body and brain. Therefore, instead of envisioning our mind "ruling" our matter; we should envision our mind "leading" our matter.

It is not mind-over-matter...It is mind-leading-matter.

By us learning to think factually, we can learn to change and improve proactively. By allowing our mind to check and balance our thinking continuously and by making changes as needed, we can train our mind to change inherently and effortlessly. For example, although we can physically work out, eat healthy, and try to slow-down our physical aging processes; the best way and the only effective means to create mind-body harmony is through awareness, understanding, and changing of our thinking-system. This means, we must bring our mind forward with the arrow-of-time in order to effectuate the improvements in our body.

As aging indicates, our physical-body is going to move forward with time regardless of what our mind does; therefore, by learning to change and move our mental-processes forward with time, our mind can lead our body to change positively, or at the minimum, to change less-negatively, by eating healthy and by being disciplined to stay active and workout regularly. No matter how much we want to eat healthy and workout to stay fit in order to minimize the effects of physical aging; if we are not in the right state-of-mind and if our mind cannot be disciplined to guide our body in eating healthy and staying active, we will not be able to have the understanding and the discipline needed to adhere to the necessary protocol. A healthy body requires a healthy mind, and a healthy mind is a mind that could change and adapt to how reality is. A healthy mind does not deal with reality as it wants reality to be, and a healthy mind does not convince itself that the dislikable reality is not really as bad as it is. A healthy mind deals with reality as reality is regardless of how dislikable reality may be.

In this example, by training our mind to seek change, our mind can lead our body into working out, losing weight, and getting fit. These physical improvements will, in-turn, get our mind excited to push us even further to improve and to maintain the improvements. However, if our mind does not like to change and if it chooses to stay stale and behind in time; our body will follow suit and become stagnant. If we think nonfactual-thoughts by justifying that we will begin to work out after the weekend or after the New-Year, while sitting on a couch eating potato chips; our mind will actually be preventing our body from changing, instead of leading it to change. In this case, by staying back in time and by not moving forward with the arrow-of-time, our mind allows our body and health to deteriorate faster as it ages. However, when our mind recognizes its tendency to procrastinate by giving excuses that it will begin a healthy lifestyle after the weekend or after the New-Year; our mind can then eliminate such nonfactual-thoughts and it can base its leadership on the remaining factual-thoughts that demonstrate why we need to eat healthy and why we must begin working out right now, and not later.

By disrupting the stagnation of our mind, we can teach our mind to seek change alongside the arrow-of-time. When our mind learns to make changes, everything else in our life will begin to change; because change will become a routine and intuitive part of our existence. As stated, as long as routines create efficiency, routines in life serve a practical purpose by minimizing variables. However, minimization of variables prevents change; therefore, routines, which inherently minimize variables should only be implemented as a means of efficiency for repetitive tasks that do not require much change. But, when routines prevent change, such routines become rituals or bad-habits. Therefore, if we make change the most important routine in our life, we can then create the best balance between routines and change.

Although routines minimize change...Routinely changing minimizes routines.

This is why, change is essential for self-improvement and for living a quality and balanced life. Self-improvement teaches us how to change with nature and with The-Universe. Conversely, resistance to change clashes with the arrow-of-time and with the natural laws-of-physics which govern The-Universe. This is not spirituality; this is physics and science clearly relating our physical and matter-based existence to The-Universe. The-Universe has been changing for 13.8 billion years; hence why, understanding how we are connected to The-Universe and to the laws-of-physics teaches us why we need to constantly change to be in balance with The-Universe. Although the arrow-of-time dictates things will change to a more disorderly state in the large scale of The-Universe; by proactively changing, this negative-change could be slowed down and even temporarily halted at the local-level of Our-Universe.

As discussed, if a building is left unused and unattended to it will begin to deteriorate and eventually collapse. This is why, it is always easier to destroy than to build. Destruction, disorderliness, and negativity require minimal to no effort; while creation, order, and positivity require effort. Hence, without effort and without input, and if left alone, change will occur naturally; but such change will result in disorder and negativity, because disorder is the default-order of The-Universe and negativity is the default-state of our existence. This is how nature operates; therefore, if left alone, things will not change favorably for us.

Disorder, is the order of The-Universe.

This is why, Theory of Self-Relativity states:

In nature, disorder, disease, and death are normal; but harmony, health, and happiness are not normal.

It is up to us to accept and understand that change is inherent to everything, and that change occurs naturally. The only thing that manages to resist change is our mind, and this mental resistance to change manifests itself negatively on our material, our mortal, and as a whole, on our Self "existence." Because, as discussed:

The only thing that could go back and stay back in time is our mind.

Our inability to accept change as a natural requirement of existence and our resistance to learn to change proactively and positively with the arrow-of-time and with The-Universe, is one of the main reasons we are unable to live a content, fulfilled, and happy life.

By understanding these facts, that change is a necessary component of our existence, and that most favorable change could only happen by us learning to think and evaluate everything factually; we can then get on the path of self-improvement. The Cognitive-Cognition-Technique teaches us how to use the binary-filter of thoughts via the process-of-elimination so that we can filter-out nonfactual-thoughts and to only retain our factual-thoughts. When we only retain factual-thoughts, we can then make decisions and take actions to make improvements in our lives based on facts and evidence and not based on any other nonfactual form of thinking that our mind tends to engage in.

Eliminating clutter and nonfactual-thoughts enables our mind to get out of its "past" stuck-mode. In order for our mind to affect our future so that our future becomes the favorable present-moment-of-now, our mind needs to first filter out all unnecessary and repetitive thoughts that keep it stuck in the past.

Therefore, it is not enough to just be mindful in the present-moment-of-now; because as discussed, such a hypothesis is not only flawed in logic, but it goes against the laws-of-physics. As further discussed throughout Theory of Self-Relativity, mindfulness is only the first step of thought-management, as mindfulness is intended to create awareness; however, awareness must always be followed by understanding, which itself, is accomplished via the process of thoughtfulness. Thoughtfulness helps us to actually understand the quality and the causes of our thoughts, so that we can then make a decision to act or inact on those thoughts.

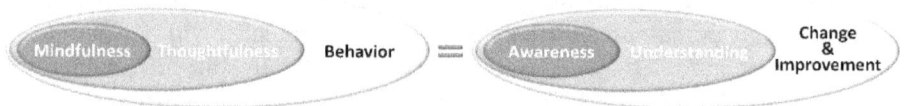

By becoming mindful we can recognize our thoughts; however, by being thoughtful we can then filter-out our nonfactual-thoughts and only keep those thoughts that are based on facts.

Unlike other methods of mindfulness which encourage to think less or to try to not to think at all; The Cognitive-Cognition-Technique teaches that by learning to only deal with thoughts that factually matter, we will not only be able to sync our Self with reality, but we will become a better multitasker, which itself is a requirement for progress in the modern-times. For example, mobile phones have created time-efficiency by enabling us to talk on the phone while driving. Likewise, thinking while driving allows us to focus on thoughts that need to be addressed. Proper thinking, just like talking on the phone and other multitasking requirements of the modern-life, is an evolving component of human evolution in the modern-times. This is why, we must learn to adapt to these faster and more efficient ways of modern-life; or else, the speed of modern-life will prevent us from changing quickly and efficiently with the modern-times. Therefore, to adapt to these modern-requirements, we must learn to think quickly and cleverly, so that our thinking-skills become more intuitive and more efficient in interacting with Our-Universe.

As discussed throughout Theory of Self-Relativity, quick and clever thinking styles could only be achieved via factual-thinking; because facts and evidence are the only definitive ways that we can trust our thinking. The solution to thinking is not to think-less; but to think more efficiently and more effectively. Likewise, efficient and focused-thinking is not the same as overthinking and over-analyzing thoughts. Efficient and focused-thinking results from uncluttered factual-thinking. This is best accomplished by only dealing with thoughts which are supported with facts and evidence; or by dealing with thoughts and ideas that have the best potential to be supported with facts and evidence.

By learning to become aware of and by understanding the factual-values of our thoughts, we can use our past-experiences to guide our future. By understanding the factualities of our thoughts, we will then be able to resolve or eliminate our unnecessary, cluttering, and repetitive thoughts by leaving them behind in the past and by moving our mind forward with the arrow-of-time. When we learn to eliminate and not carry these thoughts from the past into the present-moment-of-now; we will then be able to use the present-moment-of-now to shape our future so that when the future becomes the new present-moment-of-now, this new now is best tailored to the way we would've wanted it to be.

Furthermore, the key to living in the present-moment-of-now is to think efficiently and practically; yet to react logically and analytically, instead of reacting emotionally. This can only be achieved in knowing that our thinking is fact-based, and that these thoughts are not guided or generated by our feelings to reinforce our desire to avoid the dislikable-truth. Therefore, to live in the best present-moment-of-now, we must learn to use our past-experiences to anticipate and change our future.

Forget the now; use the past to influence and change the future.

Since change is an inherent and ever-present characteristic of The-Universe, and if we want to live the best quality and the most fulfilled and happiest life, we must learn to change along with Our-Universe; therefore, change is an inherent part of every aspect of our existence.

As discussed, Theory of Self-Relativity defines *"Self-Relativity"* as *"the interactions and relationship of the Self internally and externally with the Self, and with everything and everyone else."* Therefore, any change that we undertake will somehow relate to not only our own Self, but to other-things and other-people in Our-Universe.

Personal-change, which is the core of our Self-Relativity, could only be best achieved and experienced when change becomes an inherent part of our existence, and when such change is based on factual-thinking; because, in order to change, we must know what it is that needs to be changed. If we don't process our thoughts based on facts and if we allow our emotions to influence our thoughts, then the change that we engage in would not be based on factual-reality, and the decisions that we make and the actions that we take would be incorrect and even possibly damaging to our best interests. Furthermore, our incorrect decisions and actions could influence our relationships with others negatively.

This is why, Theory of Self-Relativity designates "desire" and "introspection" as the two non-negotiables requirements for change and improvement; because in order to change and improve, we must want to change and we must know what needs to improve, regardless of how undesirable or difficult such change may be.

Hence why, Theory of Self-Relativity states:

To change and improve, we must remain unbiased and adaptable.

Change does not necessarily mean morphing from one form to another in a drastic and obvious manner; on the contrary, some of the most fundamental characteristics of personal-change are actually cognitive and less-obvious. Therefore, when these fundamental-changes are combined together, the big picture of change takes a more comprehensive structural shape. Although according to Theory of Self-Relativity, factual-thinking is the main fundamental requirement for positive-change; the fundamental mindset that is required to connect factual-thinking to our ability to change is just as important. It is this *"Change-Mindset"* that is sometimes referred to as having an *"open-mind," or simply as "open-mindedness."*

According to Theory of Self-Relativity, the necessary fundamental characteristics which create the open-mindedness that allows our factual-thinking to lead us to change are:

$$
\text{Change-Mindset (Open-Mindedness)} \begin{cases} \text{1. Adaptability} \\ \text{2. Unbiasedness} \begin{cases} \text{a) Impartiality} \\ \text{b) Malleability} \end{cases} \end{cases}
$$

Therefore:

To be open-minded, we must remain unbiased and adaptable.

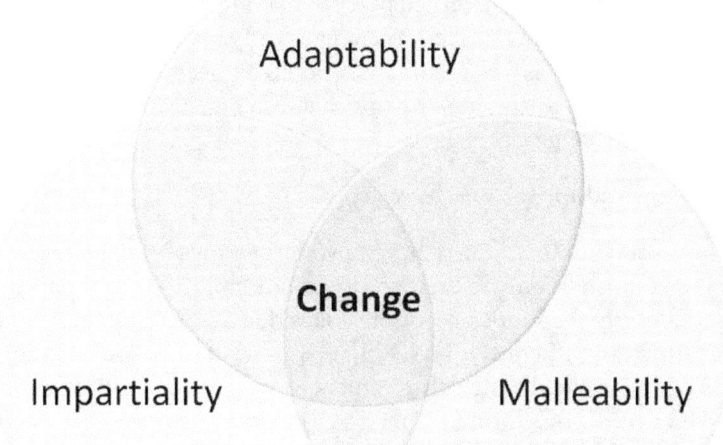

Adaptability

Change

Impartiality   Malleability

Change-Mindset
(Open-Mindedness)

Although each of the above characteristics could be defined individually and their influence on change could be described specifically; in order to reach the quickest and most stable levels of change, these fundamental characteristics should interact interchangeably and in harmony with facts and evidence. Since factual-thinking only considers facts, when it comes to change, instead of us changing to what we like, we should learn to change to what we must. Since facts are uncompromisable and are not open to interpretation; by staying impartial and unbiased to the type of change that these facts require us to implement, we can change dynamically to changing circumstances. Impartiality or being unbiased enables us to protect the cognitive work that we have done in identifying our factual-thoughts; while adaptability and malleability enable us to not remain rigid and to dynamically change our position by adapting to whatever the facts indicate.

Impartiality, adaptability, and malleability are all representatives of having an open-mind, and the main requirement for having an open-mind is to not think based on how we want to think, but to think based on how we should think. When we remove feelings, beliefs, and biases from our thoughts and when we base our thoughts on facts; we will then be able to be much more open to change. When we remove cognitive-hindrances such as preconditioned-biases and unfounded-preferences from our thought-processes; we can then become more malleable to adapting and changing with Our-Universe, while becoming less biased and more caring in our interpersonal-relationships with others.

As discussed, change is inherent and natural to everything and everyone in The-Universe. We can either learn to change by making change an inherent part of our existence[or we will be forced to change, and change made by other-things or other-people is generally not going to be as favorable for us as the changes that we make for our own Self. Therefore, to make change favorable for us, we must learn to embrace change.

Change happens…change or you'll be changed

One of the most common approaches in psychotherapy and cognitive therapy for change is to go back to our past, especially to our childhood and youth, in order to find and identify the root cause of the issues that are making our improvement and transformation difficult. It is true that past events affect our present state-of-mind and our existence; as they also influence our thinking and decision-making abilities which affect our future. Therefore, just as time is divided into the past, present, and the future; it is helpful to view our existence in our lifetime in similarly segmented time periods.

As discussed, since the arrow-of-time exists because of the Big-Bang, entropy, and motion; therefore, our arrow-of-lifetime exists because of the Big-Bang, entropy, motion, and time. Since life is inseparable from time, the analogy of segmenting our lifetime into three similar periods of time allows us to have better perception and clearer understanding of our existence. Theory of Self-Relativity recommends observing our arrow-of-lifetime in three similarly segmented periods as the arrow-of-time.

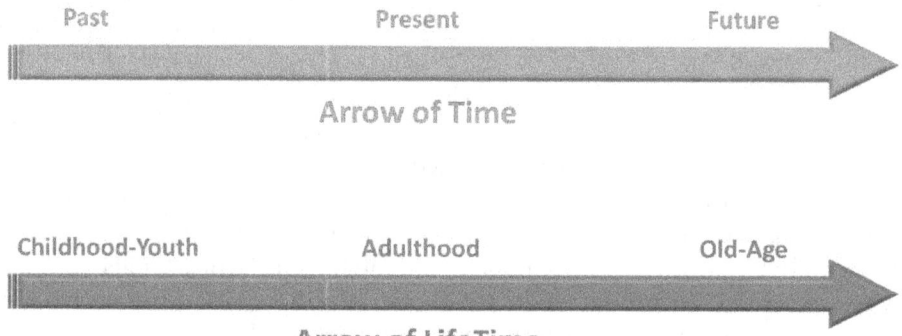

The Arrow-of-Lifetime

1. **Childhood-Youth:** Is the period when we perceive things, gather experiences, and start learning, by gaining basic and fundamental knowledge about our existence and about Our-Universe.

2. **Adulthood:** Is the period when we increase our cognitive and critical-thinking abilities in order to apply, modify, and improve our earlier life experiences, by fine-tuning and by improving the direction of our life's path.

3. **Old-Age:** Is the period when we begin to slow-down the gathering of broad knowledge and active critical-thinking, as we move onto experiential

critical-thinking by using experience and wisdom for a balanced slowing down of our life's pace.

By perceiving and by dividing our lifetime into these three time periods, we can better envision the past, the present, and the future, relative to our position in our own arrow-of-lifetime. Although perception is not necessarily a factual indication of reality; perception helps to compartmentalize non-bordered and difficult to distinguish slots of time for organization and thinking. Additionally, compartmentalization allows for piece-by-piece evaluation of facts and realities associated with each period, the significant events that occurred in any of these periods, and the effects and experiences of those events on our life. Although according to Theory of Self-Relativity, we cannot actually compartmentalize time because time is a continuum; perceived compartmentalization enables us to seg-ment time periods for better understanding, referencing, and evaluation of those periods relative to significant events.

Since the majority of our analytical and critical-thinking takes place during adul-thood, Theory of Self-Relativity considers adulthood as the period in our lifetime that is most significant for self-improvement; because adulthood is when most constructive positive-change could take place. Likewise, most who are interested in self-improvement and transformation, inquire about improvement and trans-formation in adulthood. For changing and improving, Theory of Self-Relativity considers adulthood as the most important period of our lifetime, because self-im-provement requires certain level of cognitive understanding and experience in order for it to be most effective. Furthermore, adulthood is considered to be the most significant period of our lifetime because it bridges our past to our future; whereby we can most efficiently and intellectually take constructive action by applying the experiences and knowledge that we gained in our earlier years for a better and more fulfilled old-age.

Additionally, self-improvement could also enable us to extend our period of adul-thood into the future by pushing back the onsets of certain characteristics and symptoms associated with old-age. There is nothing wrong by reaching old-age; but a prolonged and constructive adulthood will enable us to have a much more balanced, content, and secure old-age. Since humans are extending lifespans through science, technology, and medical advancements; this increase in lifespan is best lived by lengthening our adulthood. By prolonging our adulthood, we can increase the time-period which we undergo analytical and critical-thinking. Extending adulthood should lead us to make the most effective and most signifi-cant changes we make, not only in our own life, but also for others. By learning to self-improve through active-change, we can prolong our adulthood into a much more stable and even a more productive old-age. Although most people think of a secure retirement in old-age as the primary goal of change for aging; a healthy and factually-based memorable adulthood could actually add much more relative-personal-value or RPV to our old-age.

Personal-transformation through physical improvements, gaining knowledge, and improving cognitive-processes during adulthood is what will contribute to all other accomplishments and securities that we envision for our old-age. Likewise, a self-transformed person will have an old-age which will continue to be cognitively active. By continuing to gain knowledge and by keeping up our cognitive-processes in much better state than those who did not self-improve during adulthood; our transformation could continue well into the depths of our old-age.

By considering our childhood and early adulthood as our past; we can separate our younger periods of gaining awareness and experience, from periods of applying those experiences. Knowledge and experience are most powerful and effective when applied; especially when applied quickly, cleverly, and efficiently. This application of knowledge and experience is most efficient and constructive when our ability to think critically is at its highest, which is during the adulthood period. Adulthood is when we have the most potential for sound cognitive evaluation of where we came from and where we are going. Although the effects of childhood could significantly influence our perception, thinking, and decision-making abilities; to self-improve and to transform to a more balanced person, the awareness, understanding, and evaluation of our thoughts and our centered-self position in Our-Universe is what will shape our future. This awareness, understanding, and implementation is best achieved during adulthood.

As stated, to become the most efficient analytical and critical thinker, we must learn to think factually. This is best accomplished during adulthood, as adulthood is the period when we have enough experience to better understand and evaluate our existence; because what we transform in adulthood, will continue into old-age. Additionally, as our cognitive functions begin to diminish in old-age; this diminishing will take place from a higher level of cognition in comparison to those who did not learn to implement ongoing cognitive and thinking improvements in their adulthood. By learning to factually evaluate our childhood and youth, we can then identify and understand the effects of our past, alongside the relativity of everything and everyone at any present-moment as we move forward through adulthood and into old-age. Our childhood and youth were the periods that we were learning and gaining experience; thus, our adulthood is the time when we can evaluate the factuality and value of these memories and experiences, as we apply them to our life and move forward into old-age.

Adulthood is the period when our mind has the most potential for critical-thinking and cognitive-change. During adulthood, our mind has the best ability to evaluate facts and to relate them to our past-experiences in order to improve our future. Likewise, this wisdom of the mind could allow us to gain control over our perceptions, our feelings, and even our biases and superstitions, by learning to evaluate and to think based on facts and reason. Although in childhood and in adolescence we establish, absorb, and learn information about our existence; our true handle on life is reached and polished during adulthood, where we begin to apply this knowledge and experience.

It is such fact-based cognitive intellectual-ability in adulthood that provides us with the necessary tools and experiences to revisit our youth and childhood, in order to undo our incorrect and nonfactual social, familial, and personal conditionings. Because, as stated:

Childhood and early life skills and habits often become personality-traits as we age.

While heredity and genetics play a part in our psychological existence; in the absence of genetic disorders and other physical limitations which could affect our cognitive abilities, Theory of Self-Relativity contends that in the modern-times, our environment, our family, and our culture play a more significant role in establishing and shaping our emotional, psychological, and thinking states, than do our inherited traits. Therefore, in the absence of physiological and biological limitations; according to Theory of Self-Relativity, in the modern-times, nurture is more important than nature for living a fulfilled and happy life. Hence, through factual-thinking, we can change and improve our life and our existence. Since our self-identity and our sense of Self, which must be derived internally, must be reliant on "how" we think and not "what" we think; therefore, by learning "how" to think factually, we can streamline our thinking-process in a consistently applicable format. Although most people relate to the "what" or the content of their thoughts; the "what" is not as important as the "how."

Theory of Self-Relativity teaches you "how" to think; not "what" to think.

While recognizing "what" happened in our childhood and youth is essential and imperative to changing our Self; it is even more important to recognize "how" these events and experiences shaped and continue to shape our life. It is not simply enough to go back to our childhood and youth to see "what" is causing and affecting our anxiety, our negativity, or our inability to improve; as it is more important to understand "how" these events and experiences are affecting and influencing our life presently and moving forward. Hencey why, mindfulness alone, without thoughtfulness will not yield results. When we understand how we are being influenced by our past and evaluate these thoughts factually, we can then begin making changes and improvements based on the facts and knowledge of these events and experiences.

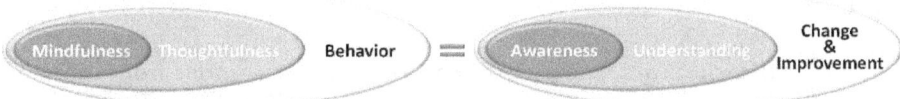

As stated throughout Theory of Self-Relativity, the "what "and the "why" are important diagnostic tools to create awareness; hence, many therapy, motivational, and self-awareness systems do that. The difficult part remains the understanding and the application of the knowledge of the cause in order to change the outcome. Knowing the cause or the purpose of an event is important; but to understand "how" a situation affects us and to learn "how" to resolve or eliminate the effects of our past negative and limiting experiences is what gives us the ability to change and improve.

This is why:

Motivation alone does not yield results.

Becoming aware and getting motivated is important in attempting to self-improve; but motivation fades out and awareness alone does not yield results. Hence why, many motivational teachings fail to consistently create change and improvement; because they fail to teach "how" to apply their teachings to our thoughts in a consistent and streamlined format. As stated throughout Theory of Self-Relativity:

Motivation alone won't get you any results. Change your thinking; change your outcome.

One of the most important influences of our conditioning and experiences from our childhood and youth is "how" our family, culture, and society shaped our thinking. Our parents are those who initially introduce us to the way they believe the world works. Likewise, during our early life, our parents introduce us to our cultural and social values and beliefs; hence, these exposures and teachings typically influence the way that we look at the world from the perspective of our family, culture, and society; for example, our religious perspective.

If we are born in The United States, we will most probably become an English-speaking Christian; however, if we are born in Iran, we will most probably become a Farsi-speaking Muslim, and if we are born in India, we will most probably become a Hindi-speaking Hindu. Yet, as a human-being, we are not born as an American, a Christian, an Iranian, a Muslim, an Indian or a Hindu. We are born a human-being, just like our other fellow humans. We become an American, a Christian, an Iranian, a Muslim, an Indian, or a Hindu by being born into the family and culture of these designations; often dictated by geography. Likewise, our thinking-system and our beliefs, which are as a result of our thinking-style, get influenced by family, culture, religion, and other social and environmental factors which are mostly manmade. It is for this reason Theory of Self-Relativity insists that our thinking must focus on the "how" we think rather than "why" or "what" we think. The "how" enables us to think based on what facts and evidence are showing; and the "how" guides us to not base our thinking on nonfactual-beliefs, baseless-traditions, or the manmade urge to find purpose, meaning and agency for things.

Cultural and societal influences are often carried over traditions from centuries and even millennia ago, which were instilled upon a society because of the thinking-system of a few influential members of that society, and based on their best understanding of the world around them. This is why, many cultural and societal traditions, values, and beliefs, which influence families and their members, are often not based on facts and scientific knowledge. While these traditions, values, and beliefs might have helped these cultures and societies to move forward in primitive and even during ancient times; in the modern-era, where we are so intertwined and reliant on technology and science, such nonfactual traditions, values, and beliefs could have severe repercussions in self-improvement, personal-transformation, and the quality of our life.

One of the strongest demonstration of the influence of family, culture, and society, and understanding the importance of "how" past events and experiences are influencing our present and our future, is dealing with trauma, PTSD, and with *"Self-Sabotage."* As discussed:

Childhood and early life skills and habits often become personality-traits as we age.

Dealing with trauma, PTSD, and self-sabotage, which is often the manifestation of unresolved trauma and low self-esteem, must be done with awareness and understanding of the facts associated with these past events and experiences that are repeated or relived; often is cycles, as one ages and moves forward in time. For example, when children are continuously cautioned, belittled, or told that they are not good enough, and that they won't amount to anything, or when the child is continuously compared to others in a devaluing way; such repetitive negative attributes, at some point, become self-fulfilling prophecies. As discussed:

Repetition enhances skill.

Although repetition can enhance positive-skills; if not careful, repetition can also enhance negative-skills. Therefore, if we are continuously repeating a mistake, which often becomes a bad-habit, we are enhancing our negative-skills; because we keep doing the same thing over-and-over again as we go through these cycles of highs, and often, extreme lows, that could last a long time, until we put in major effort to drag our Self back out of the depths of negativity, depression, and financial and relationship damages, that, once-again, we put our Self into. The reason self-sabotage, which is commonly as a result of childhood and adolescent trauma, can be so destructive is because it is subtle, nonconscious, and it happens gradually over many years of increasing chronic feelings and beliefs of worthlessness, not being good; or even, believing that we are a bad person. This is why, long-term and chronic unresolved trauma, PTSD, and negative-self-image could lead to depression, sadness, and even, suicide.

Self-sabotage occurs in not just people that have higher awareness of their own negative-self-image and negative-self-worth; but self-sabotage is even more extreme and confusing when it happens with overachievers and high-profile people. As discussed, some overachievers who became wealthy, powerful, and famous, did so as a means of compensating for their nonconscious low self-worth and negative self-image; by believing that success could make them get over their trauma and their past negative-experiences. However, unresolved and deeply imbedded experiences tend to resurface and cause more damage in the future, because the traumatized self-sabotaging individual is dealing with building more, on a foundation that is unstable. The reason people who self-sabotage have an unstable foundation is because such individuals do not have control and certainty over their trauma and past negative-experiences. Since people who are traumatized and who self-sabotage have nonconscious negative-self-image, they often become overachievers because they falsely think wealth, fame, and power will resolve their feelings of low self-worth and not being good enough. However, as discussed:

Wealth, fame, and power are simply byproducts of success; true-success is measured by the level of your fulfillment.

When an overachiever is not fulfilled because the person has unresolved self-image and self-worth issues tied to trauma from the past; the only certainty that such a person has is the certainty of knowing things will fall-apart. Therefore, traumatized people who are continuously self-sabotaging, are doing so, because destroying and damaging hard work and improvements that they accomplished is the only certainty that they have been conditioned to know; and destroying and damaging achievements is the only thing they believe they have control over.

According to Theory of Self-Relativity, another trauma and negative self-image condition similar to and often comorbid with self-sabotage is the *"Imposter-Syndrome."* The imposter-syndrome is a condition that despite being high-performing and successful externally, the person feels anxious and is not experiencing the success internally. Basically, despite even objective indications of success and its byproducts of wealth, fame, and power; the person feeling the imposter-syndrome subjectively and internally feels like a "fraud" or a "phony," and often doubts ones abilities. The awareness or lack thereof of one's imposter-syndrome could be low in consciousness or it could often be nonconscious; yet it drives the person's external performance, achievements, and relationships.

The potential for overachievement and self-sabotage is much higher in people who identify with the imposter-syndrome; because, many, become overachievers in order to feel better about themselves. As stated throughout Theory of Self-Relativity, if we have unresolved negativities, issues, and trauma, these personal matters will pull us back down into negativity regardless of how high we climbed the mountain of success and happiness. The negativity-gravity eventually pulls hard on those who feel the imposter-syndrome because these individuals were never able to create a contentment-zone to cushion their fall from naturally dissipating highs and happiness that occurs after major accomplishments.

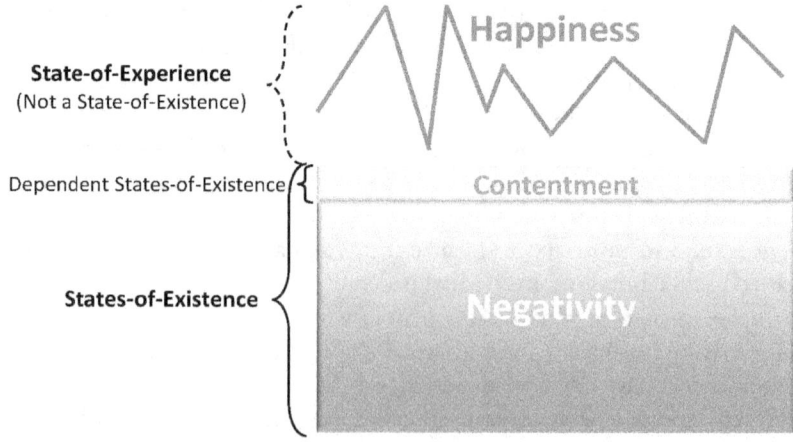

This is why, Theory of Self-Relativity is so focused on the effects of negativity on our existence; and why, we cannot achieve contentment, fulfillment, and longer-lasting happiness if we do not resolve or eliminate our negativities before attempting to reach positivities and happiness. This is further indication why positive-thinking and placebo-thinking do not accomplish lasting improvements; because those dealing with the imposter-syndrome, which almost everyone feels to a certain degree, unless they are narcissists, end up unhappy, unfulfilled, and often, they destroy what they worked so hard to build.

According to Theory of Self-Relativity, self-sabotage and the imposter-syndrome, just like Cluster-B personality-disorders such as narcissism and unstable-personality-disorder or borderline-personality-disorder, are much more prevalent in our modern-day technologically advanced societies than ever before. Many professionals, not only underestimate the hidden effects of those who are feeling and identifying with these conditions; but also, they underestimate the effects of these individuals' negative self-image and low self-worth on the people that they have interactions and relationships with. Be it in romantic-relationships or in business-dealings, having to deal with overachievers and unrealistically demanding people who are doing so as a means of their own negative self-image, becomes a difficult, conflicting, and often abusive interaction. This is why, those who become overachievers as a means of covering-up their internal weaknesses and deficiencies, often make others who have healthier sense of Self also feel low self-worth and experience negative self-image.

Therefore, in order to deal with trauma and with negative past events and experiences, it is important for us to not only become aware of and understand the causes of our trauma; but to first, stop self-sabotaging, and then, learning to change course by not only building positive-outcomes, but more importantly, by maintaining the results achieved. This is why, the "how" to move forward from trauma and how to stop self-sabotage, is more important than just knowing "why" it happened and "what" caused it. Although awareness and understanding is the required first-step; implementation, change, and improvement is how we can leave these negativities behind, and how we can bring our Self back in sync with the present-moment-of-now, on the path to improving our future outcomes.

By seeking and by understanding the facts and evidence associated with everything in The-Universe, our information and knowledge of everything about our existence has significantly changed and improved in the modern-times. We can not only have the knowledge and understanding of how to deal with past trauma and bring our Self forward in time; but, for example, we now know that a person who is going through an epileptic-seizure is having a physiological and medical reaction to a physical condition. Therefore, unlike incorrect old beliefs, we now know that the epileptic is not possessed by demons who are causing the individual to have these reactions.

When we change the way that we think and as we learn to think and evaluate everything factually; we will then learn to think and evaluate all aspects of our life in a standardized, non-judgmental, and unemotional format. By keeping our irrational emotions out of our thinking and by allowing our factual-thinking to generate our emotions, we can then allow clear thinking to guide our life; and in-turn, clear thinking will generate pure and rationality-based emotions, rather than creating emotions that are simply comforting, temporary, and irrelevant to our circumstances.

Similarly, by learning to "factually" evaluate our childhood and youth, as well as our cultural, familial, and other environmental influences; we can learn to bring the focus to our Self by refraining from blaming past-events, prior-experiences, and even, our childhood. By understanding the factuality of our past-experiences and their influences and effects on our current life; we can learn to evaluate, resolve, or dismiss nonfactual-thoughts we continuously generate, which are associated with or are as a result of those past events and experiences. By resolving or eliminating our ongoing thoughts regarding past-events, we can subsequently modify or eliminate our feelings; hence, we can change and improve our forward actions.

In therapy, visiting our childhood and our past is intended to discover and bring to the surface influential memories and unresolved experiences that we might be carrying to the present; and which are affecting our behavior. This is sometimes referred to as "family of origin issues." For example, if we were raised in a high-conflict or even an abusive family; to us, arguments and fights would be a normal part of a relationship, and it would be a representative of what we think love should be. Therefore, should we meet a high-conflict partner in our life, we might allow similar type of dysfunctionality into our relationship; hence, we could end up in a high-conflict, or even, in an abusive relationship.

In this example, psychotherapy's common perspective would be to tell people that because of how they were raised, they seek similar high-conflict and dysfunctional relationships in their future. According to Theory of Self-relativity, this conclusion is not completely true. One does not actively seek to meet someone high-conflict or abusive as one's parents were; however, should one meet someone who is high-conflict or abusive, one would be more inclined to allow a relationship with such a person to continue, because one has been brought up with the misimpression that arguments and abuse are a normal part of a loving relationship.

Furthermore, in this example, the reason for this incorrect approach is because many do not have the awareness and the understanding of the facts associated with such an upbringing. When we seek the facts and when we understand our upbringing based on what facts show us and not based on how we want to feel; we can then understand that we do not actually seek dysfunctionality, but we allow dysfunctionality to continue, if and when it enters our life. This is because we don't know how to stop something, and we don't know how to make a change into something else. Change is difficult, because understanding and accepting having been raised in a dysfunctional family upbringing is disheartening and painful. But to change for the better, we must be able to accept the difficult facts associated with an uncomfortable-reality; hence why, self-reflection and introspection are necessary, yet often painful processes.

When we become aware of the facts associated with our previous experiences, we can then take action according to those facts. In the previous example, when we get the facts and when we understand that love does not have to be a painful and argumentative process; we can then change by realizing that conflicts and arguments are not how love is expressed in other healthy relationships. Once we learn to look for facts and evidence, for example, that to love and to be loved does not mean to argue and to hurt; we can then base our thinking and reasoning on facts and evidence. After some time of practice, this fact-seeking and factual-thinking system will become inherent, intuitive, and even instinctive.

To let go of the past, we must think of the past, but not live in the past.

Filtering out our past-experiences through factual-thinking stabilizes our insecurities, diminishes our doubts, and reduces our fears; and in-turn, it brings more certainty to our future so that at old-age, we can have real peace-of-mind which is implemented during adulthood. Such balanced and peaceful old-age could only be achieved by us being able to sort out our childhood and youth carryovers during our adulthood. By resolving or by eliminating our early life's difficult experiences and incorrect conditionings, we would then have better decision-making abilities during adulthood. This, in-turn, should translate to a more secure, balanced, and certainty-based existence during old-age. As discussed, the only means of minimizing uncertainty and creating stability, not just in our old-age, but during all aspects of our life, is to live our life based on facts and evidence; because facts do not lie, and facts are not open to interpretation, therefore, facts are not open to manipulation.

Our old-age or our future is mostly dependent on the decisions that we make during our adulthood. In-turn, our adulthood is the transitional period that we can use to transform our incorrect thinking into factual-thinking. By learning to filter-out incorrect thoughts, beliefs, and perceptions of our childhood and youth, and by cultivating and by maintaining the factual aspects of our experiences during our adulthood; we can use our adulthood to seamlessly bridge our childhood and youth to our old-age, and thus, to live a satisfactory and a fulfilling life.

To experience the best present-moments of life
We must use our past experiences
To influence our future outcomes.

Index

Symbols

#1 399

10-Commandments 222, 226, 332, 337, 395, 418, 428, 501, 538, 588

10-Enemies 33, 110, 111, 116, 221, 313, 334, 351, 395, 399, 436, 522, 556, 587, 588

A

abandonment 182, 202, 211, 555, 580

absence of evidence 26, 190, 244, 245, 433

absolute 26, 30, 31, 32, 33, 93, 223, 248, 366, 412, 413, 515, 619

Absolute 30, 468

absolute-order 30, 31, 32, 33, 135, 345

abundance 112, 290, 330, 331, 332, 334, 335, 336, 396, 585, 586, 587, 590

Abundance 396, 586, 588

abuse 101, 201, 203, 204, 210, 326, 441, 498, 522, 557, 563, 684

Abuse 202

abuser 201, 202, 326

abusive 202, 203, 204, 205, 325, 326, 424, 426, 433, 441, 450, 542, 543, 554, 555, 683, 684

achievements 67, 103, 193, 290, 291, 311, 389, 437, 439, 458, 557, 578, 682

Achilles-heel 133

active-change 131, 140, 144, 596, 638, 646, 655, 656, 677

active-effort 78, 119, 137, 139, 150, 262, 263, 414, 596, 597, 599, 634, 635, 637, 639, 640, 646, 648, 649, 651, 653, 655

Active-Equilibrium 644

activism 179

adaptable 34, 97, 131, 164, 207, 213, 224, 226, 246, 255, 322, 331, 336, 379, 411, 433, 448, 510, 515, 536, 542, 561, 586, 674

addiction 191, 192, 193, 196, 197, 572

addictive 136, 170, 183, 184, 191, 193, 197, 274

admiration 551

adolescent 681

Adrenaline 473

adulthood 74, 677, 678, 679

Adulthood 676, 678

afterlife 105, 106, 107, 307, 318, 434, 636

agency 77, 226, 227, 231, 261, 295, 296, 297, 299, 301, 302, 306, 524, 528, 529, 531, 532, 533, 537, 648, 649

AI 40, 41

airplanes 650

algorithm 22, 257, 349, 384, 483, 537

allergy 298

all-or-none 322, 380

alone 16, 57, 66, 119, 120, 128, 136, 146, 150, 167, 170, 191, 200, 211, 218, 240, 256, 263, 340, 343, 382, 444, 460, 462, 464, 489, 493, 500, 540, 541, 546, 555, 562, 589, 595, 597, 599, 633, 639, 646, 651, 653, 671, 679, 680

altruism 179, 182, 427

altruistic 178

ambiguity 351

Ambiguity 350, 351

ambiguous 344, 350, 351

analytical-thinking 35, 81, 107, 382, 388, 479, 480, 535, 646, 657, 677

ancient 35, 57, 61, 62, 63, 64, 68, 107, 248, 271, 342, 343, 344, 346, 351, 352, 354, 363, 364, 497, 523, 529, 602, 628, 660, 661, 662, 680

anger 117, 172, 178, 214, 215, 217, 220, 222, 223, 224, 409, 458, 460, 548, 606

angry 115, 301, 302, 481, 506

animals 25, 36, 44, 81, 82, 83, 136, 167, 194, 195, 196, 205, 217, 252, 260, 261,

B

C

F

589, 595, 647, 653, 656, 661, 680

Motivation 16, 343, 346, 589, 595, 653, 680

motivational 16, 35, 78, 119, 121, 126, 150, 153, 239, 240, 242, 264, 307, 309, 342, 343, 346, 347, 348, 352, 353, 354, 400, 455, 481, 486, 498, 518, 522, 576, 582, 583, 584, 589, 590, 595, 596, 658, 659, 661, 662, 665, 679, 680

multitask 387, 388, 523

multitasking 65, 67, 388, 481, 672

Multiverse 70

mutual-compromise 542, 560, 561

mutual-interests 548, 549, 550

mutuality 209, 369, 428, 544

mutual-reciprocity 544, 545, 550, 551, 563, 574

Mutual-Reciprocity 544, 549

mystical 16, 23, 24, 65, 66, 71, 105, 119, 343, 346, 352, 515, 530, 582, 583, 628, 651, 655, 659

myth 264, 434

mythical 23, 24, 105, 343, 350

myths 155, 243, 248, 256, 264, 302, 651

N

naïve 354

naivety 404

narcissism 504, 683

narcissist 408, 556

narcissistic 210, 325, 408, 430, 438, 441

Narcissistic-Personality-Disorder 405, 554

narcissists 156, 211, 282, 304, 323, 324, 325, 380, 424, 427, 504, 505, 556, 683

natural 23, 31, 34, 35, 43, 54, 55, 60, 61, 71, 78, 82, 83, 105, 106, 145, 147, 262, 273, 288, 290, 295, 300, 301, 305, 308, 415, 496, 523, 526, 597, 600, 602, 610, 612, 628, 629, 630, 632, 647, 649, 652, 655, 660, 669, 671, 672, 676

natural-negativity 142

Natural-Negativity 142

natural-selection 34, 654

nature 21, 29, 35, 42, 48, 49, 51, 53, 54, 55, 62, 68, 76, 77, 83, 86, 89, 91, 118, 120, 121, 122, 124, 130, 131, 140, 142, 146, 161, 170, 174, 176, 183, 185, 191, 192, 194, 195, 196, 197, 205, 251, 263, 265, 266, 270, 284, 294, 304, 307, 308, 351, 352, 358, 374, 375, 399, 410, 413, 414, 415, 426, 430, 433, 436, 469, 476, 491, 493, 494, 511, 520, 538, 545, 553, 554, 560, 561, 566, 593, 596, 597, 600, 605, 626, 632, 635, 637, 638, 645, 646, 647, 651, 652, 660, 662, 664, 671

necessary-reinforcers 195, 196

Necessary-Reinforcers 195

neediness 97, 109, 167, 200, 201, 202, 208, 209, 224, 336, 337, 338, 339, 341, 429, 430, 440, 443, 445, 446, 522, 538, 539, 541, 542, 561, 580, 583

negative-change 494, 596, 597, 671

Negative-Consequences 432

Negative-Differentiation 118

negative-emotions 58, 123, 141, 147, 186, 188, 214, 215, 220, 222, 223, 230, 232, 255, 279, 284, 316, 374, 473, 498, 657, 660

negative-experiences 631, 681

negative-feelings 15, 18, 29, 60, 84, 86, 89, 90, 113, 114, 115, 117, 118, 120, 122, 125, 126, 134, 136, 140, 147, 157, 178, 183, 186, 187, 193, 195, 214, 215, 217, 218, 220, 223, 224, 238, 255, 260, 270, 274, 279, 294, 321, 384, 386, 397, 398, 399, 404, 405, 452, 458, 460, 461, 469, 470, 471, 472, 473, 480, 481, 487, 488, 490, 493, 494, 495, 496, 498, 548, 606, 623, 625, 660

negative-introspection 185, 186, 450, 452

Negative-Regret 292

negative-reinforcements 476

Negative-Resilience 562

negative-self-focus 526

Negative-self-focus 526

negative-self-image 681

negative-self-worth 681

negative-skills 478, 681

negative-thoughts 88, 90, 125, 134, 147, 214, 398, 406, 470, 471, 479, 481, 496, 660

negativity-bias 142, 491

Negativity-Bias 118, 491

negativity-gravity 490, 682

Negativity-Gravity 141, 490

negotiation 542

Q

R

S

391, 401, 474, 478, 479, 480, 482, 485, 503, 507, 516, 519, 520, 535, 542, 562, 563, 565, 571, 647, 661, 681

Skill 475, 478

skills 21, 22, 62, 65, 69, 92, 167, 172, 183, 188, 216, 225, 227, 256, 260, 311, 331, 332, 335, 348, 349, 359, 361, 362, 373, 382, 387, 388, 391, 401, 402, 403, 474, 475, 476, 477, 478, 479, 480, 481, 482, 484, 507, 508, 516, 520, 521, 522, 523, 525, 534, 536, 537, 562, 565, 587, 596, 655, 657, 673, 679, 681

slow-down 53, 57, 58, 62, 63, 65, 67, 68, 90, 343, 344, 349, 350, 386, 412, 413, 414, 415, 470, 472, 481, 597, 599, 609, 612, 628, 635, 637, 639, 655, 656, 659, 660, 662, 663, 665, 666, 669, 670, 676

smear 409

social-acceptability 171

social-animals 167, 340, 371

social-beliefs 243, 433

social-construct 106, 362, 363, 660

Social-construct 362

social-constructs 362, 363

social-favor 171

social-law 433, 434

social-laws 417, 433, 435

social-media 27, 28, 174, 175, 183, 184, 354, 361, 405, 438, 463, 549, 558

social-networks 174, 179, 183, 184, 191, 192

Social-networks 183

society 61, 65, 92, 95, 108, 166, 168, 169, 200, 204, 205, 237, 250, 254, 350, 352, 354, 362, 364, 416, 424, 428, 431, 433, 498, 514, 539, 562, 575, 585, 669, 680, 681

Sociopathic Personality-Disorder 554

sociopaths 282, 325, 504

Sociopathy 555

soul 43, 602, 626, 628

souls 23, 35, 39, 50, 54, 55, 351, 601

space 27, 64, 126, 165, 283, 364, 365, 366, 480, 616, 618, 619, 621, 665

SpaceTime 364, 366, 616, 619, 632

Special Theory of Relativity 364, 603, 615, 619, 665

speculators 380

speed of light 365, 415, 615, 620, 667

spiritual 23, 35, 38, 43, 57, 66, 71, 79, 105, 108, 119, 343, 344, 346, 347, 494, 524, 530, 534, 562, 602, 628, 651, 669

spirituality 23, 24, 105, 343, 355, 515, 576, 671

Spirituality 23, 245, 601

stability 88, 90, 171, 207, 216, 357, 374, 427, 433, 442, 534, 550, 551, 560, 608, 633, 634, 643, 644, 645, 646, 649, 650, 651

stars 53, 71, 596, 600, 610, 611

state-of-existence 84, 106, 120, 133, 136, 137, 140, 143, 194, 195, 215, 291, 356, 364, 408, 420, 442, 481, 487, 488, 489, 495, 497, 499, 507, 509, 513, 540, 577, 658

state-of-experience 84, 136, 194, 389, 390, 442

state-of-mind 16, 43, 65, 105, 142, 176, 186, 235, 240, 242, 251, 256, 276, 291, 325, 333, 391, 406, 411, 440, 452, 461, 477, 480, 481, 491, 494, 499, 507, 514, 515, 522, 540, 572, 576, 579, 670, 676

stationary 365, 366, 600

stealth 319, 650

stereotypical 278

stimuli 15, 29, 136, 469, 484, 517, 518, 572, 614, 615

stimulus 31, 260, 401, 517

stink 114, 145, 146, 147

stock 276, 277

Strawman-Fallacy 155

stress 85, 114, 140, 172, 202, 208, 211, 214, 215, 216, 217, 218, 221, 224, 227, 240, 255, 256, 260, 304, 313, 329, 335, 375, 401, 409, 473, 474, 481, 496, 510, 532, 550, 552, 553, 556, 606, 656, 662, 665

Stress 214, 215, 473

stubborn 289, 541

stubbornness 289

subconscious 43

subjective 20, 24, 26, 36, 106, 108, 159, 160, 243, 245, 246, 247, 248, 258, 269, 272, 278, 291, 352, 413, 417, 423, 431, 437, 461, 463, 477, 497, 567, 568, 570, 575, 579, 581, 615, 619, 620, 621, 656

subjective-interpretation 26, 258, 272, 352, 656

T

U

Y

Z

www.ingramcontent.com/pod-product-compliance
Lightning Source LLC
Chambersburg PA
CBHW060847120626
46553CB00001B/4